# SOFTWARE ENGINEERING

# SOFTWARE ENGINEERING

# SOFTWARE ENGINEERING

Gregory W. Jones
*Utah State University*

**JOHN WILEY & SONS**
WILEY

New York □ Chichester □ Brisbane □ Toronto □ Singapore

*Library of Congress Cataloging in Publication Data:*
Jones, Gregory W., 1943 –
     Software engineering / Gregory W. Jones.
                    p.           cm.
        ISBN 0-471-60882-3
         1. Software engineering.        I.   Title.
     QA76.758.J66            1990
     005.1--dc20
Printed in the United States of America
10 9 8 7 6 5 4 3 2 1

This book is dedicated to the committed researchers and steadfast practitioners of software engineering, whose efforts have made it possible.

# PREFACE

This book is intended to be an introduction to software engineering at the undergraduate level. It can be read by anyone who understands the material of the current ACM CS1 and CS2 curricula, although it will be more appropriate for those who have some experience with larger projects. To cover the material completely, one semester or two quarters are probably needed. In addition, a follow-up project, involving student-staffed software development teams, is beneficial in fostering conversion of learned material into experienced understanding.

There have been questions among the reviewers of the text about the use of Ada in examples. Some believe that students should be given more background in the language before code is thrown at them, and that the examples might better be couched in Pascal or C. I believe, first, that Ada is an important language, and that even students who are not proficient in it should be able to catch the meaning of Ada code as an issue of cultural maturity. In previous years, a cultured person was supposed to read French "a little." Today, a cultured software engineer should, at least, be able to read Ada in the same way.

In addition, software engineers are forever reading code in a language they don't fully understand. The ability to capture meaning in this fashion is an important skill in the profession. Of course, there will be situations in which a little knowledge is worse than none at all; in which ignorance of a fine point in the language will result in disaster. Nevertheless, software engineers will continue to find the need to read in unfamiliar languages, and students might as well get the point now.

I have tried to make the bibliography accessible to beginning students, and extensive at that level. *The especially useful references are flagged with an asterisk (\*).*

The problems at the end of the chapters are intentionally open-ended, as are the projects in Appendix 1. This is to allow instructors latitude in tailoring the material to their students, and to allow students some scope for exhibiting originality and judgment. This approach counteracts the students' prevailing notion that everything pertaining to software is "cut and dried." An instructor's manual is available to adopters of this book. The manual offers solutions to selected end-of-chapter problems, as well as suggested examinations and course schedules.

I originally wrote the manuscript for this book using alternating masculine and feminine pronouns. Almost all readers (of both genders) said that this tended to reduce their reading speed and comprehension. Hence, I converted to masculine only. I hope this in no way conveys a message that success at software engineering is gender-dependent; quite the opposite is true.

The staff at John Wiley, particularly my editors, Joe Dougherty and Gene Davenport, have been most kind in encouraging my work and in providing me with the opportunity to complete this book. I express my gratitude for their professionalism and enthusiasm.

I thank the many reviewers for their efforts in reading this book: Dennis Kafura, Virginia Polytechnic and State University; C.V. Ramamoorthy, University of California, Berkeley; Barry Kurtz, New Mexico State University; Frances Grodzinski, Sacred Heart University; David Gustafson, Kansas State University; Henry Etlinger, Rochester Institute of Technology; James S. Collofello, Arizona State University; Joseph E. Urban, University of Miami; Ted Tenny, Texas Christian University. They were conscientious and helpful beyond the bounds of my expectations.

If you find errors in the book, they are my fault, not theirs. I would welcome your corrections, comments, and suggestions. Mail them electronically to GJONES@CC.USU.EDU or to the Department of Computer Science, Utah State University, Logan, Utah, 84322.

GREGORY W. JONES

# CONTENTS IN BRIEF

# DETAILED CONTENTS

# C H A P T E R  1

# SOFTWARE ENGINEERING

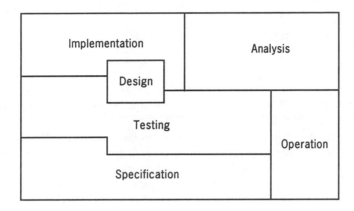

Software has become the central component in many complex activities. For this reason, the challenge of producing it requires specialized and powerful techniques. It is not possible to rely on luck, guesswork, and innate talent for dependable results. The software engineering discipline, which has grown up in response to this need, applies many of the procedural and organizational methods of traditional engineering to the challenges of developing software products. These products are quite different from other engineering artifacts — perhaps even unique.

First, software products are intangible; there is no need for physical mechanisms, structures, or processes. Second, software engineers do not use the laws of thermodynamics, partial differential equations, or most of the other concepts familiar to traditional engineers much. Their work is largely independent of natural science. Third, software products are much more complex than physical constructs. This requires special care in conceptualizing, managing, organizing, and testing them. Finally, software products are manufactured by simple copying processes, so almost all of the production effort is dedicated to design and development.

Although much of their work is based on computer science, software engineers build software products, which are much more than mere "computer programs." This book explores this difference and explains the techniques for engineering software. It

- Naïve users, with no understanding of the software.
- Careful specification of the product prior to design.
- A friendly user interface produced with user participation.
- Ability to function dependably for a naïve user.
- A lifetime measured in years, not weeks.
- Complete documentation.
- Several different configurations, meant to run on different hardware or under different operating systems.

**FIGURE 1-1**   CHARACTERISTICS OF SOFTWARE PRODUCTS

examines the major criteria that mark good software design and construction. In particular, it relates specific computer science and engineering principles to the discipline of software development and maintenance.

A frequent complaint of new university graduates (and of their employers) is that a computer science degree does not guarantee any realistic software development experience during their years in college. They may have written hundreds of programs but may never have developed a **software product**. Some of the additional characteristics of software products are outlined in Figure 1-1.

Besides these differences, software products are usually much larger, in terms of lines of code, than the programs students write to satisfy the requirements of their coursework. This forces a choice between letting one person work for years developing it or putting together a team of software people who can finish the work in a much shorter time. Practical considerations, such as market requirements, dictate the rapid completion of the product using a team. But then one is faced with all the additional problems of management, communications, coordination of effort, specialization of tasks, and verification of performance that come with group efforts. The skills needed to work in — and perhaps direct — teams are not always taught in computer science programs; consequently the new graduate may show serious deficiencies.

A mass of documents is associated with a software product: for instance, code — old, new, and variant — specification and design documents, installation and operation manuals, test data, records of modifications, schedules, committee and review reports, market surveys and cost - benefit analyses, and much more. Someone has to define the content of these documents, as well as to see that they are properly prepared and carefully preserved. This is a far cry from the "here today, gone tomorrow" practices of most students.

It *is* hard to provide a classroom or laboratory experience that approximates the real world, but far too many students are never even aware that the real world exists until they plunge into the middle of it. The purpose of this book is to provide information about that world as well as the skills that will enable the student to cope instead of panicking. In this book, the student will learn about developing software products, rather than just writing programs.

This chapter introduces the terminology and background for software engineering. It presents some of the major themes of concern currently in the profession. The first

- Accepted body of knowledge.
- Quality control.
- Foundations in science.
- Discipline.
- Product orientation.
- Use of tools.

**FIGURE 1-2**   CHARACTERISTICS OF SOFTWARE ENGINEERING

segment deals with models of the software process and how to ensure its success. The second segment looks at some of the specific activities that make software developers and maintainers more productive. Although there may not be any hope of increasing their productivity along an exponential curve, there are certainly ways of improving it by 20%, 50%, or 100%, or in a few instances perhaps even 1000%. In the third segment, ways to foster quality in both the process and the product are examined.

## 1.1 ENGINEERING THE SOFTWARE PROCESS

There is no universally accepted definition of **software engineering**, but these are usually recognized to be components in its meaning (see Figure 1-2):

there is a **methodology**, a well-defined body of knowledge and techniques, which is used in developing and maintaining software;

there is a set of recognized **criteria** for well-engineered software, such as functionality, dependability, economic viability, timeliness, ease of use, maintainability and efficiency; and methods to ensure these are met;

the recommended techniques draw from a **foundation** of Computer Science, Mathematics, Management Science, and Systems Science; recognized, scientifically sound methods are employed in studying the field;

the practice of software engineering is a **discipline**, with a defined process or system for software development and maintenance; and this discipline mirrors in many ways the traditional engineering disciplines;

software engineering produces a full **product**, going well beyond the simple and small program;

software engineers have a kit of **tools**, often automated, which are systematically used to improve productivity and the quality of the product.

The concept of "software engineering" becomes clearer upon consideration of some of the things it is not. Software engineering is not just programming; it requires an ability to express one's self clearly to nonexperts and to understand them in turn. It demands management skills and communication ability; submitting to standards and procedures and working as part of a team demands additional self-discipline, patience, and cooperativeness.

Software engineering is not an art. Accepting a systematic discipline affords a less sweeping scope for expressing individual creativity. A software engineer is constrained by user requirements, team decisions, and management instructions, and the product is seen as a common resource of the entire team, rather than one individual's private creation.

Software engineering is not a game. We respond to the economic needs of our own software organization and those of our clients. The technically superior product does not always succeed the best, and the most brilliant player does not always win. Discipline, teamwork, marketing, money management, planning, and many other nontechnical skills play a vital role in success.

Software engineering should be a recognized profession, like engineering, law, or pharmacy. Some tentative steps have been taken in that direction, but a true profession requires recognition by governmental regulatory agencies, an accepted methodology and code of ethics, an accredited educational infrastructure, and a formal examination for qualification. Many of these factors are still weak or missing. Indeed, the very use of the word "engineer," which is frequently reserved by law for licensed professional engineers, can lead to trouble in some circumstances.

### 1.1.1 The "Software Crisis"

The original impetus to develop software engineering came from a realization that we did not know how to manage large software projects. This situation was called the software crisis, and was characterized by late delivery of expensive, unsatisfactory, and unmaintainable software systems. At the same time, the inability to complete current work on time and within budget meant that needed maintenance and new development efforts were piling up.

We always seem to have prophets of ruin with us, and it is difficult not to become hardened to their pessimism. People have been worried about the software crisis for 20 years, but we have successfully avoided the actual clap of doom until now. Crises that drag out for 20 years dull our sense of danger, to say the least. Nevertheless, there is ample cause for concern, and ample reason to demand careful engineering of software products (Figure 1-3).

This concern could not be better illustrated than in the recent flurry of apprehension about the United States' Strategic Defense Initiative (SDI). SDI studies the feasibility of a missile defense system that would literally burn a wave of thousands of ballistic missiles and warheads out of the sky. Although many technologies would be necessary, advanced software is recognized to be an essential ingredient of SDI. The goals of the system would have to be severely restricted, or even abandoned, if software could not play the ambitious role planned for it.

David Parnas, a member of the U.S. Department of Defense Panel on Computing in Support of Battle Management, resigned from the panel in June, 1985 and thereafter published his reasons for doing so in *Communications of the Association for Computing Machinery* ([PAR85]). He discussed the difficulties of assuring the dependability of the proposed software, as well as the failings of software engineering as it is currently being practiced. For instance, large software products have so many different possible states

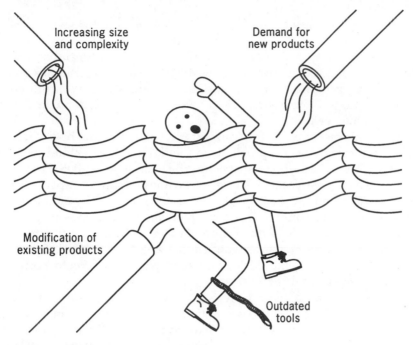

**FIGURE 1-3**  THE SOFTWARE CRISIS

that it would be very confusing for the developer to understand, remember and manage them all, if not actually impossible. If SDI Battle Management software were to work as expected, it would need to be highly distributed. This arrangement requires the developers to design large, concurrent, parallel systems, that would multiply the conceptualization problems being faced. Modifications to SDI software might be required in the field. As Parnas noted, "debugging notes can be found on the walls of trucks carrying computers that were used in Vietnam." Even in a better environment, modification of a software product containing so many interfaces and components would be extremely difficult.

In fact, personnel qualified to carry out the job might not be available. Parnas noted that "Most programmers cannot even begin to use the meager tools that are available to software engineers... Programmers cannot be trusted to test their own programs adequately." To add to the problem, demand in the U.S. for qualified personnel increases 12% each year, whereas their number increases by only 4% ([PER87]). As a result, a 20% yearly turnover of personnel is not uncommon. This turnover tends to further destabilize efforts to put together the kind of staff that can produce a quality product.

Parnas does not address one last problem — our techniques for managing software development projects are usually inadequate. Products are often late, inefficient, expensive, or unsatisfactory to users. Major product development efforts suffer from a 25% cancellation rate, that is, one in four major systems miscarry before they are born ([BUT87]). In addition, developing a large system takes between 3 and 10 years.

Brooks ([BRO87]) has a similar list of inadequacies in the state-of-the-practice of software engineering; including schedule delays, cost overruns, flawed software, software unreliability, and user unfriendliness, inflexibility, and security risks. The problem is that software is now being used to implement very complex processes—this complexity being the heart of the reason that software is used. We are hired to deal with complexity; if it were not there, nobody would want us. Our abilities, however, are frequently inadequate.

The general perception that we can best meet any difficulty by finding a computerized solution brings several problems to mind. First, the demand for new software outstrips the software industry's capacity. Musa estimates ([MUS85]) that the demand for software increases by 900% each decade, while Boehm and Papaccio ([BO88a]) puts increased expenditures to be 200%; however, the productivity of individual software engineers increases by only 35%. Second, software has become a major component in the national well-being. Ramamoorthy and others ([RAM84]) estimated that software development and maintenance would represent 13% of the U.S. Gross National Product by 1990. In 1986, the U.S. government spent $36 billion for software development and maintenance ([PER87]).

The inevitable result of the industry's inability to satisfy a rising demand is a backlog of software applications. Major corporations are now experiencing a 30-month backlog, and this has increased 50% in the last five years ([PER87]). When industries depend on software, this may cause an increasing obsolescence within vital sectors of the economy. There may be an additional hidden backlog of important applications that have not even been mentioned, since they are out of the question given the current shortage.

Another problem arises as we consider software ownership. It is, by nature, an intellectual property with no adequate protection under current laws. Three approaches have been taken toward establishing property rights in software. One, trade secret practices, has been most often used, particularly for custom built software. Once the secret information becomes common knowledge, however, no more protection is afforded. Second, the use of patents has been largely untried in the United States. The U.S. patent laws are difficult to apply to intellectual processes like software. It might be possible to patent the architectural design of software, however ([SAM88]). The third approach, copyrights, may protect software from wholesale duplication. Nevertheless, an enterprising individual may make some significant modifications to the external design and code structure of a product and change it enough that copyright laws no longer protect it. Recent U.S. court decisions have indicated that screens, menus and user interfaces may fall under copyright protection.

How do we deal with the software engineer whose error leads to radiation overdoses, closed reactors, or scrubbed space flights? The resulting losses may be enormous, and our litigious society demands that liability be placed somewhere. On the other hand, the complexity of some software applications makes it very difficult to avoid the possibility of harmful results. Whether there is blame in these cases, and if so, to what degree the software engineer must shoulder the blame, are questions that have yet to be answered fully.

Of course, all of the problems that can, and do, exist in the software industry should not lead us to the misconception that all software projects fail. There is a wide variety of successful products to emulate, ranging from telecommunications switching software, which operates months or years without failure to consumer-oriented word processors that find wide (and profitable) acceptance throughout the world to operating systems that become industry standards through sheer popularity. It is our task to learn how to make our own projects just as successful.

## 1.1.2 The Role of Software Management

Many students of software engineering dream of the day when they will graduate, rent a garage behind someone's house, and, in it, build a software product that will revolutionize the industry and make them millionaires. While this sometimes happens, the more likely outcomes are that:

The fledgling millionaire runs out of money to pay the rent on the garage before finishing the product.

The software engineer finishes the product but hardly anyone buys it.

Lots of people buy it but the developer cannot support a widely distributed product adequately. Hence, he has to hire someone to run the company. Then that person takes control of the company away from him.

The most obvious solution to the problem of late, expensive, unreliable, and unsatisfactory software is to plan better. This requires improved management techniques but is also dependent on a readiness on the part of the software engineer to exercise discipline. Software development and maintenance activities which planning should affect are shown in Figure 1-4. The important thing to recognize is that project planning is far from trivial.

Most software engineers graduate from computer science (CS) departments in which they receive extensive technical training but practically no management training. They certainly did not choose to be a CS major hoping to become managers, and

Choice of a model for the development process.

Hiring and structuring of software teams.

Purchase of hardware and software tools.

Choice of a potential product based on organizational experience, resources, and goals.

Evaluation of market information about product viability.

Estimation of cost, schedule, risk, and price of the product.

Choice of ways to report and measure project progress.

Choice of specification and design notations.

Choice of programming language(s).

Establishment of standards for documentation, coding, verification, and testing.

Choice of a configuration control mechanism.

Preparation of materials and personnel for installation.

**FIGURE 1-4**  SOFTWARE PLANNING ACTIVITIES.

Cost and effort estimation.

Assessment of the stage of software development.

Control of software development.

Performance measures for personnel.

Creation of incentives for improved productivity.

Risk estimation and reduction.

**FIGURE 1-5**   SOFTWARE MANAGEMENT CHALLENGES

most would disclaim any desire to be a manager. But somebody must manage software development efforts. Management practices based on correct understanding of cognition, individual motivation, and group dynamics may be more important to the success of large products than are technical tools and development methodologies ([CUR88]). Even so, the best candidates for manager are software engineers who understand what the enterprise is all about.

Software engineers may need someone to manage them for their own good. For instance, with respect to their resistance to the use of tools, Stucki said ([STU83]): "The software community has done an excellent job of trying to automate everyone's job except their own." If software people will not decide to improve in one particular aspect of their work, the organization has to find a way to direct them to that end.

The lack of management skills in people who do software managing may be a significant factor in the other aspects of the software crisis. The lack of an adequate management science for software enterprises alone almost qualifies for the title "crisis." Shaw ([SHA86]) lists the managerial problems shown in Figure 1-5. It is vital that we establish a management methodology to respond to those problems and that we convince ourselves of the importance of both mastering and using it.

One response, **programming-in-the-large**, refers to techniques by which large software systems can be built up out of smaller components. Probably any program over 10,000 lines of code is big — in the sense that it requires more than one developer if it is to be ready within a reasonable time. But some products are really big. IBM's OS/360 ran to more than one million lines of code. The PASS software amounts to more than a half million lines of code, and it is only one part of the overwhelmingly complex space shuttle software.

Structuring large, complex systems into components, with particular attention to interface.

Management of groups of people who are working on a common project.

Control of concurrent interacting processes.

Meeting specifications that are not straightforward, closed mathematical descriptions.

Dealing with a very large set of states in which the system may find itself.

Need for unfamiliar tools like programming environments, version control, document production, and test management.

**FIGURE 1-6**   SPECIAL CHALLENGES IN BUILDING LARGE PRODUCTS

Software products that are tens of thousands or hundreds of thousands of lines long often present challenges that simply are not seen in smaller products (see Figure 1-6) ([SHA86]).

Constraints are as difficult a challenge as size. If there were no constraints put on software development, it could be carried out just to please the developer. Some of the actual constraints that we normally find are as follows:

- The product must be profitable.
- The product must be completed within a fixed time frame.
- The product must be developed in many alternate forms and each of these may be in a different stage of development at any moment.
- The product must be developed by a group of people working together.
- Customers need to be convinced to purchase the product.

Satisfying these constraints demands management skills beyond those that are generally thought to be part of "programming."

In discussing the kinds of problems that can occur in meeting the constraints of a software project, Brooks in [BRO75] said: "Managing OS/360 development was a very educational experience, albeit a very frustrating one… The effort cannot be called wholly successful…Any OS/360 user is quickly aware of how much better it should be…the product was late, it took more memory than planned, the costs were several times the estimate, and it did not perform very well until several releases after the first."

Putnam and Wolverton ([PUT77]) wrote: "The typical 200 - 300 percent cost overrun and similar schedule slippage is no longer tolerable when the cost is measured in millions of dollars….". Enormous cost and schedule overruns were a frequent occurrence in the 1960s and 1970s. Although we have better control today, overruns still occur, and their specter continues to haunt customers.

Profit is the difference between the cost of producing, distributing, and supporting software and the income from its sale. Since we are constrained to be profitable, and we

The experience and ability of the project personnel.

The quality of the software development environment.

The degree to which our understanding of the problem and its acceptable solutions is likely to change.

The narrowness of the constraints on the product's dependability, efficiency, and interface to current products and environments.

The complexity of the eventual code.

The length of the eventual code.

The degree to which software components can be reused.

The degree of market readiness for the product.

The lifetime and degree of distribution of the product.

The amount of evolution the product will eventually undergo.

**FIGURE 1-7**  FACTORS TO CONSIDER IN COST ESTIMATION

want our commitment to a project to be based on solid information, we need to know ahead of time how much it will cost us to develop, market, and support it. These estimates of cost will depend, in turn, on our ability to estimate and evaluate several factors, as shown in Figure 1-7.

Information that goes into the estimate is often obtained from records of the organization's past history. Hence, careful observation and recording of management information improves our capacity for accurate cost estimation. This database of managerial experience may be a software organization's most valuable possession.

There are a variety of techniques for cost estimation, which range from intuition through structured debate to cookbook application of formulas. The most popular methodologies require us to break the proposed software down into conceptual modules of some kind (called a **work breakdown structure**), then assess the modules using a variety of different measures. These measurements are inserted into standard formulas, which come up with the cost estimate.

If we consider time to be an expendable asset like money, then time estimation and cost estimation tend to use the same techniques. Indeed, since labor costs constitute most of software costs, the ability to estimate time requirements is closely related to the ability to estimate cost. But scheduling goes beyond estimation. During the actual development and maintenance stages, the organization has to keep track of expenditures and plot them against budgeted expenses in different categories. Significant deviations from the budget must be corrected before they begin to spell disaster. If this is not possible, contract renegotiation or marketing plan changes have to be undertaken in order to avoid financial loss.

The ability to estimate the amount of time required for the different stages of software development, and then to maintain that schedule, promotes success in several ways.

> The success of software on an open market often depends on whether it can arrive before a competitor and thus establish a commanding market position.

> Custom software is often developed under a contract that calls for severe financial penalties if the software is delivered late. These can be avoided only by on-time delivery.

> Customer confidence and goodwill are enhanced if promised delivery dates are honored.

> The software development team itself experiences a boost in morale when it realizes that it is able to make a schedule and stick to it. Confidence that other planning aspects were correct increases.

> An adequate amount of time is spent on tests, documentation and training. In badly scheduled projects, these stages are often abbreviated or omitted.

> Movement of personnel from one project to another, as well as training and vacations, can be planned with confidence.

Management plays a vital role in the software organization. Planning, organizing, estimating, scheduling, meeting constraints, making a profit, and keeping records are

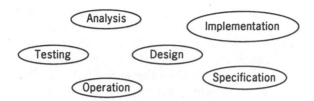

**F I G U R E 1-8**   STAGES IN THE SOFTWARE LIFE CYCLE

necessary steps to continued success. Software engineers must develop the managerial skills needed for professional achievement.

### 1.1.3 The Software Life Cycle

Software has a lifetime, just like any other commercial product. It starts as somebody's idea (or inspiration) and ends up being obsolete, unsupported, unused, and defunct. The normal stages of the software life cycle are shown in Figure 1-8. Each product passes through these stages although the duration, sequence, number of iterations, and exact effect of each stage may vary.

A **software development process model** describes how, and in what order, these stages are put together to trace the entire life history of the product. These models are discussed in the next section, where we will see that software does not generally pass through each stage in the sequence in which they appear here. In this sense, software is very different from people, who go through infancy, childhood, adolescence, maturity, senescence, and death in a predictable fashion. The stages of the software life cycle are presented in linear fashion in this book simply for want of any better organizing principle.

The analogy of building construction is often used to illustrate the stages of the software life cycle; in fact, any construct probably goes through similar phases.

Anybody wishing to put up a building will first try to determine whether the proposed structure is worth the money and effort it will require. Needs and benefits will be analyzed, preliminary costs and schedules estimated, specific functions and utility decided on, building land sought, legal implications examined and different modes of construction evaluated.

The purpose of the **analysis stage** for software is to determine whether it would be profitable to embark on the development of a new product. If so, we must assemble the necessary resources for that development effort. The analysis stage starts with conception of a new product. It is necessary to justify demand for the software by market research or by a request for a proposal from a potential client. It is also necessary to validate the desirability of the product in terms of the goals, plans, and needs of the software organization and its personnel.

If the need for the product is clear, then we must define its nature more closely. We do this by analyzing user requirements, such as: a general definition of the function of the product, and its scope, the nature of its interface to users, hardware, and existing products, and the speed, capacity, accuracy, and cost of the product. This requirements analysis provides the basis for the rest of the analysis stage. It also allows us to decide whether such a product is within the reach of our technical capabilities.

Understanding the needs to be met by the software is the first step toward its functional specification. This can be accomplished by a process often called **systems analysis**, in which representatives of the software organization consult with, interview, and observe people in the user organization. The purpose is to understand fully the needs and constraints of the possible software solution, as well as the current structure and function of user operations.

Next, it is advisable to determine the costs and benefits of undertaking the project. Cost is made up of labor, new equipment purchase, diversion of use of current facilities from other products, purchase of software components from other sources, and lost opportunities because of inability to undertake other projects. Benefits are composed of sales of the product, improvement of the organization's market stance because of the product, development of new skills within the organization, and the possibility of further product development based on this project. The risk factors, or probabilities, associated with cost and benefit calculations must be evaluated as well.

As a consequence of the cost estimation, we usually know whether the project promises to be profitable, and, if so, how many people will be needed at what points in the project. Thus, it is also possible to produce a schedule of the project, together with plans for hiring or transferring specific personnel and the acquisition of new hardware and software. If the cost - benefit analysis still looks promising, further planning is needed to establish management methods for the project. The final result will document of all the activities and results, as well as a proposal for the project. It will be accepted or rejected by the software organization's management.

Returning to the construction of our building, we must now specify the amount of square feet we require, the kinds of materials that should be used, the general style and function of the structure, its safety and security provisions, etc. These are written down

before we start to draw up blueprints, or even architect's renderings. This document is an important part of the contract between the builder and client.

The **software requirements specification stage** crystallizes a precise description of the software's function, the exact nature of the environment in which it is to function, and the constraints on its performance. This description furnishes the basis of the contract, moral or legal, between the software developer and user, and it should be accompanied by a detailed plan for the acceptance test by which the purchaser will validate the software.

By firmly understanding the user's needs and environment, the development team can proceed with a detailed software specification. This is done in cooperation with the client, if there is one, or with the marketing division of the software organization if not. Nothing can be worse than to produce the wrong software, so communication and mutual understanding at this stage are vital.

It is also worthwhile to establish priorities for the different functions and constraints of the software, to guide the development team if not all the requirements can be met initially. Finally, the plans developed during the planning phase will probably require some refinement as new information is developed.

In construction, the first product that a customer sees is usually the architect's rendering of the building. It is a pretty picture and usually includes clouds, trees, people, and cars and is usually colored. The purpose of the rendering is to give the customer a feel for what the building will look like from the outside. Additional renderings of areas within the building may show the appearance of significant interior components. The rendering is based on the specifications and on ideas that have been gathered from the customer's experience, taste and special needs. It may also require some alteration or amplification as the customer thinks about its implications.

The architect's rendering has its counterpart in the **external design** of the software, which describes exactly how the software will interact with its environment. The user interface, including the appearance of screens, the definition of command languages, the range of acceptable input, and so on, is one aspect of the external design. Similarly, the structure of permanent files used or created by the software is a matter of external design. In fact, the external design really starts during analysis, probably continues in parallel with, and as part of, the specifications, and may even extend into later design

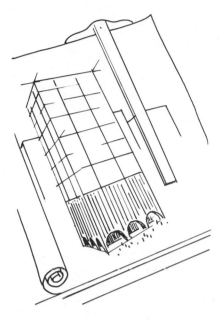

stages. It is generally important to avoid changes of the specifications after they are complete. However, if changes can be isolated to the external design, they may be tolerated and can actually be productive.

The architect would now proceed with a preliminary design. It shows the placement, relationship, and size of major areas and functions within the structure. For example, we have to decide the location of hallways, which rooms will share a common hallway, and what needs would be served by what parts of the building.

A software engineer also creates an **architectural (or preliminary) design** of a product. This design defines the general modular structure of the software, the functions provided by each module, and the internal datastreams and stores that make up the interface between modules. The software engineer, like the architect, must resist the temptation to include too much specific detail in the preliminary design. To do otherwise is to give up flexibility that is valuable at this point.

Finally, an architect must prepare (or more likely, have someone else prepare) a set of blueprints for the structure. Now the exact dimensions of each part of the structure, the placement of wall plates and door hinges, the thickness of walls, and many other details are added. Attention shifts from the conceptual structure with its interrelationships to the actual method of building it.

Software engineers carry out the **detailed design** of their product by specifying the algorithms and data structures that make up the interior of modules. Usually there are many choices possible, but choices that represent the greatest simplicity or efficiency or functionality or availability are selected, based on the relative importance of these criteria.

Besides the program design documents, the design stage should also result in (1) a user's manual, which is dependent on the external design; (2) an integration test plan, which depends on the architectural design; and (3) unit test plans, which depend on detailed design.

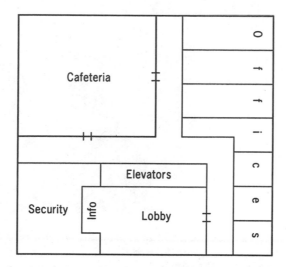

A team made up of carpenters, plumbers, electricians, and other specialists, as well as a number of unspecialized construction workers, will turn the blueprints into a reality.

The **implementation** of software is code, which amplifies the detailed design by a factor of 5 or 10 in volume. There are several issues in implementation that are independent of the specific details that must be coded. For instance, the choice of a programming language may have a significant effect on the ease with which the code is written. Standards for in-line documentation and control structures will significantly influence the ease with which the product is maintained. Optimization carried out on the code may be necessary to meet the specified performance constraints.

Another important part of implementation is that most products are meant to run in a variety of hardware and software configurations, requiring many different coded

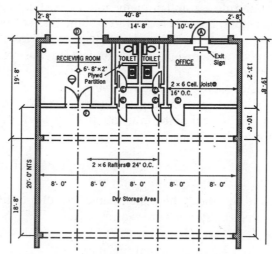

products. In order to produce a number of different implementations, the specifications and the design of the product should be as generic and portable as possible.

Beside the actual code, the implementation phase may again produce modifications of the specifications, design documentation, and unit tests to accommodate errors that have been detected. User documentation, in addition to the user's manual, will be produced. These include conversion plans for changing from whatever system is now in use to the new product, and training material to prepare personnel to use the new system.

When a construction worker frames up a wall, he makes sure that it is square, plumb, of the right dimensions, and in the right place. Local governments hire building inspectors, often with different specializations, who inspect a building, along with the architect, to approve plumbing or electrical or mechanical systems. Finally, the purchaser of a building is likely to make an acceptance tour, looking for evident defects in finish and completion.

Dependability is one of the most important attributes of good software. Good specification, design and implementation practices should reduce the number of errors in the product, but it is foolish to assume that software is perfect as coded. In most instances, testing to find and eliminate errors involves much more effort than the original coding. Refusal to accept this fact is a cause of project overruns and undependable software.

The **testing stage** goes beyond a simple effort of running a program with some input to see if it looks right. During earlier stages, a test plan must be put together, since it is too easy, in the heat of the moment, to gloss over errors. In fact, three different kinds of tests must be planned:

Unit tests, which investigate the correctness of individual modules and look for structural weaknesses in them;

Integration tests, where the interactions of modules and the functionality of integrated subsystems are examined; and

System and acceptance tests, which determine whether the final product complies with the user's original specifications.

Plans for these tests have to be created as soon as possible, and these plans include not only the data and actions to be used in testing, but also the acceptable responses of the software. Testing is carried out by those individuals responsible for the design and coding of the software as well as specially designated quality assurance personnel and representatives of the client.

The primary product of the testing stage is obviously the validated software product. Test results, however, are also very important. They will be used again as the software evolves during the next stage of its existence, to determine whether errors have been introduced into the product. Of course, a major activity of testing is the disclosure and correction of errors in the specifications, design and code; so all of the documentation produced by those stages will have to be altered in consequence of discovered faults.

Now it's time to move into the new building. Furnishings must be purchased or moved from another location. Last minute minor mismatches have to be hurriedly repaired. The power company must be informed that bills are to be sent to a new customer. Instruction on the use of elevators, heating and cooling systems, and appliances is required. The builder can sit back and evaluate what went wrong and how a bigger profit might have been obtained, while we begin to enjoy our new building...until we decide to remodel.

When software has been validated and accepted, it can be used. But first, **installation** is necessary at the customer's site. This may mean simply transporting files and manuals. However, it may be necessary to coordinate with the installation of new hardware as well. Often, some training effort will be needed beyond providing manuals to be read by client personnel. At this point, a rerun of the acceptance test may be needed to ensure that the software works as well in the client's environment as it did at the developer's.

After training, while the client organization **converts** from the previous system to the new one, the software organization has to maintain a high profile in support of their efforts. This is a critical time, when problems are bound to appear. Even if the software organization is not responsible for the difficulties, their software is sure to be blamed if they are unable to provide help. A reputation can be undeservedly lost during conversion.

It is often tempting for the development team to install the product and then try very quickly to forget it. However, a project **debriefing** process is vital to evaluate the successes and failures of the project. The purpose of the debriefing is to record what has been learned on the project in order to provide a basis for future efforts; this record is called a **project legacy**. Given the degree of job mobility among software engineers, it is not a good idea to assume that somebody will be around to remember.

It is also important the evaluate the development process at this time. The cause of both our successes and mistakes should be determined, and potential solutions to problems should be recorded. The development process itself should be assessed for its appropriateness and adequacy during the project ([HUM89]). The organization's database is also augmented with productivity and error rate information

The client will need support during the entire useful lifetime of the software. Naturally, the level of support and the effort involved decrease as the users become more expert and the client organization adapts to the new software. However, it is inevitable that problems will arise, requiring some modification of the product. Hopefully, the client will be sufficiently pleased with the work already done to pay for enhancements to the software.

This **maintenance** effort revisits all the other stages of the software life cycle in microcosm. Changes may be required to eliminate errors in the product, to provide additional capabilities or to allow the product to be used in a new environment. Each modification requires some planning, specification, design, coding, testing and installation. Some modifications may require very little effort at a given stage, but just as much attention must be given to correct methodology in maintenance as in the original development. Some changes, however, will involve so much effort that they amount to a new development project

Use of the term "life cycle" invites the question: "When does software die? As software's period of use lengthens, several things usually happen. First, the utility of the software decreases, either in absolute terms or relative to other available software. Second, repeated maintenance actions tend to complicate the original clean purpose and design of the product. Third, additional maintenance is made more expensive by this increased complexity, as well as by the departure of the original software team and the accelerating changes in the environment. As a rule of thumb, one expects a software product to be useful for at least another four years. When four additional years' worth of maintenance costs exceeds the cost of obtaining new software, then the revised product probably will not last long enough. It is time to start planning a new product and preparing to retire the old one.

## 1.1.4 Models of the Software Process

Most software development starts with an overall concept or mental model of the software development process. The model shapes and directs all our development activities. Figure 1-9 names some of the process models now being used. (Humphrey gives a formal notation for representing process models in [HUM89].)

We should understand that, even though we often talk about the software life cycle as if it *were* a predictable path from birth to death, we are really only speaking of common stages of development, without prescribing order or duration. In fact, an examination of various software engineering texts will show basic agreement about the names of these stages; but there is significant disagreement about the actual activities and products of each stage. Some different process models overlap stages, repeat them in a cycle, abbreviate them, or eliminate them altogether.

The **traditional (waterfall)** model ([ROY70]) (Figure 1-10) has held that software moves in an orderly way through each stage of its life. The software flows through a single, predetermined channel, pausing for a time in a stage, as in a pool, and then cascading inexorably into the next.

Traditional
Rapid prototyping
Program growth (incremental development)
Component reuse
Very high level (fourth or fifth generation) languages
Operational
Spiral

**FIGURE 1-9**   SOME SOFTWARE DEVELOPMENT PROCESS MODELS

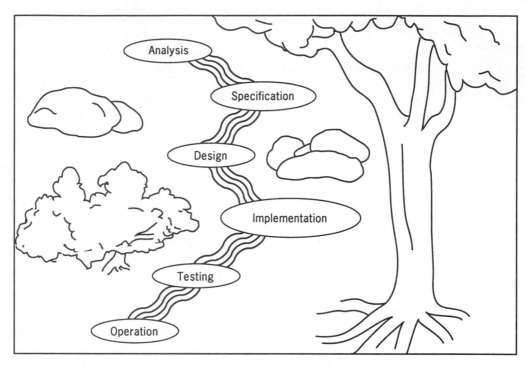

**FIGURE 1-10**  THE WATERFALL MODEL OF SOFTWARE DEVELOPMENT

The traditional waterfall model has been fertile and provides a particularly strong framework within which to develop large projects. But it also has a number of weaknesses: it does not support parallel activities well; it postpones any actual experience with the software until late in the game; it requires developers to work with software under several different guises (specifications, design, code); it puts a heavy burden of documentation preparation on developers; it does not support reuse well; it does not maintain user involvement throughout the process; and it does not support the developer's need to produce tangible results quickly.

A second process model, of considerable standing, is **rapid prototyping** ([MCC81]). In this method, a quick-and-dirty preliminary version of the software is developed, often reusing parts from other products, and making no attempt at efficiency, real accuracy or dependability. Some languages, like PROLOG, SETL, APL, and RAPID/ USE, seem to be particularly handy during the early stages of prototyping.

This first version of the software is evaluated by both the developers and the users, with the understanding that it is not a complete, final product. If the product appears to lack viability, it can be aborted at that point. If not, developers gain insight into the nature of the problem, experimenting with alternate solutions. Major interfaces can be probed. Users can sharpen their requirements and evaluate alternative solutions, communicating more easily with developers now that they have something tangible to point to. A second, or third, or as many interim versions of the product as may be needed can be developed in succession.

Each version comes closer to the efficient, accurate, complete and dependable final product. Users are involved throughout the process. Because of the feedback effect of each successive prototype's influence on the next, instead of the straight-line progress of the traditional model we travel along something more like a spiral. As we produce additional prototypes, we probably repeatedly pass through the life cycle stages of analysis, specification, design, implementation, and testing.

Prototyping, however, can be wasteful if we simply throw away each prototype after using it to gather information; and it can be sloppy if our quick-and-dirty software makes its way into the final product. Of course, as Mills says, with effort we can always make our software "quick-and-clean", by using a kind of experimental program growth model (see below). It is also hard to plan prototyped software to allow for future enhancements and interfacing to other, as yet unknown, software products. Prototyping works best in individual or small team projects, working with an interpretive language ([RUS88]).

Related to rapid prototyping is **program growth** or incremental development ([BRO87]) (Figure 1-12). Here the emphasis shifts slightly, from quick-and-dirty implementation of the bare bones of the whole project to a paced implementation of one part of the final product after another. Often, the user interface and high-level control structures are the first to be implemented. The user is thus able to evaluate the (for him) most important aspects of the product early in the development. Vital functions may at any time be represented simply by unavailable choices on a menu; but the customer has faith that they will eventually become available. Morale is certainly boosted by having some finished parts of the project early on. As time passes, the rest of the product is fleshed out.

Once again, we repeat life cycle stages many times with this model. It differs from prototyping in that each portion of the product passes through at least the design,

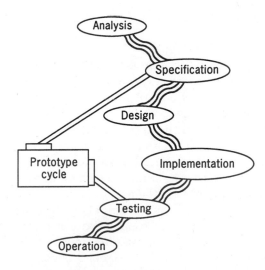

**FIGURE 1-11**   THE RAPID PROTOTYPING MODEL

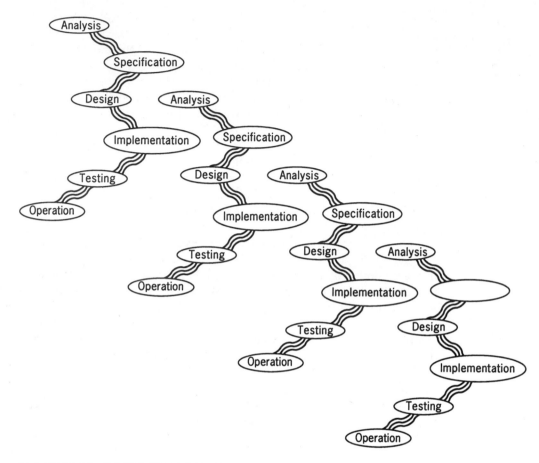

**FIGURE 1-12** THE PROGRAM GROWTH MODEL

implementation and testing stages only once, and in a traditional way. Of course, this requires a high degree of careful planning. Incremental development may suffer if there is a lack of adequate planning for the growth, since bad design decisions may become institutionalized early on in the development, only to make the rest of the growth much more difficult ([BOE88]). It is also difficult to switch methodologies or notations in the midst of an incremental development.

Program growth is basically a top-down and sideways activity, adding lower-level details and less important functions as time goes by. The bottom-up analogue is **reuse**, in which components of the product already exist and are integrated to satisfy the requirements of the software (Figure 1-13). In special cases, reuse may involve nothing more than fitting together existing code, using an interface or command language as glue. Reuse is usually the most economical method of creating new software. It also benefits from the higher dependability of components which have been previously tested and used. One big challenge is to interface the individual components in an

**FIGURE 1-13**   THE SOFTWARE REUSE MODEL

effective and reliable way; another is to make any needed modifications to individual components.

Some of the most impressive productivity gains of the last 40 years have come from the use of higher-level programming languages, which have allowed software developers to get more effect from less code and to free themselves of many of the nonessential details of their work ([BRO87]). **Very high level languages** (VHLL's) (Figure 1-14) and applications generators may represent a continuation of this trend. A single statement in these languages can provide the functionality of entire software modules in other languages. They are generally nonprocedural; that is, they are not based on the ability to state a sequence of operations; the programmer just defines the problem. By allowing him to concentrate on specifying what is to be done, rather than how, these languages reduce the amount of effort invested in the later stages of software life. Such languages usually have a direct interface to database management procedures. They are frequently accessible to end-users and represent a process that is often called "automatic programming" ([RIC88]). Among currently popular VHLLs are Focus, Oracle, Mantis, Ramis II, and dBase.

When VHLLs are applicable, they can improve productivity by a factor of ten ([MAR85]), mainly because they shrink the volume of work at the design, implementation, and testing stages. Unfortunately, at this stage they are restricted to clearly defined and well understood problem domains. They also tend to have low levels of performance ([MIS88]). Sometimes, however, they can surprise us; spreadsheet programs have many of the hallmarks of nonprocedural languages, but have been applied in a variety of unexpected ways.

The **operational** (Figure 1-15) process model ([ZAV84]) is somewhat similar to VHLLs. It concentrates on a careful and technical specification of the software, from an algorithmic, problem-oriented point of view, rather than an implementation one.

**F I G U R E 1-14**   THE VERY HIGH LEVEL LANGUAGE MODEL

Using the framework of the problem domain generally allows for a more logical and comprehensible set of requirements. Although specifications would be transformed into a design and code in a conventional development, the operational process model requires that the specifications themselves be executable. With this model, specification requires more effort, but the model provides quick results and allows earlier investigation of the product. When the specifications seem to be correct, they can be transformed into efficient code that is specific to a particular environment. Ideally, one effects these transformations as automatically as possible; in practice, they are done interactively by a software engineer using software tools.

The operational model's strengths are freedom from unnecessary detail, automatic generation of code, software portability and improved dependability. This last is because specifications are more comprehensible, closely tied to the original problem, and thus less susceptible to errors whereas transformations are carried out on the specifications by extensively tested and verified software tools. This process provides more flexibility in deciding which mechanisms, among many suitable candidates, will actually be utilized in the implementation. Finally, maintenance requires modification of the specifications with very little testing ([BAL83]). In the operational model we ideally omit the design, implementation, and testing stages. On the other hand, software reuse is not facilitated, and there is no real motivation to plan carefully. The operational model runs counter to the standard pattern of first describing "what" software does, and postponing definition of "how" as long as possible. Rather, an operational development starts right out with the "how".

Boehm recently presented a **spiral** model for software development([BOE88]). He claims that it will serve as a framework on which to hang most of the other process models mentioned in this section. As Figure 1-16 shows, development repeatedly cycles through the same stages:

- Investigate the problem and its possible solutions
- Evaluate the solutions and identify the risks.
- Resolve the risks through experimentation with a prototype.
- Develop and test the product of this cycle
- Plan for the next round of activity, including possible partition of personnel efforts or software function.
- Review the results of this round and obtain commitment to the plans for the next round.

The spiral model minimizes risk, by identifying uncertainty in the next stage and using prototypes of one kind or another to clarify the situation. It also reduces all development stages to a cycle of the four activities: set goals/constraints, evaluate and resolve risks, develop the product, and plan for the next stage. Thus, development becomes a repeated application of the same normalized activities to create increasingly complex preliminary versions of the final product. At each cycle, we may choose to conduct only those parts of the cycle which are actually needed, for instance omitting the prototypes or the simulations, models and benchmarks in Figure 1-16.

No matter which process model is chosen for development of a particular product, it will not, as Brooks points out ([BRO87]), be a silver bullet with which to slay the software crisis monster. In the end, talented and well-trained personnel are required for that. The best method for improving software productivity is probably to hire the most competent people and then support them fully within the framework of an acceptable methodology and process model. Of course, this pattern of depleting one organization to strengthen another will only produce localized success for selected managers.

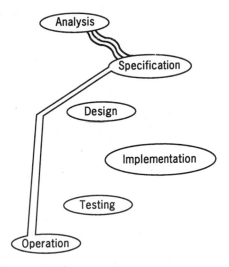

**FIGURE 1-15**   THE OPERATIONAL MODEL

## 1.1.5 Reducing the Inherent Risk of Software Development

There is no doubt that software development is a risky business. Because we work with very complex systems, and because most new products also break new ground, we never get to the point that we are working in a totally familiar environment. Mistakes can easily occur; in fact, most new software fails to achieve viability.

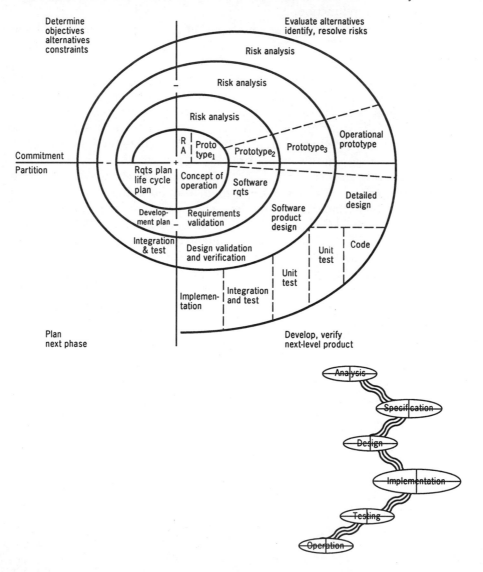

**F I G U R E 1-16**   THE SPIRAL PROCESS MODEL. (Barry Boehm, "A Spiral Model of Software Development and Enhancement," *Computer*, copyright © 1988 IEEE.)

We may add software reuse to the use of prototypes for gathering information, careful planning, and goal setting. Software reuse means that we are dealing with proven components with known characteristics and understood risk. These three principles together form the basis of the risk reduction model (Figure 1-17).

The risk of failure can be minimized in several ways:

1 Determine early in the development cycle whether the project has a chance to succeed, then quit if it does not.
2 Shift as much of the development cost as possible to the period after the success of the product is assured.
3 Obtain user input early in the design stage to avoid creating the wrong product.
4 Reduce development costs as much as possible while still guaranteeing that the product meets accepted levels of functionality, usability, dependability, efficiency, and maintainability.
5 Carry out development in such a way that the effort can be used in some future project as well as this one.
6 Speed the development process to get the software into use quickly, and thus acquire support from users. A product in development which already has an income is more secure than a nearly completed product with no income.
7 Survey initial product users, both verbally and through automatic profiling of their use of the product, to locate errors, bottlenecks and inadequacies in the product.

Notice that the first four suggestions can largely be implemented through prototyping, whereas suggestions 4 through 6 will be aided by the reuse of software components. It is particularly important to speed the arrival of the product in the marketplace. Commercial success often goes to one product rather than to a competitor simply because it arrived a few months earlier. The longer a product remains in development, the greater the risk of discouragement or boredom on the part of the team, and of disillusionment on the part of management. Long-lasting projects also begin to suffer from the disasters of resignation, retirement, reassignment, illness, and death.

Boehm proposes risk analysis as the unifying principle of his spiral model of the software process ([BOE88]). In this model, risk analysis depends on an exploration of

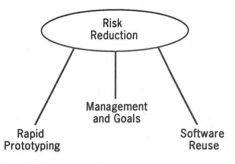

**FIGURE 1-17**  SUPPORTS FOR RISK REDUCTION

the feasibility of this stage of development. Each alternative path that we might follow is explored through prototyping, and the path combining least risk and best potential payoff is chosen. Risks are continually considered throughout the development process, so that there are no unpleasant surprises at the end. The techniques of risk analysis will be discussed in Section 2.2

### 1.1.6 Realism in the Process

"Pragmatic" means "practical, matter-of-fact" and is sometimes used in contrast to "theoretical." The reason for using the word here is to emphasize that in the real world, software is developed to be used, not for practice in or insight about the development process itself. Software engineering specialists occasionally concentrate more on the best process than the best product.

The pragmatic approach is characterized by a practical attitude: one does what works best. In the past, this kind of outlook has been condemned, since it may degenerate into temporary expediency. Indeed, bowing to the demands of the moment at the expense of long-term optimization is wrong. But it is just as wrong to set out looking for the ultimate piece of software, the conclusive machine built of gold-plated components, which will be all things to all people. Instead, one should think clearly about a product, analyze the real needs and wants of the user, and pursue a middle course between building for the moment and building for the eternities.

Beside this attitude, the pragmatic approach is distinguished by certain practices: reuse of software components, rapid prototyping of initial versions of the product, risk analysis and minimization procedures, and use of small development teams. When a very large product must be developed, the pragmatic manager recognizes its special needs and provides ample time for the significant level of learning and communication needed to work in such a context ([CUR88]). Large projects also require managers and technical people to exhibit a great deal of flexibility in negotiating with other groups, organization management, and an often fragmented mass of customer representatives.

Above all, pragmatism looks at the bottom line — profit. Among the factors that govern the profitability of software, Milne and Weber enumerate the following ([MIL83]):

- Demand for the product.
- The existence of strong competing products.
- Production costs.
- The timing of the product's entry into the marketplace.
- Protection of the product from unauthorized copying.
- The level of service the product gives.
- The degree of liability the software may incur.
- The level of customers' awareness of their own needs.

With such an array of influences, real management skills in planning and control are needed to make money.

The rationale behind the pragmatic approach is the recognition that the majority of software fails. Of course, failure comes in many packages: it was never finished; it did not work; it was not what the user wanted; it was not efficient or dependable, it was not a commercial success. Whatever the root of the problem, no one wants to spend time working on a project that is going to fail. Thus, we are faced with a dilemma: on the one hand, we cannot be in business if we do not undertake projects; on the other, failure is more likely than success. The most rational approach is to accept and minimize the risk, but at the same time minimize the cost, of failure.

### 1.1.7 Improving Productivity

The fundamental means of increasing profits is improving productivity — if each person produces twice as much this year as last, profits will nearly double. The trick, of course, is to enable each worker to produce twice as much. There are two ways of doing so. First, each worker can deliver twice as much software. An Institute of Electrical and Electronics Engineers (IEEE) workshop on productivity observed ([MUN81]):

> *[M]ajor increases in productivity for software engineering will come about only through elimination of the number of skilled man-hours required to produce new software. This reduction can occur by:*

(a) Reducing the cost of each step in the development/maintenance life cycle,

(b) Eliminating the need for a step in the life cycle,

(c) Reducing the number of iterations back through life cycle steps, or

(d) Reducing the cost of the impact of requirements changes. (see Figure 1-18.)

If we care to measure productivity in dollars, a second way of increasing productivity is not covered by these suggestions: increasing sales volume. The first copy of a software product is very expensive, but additional copies can be produced at low cost. Thus, if we can sell a million copies of a product instead of five, we are usually able to increase our profit. Hence, increased sales volume could be added as point e) in the foregoing quote.

Boehm and Standish in [BOE83] suggest a set of productivity initiatives ranging through tools, methodology, environments, education, management, incentives, and reuse. Davis et al. point out that individual productivity is the result, not only of aptitude and experience, but also of motivation ([CUR88]). Some suggestions appear elsewhere in this chapter for implementing these initiatives.

There seems to be general agreement among researchers that the productivity variation between the best and worst performance by software engineers is of the order of 5:1 ( e.g., [BOE87]). Some authors, like Mills in [MIL81] say they see a 10:1 difference between the best and worst. But, in specific circumstances, this ratio can become much more striking. For instance, a study by Sackman and others ([SAC68]) found that in some areas of effort, such as time to debug a given program, the variation was 28:1; and that overall variations of 16:1 were observed. Another source ([EVA83]) suggests that,

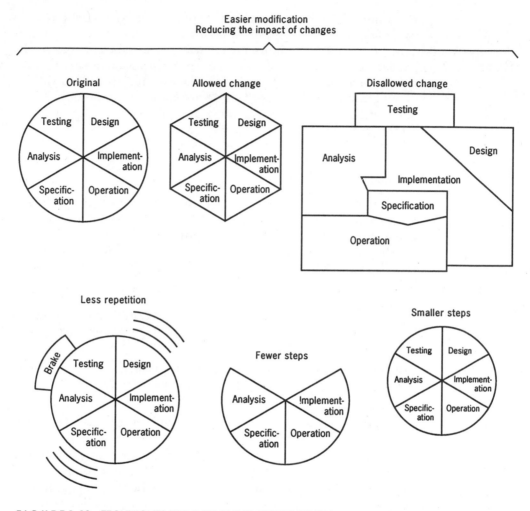

**FIGURE 1-18**   TECHNIQUES FOR IMPROVING PRODUCTIVITY

averaging over the lifetime of a project, individuals may be found to produce anything between 3 and 50 lines of code per day — again, a 16:1 productivity ratio.

Whether one aims for a 5:1 or 16:1 improvement, the profit payoff will be impressive. The trick is to identify those aspects of the entire development and maintenance process that will contribute most to that improvement, and then concentrate first with a major investment in them. Other, less impressive gains can be obtained later. To guide this decision, Boehm suggests the "opportunity tree" shown in Figure 1-19.

At a more abstract level, Mills ([MIL81]) enumerates the 10 nonnumeric indicators of software organization quality and productivity shown in Figure 1-20.

Recently, Boehm, Jones, and Brooks have all addressed the question of improving software productivity in [BOE87], [JON86] and [BRO87]. Their conclusions support each other in suggesting the following keys to improved productivity:

1 Productivity can be increased by developing software that will provide the same functionality and require the production of fewer DSI (delivered source instructions, i.e., lines of code). This can be done by: reusing existing software; eliminating "gold plating" (code that does not contribute to functionality); and programming in the highest level language available.

2 Productivity can be increased by using the best software engineers. They should be experienced, capable, and well educated. Even though their salaries will be higher, their increased production will outweigh increased labor costs. Of course, less experienced personnel must also be included in the organization as the foundation of future growth. Their efforts to improve should be encouraged by training, a good working environment, rewards for achievement, and judicious supervision.

3 Productivity can be increased by reducing the effort required at each stage of the life cycle, or possibly by eliminating a stage entirely. This can be done by the use of automation in the form of software tools.

4 Productivity can be increased by reducing the amount of rework, in which we iterate the stages of the life cycle. This follows in large part from quality assurance and from the selection and use of the most powerful methodologies for the circumstances.

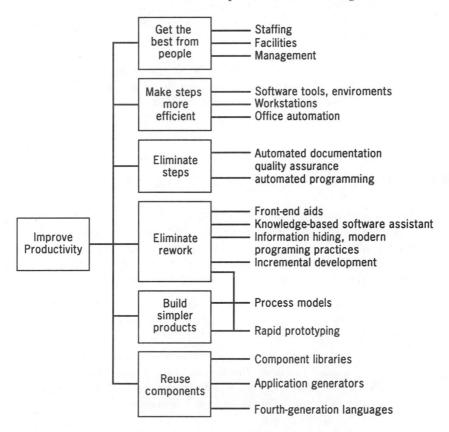

**F I G U R E 1-19**   OPPORTUNITY TREE FOR PRODUCTIVITY INCREASE. (Barry Boehm, "Improving Software Productivity," *Computer*, copyright © 1987, IEEE.)

1 Control over budget and schedule.

2 Use of good methodologies.

3 Employment of educated and experienced software engineers.

4 Their work looks easy because they are organized.

5 Low personnel turnover.

6 The ideas and viewpoints of the software engineers are valued and welcomed in nontechnical decisions.

7 Work is viewed as a profession, not a recreation.

8 Reuse of software is high.

9 Rework of material due to errors and shortsightedness is infrequent.

10 When challenged, the technical people respond by working smarter, not harder.

**F I G U R E 1-20**   INDICATORS OF PRODUCTIVE SOFTWARE ORGANIZATIONS

In all fairness, a survey reported in *Computer* magazine ([CAR80]) indicated that data processing shop managers experienced relatively little productivity increase as a result of these steps. Card et al. found that experience was the primary driver of increased productivity, and that tools and methodology had minimal impact. However, this may be the result of partial, inexpert, or half-hearted use of tools and methodology.

One final productivity suggestion often appears in the literature. We should free software engineers from unnecessary communication burdens and interruptions. Memos, staff meetings, and documentation can get out of hand. When this happens, an incredible amount of time can be consumed with very little to show for it. The solution to this problem lies in team organization, and will be discussed in Chapter 2.

## 1.2 METHODOLOGIES FOR EFFECTIVE SOFTWARE ENGINEERING

The word **methodology** means "a body of knowledge and techniques." Of course, there are many different methodologies in software engineering, each of which has its own partisans. In addition, individual techniques often go by the name "methodology." It is important to recognize some additional facts about software engineering methodologies (see Figure 1-21). A methodology should be

*Effective*   The methodology should work, should do the job that is intended, and should be economical in its use of intellect, time, equipment, money, and other resources.

*Rational*   The methodology should have a scientific foundation which has been experimentally verified. There should also be an overriding philosophy that unifies the techniques of the methodology, as well as a set of clear models (e.g., of the development process, of software structure, of software team interaction, and the like.)

*Consistent*   Individual techniques should be consistent within themselves should fit together smoothly so that the entire development process can flow from one stage to another without the need of major cutting and piecing.

*Complete*   There should be methods for successfully dealing with all the tasks inherent in software development.

*Replicable*   It should be possible for any software engineer to undertake the same task and come up with substantially the same results. The techniques and knowledge base of the methodology should be clearly and understandably stated. It should be possible to replace personnel by other qualified personnel during the development, without the need for major revision of work that is already completed.

*Automatable*   The methodology should lend itself to implementation through computerized tools, which can improve the productivity of the software engineer through improved speed, access to data, storage capacity, and representational flexibility.

Obviously, a methodology *should* be a lot of things. It is not a disgrace that no one has come up with one that meets all these criteria. This book certainly does not. These goals are being approached and are the constant aim of many practitioners and researchers in the field, but this effort is not universal and may not even be the norm. A survey ([ZEL84]) has indicated that between 1981 and 1983 that there was no widespread use of tools and methodologies which were known to be effective at the time. This bolsters the argument for improvement in the transfer of technology to the practicing software engineer.

A methodology is usually fairly restricted in its application. It may show us how to design, or test, or specify software. It may allow us to estimate the size of a product, or evaluate its degree of progress. It can form the framework within which we control software configurations or communicate with each other. Methodologies should be algorithmic, in the sense that they furnish rules for achieving their desired results. Thus, they allow work to be done quickly and surely, with relatively predictable consequences.

The task for which the most new methodologies are presented is the design of software. This topic forms the basis of Chapter 6, but it may be of interest to list some of the methodologies here, following Hailpern in [HAI86]. His point was that different methodologies are more productive when matched with languages that support them

Effective.

Rational.

Consistent.

Complete.

Replicable.

Automatable.

**FIGURE 1-21**   DESIRABLE TRAITS OF ANY METHODOLOGY

Access-oriented design.
Data-structure-oriented design.
Data flow design.
Functional design.
Imperative design.
Object-oriented design.
Parallel design.
Real-time design.
Rules-oriented design.

**F I G U R E 1-22**   SEVERAL DESIGN PARADIGMS

well. However, many methodologies can be used to code a variety of applications in a variety of languages. The word "paradigm" is frequently used in this context to mean a pattern or model for design. Figure 1-22 lists some of the different design paradigms.

New methodologies are constantly being presented to the software engineering community. Most presentations tend to be so sketchy that it is impossible to derive from them a concrete set of steps to follow. Others have limited application, within which they work well, but outside which they are less useful. It is also important to recognize that even the best methodology might not be appropriate at the moment. It might not match the needs of the project or the skills of the software engineers. Even if it does, the introduction of a novel methodology requires an investment of time and money and creates a sharp break with the past. The appropriate moment for cutting over to a new system has to be carefully chosen so as not to disrupt the software organization's activities.

Even though it is difficult to come up with a better way of carrying out any of the development tasks, it may be that the most important benefit comes from simply accepting the discipline of *any* reasonable methodology. To be methodical is essential for the practice of science. The following sections describe general areas where methodologies can be incorporated profitably.

## 1.2.1 Software Maintenance

Software engineers like to think that the major part of their work is the development of original software products. This is not true. In 1980, Lientz ([LIE80]) estimated that over one half the budget for a software product was spent on activities following its first release, whereas by 1985, Fairley ([FAI85]) believed that maintenance frequently consumed 70% of the software budget. Some published estimates go as high as 82%.

The tremendous effort expended on maintenance is, in part, the inevitable result of years of unmethodical and unplanned programming. Elshoff and Marcotty state that "...most data processing installations still have large inventories of programs that are nearly impossible to read" ([ELS82]), whereas a recent study of commercial COBOL code made by Peat Marwick indicated that 80% of the code was unstructured ([GIB89]).

Unreadable, unstructured code puts a tremendous burden on the maintenance worker.

Software engineers tend to minimize the importance of maintenance. Maintenance is less creative than development, and usually deals with problems. Users are often equally naïve, thinking that the first version of software they acquire will be perfect. This "faith" sometimes results in an overcommitment to new software without planning for the equal or greater commitment needed to keep it functional for the following 10 years or so.

Shemer ([SHE87]) estimates that 55% of all software errors must be corrected during the maintenance period. Since the cost of fixing an error at that point is 50 to 100 times as high as fixing it during the specifications stage ([BOE81]), maintenance is no time for casual or haphazard efforts.

## 1.2.2 Software Component Reuse

During the past 40 years, computer hardware has been improved to a degree that no one would have believed possible. Some components may be on the order of a million times smaller, cheaper, or faster. Software has been improved also, but not to that degree, and so it suffers in comparison to hardware. "Why can't software be like hardware?" is the nagging question in the back of many minds.

One factor in the tremendous progress of hardware design and manufacture is the reuse of previously developed components in new systems. This is most obvious in the case of integrated circuits, which have been carefully designed to carry out generally useful tasks, and can be easily plugged into a socket. If the rest of the electronic design accommodates the integrated circuit, no further effort is required.

Some steps have been taken toward the development of reusable software "chips." First, the development of libraries of reusable software components has been markedly successful in areas where the tasks are standard and well defined. Mathematical, statistical, and graphics libraries are good examples. Second, there are methodologies for the initial design of software that enhance the likelihood that it can be used again. Third, automated tools are now being developed that permit a potential user to scan through a library looking for useful software components. These tools also facilitate the modification of components to allow their use in a new setting.

However, current practice lags behind theory. The main problem is a feeling that each software use should adapt to a unique set of circumstances. Software is called "soft" rather than hard because it is viewed as being flexible. It is expected to fill the interface between the rigid design of hardware and the unyielding demands of the user environment. This demand for flexibility on the part of software may be counterproductive in the long run, but it is a fundamental aspect of the current computing culture. It certainly works against easy reuse of software components. We are still in the craft stage of professional evolution — each product is unique. Some change is being seen in the willingness of users to adapt themselves to mass marketed, packaged software for personal computers. If this trend continues, we may be able to advance into the industrial age with reusable design for cheaply duplicated parts.

Brooks ([BRO87]) claims that reuse of software components is one of two or three techniques that have any hope of improving software productivity to the same degree

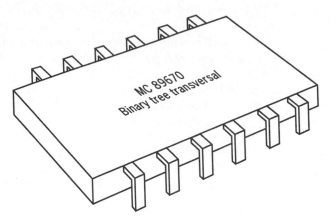

**FIGURE 1-23**   A SOFTWARE COMPONENT

that semiconductor technologies have improved hardware productivity. Reuse allows us to apply the insight of software engineers with a specialized understanding of a particular problem. As an added bonus, software reuse improves software dependability, for two reasons. First, software is, in part, validated by use; the longer and more wide-spread the use, the more likely that faults will have been detected and eliminated. Second, one of the big stumbling blocks to high dependability is cost. However, that high cost can be shared by many different software products through reuse of the dependable component (Figure 1-23).

Figure 1-24 lists some of the characteristics of well-designed reusable software components, drawn from [RAM86]. The term "software components" is somewhat ambiguous. Traditionally, one reuses a code module or subprogram of some kind. But one of the insights we have gained is that we may be able to reuse any of the work products generated during software development: concepts, plans, specifications, designs, code, test cases, or documentation. In fact, the biggest leverage will be obtained by reusing a component in as early a stage of the life cycle as possible. A second insight is that code reuse may be more efficient when the code is *not* packaged as an invoked subprogram.

We may reuse components in at least three ways. First, in the toolkit or application generator approach, existing components are put together by means of a command language. The generality of this approach usually works against efficiency, but such reuse may be invaluable in an early prototype, say during the specification or design stages. Second, as we proceed with design of the final product, we may be able to use

*General*: this component is widely needed.

*Portable*: it can be used in many different environments.

*Standard*: interface and dependencies allow integration.

*Documented*: function, effects, and dependencies visible.

*Parameterized*: automatic modification is possible.

**FIGURE 1-24**   QUALITIES OF REUSABLE COMPONENTS

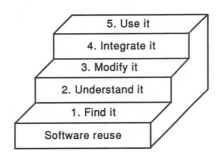

**F I G U R E 1-25**   STEPS IN SOFTWARE REUSE

the approaches or ideas of a previous design, modifying them to our current need. Finally, we may simply insert a code component with satisfactory performance characteristics into our implementation.

Biggerstaff and Richter in [BIG87] outline four tasks in traditional reuse: find the component, understand it, modify it to suit current needs, and incorporate it into the product. An inadequate methodology has, up to this point, inhibited optimal execution of these tasks (Figure 1-25).

Additional problems in reuse are the initial investment required to build up a stock of reusable components, the temptation to design software for the moment rather than for reuse (usually in response to deadline pressure), and the software engineer's fear of modifying some vital, but mysterious, part of the component.

The first task — *finding* the right component — benefits from an automated component library with an effective classification scheme. The automation should provide two functions: first, the user should be able to describe the desired component characteristics and depend on the library to select those candidates that most closely conform to the description. The actual metric used to define closeness depends on the classification scheme, as well as weights that can be assigned and tuned by the software engineer. Prieto-Diaz and Freeman have suggested a scheme based on the classifications shown in Figure 1-26 ([PRI87]). The second task of the library is to allow the software engineer to browse through the components in some intelligent fashion.

Having found one or more candidates for reuse, the software engineer now must decide which, if any, will be incorporated into the product. The following criteria, from Prieto-Diaz and Freeman [PRI87] and Tracz [TRA87], can be used in the decision:

* Does the component have the basic features that are needed?
* Is the component sufficiently small and simple that it can be used without great cost?
* Can the component be integrated easily into the product?
* Does the component (as well as its author) have a good track record for dependability?
* Is the documentation of the component good enough to be able to work with it?
* Can the component be modified easily to include new features or exclude unwanted features?

- Is the original author available (and willing) to help if needed?
- Does it appear that the cost of component understanding and modification is less than the cost of building a new component from scratch?

If one decides to go ahead with the reusable component, then it may be necessary to *understand* it fully before an attempt is made to modify it. This task will be easier for a small, simple, well documented component. In place of full understanding, we might use parameterization. In this technique, we abstract the basic function of the component, isolate and identify those aspects that are likely to vary from use to use, and provide an easy technique for the software engineer to substitute his own variable requirements for these parameters. In the words of Bassett ([BAS87]):

> Programs are variations on themes that recur again and again. A software-engineering frame is a model solution to a class of related programming problems containing predefined engineering change points.

*Modifying* the product is also easier when it is simple, small, well documented, and especially if it is parameterized, since we need only instantiate the parameter, that is, substitute new values for the parameter. Another aid to modification is the use of typed comments, that tag possible change points or segments of the component which can be extracted. Both parameterized and tagged components can be processed interactively, with the library system supporting the modification effort.

*Incorporation* often depends most on the use of predefined standard interfaces that will allow components to mesh together easily. It has been suggested that the effort of meshing components is great, and so reuse at the subroutine level makes us work on too small a scale for too little advantage. According to this argument, the real benefits of reuse will be seen when larger components, for instance, on the scale of an entire user interface, are incorporated. In addition, macro inclusion of the code, as opposed to the invocation of subroutines, provides faster performance (at the expense of space) ([LEN87]).

The foregoing comments all pertain to standard reuse techniques. There are two other methods for reuse: generating applications and transforming specifications. In the first case, the user feeds certain parameters and descriptions to the application generator, which then reuses the code stored with the generator itself to integrate the

- Function: what the component does.
- Object: what it acts upon.
- Medium: the supporting structures that hold the objects.
- System type: for example, database, compiler, scheduler.
- Functional area: application, like accounts payable.
- Setting: user organization, like advertising or auto shop.

**FIGURE 1-26**  REUSABLE COMPONENT CLASSIFICATION SCHEME

application. In the second case, methods of transforming specifications into designs and code are reused. This is discussed in Chapter 4.

### 1.2.3 Prototyping Software Products

Rapid prototyping is frequently proposed as the solution to many of the problems that arise from an unthinking selection of the traditional process model. The term is often used to describe aspects of the rapid prototyping, program growth, VHHL and operational models. In the minds of some software engineers, it is the hallmark of the new (i.e., nonstodgy) software engineering. Rapid prototyping is particularly responsive to situations that involve a significant degree of uncertainty. Prototype software can be used to validate specifications, since a user can view the prototype's action and determine whether it seems to be doing the right thing. In some cases, the prototype may provide a specification by example. In fact, there are two different specification problems that can be resolved by prototyping: we may not understand the customer's requirements, or the customer may not be sure of them either. (See Figure 1-27.).

With any ill-understood problem, there is a strong possibility that the first set of specifications will be wrong and that the more firmly we hold to them, the worse off we will be. Humphrey refers to this a the "law of software perversity" in [HUM89]. Prototyping provides a way of working from that part of the specification that we do understand to the part we have yet to learn, embodying the specifications in an executable form to evaluate and expanding them.

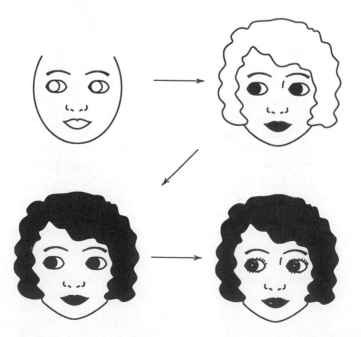

**F I G U R E 1-27**   RAPID PROTOTYPING CONVERGES ON THE END RESULT

Exploratory programming is a variant of prototyping in which the prototype becomes the product. It is used in circumstances where fixed specifications will never become available, and where a determination of feasibility is more important than abstract correctness. Exploratory programming is frequently used in expert systems applications.

A prototype can also be used to investigate the appropriateness of a major design decision, before we commit completely to the decision. Prototypes allow us to concentrate on the essentials of design without becoming enmeshed in the full complexity of a complete product. We frequently use prototypes that ignore exact formatting requirements, difficult processing cases, and exception handling.

Prototyping is most easily done in an interpretive system where reusable components can be put together quickly. UNIX tools are often given as the typical example. A more effective environment is one in which specifications can be directly interpreted and executed. Of course, efficiency is likely to be very low in such a situation, but remember that we are working with a prototype, not the end product. These specification transformation systems are hard to find, but very high level languages represent nearly the same capability so far as prototyping is concerned.

Each tool or environmental capability can add more speed to the prototyping cycle. This is worthwhile even when the particular tool or capability may not be available in the ultimate target environment. The specialized capability that helped speed up development can always be replaced by custom-built components in the final software. Any design or testing technique that supports ease of maintenance will also speed up the cycle. Luqi suggests that data-oriented design techniques are useful, since data structure is typically more stable than the algorithms used to process it ([LUQ89]). This promotes easier reuse of software components between prototypes. Object-oriented design has this characteristic, and also facilitates reuse through inheritance.

Boehm claims that there are a number of benefits of prototyping in [BOE84]. First, by concentrating on the essentials, we are able to avoid "gold-plating" our software. That is, we avoid the expense of complex and costly options that might seem theoretically desirable, but which experimentation with the prototype shows to be of little use. Second, most software engineers find it easier to design on the basis of an existing prototype rather than an abstract specification. Third, with a working version of the product in hand, we may postpone the decision on how much optimization to apply to our design and implementation until actual experience has pointed out the bottlenecks in the prototype. Those bottlenecks are frequently not where we expect them to be initially. Finally, prototyped software tends to be smaller and cheaper.

Of course, there are also some problems with software that has been prototyped. Boehm indicates that it is often less functional and robust. Of greater concern is the fact that prototyped software may not demonstrate coherence, or conceptual unity of the entire product. In this situation, the maintainability of the product may suffer. Alavi mentions that as a process model, prototyping is more effective for small than large products, and that its open-ended nature requires us to predetermine time and cost limits ([ALA84]).

Brooks suggests in [BRO75] that we should always build two versions of a product—one to throw away, that shows us how it *should* be done, and one to sell. Hoare [HOA87] said that prototyping represents an extension of this idea:

...it is advisable to throw away such models after use. The overriding need for rapid implementation gives scope for the talents of an experienced hacker rather than the formal precision of an engineer, and it is unlikely that the model can be taken as the basis or framework for subsequent development of the delivered product.

This comment is too severe, but it makes a good point. Our final version must be a well-constructed product that has the benefit of every good software engineering technique. The particular requirements of the product may allow us to use something less than the most elegant or most efficient or most dependable components. But these decisions should be made consciously, not simply because we already have something that works pretty well and we are too lazy to improve on it. Prototypes may be of the rapid, exploratory type and can point the way to the best design of the ultimate product. This is their principal usefulness.

## 1.2.4 Controlling Software Products

One of the most persistent causes of failure in software engineering is modifying the requirements after completing work that has been based on the requirements. It is necessary to freeze the requirements (and all other baseline) documents at some point, to provide a fixed, rather than fluid, foundation on which to build the remaining work products. These requirements then become the standard for further development. However, the challenges of **product control** go well beyond this.

There is an apparent contradiction between the concept of having a baselined, stable specification and conducting the kind of exploratory development encouraged by rapid prototyping. However, it is important to realize that every stage of every successful software product's development will be repeated several times; in particular, each of the designs should depend on a stable specification *for that cycle*. The fact that there will be other cycles with altered or amplified specifications does not detract from the need for freezing the specifications for this particular cycle.

The product control process is one of the ongoing tasks of software engineering and is often called "configuration management." The products to be managed fall into categories like analysis results, plans, specifications, designs, code, test plans and results, user documentation, and change requests. These documents show a high degree of logical interdependence. There must be a procedure for verifying that design corresponds to specification, that code corresponds to design, and that test results correspond to test plans.

However, at any given time these work products may exist in many forms, as they are being elaborated or modified by individual team members. Thus, the challenge grows: maintain different versions of the product in individual work spaces, but also distinguish an official project version of the work product (baseline) that can only be modified with authorization. If modifications are made to any work product, we must verify that all products depending on it undergo corresponding modifications. We must keep careful track of these modifications, perhaps archiving older baseline documents and certainly documenting the reason for and nature of any modifications (Figure 1-28).

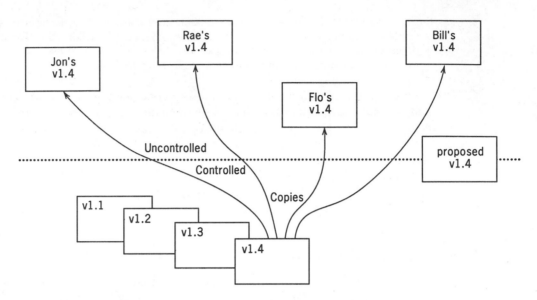

**FIGURE 1-28** CONFIGURATION CONTROL

In fact, the problem is still more complex. The eventual software product will probably be sold for execution on many different hardware configurations, running under different operating systems, and perhaps providing different functionality to its various users. Hence, we must either control many baseline versions of each work product, or provide a reliable and easy way of generating different versions of the products from a single set of baseline documents.

The end result is that there can be hundreds or thousands of different work products in current use by the software team. It is necessary to charge a team member with the responsibility for controlling all the different work products. It is also advisable to obtain a software tool that will automate much of the control process. Finally, a project needs a good message or electronic mail system, together with a framework to encourage reporting and discussion of activities between team members.

Organizations that solve the control problem for work products are able to apply a great deal of financial leverage by tailoring their software to a multitude of users and by reusing previous products in an efficient way. These organizations further avoid wasted time and effort, duplication of effort, and a host of errors caused by mismatched components or lost or incomplete modifications. Control of work products is really a key to software success.

## 1.2.5 Tools and Environments for Software Engineering

Belady observed that software engineers tend to ignore their own advice to the world ([MYE85]):

Although our salaries come from telling other people how to use computers, we have not learned to use the computer to support our own complex activities. One way of attacking the productivity problem is to look for activities that are done by software engineers, but could be done by computer.

This unwillingness to automate our own activities is gradually giving way to an appreciation of the value of available **software tools** and environments. We are still far from that goal. Our tools have tended to be narrow in their application in three ways: First, tools can be used in a very limited portion of the life cycle; second, they restrict their users to a single technique; and third, they lack portability to new hardware and applications. In addition, some widely used tools are not yet automated but exist only as forms and paper notations.

Many benefits can be gained from the use of software development tools:

* Good tools will improve productivity, at least doubling it, perhaps by as much as a factor of 7 ([MYE87]).
* Well-designed tools can serve the entire development and maintenance team, sometimes being used in unexpected but highly productive ways.
* Aside from actual increases in power and speed, tools may make a software engineer's job more enjoyable.
* By assuming the burden of the mechanical tracking of details, tools should reduce errors and improve software quality.
* Using tools should submit work products to better control and higher visibility and should provide a medium for communication and learning throughout the software team.

Tools may be able to speed up our work by making data available more widely and more quickly and presenting and processing data in formats more closely suited to the way people think. This added convenience represents much of the productivity gain we can currently expect from automation, since few tools carry out massive amounts of processing. Another benefit of tools is the chance to encourage use of new methodologies, rather than allowing the software engineer to continue using techniques that are familiar but suboptimal.

Of course, there are costs involved in the use of software development tools. A decision to use tools involves a high initial investment, and the tools do not pay for themselves for some time. Tool users need to spend time learning to operate them effectively. Without careful planning and preparation, tool introduction can throw an ongoing project into chaos. Finally, even the best tools tend to direct users into a specific methodology, which might not be the most appropriate for a given application.

Many of the earlier software tools tended to be analytical in nature. That is, they were used to provide insight into existing designs or code. Our current need is to use tools to help with the synthesis, or building, of software. (One of the most commonly used and most effective tools, — the compiler — is synthetic.) A tremendous number of software tools are referred to in the literature. Some are of marginal interest, and some have very limited application. Software engineers have concentrated too much on tools of limited application; instead, they need to provide tools that are independent of specific life-cycle stages ([RAM86]). These tools should focus especially on information abstraction and complexity reduction. The result would be an increased manageability of software products at all stages of development.

Of course, there are many tools available in the commercial market, only some of which would be useful on a given project. Firth et al. ([FIR87]) give a checklist for deciding whether a given tool should be employed . Is the tool easy to use (tailorable, helpful, predictable, dependable, integratable)? Is the tool powerful (capable, work saving, storing state, fast)? Is the tool robust (consistent, flexible, dependable, easy to debug)? Is the tool functional (complete for methodology, correct)? Is the tool easy to integrate (learning, into environment)? Is the tool well-supported (good track record, maintenance, training and documentation)?

The tools listed in Figures 1-29 to 1-35 all seem to have proved their worth in actual use. For most of them, we defer discussion of their nature and application until they are discussed in Chapters 3 to 9. The tools that, in some sense, represent the minimal set are marked in Figures 1-29 through 1-35 by an asterisk. The division of tools into different stages in the tables is somewhat artificial. In particular, design, implementation, and testing tools can often cross over each other's boundaries.

Three of the tools in Figure 1-29 need some explanation. The software project database system is the mechanism that transports the product from inception to

* Operating software.
* Software project database system.
* Text editor.
    Spelling checker.
    Thesaurus.
    Style analyzer.
    Table of contents and index generator.
* Electronic mail system.
* Data dictionary manager.
Windowing system.
Graphics editor.
Toolboxes.
    Graphics.
    Database.
    Mathematics and statistics.
    Expert systems.
    Natural language processing
Formatter/typesetter.
Screen history scribe.
Outline editor.

**F I G U R E 1-29**   GENERAL TOOLS WHICH ARE USEFUL IN ALL LIFE CYCLES

* Cost estimation system.
* Organization's historical database.
* Project scheduler.
Spreadsheet software.

**F I G U R E 1-30**   TOOLS THAT ARE USEFUL DURING THE ANALYSIS STAGE

completion. The objects manipulated by the system are software, where each software entity is seen as a single object in various forms (specification, design, etc). This view of software promotes our ability to trace requirements smoothly from the initial to the final stages of the product. It also allows the product to be seen in full visibility by the entire software team.

The data dictionary manager is a subset capability of the project database system. It allows us to define individual and composite data entities, specify their attributes, and trace them through the entire project, while correlating access, interpretation, use and modification of these entities by different parts of the software. Along with the project database and the electronic mail system, this tools allows really large software teams to maintain communication and coordination.

A screen history scribe allows us to capture a faithful history of any interaction between the computer system and the software engineer. It may be used to document activities, register important events and record scripts of activities to be replayed later.

## 1.2.6 Software Development Environments

A software engineer's environment is the surroundings in which he works. Software engineers are surrounded by hardware, software and an organization, and each of these elements can create more or less productivity. Relatively modest investments can improve the quality of the environment and pay back handsome dividends in increased efficiency and capability.

The 1990s will be a decade in which there will be a large increase in the number and range of tools available to software engineers. Some of these tools will be created for the

Formal specification language and editor.
Specification consistency checker.
Specification completeness checker.
Specification transform system.
Applications generator.
Library of reusable specifications.
Prototyping language.
Specifications executor.
* Cross-reference generator.

**F I G U R E 1-31**   TOOLS THAT ARE USEFUL DURING THE SPECIFICATION STAGE

computer-aided design of software. Other tools will provide automatic retrieval and adaptation of reusable software modules from large libraries. Additional tools will implement many of the planning and other management tasks that are of secondary interest to most software people.

Just as we have repeatedly heard the claim in recent years that every worker must know how to use computers, we will find that top-flight software engineers will have to know how to use computers even more. It is debatable whether automation can take over the most important tasks of the software engineer, especially conceptualization, which Brooks states is central to our role. Brooks ([BRO87]) and Parnas ([PAR85]) are

* Formal design language and editor.
* Library of reusable designs code.
Module interface verifier.
Modularity analyzer.
Design language interpreter handling incomplete design.
Design amplifier.
User interface development system.

**FIGURE 1-32** TOOLS THAT ARE USEFUL DURING THE DESIGN STAGE

* Compiler.
Optimizer.
Macro capability or preprocessor.
Incremental compilation.
Conditional compilation.
* Linker.
* Library of reusable source and object code.
* Cross-reference generator.
Browser.
Syntax-directed editor.
Interface generator (menu, form, mouse).
Coding standards auditor.
* Pretty printer (code beautifier).
Documentation extractor.
Assertion verifier/termination prover.
Static analyzer.
Execution profiler

**FIGURE 1-33** TOOLS THAT ARE USEFUL DURING THE IMPLEMENTATION STAGE

* Debugger.
* Test manager.
* Static analyzer.
* Test data generator.
Symbolic executor.
* Execution profiler/test coverage analyzer.
* Test harness.
Environment simulator.
Multiple view execution animator.
* Code comparator.
Assertion checker.

**FIGURE 1-34** TOOLS THAT ARE USEFUL DURING THE TESTING STAGE

(tools from all other stages)
* Source code control.
* System building.
Validation suite automation.
* Code comparator.
Porting automation.

**FIGURE 1-35** TOOLS THAT ARE USEFUL DURING THE MAINTENANCE STAGE

somewhat pessimistic about the impact expert systems will have on software engineering, while Frenkel ([FRE85]) is very optimistic. The majority opinion is that tools and methodologies will provide incremental, rather than sudden leap, improvements in our ability to produce quality software.

Some very good software tools have been available for more than 10 years. These tools usually lack integration; they do not fit together into a seamless system, a single, unified product that supports all the stages and activities of software engineering. For instance, we would like the requirements specifications to be a good basis for design. However, we may be faced with using a specification analysis tool that verifies the consistency of the specifications; using a design tool that sharpens our understanding of the product; and finding that the notations required by these tools are totally incompatible.

Typically, three specific aspects of different tools should be consistent. First, a unified database should be maintained, in which all the relevant information about the project is stored. These data should be available so that they are useful to any tool that needs the data. Second, the user interface should be consistent between tools so that a software engineer does not have to spend unnecessary effort in "shifting gears" while moving from one tool to another. Third, a single model of the software development process should form the basis for all the tools. The major quality attributes of an environment are its functionality, friendliness, adaptability, support for productivity and good methodology, breadth of coverage, degree of automation, and integration ([PEN88], [HUM89]).

Most software environments choose to support either the analysis - specification - design portion of the life cycle, or the design - implementation - testing portion. The former are often called *software engineering environments* whereas the latter are termed *programming support environments* (PSEs) (Figure 1-36).

The choice is between language-independent generality in the first part of the life cycle and the need to support specific programming languages in the last portion. Some design methodologies are better adapted to implementation in a particular language, whereas most languages are best used in certain applications. This being true, a specialized, rather than generalized, environment will most likely be chosen during the last half of development.

Some of the language-specific capabilities of PSEs are language-sensitive editing and syntax tree execution. Language-sensitive editing is obtained, in part, by including templates for control constructs in the editor. A user typing "if" would then see the following format on the computer:

```
IF  []
   THEN
   BEGIN
   END
ELSE
   BEGIN
   END;
```

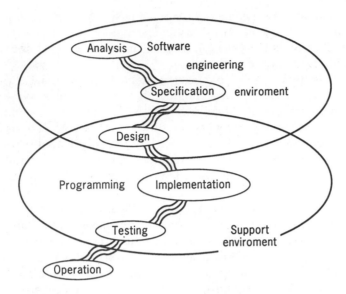

**FIGURE 1-36**  DOMAINS FOR PSES AND SEES

with the cursor in position to type in the condition. Function keys or mouse interaction would allow movement to other parts of the statement that need input and omission of the ELSE part, for example. A second, and more useful feature of such a system is coupling the editor to the front end of a compiler for the language. This allows syntax errors to be detected and rejected as they are created.

It has long been recognized that code interpretation is superior to compilation during the coding and debugging process. This is because the break caused by waiting for compilation interrupts the smooth flow of thought processes, and also because translating the code into another (machine) language can introduce subtle differences that alter its structure and make debugging more difficult. The trouble with interpreting is that execution of the code is slow. However, with a compiler front end in place for syntax-directed editing, interpreting the resulting intermediate code (usually syntax trees) is considerably faster. This speed is another important capability of some PSEs.

The Ada[1] Programming Support Environment (APSE) is a particularly well-defined programming support environment. Like Ada itself, an APSE has to meet certain U.S. Department of Defense specifications for its structure and behavior. These specifications were created mainly to ensure that the APSE (and its user) is portable. Myers ([MYE87]) investigated the initial experience with Ada and APSEs. He found that users of industrial-strength APSE's were reporting significant improvements in productivity, in some cases a 500% increase over industry average levels. It should be noted that the programming environment is given only some of the credit for this increase. The inherent nature of Ada and the capabilities of Ada compilers also have an effect.

---

[1] *Ada is a trademark of the Department of Defense (Ada Joint Program Office)*

Analysis, specification, and design can be done in a uniform manner, independent of the specific programming language eventually used for implementation. For this reason, software engineering environments often concentrate on the earlier stages of software life cycle activities. In these instances, the major focus of the environment is a support of the analysis and specification activity and semiautomatic translation of specifications into a design notation.

Such a product is likely to be tied to one specific development process model and to one specific design methodology. Although this can be useful, it is probably more restrictive than necessary. Overspecialization of software tools ends up requiring the software engineer to be an expert in the use of many tools that perform similar tasks.

A better viewpoint on software engineering environments is that they will add to a Program Support Environment (PSE) whatever tools are missing to provide full computer-aided software engineering (CASE) (refer to the March 1988 issue of *IEEE Software* for a summary of the status of CASE). These will include front end tools for analysis, specification, and design. However, there are also tools for project management, testing, document production, configuration control and team communication. Underlying this is a carefully designed database that allows all tools to manipulate the work products appropriate for their mission as well as to provide a smooth transition of the developing software as it moves from tool to tool. There will still be a specific development model overarching the entire process.

There is presently no environment that includes the bulk of the tools listed in Section 1.2.5 and that is available to the public.

The Software Engineering Institute (SEI) at Carnegie-Mellon University in Pittsburgh has initiated a project to identify, evaluate, and nurture new environments.

The SEI evaluation group has classified existing environments into four groups ([DAR87]):

*Language-Centered*   This type tends to be an exploratory environment where one designs and even specifies experimentally. The code is generally interpreted, and there is no context switch between creation and execution of programs. The environment itself represents a tool kit to be utilized by the application being developed. Specialization to a single language allows semantic understanding of the code to be accessible for **browsing,** that is, navigating through the code and responding to queries about it.

*Structure-Oriented*   This type centers around a syntax-directed editor, which provides a basis for editing, understanding, executing, and debugging. Programs can be viewed as source code, but also as language-independent objects such as abstract syntax trees. Incremental development of programs is usually supported.

*Tool kit*   This type is not an environment per se, since it tends to be available through the interface of an operating system command language. However, it is possible to create a command language shell to simulate a more unified environment. Tool kits tend to be language independent and to depend for integration on some simple interface between tools. They foster reuse of code and portability.

*Method-Based*   This type tends to be more a software-engineering environment rather than a programming support environment. Although these environments lack the implementation specific tools of the other three kinds, they include special capabilities for project management, task management, communication management, and process modeling. Some older environments like SREM, SADT, SDL, and PSL/PSA provide editing, display, and cataloging capabilities but are weak in actual verification and validation. Newer environments of this genre depend on a more formal notation and set of design procedures and can provide a stronger support for the underlying methodology.

Penedo and Riddle ([PEN88]) presented an alternate classification of environments (virtual machine, network, database, and control-centered). In addition to these categories of environments, one ought to consider transformation systems ([PAR83]). Transformation systems allow the software engineer to develop software specifications, and then use tools to automatically transform the specifications into executable code. Transformation abolishes or greatly diminishes the design, implementation, and testing stages of software development by automating them.

Since there is no current standard for either the structure or function of a CASE environment, let alone for individual tools, no attempt is made here to explain the specific commands necessary to operate any of them. There are far too many variations to be able to cover them all, and no single one has a significant prominence over the others. Here, we limit ourselves to the more productive task of understanding why certain tools are useful and how they are employed in a general sense.

A good hardware configuration currently available to a software engineer would probably include the items shown in Figure 1-38. These items embody the capabilities of the powerful, graphics-oriented workstations that first became available in the mid-

| | |
|---|---|
| Aloe | ISTAR |
| Ariadne | MENTOR |
| CASE2000 | Pecan |
| Cedar | PCTE |
| Cornell Program Synthesizer Development System | DCDS/TAGS |
| Refine | |
| Draco | SADT |
| DSEE | Smalltalk-80 |
| Excelerator | Software Through Pictures |
| Gandalf | SREM |
| Garden | Teamwork |
| GIST | Unix/Programmer's Workbook |
| Higher Order Software | VMS Tools |
| Interlisp | |

**FIGURE 1-37**   SOME CURRENTLY AVAILABLE ENVIRONMENTS

A single-user system with:

A full 32-bit architecture.

4 to 8 megabytes of memory.

A 100 megabyte hard disk.

A large dimension 1028x1028 bit mapped display.

A variety of built-in character fonts.

Color or, at least, variable intensity.

A high-density floppy disk drive.

A three-button mouse or a tablet.

Audio input/output capability.

A dot-matrix printer.

Connection to a local area network with:

A high resolution laser printer.

A tape drive for disk backup.

Gateways to computer (long-haul) networks.

Access to the target machines of the software project.

**F I G U R E 1-38**    HARDWARE ENVIRONMENT FOR A SOFTWARE ENGINEER

1980s. Of course, something more modest is quite common; failure of an organization to provide this much hardware is not necessarily a reason to quit the firm. On the other hand, one would think twice (or three times) about signing on with a group that furnished no more than shared access to a terminal attached to a time-shared computer.

## 1.3 FOSTERING QUALITY IN THE SOFTWARE PROCESS AND PRODUCT

There is an increasing penetration of software into new application areas. The home computer user might want to be an electronic commuter, performing tasks that originally required his presence at the office, and expecting to use all the professional tools previously available in the workplace. Industry expects software to control dangerous processes, to enable the use of robots on the assembly line, to provide tools for the design and manufacture of mechanisms, to balance the load of automobiles in the parking lot, and to schedule workers to meet varying demands.

The government expects software to locate criminals but not to infringe on individual rights of privacy. Their software must also model fragile ecosystems in order to make the decision whether to build a dam. Software has to fly fighter aircraft at speeds and altitudes that make human control impossible, and software has to guide and secure the exchange of billions of dollars worth of assets.

This frequent use of computers in a bewildering variety of applications, from the trivial to the vital, means that software failures have both deep and widespread effects. How does the software developer satisfy the legitimate demand for consumer rights?

Warranties, like those known in other industries, are unknown. If one copy of software has a bug, all copies have a bug, so a replacement policy would be useless. A promise to correct any bugs that customers find would be foolish, since one person's bug is another person's feature (Figure 1-39). A money-back guarantee would invite some users to make and use a backup copy of the software while returning the original for a refund. The best alternative is to engineer high quality into the product right from the start.

There are quality attributes other than functionality and dependability. Software should also be reasonably priced and easy to use; it should multiply the user's abilities in the same way that physical tools do and it should be easy to maintain over its entire lifetime. Although the software organization will have specific members assigned to perform quality assurance tasks, these members cannot be solely responsible for them. It must be the concern of every member of the staff, and that concern must be operative starting with the earliest planning and throughout the entire software life cycle.

All these problems point out the need for high quality software products. We need to start by building sufficient dependability into the product that it will not fail in any serious way.

There are four techniques available for preventing failure. One is **fault avoidance**, a combination of careful specification, design, and implementation. The second is **program verification**, which promises to produce even better results: programs can be shown to be correct, rather than just carefully crafted. The third is **fault tolerance**, the introduction of sufficient redundancy into software to allow for correct function even in the face of active errors in some of its components. Fourth, **error removal** detects and corrects errors during testing before the software is put into service (see Figure 1-40).

In Section 1.3.1, we look at one method for providing dependability in software — fault tolerance. The other techniques are examined in the chapters that follow. We will see how a quality assurance organization must be responsible for controlling the development of the product. Among their activities are measuring quality attributes

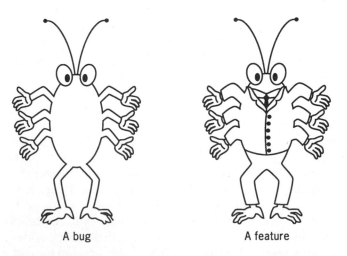

A bug                                   A feature

**FIGURE 1-39**   THE DIFFERENCE BETWEEN A BUG AND A FEATURE

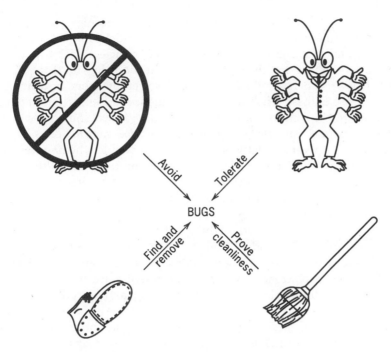

**F I G U R E 1-40**    RESPONSES TO SOFTWARE FAILURE

and the verification and validation process, by which we make sure that both our process and our product are correct.

### 1.3.1 Software Dependability

Dependability is a fundamental concept of software engineering. We would like to count on our product to function correctly, consistently, predictably, and without undue delays. If the product should fail in some way, we want it to do no permanent damage. Almost anybody can accept game software, meant to run on a home computer, which fails to work properly once in 1000 times. If the software were made for an arcade game, and users had to place a coin in a slot to play it, there might be some hesitation. If the software were an accounts payable package that lost 1 bill in 1000, the user would be in the market for replacement software very soon. If the software were intended to monitor the vital signs of a patient in an intensive care ward, nobody would think of using it.

Software engineers must do more than plan for a reasonable level of dependability in their software and then add an extra margin of safety. Because software engineers participate in the creation of systems whose effects can be far-reaching and vital, they, themselves, must take the responsibility of determining exactly what effects the system will have. At that point, software engineers can choose to "do what they are told to do"; but they must understand *what* they are doing first.

For example, an incomplete understanding of astronomical facts and formulas led to an early warning system that signaled a massive nuclear attack when it spotted the rising moon and to a 100-mile error in a space vehicle splashdown when nobody thought about the fact that the earth revolves around the sun ([BOR87]). Unreliable programs leave us open to failure if they are rejected by users, but harmful programs like these expose us to legal liability if our negligence causes serious damage to life and property and to the remorse of having carelessly caused someone's death; *it is very difficult to be absolutely sure that a particular product does not entail this kind of risk.*

As computing power and activities spread from people who have technical training to those who have not, potential damage from undependable software increases, simply because the user has fewer resources available to correct problems. This puts additional pressure on the software engineer to verify that the software will function correctly and will pose no danger to users. Assuring that software is dependable is probably the second most important thing (after assuring usefulness) that can be done to guarantee a successful product.

Unfortunately, high levels of dependability do not come free. Dependability requires a heightened awareness on the part of the software engineer, more careful use of tools and methodology, longer periods of testing, and less efficiency in the running software. The degree to which these costs are acceptable is governed by the amount of damage that can be caused by faulty software. Dependability must be built into the product from the very start. It is difficult to modify an existing product to substantially increase the amount of reliance that can be placed in it. This is why the required dependability level of the eventual product must curb our ambitions for the scope of the product. We should not try to go further than our abilities, resources, and methodologies will allow us.

Reporting on software failures that have enormous repair costs seems to be one of the favorite pastimes of the media. Here are some recent examples.

1 An error in software used to design nuclear reactors caused five unsafely designed reactors to be built, then later shut down as earthquake hazards. The problem was mistaken use of signed, rather than absolute, values [LEV86].
2 A man was killed by a huge overdose of therapeutic radiation. This was the result of a software error that allowed improper echoing of keyboard commands on the video display of the computer controlling the machine [BOS86].
3 The first attempted launch of the U.S. Space Shuttle had to be aborted because of faulty software coordination. This was due to a valid design "assumption" that was invalidated by later changes in the software [SPE84]. Despite the great care taken in development, the error occurred as a result of maintenance of portions of the software designed to provide additional fault tolerance through redundancy [BOR87].

*Software Engineering Notes,* a journal published by the Association for Computing Machinery's Special Interest Group on Software Engineering, carries descriptions of frightening incidents; in fact, they are indexed in the January 1987 issue.

Laprie has given the following definitions of the terminology of dependable software ([LAP85]). **Dependability** in software represents the degree to which reliance

**FIGURE 1-41** A NOT-SO-SERIOUS SOFTWARE FAILURE. (Doonesbury, copyright © 1970, G.B. Trudeau. Reprinted with permission of Universal Press Syndicate. All rights reserved.)

can reasonably be placed on its service. This service is usually measured by **reliability**, which normally is represented by the length of time we can expect the software to function correctly before it fails. Another measure of service is **availability**, which indicates the percentage of elapsed time during which the software functioned correctly.

Software undependability starts with a **fault**, which is the software engineer's design mistake. This fault creates an **error** in the software, which, for the time being, is latent. When a combination of circumstances and input data activate the error, the result may be a **failure**, the deviation of the software from its specified delivery of service. The failure may be manifested in terms of wrong output or incorrect timing of output.

The principle methods of software fault tolerance are checkup, rollback and redundancy. **Checkup** refers to a variety of techniques used to assure that hardware, input data, and user interaction are within the limits of acceptability. **Rollback** is the method of restoring the computational state to a previously encountered configuration that is known to be correct. Unlike the situation with checkup, it is necessary to lose some time and effort and, possibly, data. **Redundancy** involves the use of multiple resources. These might be several processors running in parallel, checking each other's results; duplicate copies of stored data or execution of multiple distinct procedures to carry out the same task.

Software handling of an error must start with the *detection* of the error. This can be followed by measures to *confine* the error and to categorize the nature of the error. Next follow efforts to *recover* from the error, which might involve either *forward* or *backward* techniques. Finally, the error and its context must be *logged*.

**Forward recovery** techniques are always specific to the error and the context. They involve correction of the system state to achieve what the user intended all along. Obviously, each software procedure to implement forward recovery is likely to be unique. **Backward recovery**, on the other hand, is accomplished by rollback methods and can be accomplished by generic procedures, although at the cost of lost time or effort.

Sometimes, it is impossible to recover from an error. The software may then *reconfigure* the system by continuing to perform a smaller set of functions that are still within its capabilities. At least, this fail-soft technique avoids needless loss of parts of the system that could still be used legitimately.

Failures can originate in bad data, bad user interaction, bad hardware, or bad software. There is a kind of double standard in our attitudes. Although software engineers agree that they should be on the lookout for hardware, data, and user-induced errors, they sometimes argue that we ought to ensure that our own software is totally correct. Tolerating faults in software design smacks of defeatism. But formal proofs of correctness are usually difficult, fallible, and incomplete. We might as well be realistic and augment our fault-avoidance efforts with some fault tolerance.

## 1.3.2 Verification and Validation

Quality assurance is a technical activity whose purpose is to assess the product and the process during the development stages, and enforce whatever measures may be needed to guarantee a specified level of quality. Quality assurance is often referred to as verification and validation and will be dealt with in greater detail in the next chapter. Quality assurance is one of the important themes of software engineering.

**Verification** is making sure that we are "building the product right." That is, we verify that the process of software development is correct. The main way of doing this is to compare each work product with its predecessor, to make sure that each part grows correctly from its prior form. We also verify the process by making sure that we are complying with all the established organization standards.

**Validation** is making sure that we are "building the right product." This is done by comparing the product in its current form with the original user requirements. Users may be able to inspect some work products, particularly prototypes, to determine that

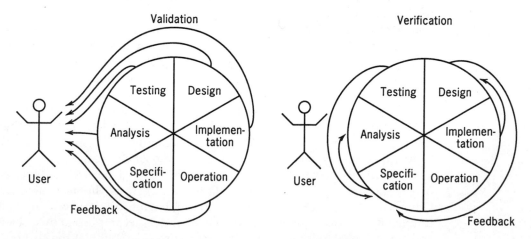

**FIGURE 1-42**   FEEDBACK LINES IN VALIDATION AND VERIFICATION

what they see is what they want. However, most of the validation effort comes at the end of the development period, when we test the product to see that it matches its requirements (see Figure 1-42).

The first step in verification is to make sure that there are no faults in the product. The cheapest method of doing this is through fault avoidance, particularly through inspections during the early phases of software development or maintenance modification. The cost of avoiding an error may be 1% of the cost of error removal after the software goes into service. If the development process is correct, then most errors will indeed be avoided.

Testing and debugging the implementation can easily consume 40% of the resources used during development ([DEU82]). Careful quality assurance reduces the number of errors introduced into the software and promotes an earlier termination of testing, thus saving a significant amount of money. It is a well-known paradox that spending more time analyzing, specifying and designing will actually shorten the entire development effort.

Continuous quality assurance activities can provide ongoing information about the progress of software development and the quality of the product. An increasingly accurate picture of the eventual dependability and performance characteristics of the software emerges from this effort. Management can utilize verification and validation activities to gather information that will aid in controlling the current project and improve planning for future projects.

Standards are a very important consideration in verifying the software engineering process ([BRA84]). Each software organization or working group should establish standards for the content, organization and style of all the work products that together make up the software product and for the process that creates them. Some of the benefits of the standards are outlined in Figure 1-43 and are amplified in the following paragraphs.

Standards should generally embody the methods and judgments that have been most successful in producing quality software. Since new methodologies continually arise, standards need to be reviewed periodically to determine their continued utility. By including software engineers in the review process, their cooperation and commitment can be enlisted. The software organization itself must also show commitment to the extent of modifying procedures and providing tools to support standards observance.

A fixed foundation on which to build.

A way of assessing the quality of the product.

A protocol for standardized communication.

A vehicle for control of product quality.

A framework for constructing the product.

A method for promoting continuity in development.

A guarantee of required content in the product.

A road map to those who use the product.

**FIGURE 1-43**  BENEFITS OF STANDARDS

Standards for the format and contents of documents have been published in various sources ([BRA84]). One can obtain copies of ANSI/IEEE standards from the IEEE, and copies of the FIPS (Federal Information Processing Standards) and the MIL-STD (military standards) from the U.S. government, for example. The ACM has a special interest group for systems documentation, SIGDOC. Its newsletter and conference reports provide further information about the content of standard documents and methods for producing them.

If we have established standards for what work products must be constructed, their content, and the point at which they must be available, then that information is sufficient to determine how the product is shaping up and to control its quality. The existence of certain standard documents will help ensure the continued life and success of the product.

Standard content, organization, and format in a document serves both the authors and users. Authors have a framework already set out on which to hang their ideas. Users do not have to guess where to find information, since the organization of the document is probably already familiar to them. Technical users, in particular, find their use of standardized documents is optimized, since they can browse for pertinent information in a highly directed manner.

Of course, uniform observation of documentation standards does not come naturally. Someone in the software organization has to serve as documentation coordinator to enforce adherence to the rules; but documentation standards can be automated. Posten ([POS85]) outlined the expenses associated with information as the costs of recording, storing, retrieving, producing and using documents. Integrating documentation production into a software engineering environment allows computers to minimize storage, retrieval, use, and production costs. Automated configuration management can help enforce the documentation standards themselves. Intelligent word processing software that can interface to the environment database will reduce the cost of recording.

### 1.3.3 Software Metrics

It is common to find a non technical manager struggling to measure the real productivity of a technical section or team. Without understanding their work, the manager can only take the team's word for the intensity of their effort and the magnitude of their success. This situation generally leads managers to choose one easily measured and quantifiable aspect of the job and base their entire decision on that one aspect. Then everybody complains that the manager is more worried about numbers than quality.

Even the technical people who make up the quality assurance group need to be able to measure the product objectively. One of the major activities of software engineering is a search for appropriate **metrics**, or measuring sticks, for the various products and processes seen in software development. If we cannot measure our activities and products, we do not know how good they are, whether they are changing, or how to do them best. A summary of potentially useful metrics can be found in [WAG87] and [MIL88].

Measurement is the beginning of science. Lord Kelvin said, "...when you can measure what you are speaking about, and express it in numbers, you know something about it; but when you cannot...you have scarcely in your thoughts advanced to the stage of science." However, there is widespread concern that current a use of metrics lacks both a theoretical foundation and clear-cut goals ([BAS88]). Therefore, we also need to be sure why we measure and for what purpose we measure.

It is possible to evaluate the quality of the software built by a team using broad measures such as utility, reusability, dependability, maintainability, flexibility, clarity, and performance. Although some of these attributes may not be easily quantified, they have a large impact on any evaluation of the productivity of the software engineers who produced the software. People who can write a large volume of low-quality software are not as productive as those who produce fewer, but better, lines of code.

Despite the foregoing, or in addition to it, most managers would still like to be able to graph production just as a sales manager graphs dollar volume of sales, or a coal mine operator graphs tons of coal ([GRA87] is a good example of these kinds of useful measures). The question is, what is the appropriate unit of measure for software? You cannot measure it in either tons or dollars. Of course, the manager is likely to pick completion of scheduled tasks as a primary measure. The danger here is that the software team will respond by finishing poor quality software on schedule and feel good about it. It is a truism that whatever behavior is being measured will improve according to that measure.

Boehm ([BOE87]) makes a strong case for using delivered source instructions (DSI) as a measure of software, and DSI per man month as a measure of individual or team productivity. In this measure, "delivered" excludes the software that was developed in support of the main effort; the software that was developed and discarded; and the software that served as scaffolding for the testing of delivered software. "Instruction" excludes comments. However, once we standardize the definition of DSI, actually counting it can be done automatically; this can be part of the output of a tool that will also ensure that standards of coding style are met. Similarly, we need to make clear exactly who contributes man-months to the effort: do we include computer operators, managers, secretaries, custodians, etc? Furthermore, do we count activities like planning, training, and management as software effort?

Of course, some of the striking comparisons may be artifacts of different methods of calculating productivity. In particular, different organizations may include (or not) comments in reporting lines of code production. Similarly, counts can be dramatically affected by deciding to count reusable code only when it is first produced, or on its first use, or for every reuse.

One drawback of the DSI measure is that it creates an apparently lower productivity among those who use higher-level languages. Jones ([JON86]) indicates that the same program might be written in one-tenth as many lines of code using APL as opposed to the assembler language. When we compare efforts using different implementation languages, it is necessary to normalize the DSI measure by using a multiplier representing the density of functionality of the language. Both Jones in [JON86] and Boehm in [BOE81] present appropriate multipliers for language level and rules for the definition of "delivered source instructions" and "man-months."

Several techniques for standardizing the volume of software and making it independent of the implementation language are available. These include Halstead's "software science" measures, the McCabe program flow complexity metric, Albrecht's function points ([ALB83]), and counting object code instructions rather than source code instructions. These metrics are described Chapters 6 and 7. Although each of these techniques may show localized advantages, there seems to be no evidence that their overall value is greater than that of the simpler DSI measure.

## 1.4 FUTURE SOFTWARE ENGINEERING METHODOLOGIES

In its early days, software engineering concentrated on three major problems: eliminating errors, programming-in-the-large, and the maintenance burden, but Shaw ([SHA86]) identifies some of the directions that software use and development will follow in the 1990s. They include nontraditional programming languages, parallel computing, real-time and embedded systems, and expert systems. We must expand the software engineering discipline to support these new activities.

The first languages taught to students (Pascal, C, Modula-2, Ada, Fortran, PL/I, Basic, or Cobol) are quite similar to one another. Software engineering has been developed largely under the implicit assumption that products will be implemented in these languages. Although one would hope that software engineering techniques could be used just as effectively in conjunction with *any* programming language, this is not true.

There are many other implementation languages, differing markedly from the traditional procedural languages in style and application. Occasionally entire specialized environments have grown up to satisfy users of these languages.

Several environments implementing specific methodologies for specification and design to support logic programming languages, like Prolog, have come onto the market. Early experience, however, indicates that customer expectations exceed the actual capabilities of these products. InterLisp, however, is a less ambitious and more successful programming support environment. It may be that its success is because Lisp has been around for decades and people already know how to work with it. Smalltalk-80 is another environment, this time for object-oriented design, which is quite successful. More recently, C++ and object-oriented Lisp have been the platforms from which current environments are developing.

Some of the new process models are adapted to the new fourth-generation languages. The VHLL process model suggests that programming in the applications or problem oriented fourth-generation language is so straightforward that the need for a careful and disciplined use of methodology is largely eliminated. This seems quite unlikely; instead, it would seem that such languages have not yet been used to implement sufficiently complex applications to demonstrate the need of a methodology.

Product development in the more radical of the nontraditional languages is demanding. We should consider ourselves lucky to be able to use a significant part of current design, implementation, and testing methodologies, not to mention existing programming support tools. New languages appear frequently, and most of them do not catch on. For nontraditional languages that do last, developing appropriate methodologies and corresponding tools will be a significant and ongoing challenge.

Software engineering has also grown up in the Von Neumann world of procedural languages and single-processor architectures. It appears certain that computers, if they are to continue their spectacular progress, will have to use multiple-processor architectures. Of course, "multiple processor" represents an entire range from the lockstep processing units in a single-instruction multiple-data machine to the cooperating, but independent and heterogeneous, computers in a network.

Among the potential benefits of truly distributed software products are much faster processing, additional fault tolerance possibilities, fail-soft capabilities, and the ability to handle dramatically increased processing loads without redesign ([SHA87]). There are several specification environments, including PAISLey and SREM, which deal with some of the special problems encountered during development of parallel systems. The typical design approach includes partitioning data into files and functions into processes. These files and processes are later optimized through allocation to specific processors in the distributed system.

However, current methodologies for parallel systems are far from adequate. As Parnas notes ([PAR85]), "Any attempt to design these programs [for parallel systems] by thinking things through in the order that the computer will execute them leads to confusion and results in systems that nobody can understand completely ... There are so many possibilities to consider that only extensive testing can begin to sort things out. Even after, we have incidents ...." We lack effective methodologies for designing, implementing, and testing programs with concurrency mechanisms. Even specification may be a problem. When systems are so complex that initial specifications are necessarily incomplete and perhaps inaccurate, there should be prototyping tools to support frequent modification of specifications and automatic change of work products affected by the modification.

Most current design notations intentionally avoid representing causality, timing, and concurrency (Petri nets are one exception). This notational lack mirrors the inability of most design methods to deal with parallel processes. When parallel processes *are* designed, it is often done by using a kind of pseudocode which mirrors the particular concurrency constructs of the implementation language. Functional programming languages and design methodologies may solve this problem, since they do not involve software engineers in concepts of timing and concurrency.

Since the mid-1960s we have been preoccupied with the challenges of programming-in-the-large. Having gotten a grasp on that problem, we are now free to attack the ever more insistent demands for the "program-as-component." This refers to applications in which software is used either to control complex and time-critical physical processes (real-time systems) or in which software is designed for a processor that is only part of a larger physical system (embedded systems).

Real-time software is usually composed of parallel processes running on a single-processor system. If it is run on a multiple processor system, it is typically one with shared memory and communication on a bus or channel, all the processors being homogeneous. Real-time systems are used to control physical processes like the refining of petroleum products, the control of air traffic, or the capture and analysis of data. In these instances, the software must keep up with actual events, that is, operate under the constraints of real, rather than processor, time.

Embedded software usually runs on a processor that is one component of a very complex system. A space shuttle vehicle contains many components, several of them processors, that cooperate in the control and function of the device. Embedded software faces the challenges of parallel as well as real-time programming.

Some of the specific challenges of real-time and embedded systems are maintaining an adequately low response time to external events and signals, maintaining a high level of dependability, and responding to interrupt signals. The software engineer must learn to interface to and integrate software with disparate physical devices, to deal with a physically distributed database, and to adjust to system reconfiguration should devices fail.

Testing systems that are meant to be connected to other systems or physical devices can be very difficult indeed. Systems must either be tested while connected with the actual devices, which sacrifices the benefits of problem decomposition, or they must be tested in a simulated environment, which involves creating complex tools that we can never be sure do an adequate job of representing the real environment. This represents a particular problem in the case of life-critical software for which a testing environment cannot exist — for instance, the SDI software.

Expert systems use well-developed techniques for searching a knowledge base to find applicable rules in a problem situation. Applying these rules may then transform the problem into a solution. Search techniques are often heuristic, rather than absolute, and as a consequence solutions are not always optimal. One of the prime goals of artificial intelligence is to allow the expert system to modify its knowledge base in accordance to the results of its own use. That is, we would like the expert system to "learn" by including experience in its knowledge base.

Shaw refers to the challenge of expert system development as learning to produce the "program-as-deputy" ([SHA86]). The program acts in place of humans carrying out activities that we think of as uniquely human. There are two major challenges for software engineering in learning how to use programs as deputies.

First, we need better methods for developing and maintaining expert systems. The specification stage of expert system development requires an intensive and highly technical analysis phase in which the knowledge of one or more experts is transferred into a knowledge base. Current tools are not standardized and are in a state of continual flux. Methodologies are under development but tend to be personal or proprietary, rather than ratified by general acceptance. The algorithms for creating inferences on the basis of rules, as well as the data structures for representing rules, need further analysis and development. Implementation languages are still difficult to use and are frequently in flux. Testing expert systems is particularly weak.

The second challenge, referred to in [SHA86] and [BRO87], is applying expert systems technology to software engineering itself. It has already been pointed out that tools are one fundamental solution to the software engineering crisis. Given the lack of personnel in the field, what better way to use tools than to relieve people of judgmental as well as bookkeeping duties? Artificial intelligence will provide the engine that drives much of the improvement in software engineering during the next 20 years.

**F I G U R E 1-44**   AN EXPERT SYSTEM. (Doonesbury, copyright © 1984 G.B. Trudeau. Reprinted with permission of Universal Press Syndicate. All rights reserved.)

Such tools have been incorporated into environments like the Programmer's Apprentice ([RIC79]) but are still a long way away from widespread acceptance. Expert tools will make heavy use of existing solutions and techniques, which will form a part of the knowledge base. Thus, another challenge will be to improve our methods of reuse to the point that they can be carried out by our deputies.

## 1.5 SUMMARY

This chapter has been an orientation to the current state of software engineering. The general software life cycle, with its six stages of analysis, specification, design, implementation, testing, and operation, provides the framework for continued discussion throughout the book. Software engineering has been necessitated by the "software crisis." Working with very large products, maintaining a large mass of current software, fostering quality in the process and the product, and learning how to manage software projects are challenging, but some solutions can be found in planning, tools, methodologies, and new process models.

Success factors for software development go far beyond a talent for programming. Management skills are needed to allow software project budgeting and scheduling, as well as control of product and personnel. The proper climate for productivity can be created, if we understand how to measure it and foster it. Productivity is also supported by accepting the discipline of the software development process. This includes a high degree of component reuse, the liberal use of prototypes in developing the ultimate product, and an effort to minimize the risk of failure. In particular, the use of tools can improve productivity, allowing us to create a software assembly line. Specific kinds of tools, as well as some integrative environments were presented. Unfortunately, no complete and seamless environment is available yet for general use.

We will never be good at software engineering unless we develop a methodology to guide our activities. Using the correct techniques and body of knowledge is the mark of a professional. Standards should always be established for the format and content of documents, as well as for code; together they form the entire software product. Some of the standard, but neglected, attributes of good software are maintainability, dependability and reusability. Prototyping is one technique for evaluating software attributes while there is still time to alter the product. Fault tolerant software uses checkup, rollback, and, especially, redundancy to allow software to continue to function correctly despite residual design faults, as well as data, user, or hardware faults.

Fostering quality in our process and product depends on an ability to measure and manage, which goes under the rubric of quality assurance. We mentioned some of the metrics by which we can evaluate our work products, and ongoing programs to verify the correctness of each step in the development process, as well as to validate our compliance with user requirements and needs.

Software engineering has developed many useful techniques and theories, but is far from a completed discipline. Some of the challenges for which the discipline has as yet no complete solutions are learning how to use new languages, dealing with parallel and embedded systems and integrating expert systems. The solutions for these challenges are the goal of current work in the field.

## BIBLIOGRAPHY

[[ALA84]    Alavi, M., "An Assessment of the Prototyping Approach to Information System Development," *Communications of the ACM*, 27(6):556 – 563.

[ALB83]    Albrecht, A.J. and J.E. Gaffney, "Software Function, Source Lines of Code and Development Effort Prediction," *IEEE Transactions on Software Engineering*, 9(6):639 – 648.

[BAL83]    Balzer, R., T.E. Cheatham, and C. Green, "Software Technology in the 1990's Using a New Paradigm", *Computer* 16(11):39 – 45.

[BAS87]    Bassett, P.G., "Frame-Based Software Engineering," *IEEE Software*, 4(4):9 – 16.

[BAS88]    Basili, V.R. and H.D. Rombach, "The TAME Project: Towards Improvement-Oriented Software Environments," *IEEE Transactions on Software Development*, 14(6):758 – 773.

[BIG87]*   Biggerstaff, T. and C. Richter, "Reusability Framework, Assessment and Directions," *IEEE Software*, 4(2):41 – 49.

[BOE81]*   Boehm, B.W., *Software Engineering Economics*, Prentice-Hall, Englewood Cliffs, NJ.

[BOE83]*   Boehm, B.W. and T.A. Standish, "Software Technology in the 1990's Using an Evolutionary Paradigm," *Computer*, 16(11):30 – 37.

[BOE84]*   Boehm, B.W., T.E. Gray, and T. Seewaldt, "Prototyping vs. Specifying: A Multiproject Experiment," *IEEE Transactions on Software Engineering*, 10(3):290 – 303.

[BOE87]*   Boehm, B.W., "Improving Software Productivity," *Computer* 20(9):43 – 57.

[BOE88]*   Boehm, B.W., "A Spiral Model of Software Development and Enhancement," *Computer*, 31(5):61 – 72.

[BO88a]    Boehm, B.W. and P.N. Papaccio, "Understanding and Controlling Software Costs," *IEEE Transactions on Software Engineering*, 14(10):1462 – 1477.

[BOR87]    Borning, A., "Computer System Reliability and Nuclear War," *Communications of the ACM*, 30(2):112 – 131.

[BOS86]    *Boston Globe*, June 20, 1986, p. 1.

[BRA84]    Branstad, M. and P.B. Powell, "Software Engineering Project Standards," *IEEE Transactions on Software Engineering*, 10(1):73 – 78.

[BRO75]*   Brooks, F.P., *The Mythical Man-Month*, Addison-Wesley, Reading, MA.

[BRO87]*   Brooks, F.P., "No Silver Bullet: Essence and Accidents of Software Engineering," *Computer*, 20(4):10 – 19.

[BUT87]    Butler, J., "CASE: How Real Is It?" *IEEE Software*, 4(6):94.

[CAR80]    Card, D.N., F.E. McGarry, and G.R. Page, "Evaluating Software Engineering Technologies," *Computer*, 13(7):845 – 851.

[CUR88]*   Curtis, H., H. Krasner, and N. Iscoe, "A Field Study of the Software Design Process for Large Systems," *Communications of the ACM*, 31(11):1268 – 1287.

[DAR87]*   Dart, S.A., R.J. Ellison, P.H. Feiler, and A.N. Habermann, "Software Development Environments," *Computer*, 20(11):18 – 28.

[DEU82]    Deutsch, M.S., *Software Verification and Validation*, Prentice-Hall, Englewood Cliffs, NJ.

[ELS82]    Elshoff, J.L. and M. Marcotty, "Improving Computer Program Readability to Aid Modification," *Communications of the ACM*, 25(8):512 – 521.

[EVA83]    Evans, M.W., P. Piazza, and J.B. Dolkas, *Principles of Productive Software Management*, Wiley-Interscience, New York.

[FAI85]    Fairley, R., *Software Engineering Concepts*, McGraw-Hill, New York.

[FIR87]    Firth, R., V. Mosley, R. Pethia, L. Roberts, and W. Wood, "A Guide to the Classification and Assessment of Software Engineering Tools," Software Engineering Institute, Technical Report CMU/SEI-87-TR-10.

[FRE85]*   Frenkel, K.A., "Toward Automating the Software-Development Cycle," *Communications of the ACM*, 28(6):579 – 589.

[GIB89]    Gibson, V.R. and J.A. Senn, "System Structure and Software Maintenance," *Communications of the ACM*, 32(3):347 – 358.

[GRA87]*   Grady, R.B., "Measuring and Managing Software Maintenance," *IEEE Software*, 4(5):35 – 45.

[HAI86]    Hailpern, B., "Multiparadigm Languages and Environments," *IEEE Software*, 3(1):6 – 10.

[HOA87]*   Hoare, C.A.R., "An Overview of Some Formal Methods for Program Design," *Computer*, 20(9):85 – 91.

[HUM89]*   Humphrey, W.S., *Managing the Software Process*, Addison-Wesley, Reading, MA.

[JON86]*   Jones, T.C., *Programming Productivity*, McGraw-Hill, New York.

[LAP85]    Laprie, J.C., "Dependable Computing and Fault Tolerance," Proceedings of the IEEE International Symposium on Fault-Tolerant Computing, No. 15, pp. 2 – 110.

[LEN87]    Lenz, M., H.A. Schmid and P.F. Wolf, "Software Reuse Through Building Blocks," *IEEE Software*, 4(4):34 – 42.

[LEV86]    Leveson, N.G., "Software Safety: Why, What and How," *Computing Surveys*, 18(2):125 – 163.

[LIE80]    Lientz, B. and E. Swanson, *Software Maintenance Management*, Addison-Wesley, Reading, MA.

[LUQ89]     Luqi, "Software Evolution Through Rapid Prototyping," *Computer*, 22(5):13 – 25.

[MAR85]     Martin, J., *Fourth-Generation Languages*, Vol. 1, Prentice-Hall, Englewood Cliffs, NJ.

[MCC81]     McCracken, D.D., "A Maverick Approach to Systems Analysis and Design," *Systems Analysis and Design: A Foundation for the 1980's*, Elsevier-North Holland, New York.

[MIL81]     Mills, H.D., "Software Productivity in the Enterprise," in Software Productivity, Little, Brown, Boston.

[MIL83]     Milne, F. and R. Weber, "The Economics of Designing Generalized Software," *Communications of the ACM*, 26(8):582 – 589.

[MIL88]     Mills, E.E., "Software Metrics," Software Engineering Institute, Curriculum Module, SEI-CM-12-1.1.

[MIS88]     Misra, S.K. and P.J. Jalics, "Third-Generation vs Fourth-Generation Software Development," IEEE Software, 5(4):8 – 14.

[MUN81]     Munson, J.B. and R.T. Yeh, report by the IEEE Software Productivity Workshop, 1981.

[MUS85]*    Musa, J.D., "Software Engineering: The Future of a Profession," *IEEE Software*, 22(1):55 – 62.

[MYE85]*    Myers, W., "MCC: Planning the Revolution in Software", *IEEE Software*, 2(6):68 –73.

[MYE87]*    Myers, W., "Ada: First users — pleased; prospective user — still hesitant," *Computer*, 20(3):68 – 73.

[PAR83]*    Partsh, H. and R. Steinbruggen, "Program Transformation Systems," *Computing Surveys*, 15(3):199 – 236.

[PAR85]*    Parnas, D.L., "Software Aspects of Strategic Defense Systems," *Communications of the ACM*, 28(12):1326 – 1335.

[PEN88]     Penedo, M.H. and W.E. Riddle, "Software Engineering Environment Architectures," *IEEE Transactions on Software Engineering*, 14(6):689 – 696.

[PER87]     Perrone, G., "Low-cost CASE: Tomorrow's Promise Emerging Today," *Computer*, 20(11):104 – 110.

[POS85]     Posten, R.M., "Selecting Software Documentation Standards," *IEEE Software*, 2(3):90 – 91.

[PRI87]     Prieto-Diaz, R. and P. Freeman, "Classifying Software for Reuse," *IEEE Software*, 4(1):6 – 16.

[PUT77]     Putnam, L.H. and R.W. Wolverton, *Quantitative Management: Software Cost Estimating*, IEEE, New York.

[RAM84]*    Ramamoorthy, C.V., A. Prakash, W.-T. Tsai, and Y. Usuda, "Software Engineering: Problems and Perspectives," *Computer*, 17(10):191 – 209.

[RAM86]     Ramamoorthy, C.V., V. Garg, and A. Prakash, "Programming in the Large," *IEEE Transactions on Software Engineering*, 12(7):769 – 783.

[RIC79]     Rich, C., H.E. Shrobe, and R.C. Waters, "Overview of the Programmer's Apprentice," Proceedings of the 6th International Joint Conference on Artificial Intelligence.

[RIC88]*    Rich, C. and R.C. Waters, "Automatic Programming: Myths and Prospects," *Computer*, 21(8):40 – 51.

[ROY70]     Royce, W.W., "Managing the Development of Large Software Systems: Concepts and Techniques," Proceedings WESCON.

[RUS88]     Russon, M.B., S. Maass, and W.A. Kellogg, "The Designer as User," *Communications of the ACM*, 31(11):1288 – 1298.

[SAC68]    Sackman, H., W.J. Erikson, and E.E. Grant, "Exploratory Experimental Studies Comparing Online and Offline Programming Performance," *Communications of the ACM*, 11(1):3 – 11.

[SAM88]    Samuelson, P., "Is Copyright Law Steering the Right Course?," *IEEE Software*, 5(5):78 – 86.

[SHA86]*   Shaw, M., "Beyond Programming-in-the-Large," Software Engineering Institute, Technical Memorandum SEI-86-TM-6.

[SHA87]    Shatz, S.M. and J.-P. Wang, "Introduction to Distributed-Software Engineering," *Computer*, 20(10):23 – 31.

[SHE87]    Shemer, I., "Systems Analysis: A Systemic Analysis of a Conceptual Model," *Communications of the ACM*, 30(6):507 – 512.

[SPE84]    Spector, A. and D. Gifford, "The Space Shuttle Primary Computer System," *Communications of the ACM*, 27(9):874 – 900

[STU83]    Stucki, L.G., "What about CAD/CAM for Software," Proceedings of SoftFair (IEEE), New York, 1983.

[TRA87]*   Tracz, W.,"Reusability Comes of Age," *IEEE Software*, 4(4):6 – 8.

[WAG87]    Waguespack, L.J. and S. Badlani, "Software Complexity Assessment: An Introduction and Annotated Bibliography," *Software Engineering Notes*, 12(4):52 – 71.

[ZAV84]*   Zave, P., "The Operational versus the Conventional Approach to Software Development," *Communications of the ACM*, 27(2):104 – 118.

[ZEL84]    Zelkowitz, M.V., R.T. Yeh, R.G. Hamlet, J.D. Gannon, and V.R. Basili, "Software Engineering Practices in the United States and Japan," *Computer*, 17(6):57 – 66.

## PROBLEMS

1 Why is it impossible to develop a "software management science" without metrics? What metrics should ideally be available?

2 Rank the items in Figure 1-7 according to their importance in determining development cost. Justify your ranking.

3 Some models eliminate or reduce the effort needed for some stages. Which models eliminate which stages, and how do they do it?

4 What legal issues do you think a software engineer needs to be aware of? How can ignorance of each issue threaten the success of the organization?

5 What elements of expert system technology increase our risk of liability? What can we do to avoid the risks?

6 Describe a way of combining a single-methods-oriented environment with a set of alternative language-based environments.

7 What are the potential benefits and drawbacks to an organization that arise from taking "responsible," "ethical," or "socially relevant" factors into account in choosing projects?

**8** How many lines of code of finished product do you generate each hour? The industry standard is about 2 DSI/hr. Are you that much better? If not, can you explain the disparity?

**9** Study a documentation standard from an industry organization and outline its salient features.

**10** Why does fault tolerance necessarily depend on redundancy?

**11** Is the packaged or the custom software industry larger in terms of income? In terms of work force?

**12** List some of your own work habits that contribute to the software crisis. What can be done to solve this problem?

**13** Study *Software Engineering Notes* and report on the most deadly and the most costly software errors.

**14** Research and report on a successful use of prototyping. Was there anything special about the application that made this process model effective?

**15** The analogy of commercial construction to the traditional process model works pretty well. Find an equally good analogy to illustrate the spiral model.

**16** Use data from your community to determine labor costs, other organizational costs, and labor scarcity and turnover in the software industry.

**17** Several different desirable attributes of software have been mentioned in this chapter. List and rank them from the most to the least important. Give reasons for your ranking.

**18** Find published accounts of or interview software people who have experienced the following problems:

an unreasonable maintenance burden

a project team of more than 100 people

a failed project

Report the insights you gain about these problems and their remedies.

**19** Suppose you are going to develop a tool to aid in reuse of software components. List the tool's different functions.

**20** Suppose you are going to develop an expert system to aid in software development. List the system's different functions.

**21** Sketch ideas for data structures to implement a software project database.

**22** Outline the pro- and con- arguments for copying and using software that was purchased by someone else.

**23** Choose the five leaves from the tree in Figure 1-19 that you would implement first. Justify your choices.

**24** Read about (or, if possible, experiment with) one of the environments listed in Figure 1-37 and report on it.

**25** What percent of the tools marked with an asterisk in Figures 1-29 through 1-35 are available to you? What three tools would you add? Why?

**26** If you were to create several different prototype versions of a product, would you use the same language to implement each one? Why or why not?

**27** The suggestion that we get to market as soon as possible with a product seems to contradict the desire to come out with a polished product. In what way would the feasibility of this strategy depend on the intended clientele?

**28** At what point should a work product be baselined?

**29** Which is more important to the eventual success of a product: validation or verification? Why?

# C H A P T E R  2

## SOFTWARE MANAGEMENT

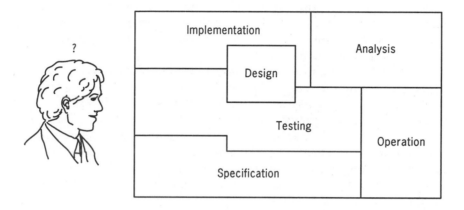

In Chapter 1, we learned that good management was essential to success in software engineering. Even though management is not taught in most university computer science departments, the software engineer is still in the best position to understand the problems, develop the expertise, and undertake the management of the software organization. This software manager has a tremendous advantage in working with self-motivated, intelligent professionals who are doing what they most enjoy. This offsets many of the problems one might otherwise anticipate. On the other hand, these same professionals may become so involved in the process that it becomes an end in itself.In this instance, it is up to the manager to introduce a note of realism into the software team. He must manage the process and the products so that deadlines are met, quality is assured, resources are used wisely, and everything is in its place ([COO84]). The manager has a special responsibility to control the amount of risk the organization takes by assessing the economic and technical feasibility of the project, analyzing the risks, and making intelligent decisions.

A manager must also understand the people who work under his supervision. The manager must be able to understand the psychology, and the strengths of individuals, and match them to the job descriptions of various team roles.

Finally, the manager must be able to supervise the project's work, schedule and budget the resources, arbitrate disputes, hire and fire, set goals, and motivate. This chapter is not meant to train a software engineer in all those skills, but it covers some of the main points.

## 2.1 MANAGING THE SOFTWARE PROCESS AND PRODUCTS

We engage in two kinds of activities during the software process: **staged** activities occur during a single stage of the life cycle, whereas **longitudinal** activities are carried on pretty uniformly throughout the entire process. Similarly, there are work products that are created at only one stage and others that are generated at every stage. The first two sections of this segment deal with staged and longitudinal activities and work products.

Among the most important longitudinal activities are those that promote quality. It is necessary to plan these activities; they often cover several projects, and, therefore, planning them is done outside any individual analysis stage. This chapter covers three quality control activities: (1) quality assurance, which measures, records, and evaluates the process and the products; (2) project accounting, which ascertains the state of the project on an ongoing basis and makes progress visible for management purposes; and (3) product control, which manages all of the varied work products so that nothing is lost, mismatched, or modified improperly.

### 2.1.1 Staged Activities and Work Products

Figure 2-1 lists some of the activities and work products, which are separated into the stages in which they are typically completed. There may be some reasons to vary this pattern in particular circumstances, but the outline given is fairly standard and would be appropriate in almost all instances.

### 2.1.2 Longitudinal Activities

Beside the activities that fall into specific stages, we must plan for activities that are carried on throughout the entire process. It is a frequent error of software engineers to become so tied to the life cycle concept that they forget about the vital longitudinal activities. By concentrating on the needs of the moment, software engineers neglect the unifying actions that impart continuity and quality to their product.

These longitudinal activities are often carried out by software engineers who have specialized responsibilities. In some organizations, there may be entire departments devoted to project management, quality assurance, and the like. In other organizations, these activities may be the responsibility of each software engineer. Figure 2-2 outlines some longitudinal activities and their associated documents.

The project plan includes standards, testing and quality assurance, product control procedures, and project accounting (management). This is done so that a complete list of policies and procedures for software development are contained in each individual project's documentation.

| **Analysis Activity** | **Analysis Document** |
|---|---|
| Systems analysis | Project plan |
| Requirements definition | |
| Size, cost, schedule estimate | |
| Feasibility analysis | |
| Project goal determination | |
| Selection of procedures | |
| Management review | Minutes of review |

| **Specification Activity** | **Specification Document** |
|---|---|
| Requirements specification | Requirements specification |
| Technical review | Minutes of review |
| | Software verification plan |
| | Acceptance test plan |

| **Design Activity** | **Design Document** |
|---|---|
| External design | External design document |
| | Preliminary user's manual |
| Architectural design | Architectural design document |
| Preliminary design review | |
| Minutes of review | |
| Detailed design | Detailed design document |
| Minutes of review | |
| Critical design review | |
| | Unit test plans |

| **Implementation Activity** | **Implementation Document** |
|---|---|
| Coding | Source code |
| Code inspection | Minutes of inspection |

| **Testing Activity** | **Testing Document** |
|---|---|
| Unit testing | Unit test results |
| Integration testing | Integration test results |
| System testing | System test results |
| | Principles of Operation |

| **Operational Activity** | **Operational Document** |
|---|---|
| | Installation manual |
| | Installation training manual |
| Training | |
| Project debriefing | Project legacy |
| | Maintenance procedures |
| Maintenance | Software problem report |

**FIGURE 2-1**   ACTIVITIES AND PRODUCTS BY LIFE CYCLE STAGE

| Activity | Document |
|---|---|
| Management | Progress reports |
| | Policies |
| | Individual goal statements |
| Documentation | All documents |
| | Personal journals |
| Quality assurance | Standards |
| | Minutes of reviews |
| Product control | Versions of software product |
| | Build descriptions |
| Communication | Electronic mail logs |
| | Telephone logs |

**FIGURE 2-2**  LONGITUDINAL ACTIVITIES AND DOCUMENTS

## 2.1.3 Planning a Quality Product

Producing high-quality software increases both the cost and income of development. Obviously, it is more expensive to produce quality, but higher quality should imply greater user satisfaction, thus improving the overall profit. Improved quality reduces the potential liability for careless software engineering practices or substandard software products. The extent to which quality control adds to costs or improves income varies in each individual case. It is always necessary to select an appropriate level of quality control to optimize a given development effort.

Quality cannot be added to a product at the end of its development. From the beginning we have to establish set procedures for activities that will lead to quality. We must then systematically enforce those procedures throughout the entire development and maintenance cycle. Some useful quality control procedures are inspecting work products as milestones are reached, controlling work products so that they remain stable after their milestone, selecting and monitoring work product metrics throughout the life cycle, and assigning personnel to monitor, record, and analyze all quality assurance activities. The result is software that achieves the requirements and goals that have been set.

There are three different formal activities designed to promote software quality: (1) **quality assurance** tells us whether standards are being observed and whether the developing product is meeting our expectations, (2) **project accounting** ensures that cost and schedule targets are being met, (3) **product control** provides that all portions of the product are kept current, that changes occur only when they are in the best interests of the product and the user, and that different versions of the product are correctly identified and correlated.

In discussing how to plan for quality, Basili and Rombach ([BAS87]) suggest that, during the analysis stage, four decisions have to be made: *what* attributes of the product and the process manifest quality; *how* are we to measure quality; *when* do we evaluate the product and process and carry out other quality-promoting activities; and *who* is

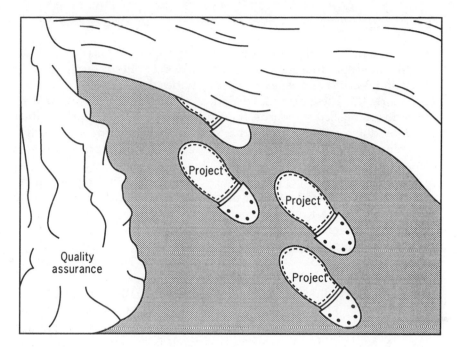

**FIGURE 2-3**   A QUALITY ASSURANCE GROUP CAN PROVIDE CONTINUITY

responsible for carrying out the process. Basili and Rombach point out that objective measurement is fundamental to our ability to evaluate and that ultimate, direct measures of quality may not be available until after the product is complete. For this reason, criteria that *are* measurable and available during development and that predict eventual quality need to be monitored.

Basili and Rombach also strongly recommend that the question "Who is responsible?" be answered this way: "An independent software quality assurance group within the software development organization." This kind of group can provide the independence needed to enforce standards when the pressure of expediency might lead us to ignore them. Also, a quality assurance group provides the continuity and focus needed to analyze performance in past software projects and initiate plans for improvement in the future. Although projects come and go, like footprints on the beach, washed away by the tide, a strong quality assurance group can provide lasting stability and keep the imprint of the project from disappearing (Figure 2-3).

When the appropriate kind of planning for quality is done, and the established procedures are systematically observed, the results are impressive. For instance, Mills, Dyem, and Linger ([MIL87]) indicate that the "clean-room" methodology, which depends on meticulous design and extensive formal verification, results in a 30% increase in overall productivity, a 50% decrease in software faults, and increased ease in locating errors that do occur. Careful planning and attention to quality resulted in much more dramatic productivity and dependability increases in the project reported in Posten and Bruen ([POS87]).

### 2.1.4 Quality Assurance

Quality assurance embraces the technical, as opposed to managerial, activities necessary to achieve product quality. These activities are often referred to as verification and validation. Verification refers to those activities that ensure that we are "building the product right". These activities include appraising all work products to be sure they meet the established standards, tracing all portions of the work products back to the previous documents to verify that development continues correctly and that all requirements are being met, and examining or testing all work products to see that they contain no faults.

Validation, on the other hand, ensures that we are "building the right product." This process involves activities that guarantee that the product meets the customer's needs. Specification is the first validation activity and the acceptance test is the last. In between, however, quality assurance personnel confirm that the software is meeting all the constraints that are outlined in the project plan and that the work products seem to meet the reasonable demands of the customer. This may involve obtaining user feedback on the project as it progresses.

Reifer, using a different terminology, divides quality assurance into four separate areas [REI79]: auditing, inspection, verification, and testing. **Auditing** is the rather mechanical inspection of work products for completeness and compliance to standards. It should utilize software tools as much as possible. **Inspection** is the examination of work products to locate errors. **Verification** is the tracing of each element back to previous documents. A good software engineering environment database system provides support for verification. **Testing** is executing the code to find errors and determine reliability. Testing methodologies and tools are discussed in Chapter 8.

Inspecting locates and removes problems in the software and documentation, provides information about the current status of the work products and the process as a whole, motivates staff to greater effort, and promotes a timely conformity with the organization's standards. Ackerman, Buchwald, and Lewski ([ACK89]) cite evidence that inspections are a more economical way of removing defects than testing. This idea is compatible with the concept that it is cheaper to remove errors earlier in the life cycle.

Formal Inspection–
People with clipboards
looking at documents

Review–person presenting
information to group from
lectern using blackboard

Walkthrough–
three people at table with
documents in animated
discussion

**FIGURE 2-4**   VERIFICATION BY INSPECTION, REVIEW AND WALKTHROUGH

Several different roles may be played during inspection: the moderator who conducts it, the recorder who documents it, a designated reader who focuses on details, individual inspectors who examine the product under review, and the producer of that product.

The inspection task can be organized in various ways. Weinberg and Freedman in [WEI84] suggest that an inspection be carried out in a **formal** way, using a checklist of items to be verified. Such inspections deal solely with the product itself; its producers are not included. Inspections are usually carried out by quality assurance personnel; the results are subsequently transmitted to the development team, and a separate summary of results is sent to the project manager. Thus, inspections locate technical problems within the work product and feed back information about the work status to management.

Fagan in [FAG76] suggested that there be six tasks during an inspection. Following a **planning** effort, part of which is a determination that all prior work products have been approved and are available, there is an **overview** session in which the producer brings other members of the inspection team up to speed. The team then engages in **preparation**, using complete and precise copies of the work product to be inspected. During the actual inspection **meeting** problems are found, listed, and classified. Then, there is **rework** on the part of the producer and **follow-up** to ensure that the problems detected during inspection have actually been solved. Fagan's view was that inspections should include the producer so that he could answer questions.

An alternate method of inspection is to hold a **review**. This is a less directed activity; instead of a predefined item checklist, topics are suggested and questions are asked by the people attending the review. One method of imparting some organization is to have the software engineers responsible for the product "walk" the participants through it, highlighting important points. There should be a specific moderator for the review, and a clerk should take minutes ([FAG76]).

The purpose of an informal **walkthrough** is not to attack, nor is it to solve problems in a work product. Instead, it should allow the producer to lead a few of his peers through the product, inviting the participants to ask questions and make suggestions. Questions raised during the walkthrough should be responded to at a later date, and a summary should be furnished for management purposes.

Inspections can occur at many levels; some deal with the entire project, others with small facets of it. A preliminary design review is an example of the first kind, and most of the software team would like to attend it. An inspection to determine completeness of testing for a single procedure would include very few people. Similarly, the preliminary design review would be a very formal and organized meeting, while a code walkthrough for a few procedures should be informal and should progress according to the needs of the moment.

Each project should be operating under a software quality assurance plan that specifies the responsibilities and required tasks of the quality assurance team. This includes the types of inspections to be performed, the standards that each work product will meet, the authority to enforce correction of deviations, the method of record keeping and archiving, and the tools and methodologies to be used in quality assurance.

### 2.1.5 Project Accounting

Determining the state of the various parts of the project to better direct the project is a managerial quality assurance task. The primary quality attributes important for management are progress, cost, schedule, completeness, dependability, and documentation. Progress, cost, and schedule should be tracked for individual parts of the product as defined by the work breakdown structure created for cost estimation. They also need to be summarized for the project as a whole.

It is very important to obtain objective measures of progress; usually we depend on a milestone for this purpose. A **milestone** is a specific action, like holding a review or submitting a completed and audited document. As we pass a milestone, we can be relatively sure of the state of the work product involved.

On the other hand, if we just ask a software engineer how a particular assignment is shaping up, we will be told that it is about 90% complete. This answer is usually more a product of optimism than realism. In fact, in the eyes of software engineers every task seems to be 90% complete for 90% of the duration of the task. This unwarranted optimism is sometimes called the "90% syndrome" (Figure 2-5).

Progress, cost, and scheduling are generally best represented graphically, although one might use tabular forms (or spreadsheet software) to gather and store individual data. The chart shown in Figure 2-6 gives the schedule for completion of four different modules in a software package. The chart indicates actual events that have occurred (top of line, black triangles) as well as scheduled events yet to occur (bottom of line, open triangles). The numbers below and above the lines represent budgeted and actual person-days.

Figure 2-6 also indicates project progress. This project seems to have passed milestones indicating completion of 21% of the work at a time when we had anticipated that 27% of the effort would be made. There are two possible reasons: first, we may be working less productively, thus achieving 21% progress with 27% of the effort; or second, we may have worked less time; by expending 15% of the budgeted effort, we have achieved 21% of the progress in the time allotted for 27%. We really need several

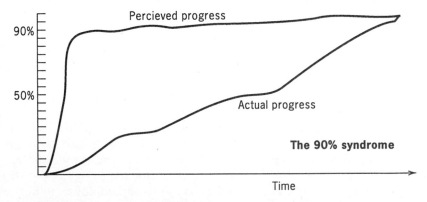

**FIGURE 2-5**   ACTUAL VERSUS PERCEIVED (OR CLAIMED) PROGRESS

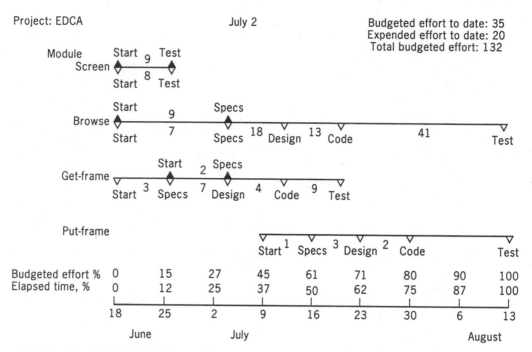

**FIGURE 2-6**  CHART FOR ACTUAL AND SCHEDULED EVENTS

different ways of measuring project status, to get a clearer picture of what is going on.

A manager, looking at Figure 2-6, would want to be sensitive to variations of actual progress from scheduled progress and of actual effort from the effort estimated for that stage of progress. Any significant deviation should be verified by using some alternative or subsidiary measures. The manager should then analyze affairs to determine the cause of the variation. Possibly, this is just an example of bad estimation; if so, that fact should then be fed back to the estimation methodology. Possibly, productivity and performance are really ahead of what was reasonably expected; if so, this secret needs to be uncovered and used in the future. If there is a significant loss of productivity or progress, the cause needs to be found and the situation corrected (Figure 2-6).

To sensitize the manager to critical variances from expectations, it might be better to chart progress as the difference between the expected and the actual, as shown in Figure 2-7. This still does not answer the question of whether the progress variance in June on the chart is due to a lack of effort or to unanticipated difficulties. Figure 2-8 helps to answer that question by charting three different cost graphs. (Since cost is overwhelmingly made up of labor, we actually chart hours worked.) Estimated and actual expenditures are shown, but the third line represents earned hours. These hours are found by multiplying the fraction of total expected progress actually made so far by the total number of hours budgeted for the task.

These measures all depend on milestones and person-hours. Doerflinger and Basili

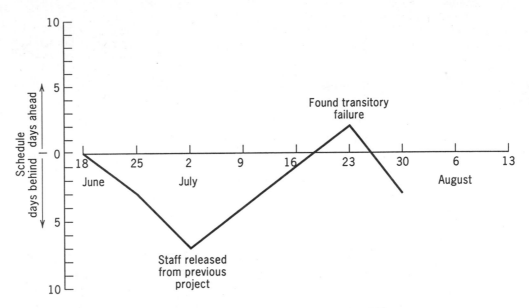

**FIGURE 2-7**   DIFFERENCE BETWEEN ACTUAL AND PLANNED PROGRESS

([DOE85]) suggest other variables that might be used to give an indication of progress, such as the number of computer runs executed, CPU time expended, the number of changes to code, and the number of lines coded but not inspected or reviewed. These variables can be particularly revealing when seen as ratios. For instance, a high changes/(lines of code) ratio is usually an indication of careless design or volatile specifications. Once again, a unified project database will be a tremendous tool in providing these charts and measures automatically, and keeping them up to date.

A chief goal of project accounting is to make the product visible. Since software is an intellectual artifact, it is sometimes hard to decide exactly what its status is. The objective measures mentioned above provide visibility, although their interpretation is sometimes challenged. The other primary visibility is of completed work products; they are the tangible evidence of progress, particularly when they have passed inspection.

The software engineering environment database provides storage and access to all work products. Some of these products, such as the project plan, the software requirements specification, the external design and integration test plans and results, are single documents describing the entire software package. Other work products describe only part of the entire software; but all products concerned with a particular program unit should be stored together, perhaps organized by the work breakdown structure. The contents of the project plan and the work breakdown structure are explained in Chapter 3.

A file of related documents is often called a unit folder. It contains the work products themselves, as well as inspection results and sign-off documents indicating satisfactory completion of the product and authorizing initiation of the next stage of development.

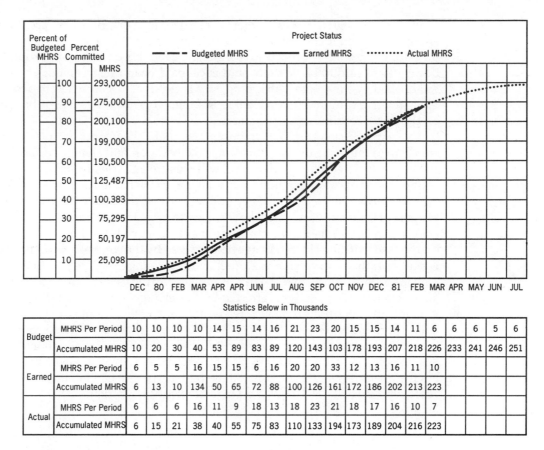

| | | | | | | | | | | | | | | | | | | | | |
|---|---|---|---|---|---|---|---|---|---|---|---|---|---|---|---|---|---|---|---|---|
| **Budget** — MHRS Per Period | 10 | 10 | 10 | 10 | 14 | 15 | 14 | 16 | 21 | 23 | 20 | 15 | 15 | 14 | 11 | 6 | 6 | 6 | 5 | 6 |
| **Budget** — Accumulated MHRS | 10 | 20 | 30 | 40 | 53 | 89 | 83 | 89 | 120 | 143 | 103 | 178 | 193 | 207 | 218 | 226 | 233 | 241 | 246 | 251 |
| **Earned** — MHRS Per Period | 6 | 5 | 5 | 16 | 15 | 15 | 6 | 16 | 20 | 20 | 33 | 12 | 13 | 16 | 11 | 10 | | | | |
| **Earned** — Accumulated MHRS | 6 | 13 | 10 | 134 | 50 | 65 | 72 | 88 | 100 | 126 | 161 | 172 | 186 | 202 | 213 | 223 | | | | |
| **Actual** — MHRS Per Period | 6 | 6 | 6 | 16 | 11 | 9 | 18 | 13 | 18 | 23 | 21 | 18 | 17 | 16 | 10 | 7 | | | | |
| **Actual** — Accumulated MHRS | 6 | 15 | 21 | 38 | 40 | 55 | 75 | 83 | 110 | 133 | 194 | 173 | 189 | 204 | 216 | 223 | | | | |

**FIGURE 2-8**　ESTIMATED, ACTUAL, AND EARNED EFFORT. (Norman Howes, "Mananging Software Development," *IEEE Transactions on Software Engineering,* copyright © 1984, IEEE.)

Unit folders help to establish visibility for the product and individual accountability.

The strength of the unit folder approach becomes evident when the only measures of progress and effort gathered are cumulative and measure the performance of an entire group of people; it is hard to manage individuals. A unit notebook makes it possible to determine whether people are meeting their individual goals and working hard for the project.

## 2.1.6 Product Control

Product control consists of a set of procedures meant to identify, control, provide, and log the various work products of a software project ([BER84]) and is more frequently called **configuration management**. Its purpose is to identify and store "official" copies of all products that might be needed by the project or by customers and to provide these when requested.

During the initial stages of their construction, work products are not yet stable enough to warrant control of this nature. But when they have passed an inspection milestone, they are "officially recognized" and become group property. Such a document is said to be "frozen" and is called a **baseline**, in analogy to the baseline established by surveyors in mapping out a large area. Just as property descriptions are given relative to a surveyor's baseline, so other work products will be built depending on the fixed, baseline work product.

As the product is frozen, it comes under established control procedures. The first step is to identify the product. Since it is likely that it will change somewhat, and it is possible that alternate versions of it will exist for alternate implementations of the product, identification includes a version and implementation designation.

Should changes to a controlled product become necessary, then the first step is to propose the change and notify the software team of the proposal. Everyone is given a chance to respond, listing the ramifications of such a change along with points in favor or opposed to it. Should the change be approved by the control board, then notification is sent out, the new version is stored, and the change itself is documented with the reasons, ramifications, and the like. Product control is also responsible for seeing that all other controlled products affected by this change are updated (Figure 2-9).

Controlled products represent read-only information for most of the team. They are able to obtain any version of any product, but changes have to come through the control board. During planning it is necessary to decide which work products *will* be controlled and to select a software tool to assist in product control. If a software engineering environment is being used, this will be part of the project database system. In other cases, a product like SCCS (Source Code Control System) in the UNIX environment can be used.

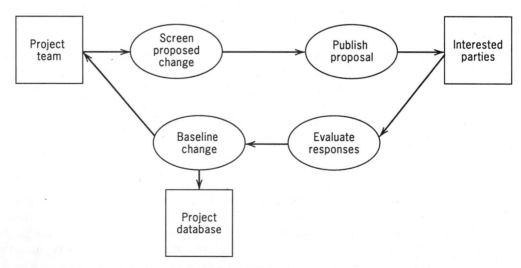

**FIGURE 2-9**   CHANGING A BASELINED DOCUMENT

All versions of work products that are under product control should be archived by the system. These persistent objects in the project database may represent a large mass of data, but appropriate management systems, incorporating change control tools, allow us to record no more than the modifications to previous versions, rather than store the new version in its entirety. When it is necessary, the tools can then build the newer version. Such tools can also identify, and in some instances automatically update, dependent products.

Each project should be operating under a software configuration management plan that specifies the responsibilities and required tasks of those involved in product control. It includes the naming scheme for work products, the relationship of various products to each other, the authority to receive and control products, the method of authorizing changes, and the tools and methodologies to be used in quality assurance.

## 2.1.7 Software Documentation

A software product is composed of code and documentation. Documentation consists of all the information about software, except the code itself. In size, the code is by far the smaller part of the product. The production of effective documentation is sometimes overlooked, but it is vital to the success of software engineering. Documentation is aimed at three different audiences: the software engineer, who will depend on documents from previous life cycle stages to guide continued development and maintenance; the manager, who will use documents from past projects to plan and understand current projects; and the user, who will learn how to use the software from documentation.

Within the organization, decisions have to be recorded in some permanent fashion, forming a baseline for continuing development of the product. Such a baseline document can only be changed with special authorization, and in that case automatic notification of those most interested will result. Thus, documentation provides information in a more efficient and less intrusive way than shouting down the hall. This is particularly true when documentation forms a part of the project database. Such a repository allows us to access the right information quickly, always provides exactly the same information to whomever asks, and gives needed visibility to the progress of the project.

It often seems unfair to the software engineer that a user judges the product on the basis of its documentation rather than the performance of the code. From the engineer's limited viewpoint, he fails to see that the best program in the world is useless if one does not know how to operate or maintain it. The fact is that quality documentation is considered to be the hallmark of desirable software. The purchaser of packaged software often has little on which to base his decision except the quality of the accompanying documentation. Consider these two quotes ([EVA83], [COV85]):

> The most critical aspect of software development is the creation of excellent documentation, not the production of elegant code.
>
> — *M. W. Evans, P. Piazza, and J.B. Dolkas*

Documentation is arguably *more* important than programming. After all, the program becomes usable only through documentation.

— *M. K. Covington*

In preparing documentation, careful consideration has to be given to a number of factors. First, documentation should be *complete*: all known, pertinent information should be given somewhere. Second, documentation should be *consistent*; inconsistency will destroy the reader's confidence in the documentation. The biggest challenge is not consistency in the original documentation but maintaining consistency through all the changes the product may undergo. There are situations in which we must produce an individual document with extra care, including writing baselines on which an entire project will depend, documents that have multiple authors, and documents that will be delivered to the customer.

Third, documentation has to be pitched at the *right level* for its intended audience. A training manual cannot demand as much from its readers as a design document can. Hence, we have to identify the audience, determine its characteristics, background, and needs, and plan accordingly. We should use an appropriate level of formality, and an appropriate vocabulary in our presentation.

Finally, we need to select the *right approach* in presenting information so that it will be readily understood. This certainly includes a choice of format: text, technical manual, workbook, tutorial, video or audiotape, online help package, and so on. Illustrations and tables are very important, since they organize and present large

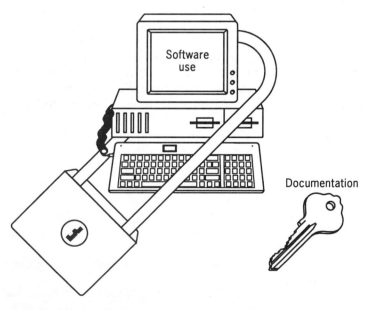

**FIGURE 2-10**   DOCUMENTATION PERMITS SOFTWARE USE

amounts of material for quick comprehension. We should also consider the need for adjunct material like indices, exercises, bibliographies, appendices, and glossaries.

The documentation task consumes a large part of the total effort on a software project. Documentation's share of effort is estimated at 30% in [BOE81], while [EVA83] indicates that it might exceed 50%. As a rule of thumb, very large projects, particularly those that provide software of the U.S. Department of Defense, budget more effort for documentation than for code development. Obviously, we cannot leave a job of that magnitude to do itself. At a minimum, we will require someone to act as a documentation coordinator, who will follow the production of documentation and make sure that standards are being followed. Large organizations may hire editors, graphics designers, and printers; small organizations may contract these services out. The advance of computer text processing, graphics, formatting, and typesetting technologies has allowed many software engineers to develop expertise in documentation.

Publishing a high-quality document involves many different skills and steps. Although software for desktop publishing is becoming more sophisticated each year, many software engineers lack the necessary skills to do a good job of writing documentation. Technical writers, employed by the software organization, can work with the software engineer in producing documentation. Technical writers function best when they themselves understand the subject matter of the documentation, so they should be hired with that in mind or trained in house.

There are two reasons for the almost universal dislike that software engineers have for producing documentation. First, they do not see the need for it, and second, they do

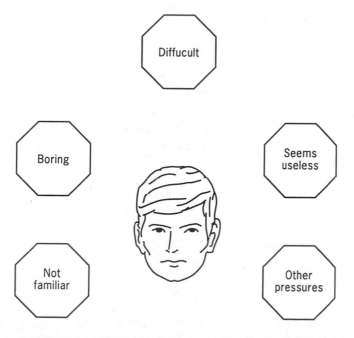

**FIGURE 2-11**   WRITER'S BLOCK IN SOFTWARE ENGINEERS

not feel capable of doing it. The need has already been outlined; failure to understand it indicates either that one is new to the profession and hasn't yet had time to appreciate the benefits of documentation, or that one is so wrapped up in the pressures of the moment that long-range goals have become obscured.

As for not feeling capable, there is a lot to be said for that argument. It is the reason that so many organizations hire documentation experts to assist software engineers. There are a number of good books that help train or guide technical people in writing skills (e.g., [ADA83], [BIR85], [BRO84], [FOE86], [POS84], [SOM89], or [STU84]). Sometimes, the feeling of inadequacy derives not so much from being unable to express one's self as from an inability to talk about technical subjects with nontechnical people. However, if a sufficient amount of willingness is present, this can be overcome.

The unfortunate result of this resistance is that the documentation task becomes low priority. If standards are not enforced, then documents may be sketchy and incomplete or delayed until later. Of course, a delayed task becomes ever more difficult to start. Even worse, as the work becomes more remote in time, our recollection fades and documentation actually grows harder. If the pressures of a tight deadline are added to this mix, we may find that documentation is never done. This *may* help us move the product out the door sooner, but it will surely shorten the useful lifetime of our software.

One way by which the software engineer can assist the technical writer is in providing examples of correct use of the software. These are data sets for input, together with the response of the software to the data. An explanation of the meaning of the output and its relationship to the input must be provided. Where errors are indicated, corrected input data should follow so that users can see how to resolve their mistakes. Examples should be carefully selected to provide insight into correct and incorrect use of the system. Users will frequently want to try these "safe" scripts out on their own as part of their learning.

## 2.2 Managing Risk

An important part of choosing a strategic plan for a project is deciding whether that strategy can succeed. The feasibility of any alternative plans needs to be assessed from economic and technical angles and then risk must be calculated. If the plan does not seem likely to work, it needs to be discarded. One of the remaining alternatives is then selected for the same feasibility analysis.

Feasibility is evaluated by determining whether the strategy meets the goals and requirements that have been chosen within the constraints that have been set by the user. We can increase the precision of our study by asking, not just "Can it succeed?" but "How much will it benefit us?". The latter question is frequently investigated by means of cost/benefit analyses and risk analyses.

### 2.2.1 Economic Feasibility

Basically, the evaluation of economic feasibility depends on knowing the costs and benefits of the proposed solution. If these can be measured in common units (dollars?), then a feasible solution is one in which the benefits are larger than the costs, while the best solution, from an economic standpoint, is the one which produces the largest profit.

Unfortunately, there are many ambiguities in trying to measure cost and benefits. Even with fairly detailed costing methods, which will be outlined in Section 3.3.3, the resulting cost estimates are notoriously unreliable. This problem can be partly resolved by using several different cost estimating techniques, and proceeding only if they are in rough agreement; but even this method is not perfect.

Another source of ambiguity is the fact that benefits may be tangible or intangible. Tangible benefits, like the salary saved by replacing a single worker with an automated system, are fairly easy to quantify. Intangible benefits, such as "improved customer confidence resulting from the impression that automation means we are up to date," are harder to quantify. This does not mean that intangible benefits should not be considered — simply that it is harder to incorporate them into an economic feasibility study. Typical costs and benefits encountered in software engineering are shown in Figure 2-12.

It is important to notice that the point of view in Figure 2-12 extends beyond the interests of the software organization to those of the customer. There are two reasons for this. First, for contract software, the cost/benefit analysis is often used to help convince the customer that the software should be purchased. Second, the software engineer has an obligation to consider the needs of the customer as well as his own. This will increase his success in the long run, although it might cause him to reject a solution that would be personally more profitable, selecting one that is socially more responsible ([BOE81]).

If it is impossible to reduce all benefits to monetary units, it may still be possible to compare alternative solutions through limited cost/benefit ratios. In such a case, a measure of a benefit under different alternatives (e.g., total control of inventory, weekly assessment of inventory, no control of inventory) can be associated with costs of providing those alternatives ($100,000, $12,000, $0) to get a feeling for the degree of

| Costs | Benefits |
|---|---|
| Labor during development | Use of existing labor |
| Labor during operation | Reduced operational labor |
| New equipment (purchase, maintenance, depreciation) | Replacement of equipment maintenance (sale, maintenance, depreciation) |
| New software purchases | Other use of new software |
| Conversion from old system to new | Improvement of system |
| Increased data gathering | Increased control |
| Employee discontent | Employee satisfaction |
| Training for employees | Increased productivity |
| Lost opportunities | Increased capacity |
|  | Better market stance |
|  | Basis for further growth |

**FIGURE 2-12**   SOME COSTS AND BENEFITS ASSOCIATED WITH NEW SOFTWARE

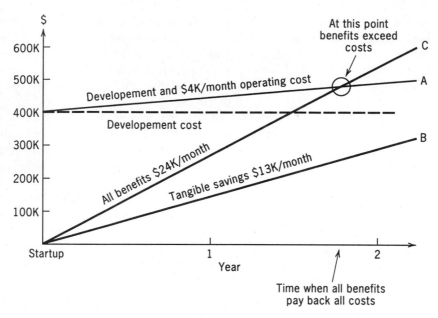

**FIGURE 2-13** A PAYBACK SCHEDULE

benefit per dollar cost. The entire set of cost/benefit ratios can then be examined to decide on a strategy to pursue.

Another question that influences the choice of a strategy is the timing of the benefits and costs being considered. If all the costs are immediate, whereas the benefits will be delayed for many years, then the solution does not seem as attractive. This analysis is usually represented by a payback schedule, such as the one shown in Figure 2-13 ([KIN84]). The lines shown in the figure represent total development costs, which do not change in time and are thus constant; development costs plus operational costs over time; tangible benefits over time; and tangible plus intangible benefits over time. The point at which a benefits line crosses a costs line is called a pay-back point.

## 2.2.2 Technical Feasibility

In some situations, the technical feasibility of a proposed product is obvious; for instance, if the software organization has already produced a C compiler for a particular machine, then there is little doubt that it can produce a Fortran compiler for the same machine. In other instances, technical feasibility may be more in doubt.

The first question to ask is about expertise: do the software engineers know how to develop this kind of product? The next question is of experience: have they done it before? Next is the question of resources: are enough people, computers, software tools, and time available to complete the job within schedule? Finally comes the question of motivation: will everybody concerned cooperate enough to bring the project to a successful conclusion?

Now, what happens when some of the answers are "No"? For instance, it is often necessary to develop a new product for which no proven technology, let alone previous experience, exists. In this case, a development process model that emphasizes proto-typing may be best, since product development can be authorized one stage at a time. The feasibility of each succeeding stage is confirmed by the success of the prototype developed at that stage.

Another technical feasibility question is whether the proposed solution will indeed meet the requirements and constraints developed during systems analysis. Again, extensive experience with this type of product may already make the answer obvious. In other instances, modeling the solution may be a way to establish its credibility.

At the lowest level, a software product can be modeled by developing mathematical formulas that represent its purported function. The model will depend on a few parameters that are judged most important to the software's operation and will provide a few variables judged most important in the software's success. The model can be evaluated not only for attainment of the software's required performance but also for its sensitivity to changes in the input parameters. This sensitivity analysis may allow us to fine tune the design goals of the product.

At a higher level, software can be modeled by a simulation, using more complex or time-dependent relationships between the input parameters and elements of the product. Such a simulation can again be evaluated for success and for sensitivity, just as the simpler mathematical model was. Finally, it may be necessary to model a proposed product with a prototype. In this situation, we usually choose to evaluate the feasibility of a few crucial technical aspects of the software. Such a prototype produces the greatest insight into the feasibility of the proposal but also costs the most.

## 2.2.3 Risk Analysis

One of the principles of pragmatism in software development is the minimization of risk. Risk in software development arises from uncertainties in our plans. Risk can come from several different directions, as indicated in Figure 2-14. The technique for managing risk involves recognizing areas of uncertainty, evaluating the costs of best- and worst-case performance in these areas, and estimating the probability of best- and worst-case outcomes.

Risk analysis is conducted as an extension of cost/benefit analysis. Costs and benefits are estimated in monetary units for the best- and worst-case eventualities, and then these values are multiplied by the probability of those eventualities, giving the expected value of each case. For instance, if there is a 20% chance of a moderate schedule slip, which would cost $15,000 and a 7% chance of a severe slip costing $45,000, the estimated cost of slips would be $0.2 \times \$15,000 + 0.07 \times \$45,000 = \$6150$. This is done for each of the alternative strategies, and then a single strategy is chosen.

There are two ways in which this choice can be made. The most reasonable and pragmatic method is to choose the outcome for which the worst-case loss is minimized (or, if worst-case results in a gain, the gain is maximized). A riskier approach is to choose the alternative for which the best-case gain is maximized.

The reason for minimizing possible loss rather than maximizing possible gain is that

| Economic | Technical |
|---|---|
| Low market demand | Poor software dependability |
| High development costs | Low software dependability |
| Contract penalties | Excessive resource use |
| | Loss of key personnel |
| | |
| | Schedule slips |
| Liability for damages | Stiff competition |
| Contract dispute | Pirating |
| Infringement claims | Inflationary costs |
| **Legal** | **Management** |

**FIGURE 2-14**   SOME SOURCES OF RISK

loss and gain are not usually evaluated as being equally important to an organization. That is, a loss of $50,000 can hurt one's career more than a gain of $50,000 can help it. Of course, if the potential best-case gain far exceeds the worst-case loss, then it might well be worth taking a chance on it.

One other note should be made in connection with risk analysis. Its difficulty is usually due in part to our lack of precise information about the product. Boehm ([BOE84]) points out that prototyping and other exploratory methods are ways of "buying" information, on which to build our plans more solidly. This is, in fact, the basis of the spiral model.

But buying information may not always be a bargain. To ensure the value of exploratory techniques, four circumstances must hold. First, there have to be several viable and relatively likely alternative courses of action. Second, we have a good chance of evaluating the benefits of each alternative. Third, the cost of investigating the alternatives ought to be is relatively low. Fourth, there should be some side benefits from the investigation.

## 2.3 MANAGING PEOPLE AND THE ORGANIZATION

Some software engineers choose the profession to escape personal interaction; they're more comfortable with predictable machines than with other people. But, in fact, for each successful software hermit, happily programming alone in his windowless basement office or mountaintop cabin, there are a hundred unsuccessful hackers who cannot deal with people and whose work is unsatisfactory to employers and customers alike. "People skills" *are* important.

The software engineer relates to people in many ways. The user is human, and software must be carefully designed to take into account users' psychological weaknesses and strengths. The customer will demand understandable documentation and continued support and hand holding. A software manager has to deal with all the personality quirks of his fellow professionals. Few software projects can be developed

**Manager**

| | | |
|---|---|---|
| Schedule and monitor work. | Budget. | Motivate. |
| Hire, fire, and evaluate. | Purchase. | Arbitrate. |
| Reward. | Maintain equipment. | Interface. |

**Analyst**

| | |
|---|---|
| Interview customer personnel. | Transmit customer requests. |
| Understand customer needs. | Explain customer environment. |
| Define new software function. goals. | State software requirements. |

**Designer**

| | |
|---|---|
| Choose or create software structure. | Choose or devise algorithms. |
| Choose or create subsystem interfaces. | Design test procedures. |
| Choose or devise data structures . | Direct detail workers. |

**Detail Worker**

| | |
|---|---|
| Follow and flesh out design. | Debug program units. |
| Write compilable code. | Exhibit self-discipline. |
| Have complete grasp of the programming language. | |

**Tester**

| | |
|---|---|
| Believe in quality assurance. | Test software systems. |
| Enforce standards pleasantly. | Cope with complexity. |
| Develop test data. | |

**Librarian**

| | |
|---|---|
| Make work products publicly available. | Organize materials. |
| Control changes to work products. | |

**Whiz**

Provide prototype software quickly.
Interface to system software.
Give advice on language nuances.

**F I G U R E 2-15**   TASKS CARRIED OUT IN SOFTWARE ROLES

by one person and still arrive on the market soon enough to compete. The simplest commercial projects probably require one person-year of effort, whereas the most complex may involve thousands of person-years. Teamwork means depending on others and being dependable yourself. It also means spending a sizable part of your time in meetings or reading and writing memos. A reasonable estimate is that a software engineer spends half his time interacting with others.

Of course, the only reasonable way to use many people together on a single project is to have them specialize their activities; Figure 2-15 shows some of the tasks undertaken by software personnel in their various roles. Do not assume, however, that people will function purely in any one of these roles. Instead, they will often have some concurrent responsibilities under various roles. The manager's role is the most complex and unfamiliar and is discussed a later in this chapter.

### 2.3.1 Software Roles

The **analyst** serves as the project pioneer and contact man with the customer. He frequently needs to wear business attire, although he would be more comfortable dressed in a software engineer's traditional garb. Without the analyst, software people would continually find themselves designing the wrong software in the wrong way, and then wondering why nobody wants to use it. The analyst has duties in two different places: the customer's environment and the software environment, and serves as the bridge between the two.

Although we often speak about "the customer," many software organizations do not have the luxury of a contract with a specific customer who has agreed to purchase the software product under development. Rather, they are forced to determine what market exists for new software products and what form the products should take. This can be done by market surveys, including interviews of typical users of the proposed software and evaluation of similar products already on the market. In any case, it is the analyst that connects the outside world with the software development team.

**FIGURE 2-16**   THE PERILS OF TECHSPEAK. (Doonesbury, copyright © 1984, G.B. Trudeau. Reprinted with permission of Universal Press Syndicate. All rights reserved.)

To play this role, the analyst must first speak the customer's language. This requires a reading background in the user environment as well as a willingness to put aside the technical jargon of computer science. Too often, a precise technical statement is heard by the customer as "megabyte blocks per binary sort frame in the parity channel," technical jargon. The customer only wants to talk about inventory or music or machine tool design.

Coupled with the ability to speak the language, the analyst needs to be a talented interviewer. This requires a mixture of patience and the ability to direct a conversation into productive channels, as well as taking highly structured and organized notes. Sometimes a tape recorder can help. It is usually necessary to interview people, then come back to them again. In subsequent interviews the analyst reviews their conversation and explains what he has understood from it. This may prompt the user to amplify and extend the previous information.

Going beyond language, the analyst must be able to absorb quickly the essentials of the operation to be automated by the software. This requires an open mind, a quick understanding, and the ability to distinguish between the essential and the irrelevant. Surprisingly, users frequently do not understand what they really need. They may dwell on nice, but very minor points, while forgetting to mention fundamental issues; or they may be so concerned about a problem that has been bothering them that week that they dwell on it and give it undue importance.

Another problem arises from the unbounded expectations of users. They feel they have nothing to lose in asking for the moon, since software very often seems like magic to them. The analyst interviews before any cost estimates have been prepared, so the user is not yet deterred by expense. The analyst can correct this problem by helping the users to establish priorities among the various functions to be performed by the software, as well as the performance (speed, size, reliability) requirements.

The analyst is the software organization's representative with the customer (Figure 2-17), and will maintain that relationship throughout the development of the product.

**FIGURE 2-17**    THE ANALYST IS THE BRIDGE BETWEEN TWO ENVIRONMENTS

The analyst will serve as a pipeline for information flowing back and forth between the two parties. He will also be a filter, shaping the nature of the software by focusing on the important parts of the task and winnowing out the unimportant.

From the software organization's point of view, the analyst practically *is* the user. He transmits requests for software features to designers and explains the background behind these requests. Later on, when the time comes to write the software requirements specifications, the analyst will play a large role in putting the user's requirements into language technical enough for designers to base the software on. In fact, the analyst will largely determine the external appearance and functionality of the software.

The analyst experiences both the good and the bad of being a go-between. On the one hand, he has great influence on the eventual shape of things. On the other hand, he is truly caught in the middle — looking like "the other person" to both the customer organization and the software organization. It takes very strong communication and adaptive skill to fill this role.

The **designer** comes closest to what you envision when you hear the title "software engineer." It is the designer's duty to take the user's specification of the external function and appearance of software and turn it into running software. Usually the designer is helped by detail workers, but the ultimate responsibility is his alone. The designer also has the most obviously creative role in the development of software. An outstanding designer possesses deep understanding of the application environment, good communicational skills, and a compelling drive to achieve. The designer is the one who powers the project and is its nexus for communication and decision making ([CUR88]).

On the other hand, creativity does not come cheap. If you look at the verbs in Figure 2-15, they generally include "choose" along with "create." In almost any software project, economics is the driving force. Designs that already exist are usually much less expensive than newly invented ones, even if they are also less fun. Hence the designer often has to swallow his artistic aspirations and do things in the same old way.

The major task of the designer is to create a software structure and the accompanying interfaces between software modules. This requires the logical skill of dividing a process into well defined and independent subprocesses; it also involves the insight necessary to determine the exact amount and structure of information that must be passed between the modules. This is compared to the job of the architect, who must design structure, form and function, but rarely (in the role of architect) gets involved in the details of drawing actual blueprints. Since the designer of software will largely "farm out" the design of individual modules, the designer only gets involved with detail in designing the interface between modules. Since detail workers will take this interface as their starting point, it must be precise and complete.

Creating or choosing appropriate data structures and algorithms to be used within specific modules is a secondary design task. Designers have to correctly balance complexity in the data structure and the algorithm, since this balance has the effect of minimizing the overall software complexity. More often than not, these choices are fairly obvious to someone with broad experience in software design. It is always desirable, and sometimes possible, to use existing modules "off the shelf." Usually, existing software will require some reworking before it can be used in the current context. The designer must compare the effort of creating the ideal data structure/ algorithm configuration with the ease of using an existing configuration, then choose the best compromise between the two.

A designer must also be prepared to specify the ways in which the program modules will be tested and validated as they are put together. Detail programmers will be responsible for the individual modules, but they may have incomplete understanding of the system as a whole. They will work under the direction of the designer, but he will be the one to say that everything fits together in a reliable and seamless fashion. This forces the designer to help produce a set of tests that will confirm that the software meets the requirements of the specifications, that there are no hidden time bombs buried in it, and that it performs with acceptable efficiency.

Design is fun and frustrating at the same time. It is the role for which most people are prepared by conventional computer science curricula, and is probably the most coveted position in the software organization. Those who do it well often end up continuing in the role for the span of many projects. Those who do it badly must learn to develop usable talents in other tasks.

The **detail worker** is the one who actually gets the work done. Others prepare, evaluate, assess, explain, administer, and plan. But somebody has to *do* it in the end. The detail worker does it. He corresponds to the carpenter, the assembly line worker, or the auditor. The detail worker is the one who *manufactures* the product.

The primary duty of a detail worker is to faithfully implement the design of individual program units. This frequently involves amplifying the architectural design by adding those details that it glosses over. Such design work is followed up by the actual writing of code in some programming language. At other times, the detail worker is involved in the modification of existing software to make it fit the interface defined for it, thus bypassing any significant design steps. This work is straightforward and sometimes tedious. It is rarely challenging in the creative sense.

Of course, to do these things requires a relatively complete knowledge of the programming language being used for the implementation. Knowledge of this language and experience with it are fundamental skills for the detail worker. Even more important is the ability to debug the software that is produced. This involves an ability to trace execution, to hypothesize likely causes of failures, and especially to consider systematically a very large set of possible states and circumstances. Contrary to intuition, debugging often requires more time and effort than detailed design and coding.

The detail worker is called on to cooperate with the overall plan and philosophy of the project. The production of software is not an individual effort but part of a team accomplishment. It requires self-discipline to take directions without resentment. If this is done, the resulting product will demonstrate a unity of concept and presentation that will be important during the operational stage. Self-discipline is also important in the day-to-day efforts of the detail worker. Files must be kept up to date, communication with others is always going on, debugging must resist the momentary expediency of a quick fix (called a **kludge**) and careful documentation of unit testing is vital. These and 100 other jobs have to be performed on time, according to standards and under the shadow of failure when one becomes disorganized.

An unfortunate reality of software engineering is that the **tester** is frequently the

**FIGURE 2-18**   THE TESTER ENFORCES STANDARDS WITHOUT FEAR OR FAVOR

pariah of the organization. The tester's task is to evaluate and correct the work of others. Nobody likes a critic, so it takes a special person to do this job right. The first criterion is a firmly held belief that quality assurance is vital to the success of the organization ([BUC84]). This means constant vigilance to see that standards are met during all phases of software existence. The tester applies these standards to all work products beginning with the initial analyses and continuing through the modifications made during maintenance.

The tester has to have an uncompromising sense of duty, unquestioned integrity, unflinching courage, and rigid discipline; yet he cannot be overly rigid. Standards must be applied in a way that encourages cooperation rather than resistance and ridicule. It takes real talent to convince people to make efforts when they appear to delay unnecessarily an already late assignment (Figure 2-18).

The tester's responsibility is to test entire software systems as they are integrated from the individual units created by detail workers. The first need is a well-conceived set of data that will exercise the software in all its aspects. Development of test data requires a deep understanding of the requirements of the software, as well as familiarity with the actual software design. The software designer and detail workers cooperate closely with the tester, providing a test plan and guidance in choosing the best test data. Second, the tester may have to create a fair amount of **scaffolding**, code which takes the place of missing program units to allow the testing of one part of the complete system at a time.

Testing is a major part of the development task, often surpassing the design and implementation phases in the effort and time it requires. The tester must organize this very complex task by keeping careful records of the results of all tests, and the changes that may have been dictated by test results. Detail and design workers usually provide much of the testing manpower needed during this stage.

The **librarian**'s job is to make sure that all the documents, test data, test results, code, and logs for the project are in good order. Of course, this usually means a particular directory on a disk rather than a room; but paper documents also need to be kept by the librarian. Product control is the librarian's principal task. Of course, a really good project database system can serve in place of a human librarian.

The **whiz** is known to anyone who works in an organization. He always knows the secrets of how the (computing) system works. Among the whiz's other talents is that he is typically a very fast code writer. The designer often uses the whiz to test out ideas for data structures and algorithms by rapid prototyping. The whiz spends a good deal of time giving advice to others when an obscure question troubles them. This may deal with the nuances of how a language is actually compiled or with the structure of files or how the system does buffering or paging. The whiz is often called on to implement code with extensive interfaces to system facilities. Although most detail workers aspire to be designers, some fall in love with systems and feel successful when they have become whizzes. In some cases, whizzes are grownup hackers.

There are also a lot of **extras**. These people provide vital services to the software team, although their expertise is not in the software area. They are the **operators** and **field engineers** of the equipment. They provide **secretarial** and **janitorial** services. Some do **data input** for the software team, whereas others are **technical writers.** Beyond them are the money people, the salespersons, the receptionists, and all the rest who exist in any organization, but who do not work on a daily basis with the software engineers.

### 2.3.2 Software Team Organization

It is a truism that the best government is no government. But we seldom find ourselves in a situation where we are able to dispense entirely with the trappings of government: supervision, authority, and regulation. A few excellent software projects have been able to do so, and more power to them. Most frequently, the software engineer finds himself working within a definite organization and submitting to the authority of others.

From the description of the roles played by software people, one can deduce an **obvious** organization, as shown in Figure 2-19.

This organization shows two separate groups, under the control of the designer and manager, plus the semiautonomous analyst. The division between manager and designer is largely on the grounds of technical versus general activities, except for the

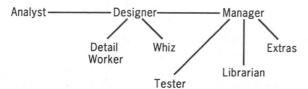

**FIGURE 2-19**   THE "NATURAL" SOFTWARE TEAM ORGANIZATION

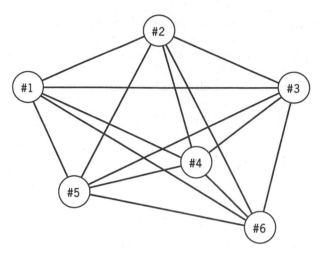

**FIGURE 2-20**   AN ANARCHISTIC TEAM

tester. Since the tester's job is to find errors in the design and implementation of the software, it is better to insulate him somewhat from the people who have done the design and implementation. Hence, the tester reports to the manager.

The designer, however, may find himself bogged down in the communication overhead of his job. Supervising three or ten detail workers, plus the whiz, can require a great deal of time. Added to this, the designer is undertaking supervision tasks that the manager might be better able to undertake. The result is that this normal and intuitive structure may not be the best.

The idealized, **anarchistic**, organization has proved effective in some circumstances (Figure 2-20). In these instances, team members have been highly competent and highly motivated. They have voluntarily chosen to fill any specialized roles that they assumed. They have worked in an atmosphere of frequent intercommunication and public discussion of their work. Individual goals have been melded into a group unity and purpose, and individual egos have been forgotten. Figure 2-20 illustrates the anarchistic environment. Notice that the dotted lines in the figure represent the necessary lines of communication. This organization has the worst communication overhead, since everybody has to talk to everybody else. In fact, the lines of communication are proportional to the *square* of the size of the team.

Many factors that contribute to the success of anarchistic groups are worthwhile. For instance, Weinberg has promoted egoless programming ([WEI71]). This type of software development divorces the work product from the individual who produces it. Work products become the joint property and responsibility of the entire team. This fosters constructive criticism and standards and avoids unpleasant surprises; the latter occurs when you find out what your colleague has actually been doing all this time. Criticism is of the product, not the producer. There is no individual blame. The real foundation of success in egoless programming is simply the decision by each member of the team that the team effort is more important than individual achievements.

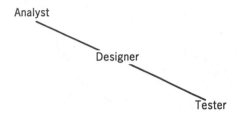

**FIGURE 2-21**   PHASES OF DEMOCRATIC LEADERSHP

Anarchistic teams do present problems, however. They may suffer from a lack of direction. It is difficult to maintain sufficient motivation to keep everybody working hard in the absence of authority. Anarchistic teams suffer from a high communication overhead; this is because everybody has to know everything that is happening, since all decisions affecting the group as a whole have to be made by the group. It is thus impossible for anarchistic teams to get very big, which in turn limits them to relatively small software projects. Finally, bringing together the right people for an anarchistic team is chancy at best; we cannot count on its happening.

A more dependable organization is the **democratic** one. Once again, it requires the cooperation of team members in making major decisions. But authority is vested in some of them (perhaps on a rotating basis) to make minor decisions and enforce them among the rest of the team. Frequently, team leadership rotates from the analyst to the designer to the tester as different phases of development are reached, as illustrated in Figure 2-21. Like the anarchistic team, the communication overhead of decision making limits the democratic team to relatively small projects. On the other hand, this structure may be ideal for difficult or experimental projects, since small groups work best for problem solving ([MAN81]).

One answer to size limitation is the **bureaucratic** organization. Here different working groups are organized as the leaves of a tree, with nodes above them being occupied by supervisors (see Figure 2-22). These are usually people functioning in a blend of the analyst, designer, and manager roles. By partitioning the software effort into relatively independent subsystems, they are able to reduce communication to a few channels. Although this allows the construction of large software systems, it also creates a tendency to authoritarianism, at least above the individual team level (and probably there, as well, by emulation). Such organizations may exhibit the fatal tendency of having good news flow upward and bad news downward. That is to say, managers are always given an unrealistically rosy picture of progress and respond to the eventual problems by heavy handed interference in matters about which they know too little. Though less effective than small teams, there is no alternative to the large bureaucratic team when really large products are developed.

Another suggested organization, due to Mills and Baker ([BAK72], [BAK73]), is the **chief programmer team**. In one current modification, it takes the obvious organization, described at the beginning of this section, inserts an "alter ego" and reorganizes the structure as shown in Figure 2-23. The individual designer at the top of the structure

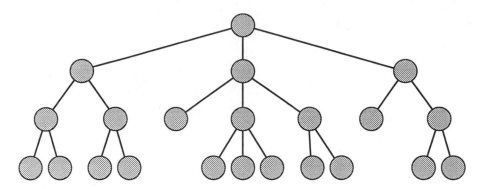

**FIGURE 2-22** THE BUREAUCRATIC TEAM

is referred to as the chief programmer. The fundamental goal of the chief programmer team is to reduce the communication and administrative load on the designer as much as is possible, allowing the designer to concentrate on what he does best, designing and implementing software. The alter ego and the manager serve to communicate the chief programmer's needs to the rest of the team. The manager picks up all purely administrative tasks, whereas the alter ego provides research assistance and a sounding board for ideas (and a backup in case of heart attack). A very talented person can be extraordinarily productive in the role of chief programmer ([BRO75], [MIL83]). Chief programmer teams are a good choice when a relatively large and difficult job must be completed within tight time constraints ([MAN81]).

When the chief programmer organization works, it is by using extreme specialization, similar to that exhibited in a surgical team. The result is a software package that shows a high degree of philosophical and stylistic unity. Such software is much less costly to maintain as the years go by. Unfortunately, people with the talent necessary to make this organization function correctly are rare.

An obvious difficulty exists when we talk about "the team" that produces and maintains software. Different roles are needed during different phases of the software's existence. The analyst is used heavily up front, the tester and detail workers in the middle, the maintainer at the end. Are these people callously hired and fired at strategic moments? Or do they sit on their hands or wander around looking for useful

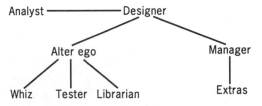

**FIGURE 2-23** THE CHIEF PROGRAMMER TEAM

things to do when they aren't needed? The software organization might hire people as temporary employees from some organization that specializes in this kind of placement. Small organizations have greater difficulty doing this, since they depend so heavily on establishing team spirit.

A partial solution, which preserves the fundamental team structure, is found in allowing the same person to fill various roles on the team at different times. The analyst could also be a tester, while everybody serves as a detail worker as needed. Perhaps one of the detail workers could be kept on for maintenance. Although this technique serves a useful purpose in allowing people to experience variety, shed their parochial attitudes, and develop many talents, it does not develop the efficiency that is a frequent result of specialization.

Typically, a larger organization (50 or more software people) can shift employees from project to project or share them on two projects at once. This maintains a constant level of employment for the organization while also assigning staffs of varying size to projects. In these **matrix** organizations, each software engineer is part of an individual project and of a permanent department — analysis, planning, design, implementation, testing, documentation, or maintenance. A more drastic solution involves abolishing the concept of the team altogether. Instead, the software organization is grouped into specialty departments. A software product moves from department to department as it travels through life, shepherded by a project manager. This method certainly provides for specialization, but suffers from a lack of continuity. Expertise gained with the product during design is lost by the time it reaches different people in testing. Also, workers may feel trapped in a rut if they are forced to work in one department for more than a year or two.

An even more severe penalty is paid in terms of lost loyalty and enthusiasm for the project. Only the project manager nurses it through its entire history, and he is seen as

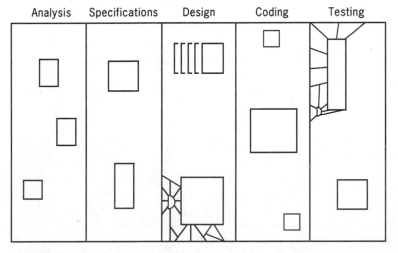

**FIGURE 2-24**   SOME PROJECTS CAN BENEFIT AT THE EXPENSE OF OTHERS

an outsider in every department. Projects can be put on the back burner by any department supervisor, and department members then find themselves caught between two bosses, the supervisor and project manager (Figure 2-24).

None of these organizations or structures is *the* answer ([MAN81]). Circumstances, the history of the organization, the quality of available personnel, and the size of the product will all influence our choice. All other things being equal, team organization is preferable to departmental organization, and something approaching the democratic team is most practical.

As part of the pragmatic approach to software engineering, we should seek to work on small projects as the opportunity arises. There are several benefits of small teams that will contribute to their success. First, small software teams have the potential of developing a real esprit de corps, which is normally missing in the faceless mobs of the really large projects. The feeling that one is part of a select group of people, and the enjoyment of working closely with others, improve job satisfaction.

A small team reduces the overhead of management and team communication. The result is that a larger proportion of the team's effort can be spent on developing software. Small projects can also be completed more rapidly, especially if we employ reuse and prototyping. This short span, together with team spirit and less organizational overhead, may allow us to keep the real hot-shots interested in the project. These highly productive software engineers are also highly mobile. If they get bored with a project they have the ability to find another job, not only removing a very useful team member but also disrupting the progress of the team until a replacement is found and trained.

### 2.3.3 The Psychology of Software Engineers

What kinds of people do you encounter working as software engineers? You might see a mixture of all possible psychological profiles, but there are certain traits that seem to prevail among software engineers, some of which are particularly troublesome for them.

**FIGURE 2-25**  A SOFTWARE ENGINEER MUST COPE WITH ADVERSITY. (Doonesbury, copyright ©
1972, G.B. Trudeau. Reprinted with permission of Universal Press Syndicate. All rights reserved.)

A software engineer gets impatient at least several times a day — with a slow machine, an obstinate colleague, a customer who does not understand things, a supervisor who demands too much, and most of all with himself. Software engineers live with the most complex mechanisms devised. Something is always going wrong or being changed. There is always pressure to get more done faster. Everybody gets impatient, but some are more sensitive to frustration and opposition than others. This is no profession for someone who cannot cope with hindrances and stress.

Along the same lines, flexibility can be invaluable in a software engineer. He must adapt to the needs of the user and the wishes of his colleagues. New methodologies and technologies arise frequently in the field, and he must accept them as they come. New machines and tools replace old ones and new assignments on different projects come regularly. A software engineer's career is an evolution, and adaptation is the tool by which the fittest succeed.

An almost universal characteristic of programmers is their unfounded optimism. They believe, despite years of experience to the contrary, that changes to software can be implemented in just a few hours (or days or weeks). This must come in part from the realization that software is essentially an intellectual construct and in part from a belief that the powers of their intellects are unbounded.

At any rate, software engineers chronically underestimate the effort needed to produce software. At any time following the second week of design, engineers will tell you that the package is "about 90% done"— after all, the rest is just details that can be cleared away in a few afternoons' work. Testing will take very little time, since their software does not contain any errors. Integration will be a breeze because of the skill with which interfaces were designed. Of course it is not so, but they believe it, year after year.

Since software is an intellectual creation, some designers tend to look on it as an expression of creativity, cleverness, and artistic ability. They become attached to their product and exhibit real possessiveness about it. This is counterproductive in team situations which require adaptation of their work. Hearing these people in a walkthrough of their design, one is reminded of a father defending the beauty of his baby's nose and ignoring the mole on its cheek. Egoless programming is the answer to this attitude; it has the additional effect of making work products less private and more the public property in the team ([SHN80]).

It should be obvious that communication talents are vital to a software engineer. He communicates with other people directly during meetings, conferences and telephone calls and indirectly through documentation, memos and mail. It is not unusual for a software engineer to spend as much time at a keyboard writing documentation as programming, and to spend as much time in meetings as at a keyboard. Every effort should be exerted to develop writing and speaking skills during the software engineer's schooling. But beyond these skills, a software engineer must have the patient interest in other people that will make him an effective communicator.

Analytic thinking is another vital talent for the software engineer. He will spend much of his professional life taking problems apart, understanding their true nature, and matching up solutions. The ability to organize, see patterns, subdivide problems, and distinguish the forest from its constituent trees is essential. This ability has been described by Soloway ([SOL86]) in terms of *goals* and *plans*. Goals represent the desired behavior or specifications for software. Plans are standard algorithms or code segments which achieve these goals. The analytic technique of stepwise decomposition of problems represents the subdivision of goals to the point that plans for the small subgoals exist and can be *composed* synthetically into a software package.

## 2.4 THE SOFTWARE MANAGER

The **manager's** primary task is to keep the organization running smoothly, so that the other software engineers can concentrate on developing software. Management is one of the prime determinants of whether one's job is a source of joy or misery. The manager's tasks within the software team fall into three categories: supervising, motivating, and hiring.

The manager also serves as the business interface between the project team and the rest of the organization, as well as the users and customers. So far as the organization is concerned, his biggest task is being a salesperson: writing proposals, convincing others that this project is worthwhile and developing it successfully; promoting the reputation and influence of the group; obtaining budget increases and freedom from organizational oversight. The manager should cultivate opportunities to present a realistic, but positive view of the group to the organization.

For the customer and user, the manager is a facilitator. He sees to it that requests for service and support are routed to the appropriate personnel and that responses are timely and thoughtful. Additional efforts must be taken to maintain contact with customers. These will provide a continuing flow of business and an awareness of changes in the marketplace. Individual staff members, particularly the analyst and the customer support person, can be used to assist in these tasks.

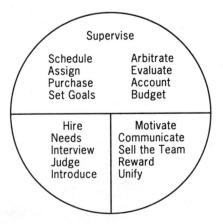

**FIGURE 2-26**  RESPONSIBILITIES OF THE SOFTWARE MANAGER

It should be evident from the foregoing list of duties that the manager's role is varied and that it requires significant interpersonal skills. Managers have to understand technical questions, show management expertise, be salespersons, cheer others up, and stay cheerful themselves. It is not a role to be underestimated, even though some organizations choose managers at random. Good management requires exceptional skills and understanding. It is not enough to promote an excellent technician to management; without the skills, a good technician can be lost and an inferior manager gained.

## 2.4.1 Supervising

We have discussed planning and control for three resources: money, time, and work products. Of course, the real value in a software organization lies with its personnel. The most effective planning and control we can conduct is in reference to people.

It is necessary to examine the schedule to determine how many people will be needed during each stage of development and maintenance. Being able to provide the right number of qualified software engineers at each stage may be difficult, but will certainly help optimize profits. If more people are on the project at any time than can be effectively utilized, productivity falls. If we are shorthanded, then schedules slip.

On a long term basis, the manager needs to move employees from role to role. This is most easily done as projects wind down. Employees should be left in a role long enough to develop and productively use the role's specialized skills, but not so long that boredom or the feeling of being at a dead end take over. It is beneficial for employees to acquire experience in all areas of the profession. They will be better able to communicate with each other and support each other's activities; and they can fill

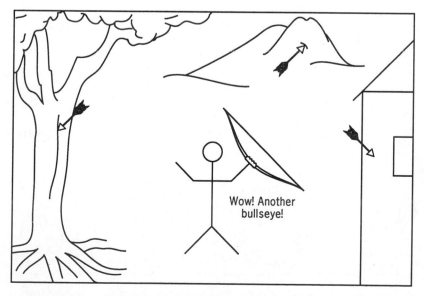

**F I G U R E 2-27**   TARGET SHOOTING WITHOUT THE TARGET

in for each other during an emergency. They also feel a greater sense of participation and power within the organization.

Professional employees want to work, and resent having their work held up by lack of resources. During the planning of a software project the hardware and software resources required for completion of the project must be determined. The manager must ensure that these have been ordered or scheduled and are in place by the time personnel are assigned to work on the project. After that, hardware maintenance must be scheduled periodically, and software updates must by installed, usually at the manager's direction.

But supervision skills go far beyond the ability to provide the right people and resources at the right time. A supervisor would be well served by an understanding of small-group psychology and dynamics. For instance, it is necessary for a supervisor to facilitate goal-setting for the entire group. He must also assist individuals in setting their own goals, and then monitor them as they work toward these goals. The supervisor's purpose is only secondarily to reward or to punish; more important is providing feedback on how well one is doing. Goal setting and evaluation are vital to success. Indeed, how do we measure success if we have no goals? Conversely, if we have no target, we are almost sure to hit just that — nothing (Figure 2-27).

The supervisor plays an important role for team members who are not achieving their goals. Understanding and encouragement, suggestions and relief may all be needed. Occasionally, of course, there is no way to remedy the situation. It is then the supervisor's challenge to terminate the activity (or worker) in such a way that the experience still provides additional understanding and growth.

Standard methods of employee evaluation are needed, both to ensure fairness and to avoid the possibility of complaint or even lawsuit. Management by objective is done by sitting down with the employee periodically and coming to an agreement about goals and responsibilities for the near future. At the same time, success in achieving the goals and meeting the responsibilities of the last period is evaluated. This provides an immediate technique for assessing the performance of employees. Software engineers

**FIGURE 2-28**   COMPUTER OPERATOR BENEFITS. (Doonesbury, copyright © 1972, G.B. Trudeau. Reprinted with permission of Universal Press Syndicate. All rights reserved.)

can be managed by objective and their work assessed every three months. Employees who show poor performance, may need to be motivated or may need to be fired.

Nonprofessional employees (e.g., like computer operators, janitorial and clerical staff) sometimes need more supervision. Their work is not usually as compelling or rewarding. Although professionals are used to working in a relatively unsupervised fashion, hourly employees have often come to expect and need more specific management. Similarly, these employees require more immediate evaluation and reward and more specific benefits, including fixed working hours and conditions and scheduled pay raises.

The manager must control the monetary resources of the project. These are generally budgeted in two categories: equipment and personnel. Equipment budgets are relatively straightforward, as long as maintenance, supplies and depreciation are included. Personnel budgets are calculated by taking the salaries of all professional employees and multiplying by a factor for benefits (benefits = salary x 0.25) and another factor for support (support costs = salary x 0.5) ([TUR84]). Support costs include items like space and furniture, utility costs, non-professional staff services, supplies, travel and professional development. The personnel budget is then the sum of salaries, benefits and support.

Trained, scarce, and irreplaceable human labor tends to be rather expensive, and labor costs are a large majority of software costs. When employee benefits and support costs are added to a relatively high salary, a small software team can cost upwards of half a million dollars a year. At prices like these, software engineers need to be very productive, or the software must have a very wide distribution, or it must be vital to someone. Otherwise, it cannot be justified.

Sometimes, legitimate individual goals and desires are hard to satisfy. At this point, the supervisor needs to arbitrate and to make final decisions. If the supervisor's leadership capabilities are strong enough, team members will accept these decisions and work with them, rather than continue to complain and undermine further progress. This last can be detected by complaints or simply by a drop in productivity. Here are some principles to observe in handling conflict.

1 Stay in contact with people, to learn quickly of conflicts.
2 Spend plenty of time listening before drawing any conclusions.
3 Attempt to find a solution of the conflict that can benefit all parties involved (a win-win situation).
4 Focus on constructive suggestions. Where criticism is needed criticize actions, not people.
5 Be patient and expect patience and tolerance from others.

In cases of ongoing incompatibility between team members, the supervisor often has to provide most of the cohesion for the project.

Many people consider being supervised as slavery; and, in truth, this feeling can be the result of inexpert supervision. Nevertheless, capable supervision promotes freedom instead. People are free from many of the burdens of personal relationships and can perform the work for which they were hired. Workers receive support, encouragement, and directions when needed. There is much to be said for good supervision, and many organizations have failed because of a lack of it.

### 2.4.2 Hiring

One of the keys to success is the ability to hire experienced and capable software engineers. This depends to an extent on the salaries and benefits that are offered; software project managers may have little control over these. However, careful study of the organization's needs, along with diligent recruiting, is within the scope of every manager. Likewise, innovative and significant projects, and a reputation for producing excellent products, will tend to attract the best personnel despite less than excellent salaries. These *are* within the manager's scope of influence.

Job applicants can be evaluated using the following criteria:

1  Does the applicant have the technical and communication skills needed to fill the job, as evidenced by his prior work record and/or academic record?
2  Does the applicant show appropriate personality traits: cooperation, adaptability, ability to handle stress, persistence, and independence? These can be determined by a job interview, by the candidate's past history of job changes, by letters of reference, by telephone calls to references, and even by the administration of standardized tests.
3  Do the applicant's stated professional and economic goals fit in with the goals of your organization? Is he likely to be happy here, or will the applicant want to move on in a short period of time?

Most managers are reluctant to fire an employee, since it usually means losing a considerable investment in training and experience. The best way to make the decision is to outline the dollar cost of continued poor performance against the cost of replacing the employee, and then, if the decision is not clear, to keep the employee on out of loyalty. All employees will be aware of this and will generally respond with a return of loyalty to the organization.

The demand for software personnel always seems to exceed the supply. The U.S. Bureau of Labor Statistics has for years published lists of jobs in highest demand, with programmers and systems analysts usually heading the list. During boom years, staff raids are systematically organized, as one company tries to lure away another's employees. During bust years, new graduates may need to go out and look for jobs, rather than waiting for recruiters to come to them. But still, they all seem to find employment.

Barry Boehm ([BOE83]) estimates that by 1990 the United States will face a shortfall of 1 million workers in production of software engineers and computer scientists. This shortfall represents the difference between the personnel that the economy would use if available and the number actually available. There are many reasons for this shortfall, most rooted in the U.S. educational system, which frequently fails to train students in those basic skills needed for the study of software engineering. Software engineering does not pretend to address the problem directly, but rather attempts to make the available personnel more productive, thus softening the effect of the scarcity of trained labor.

Still, labor costs have a tremendous impact. The software industry, unlike many others, is still labor intensive. Frenkel ([FRE85]) believes that the demand for new software is growing exponentially which, if true, means that we must either find a way of producing it that does not require a lot of labor, or do without much of the software we desire. Tools exist, and should be used where possible, but "The essence of a software entity is a construct of interlocking concepts" ([BRO87]). Conceptual constructs are born in people's minds, and Brooks points out that no advances now on the horizon will allow us to automate software production as we have hardware production.

This means that software costs will continue to be largely determined by labor costs, and the feasibility of a project will often be determined by what employees are available. Each software manager should be constantly monitoring an organizational plan for hiring, training, and developing staff. This is the only way of staying ahead of the very competitive game of developing quality software engineers.

### 2.4.3 Motivating

The ability of a manager to influence people comes to the fore in the motivation task. Professionals are usually motivated by the knowledge that they are doing good work, and that their work is appreciated. The manager should spend some time weekly, or even daily, checking in with the staff to determine how things are going. This is the moment to find out about success as well as failure, to develop a friendly relationship, and to let the employee emerge from his personal worry space to see the larger picture of the organization's progress. The manager should give appreciation for success, and understanding and support for difficulties. A manager can tell that he is spending too little time with the employees if the reaction when he steps up to somebody's desk is "Oh no. What have I done wrong? What does _he_ want?"

It is also the manager's duty to apportion rewards to employees. These can take the form of pay increases, special equipment like workstations, better office space, and educational opportunities. Since most software engineers are motivated by success, special equipment to improve productivity often increases satisfaction significantly. In the same light, success and satisfaction are enhanced by educational opportunities (attendance at conferences and seminars, paid tuition or time off for classes). As professionals, software engineers are expected to work as much as is needed to accomplish assigned tasks; there is no eight-hour day. On the other hand, wise managers provide compensating time off after a period of exceptional effort and always manage to schedule vacations for their staff. Overtime pay is not a positive reward, since it does not give a break from the burden. But of course, overtime pay is better than no reward at all.

Management policies affecting software engineers can enhance their motivation, by making work easier or harder, more or less pleasant. The most important of all policies is one that encourages sharing of responsibility and rewards with employees. This policy rests on making sure that the organization's status and plans are openly discussed with employees. Their cooperation in management-oriented tasks (like process data accumulation) should be acquired by convincing them of the benefits (of gathering data) as an investment in the future. Their ideas and opinions should be sincerely considered in making decisions. Whether an actual democratic vote is taken is beside the point. Software engineers are competent and well educated and need to feel that they are able to influence the course of their professional lives.

Management policies can often debilitate esprit de corps by fostering jealousy, secretiveness, and mistrust. Of course, the manager must guide meetings to ensure that communication between the staff is constructive and not competitive. A policy that fosters the team spirit and mutual respect will improve employee satisfaction and productivity. Even the physical layout of work areas can be designed to provide privacy without forbidding interaction. To strengthen trust and respect, managers should always be meticulous in observing their own rules. If they demand quality work, their own memos should be correctly written, with no spelling mistakes; if they demand responsibility, their meetings should start and end punctually.

## 2.5 MANAGING YOUR OWN FUTURE

It is a major challenge in any profession to keep up with the changes in the field. The rapid development of the software industry only aggravates this problem for software engineers. No matter how much you learn in school, much of that knowledge will be out of date in ten years. No matter how hard you work at developing and maintaining software, you will not generate, on your own, a fraction of the new knowledge being discovered elsewhere. It's up to you to keep in contact with the field.

Keeping current is not just a professional responsibility. As a person's knowledge becomes more dated, his productivity and skills decline in comparison to others'. Eventually, this fact becomes obvious to everybody, and the person's achievement begins to tarnish. So keeping up to date is one of the keys to personal success.

There are two large organizations in the United States to which software engineers belong: the Association for Computing Machinery (ACM), and the Computer Society of the Institute of Electrical and Electronic Engineers (IEEE). ACM leans more to software, whereas IEEE is more interested in hardware. Through the media of national conventions, journals, tutorials, and proceedings, they can inform you of the latest developments in software engineering. Both organizations sponsor local chapter activity that can put you in touch with other professionals in your area.

Within these organizations there are smaller groups with a more concentrated mission. There are currently 31 special interest groups (or SIGs) in the ACM, and 33 technical committees (or TCs) in the IEEE Computer Society. They both publish newsletters and often jointly sponsor conferences, which are advertised in the parent organizations' journals. In particular, SIGSoft (ACM) and the Software Engineering Technical Committee (IEEE) should be of interest to software engineers.

Finally, there are numerous user groups associated with particular brands of hardware or software products. The supplier of the hardware or software can inform you about membership in user groups. Once again, there will probably be national conventions held annually for most user groups.

You should take every opportunity to continue your education after leaving school. At a minimum, tutorial books and text books can be obtained from professional organizations and bookstores. More to the point, it is usually possible to continue taking classes at a nearby university. Although these classes may not lead to any advanced degree, they will certainly enhance your abilities. In all likelihood, your employer will be willing to pay tuition costs, and may even provide time off for attending classes.

If you belong to either the ACM or the IEEE, your name will find its way onto a multitude of mailing lists. You will then receive announcements of professional seminars on an almost daily basis. These seminars and courses vary widely in their usefulness. The best way to judge them is to talk to someone who has attended one and to consider the real experience of those who offer and teach them.

Some of the best seminars are given by nationally recognized universities, often as part of their continuing education efforts. Hardware manufacturers also provide worthwhile courses, although one has to investigate the level at which they are taught before attending. Finally, the professional organizations often sponsor tutorials preceding and following their national conventions, and these are usually excellent.

The journals of the ACM and IEEE are valuable resources, and many people belong to the organizations for no other reason than to subscribe to them. The bibliographies in this book refer to some of the journals that you might be interested in. In addition, there are a number of trade-related magazines, like *Byte* and *Datamation*.

Publications like *Computing Reviews*, *Guide to Computing Literature*, and *Computer Abstracts* can provide useful pointers when researching particular subjects. You should also pay attention to the references made in articles you find; these may lead you to other publications of which you were previously ignorant.

Don't ignore one of the best sources of information and learning available to you — your own colleagues. Foster the ability to talk with others in your organization, and be humble enough to take their suggestions seriously. Study the work of others and try to incorporate its best features in your own efforts. Form contacts outside your organization, and take the trouble to consult with these people when you need help. Being part of this kind of network not only provides learning and updating, but it may some day help you to find that perfect job you've been waiting for.

A continuing organizational development policy should be in place to facilitate constant updating of the software engineer's understanding. Such a policy should require a minimum number of classes or seminars during each year. The organization should also be willing to provide new technology (tools) to support the new methodologies being learned by employees. As a corollary, opportunities for different kinds of work within the organization should be provided for software personnel. Employees should be consulted periodically about different assignments, allowing them to try their wings at something new. Sometimes an entire project will be chosen to satisfy the professional development goals of a group of software engineers.

## 2.6 SUMMARY

Management is not one of the skills cultivated in typical computer science coursework, but it is vital to the success of software organizations. The choice is to use a technical person with managerial ability, or to hire a management person; the former is preferable. The most obvious, and easiest, managerial task is to schedule and track those technical tasks that comprise the staged and longitudinal activities of software development and operation. In particular, planning for, and inculcating, quality in the product is a primary management goal.

It is also up to the manager to consider the sources of strength and weakness in a project. These can be used, along with cost/benefit analyses, to estimate the risks we are undertaking. Risks should be minimized insofar as possible, if we are approaching the software business pragmatically.

Software engineering is not a haven for the socially maladapted. Human issues are paramount to success in this endeavor. Software engineers exhibit certain typical personality failings like unjustified optimism and possessiveness. Other traits like flexibility, patience, communication, and analytic skills are desirable and should be hired or fostered.

Teamwork is the only way in which large projects can be created, and team roles should be assigned in accordance to the talents and preferences of individuals. Team organization is the key to working together efficiently, and choosing the right organization for a particular project and set of people can make all the difference in the world. Managers, in particular, need to understand and manage different personality types effectively. To be able to deal with human issues is a large step toward success in software engineering.

The manager's role consists of many tasks, but primarily they involve supervision, hiring, and motivation. Of course, many of the planning, administrative, and tracking activities of the project may also devolve on the manager.

Finally, we have seen that it is one's personal responsibility, as well as being to one's personal advantage, to keep up with the field. This can be done by taking advantage of educational opportunities, professional organizations, journals, conferences, and the knowledge and experience of colleagues.

## BIBLIOGRAPHY

[ACK89]     Ackerman, A.F., L.S. Buchwald, and F.H. Lewski, "Software Inspections: An Effective Verification Process," *IEEE Software*, 6(3):31 – 36.

[ADA83]     Adams, K.A. and I.M. Halasz, "25 Ways to Improve User Manuals," *IEEE Proceedings of the Conference on Software Development*, New York.

[BAK72]*    Baker, F.T., "Chief Programmer Team Management of Production Programming," *IBM Systems Journal*, 11(1):56 – 73.

[BAK73]     Baker, F.T., and H.D. Mills, "Chief Programmer Teams," *Datamation*, 19(12):58 – 61.

[BAS87]     Basili, V.R., and H.D. Rombach, "Implementing Quantitative SQA: A Practical Model," *IEEE Software*, 4(5):6 – 9.

[BER84]*     Bershoff, E.H., "Elements of Software Configuration Management," *IEEE Transactions on Software Engineering*, 10(1):79 – 87.

[BIR85]*     Birrell, N.D., and M.A. Ould, *A Practical Handbook for Software Development*, Cambridge University Press, New York.

[BOE81]*     Boehm, B.W., *Software Engineering Economics*, Prentice-Hall, Englewood Cliffs, NJ.

[BOE83]*     Boehm, B.W., and T.A. Standish, "Software Technology in the 1990's using a Evolutionary Paradigm," *Computer*, 16(11):30 – 37.

[BOE84]      Boehm, B.W., "Software Engineering Economics," *IEEE Transactions on Software Engineering*, 10(1):4 – 21.

[BRO75]*     Brooks, F.P., *The Mythical Man-Month*, Addison-Wesley, Reading, MA.

[BRO84]      Browning, C., *Guide to Effective Software Technical Writing*, Prentice-Hall, Englewood Cliffs, NJ .

[BRO87]*     Brooks, F.P., "No Silver Bullet: Essence and Accidents of Software Engineering," *Computer*, 20(4):10 – 19.

[BUC84]*     Buckley, F.J., and R.M. Posten, "Software Quality Assurance," *IEEE Transactions on Software Engineering*, 10(1):36 – 41.

[COO84]      Cooper, J., "Software Development Management Planning," *IEEE Transactions on Software Engineering*, 10(1):22 – 26.

[COV85]      Covington, M.A., "Documentation That Works," *PC Tech Journal*, January 1985.

[CUR88]*     Curtis, B., H. Krasner, and N. Iscoe, "A Field Study of the Software Design Process for Large Systems," *Communications of the ACM*, 31(11):1268 – 1287.

[DOE85]*     Doerflinger, C.W., and V.R. Basili, "Monitoring Software Development Through Dynamic Variables," *IEEE Transactions on Software Engineering*, 11(9):978 – 985.

[EVA83]      Evans, M.W., P. Piazza, and J.B. Dolkas, *Principles of Productive Software Management*, Wiley-Interscience, New York.

[FAG76]*     Fagan, M.E., "Design and Code Inspections to Reduce Errors in Program Development," *IBM Systems Journal*, 15(3):219 – 248.

[FOE86]      Foehr, T., and T.B. Cross, *The Soft Side of Software*, Wiley / Interscience, New York.

[FRE85]*     Frenkel, K.A., "Toward Automating the Software-Development Cycle," *Communications of the ACM*, 28(6):579 – 589.

[KIN84]      King, D., *Current Practices in Software Development*, Yourdon Press, New York.

[MAN81]      Mantei, M., "The Effect of Programming Team Structure on Programming Tasks," *Communications of the ACM*, 24(3):106 – 113.

[MIL83]      Mills, H.D., "Chief Programmer Teams: Techniques and Procedures," *Software Productivity*, Little, Brown, Boston.

[MIL87]*     Mills, H.D., M. Dyer, and R.C. Linger, "Cleanroom Software Engineering," *IEEE Software*, 4(5):19 – 25.

[POS84]      Poschman, A.W., *Standards and Procedures for Systems Documentation*, American Management Association, New York.

[POS87]      Posten, R.M., and M.W. Bruen, "Counting Down to Zero Software Failures," *IEEE Software*, 4(5):54 – 61.

[REI79]*     Reifer, D.J., "Software Quality Assurance Tools and Techniques," in *Software Quality Management*, Petrocelli, New York.

[SHN80]*     Shneiderman, B., *Software Psychology*, Winthrop, Cambridge, MA.

[SOL86]      Soloway, E., "Learning to Program: Learning to Construct Mechanisms and Explanations," *Communications of the ACM*, 29(9):850 – 858.

[SOM89]* Sommerville, I., *Software Engineering*, Third Edition, Addison-Wesley, Reading, MA.

[STU84] Stuart, A., *Writing and Analyzing Effective Computer System Documentation*, Holt, Rinehart and Winston, New York.

[TUR84] Turner, R., *Software Engineering Methodology*, Reston, VA.

[WEI71] Weinberg, G.M., *The Psychology of Computer Programming*, Van Nostrand Reinhold, New York.

[WEI84]* Weinberg, G.M., and D.P. Freedman, "Reviews, Walkthroughs and Inspections," *IEEE Transactions on Software Engineering*, 10(1):68 – 72.

## PROBLEMS

**1** What are the advantages and disadvantages of filling software management positions with software engineers? With people trained in management?

**2** Use data from your own community to determine what proportion of total software costs are overhead, above labor and benefits costs. Of labor costs, what proportion is for technical, and what proportion is for nontechnical positions?

**3** Conduct research to determine the relative pay scales of software engineers who possess bachelor's, master's, and doctoral degrees.

**4** Evaluate five different professional publications.

**5** Survey help wanted and full-page ads in newspapers (particularly for large metropolitan areas), trade journals (like *Computerworld*), and professional journals (like *IEEE Software*). What roles seem to be most in demand? Give statistics on which publications have how many jobs, what the typical requirements are, etc. Share this information with your class.

**6** Can you think of a team organization used in some other field (such as sports teams, flight crews, or organized crime) that is unlike any described in this chapter but that could be used? Describe one in detail.

**7** Make a list of the 10 attributes you would look for if you were hiring a software engineer, together with justifications for the importance of each. Make a list of your own ten strongest personality attributes, which you would mention to a prospective employer. Are they the same? If not, why not. What can you do about it?

**8** Software engineers can be either specialists or generalists in terms of the roles they play. Choose one and defend it as the most productive and useful.

**9** Should a person playing the manager role be involved in the technical aspects of software production and maintenance? Why?

**10** Suppose there is no separate individual to carry out the testing role. Who should perform the tester's tasks? Why? What problems might occur in this case?

**11** How can a small organization (e.g., with 10 software people) handle the fact that projects require a much smaller staff at the planning and maintenance stages than at the implementation and testing stages?

**12** List possible measures for estimating a software engineer's capability.

**13** The structure of the chief programmer team as it is described in various publications differs in the presence of detail workers. Is it better to have them or not? How many can there be?

**14** The systems analyst does not have to be an in-house person. He or she could come from the customer organization or a third party organization, like a consulting firm. What are the benefits and drawbacks of each?

**15** Add new sources of risk to Figure 2-14. Are there any other quadrants that need to be added?

**16** Describe a disaster within the software organization that might occur because of poor product control. Are there any which might result from *too much* product control?

**17** What are the complementary advantages and disadvantages of formal inspections, walkthroughs, and reviews?

**18** Are there other important longitudinal activities that were not mentioned in the chapter? What are they, are they universal, and how important are they?

**19** It is possible to evaluate individuals by surveying the opinions of their co-workers. What would be the disadvantages or advantages of this kind of evaluation? Would it be equally valuable as a technique for evaluating managers?

**20** How might an electronic mail system be optimized for use within a software organization?

**21** What role should the quality assurance group have in making management decisions for the software organization?

**22** Give examples of how parts of a proposed database management system might need to be modelled by formulas, by simulation and by prototyping.

**23** In many organizations, detail workers tend to want to be promoted to designers or to analysts. Where do whizzes and testers come from?

**24** Are there certain kinds of software organizations which might find departmental organization more effective than team organization? What are their characteristics?

**25** The frequent optimism of software engineers has been pointed to as a source of problems. Is it also a strength? Why?

**26** What quality assurance procedures should be implemented as a project starts.

**27** Examine the operating system manual for the computer system you normally use. Evaluate it as written documentation in the following categories:

Organization

Layout

Graphics

Clarity of objectives

Examples

Ease of searching for a particular topic

Clarity

Error recovery procedures

# CHAPTER 3

# THE ANALYSIS STAGE

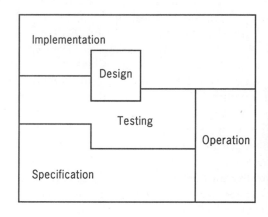

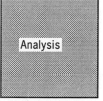

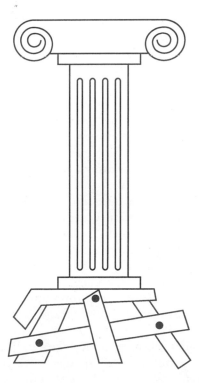

In this chapter, we begin to follow software development and maintenance activities through each of the stages of the software life cycle. It is important not to let the linear order of the book influence your thinking about the actual order of software activities. Remember, *only the traditional process model proceeds in an even, linear fashion from analysis to maintenance.*

The analysis stage, as the first step in the process, will set the scene for success or failure. Euripides stated this fact succinctly when he said "A bad beginning makes a bad ending," but the Bible paints a more colorful picture: "[A] foolish man...built his house upon the sand: and the rain descended, and the floods came, and the winds blew, and beat upon that house; and it fell: and great was the fall of it."

A beautiful column on a weak foundation is at best foolish, and at worst dangerous.

## 3.1 THE ANALYSIS PROCESS AND PRODUCTS

Orienteering is a little-known and demanding sport. In principle, it is a competition in which participants are transported into a wilderness area, given maps with their current location and their goal marked, a compass and other outdoor gear, and then left to find their way to the goal as best they can. Those who arrive most quickly win. Contestants must complete three tasks before they can start toward the goal: they must study their actual surroundings and correlate them with the map; they must discover what barriers (cliffs, dense underbrush, rivers, etc.) might hinder their progress toward the goal; and they must choose the path that is the quickest and easiest.

The software team — and particularly its point man, the systems analyst — is in approximately the same position as it faces a problem at the start of a software project. Given a map (experience and professional knowledge) and equipment (methodologies and tools), the team must find out where it stands (problem analysis), locate the barriers to progress (customer, environmental and software organization constraints), and choose a path (the project plan) that will lead to the goal while consuming the least time and money. The apparent simplicity of the task should not deceive us, however; managers chronically underestimate the cost of gathering information ([CUR88]).

The major document developed during this stage is the project plan, outlined in Figure 3-3 (see [COO84]). The plan (and all other work products) results from a cycle of goal setting, writing, evaluating, and rewriting until it is correct. The first version of the project plan is unlikely to be acceptable.

### 3.1.1 Purpose of the Analysis Stage

The basic purpose of the analysis stage is to define the requirements of the proposed project. These requirements range widely, from what the customer expects the software to do, to what the goals and expected benefits to the software organization are, to how many people and how much time will be required before the project is done. Planning the project and establishing procedures and an organization are important secondary purposes.

None of us wants to see the software we are building collapse into a heap. We must be sure that the foundation, the first stage of our construction, is secure. The analysis stage prepares the necessary plans for completing a successful software project. We need to understand the user environment and the way things are done there, as well as the specific needs that have convinced the customer to purchase the software product. The three major problems with large projects are lack of understanding of the application environment, requirements volatility, and ineffective communication and coordination ([CUR88]). All these problems can be minimized by effective customer relationships during this stage.

Customer needs and interest are not a sufficient reason to undertake a project. For this reason, we also need to decide whether the venture will be advantageous to our organization. This depends on what our goals are. Hence, we need to decide whether we can produce the software at all, what the risks are, what the goals of the organization are and whether we can meet the constraints that the customer wants to put on the project.

Getting oriented
Determining the function of the product
Conducting feasibility studies
Setting goals for the project
Choosing a development model
Cost and schedule estimation
Planning for software quality

**FIGURE 3-1**  TASKS ACCOMPLISHED IN THE ANALYSIS STAGE

Assuming that the answers to all these questions still indicate that we should continue with the project, next we have to choose a model of the development process. This will form the framework for our estimates of the effort that will be required, the number and type of software engineers who will be needed, and the duration of the project. Finally, we have to establish the quality assurance, product control, and project accounting procedures that will enable us to achieve a quality process and to create a quality product.

| | |
|---|---|
| **Orientation** | Market Research |
| | Selling Ourselves to the Customer |
| **Analysis** | Studying Documents |
| | Interviewing |
| | Observation |
| | Surveys |
| | Customer Goal Setting |
| **Feasibility Study** | Cost Estimation |
| | Benefit Estimation |
| | Risk Analysis |
| | Modeling/Simulation/Prototyping |
| **Goal Setting** | Constraint Definition |
| | Software Organization Goal Setting |
| **Model Selection** | Product Profiling |
| | Strategic Planning |
| **Cost/Schedule Estimation** | Work Breakdown Study |
| | Delphi Analysis |
| | Project Modeling |
| | Bidding |
| **Planning for Quality** | Standards Selection |
| | Staff Assignment |

**FIGURE 3-2**  ANALYSIS ACTIVITIES

### 3.1.2 Activities During Analysis

In accomplishing the tasks shown in Figure 3-1, we must perform a number of activities. These are listed in Figure 3-2.

At the end of the analysis stage, the project plan has to pass a *management review*. If the software is being developed under contract, customer representatives should be part of the management review team. This review determines whether the plan is sufficiently complete and accurate, and whether the planned project is likely to be advantageous to the parties involved. A decision to continue with the project is based on its potential benefits, not its technical feasibility. Hardly anybody is in business to produce software just because it can be done.

### Project Plan

**Introduction**
  Description of the problem
  Description of the problem environment
  Client and software organization goals
  Proposed solution and its scope

**Proposal**
  Functions provided through the proposed solution
  General strategy for developing the solution
  Role of users and hardware in the solution
  Advantages and drawbacks of the solution

**Constraints**
  Customer Priorities
  Profile of users and tasks
  Expected lifetime of the product
  Dependability requirements
  Performance requirements
  Existing data interface and hardware environment
  Future extensions of the product
  Required implementation language, if any
  Training, installation, and documentation requirements
  Availability of customer environment

  Alternative solutions
  Feasibility of proposed and alternative solutions

**Estimates**
  Work Breakdown Structure
  Schedule
  Staffing and organization
  Budget
  Cost - benefit analysis
  Risk analysis
  Deliverable tools needed

**Procedures**
  Process model
  Methodologies and notations
  Standards and quality assurance
  Accountability monitoring
  Product Control
  Testing and source of test data
  Acceptance criteria and method of payment

**Reference**
  Documents used in developing the plan
  Glossary of terms
  Proposed contract (if any)

**FIGURE 3-3**  CONTENTS OF THE PROJECT PLAN

### 3.1.3 Analysis Documents and Deliverables

The project plan, which is the major deliverable of the analysis stage, is the foundation document of the entire project. It contains a proposal for the product itself, as well as a description of the environment in which it is to be used and plans for developing it. Those plans indicate the schedule, budget, and procedures of the project.

The working documents (on-site interview reports, market surveys, rejected strategy developments) that lead to the plan and the minutes of the management review, together with any follow up documents that result from its decisions, are the minor documents created during the analysis stage.

This pattern of having working documents leading to a major document that is reviewed and approved before continued product development is followed throughout all the stages of the software life cycle. Indeed, each stage is pretty much defined by an iteration of the pattern, as shown in Figure 3-4.

## 3.2 ANALYSIS PRINCIPLES

Sections 3.2.1, 3.2.2, and 3.2.3 outline principles of good analysis. First, there is a discussion of goals the software engineer should have in mind in conducting analysis. These are not the goals we have for the entire project, but some goals of the analysis process itself. Next, we consider some of the characteristics of a good project plan, including clearly stated purposes for the project, accuracy, completeness, and a solid underpinning. Finally, we discuss a special topic, which is not seen too often in treatments of software engineering: how to determine the needs of anonymous

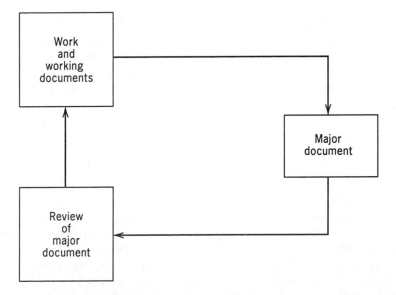

**FIGURE 3-4**  THE PATTERN OF DEVELOPMENT, PROPOSAL, AND APPROVAL

customers, how to sell a product to them, and how to bid on a project announced in a request for proposal.

### 3.2.1 Goals for the Analysis Stage

It is tempting to say that user satisfaction is <u>the</u> key to success in software development. After all, success is most often measured by commercial standards; the products that are most satisfactory to customers are usually the ones purchased most often. These products, in turn, are the ones that usually provide the greatest profits. The foundation of all this success is the ability to determine what the customer wants and what will satisfy him. The analysis stage is centered around the customer — discovering the customer's wants and needs, restrictions, and goals. Obtaining a true picture of these customer-oriented requirements is the first goal of analysis.

Users are often unjustifiably dissatisfied with a product, when their problem is just that they have no confidence in it; they may be people who base confidence on appearances. Thus, user satisfaction may depend on whether the user likes the looks of the software and its developers and documentation. For this reason, we should pay attention to those aspects of the organization on which customers might base their judgment. If dress, grooming and behavior of the personnel conform to what customers expect, the customer will be more disposed to be favorably impressed by the product. If the organization's business is conducted in a timely and professional manner, they will be doubly impressed. First-rate documentation and advertisements are also important.

It is also true that automating previously manual processes creates a more boring and isolated working environment. Since the analysis stage is the period that throws us into the first, and greatest, contact with customers, we have to be careful to put our best foot forward, allaying their anxiety about the impact of our project. It is vital that we feel sincere concern for the users, and demonstrate our willingness to help them.

After installation, users will seek help from the software engineers who produced their software in two ways: by consulting manuals and by direct contact with the software organization to obtain **technical support**. From the organization's point of view, a single extended phone call can be much more expensive than the cost of printing a single manual. Thus, expenses are minimized by deciding, right now, that the user's needs will be met, insofar as is possible, by published documentation.

Even with the best documentation, there are bound to be questions that require an expert answer. Software providers usually furnish telephone and correspondence consultation to users. Since this can be a very expensive activity, there may be rules that assess fees for technical service, immediately or after some initial amount of free time. On the one hand, the software organization does not want its best people tied up on the phone all the time. On the other hand, dissatisfied customers may be the kiss of death. Still, the software engineer has to choose between spending time developing the software, documenting it, or answering questions (Figure 3-5).

One way of reducing the time required for technical support is to shift some of the questions to correspondence, in which the user submits bugs or questions on magnetic media or through electronic mail networks. Another method for reducing consultation

**FIGURE 3-5**   CHOOSING THE LESSER OF EVILS

and improving customer satisfaction is planning for an **open software architecture**. In this situation, the customer is given sufficient information to understand the system by himself, and will be able to make his own modifications, perhaps using tools we provide to customize the software to his own needs, including capabilities for establishing new input and output formats, changing prompts and command names, changing defaults, adding new commands, modifying the content and frequency of appearance of menus and help screens, and modifying the hardware requirements of the software.

Finally, it is important not to underestimate the effect that one's self-confidence has on others. This has to be the most tenuous basis for being satisfied with a product, since self-confidence can be radiated by someone who has no real ability. Nevertheless, few people will believe in you or your product, unless you seem to believe in yourself.

However, although user satisfaction is fundamental, it alone cannot guarantee success. Too many software products have been wonderful to use but have still failed because they had too low a profit margin, were too expensive, could not be obtained easily, were unmaintainable, or were behind the times. Hence, we have to take steps during planning that will reduce the risk of failure because of these or other causes. In fact, risk and uncertainty reduction are major goals of the process. It is not easy to read the future, but we will see some methods for doing so.

On the basis of our understanding of user needs and the risks of the proposal, we can then erect a framework within which to build the product itself. It is our goal to make this framework as strong and supportive as possible, consisting of schedules, work assignments, procedures, standards, resources, and goals that we establish for the project plan.

### 3.2.2 Characteristics of Good Analysis

Accuracy and completeness are the primary characteristics of good analysis. We will build every other major work product — the specifications, design, code, and user documentation — by referring them back to the plan. A fault at this stage will propagate errors throughout the entire product. For this reason, market research, customer interviews, workplace observation, and the like, must be scrutinized and crosschecked. Cost and schedule estimates should be obtained in more than one way; if they agree, we might be able to trust them. Risk analyses should be reviewed by qualified people other than their creators.

For the same reason, the project plan should be complete, since missing information simply represents an error by omission. Checklists can help in this respect; they can be gathered by surveying the plans of previous projects. Customers can also provide valuable help by reviewing the plans and looking for oversights. At the same time, we should attempt to validate the realism of the estimates, analyses, and constraints.

During analysis we should select clear-cut, rational, measurable goals for the product and the process to help us in setting priorities. Product goals establish the worth of each attribute and function of the product, so that they can be ranked in importance. Although this practice is eminently sensible, it is often ignored. These priorities guide team management in allocating effort during development. This may be needed to schedule the incremental development of the product. Priorities ensure that, if we estimate badly and need to deliver a smaller product than originally intended, at least we will deliver the most important part.

A second reason for priorities is to avoid the production of gold-plated software, which occurs when no value is put on functions and attributes. Users are likely to ask for the moon if no limits are set on their desires. The resulting system may be exceptionally functional and beautiful, but its expense far outweighs its usefulness. In fact, like a one-person band, it may attempt to do so much that its actual usefulness is impaired.

Having clear process goals is also vital. The degree to which we achieve our goals will determine whether the project was successful in the end. It is usually easy to evaluate our success in satisfying a testable requirement, like delivering the product on October 1, or using less than 256K of internal memory. It is somewhat unfortunate that fuzzy goals, such as a high level of customer satisfaction or development of proficiency in database architecture, are both more important and more difficult to evaluate.

We sometimes become so focused on the product — its quality, performance, and dependability — that we forget that the process — how we create the product — is also important. In the past, for instance, some successful products have been created by unplanned and careless design methods. There were lengthy periods of hit-and-miss testing and even lengthier periods of failure-ridden use, until finally the product seemed to satisfy its customers — but at what expense!

Concentrating on the product to the exclusion of the process is typical of the skills of programming where the desired product is the only goal. The study of the process — *how* to achieve the product — is more the domain of software engineering. However, software engineering has its own weak spot: it is possible to over-engineer, to become

| **Product** | **Process** |
| --- | --- |
| Functional | Economical |
| Dependable | Timely |
| Usable | Open to suggestions |
| Efficient | Well managed |
| Maintainable | Communicative |
| Documented | Complete |
| Portable | Meticulous |
| Extensible | |

**F I G U R E 3-6**   PRODUCT AND PROCESS ATTRIBUTES VITAL TO THE CUSTOMER

so enamored with the process that the real goal — the product — is neglected.

In fact, both the process and the product are important. A quality product is what we are working for; but if the process is inefficient, error prone, badly planned and managed, then we will not be in business long enough to create the next product.

The customer usually has some very definite goals in mind for both the product and the process (see Figure 3-6). These include cost, delivery date, general functionality, and performance. For custom software, it is important to help the customer solidify these expectations, as well as those for dependability and usability (user friendliness).

The organization should have additional goals for both product and process that go beyond those of the customer. First, the software organization should have a better and more complete concept than the customer of what constitutes a good product and a professional process. Second, the software organization should be planning for its own progress and growth, independent of the customer.

The primary goal is to run a profitable project. This depends both on the product, if it is to be marketed, and on the process. In the first situation, the product must find a lot of demand in the marketplace; every copy sold after costs are recovered will be almost entirely profit. In the second situation, particularly for custom software, profit will depend on keeping the development (process) cost below the anticipated income.

Projects are often chosen for the good they will do within the software organization.

| **Product** | **Process** |
| --- | --- |
| Achieve market acceptance | Turn a profit |
| Develop reusable components | Develop new skills |
| Establish a reputation | Test new methodologies |
| Start a new product line | Provide useful experience |
| Test a new design | Change of pace |
| Establish a market presence | Foster esprit de corps |
| Use the highest professional standards | |

**F I G U R E 3-7**   INTERNAL GOALS IN ADDITION TO THOSE OF FIGURE 3-6

There may be software engineers who need to develop new technical or managerial skills; others might be new to the organization and need a carefully chosen environment in which to gain experience; still others may need a fresh task after lengthy service in some other mode. Although one might not choose a project just to cement relationships among the team, fostering a team spirit is certainly a worthy adjunct goal to the development process.

Every organization needs to grow or change if it is to thrive. Software projects are often chosen because they provide an opportunity to try out a new methodology for design, configuration management, or testing. Similarly, it may be important to experiment with a new design for a particular application that has been in the back of our minds. Finally, the software product may have future as well as present utility; we may be able to effectively reuse parts of the product in a number of profitable projected offerings.

Some of our goals relate to the software organization's position in the market. A well-designed product may establish a reputation that will pave the way for future software. We may have decided to begin developing a new product line, either in terms of the application or the environment in which it runs, or we may be taking advantage of an opportunity to establish a credible presence in an area where we have not previously penetrated, in the hopes of attracting future business.

Professional pride and responsibility urge us to display state of the art skills in creating a software product. However, this goal is subsidiary to others; we should not let it guide us into creating unsatisfactory or unprofitable products. Although we have a duty to customers, the bottom line is that we also have a responsibility toward our own organization. The choice of projects and goals should benefit both customers and software engineers. A software organization that decides that the customer is the only king may experience transitory success, but is probably doomed to eventual failure.

### 3.2.3 Market Research, Marketing, and Bidding

It is a bit facile to say that the marketing department stands in the stead of the customer for an organization developing packaged software. After all, how does the marketing department know what the customer wants? How will they identify the customer and deliver the product once it is ready? Market research is the answer to the first question, and marketing is the answer to the second.

The purpose of market research is to gather information, much like that obtained by customer interviews in the case of custom software, for a proposed packaged software product. The software organization's bright idea has to be verified among potential users. Interview and survey techniques can be utilized, coupled with statistical analysis. Market surveys must determine what features might be desirable in the product and how much people would be willing to pay for them. It may be that the research is carried out with an actual prototype, gathering user reactions at the source.

An important consideration is identifying the niche into which the product would fit. A niche is often a group of users wanting to apply existing hardware to a given purpose. Mailing lists, lists of hardware owners, and existing user and professional groups are possible sources that can provide market information.

It is also important to know what other products exist in the niche and to estimate

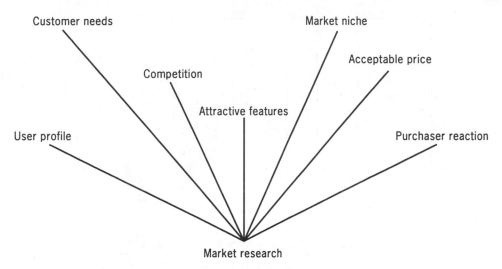

**FIGURE 3-8**   INFORMATION GATHERED DURING MARKET RESEARCH

the success of your potential product in competing with them. Frequently, these products are themselves under development, and it may be difficult to identify them. Marketing organizations and hardware manufacturers may help with this.

The best product in the world will not be profitable if no one buys it. There is no truth in the supposition that building a better mousetrap will cause the world to beat a path to your door. Although product quality is a vital factor in success, one must also attract customers. If one is producing packaged software, it is necessary to advertise and sell the product to potential customers. For relatively inexpensive software, the developing organization sets up a distribution network, either mail/phone order or through retail outlets, in place of a professional sales force.

There are several innovative marketing techniques for software, including the following:

- Software publishing, in which a product is turned over to an entirely separate organization for marketing.
- Using bulletin boards and other electronic communications capabilities for software advertising and distribution.
- Free distribution of object software that would allow a limited number of uses, after which it self-destructs. This allows potential users to try it out and buy it if they like it.
- Freeware, in which software is distributed free, probably through a bulletin board, and through which users are invited to send a payment in appreciation, or to obtain documentation and support.
- Special relationships with hardware manufacturers who will highlight or authorize software products not their own.

One particularly creative marketing strategy is used by a text editor which is

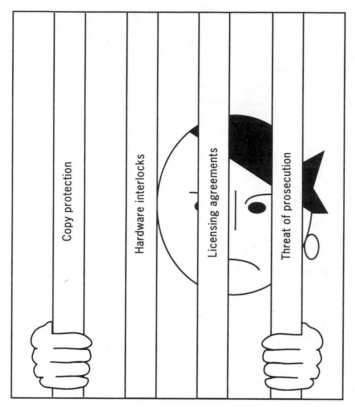

**FIGURE 3-9**   DETERRENTS TO SOFTWARE PIRACY

distributed free, but which periodically interrupts processing to display an advertising screen. Users who like using the product may be willing to pay for a version that eliminates "commercial interruptions." Despite all these innovative alternatives to standard marketing, however, the mainstays of the industry still seem to be advertising in special-interest magazines and catalogues and by word-of-mouth through electronic media and user groups.

There is another issue in marketing: how to minimize software piracy (Figure 3-9). Each version of software that is obtained without payment represents a loss to the developing organization. Copy protection, using variant disk and directory organization or weak bits, works for a while; but more powerful copy software always seems to catch up with this technology. Hardware solutions tend to be cumbersome, and users resent them. Licensing agreements depend on the goodwill of customers or on the threat of litigation that may be prohibitively expensive to developers. Freeware vendors have decided not even to try to protect their investment. There are as yet no really good solutions to the problem.

Custom software developers do not face the piracy problem to the same extent, since they have a contract that should guarantee sufficient payment to cover development costs and still provide a profit. If the developers continue to hold rights to the product after delivery, it is not as hard to prove infractions of licensing agreements. However, although custom developers may escape the piracy problem, marketing is still necessary.

In the custom software world, software engineers usually learn of a potential customer organization when they hear about a request for proposals (RFP) in which the customer specifies the job to be done. The software organization can respond by presenting a proposal. For public entities, the RFP may be published; in other cases, it is important for the software organization to foster its reputation and visibility in the marketplace so as to receive enough RFPs to keep its business volume up. First, the organization must be known to the customer. This still depends on advertising and word of mouth. Second, the organization must have credibility. This depends on past success, marketing presentations, and reputation.

If one is producing custom software, it is necessary to be chosen during a bidding process. Since preparation of a proposal is expensive and time consuming, it is in the software organization's interest not to undertake it unless there is a fair chance of success. After all, the software organization must take the customer's original request for a proposal and build an entire project plan from it. This represents a significant effort, which will be wasted if the bid is not won. To compete, the software organization must prepare to produce software at a lower cost than its competitors — but still at a profit. This depends on very good cost estimation techniques coupled with good sense, efficiency in the organization, and familiarity with the customer's needs.

The software organization's management must understand the customer environment, be able to talk their language, and elicit information from them. The chance of winning the bid can be improved if management is able to determine the exact nature of the desired software through informal contact with the customer organization. To use this kind of grapevine information, we must carefully cultivate our access to the vine. This seems to be particularly true in the environment of large government contracts. The trouble with the practice is that it borders on, and sometimes steps over, the bounds of legality.

## 3.3 ANALYSIS METHODOLOGIES AND TOOLS

Three kinds of analysis methodologies are profiled in the sections that follow. First, we will see the techniques used by systems analysts in determining user wants and needs, constraints, and expectations. Few of these are automated, and most analysts use no more tools than a word processing system or graphics editor.

Next, we consider techniques for strategic planning in software enterprises. Strategic planning is neither short- nor long-range; it encompasses the length of the software project. Strategic planning allows us to make correct decisions about the project being worked on.

Finally, we consider methods for estimating the cost, duration, and staffing needs of the project. We will not be able to submit a bid, or tell whether we will recover the cost of developing packaged software, if we do not know how much it is going to cost us. There are quite a few tools for us to use in determining cost estimation, scheduling, and staff assignment. There are also other tools that are used for feasibility and risk analysis — principally simulation and prototyping systems.

### 3.3.1 Analysis Methodology

The project plan contains a detailed and explicit budget, and schedule and staffing estimates. To obtain this information, we need data about the product. Some of these data take the form of functional requirements. The functional requirements provide a very limited view of the planned project. Although these requirements give us a general picture of the product's external behavior, as seen by the users, the requirements tell us nothing about its real internal structure. That is, the requirements may describe *what* the product does, but they do not specify *how* it is to be done.

The use of words like "limited" and "general" attempts to point out that these functional specifications are *not* the basis on which the product will be designed. Design depends on the more complete and much more formal software requirements specification. Functional requirements are stated in a natural language, in a rather informal fashion, and are for the purpose of analysis. As with the constraints mentioned in Section 3.3.2, functional requirements should be described in quantitative terms wherever possible. This will not only help us to clarify our thinking but will also provide us with a firmer basis for analysis and formal specifications.

The job of the analyst is to take the lead in the orientation and functional requirements activities. He must become familiar with the current and projected application environment, determining how to transform the existing system into one that either provides more function (this is the most common goal by far) or provides the same function at a lower cost. There is always a possibility that analysis will determine that no change should be made. The analyst's techniques are shown in Figure 3-10.

Understanding the user's needs is fundamental in determining software requirements. We must identify the user's work habits, job stability, skills, expectations, problem-solving skills, experience level, willingness to use manuals, tolerance of delays or effort, and the tasks to be performed and how often the user will perform them ([GOU85], [POT87]). Creating this user profile and task analysis allows us to optimize the product for usability and friendliness.

The user profile should categorize subjects as being novices, or as intermittent, frequent, and power users. A power user customizes the software and makes full use of all its features. User tasks should be considered at the high, mid, and atomic levels.

- Observation of user operations
- Practice in the application area
- Interviews with customers
- Surveys of user opinion
- Research into the theory and practice of the application
- Analogy with other systems

**FIGURE 3-10**  TECHNIQUES USED BY SYSTEMS ANALYSTS

A high-level task might be checking the spelling of a document, whereas an atomic task might be correcting a single mistyped character. If the software supports an overabundance of atomic tasks, then reasonably substantial tasks require far too many steps. On the other hand, if the concentration is on high-level tasks, then each task may require a confusing glut of options to make up for missing atomic actions ([SHN87]).

**Observation** requires that the analyst spend time in the actual application environment, watching the way in which tasks are being performed. This exercise familiarizes the analyst with the system, pinpoints problems and inefficiencies, points out additional valuable functions that could be performed, and conceptualizes the entire system. The conceptual model is used to design the eventual product. Various notational tools such as flow diagrams, control hierarchies, written procedure descriptions, document formats, and the like, may be used by the analyst in studying the system.

**Practice** involves the analyst actually functioning as a part of the system. Practice has its good and bad points. On the plus side, the analyst gains a deeper and clearer view of the system as it now exists. On the negative side, the analyst loses perspective, since the existing system may loom too large and close to allow understanding of how things *should* be, as opposed to how they are.

This situation is a risk for the analyst. He must maintain a certain independence of, and distance from, the existing system at all times. Independence allows the analyst to look at the entire project and not just its details. The analyst will then feel less commitment to the current structure of the system and less pressure from customer personnel who think they already know the solution. In fact, the analyst should have as few *a priori* opinions as possible. Even the decision whether the system should be changed, and whether software should be part of the solution, can only be made after the system is analyzed.

Although the customer organization can sometimes give a full set of specifications right away, the organization more often is not quite aware of what it wants or needs. The requirements definition, then, is obtained by a series of **interviews** with members of the customer organization; this is an important part of systems analysis. There are several items to be discovered by interviewing (see Figure 3-11).

Some people are sufficiently skilled at interviewing that they are able to elicit full information while maintaining a free-wheeling and informal interview style. For most of us, however, the quality of interviews is improved by using fairly structured and

- Customer needs
- Customer desires
- Priorities among needs and wants
- Current functions (and personnel?) to be replaced
- Environment to which the software must interface
- Willingness to accept change in the customer organization
- Source of support for the new software
- Source of decision-making power in the customer organization

**FIGURE 3-11**  ITEMS TO BE DISCOVERED IN INTERVIEWS

formal interviewing techniques. This can be done with a checklist, with the name of the interviewee, his position in the organization, the date, the purpose of the meeting, and individual questions and points to be cleared up.

Another important structure is that of repeated interviews. There should be an *initial* session, in which the scope and purpose of the information and cooperation needed is outlined and friendly relations are established. In *detail* sessions, the interviewee is questioned about specifics, sometimes being asked to amplify or clarify information that has already been given. An *exit* session provides feedback to the interviewee and allows for comment (and the relief of knowing that the task is done).

While conducting interviews, it is well for the interviewer to be aware that not everything spoken is the truth. Sometimes people lie; more often they forget; most often, they speak from their own ignorance or point of view. These problems are best combatted by interviewing many people. Ignorance and forgetfulness are also overcome by carefully structured interviews and by multiple interviews. It is always important for the interviewer to step back from an interview and to exercise common sense in the light of experience so that he can evaluate what he is hearing.

Some specific skills and attitudes enable a systems analyst to improve interview productivity. The interviewer should always exhibit *interest* in, and *really listen* to, what the interviewee says. The interviewee should understand that the analyst's expertise is available to serve the user. Enough *time* should be scheduled in a quiet place so that the interview is not rushed or constantly interrupted. The interviewer should maintain a neutral attitude and avoid shutting off or condemning the interviewee's ideas. Apparently difficult requests should not be discarded without careful consideration ([POT88]). The interviewer should provide feedback in terms of his own understanding to clarify information, extract the most salient points, and avoid misunderstanding. Feedback should be carefully prepared and should include written descriptions, procedures, and requirements, as well as easily understood graphical models of systems, data, data flows, organizations, and the like.

Finally, the interviewer should watch for verbal and body language cues that any animosity or duplicity is present. In such a situation, the information gathered has to be judged accordingly. Franz and Robey in [FRA84] give an example of the familiar kinds of power games played by customers with hidden agendas relating to power and control. The software system becomes a pawn in the conflict, with the development team left holding a bag full of impossible requirements. These hidden agendas may occur when the new software will threaten someone's control, reduce some department's staff, or make a previously indispensable staff member superfluous ([MAR83]).

It can also happen that customers wanting a better bargain will continue to change their requirements to the point of destabilizing the project. This can especially be a problem with large projects and diffuse, fragmented, or remote customers ([CUR88]). For instance, if the software is subcontracted through a hardware manufacturer and the software team has no established liaison with the ultimate customer, and if the customer has several committees trying to specify portions of the software, the project may never stabilize.

Interviews and surveys allow users to make their experience and feelings part of the analysis. Users should continue to be involved throughout the analysis stage, and their

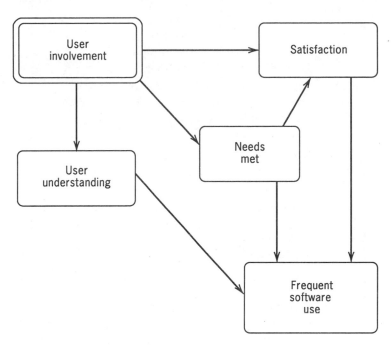

**F I G U R E 3-12**   PROPAGATED BENEFITS OF USER INVOLVEMENT

reaction to the progressing plans should be considered seriously. Baroudi et al. ([BAR86]) measured some valuable benefits derived from user involvement in system planning. They found that user involvement leads to a system that better meets user needs and that is better understood by the users. In addition, such systems are employed more often, and are more satisfactory(Figure 3-12).

**Research** has the analyst studying documentation provided by the customer organization, as well as more general information about the application area. Research may provide some of the independence that the analyst needs by allowing him to see a more general picture of the problem. The researcher spends significant amounts of time in the library using on-line abstraction software, as well as reading product descriptions, reviews and guides, and professional journals and books.

This **reasoning by analogy** to other systems may provide important insight, but it cannot be allowed to obscure the facts that are gathered by actual observation and other firsthand techniques. They will remain the foundation of the analysis. Specific information is usually more useful than general understanding and should be given greater weight in making decisions.

Shemer outlined the items of information that a systems analyst has to gather to understand the system under study ([SHE87]). With the information outlined in Figure 3-13, the analyst can form a conceptual model of the system. Comparing the conceptual model with the actual observed system will point out problems that currently exist and will suggest ways of improving the system. The analyst finds that certain kinds of

- Purpose of the system
- Goals of the organization
- Priorities of the organization
- Components of the system
- Interactions of the components
- Cause/effect relationship of different component functions
- Effectiveness of component functions
- Input and output used by the system
- Flow of data in the system
- Resources used by and available to the system
- The system's environment
- Constraints placed on the function of the system
- Pivotal data, functions, or people in the system

**F I G U R E 3-13**   INFORMATION TO BE GATHERED DURING SYSTEMS ANALYSIS

problems recur constantly and learns to watch for them: confused division of responsibility and function among components, inefficient function, inadequate control,
duplication of effort and data, and incomplete procedures.

Vitalari and Dickson ([VIT83]) list the most important attributes of a systems
analyst, including the ability to reason by analogy, planning and strategic skills,
dealing well with alternative hypotheses, having a heuristic capacity, and dexterity in
facilitating communication. Systems analysis is often taught using checklists, diagrams, and step-by-step procedures. This may help clarify what is a frequently
confusing task, but it may also obscure the already fuzzy nature of the analyst's
domain. Few things are clear cut; procedures are frequently not documented; user
opinions and viewpoints differ; control is often not where one would expect it to be. It
is well to remember that the analyst puts together a puzzle rather than running through
a cut-and-dried process.

### 3.3.2 Strategic Planning

The purpose of strategic planning is to get you to your goal in the most efficient fashion.
Imagine your chagrin if you were to develop an entire, functional software product,
deliver it, and be told "No, that will not do. We need a system that will...." This sort of
thing actually happens and represents one of the software team's worst nightmares. It
is sort of like an orienteering contestant who arrives in a farmer's field only to be told
that the farmer saw everyone else waiting at a campground, eight miles away.

The analyst needs to determine, up front, exactly what the constraints on the project
will be. From the user's point of view, the most important of these are the *acceptance
criteria*. These criteria are demonstrated in an acceptance test, the nature and timing of
which is defined in the project plan. The acceptance criteria, together with commit-
ments about cost, schedule, and services like training, installation, and support, are the

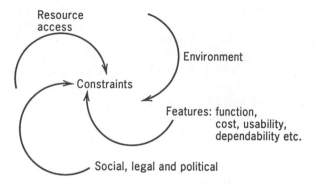

**FIGURE 3-14**   CONSTRAINTS ON THE DESIGN OF SOFTWARE

contract between the customer and software developer. Even in instances where software is being developed for internal use or for a marketing department, drawing up acceptance criteria as a "pseudo-contract" is an excellent idea.

Of course, the most obvious criteria for acceptability of the product are those that describe software's most important attributes: functionality, cost, dependability, maintainability, usability, and efficiency. All such criteria must be specified and prioritized during the analysis stage, and the analyst must first determine the customer's desires with regard to them. An important — but sometimes overlooked — aspect of software is its storage capacity and throughput. Since solutions do not always scale up effectively, these need to be determined as soon as possible (Figure 3-14).

The product must function within an environment that may impose additional constraints. First, it will probably have to interface to existing procedures, data files, and forms from the user organization. Second, it will likely run on hardware that is already purchased and being used for other tasks. The product cannot require more change and adjustment on the part of its users than they are willing to supply.

Sometimes a software product is developed as part of a larger system that includes hardware and policy components as well as the software. In these cases, the software is probably subcontracted by the organization responsible for the development of the entire system. This situation usually produces a large number of inflexible constraints that the software product must meet. In fact, software is often supposed to be the glue that holds everything else together but must take second priority in overall system design. This kind of project also distances the end user from the software organization, forcing software engineers to accept the analysis performed by the primary developers.

Next, there may be social, political and legal constraints. For instance, automation usually displaces workers. If workers are unable to function in any other place in the customer organization, they may lose their employment, a result that the customer (not to mention labor unions) might find unacceptable. In another case, an information system might be under legal restraint in terms of the right to privacy of individuals whose data are held by the system.

Finally, we must consider *access to resources* needs. If the software needs to run on hardware that only the customer possesses, windows of availability of that equipment for testing the new software need to be determined. Certain personnel in the user organization may need to be consulted; their availability, too, has to be considered. Needed tools, software components, even hardware may not be obtainable until sometime in the future. If there is any doubt about these objects being provided, then contingency plans have to be developed.

All of the constraints mentioned here should be quantified as much as possible. Instead of referring to "high dependability," a constraint should specify "no more than 0.01% lost transactions," for example. It is not enough to say that output data must be used by another, existing program. Instead, the exact format of the output should be written down. Legally acceptable uses of personal data should be listed in place of the vague "respect the right of personal privacy."

Having analyzed the nature of the problem space and recorded the constraints on a solution to the problem, the software team is now ready to sketch a strategy for solving the problem. Of course, this strategy has to be rather general. It is much too soon to firm up details about the nature of the product. But the general approach — the development process model, the methodologies to be used — can be chosen now.

The solution strategy will be chosen from among several possibilities. It is a serious error to accept the first idea that comes into one's mind, particularly at the formative stage of the product. To cover the range of possible solutions, the team should not be too concerned just yet with the constraints that were discovered earlier. Instead, they should brainstorm — throwing out all sorts of suggestions and perhaps even wild ideas. These suggestions should be heard by everybody, with no criticism or evaluation, and they should be recorded.

- Is the problem complex?
- Is the problem new or unusual?
- Will the product be widely distributed?
- Will the product run in many distinct environments?
- Does the problem require concurrent access?
- Does the problem require concurrent processes?
- Does the problem require interactive processing?
- Does the problem require real-time response?
- Does the problem require distributed processing?
- Does the problem require large amounts of data?
- Is the data structure complex?
- Does the problem require high security?
- Are there hardware dependencies?
- Are acceptance criteria established?
- Are user expectations high?
- Is the software team experienced?

**FIGURE 3-15**   QUESTIONS WHICH HELP DEFINE THE SOLUTION STRATEGY

Once all the conceivable strategies have been listed, we next trim the list down to the ones that are possible. This is done by looking at the constraints and seeing whether a proposed strategy will work within them. Following that, a series of questions, outlined in Figure 3-15 (taken in part from [PFL87]), should be answered, in order to better define the profile of the problem.

The answers to these questions may give a fairly detailed picture of the product, say a highly reliable, low-cost, nondistributed batch process with large amounts of simply organized data, interfacing to specific equipment, used in a single operation, and using known techniques. When the answers are not entirely clear, we may again try to reason by analogy, comparing the current problem with others we have seen in the past. The product profile thus arrived at further cuts down the list of viable solution strategies.

If there are several candidates left (we hope there is at least one), then we conduct an analysis of economic and technical feasibility, as described in Section 2.2.3. If there is still a choice to be made, we may decide on a single strategy according to the interests of the software team. It is important at this point to document the rejected strategies, together with the reasoning behind the decision. Someone may ask, at a later date, "Why didn't they do this instead?" If this person does not understand the reason, he may make some inappropriate decisions.

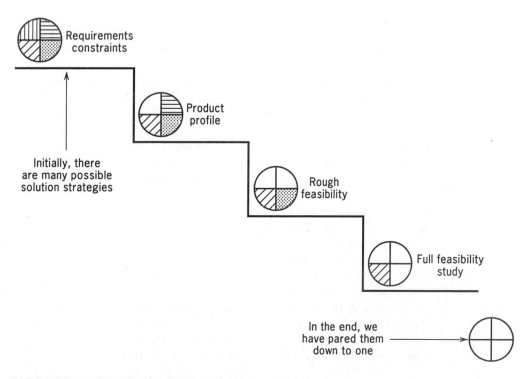

**FIGURE 3-16** STEPS IN SELECTING A SOLUTION STRATEGY

The treatment in the previous paragraphs may make it unclear whether a full cost / benefit and risk analysis should be undertaken for each alternative solution strategy that is proposed. Since these analyses are time consuming and expensive, it would be better to conduct them only to verify and bolster the best solution. On the other hand, without a detailed analysis, the best solution may slip through the cracks of the process.

This rule works effectively: first consider the constraints and requirements for the software; then eliminate any solutions that do not meet them. Next, create a profile of the product, and, reasoning from prior experience or analogy, eliminate those solutions that are in sharp contrast with the profile. Rough feasibility studies should be conducted now to choose a best solution, and this should be supported by a full feasibility study. If the full study throws any doubt on the chosen solution, other solutions should receive a complete feasibility treatment (Figure 3-16).

Finally, remember that one particular solution should always be kept in mind: do nothing. Our natural desires to keep busy, make progress, modernize, or venture forth all tend toward a decision to implement some new software solution for an existing problem. But all too often the cure is worse than the sickness, and we discover that we should have left well enough alone.

As part of the functional requirements, we must indicate what portion of the function of the entire new system will be carried out by software, and what parts fall under the responsibility of hardware and of personnel. The systems analyst needs to view the entire system — people, machines, and programs — even though the software team will only be involved in one sector. In particular, the analyst must always remember that *people* are a vital part of the entire computing system. It may be that the software organization is asked to provide advice about hardware purchases or personnel development, but this is apart from the issues dealt with in this book.

The decision of what functions should be exercised by each sector of the system depends on the tradeoffs between them. Hardware solutions tend to be faster and more dependable, but they are also less flexible and slower to implement. Software is cheaper than hardware but is frequently more expensive than personnel in the short term. Software has a lot of flexibility but little intelligence. People think better than the other two, but are slow, expensive in the long run, and not very dependable. Although these generalizations may not be true in the specific case under study, certainly there are tradeoffs that can be quantified and set so as to maximize the benefit of the new system.

One important condition of the allocation of function, and of the functional requirements as a whole, is that the division of function be complete, consistent, clear, and rational. That is to say, every important function should be accounted for, the different parts must mesh together, there should be no question as to where a function will be performed, and the division should be made for maximal effectiveness.

As mentioned in Chapter 1, the process model shapes all of software development. This model must be carefully chosen to fit the needs of the occasion. The experience and preferences of the software team will influence the decision significantly. In addition, it would be wrong to think that the choice cannot fall on a composite of more than one of the models (listed in Figure 3-17). Nevertheless, a conscious decision about the model, whatever it is, must be made during the analysis stage.

| Model | Reasons for Selection |
|---|---|
| Traditional | Well understood application, few reusable components or software generation tools available, predictable environment cycle |
| Rapid prototyping | Experimental development, small product, sophisticated customer anxious to be involved, open ended schedule or budget, fluid requirements |
| Program growth | Budget or schedule pressure, fixed requirements, software team unsure of itself, lack of customer confidence |
| Reuse | Familiar application, reusable components available, budget or schedule pressure |
| VHLL | Standard application area, available tools, low priority on product efficiency, budget or schedule pressure |
| Operational | General application, available tools, fluid requirements |
| Spiral | Uncertain or experimental development, high degree of risk or uncertainty, internal use or sophisticated customer |

**F I G U R E 3-17**   SELECTING A SOFTWARE DEVELOPMENT PROCESS MODEL

It is also necessary to select the specific methodologies (and tools) to be used in the various tasks that compose the entire development and maintenance process. Methodologies and tools are intimately connected, since the tools usually implement specific methodologies. Tasks that need to be covered as we choose methodologies and tools are listed in Figure 3-18. Even when the task may not occur for some time, it is necessary to obtain tools or training in advance; sometimes a methodology can only be used if the appropriate steps were taken at earlier stages to prepare for it. Specific methodologies and tools, along with the criteria for selecting them, are discussed along with the tasks to which they relate.

- Project management
- Project communication
- Quality assurance
- Product control
- Project accounting
- Requirements specification
- Architectural design
- Detailed design
- Coding
- Debugging and unit testing
- Integration testing
- Maintenance

**F I G U R E 3-18**   TASKS FOR WHICH THE METHODOLOGY/TOOL CHOICE IS MADE

Associated with a selection of methodologies and tools is the choice of notations in which to represent the various work products. Most important of these is the choice of an implementation language. This may be constrained by the customer or application environment. If not, then the methodologies and software team preferences will govern the choice. But notations for configuration, accounting, specification, and design are also decisive. The importance of choosing the right notation was emphasized by Iverson ([IVE80]) in these quotes:

> By relieving the brain of all unnecessary work, a good notation sets it free to concentrate on more advanced problems, and in effect increases the mental power of the race.
>
> — *A.N. Whitehead*

> The quantity of meaning compressed into small space by algebraic signs, is another circumstance that facilitates the reasonings we are accustomed to carry on by their aid.
>
> — *Charles Babbage*

One of the principles of common sense that we learn at an early age is to work on the broad sweep of a problem first, then fill in the details later. A sculptor, faced with a large block of marble and wanting to create a human figure, does not bore some distance down into the rock and fashion a perfect ear. Instead, the sculptor begins chipping away at the whole block, removing chunks that do not belong, bringing out a vague shape, refining it, refining it some more, choosing now and then a specific part to finish.

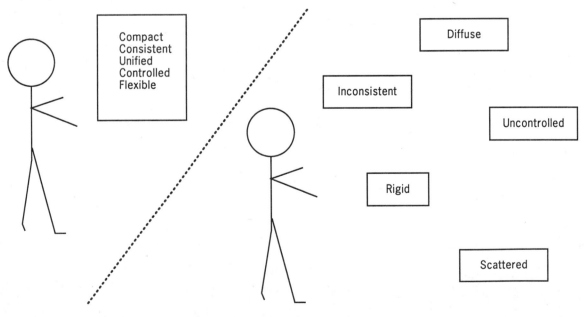

**FIGURE 3-19**    BENEFITS OF DEFERRING DETAILS

Similarly, the software engineer, although no artist, liberates his skills and avoids future grief by planning the product in a rough form initially, then gradually shaping it to plan, working on specific portions and detailing the product at the end. One example of this is the use of only general and limited functional requirements.

This powerful and time-honored technique of deferring decisions about details produces several benefits (Figure 3-19). First, there is the question of *unity*. A fairly large project that is defined in detail, right at the start, will likely suffer from a lack of unifying principles and philosophy. There will simply be too much to do all at once for the definition to be rational. A lack of conceptual unity will make the product harder to understand. Both design and maintenance will suffer as a result. Users may be especially confused by the hodge podge presented by a disorganized product.

Second, but related to the question of unity, is *consistency*. It may be very difficult to make all the pieces fit together in a workable product, when they are all designed in detail at once. Like a jigsaw puzzle, it is easier to plan software as a unit and then cut it apart, than it is to plan the parts individually and put them together.

Third, and still related to unity and consistency, is *control*. There may be too much going on in a fully detailed product for a single software engineer to maintain intellectual control of it. But at the early stages, the product still has to be treated as a single unit — it cannot be effectively planned and specified in parts.

Finally, and perhaps most important, is the question of *flexibility*. By choosing to accept the details of the solution early in the development process, we may make it impossible to correct any errors, optimize the solution on the basis of future experience, utilize reusable software components, develop the product incrementally, or adjust to changing requirements.

All of these arguments are also made in connection with a specific design technique (top-down design) to be covered in Chapter 6. But do not confuse deferring detail with top-down design. Details should be deferred during the analysis and specification stages regardless of the design methodology that has been chosen. Deferring details is particularly important when using the pragmatic approach to software development.

### 3.3.3 Project Cost and Schedule Estimation with COCOMO

There are a number of simple and explicit procedures for estimation; however, none of them is foolproof. In fact, there seems to be considerable doubt as to whether any of them is even valid for the broad range of software projects. The estimation methodologies problems discussed in the literature range from a need for additional calibration through limitation to a single application area on up to error in the foundational assumptions. For example, Boehm in [BOE81] states that the COCOMO (Constructive Cost Model) estimation technique (developed for large aerospace applications) works for small projects as well, if it is adjusted to take project overhead into account. Boehm ([BOE81;84]) developed COCOMO based partly on his experience at TRW (Thompson, Ramo, Wooldridge), a defense contractor and aerospace company.

Baskette asserts that many of the leading estimation techniques fail when applied to projects developed using Ada design and implementation [BAS87]. Kemerer [KEM87] noted a similar limitation when he showed that a technique developed for business applications works best in estimating the size of business applications. Kemerer further noted that several prominent methods fail to make reasonable adjustments to estimates on the basis of productivity ratings of the software team.

Finally, Abdel-Hamid and Madnick [ABD86] claim that no estimation technique will be entirely accurate, since the estimate is fed back into project management, thus altering the behavior being modeled. As Boehm says in [BOE84], "[T]here is no royal road to software sizing. There is no magic formula that will provide an easy and accurate substitute for the process of thinking through and fully understanding the nature of the software product to be developed."

The result is that the state of the practice in estimation is not yet adequate to our needs. We will compromise by hedging our bets. We start with a presentation of the COCOMO method, which seems to be accepted more than any other formal technique, with the caveat that it was designed only for the traditional process model. Then we briefly describe several other methods, with the recommendation that repeated estimates should be made for greater assurance.

COCOMO's constructive aspect depends on the existence of a work breakdown structure, which divides and subdivides the product into functional segments until the segments are small enough for us to estimate their size on the basis of prior experience.

The size of each such segment is measured in KDSI (Thousands of Delivered Source Instructions). Recall that this measure excludes nondelivered software, like test scaffolding, source code comment and blank lines, and reused software that was not modified for this project. All other source and job control instructions are counted, but modified reused software must be prorated with an estimate of the fraction of original development effort expended in modification.

Of course, we must be able to estimate the actual size of a functional segment based on previous experience. Although this seems to imply an imprecise foundation for what should be a scientific estimation method, a fine-resolution work breakdown structure does make the task of guessing about small functional segments rather easy. Also note that a high level of abstraction in our description of the original functionality of the product makes it more difficult to come up with the work breakdown structure.

It is also important to note that the COCOMO equations cover the effort expended in the design, implementation, and testing stages of the software life cycle. The added effort of the analysis and specification stages is easily calculated according to the model, but installation and training effort varies too widely to estimate effectively. Separate formulas can be used to estimate maintenance effort.

Once the work breakdown structure is fine enough for us to estimate and sum up the sizes of individual components, three basic COCOMO equations can be used for estimating the effort (measured in person-months) of software projects. The three equations are for three different kinds of product: organic, semidetached, and embedded.

$$\text{Effort in person-months} = 3.2 \, (\text{size in KDSI})^{1.05} \text{ (organic)}$$

$$\text{Effort in person-months} = 3.0 \, (\text{size in KDSI})^{1.12} \text{ (semidetached)}$$

$$\text{Effort in person-m,onths} = 2.8 \, (\text{size in KDSI})^{1.20} \text{ (embedded)}$$

Basically, organic products are well-understood, nondemanding, loosely constrained software, for example, a scientific application. Semidetached products may be less familiar, more constrained, or have a significant interface to the hardware or operating software; a new database management system is an example. Embedded software will have significant constraints, heavy hardware, and real-time requirements, complex control needs, and the like. A large operating system for a new multiprocessor architecture would be embedded.

Notice that the formulas are nearly linear in program size, the difference being negligible for relatively small products. However, as product size grows, the required effort grows more, in something between linear and quadratic fashion. Thus, for embedded products A and B, with B 10 times larger than for A, the effort needed to produce B is 16 times greater than for A. This is the result of greater difficulty in maintaining coherence among the different parts of B, as well as the greater effort expended in communication and management.

The appropriate equation can be used with the size estimate for the sum of all individual segments of the product. For example, if a semidetached project were

| Cost Drivers | Ratings | | | | | |
|---|---|---|---|---|---|---|
| | Very Low | Low | Nominal | High | Very High | Extra High |
| **Product Attributes** | | | | | | |
| RELY Required software reliability | .75 | .88 | 1.00 | 1.15 | 1.40 | |
| DATA Data base size | | .94 | 1.00 | 1.08 | 1.16 | |
| CPLX Product complexity | .70 | .85 | 1.00 | 1.15 | 1.30 | 1.65 |
| **Computer Attributes** | | | | | | |
| TIME Execution time constraint | | | 1.00 | 1.11 | 1.30 | 1.66 |
| STOR Main storage constraint | | | 1.00 | 1.06 | 1.21 | 1.56 |
| VIRT Virtual machine volatility[a] | | .87 | 1.00 | 1.15 | 1.30 | |
| TURN Computer turnaround time | | .87 | 1.00 | 1.07 | 1.15 | |
| **Personnel Attributes** | | | | | | |
| ACAP Analyst capability | 1.46 | 1.19 | 1.00 | .86 | .71 | |
| AEXP Applications experience | 1.29 | 1.13 | 1.00 | .91 | .82 | |
| PCAP Programmer capability | 1.42 | 1.17 | 1.00 | .86 | .70 | |
| VEXP Virtual machine experience[a] | 1.21 | 1.10 | 1.00 | .90 | | |
| LEXP Programming language experience | 1.14 | 1.07 | 1.00 | .95 | | |
| **Project Attributes** | | | | | | |
| MODP Use of modern programming practices | 1.24 | 1.10 | 1.00 | .91 | .82 | |
| TOOL Use of software tools | 1.24 | 1.10 | 1.00 | .91 | .83 | |
| SCED Required development schedule | 1.23 | 1.08 | 1.00 | 1.04 | 1.10 | |

[a] For a given software product, the underlying virtual machine is the complex of hardware and software (OS, DBMS, etc.) it calls on to accomplish its tasks.

**FIGURE 3-20** COCOMO EFFORT MULTIPLIERS. (Barry W. Boehm, *Software Engineering Economics*, copyright © 1981, p. 118. Reprinted by permission of Prentice Hall, Inc., Englewood Cliffs, N.J.)

broken down into 19 subsystems, and the total of their individual estimated sizes were 47.3 KDSI, then the nominal effort would be $3.0 \times 47.3^{1.12} = 225.4$ person-months. The effort amounts obtained are only nominal; that is, specific characteristics of the software and our development environment, like performance constraints or the availability of tools, would cause us to decrease or increase them. If the software as a whole has the same characteristics, then we can deal with the product as a whole. If not, then we should calculate effort on a segment-by-segment basis, using the different characteristics of the different segments.

A list of the multipliers to be used is shown in Figure 3-20. A multiplier is chosen for each characteristic of the segment, and then the nominal effort is multiplied by all of the factors to give the true effort estimate. Criteria for deciding which rating to give the product in each characteristic can be based on experience, or we can use those found in [BOE81] and [BOE84]. Generally, Boehm and Papaccio ([BOE88]) consider the order of importance of these factors to be size, management, ability, complexity, reliability, database size, and requirements volatility. All of this work should be carried out by using a software tool. Until recently, one such tool, called WICOMO, was available from the Wang Institute.

For our postulated project, we might judge it to be of very high complexity and high time constraint and the personnel to be highly experienced. The rest of the product and project attributes could be nominal. Since the three applicable multipliers are 1.30, 1.11, and 0.91, the effort value becomes $1.3 \times 1.11 \times 0.91 \times 225.4 = 296$ person-months.

Boehm suggests that the additional effort of analysis and specifications is found by multiplying the true effort by 0.06 for organic products, by 0.07 for semidetached, and by 0.08 for embedded. In our case, this would give a total of $1.07 \times 296 = 316.7$ person-months. The additional effort of installation and training will vary, depending on the nature of the product. Typical values of multipliers range from 0 to 0.25. These should be added to the true effort to obtain the total effort for the development stages of the product. Of course, some of this effort, perhaps 3% to 5%, has already been expended by the time the estimate is made. Finally, the effort must be adjusted to reflect possible sick leave and vacation time. This might cause an increase of 10% in estimating actual person-months. In our example, if we calculate 5% training and 10% sick/vacation leave, the total effort becomes $1.15 \times 316.7 = 364.2$ person-months.

It may not be necessary, or even possible, to estimate maintenance effort at this point. For a packaged product, the extent of maintenance will depend in part on the sales volume, which is still conjectural. For a custom product, the COCOMO calculations basically prorate the entire development effort by the fraction of the product that will be modified in any given year, to get the effort required in that year. Again, this estimate depends on the lifetime of the product, but it typically ranges between 100% and 200% of the development costs.

Labor represents the bulk of software costs; for this reason, the COCOMO model has us estimate cost on the basis of effort, measured in person-months. To calculate actual cost, we must use monthly salary levels and include benefits costs, either averaged over the organization or for specific personnel who will be assigned to the project. If we follow the second pattern, then cost estimation has to wait until staffing assignments have been made, as is shown in Section 3.3.4.

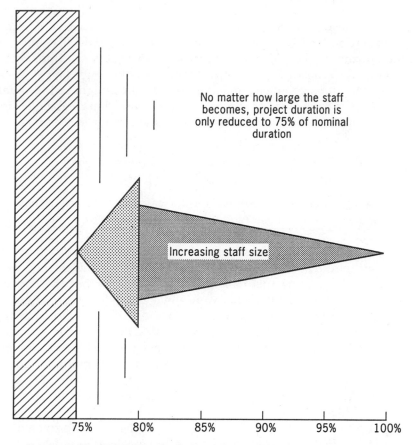

No matter how large the staff
becomes, project duration is
only reduced to 75% of nominal
duration

Increasing staff size

75%    80%    85%    90%    95%    100%

**F I G U R E 3-21**   PROJECT DURATION HAS AN ELASTIC LIMIT

There will be additional costs: the cost of providing work space and computers, heat and air conditioning, electrical power, secretarial and custodial support, supplies, training, and travel. Turner ([TUR84]) estimates that these might increase the dollar cost from salaries and benefits by about 50% . Assuming benefits at 25% of salary, the result is that software development cost can be roughly calculated at

cost = 1.75(average monthly salary)(actual person-months).

How long will it take to get a finished product? How long will each stage last? Of course, the duration of the project will depend on the size of the software team, to an extent. More people should result in faster progress. But there are limits to the degree to which we can speed up a project. As the saying goes, "The fact that one woman can produce a baby in nine months does not imply that nine women can produce a baby in one month." In fact, the addition of too many people to a project may actually lengthen its duration.

The formulas for project duration are independent of staff size, but increasing staff size by 25% beyond the nominal amount suggested by COCOMO might decrease project duration by 25%. Additional staff increases probably would not decrease duration further, and could even increase it, because of the additional confusion and management overhead. For complementary reasons, decreasing staff might not increase duration to a commensurate degree, and thus might reduce total effort. But lengthy projects have other problems, as was discussed in Chapter 2 (Figure 3-21).

The appropriate development duration formulas from COCOMO are:

Duration = 2.5(effort in person-months)$^{0.38}$ (organic)
Duration = 2.5(effort in person-months)$^{0.35}$ (semidetached)
Duration = 2.5(effort in person-months)$^{0.32}$ (embedded)

Once again, the effort represents the value calculated before we have added in the values for analysis, specification, and installation. Hence, these formulas give the duration of the design, implementation, and testing stages.

Given the duration of the design-implementation-testing portion of the project, we can estimate the duration of each stage by using the COCOMO method, as is illustrated in Figure 3-22. In using this table, we need to remember that the analysis and requirements specifications stages were not included in the duration; thus, their percentage of the total duration is in excess of the 100% represented by the entries for design, programming, and test. There are no COCOMO estimates for installation and training, but these estimates should be fairly easy to estimate on a case-by-case basis. Training duration, in particular, is usually specified in a contract.

Using the table, for instance, we can see that our 47.3 KDSI semidetached project, with a calculated effort of 296 person-months (after multipliers for characteristics) and a duration of 18.3 months, would actually require 18.3 x 0.2 = 3.7 additional months for analysis and specification, while the basic 18.3 months would be divided into 18.3 x 0.26 = 4.7 months design, 18.3 x 0.48 = 8.9 months implementation and unit testing, and 18.3

| | Schedule distribution | 2 KDSI | 8 KDSI | 32 KDSI | 128 KDSI | 512 KDSI |
|---|---|---|---|---|---|---|
| Organic | Plans and requirements (%) | 10 | 11 | 12 | 13 | |
| | Product design | 19 | 19 | 19 | 19 | |
| | Programming | 63 | 59 | 55 | 51 | |
| | Integration and test | 18 | 22 | 26 | 30 | |
| Semidetached | Plans and requirements (%) | 16 | 18 | 20 | 22 | 24 |
| | Product design | 24 | 25 | 26 | 27 | 28 |
| | Programming | 56 | 52 | 48 | 44 | 40 |
| | Integration and test | 20 | 23 | 26 | 29 | 32 |
| Embedded | Plans and requirements (%) | 24 | 28 | 32 | 36 | 40 |
| | Product design | 30 | 32 | 34 | 36 | 38 |
| | Programming | 48 | 44 | 40 | 36 | 32 |
| | Integration and test | 22 | 24 | 26 | 28 | 30 |

**FIGURE 3-22** SCHEDULE DISTRIBUTION. (Barry W. Boehm, *Software Engineering Economics*, copyright © 1981, p. 90. Reprinted by permission of Prentice Hall, Inc., Englewood Cliffs, N.J.)

| Mode | Effort distribution / Phase | Size | | | | |
|------|------|------|------|------|------|------|
| | | Small<br>2 KDSI | Inter-<br>mediate<br>8 KDSI | Medium<br>32 KDSI | Large<br>128 KDSI | Very<br>Large<br>512 KDSI |
| Organic | Plans and requirements (%) | 6 | 6 | 6 | 6 | |
| | Product design | 16 | 16 | 16 | 16 | |
| | Programming | 68 | 65 | 62 | 59 | |
| | Detailed design | 26 | 25 | 24 | 23 | |
| | Code and unit test | 42 | 40 | 38 | 36 | |
| | Integration and test | 16 | 19 | 22 | 25 | |
| Semidetached | Plans and requirements (%) | 7 | 7 | 7 | 7 | 7 |
| | Product design | 17 | 17 | 17 | 17 | 17 |
| | Programming | 64 | 61 | 58 | 55 | 52 |
| | Detailed design | 27 | 26 | 25 | 24 | 23 |
| | Code and unit test | 37 | 35 | 33 | 31 | 29 |
| | Integration and test | 19 | 22 | 25 | 28 | 31 |
| Embedded | Plans and requirements (%) | 8 | 8 | 8 | 8 | 8 |
| | Product design | 18 | 18 | 18 | 18 | 18 |
| | Programming | 60 | 57 | 54 | 51 | 48 |
| | Detailed design | 28 | 27 | 26 | 25 | 24 |
| | Code and unit test | 32 | 30 | 28 | 26 | 24 |
| | Integration and test | 22 | 25 | 28 | 31 | 34 |

**FIGURE 3-23** EFFORT DISTRIBUTION. (Barry W. Boehm, *Software Engineering Economics*, copyright © 1981, p. 90. Reprinted by permission of Prentice Hall, Inc., Englewood Cliffs, N.J.)

x 0.26 = 4.7 months integration and system testing. Section 3.5 gives an additional example of project estimation.

Knowing how long a particular stage will last does not tell us yet how much effort it will consume. The initial stages of software development do not benefit from large staffs, since the analysis, planning, specification, and initial design tasks need to be under the control of single individuals as much as possible. This should impart coherence and philosophical unity to the product. As can be seen from Figure 3-23, the staff size can triple from the analysis to the implementation stages.

Using this figure for the same 47.3 KDSI semidetached project, the 20.7 + 296 person-months of effort would be distributed as 20.7 person-months in analysis and specification (not included in the 296), 296 x 0.17 = 50.3 in design, 296 x 0.58 = 171.7 in programming, and 296 x 0.25 = 74 in testing, for a total of 316.6 person-months. Dividing the efforts for each stage by the duration of each stage gives the staffing levels as follows:

| | |
|---|---|
| Analysis and specification | 20.7 p-m/3.7 m = 5.6 persons |
| Design | 50.3 p-m/4.7 m = 10.7 persons |
| Implementation | 174.6 p-m/8.9 m = 19.6 persons |
| Testing | 71.0 p-m/4.7 m = 15.1 persons. |

Just how to come up with 0.6 persons is left to the reader. In practice, one either rounds to the nearest integer, or splits a person's time between two different projects. Staffing for maintenance can be calculated by taking the effort values estimated above and dividing by 11 months per year, giving the number of people needed during that year for maintenance.

### 3.3.4 Other Estimation Methods

Brooks ([BRO75]) gives one of the best reasons for planning staffing levels in advance: "Adding manpower to a late software project makes it later." This is partly a corollary of the rule that duration cannot be shortened beyond 75% of its nominal length. In part, it recognizes the tremendous overhead of training and integrating new staff on a project that is already near completion. In any case, we cannot solve a staffing problem *ex post facto*. Any staffing has to be planned in advance.

Abdel-Hamid and Madnick ([ABD86]) suggest that the simple effect of setting a scheduled duration and telling the software team affects their performance. First, there is the well-known deadline effect: productivity increases as deadlines approach. Thus,

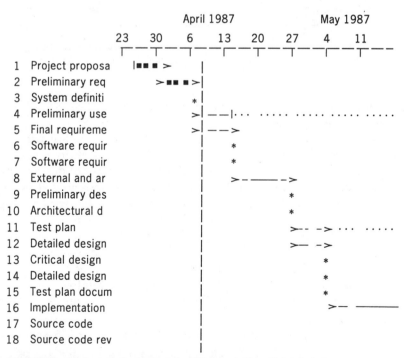

**FIGURE 3-24**   A GANTT CHART SHOWING SCHEDULED ACTIVITIES

creation of a detailed schedule with numerous reviews and milestones should improve productivity and shorten project duration through repeated application of deadlines. On the other hand, a feedback effect of scheduling can lengthen its duration. This occurs when the project falls behind schedule toward the end. Managers, familiar with Brooks' law, are reluctant to hire additional staff, knowing that they are at the end of the project. Hence, schedule slips are maintained.

Another scheduling and staffing difficulty arises from the concept of slack time. This is the time used by personnel for tasks that have no direct relationship to the project, such as reading professional journals and reorganizing their files. If deadlines are not near and the project is perceived to be in good shape, more slack time will be expended. Also, if a worker divides his time between two projects, he may decide to spend all of his slack time on one of them, rather than the other. How to deal with the slack-time phenomenon in a professional setting is unknown.

Although the process model we have chosen defines the coarse dependencies between stages, there may be many finer features in our schedule than a simple knowledge that specifications come before design. The acquisition of equipment and software tools, and the hiring of additional personnel, if required, will have to precede activities that make use of the tools, equipment, or personnel. If development of the product is to be broken out into development of separate modules by separate teams, then each module will have a separate schedule, but there may be dependencies between them. The timing of all these interrelated events can be represented by a weighted precedence graph and analyzed by the critical path method. The result of this can be a Gantt chart, showing a sequence of overlapping events, with start and finish times for each. An example Gantt chart is shown in Figure 3-24.

The Gantt chart can be used to schedule sufficient people to achieve the tasks indicated while ensuring that the same person is not scheduled for two concurrent tasks. For motivational and project accounting purposes, the milestones on the chart should probably occur every two to three weeks. Equipment and other facilities can be scheduled in the same way. Again, a tool should be acquired for this job; Figure 3-24 was produced by a tool called Schedule.

It should be evident from the discussion in the preceding sections that any general model, as careful as it might be, still would not produce precise estimates for a given project. There is too much variation in ability and circumstance to allow entirely reliable estimates. A study of U.S. Air Force management personnel revealed that they customarily tried to protect themselves by adding a "fudge factor" to their estimates ([ABD86]). This averaged 15%, but in some instances was as high as 50%.

A more realistic approach is suggested within the context of the COCOMO model. As Boehm says ([BOE81]), an actual database of software development experience in a specific organization can be compared to the standard COCOMO values, and "differences fed back into an improved cost-estimation model calibrated to the organization's experience." The easiest way to calibrate the model is to change the multipliers that appear in Figure 3-20 and in each of the basic formulas for effort and duration. The percentages in Figures 3-22 and 3-23 can also be easily modified on the basis of local experience.

COCOMO, however, was developed to be used with a traditional process model, and it might not be tunable for another model. For instance, [BAS87] indicates that its effort and schedule distribution tables are entirely off for a specific project, and by implication, any project implemented in Ada and using an Ada Programming Support Environment (APSE). Most of the criticism of COCOMO, however, has been of the specific tables and multipliers defined by its database, rather than the basic methodology and formulas.

Two fundamental criticisms have been levied. The first is that the set of effort multipliers is incomplete. Other estimation techniques might be examined for candidates to amplify the COCOMO set. Second, Gaffney thought ([GAF86]) that the KDSI measure might be appropriate for the implementation stage but that other stages are independent of the implementation language and their effort should be measured in a language-free way.

One way of doing this is to use Albrecht's **function point** calculations ([ALB83]). These calculations attempt to describe the size, not of the code, but of the functionality of the product. The calculation is based on a count of how many external input, output, interface, and inquiry types occur in the software, as well as how many internal file types there are. These counts are then modified by effort multipliers, and the resulting size is used in calculations similar to the basic COCOMO formulas. The major algorithmic estimation methodologies are listed in Figure 3-25. The first five are similar in nature to COCOMO, while ESTIMACS is more like Function Points.

There are some nonalgorithmic estimation techniques of interest. The first, and most widely used, is expert judgment. This is, in fact, the fundamental basis of methods like COCOMO, where we estimate the size of functional segments of the software using our experience. Expert judgment simply skips the formulas and multipliers and comes up immediately with estimates of total effort, schedule, cost, and staffing needs. As with any effective estimation technique, the expert must at least take into account the experience and ability of the personnel, the application environment, and the stringency of standards and constraints.

A generalization of expert judgment uses the **Delphi** technique. Delphi was a town in ancient Greece where people went 2500 years ago to get answers to their questions from the oracle of the god Apollo. The modern Delphi technique requires a panel of

- COCOMO [BOE81]
- COPMO [CON86]
- Price-S [FRE79]
- SLIM [PUT78]
- SoftCost [TAU81]

---

- Function Points [ALB83]
- ESTIMATES [RUB83]

FIGURE 3-25   MAJOR ESTIMATION METHODOLOGIES

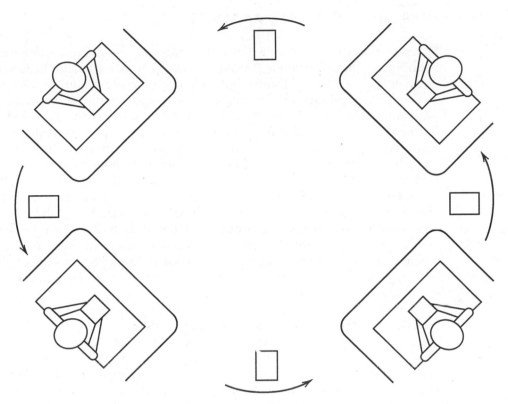

**FIGURE 3-26** INFORMATION FLOW IN DELPHI ESTIMATION

experts to render (anonymous) judgment on a proposed product, along with brief reasons and explanations of their thinking (Figure 3-26). Anonymity is supposed to ensure that the estimates will be made without fear or favor. These estimates then go through several rounds of joint evaluation and reconciliation by the panel, until some kind of consensus estimate is achieved. An example of a series of Delphi evaluations is given in Figure 3-28.

Boehm suggests another cost estimation method, called **price-to-win**. Used with custom software, it estimates the highest price guaranteed to come in below competitive bids and ensure obtaining a contract. The actual price is negotiated later, once the customer is locked into the software organization and is presented with evidence of potential cost or schedule overruns.

The very imprecision of estimation techniques suggests that the software organization should use several different methods, refining the various estimates in the Delphic manner until a reliable prognosis can be obtained. As a suggestion, one might try COCOMO, SoftCost, Function Points, and a few expert judgments.

## 3.4 FOSTERING QUALITY DURING ANALYSIS

There are three major activities that foster analysis quality: (1) measurement of process attributes, (2) verification and validation, and (3) management. In fact, these three themes will be followed throughout each of the succeeding life cycle stages.

We are in a paradoxical situation when we try to measure accuracy, completeness, and rationality, the attributes of analysis. We really will not know how well analysis has succeeded until the end of the project. It will be very useful, however, if we compare the predicted schedule, cost, feasibility, market acceptance, staffing needs, and so forth, with the actual figures. This can be done as part of the project debriefing, and any variances between planning and actuality can be fed back into the analysis methodology.

Verification during analysis can be performed by making sure that functional requirements and constraints, as they appear in the project plan, follow from customer requests that were determined during systems analysis. It is also important to verify risk analysis, cost estimation, strategy and model selection, and so on, by comparing them with the results of independent methodologies or previous projects. Validation can be performed by allowing users to review the project plan and experiment with prototypes.

Although there are no exceptional challenges in managing the analysis stage, it is at this point that the most important management decisions for the rest of the project will be made. Thayer et al. ([THA81]) report a survey of software organization managers. The major management deficiencies listed in the survey were incorrect schedules, incorrect cost estimates, inadequate accountability procedures, inadequate quality assurance procedures and imprecise goals and success criteria — all products of the analysis stage.

## 3.5 AN ANALYSIS EXAMPLE

This section presents an abbreviated example of analysis for a small- to medium-range product. Sufficient detail is given here to understand what is going on, but more details would be needed to produce the actual project plan. Steps are presented in the order in which they would probably occur: orientation, goal determination, functional requirements, estimation, feasibility, model selection, and quality planning. The software product is to be called Experimental Data Capture and Analysis (EDCA).

### 3.5.1 Orientation

A large research organization with its own software development section has signed a contract with a government agency to design and furnish an experimental observation device. This is an extremely sophisticated and complex piece of equipment, which produces a stream of data representing signals from various detectors as well as information about the internal state and housekeeping functions of the device. A receiving station is also to be built, which will include a minicomputer capable of storing the data stream on magnetic tape and, during periods in which the device is not transmitting, provide batch analysis of its signals as well as browsing through the data stream.

The software development section is required to develop a software product, EDCA, for the receiving station. EDCA will perform the data capture, storage, processing, and browsing functions. The customers are the team designing the receiving station; this group consists of four research electrical engineers, all self-taught so far as software is concerned. The actual users are technicians and operators with no software training.

Although all four of the research engineers are supposed to provide input for the systems analysis, interviews with them quickly make it clear that the lead (and senior) engineer will, in fact, determine the nature of EDCA. He has developed a similar product for his own use in the past. That product was written in BASIC and served a data collection system that had much lower throughput and volume. The lead engineer is able to specify quite precisely the basic function of the proposed product. Unfortunately, he can also imagine many more functions that would be "nice" or "useful," some of which he cannot define now, but will be able to think of "once he gets a look at how EDCA is shaping up." In addition, he has already decided (on the basis of his past experience) which algorithms would be appropriate for the processing functions.

The minicomputer has already been chosen, and has been provided with a Unix-type environment. Fortran 77 is the mandated language in the research organization, and a typical basic Unix toolset is available. Documentation for the minicomputer system is rather poor. On the positive side, the minicomputer will be available to the software team for almost all of the development period. The design of the rest of the receiving station is not entirely stable, and there is a significant possibility that the design will change during or after EDCA development. In particular, timing problems with some memory chips in the receiver are known to cause unpredictable and variable-length gaps in the data.

The lead engineer believes that, once functioning, EDCA will require little maintenance. He does not anticipate that the technicians and operators will need more than a day's training in the use of the software; in any case, his team will take responsibility for it. Although the data being captured are important, the device has such high throughput that transitory software failures at any point can be recovered simply by resetting all the devices, restarting the software, and trying again. Software failures lasting longer than a minute would be serious. The actual cleaning of the signals to detect gaps and resynchronize the data stream has to be handled very carefully, but it is not a real-time operation. Data processing is largely carried out by accumulating large amounts of data and analyzing them statistically; since this process could be run at little cost, its dependability can be relatively low.

EDCA, in its capture mode, will have to process and store 22 kilobytes of data per second (on magnetic tape). Data capture *must* proceed in real-time. Raw data will have to be saved for about 3 months, and even though data capture will last less than an hour each day, this means storing and manipulating 4 gigabytes of data on about 100 tape reels. Thus, it is important that archived data be compressed as much as feasible. The software will also have to assist significantly in the identification and retrieval of separate data tape files.

Contractual obligations require that EDCA be completed within 7 months, and there are only three software engineers and one trainee in the software development section. There are other individuals, however, who will perform secretarial, custodial and documentation tasks.

### 3.5.2 Goals

The primary goal of the customers is to have a working EDCA at the end of 7 months. They have established priorities among its various functions, as is shown in Section 3.5.3. They would like to minimize the cost of the product, as charged to their internal account, and are willing to sacrifice both user friendliness and functionality for this purpose. In particular, they are unwilling to consider subcontracting the development to some organization other than the in house development team. The most important criterion for EDCA is that it handle the high throughput of the system and provide the basic statistical and graphical output.

The software development team would like to guide the project to allow for the reuse of several existing products that might provide utility routines within EDCA. They believe that manipulation of the data stream has some similarity to parsing and are anxious to try out some compiler writing technology and tools. Finally, they are most anxious to protect themselves from the apparent volatility of the design of the receiving station. Related to this is the lead engineer's apparent desire to add functions at a late date in order to experiment with the system. Thus, although the customer does not believe maintenance is a factor, the software team believes that modifiability will be very important.

### 3.5.3 Functional Requirements

The functions envisioned for EDCA are outlined in Figure 3-27, starting with the aspects that are most important to the customers at the top of the list shown there. These

- Device drivers for the data stream receptor interface
- Real-time capture and storage
- Data stream cleaning and resynchronization
- Signal processing
- Statistical analysis
- Plotter graphics
- Batch processing control
- "Other things we might need"
- Screen graphics
- Interactive control for browsing
- Screen form generation

**FIGURE 3-27**   REQUIRED FUNCTION OF EDCA IN ORDER OF PRIORITY

| Oracle | Estimate | Reasons |
|--------|----------|---------|
| A | 40 person-months | Standard kind of project with high degree of specification volatility |
| B | 24 person-months | Low reliability |
| C | 29 person-months | Not too many challenges except real-time portion and device driver for interface |
| A | 33 person-months | Little documentation, specification volatility, difficulty in real-time and interface drive, but there are still significant reliability challenges in the real-time portion |
| B | 30 person-months | Not too many challenges, but the volatility is an important issue. The lead engineer wants to keep things open-ended |
| C | 29 person-months | I haven't had to change my opinion |
| A | 34 person-months | Open-endedness is an important issue |
| B | 30 person-months | I haven't had to change my opinion |
| C | 32 person-months | I agree on open-endedness |

**F I G U R E 3-28**    DELPHI ESTIMATION ON EDCA IN THREE ROUNDS

functions have to be defined in considerably more detail than we have space for, but we will explain somewhat here.

The minicomputer inputs information from the receiving station in real time, and a special pair of interface boards for it has been designed. These are put onto the computer's bus, and as a bus device, we need to write device drivers to control the interface and access data from it. Data will be captured and stored on temporary magnetic tapes as it is received. During slack periods, this data will be examined, gaps and partial data frames removed, and a **cleaned** data stream, with no gaps and synchronized, complete frames, will be archived permanently.

Signal processing will attempt to obtain meaningful observations from the data stream. The output of some detectors represents frequency information and will be put through a Fourier transform to obtain positional data. The output of other detectors must be filtered to eliminate a large amount of noise inherent in their function. Statistical analysis will take this second kind of data and provide standard statistical measures.

The positional data will be represented by three-dimensional curved surfaces, and it will be necessary to use plotter graphics routines to display it as seen from any selected viewpoint.

Batch control will oversee the non-real time processes of cleaning, signal processing, plotting, and report generation. Although data capture will be constantly supervised by a technician, we hope that batch processing can proceed with little or no operator intervention. An important part of batch control will be managing the storage and retrieval of archival data files.

Are multipliers to be calculated separately for each component? y

Component 1 mode? s

Module 1.1? Capture          KDSI? 2.0

Module 1.2? Interface driver   KDSI? 0.4

Module 1.3?

NOMINAL EFFORT = 8.0 MAN-MONTHS

Reliability? 1

Database size? vh

Product complexity? n

Execution time constraint? n

Main storage constraint? 1 (WARNING: no low value, using nominal)

Virtual memory volatility? vh

Turnaround time? 1

Analyst capability? h

Applications experience? 1

Programmer capability? h

Virtual; machine experience? 1

Programming language experience? vh (WARNING: no very high value, using high)

Use of modern programming practices? h

Use of software tools? n

Required development schedule? vh

COMBINED MULTIPLIER = 1.19

TOTAL EFFORT = 9.5 MM DURATION = 5.5 M MAX STAFF = 2

Component 2 mode? o

Module 2.1? Cleaning          KDSI? 0.8

Module 2.2? Batch Control     KDSI? 0.8

Module 2.3? Interactive Control  KDSI? 1.0

Module 2.4? Screen Form Generation KDSI? 0.5

Module 2.5? Signal Processing    KDSI? 1.2

Module 2.6? Screen Graphics  KDSI? 1.1

Module 2.7? Plotter Graphics  KDSI? 1.8

Module 2.8? Statistical Analysis  KDSI? 0.7

Module 2.9? Other things       KDSI? 2.0

Module 2.10?

NOMINAL EFFORT = 35.5 MAN-MONTHS

Reliability? 1

Database size? vh

Product complexity? n

Execution time constraint? n

Main storage constraint? n

Virtual memory volatility? vh

Turnaround time? 1

Analyst capability? h

Applications experience? h

Programmer capability? h

Virtual; machine experience? 1

Programming language experience? vh

Use of modern programming practices? h

Use of software tools? n

Required development schedule? vh

COMBINED MULTIPLIER = 0.74

TOTAL EFFORT = 26.3 MM DURATION = 8.7 M MAX STAFF = 3

**FIGURE 3-29**  COCOMO ESTIMATION FOR EDCA

"Other things we might need" are the variant or additional functions the lead engineer thinks he will require as he is putting together a working system. During his previous experience, he was accustomed to tailoring or modifying his BASIC programs to experiment with the system and to debug the hardware.

Screen graphics will allow engineers to browse through any archived data stream and see two- and three-dimensional plots of the data before and after signal processing is applied. The interactive control module will implement the browsing capability, whereas screen form generation will be used to display digital data, particularly the housekeeping functions of the device.

## 3.5.4 Estimation

The first effort estimation is made by using the three software engineers on the software development team as a Delphi panel. They each write an estimate with justifications to a shared file. For two days thereafter, they read the file and refine their own estimates on the basis of the others. When no new ideas surface, the process is complete. An abbreviated form of the estimation is shown in Figure 3-28. The end result is an effort estimation of 32 person-months.

To back up the Delphi estimation, a COCOMO tool is used. The results are shown in figure 3-29; for mode, the abbreviations are o(rganic), s(emidetached), and e(mbedded); for multipliers they are v(ery)l(ow), l(ow), n(ominal), h(igh), v(ery)h(igh), and e(xtra) h(igh). We need to increase the effort by 2.3 person-months to account for analysis, thus raising the total to 38.1 person-months. The duration including analysis will be about 9.5 months if we can achieve maximal overlap of the two components.

## 3.5.5 Feasibility

In one sense, economic feasibility is not an issue here, since the contract was already signed and the research organization is committed to providing this software. However, with a 7-month time limit and a four-person staff, it is hard to see how to fit in a project lasting 9.5 months and needing five persons. It is also a little disturbing to see that the COCOMO effort calculation comes in 12% higher than the Delphi estimate.

In thinking about this disparity, the software team notices that the Delphi estimates were made under the assumption of significant reuse of software for the signal processing, plotter graphics, and statistical modules. It is felt that the real effort in reusing these components will be only about 30% of their nominal effort. In effect, this reduces the total effort in the COCOMO calculations by 6.6 person-months, while the duration is reduced by more than one month.

It is decided that the new COCOMO effort estimate is very close to the Delphi estimate, but that the duration of 8.4 months is still very dangerous. However, the software team notes a combination of favorable factors: having all four software people available through the entire duration; the fact that the offset stages of the two segments of the project will allow shifting of assignments; the relatively informal documentation requirements and the availability of additional editorial assistance; and finally the fact that the customer is relatively sophisticated and can help in the design. The engineers hope that the combination of these factors makes the 7-month deadline possible.

The only technical question is whether the minicomputer will be able to process data at a high enough throughput to handle the data stream in real time. However, some experimentation with disk to tape transfers indicates a potential for significantly higher transfer rates, especially considering that the special interface is expected to be faster than the disk interface card.

The major risks involved are whether the deadline can be met; the possibility that equipment will suffer a prolonged down time during development; and the possibility that the problems with the timing in the receiver will cause major modifications to the software specifications. A minor risk is that the lead engineer will continue to ask for "other things" beyond the amount we have estimated; this will have to be handled through management.

### 3.5.6 Model/Methodologies/Tools

The process model suggested is that of rapid prototyping. This seems to fit best with the uncertainty of the specifications, the sophistication of the customer, and the experimental nature of the project as a whole. Heavy reuse of software components for the signal processing, plotter graphics, and statistical modules, along with associated test sets and documentation, will lighten that part of the burden.

For design, we will use dataflow techniques at the architectural level, with pseudocode and finite state machine notations at the detailed level. The latter is suggested by the compiler writing technology. Data stream cleaning and screen form generation will be driven by tables, which are already available from the hardware design effort.

Other possible models have been considered and ruled out. The traditional model does not adapt to the experimental nature of the problem. The program growth model does not take advantage of either the software engineers' or user personnel's expertise. The spiral model is somewhat irrelevant, since the software *must* be provided, and management is unwilling to spend too much money in making decisions.

### 3.5.7 Planning for Quality

The massive database, together with dropout problems, can be made more manageable by the use of self-identifying structures, whose type can be identified by examining their contents. This includes text prologues within files, which will identify many of the environmental factors at the time of the data capture. Similarly, the names of the cleaned data files will be unique and dependent on the date (down to the second) of data capture. File extensions will be used to classify the nature of various related files of processed data. All processing will create auxiliary log files to document the events.

Tools will be created to assist in the design of time-series filters, Fast Fourier Transform (FFT) routines, and screen forms. Additional tools needed include a specification and design tool with a data dictionary, electronic mail, Schedule, CO-COMO, Fortran editor and optimizing compiler, linker with cross-reference capability, debugger (which can act as a test harness), static analyzer, and comparator.

Documentation and coding standards already exist for several development modes in the organization. We will use the low-volume documentation standards. The trainee will conduct quality assurance activities; this will give him a chance to learn from the activities of the others. In particular, the trainee will control all frozen work products and will arrange for staff reviews twice a week. From these he will produce progress and Gantt charts to make visible the current status of the project.

Seventeen sets of test data are available from previous work by an independent consultant. These sets will be used to develop test data for units where possible, and certainly for integration. Finally, the actual observation device and receiving station will be available to compare processed data against the output of calibrated physical sources. There will be no acceptance test, but a single day is scheduled for demonstrations, to be attended by the hardware and management people.

## 3.6 SUMMARY

This chapter has sketched out the steps that must be taken to change an idea into realistic plans for a profitable software project. The analysis process includes systems analysis, feasibility studies, and goal and process selection; the end result is a project plan. Some of the principles of good analysis are to provide a solid framework for development, to minimize risk and uncertainty, and to develop customer satisfaction and confidence.

The characteristics of quality in analysis include accuracy, completeness, rationality, and a set of clear-cut goals. During this stage, we conduct market research, advertise and sell the product, and engage in the bidding process for contract software. Techniques for systems analysis, including interviewing, are vitally successful to the success of our activities. This is one of the primary analysis methodologies, but cost and schedule estimation are also important. Strategic planning, comprising constraint identification, feasibility analysis, strategy, and model selection round out the list.

Although it may seem that one might minimize or skip the analysis stage, it is the best foundation for subsequent success. Once adequate planning has taken place, we can proceed to the more technical (and probably more familiar) task of specifying the exact requirements for the software.

## BIBLIOGRAPHY

[ABD86]*   Abdel-Hamid, T.K., and S.E. Madnick, "Impact of Schedule Estimation on Software Project Behavior," *IEEE Software*, 3(4):70 – 75.

[ALB83]   Albrecht, A.J., and J.E. Gaffney, "Software Function, Source Lines of Code and Development Effort Prediction," *IEEE Transactions on Software Engineering*, 9(6):639 – 648.

[BAR86]   Baroudi, J.J., M.H. Olson, and B. Ives, "Impact of User Involvement," *Communications of the ACM*, 29(3):232 – 238.

[BAS87]*   Baskette, H.J., "Life Cycle Analysis of an Ada Project," *IEEE Software*, 4(1):40 – 47.

[BOE81]*   Boehm, B.W., *Software Engineering Economics*, Prentice-Hall, Englewood Cliffs, NJ.

[BO81a]*   Boehm, B.W., "An Experiment in Small-Scale Applications Software Engineering," *IEEE Transactions on Software Engineering*, 7(5):482 – 493.

[BOE84]*   Boehm, B.W., "Software Engineering Economics," *IEEE Transactions on Software Engineering*, 10(1):4 – 21.

[BOE88]*   Boehm, B.W., and P.H. Papaccio, "Understanding and Controlling Software Costs," *IEEE Transactions on Software Engineering*, 14(10):1462 – 1477.

[BRO75]*   Brooks, F.P., *The Mythical Man-Month*, Addison-Wesley, Reading, MA.

[CON86]*   Conte, S.D., H.E. Dunsmore, and V.Y. Shen, *Software Engineering Metrics and Models*, Benjamin Cummings, Menlo Park, CA.

[COO84]   Cooper, J., "Software Development Management Planning," *IEEE Transactions on Software Engineering*, 10(1):22 – 26.

[CUR88]*   Curtis, B., H. Krasner, and N. Iscoe, "A Field Study of the Software Design Process for Large Systems," *Communications of the ACM*, 31(11):1268 – 1287.

[EVA83]    Evans, M.W., P.H. Piazza, and J.B. Dolkas, *Principles of Productive Software Management*, Wiley-Interscience, New York.

[FAI85]    Fairley, R.E., *Software Engineering Concepts*, McGraw-Hill, New York.

[FRA84]*   Franz, C.R., and D. Robey, "An Investigation of User-Led System Design: Rational and Political Perspectives," *Communications of the ACM*, 27(12):1202 – 1209.

[FRE79]    Freiman, F.R., and R.D. Park, "PRICE Software Model — version 3," *Proceedings of IEEE-PINY Workshop on Quantitative Software Models*.

[GAF86]*   Gaffney, J.E., "The Impact on Software Development Costs of Using HOL's," *IEEE Transactions on Software Engineering*, 12(3):496 – 499.

[GOU85]    Gould, J.D., and C. Lewis, "Designing for Usability," *Communications of the ACM*, 28(3):300 – 311.

[IVE80]    Iverson, K.E., "Notation as a Tool of Thought," *Communications of the ACM*, 23(8):444 – 465.

[KEM87]*   Kemerer, C.F., "An Empirical Validation of Software Cost Estimate Models," *Communications of the ACM*, 30(5):416 – 429.

[MAR83]    Markus, M.L., "Power, Politics and MIS Implementation," *Communications of the ACM*, 26(6):430 – 444.

[PFL87]    Pfleeger, S.L., *Software Engineering*, Macmillan, New York.

[POT87]    Potosnak, K., "Where Human Factors Fits in the Design Process," *IEEE Software*, 4(6):90 – 92.

[POT88]    Potosnak, K., "Ten Tips for Getting Useful Information from Users," *IEEE Software*, 5(4):89 – 90.

[PUT78]    Putnam, L.H., "A General Empirical Solution to the Macro Software Sizing and Estimating Problem," *IEEE Transactions on Software Engineering*, 4(4):345 – 61.

[RUB83]    Rubin, H.A., "Macroestimation of Software Development Parameters," *SOFTFAIR Conference on Software Development, Tools, Techniques and Alternatives*, IEEE, New York.

[SHE87]*   Shemer, I., "Systems Analysis: A Systemic Analysis of a Conceptual Model," *Communications of the ACM*, 30(6):56 – 512.

[SHN87]*   Shneiderman, B., *Designing the User Interface*, Addison-Wesley, Reading, MA.

[TAU81]    Tausworthe, R.C., "Deep space network software cost estimation model," Publication 81-7, Jet Propulsion Laboratory.

[THA81]*   Thayer, R.H., A.B. Pyster, and R.C. Wood, "Major Issues in Software Engineering Project Management," *IEEE Transactions on Software Engineering*, 7(4):333 – 342.

[TUR84]    Turner, R., *Software Engineering Methodology*, Reston, Reston, VA.

[VIT83]*   Vitalari, N.P., and G.W. Dickson, "Problem Solving for Effective Systems Analysis," *Communications of the ACM*, 26(11):948 – 956.

## PROBLEMS

1 Pretend that you are the analyst and that the customer is an educational software publisher who is planning to market a general-purpose text editor for use in grade schools. List the 20 most important questions to which you must have an

answer. Then place in order from the most important to the least important the following software attributes:

> Consistency
> Efficiency
> Friendliness
> Robustness
> Security
> Simplicity
> Versatility

**2** The systems analyst does not have to be an in-house person. He could come from the customer organization or a third-party organization, like a consulting firm. What are the benefits and drawbacks of each?

**3** What would be the benefits and drawbacks of placing a cost in dollars on each constraint raised by the customer and then allowing the customer to decide whether to buy that constraint?

**4** Functional requirements that become too detailed begin to infringe on the specification stage. Is there some way to draw the line, or are we being too arbitrary in trying to separate the analysis and specification stages?

**5** Conduct a Delphi analysis for the EDCA project among members of the class. How long did it take to reach a conclusion? Were there oracles who were outliers — whose estimates were usually distant from the body?

**6** Give four reasons why it would be difficult to compress a project to less than 75% of its nominal duration.

**7** The amount and detail of analysis might reasonably be different for different kinds of projects. Describe how size, type of user, risk, criticality, and other attributes you might think of would affect analysis.

**8** Can you think of additional multiplier types which should be added to Figure 3-20?

**9** How should COCOMO be adapted to deal with the software reuse process model?

**10** You need a product. You could develop it in house, contract it out to a software development organization, or purchase it (in not completely satisfactory form) as a package. What questions need to be answered before you are able to make a reasonable decision?

**11** Use tools available to you to carry out the estimation of effort, schedule and staffing for EDCA.

**12** Imitate Section 3.5 for a project on which you have worked. How well does your planning correspond to the actual project? Why?

**13** Research and report on sources of information (e.g., *Commerce Business Daily*) that describe potential government contracts. Report on three such requests for proposals (RFPs).

**14** What conditions would justify the software organization in discontinuing a proposed project after receiving the analyst's report of customer interviews.

**15** Perform a work breakdown study for the EDCA project.

**16** Give 10 examples each of short- and long-range planning in a software organization.

**17** Ideally, documentation should be available on-line, as well as in printed form. List the functionality of an on-line documentation browser. How does this differ from a help package?

**18** Come up with an idea for a new product. Conduct market research among your fellow students and by researching publications and existing products. Report on the result.

**19** Read "An Investigation of User-Led System Design" by Franz and Robey in *Communications of the ACM*, 27(12):1202 – 1209. Pick at least one reference in the article and read it. In what ways can user involvement beyond the analysis stage create difficulties for the software organization? How can these difficulties be avoided?

**20** Is there any kind of detail that *cannot* be deferred?

**21** Choose one of the eight potential projects listed below and conduct all or some portion of the analysis stage activities for it.

PLAGIARISM CHECKER — a tool to detect plagiarized source code. It should look for simple substitution of identifiers, structural similarities, and similar McCabe and Halstead measures (see Chapters 6 and 7 for discussion).

MEMO FILTER — a tool to analyze memos received through electronic mail to prioritize and to sort them according to the individual's interests and duties. Memos must be identified through some classification scheme, but memo contents should also be scanned for keywords.

ESTIMATION TOOL — a tool to estimate effort, duration, and manpower for software projects. It can be based on COCOMO or any other pricing model.

CROSS-REFERENCE ANALYZER — a tool to create a cross-reference table for a text document. It should attempt to distinguish definitions from uses of terms, as well as eliminate words that appear in a common, non-technical vocabulary.

FLOWCHART GENERATOR — a tool to create an on-line flowchart from pseudocode. It should provide scrolling capabilities for flowcharts whose size exceeds the screen.

SYNTAX-DIRECTED EDITOR — a tool for input of source code in a specific programming language. It should provide structure templates with defaults, automatic indentation, prologue creation, syntax checking, visual distinctions between keywords and identifiers, and creation of intermediate code.

TEST HARNESS — a tool that allows the execution of single program units in a specific programming language. A test harness should allow its user to generate scripts that will contain specific test cases and anticipated results, or specifications of test case domains for which the harness will randomly generate data and display results.

PROFILER — a tool that will instrument source code in a specific programming language. It should monitor execution of the object code under user control and then provide tables, statistics, and graphs indicating traces, branch and program unit execution counts, CPU time expenditure, and the like.

# CHAPTER 4

# THE SPECIFICATION STAGE

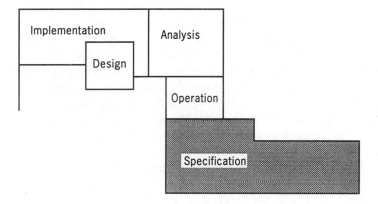

During the specification stage of software development, we translate the requirements and constraints, which were outlined by the analysis stage, into a set of explicit, detailed specifications couched in a technical language. This is the stage in which the major product is described in terms of the software environment as well as the user's environment. In the traditional model of the software process, the specification stage is also the last stage at which there is a significant user involvement before the actual product is available for acceptance.

Recent developments in software engineering have strongly reinforced the importance of the specification stage. Research indicates that increased effort and care during specification will pay handsome rewards in terms of dependability, maintainability, productivity, and general software quality. This research particularly highlights the importance of formalizing the specification process and products. This includes the use of formal specification notations and languages, conformity to set standards of quality and content in the work products, and careful observance of rules for the verification and validation of the specifications.

## 4.1 THE SPECIFICATION PROCESS AND PRODUCTS

The purpose of the specification stage is to transform the requirements developed during the analysis stage into a precise form that is oriented to the needs of software engineers. This, in turn, serves as the basis for the design of a software product. To quote the ANSI/IEEE standards, "The Requirements Specification shall clearly and precisely describe the essential functions, performances, design constraints, attributes, and external interfaces. Each requirement shall be defined such that its achievement is capable of being objectively verified...."

One of the trends in current software engineering practice is to shift more of the effort toward the analysis and specification stages. The underlying principle is that careful groundwork makes actual construction easier and less prone to errors. Such a shift also supports automated design, implementation, and testing methodologies and may result in a smaller overall project cost. But it is not enough just to spend more time; we also have to change the way in which we do specifications. In particular, the employment of formal specification methodologies with the accompanying tools and/or environments is vital if we are to reap the full benefits of the specification stage.

There are three major work products during the specification stage. First, and most important, is the **Software Requirements Specification** itself. It formalizes our view of the eventual product. Second are the **Software Verification Plan** and **Acceptance Test Plan**, which will guide the software team in assuring the integrity of each successive stage's work product and in validating the completed software product. Third is the preliminary **User's Manual**, which describes the external functionality of the product's function from the user's point of view.

### 4.1.1 Purpose of the Specification Stage

There are three major reasons for the activities of the specification stage. (1) We need to translate the user-oriented requirements into a form that is meaningful to the software organization. (2) We need to set the stage for a methodology and tool-intensive development of the product. (3) We need to commit ourselves and the customer to a set definition of the product.

The specification process is largely one of translation of the requirements from one form to another. The first form is found in the Project Plan. It reflects the *user's* vision

| **User Requirements** | versus | **Specifications** |
|:---:|:---:|:---:|
| User | | Software engineer |
| Natural language | | Formal language |
| Imprecise | | Precise |
| Nontechnical | | Technical |
| Application terminology | | Software terminology |

**FIGURE 4-1**   THE DICHOTOMY BETWEEN USER REQUIREMENTS AND SPECIFICATIONS

of the software, and is expressed in a natural language like English. Potentially, these requirements could display a high degree of ambiguity and a broadly expressive style. This tends to make the requirements easier for users to understand and work with. However, ambiguity and nontechnical usage are not a very good way to start out a technical project (Figure 4-1).

The new form of the requirements—the specification—is written for the software team. It will have much the same information as the proposal and constraints sections of the Project Plan, but the information will now be couched in a technical language, designed expressly for the use of software engineers.

If the specification is a reformulation of information already present in the Project Plan, why don't we just use that information as it already exists? If it's because the information is not sufficiently precise, then why not write it precisely in the first place and avoid this extra step? Although some models of software development do almost that, it is not a wise practice in general.

The problem is that software is a product being sold by people of a technical culture to people from a user culture. The disparities between the two are not as obvious as, for instance, when sixteenth-century European explorers traded with South Pacific islanders. But the similarities between the user and the software developer can make us underestimate the very significant risk of misunderstanding.

The software market is not sufficiently mature to have produced a set of industry-wide standards of quality and professional practice. Customers know that software products should be surrounded by signs: "Buyer beware!" So, like any wise person, we want the documents drawn up in both languages, just to make sure. Then each party can examine his own documents to see that they are satisfactory. After that, the remaining issue is the less challenging one of correct translation.

This is not to say that the user should not be involved in the specification process simply because of a lack of technical expertise. On the contrary, just as the software engineer learns much by interacting with the user environment during analysis, so also the user can learn and understand much by participating in the specification. Typically, user involvement will be less intense during this stage, and will continue to decline as product development continues.

User satisfaction will be heightened by involvement in specification; the user feels that attention is being paid to his desires, and that he has some influence over the development of the product. In addition, mistakes in the Product Plan may be discovered, and the software engineer can obtain additional clarification of details. Finally, if specifications are executable, either directly or through construction of prototypes, the user's reactions to this preliminary product can influence the final form of the specifications.

The second reason for specification is to set the stage for a methodical development of the software product. This implies that the work will be produced in an artificial or *formal* language. We will thus be able to use methodologies and to apply algorithms to the work product, much as we are able to work with physical phenomena by using the language of mathematics.

Formal specification languages not only allow us to be methodical; we can also automate the methodology as a tool, and let a computer do part of the work for us. We are familiar with tools like compilers that analyze software and translate it from one form to another. It is far easier to do this when the software is expressed in a carefully designed formal language than when it is expressed in some loose form.

Besides this, a carefully chosen formal notation allows for a precise statement of specifications in a form specialized to both the nature of the application and the needs of software design. The syntax of a specification language can discourage the inclusion of unnecessary detail while it obligates us to provide the essential information. Iverson points out many of the ways in which notation actually shapes our thought and work in [IVE80]. Among his arguments is the fact that notations like the formal specification languages allow us to reason about the behavior of the software and even to prove certain kinds of software theorems.

The third purpose of specification is to provide a point of explicit commitment to the product. There are points in our lives when we stop, draw a deep breath, and think carefully before taking the next step. We do this because we are committing ourselves to a course of action that will have important consequences. Specifications represent just such a commitment in the software development process. We are bound to follow through on our plans now or suffer unpleasant consequences.

Humphrey suggests several characteristics of an effective formal commitment procedure in [HUM89]. All parties should be willing to accept agreed-on responsibilities. The agreement should be made publicly and should represent the sincere and carefully considered judgment of all concerned. Finally, there must be a mechanism for reporting and dealing with problems that might later surface in the agreement.

Like all such resolutions, there is a substantial cost and a commensurate reward associated with software requirements specification. On the one hand, we are now constrained to follow a certain strategy, conform to established data formats, limit ourselves to the stated functions, and so forth. Even if a better way of doing things surfaces, we can only use it at the cost of substantial backtracking and loss of effort. We will have to exercise considerable discipline to conform ourselves to the specifications.

On the other hand, by establishing and following specifications, we free ourselves from constant worry about whether we are doing things in the best way possible. We can improve productivity by devoting our energies to the task at hand, rather than wasting them on second thoughts. If the specifications have been carefully and completely developed, we should be able to avoid false starts, minimize rework, and reduce the incidence of faults in the software. Indications are that careful attention to specifications may improve overall productivity significantly ([MIL87], [POS87]).

### 4.1.2 Activities During Specification

Unlike the changes that occur during design, specification does not modify the fundamental nature of the work product. Instead, it *formalizes* what we already have by making it more precise and adding details where needed. The informal requirements determined during analysis remain requirements, and the testing criteria are still just testing criteria. But instead of being conceptual, they become technical; rather than suggestions, they are specifications.

The basic technique for formalization is simply to go over the requirements point by point, translating them into the formal notation that we have decided is best suited to expressing them. At the same time we maintain constant vigilance to make sure the translation correctly expresses the requirements, that it is complete with all the details that will be needed, and that the resulting Software Requirements Specifications are clear, precise, and consistent. Additional attributes of good specifications are listed in Section 4.2.2.

This is the first stage at which it is possible to reuse software components. If, for instance, we find that part of our product involves the parsing of a command language, there is a good chance that the language will be quite similar to one that has been used before, and that the specifications we are writing for it are straightforward modifications of a portion of a specification that is available to us. At another time, we might be defining communications protocols or validation logic for complex records; in that case, existing tables used in previous products could form a framework for our new specification.

The important thing to remember is that the sooner a reused component is introduced into the development process, the more efficient and productive reuse becomes. It is definitely a mistake to wait until implementation and then look around for some existing module that we can drop into place. First, if such a tailor-made module exists, then it should have accompanying specification and design documents that are also tailor-made and need not be duplicated by current effort. Second, if there is no perfect match at the code level, it is quite possible that additional constraints, created while specifying and designing without considering what code *is* available, will make it impossible to fit the existing code into our product at the implementation stage.

Since a lack of maintainability is one of the prime problems in current software engineering practice, special attention must be given to specifying software in such a way that its maintainability is enhanced. In part, this goal is met simply by making certain that a good specification in a formal notation exists. This will allow maintenance to be carried out on the appropriate part of the product. That is, all perfective and adaptive changes to software, as well as many corrective changes, are made because the product *as specified* is not satisfactory. The logical place for the modification is in the specifications. Subsequent alterations to the design and code, as well as verification and validation of the modifications, can then be carried out using standard development techniques (Figure 4-2).

But there are other specification-stage activities that will promote the maintainability of the product. A careful statement of requirements will avoid any unnecessary or illogical mixing of function. This groundwork will then promote modularity in the design and implementation, and will thus enhance maintainability. Similarly, the quality of the verification plan and the testing data developed now will influence the ease with which a modified product can be retested to verify its continued conformity to specifications. It is very difficult to retest software without adequate test plans and at a distance of several years from the original development.

Prototyping during the specification stage can be used for validation of the specifications. This is done by allowing the user and the software team to see the software in action, noting aspects that fail to meet the requirements. Of course, it is not generally possible to prototype the entire product, unless one is working with an executable

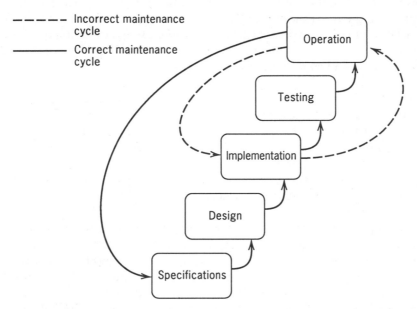

**FIGURE 4-2**   MAINTENANCE REACHES ALL THE WAY BACK TO SPECIFICATIONS

specification language. There is also the risk that the prototype will not match the specifications exactly, since it is usually put together with less care than a final product. Nevertheless, the value of prototyping outweighs its drawbacks.

Along with the Software Requirements Specification, we also need to develop the Software Verification Plan and Acceptance Test Plan at this time. With a technical specification of the software in hand, it is possible to transform the acceptance criteria of the Project Plan into a set of input data with the expected system response. The specification of tests is usually done in a simple tabular format, but formal notations can be used. A good example of formal test specification can be seen in Hayes ([HAY86]).

Acceptance testing is a validation function — it shows that we built the right product. But we also need to verify — to see that we build the product right. Software Verification should be conducted by the team member(s) assigned to the testing role and forming the quality assurance arm of the team. Quality assurance procedures have already been outlined in the Project Plan. Now that technical specifications exist, we can list each requirement together with specific methodologies for verifying compliance during the design, implementation, and testing stages.

In particular, we need enough data to test the finished product thoroughly in all its behavior. These data will far exceed the amount to be used in acceptance testing, since the software organization will want to ensure against as many potential disasters during the operational stage as possible. Selection of test data should be guided by two principles: first, emphasize the testing of critical and vital parts of the product; second, choose data to test all parts of the software to some predetermined degree of thoroughness. Chapter 8 discusses test case selection methodologies.

Finally, a preliminary version of the User's Manual will be produced during specification. This represents the bulk of the planning and writing of user documents and may require the participation of specialists in technical writing and instructional methods. The preliminary User's Manual, like prototyping, represents an avenue for early validation of the product. Since it is a document specially prepared for the users, the Manual is more understandable to them than the specifications. On the other hand, as with prototypes, there is always the danger that the User's Manual does not, in fact, mirror the actual specifications.

A review is conducted at the end of the specification stage, in order to examine the documents we have produced for correctness and quality. This is a technical review and is conducted by the software team. If the customer has some representative who is capable of evaluating the technical nature of the specifications, then he is included on the review team. The documents developed during specification are submitted to configuration control following successful completion of the review. Subsequent changes to them must go through the standard approval process established in the product control policies.

If the specifications represent a software organization's contract with the customer, then the specification review is the contract signing ceremony. It is the last time when one can raise major objections to or questions about the product as a whole. For this reason, planning in preparation for the review and formality in conducting it are particularly important. When carefully handled, the specification review not only improves the quality of the eventual product but also raises the level of feedback, understanding, and commitment among all the participants.

In most cases, the management review that finalized the analysis stage determined that we *will* develop the product. However, there are some circumstances, particularly for large contract software, when the Software Requirements Specification has to be developed before the contract is awarded. In that instance, some of the nonrequirements parts of the Project Plan may be written after specification but before design. It may even happen that separate contracts are awarded for the development of specifications and of the final product, in which case there will be no follow-up activities on the part of the organization that develops the specifications.

### 4.1.3 Specification Documents and Deliverables

Three major documents are produced during the specification stage. The first, and most important, is the Software Requirements Specification, which is outlined in Figure 4-3.

The introduction will be similar to the corresponding section in the Project Plan; it sets the stage for the rest of the specification. There is a description of the user environment and of the problem that is to be solved by the software product. An understanding of the concerns, abilities, and functions of users will help in developing the product, enabling us to understand how the product fits in with other activities in the environment. Instructions on how to interpret and to use the formal notations appearing elsewhere in the document may be necessary. Finally, internal and external goals for the project will help guide the design and other subsequent stages.

**Introduction**
> Problem overview
> Application environment, user characteristics
> Notations used in the specification
> Goals of the project

**Software functions**
> Process descriptions
> Function pre- and post-assertions
> Data descriptions
> Data relationships
> Priorities for implementation

**Constraints**
> External interfaces (hardware, operating system, user, data, network)
> Compatibility with previous products
> Timing and processing rates
> Code and data size, and processing volume
> Dependability
> Accuracy
> Maintainability
> Security and Safety

**Exceptions**
> Forbidden Behavior
> Hardware failures and responses
> Software faults and responses
> Data faults and responses

**Software life cycle**
> Process model, standards and methodologies
> Predicted modifications and maintenance

**Reference**
> Documents used in developing the specifications
> Glossary of terms

**FIGURE 4-3**   THE SOFTWARE REQUIREMENTS SPECIFICATION

Although much of the first section will still be expressed in English (or some other natural language), the vocabulary will probably shift from that of the application environment to that of software engineering. This is in keeping with the fact that the software team is the primary user of the specifications.

The second section, however, should be phrased in one or more formal notations. The purpose of this section is to describe what the software is to do, and the exact structure and relationship of input and output data. Some appropriate notations are outlined in Section 4.3. Preassertions and postassertions are formal descriptions of the

**Unmeasurable Constraints**

"Should conform to the earlier Mark II editor language"

"Should handle a high volume of transactions"

"Should report readings accurately"

"Should protect all data from unauthorized inspection"

"Should show a high level of dependability"

**Measurable Constraints**

"Must process all Mark II commands identically to the original"

"Must handle 1200 random update transactions per hour"

"Must report pressure within 0.05 PSI of the calibrated source"

"Must encrypt all network messages using the DES algorithm"

"Must perform for an average of more than 96 hours between failures"

**F I G U R E 4-4**   INCORRECTLY AND CORRECTLY STATED CONSTRAINTS

state of the software system before and after the function is executed. They will be used to judge the correctness of the design and implementation of the function during later stages of development. The priorities tell us which functions will be basic to the product, and which will be added later.

The constraints need not use any specialized formal notation, but they must be made precise and testable (see Figure 4-4). If we cannot state a constraint precisely, we will never know if it is being adhered to.

The exceptions section outlines those unusual events that the user, the analyst, and the software designer can imagine happening. Forbidden behavior refers to those things that under no circumstances may be allowed to occur. This information may relate to the safety constraints, but it is good to list it separately. Along with an identification of the event, the specifications have to state precisely how we will know the event has occurred, and what measures are to be taken by the software in response. A complete treatment of exceptions in the specifications will make for much more dependable software. Additional suggestions for dependability will be given in Section 4.2.4.

The software life cycle section reviews material dealing with strategy from the Project Plan. In addition, it tries to foresee the probable course of the product, both in terms of its evolutionary changes during maintenance, and also in terms of the frequency, nature, and level of support for maintenance. This information will be useful in designing the product, to create sockets where additional functions can be plugged in or to facilitate the kind of maintenance that is expected.

Figure 4-5 shows an outline of one section of the Software Verification Plan; an abbreviated form of this document can also be used for the Acceptance Test Plan. These documents are organized to parallel the Software Requirements Specifications. Each separate requirement will have a corresponding section of the Verification or Acceptance Plan. The section is broken down into a restatement of the requirement as it appears in the Software Requirement Specification, a description of how the design

Requirement (restates specification)
Design verification methodology, schedule, responsible party
Code verification methodology, schedule, responsible party
Test data and responses, schedule, responsible party

**FIGURE 4-5**   THE SOFTWARE VERIFICATION PLAN (ONE SECTION)

document will be verified to meet the requirement, how the code will likewise be verified, and how the code will be validated through testing.

The last document produced during the specification stage is the preliminary User's Manual. Since we have a specification of the input, function, and output of the software, we are already in a position to tell the user how it will work. However, specifications will need amplification and tuning during design and implementation, and screen and hard copy images are not yet available for illustration. Thus, some details, particularly as they describe the user interface, will be missing from the preliminary document. It would be premature of us to invest a great deal of effort in a high quality production. Hence, the document is somewhat informal at this point. An outline of the User's Manual is given in Figure 4-6.

## 4.2 Specification Principles

In this section we discuss some of the principles that should guide the specification process. First, choosing appropriate goals will help direct us to the desired end. The three goals outlined are: (1) use of formal notation for easier transformation of specifications into design, (2) restriction of specifications to functional rather than procedural representation, and (3) maximal use of tools during specification.

Next, we consider some of the characteristic attributes of good specifications. These attributes will help us to evaluate our specifications as we determine their quality. If the work product displays these characteristics, then there is a good chance that we are on the road to a successful product.

The third topic deals with the cost of errors in software and the importance of catching and eliminating them as soon as possible. This is particularly appropriate for discussion now, since the majority of the errors in software are usually present in the specifications ([BOE81]). Finally, we consider some of the ways by which residual errors, which have not been eliminated despite specification, can be tolerated within the final software product.

## 4.2.1 Goals for the Specification Stage

It may seem that the emphasis on formal versus informal specifications is largely academic but, in fact, the use of a formal specification language provides a very practical payoff. First, formal specifications seem to exhibit fewer errors that are propagated into the design ([MIL87]). Second, it costs less to rework formally specified software, either for repairing an error or for use during subsequent maintenance

**Introduction**

    Purpose of the software product

    Operating environment

    General functionality

    Special features

    Limitations

    Conventions used in this document

**Installation**

    Physical requirements

    Copying and backing up

    Software installation procedures

    Customizing the product

**Tutorial**

    Walkthrough of an example

    Explanation of the example

    Elaboration of the basic example

    Use of on-line help package and manuals

**Detailed instructions**

    Output of the product

    Input to the product

    Operation of the product

    Error handling

    Specific functions

        How to invoke this function

        Input data needed

        How to interpret the results

**Technical details**

    Principles of operation

    Advanced features

    Major algorithms

    Major data structures

    Modification of the product

    How to get support and further information

**FIGURE 4-6**   OUTLINE OF THE USER'S MANUAL

activities. Third, automation of the specification stage, and the resulting gains in productivity, can only occur when they are based on some formal notation. Fourth, formal specifications are more precise and less ambiguous — in fact, they are a better scientific basis for software development (Figure 4-7).

Besides the issue of phrasing requirements in a language understandable to the software team, there are several reasons why natural languages are not a satisfactory

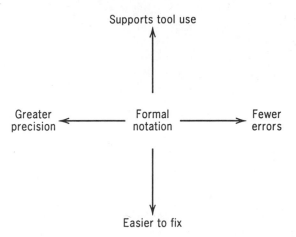

**FIGURE 4-7**   THE BENEFITS OF USING FORMAL NOTATIONS FOR SPECIFICATION

basis for the following stages of development. The very fact that natural languages are so powerful and are capable of such subtle nuances of meaning, brings in train the possibility of varying interpretations of intention. Ambiguity may be a wonderful way to buffer people's feelings during emotional interchanges, but it does not provide much of a framework for verification of software. It is also very difficult to build software tools that will transform, or even fully analyze, specifications written in a natural language.

We will consider about a dozen notations and methodologies that can introduce formality into specifications. In addition, there are many different complete formal specification languages. Almost all of them are supported by tools for analysis, execution, and/or transformation, and some are supported by full software engineering environments.

In situations where it is impossible to utilize a formal specification language, Posten has some suggestions that will improve the utility of natural language specifications ([POS85]):

1 Limit the structure of paragraphs to a list of individual sentences.
2 Limit the structure of each sentence to a simple sentence using noncompound verbs and objects.
3 Limit the verbs and objects in the sentences to a small set, with a single specified definition for each word.
4 Limit the verbs and objects to terms that are common to the end user of the product.
5 Limit the verbs and objects to actions and items that are visible in the product's external environment.

Following these rules will increase the completeness, verifiability, comprehensibility, and modifiability of natural language specifications while reducing their ambiguity.

An obvious extension of the idea of transformation of specifications into code is that of transformation of functional requirements and other analysis stage work products into code. Balzer describes his hope for such a system in [BAL85], although it has only been used on relatively small products. It provides a tool, called **SAFE/TI**, for acquiring, understanding and formalizing natural language requirements, as well as disambiguation and dynamic interpretive execution of the resulting formal specifications expressed in the Gist language. A verification tool can be used for proving properties of the specifications, whereas symbolic execution provides some testing capabilities for the specifications.

A similar system, developed as part of the **PSI** project at Stanford University in Palo Alto, California, is described in [FRE85]. Here the "natural language" specifications can be expressed in a mixture of English, graphics, examples, and formal notations. Tools are proposed for transformation, analysis, validation, and optimization of the resulting code.

Another goal of most specification methodologies is to maintain the distinction between *functional* and *procedural* descriptions of software. Although we need to have firm specifications, these generally refer to the external behavior and appearance of the product — a functional description. We are still specifying *what* the software will do, and not *how*. The "how," or procedural details, will be gradually filled in as we continue through the design and implementation stages. Some specification methodologies suggest that detailed descriptions of processing, like Nassi — Shneiderman boxes, or flowcharts, or HIPO diagrams, should be provided during specification. Such detail is usually premature, and frequently suffocating. The operational process model requires just the opposite — all of the "hows" are included in the specification. This is because the software engineer will have very little more to say about the function of the software after the specification stage (Figure 4-8).

Parnas recommends ([PAR83]) that specifications provide all of the information needed to design software *but nothing more*. In particular, functional specifications should be formalized without any procedural details — they simply tell what the output will be for a given set of input. This minimalist approach gives the designer full rein in choosing a specific implementation of the function being specified. Also, a functional specification can be validated and analyzed before design begins, thus reducing the possibility of undetected specification errors, which are more costly to eliminate at later stages of development. Of course, the formal specifications can be amplified by other, informal descriptions, as long as these are not taken as the basis for further development of the product.

In reporting the Fourth International Workshop on Software Specification ([ZAV88]), Zave points out that formal process specification methodologies can usually be classified as operational (procedural) or mathematical (functional). Operational specifications are understood in terms of some execution model, whereas mathematical specifications are understood in terms of what can be proved about them in some mathematical system. Operational specifications have the advantage of being more easily transformed into code, whereas mathematical specifications tend to be more implementation independent. In keeping with the principle that specifications should deal with "what" rather than "how," mathematical specification methodologies should be considered superior.

If a module is really a black box.............

...........then specifications should only describe its exterior

**F I G U R E 4-8**   WE SHOULDN'T SPECIFY THE WORKINGS OF SOFTWARE

On the other hand, we must realize that there is an inevitable interdependence of specification, design, and implementation. Swartout and Balzer point out in [SWA82] that our knowledge during the specification stage is necessarily incomplete and our foresight may not be acute enough to show us all of the consequences of the specifications. Thus, design and implementation experience may cause us to return to, and modify, the specifications. This is, of course, simply the principle of prototyping.

There is nothing wrong with changing specifications, assuming that the customer and developer agree to the changes and that the benefits justify the cost. We must be sure, however, that we have adequate control over all work products, so that changes in the specification are fully reflected by changes in the existing design, code, and other documents. More to the point, we must control changes so that they cause the product to evolve into something better than it was. It is *uncontrolled*, ill-considered change that most likely jeopardizes the product at this stage.

Another goal of the specification process is to support the use of appropriate tools. Specification tools generally provide three different kinds of capability. First, some tools allow us to investigate the specifications, with the purpose of understanding them better. Second, other tools allow us to analyze the specifications, to determine whether they possess all the quality attributes outlined in Section 4.2.2. Third, some tools help us in transforming specifications into design or even code. Each of these capabilities is discussed in Section 4.3.4, while Section 4.3.5 describes some semi-integrated environments now available commercially.

### 4.2.2 Characteristics of Good Specifications

The quality of the Software Requirements Specification can be evaluated with regard to several different attributes that it should possess. The level of these attributes in a given specification will determine its appropriateness and usefulness for the task. The attributes are listed, more or less in the order of their importance, in Figure 4-9. They are explained more fully in the paragraphs that follow.

The first — and by far most important — attribute is **correctness**: requirements that are important to the customer and that are stated in the Project Plan must appear in correct form in the Software Requirements Specification. Unfortunately, since the customer's requirements were probably stated in an informal language, there is no formal method for verifying the correctness of the Software Requirements Specification. This specification can, however, be validated by allowing the user to exercise the specified product, either through the use of an executable specification language or by means of a prototype. In addition, customer requirements should have been checked to see that they are appropriate from a technical viewpoint and that they can be realistically achieved within the constraints and context of the software project.

The attributes of being **consistent, complete,** and **unambiguous** all group together logically. With consistency, we can be sure that requirements that are correct in isolation can still be achieved when taken together. Completeness guarantees that no important requirements have been left out. Freedom from ambiguity assures us that

- Correct.
- Consistent.
- Complete.
- Unambiguous.
- Minimal.
- Formal.
- Verifiable.
- Transformable.
- Modifiable.
- Traceable.

**FIGURE 4-9**  ATTRIBUTES OF A GOOD SPECIFICATION

everyone on the project (and among the customer and users, if they are familiar with the specification notation) will agree on the exact meaning of the specification.

**Minimality** touches on the concept of deferring details. We must guard against overspecifying the software at this point. In particular, specifications should be functional. Another kind of minimality is obtained by the use of a notation that supports us in saying just what we want, with no additional, redundant, or distracting verbiage. Wordiness tempts software engineers to skim through specifications; they do not want to spend a lot of time wading through superfluity. Meyer points out in [MEY85] that we tend to specify and then respecify portions of the requirements that we recognize to be ambiguous or incomplete. This kind of redundancy adds confusion, not certainty, to the document. As a corollary, the specification format should not require that the same information appear in separate locations, since this makes it more difficult to maintain consistency.

**Verifiability** is the capacity of determining that requirements are met at each stage of development; it depends on precise, unambiguous, and concrete statements of constraints, exceptions and software functions. Unfortunately, verifying that design and code follow from specifications is easier when specifications are procedural rather than functional. This puts a constant tension between the attributes of minimality and verifiability.

**Transformability** describes the characteristic of specifications that provide for a smooth processing to create a design, the working product of the next stage of the life cycle. This smooth transition will minimize the amount of "rework" and adjustment needed to prepare for the design process. For this reason, the specification notation should be compatible with the methodology and tools used during design.

**Modifiability** refers first to the ease with which changes can be made to the specifications themselves. Of course, the first step in guaranteeing modifiability is to create and to store the specifications electronically in a project database. Beyond that, minimality helps ensure that a change only needs to be made in one place, rather than in several redundant locations. Finally, modifiability will be promoted by modularity in the specifications with a minimum of cross-connections and dependencies between different requirements.

**Traceability** is the inclusion of sufficient pointers, cross-indexes, references, and the like. to allow us to go forward from a requirement to find those parts of a subsequent work product that satisfy the requirement, or backward from a portion of the work product to find the requirements that give rise to it. Of course, traceability also refers to our ability to correlate the specifications backward to the requirements analysis (Figure 4-10).

**Formality,** as was mentioned above, is the key to much of the specification process. Software engineers often resent the time spent in formal specification, believing that it simply delays the moment when they can begin their "real" work. But most of the essential attributes of good specification can be supported most easily when we use formal specification languages. These languages are designed to be minimal — they include nothing that is not needed. Formal languages also allow for a high degree of organization, often hierarchical, in the specifications. Organization is vital when we are working with the specifications for a very large project. Minimality and organization

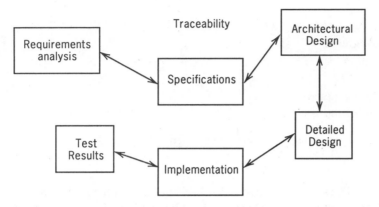

**FIGURE 4-10**   TRACING SPECIFICATIONS TO OTHER WORK PRODUCTS

make the requirements easier to scan so that incompleteness is more likely to be spotted.

Formal notation directly supports automatic evaluation of consistency and a partial automation of completeness analysis. Some types of verification of subsequent work products can be carried out automatically on the basis of formal specifications, as will be seen in Section 4.3.4. Tracing software features forward from or back to requirements is also automatable. Finally, some kinds of formal specifications can be executed. At the least, prototype creation can be aided by software tools acting on formal specifications.

In connection with formal specification notations, Roman has suggested in [ROM85] an alternative list of attributes to those found in Figure 4-9. These are as follows:

| | |
|---|---|
| Appropriateness | Analyzability |
| Cleanliness | Formality |
| Constructability | Testability |
| Structuring | Traceability |
| Ease of access | Executability |
| Precision | Tolerance of incompleteness |
| Lack of ambiguity | Adaptability |
| Completeness | Economy of expression |
| Consistency | Modifiability |

Several of these (constructability, ease of access, analyzability, traceability, executability, and modifiability) refer to capabilities that we would expect from a good environment and software project database supporting specification. Others, like cleanliness, precision, lack of ambiguity, testability, and economy of expression, are natural qualities of good formal notations. Appropriateness refers to the ability of a particular notation to capture the concepts and activities of the customer's environment.

- Noise.
- Silence.
- Overspecification.
- Contradiction.
- Ambiguity.
- Forward reference.
- Wishful thinking.

**FIGURE 4-11**   ATTRIBUTES THAT SPECIFICATION *SHOULDN'T* HAVE

Berzins and Gray also suggest a similar list of attributes in [BER85]; they add that a specification notation should support the abstraction of concepts and that specifications should be modular. These attributes will help substantially in the reuse of specification components.

Of course, specifications can also be described in terms of attributes they *shouldn't* have. Meyer ([MEY85]) presents the list in Figure 4-11. Silence, contradiction, and ambiguity are the opposites of completeness, consistency, and unambiguity. Overspecification and noise are the opposites of minimality. Forward reference is the use of features of the problem that have not yet been defined at the point of use as part of the specifications. Wishful thinking is the inclusion of requirements that cannot realistically be met. Meyer also asserts that very long specifications, which frequently occur in the acquisition of software by the U.S. Department of Defense, represent a misuse of the requirements process. Words are multiplied and concepts are reiterated simply in the hope of avoiding any incompleteness. This redundancy is more likely to cause confusion than to solve problems.

Part of the review process at the end of the specification stage deals with verifying that appropriate methodologies and notations have been chosen for the specification. Most especially, the quality of the specification should be assured by determining that it has all of the attributes listed in this section.

## 4.2.3 Reducing the Cost and Impact of Errors

A common truism in software engineering is the observation that errors committed in software development are cheaper to fix if they are discovered immediately, and that the cost of correcting errors rises rapidly as we go to later and later stages. The traditional, or waterfall, software process model recognizes this fact by providing immediate feedback flows from each stage to the previous one. These are simply corrections of errors caught early. The problem with waiting longer is that the effects of errors are propagated more widely, either as time goes on or through the more extensive, complex and widely distributed work product of later stages.

Figure 4-12, from Boehm ([BOE81]), illustrates the relative cost of fixing requirements errors during different stages. It is evident that the cost of repairing a requirements error during operation is about 100 times the cost of correcting it as it occurs. This is because we must move forward through all the work products, changing them to

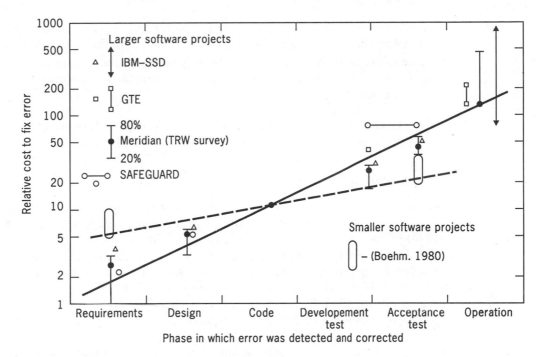

**FIGURE4-12**   THE RELATIVE COST OF FIXING ERRORS (Barry W. Boehm, *Software Engineering Economics*, copyright © 1981, p.40. Reprinted by permission of Prentice Hall, Inc., Englewood Cliffs, N.J.)

reflect the corrected specifications, and then modifying all versions of the software that have been distributed for use. In addition, the mechanism for reviewing and approving requests for changes of a controlled document is much more costly at later stages. Finally, there may be a significant impact on people, who might need to rethink their development plans or to relearn ways of using operational software.

Unfortunately, it becomes easier to detect errors as work products become more concrete; an error has less reality to us in the specifications than when it appears in a running program. Posten cites data in [POS85] that indicate that 55% of all faults occur during requirements analysis and specification, whereas 43% of all faults are not found until after the testing stage. That is, most software errors are introduced early in the process and are removed relatively late. Thus, the best strategy, which is to avoid long-term errors (created in specification and detected during use) and to correct specification errors during the specification stage, has been difficult to achieve in practice.

There are four procedures that will help to remedy this, however.

1 We should combine formal specification notations and the use of software tools with a careful inspection of the specifications to analyze them for errors.

2 Increased use of prototyping will help us to visualize and to actualize the product, thus giving us new ways to detect errors at an early stage. In particular, the help of users in validating the specifications should be actively sought during this stage.

3 We should make the development of the software product as modular as possible to minimize the propagation of a single error throughout the work product.

4 Traceability of the specifications (hopefully built into the project database system) and configuration management tools can automate the modification of subsequent work products

This kind of careful attention to fault elimination can reduce errors to 1% of their former rates, even for very large software systems ([MYE88]).

### 4.2.4 Specifying Software Dependability

In Chapter 1, we learned that, even with the best will and extensive testing, it is not always realistic to assume that we can either remove or avoid all errors in our product. Although, this risk may be acceptable in some instances, software that demands an extra degree of dependability cannot tolerate it. For this reason, it is necessary to consider the inclusion of fault tolerance as one of the requirements during specification. There is a wide spectrum of techniques for providing this added level of dependability ([AND81], [KIM84]). The techniques listed below are arranged from the simple to the complex end of that spectrum (Figure 4-13).

The simplest of all fault-tolerance measures is to provide the user with some **restart** capability ([REE74]). This is used in situations where the software has failed to handle an error and the user becomes aware of a failure. The user then has the capability of terminating execution, or of signaling a decision to restart execution from a prior point. Although most operating systems allow for a control character to abort execution, this may not work, for instance in circumstances where the software is in a tight loop with no READ statements.

Once an error is activated in software, it is desirable that the error not propagate through a multitude of data structures and files. This objective can be implemented through the localization techniques of **code and data modularity** ([WUL75]). Carefully designed interfaces that check the correctness of data passing between the modules are

**Fault Tolerance Measures**

|          |    |                                |
|----------|----|--------------------------------|
|          | 1. | Restart                        |
| basic    | 2. | Code and data modularity       |
|          | 3. | General error handling procedures |
|          | 4. | Checkpointing                  |
| moderate | 5. | Careful replacement            |
|          | 6. | Handshaking                    |
|          | 7. | Self-identifying structures    |
| advanced | 8. | *N*-version software           |
|          | 9. | Recovery blocks                |

**FIGURE 4-13**  LEVELS AND TECHNIQUES FOR SOFTWARE FAULT TOLERANCE

vital to error containment and, indeed, to provide the principle method for error detection. In programming languages that do not contain the ability to do this kind of checking, it is necessary to check preassertions on the incoming data to determine their suitability. A simple example of this is represented by the prompt-input-test procedures of Section 5.3.2. Here, the interface being protected is between the user and the software.

If it is possible to use **generalized procedures for error handling**, this should be done. As mentioned previously, rollback methods are usually amenable to standardization; so are error reporting and logging. It is particularly important to select a set of error condition codes that will give an adequate basis for later correction of the software (since we will surely try to remove the fault) and that will give the user an idea of what has been going wrong. Error handling should be merged with exception handling ([GOO75]). This is particularly attractive in a language like Ada, which permits exceptions to be declared and raised.

**Checkpointing** the system state, or at least the part of it that will be needed for rollback, can be a very expensive task. Some operating systems were devised that automatically did this periodically, perhaps every 15 minutes. The overhead was more than users were willing to pay. It seems more acceptable to provide a snapshot function within software, and to allow the software engineer to invoke it where it might be needed to save the program state. Of course, it is necessary to verify the correctness of the state before saving it, since rollback to an error state is no solution at all.

**Careful replacement** is a method by which old data are maintained in parallel with new data until the new data are fully certified ([VER78]). Only then are the old data replaced. This is sometimes implemented by using differential files in addition to the basic data files. When a change of data is made, the record is marked "outdated" in the basic file, and a new record is inserted into the differential file. In this way, if the update turns out to be incorrect, the original is easily reclaimed. The inverse operation is keeping an audit trace, where the old records are stored in a history file.

**Handshaking** is a technique by which independent processes or devices attempt to verify the viability of their interface. It consists of passing messages back and forth of the type:

"Are you there?" and "Yes, I'm here."

or

"Here's the data, repeat it back." and "OK, here it is."

Handshaking must be combined with a timeout facility that allows the signaling process to continue with an alternate path if no response has been received within a reasonable amount of time.

A specialization of handshaking is found in **self-identifying structures** ([DEN76]). It sometimes occurs that software can get mixed up and use an incorrect pointer to data. We then run the risk of corrupting some other structure rather than updating the one we want. For prudence, a field in the structure should identify it, and should be confirmed before an update. For example, if the key field in a record is a name, and we think we are pointing to the right record, we should still verify that the name in the record is the one we are looking for.

The **N-version technique** ([AVI85]) requires that several procedures of the same functionality but independent design be provided. The different versions are then run in parallel and the results are voted on. This technique is good for real-time systems that must be fast and dependable. However, some doubts have been cast on the techniques for obtaining independent designs. A hardware-related example of this problem was demonstrated in the Brown's Ferry reactor accident, where a fire in a cable tray disabled a number of redundant systems simultaneously ([BOR87]).

One method of obtaining software independence is to partition the instruction set of a computer and to allow each version to use just the instructions of its cell in the partition. This is clearly inappropriate. Nor is it certain that simply giving the same specifications to $N$ different design groups and forbidding them to communicate will result in independent designs. A test by Knight and Leveson ([KNI86]) indicates that even totally independent programmers naturally choose the same plans to meet the goals of the specifications. Hence, designs are, in fact, *not* independent.

Another technical difficulty arises from small differences between values calculated in equivalent ways by different versions. These differences are because of rounding and other finite-precision arithmetic problems. If the values are on the boundary between true and false for a conditional, the differences can cause two different decision paths to be taken by two different versions. These can continue to propagate through other decisions until $n$ different versions come up with $n$ different values for the function. In this instance, no majority is present, and voting is deadlocked. A partial solution to the problem can be obtained by allowing each version to signal that a *close* decision was made ([BRI87]). The entire system can reserve judgment if most of the versions signal *close* and no majority is obtained. If the system reestablishes agreement shortly thereafter, the problem can be ignored.

The **recovery block** ([RAN78]) has been suggested as a new construct in programming languages. Its syntactic form is as follows:

```
ensure postassertion
      by procedure-1
      else by procedure-2
      . . .
      else by procedure-n
      else error.
```

It appears to be a type of $n$-version software, but here the different procedures are executed sequentially. The semantics of the recovery block are that procedure1 is executed, at which point the postassertion is tested. If it fails, then the data are restored and procedure2 is tried. Procedure2 has the same functionality as procedure1, but its form is quite different. It is probably more dependable but less efficient. If errors continue to occur, we try the remaining procedures and finally signal an error. A recovery block can easily be coded in any programming language, but the cost of saving the data space and rolling back to it each time can be tremendous. However, we can implement a recovery stack containing a frame of changed data for each nested recovery block, just as a system stack might contain call frames for recursive procedures. If, at the end of execution of procedure$i$, the postassertion is met, then the changes in the change frame can be recorded permanently. Otherwise, the frame can be popped, and procedure$i+1$ can start its own frame (Figure 4-14).

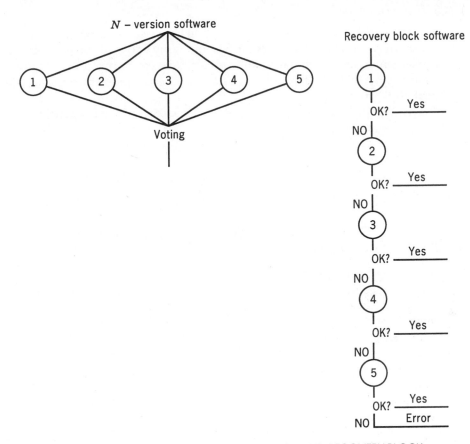

**FIGURE 4-14** THE DIFFERENCE BETWEEN N-VERSION AND RECOVERY BLOCK

$N$-version and recovery techniques can be combined into a **consensus recovery block** mechanism. All $N$ versions execute in parallel, avoiding the need of a recovery stack for rolling back values. After execution, if the outputs of two or more versions agree, a plurality decides which outputs are to be used. If not, outputs are tested in a standard recovery block ordering, giving priority to the earliest set of outputs that satisfy the postassertion.

The specific methods presented here form a spectrum of possible responses to faults. Some software might require us to use the full armory, whereas other situations call for nothing more than pushing the system reset button. The degree of dependability is established in the Software Requirements Specification, and we must have some idea of what methods will be required to provide that level of protection.

As a rule of thumb, the methods of restart, localization, and generalized error procedures should be used in all software. The techniques of checkpointing, careful replacement, and handshaking are typically found, where applicable, in software of moderate dependability. Self-identifying structures (in their full extent), $n$-version software, or recovery blocks are likely to be used only in products that have a very high level of specified dependability.

Careful specification of the software will give rise to a large number of anticipated exceptions. These are the basis for design of any forward recovery techniques to be implemented in the software. Unfortunately, the eternal optimism of software people leads them to slide by both the specification of errors and the construction of code to deal with errors.

Finally, note that, judging by experience, the parts of software most likely to contain errors are those that are designed to handle errors. Optimism probably plays a part here, since we believe that these code segments will be seldom, if ever, executed; thus, we invest less time in their careful design. But the testing of error-handling code is quite difficult, since in the normal course of events it is difficult to generate errors. Hence, inadequate testing makes the fault-tolerance portions of our software more vulnerable to faults.

## 4.3 Specification Methodologies and Tools

Since specification is largely a process of translating and expressing the functional requirements portion of the Project Plan, specification methodologies tend to concentrate on the best way to represent the various components of a software product. In general, these components will be *processes*, which eventually become executable code, and *data*. In addition, since data can have very complex organizations, we need special ways to describe *relationships* between data (Figure 4-15).

In specifying processes, we will represent both function and system behavior. Processes are the first thing we think about in connection with software. For our purposes, a **process** is simply a set of executable actions that have a single unified aim. We cannot afford to sacrifice flexibility, however. Hence, our representation techniques should avoid the writing of actual algorithms in favor of less constricting and more functional process notations.

Davis gives a brief comparison of various process specification notations in [DAV88], emphasizing that they only describe the *external* behavior of the product. This does not mean that procedural specifications should never be allowed — just that the use of them should be examined very carefully and critically. Process specification methods usually possess a functional aspect (what happens?). Some are control driven (when does it happen?), whereas others are data driven (how are inputs transformed into outputs?).

Data definition is vital to a specification of both input and output of the product. Since these data may represent an important interface to parts of the applications environment, conforming to their specified structure may be vital. The structure and content of data are of particular interest to users and need careful attention. Data relationships are particularly useful in describing allowable data, data-induced exceptions and correct implementation of processes. Data specification methods are usually nonfunctional, describing states or structures rather than changes in state or structure. However, the functional description of how to generate some data (e.g., languages generated by production grammars) lies very close to the surface.

Constraints must also be represented, but most of them do not have any actual existence within the product. Thus, they can be represented by precise and verifiable natural language statements. However, Ada is an exception to the rule of inexpressi-

The three facets of software specification notations

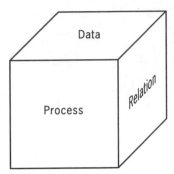

**FIGURE 4-15** PARTS OF SOFTWARE WHICH CAN BE SPECIFIED FORMALLY

bility of constraints in code. Ada's highly modular structure and its ability to represent tasks, modules, objects, and other design constructs have led to the development of special Ada specification methodologies. For instance, Anna ([LUC85]) is an extension of Ada and allows specification in terms of a combination of Ada declarations, virtual Ada text, and annotations that express various aspects of specification. An Anna specification is a precise description of the eventual product and is machine processable, allowing for transformation of assertions into code.

## 4.3.1 Process Specification

The most useful process notation at the specification stage is the *data flow diagram*. Processes are represented by an input-procedure-output model. Data are shown as flows between processes, the output of one flowing as input to another. Processes themselves are viewed as black boxes with no procedural information attached.

Data flow diagrams have been used as the basis for a number of design methodologies ([YOU79] and [DEM78]); hence, their use during specification facilitates an easy transformation of specifications into design. Data flow diagrams have the advantage of omitting actual procedural details and also emphasize the central role of data in structuring the eventual design and code. Since the data are more likely to be user constrained than are the processing details, a data flow notation better supports a methodical and reproducible transformation of user requirements into a software product. In addition, data flow diagrams easily incorporate the notion of top-down and modular description. Each process can be selected for additional, more detailed elaboration as an entity separate from every other process at its level.

Typically, data flow diagrams contain data flows, processes, databases, and sources or sinks of data. The connection with hydraulic engineering diagrams is fairly obvious, both in the notation and the terminology. The idea is much the same — data originate in several sources outside the system and flow in specified paths through processes that transform the data in various ways. Data may be stored temporarily, but eventually

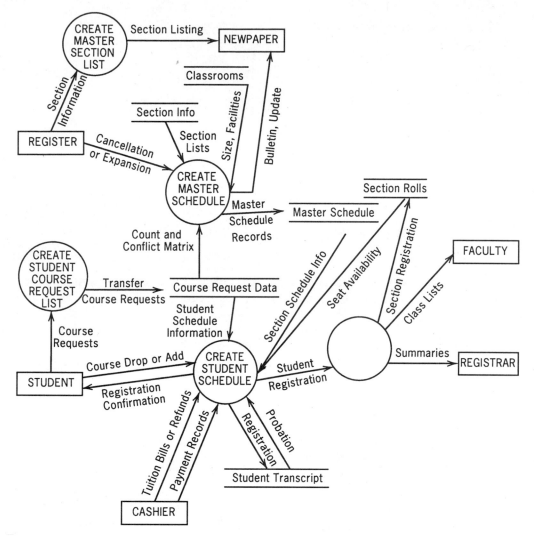

**FIGURE 4-16**   A DATA FLOW DIAGRAM

data finds the way out of the system to the users. In Figure 4-16, sources and sinks are represented by rectangles, processes by circles, data flows by arcs, data objects by arc labels, and databases by parallel lines.

The data flow diagram of Figure 4-16 describes a student registration system. Prior to registration, the registrar advertises a list of the course sections to be taught, along with minimum and maximum sizes for each section, special facilities needs, and so on. Students provide preregistration information about the courses in which they wish to enroll. Student requests are counted, and a conflict matrix tallying joint requests of all pairs of courses is stored. These are combined with the section information to determine the time and place of each section; at that point, student preregistrations are honored. Subsequently, the registrar can offer more sections or cancel sections, whereas students can drop or add to their registration. At the end of the registration period, instructors receive class lists, and the registrar receives management reports.

Data flow diagrams lack any way of indicating the conditions that may control or initiate processing of data as data become available along a data flow. One extension of the data flow diagram, utilized with the SADT tools outlined in Section 4.3.5 ([ROS85]), contains references both to control data (coming in at the top of process boxes) and mechanisms for processing (coming in from the bottom). This is illustrated in Figure 4-17.

This figure expands one node of the data flow diagram in Figure 4-16. The original Create Master Schedule node is expanded from the inset at the bottom to the three nodes shown at the top. First, courses are prioritized according to the number of

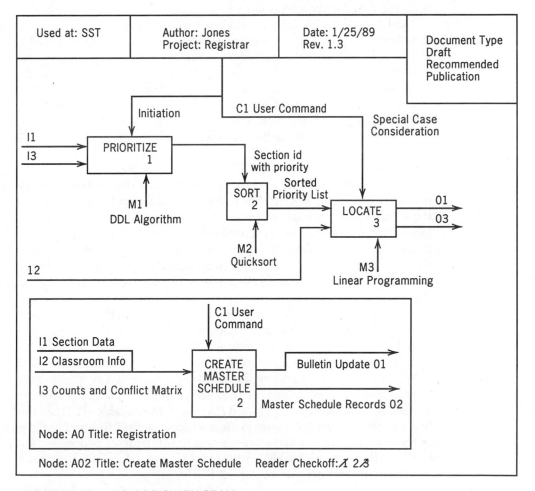

**FIGURE 4-17**  AN SADT FLOW DIAGRAM

requests for them, the degree to which they are jointly requested, and their special facilities needs. Next, they are sorted from the highest to the lowest priority. Finally, classrooms are located for them.

It may be argued, quite correctly, that this second level expansion infringes on the design stage of software development. Normally, the choice of specific algorithms (mechanisms above), would only be made during the specification stage if it were mandated by the customer. In this instance, the registrar happens to be trained as a computer scientist, and has done just that.

One of the significant advantages of the SADT notation is the degree of control over documents and the standardization of presentation it provides. First, the inset gives the context, at the next higher level, of the current data flow. Both the higher level and this level are named in a systematic way. The degree to which the document has been baselined is indicated. Space is given for readers (reviewers or inspectors) to check off. All of the inputs, outputs, commands, and mechanisms are numbered and correlated with the next higher level node.

Real-time systems, which must react to their external environment within fixed timelimits, require extensive representation of both timing and control information. Bruyn et al. in [BRU88] have suggested an extension of data flow notation called the *Extended System Modeling Language*. ESML models data flow as being either continuously or intermittently available, and allows for intermittent control signals. Timing information is represented by different kinds of control prompts, including enable, disable, trigger, suspend, and resume. There are rules that allow or disallow application of certain kinds of control to processes, or "transforms" as the authors refer to them.

Figure 4-18 shows a model of an automobile cruise control (CC) mechanism in ESML. The solid lines and boxes represent the data flow, whereas the dotted lines and boxes are for control signals. The triangle and diamond arrowheads indicate whether the signal is continuously or intermittently available. Circle arrowheads encode the kinds of control signals by one transform on another. For example, the "control speed" transform will be activated by the "monitor CC status" transform and, in turn, triggers the "capture current speed" data transform. "Capture current speed" is triggered intermittently, as indicated by the arrowhead going to the data store for desired speed (Figure 4-18).

Another data flow notation, which also emphasizes the way in which processing is coordinated, synchronized, and triggered, was originated by Carl Petri. *Petri nets* allow us to look at a moment in the lifetime of the data flow, indicating the presence of data by tokens (the solid circles in Figure 4-19). Tokens are held in places (the hollow circles below) analogous to processes. Data flows are controlled by transitions (the short lines intersecting the arcs). When the processes can make data available on all of the arcs leading into a transition (say, $P_1$ and $P_2$ make data available at $t_1$) then the transition can fire, and the data are passed on to the next process. Splitting and merging of tokens (as in the $t_3$ and $t_2$ transitions) allows a synchronization of processes. The two parts of Figure 4-19 represent the net before and after the firings at transitions $t_2$ and $t_3$. A full treatment of Petri nets can be seen in [PET81].

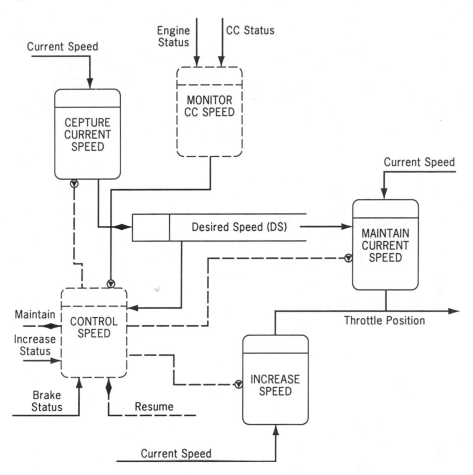

**FIGURE 4-18**   AN ESML FLOW DIAGRAM (By permission of the ESML Working Group.)

Tables are a good general notation for representing the functional part of the transformation of input to output. *Function tables* generally list input and output as pairs, without any indication of the procedure (other than simple lookup) that is used to determine output when given input. *Truth tables* are one commonly seen form of function table. Another is the *transition table* used to define finite automata and other finite state machines. Figure 4-20 shows a transition table for an automaton that recognizes nonnegative multiples of three written as binary numbers and that read from most significant to least significant bit. The initial state is the first row in the table. Finite state machines are particularly useful in specifying the sequence of events necessary in responding to user commands in a direct manipulation user interface ([MYE89]).

A combination of data flow diagrams and transition tables, called *finite state mechanisms*, was suggested by Babb and Tripp in [BAB80]. This involves the labeling

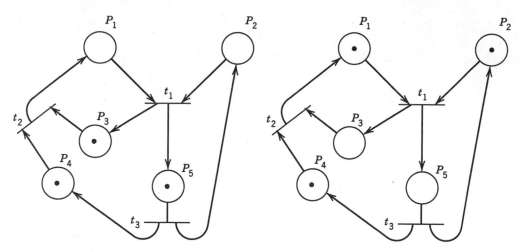

**FIGURE 4-19**  A PETRI NET, BEFORE AND AFTER FIRING

of arcs by data structure notations (Figure 4-21 uses regular expressions, defined below) and the defining of the processes by means of transition tables. Although this amount of process specification nears the limit of what is acceptable at the current stage, it is still free of implementation details. Figure 4-21 represents a small part of a data flow

| State \ Input Bit | 0 | 1 |
|---|---|---|
| null string | 0 mod 3 | 1 mod 3 |
| 0 mod 3 | 0 mod 3 | 1 mod 3 |
| 1 mod 3 | 2 mod 3 | 0 mod 3 |
| 2 mod 3 | 1 mod 3 | 2 mod 3 |

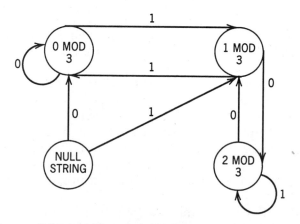

**FIGURE 4-20**  A TRANSITION TABLE

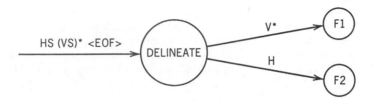

| Present State | Input | Actions | Output | Next State |
|---|---|---|---|---|
|  | H | Open F2 | H: F2 | S1 |
| S0 | other |  |  | S0 |
|  | S | Close F2 |  | S2 |
| S1 | other | Delete F2 |  | S0 |
|  | V | Open F1 | V: F1 | S3 |
| S2 | <EOF> |  |  | S0 |
|  | S |  |  | S4 |
| S3 | other | Delete F1 |  | S0 |
|  | V |  | V: F1 | S3 |
| S4 | <EOF> | Close F1 |  | S0 |
|  | other | Delete F1 |  | S0 |

**FIGURE 4-21**   FINITE STATE MECHANISM NOTATION

diagram in which a stream consisting of a header and a synchronizing signal, followed by a sequence of pairs consisting of a valid data frame and a synchronizing signal, is separated into two flows. The two types of block, header, and frame, are directed toward two different files.

*Decision tables* allow a schematic and organized way of representing actions that will be taken on the basis of sets of conditions. They can be used to describe software functions that tend to get bogged down in a lot of *if*'s, *then*'s, *or*'s and *and*'s when stated in a natural language. Within the decision table are listed a number of different conditions, which can have values that are true or false. A separate column is created for each combination of these Boolean values (just like a logic truth table), and then each of these columns (a rule) is flagged with the particular actions that are to be taken. Figure 4-22 shows natural language instructions and a decision table for cooking vegetables. Sometimes there is a tendency to omit or combine rules; this usually ends up costing much more in the potential for errors through incompleteness and inconsistency than it ever saves in having a smaller specification.

Vessey and Weber ([VES86]) recommend *decision trees* as being superior to decision tables for demonstrating complex conditional logic. Figure 4-23 shows the same logic, but now represented as a tree.

As a final example of process specification, *event tables* extend the decision table notation by allowing compression and sequencing of actions. Rather than having a different row for each action, rows are defined by events that might occur, and the corresponding actions are placed at the intersections of conditions and events. Figure

Crispy, leafy vegetables that are juicy but not tall, are fried if they are red; otherwise they are steamed. Crispy vegetables that are juicy but neither tall nor leafy are grilled. Noncrispy vegetables that are not tall but are juicy are prepared in two steps: they are first peeled, and then if they are hard they are boiled, otherwise they are chopped. The recommended method of cooking all vegetables that are not juicy is roasting. Juicy vegetables that are tall are chopped.

| Juicy | Y | Y | Y | Y | Y | Y | N |
|---|---|---|---|---|---|---|---|
| Tall | Y | N | N | N | N | N | — |
| Crispy | — | Y | Y | Y | N | N | — |
| Leafy | — | Y | Y | N | — | — | — |
| Red | — | Y | N | — | — | — | — |
| Hard | — | — | — | — | Y | N | — |
| | | | | | | | |
| Fry | | X | | | | | |
| Steam | | | X | | | | |
| Grill | | | | X | | | |
| Peel | | | | | X | X | |
| Boil | | | | | X | | |
| Chop | X | | | | | X | |
| Roast | | | | | | | X |

**F I G U R E 4-22**   A DECISION TABLE (Vessey and Weber, "Structured Tools and ..." *Communications of the ACM,* copyright © 1986, Association for Computing Machinery, Inc. Reprinted by permission.)

4-24 shows part of an event table for interrupt management. In this illustration "THEN" expresses sequential action and "&" represents parallel or concurrent action. The notation "NA" means "no action."

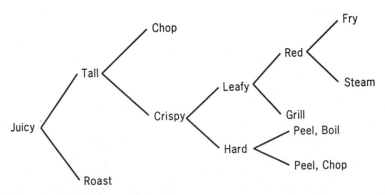

**F I G U R E 4-23**   A DECISION TREE

| Conditions | | | | |
|---|---|---|---|---|
| Events | 1 | 2 | 3 | 4 |
| 1 | A1 THEN A4&A5 | A1 THEN A4&A5 | A1 THEN A4&A5 | A5 |
| 2 | A1 THEN A2 | A3 | A1 THEN A2 | A2 |
| 3 | A3 | A3 | A1 THEN A2 | A2 |
| 4 | A6 | A6 | NA | NA |

**KEY**

| Events | 1 | Power failure |
|---|---|---|
| | 2 | Disk controller interrupt |
| | 3 | Terminal controller interrupt |
| | 4 | I\O completion |

| Conditions | 1 | Disk I\O in progress |
|---|---|---|
| | 2 | Terminal I\O in progress |
| | 3 | User process in progress |
| | 4 | Idle |

| Actions | A1 | Stack current process |
|---|---|---|
| | A2 | Service interrupt |
| | A3 | Queue interrupt |
| | A4 | Flush user buffers |
| | A5 | Save stack |
| | A6 | Unstack process |

**FIGURE 4-24**   AN EVENT TABLE

### 4.3.2 Data Specification

Most data representation notations are used to depict the structure of composite data or the rules by which data may be recognized or validated. Occasionally, some of them have proved so worthwhile that they have found their way into design methodologies (e.g., Warnier diagrams) or programming languages (e.g., PIC in COBOL). In some instances, like the Jackson Structured Programming methodology, data structure representation is the foundation for the entire development process.

To start out, the *PICTURE* notation from COBOL can be used to describe character-encoded data. For instance, the picture BBAAAAS999V99 indicates a 13-character string, with two leading spaces, four alphabetic characters, an optional sign, three digits, a decimal point and another two digits. The PICTURE was both more compact and more understandable than the English description that followed. If we know during specification what the eventual implementation language will be, the format descriptors from that language can be used in the same way to describe simple character strings.

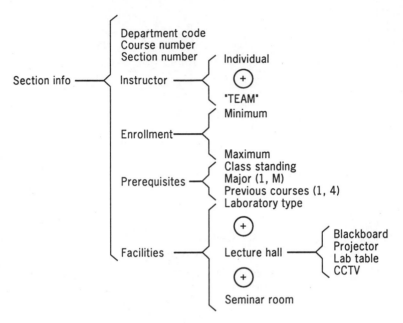

**FIGURE 4-25**   A WARNIER DIAGRAM

*Warnier diagrams* ([WAR74]) are used to indicate hierarchical structures in which records are divided into subrecords and so on down to individual fields. Braces delimit records, with subrecords listed in sequential order. The number of repetitions of a specific subrecord can be represented by a number in parentheses, whereas conditional appearance of subrecords is indicated by a range in parentheses. In Figure 4-25, each section information record is made up of seven fields. The instructor will be either an individual or the string "TEAM." There may be up to $M$ majors listed that will enable a student to register for the course, as well as up to four prerequisite classes.

Command = (Command_String)*Delimiter
Command_String = NameSeparation(Options(Separation))*Params
Options = DashLetter(DashLetter)*
Params = Name(SeparationName)*
Name = Letter(Letter+Digit)*
Separation = Space(Space)*
Space = ' '
Dash = '-'
Delimiter = EOL

**FIGURE 4-26**   REGULAR EXPRESSIONS FOR UNIX COMMANDS

Two notations have been borrowed from automata theory ([COH86]) to represent generation, and hence recognition, techniques for strings. These are particularly useful in specifying messages, command languages, and programming languages. *Regular expressions* build on atomic elements of the language being defined, by utilizing three operations: sequence, selection, and iteration. Figure 4-26 shows the layered definition of a command, starting with the individual space, dash, and EOL characters and the generic descriptions "letter" and "digit." The asterisk is used to specify repetitions, the "+" indicates selection between alternatives, and sequence is represented by concatenation. For example, the Unix command "ls -t-s new old<EOL>" has a single command string with two options and two parameters.

Figure 4-27 defines the same Unix commands using *production grammar* notations; this particular format is called Backus–Naur form and is frequently used to specify programming languages. The words at the extreme left are just comments. Each production indicates that the nonterminal symbol on the left can be replaced by the string on the right. The vertical bar, | , indicates selection between two alternatives, . is the EOL character, *09* is any digit, *az* is any letter, *b* is a blank space, and *epsilon* is nothing, the empty string.

We can see how a generic command symbol, C, can be turned into an actual command by repeated application of the productions. The command "ls -t-s old new<EOL>" can be derived thus (some steps have been joined together):

```
C       ==>  Cs<EOL>
        ==>  NSOsP<EOL>
        ==>  lsSOsP<EOL>
        ==>  ls OsP<EOL>
        ==>  ls -azOsP<EOL>
        ==>  ls -tOsP<EOL>
        ==>  ls -t-azOsP<EOL>
        ==>  ls -t-s P<EOL>
        ==>  ls -t-s NPl<EOL>
        ==>  ls -t-s oldSNPl<EOL>
        ==>  ls -t-s old NPl<EOL>
        ==>  ls -t-s old newPl<EOL>
        ==>  ls -t-s old new<EOL>
```

The production grammar version of this definition appears to be more complex than the regular expressions; this is not always true, but it is true that grammars of this type are a more powerful specification tool. In general, the uses of regular expressions and production grammars are outlined in books dealing with finite automata, compiler construction, or programming languages.

The *data dictionary* contains information about all the data defined for the system. It should be maintained and accessed through the project database of the software engineering environment. It can take a form like that shown in Figure 4-28, where it is expanded to include processes and their relationship (creates, uses, modifies, and so on) to individual data items. These individual data items, in fact, can be compounded from simpler items that also appear in the dictionary. We may also exclude processes.

Command C -> Cs.
Command string Cs -> NSOsPCs | *epsilon*
Option string Os -> -azOs | S
Parameter P -> NPl | *epsilon*
Parameter list Pl -> SNPl | *epsilon*
Name N -> *az*Nl
Name list Nl -> *az*Nl | *09*Nl | *epsilon*
Separator S -> *b*Sl
Separator list Sl -> *b*Sl | *epsilon*

**FIGURE 4-27**   PRODUCTION GRAMMAR SPECIFICATION OF UNIX COMMANDS

It is frequently handy to create an additional column in the data dictionary for notes in which peripheral information can be kept.

One desirable trait of a data dictionary is that it be nonredundant with respect to other specification notations. This means that the relationship information, which is also found in the data flow diagram, should be omitted. However, it is often useful when utilizing paper documents to repeat information as is done here. A project database would allow us to store such information in only one location but to show it in two.

### 4.3.3 Data Relationships

Relationships between data items need to be specified in several contexts. For instance, we may need to specify correct output as a function of input. In its simplest form, this may be done by writing explicit **equations,** like the following.

$$\sigma = \sqrt{\frac{\sum (xi - x)^2}{n-1}}$$

This is the formula for calculating the standard deviation of a nonempty sequence of $n$ reals, assuming that $x$ is the average of the sequence.

We may also utilize implicit equations like

$$dx/dt = Kx(M\text{-}x)$$

This differential equation is for a logistic curve, shaped like the following:

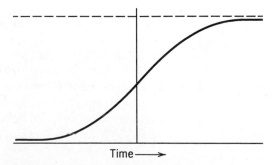

Time ——>

| Entity | Type | Relationship | Contains |
|---|---|---|---|
| Instructor | atomic field | part of Section Information | staff id number |
| Section Information | record | input to Create Master Schedule | Department Code Course Number Section Number Instructor Enrollment Prerequisites Facilities |
| Create Master Schedule | process | inputs: Section Information Classroom Information Counts and Conflict Matrix outputs: Bulletin Update Master Schedule Records | Prioritize Sort Locate |

**F I G U R E 4-28**   PART OF A DATA DICTIONARY

It might be a representation of the sales rate of a new, durable consumer item. Initially, when $x$ is small, people only buy the item because they know someone who has one, hence, the sales rate is approximately proportional to $x$. Later on, when everyone is familiar with the item, our sales are approximately proportional to the number of people who do not have one yet, $M$-$x$, where $M$ is the total population. Implicit equations like this one are much harder to solve (i.e., write in explicit form) but may be used directly in iterative computations.

Another iterative type of computation can be based on recurrencies like this one:

$$v(0) = 100$$
$$v(t+0.01) = v(t)-0.01 \times v(t)^2$$

This set of recurrence equations might represent the velocity of a body that enters a viscous fluid at a speed of 100 but then is slowed by friction. Obviously, we can calculate $v(20)$ either by iterative or recursive means.

Boolean functions can be represented by Boolean equations or, if these become too complex to comprehend, truth tables. Equations like the preceding ones define the exact outcome of single applications of a function. However, implicit or recursive equations are often difficult for readers to comprehend.

Formal verification of code, discussed in Section 4.4.2, often requires that we reason about assertions involving equations and that we combine such assertions across uses of control operators like if-then-else and while-do. Assertions may also use comparison operators, like <, and quantifiers, like "there is" or "for all," sometimes in a hidden form. In fact, the *predicate logic* can be used as a fairly comprehensive specification language. This is recommended in [MEY85], [BER82], and [PAR83].

It is true that many useful assertions are stated in a rather careful natural language form, rather than a formal language. However, this prohibits use of automated assertion verification systems. Such a set of assertions, from Chapter 6, is shown in Figure 4-29.

Note that, by themselves, equational specifications suffer the drawback of only describing correct behavior. There is not much framework for defining exceptions and determining the corresponding actions to be taken for them. Usually, equational specifications for a module will at best allow the reporting of exceptions; dealing with them becomes the responsibility of the calling routine.

*Abstract data types (ADTs)* are mathematical models, consisting of sets of data elements, operations on those elements, and axioms defining the appropriate relationships between elements and operations. As an example, Figure 4-30 illustrates a definition of binary trees with "items" of some previously defined type located at the nodes. Using these axioms, we are able to describe the relationship between trees and the elements at their nodes; for example, how to find the data at the root of the left child. Additional relationships could be added to describe, say, a binary search tree.

In this definition of binary trees, we note that newly created trees are empty. A tree with a single node could be made from two empty subtrees, and the item to be stored at the root. The operations on this recursive structure (trees are defined as being composed of two smaller trees plus a root) are obviously candidates for recursive design.

Algebraic specifications of this type have some drawbacks. As Berg et al. note in [BER82], most abstract data types require hidden, or private, functions for full specification. For example, in defining a stack as an ADT, one might use a hidden stack pointer and depth limit to be sure that an error is generated in pushing onto a full stack. The reason, however, that this kind of function is hidden is that it does not represent externally observable behavior — it is a "how," not a "what." With complex ADTs we may find that the bulk of the specification involves the hidden functions, and thus concentrates on design and implementation issues rather than specification.

Abstract data type representation can be formalized by using a language like those available in the Larch family ([GUT85]). The family centers around a core, which provides a common notation for representing "traits," which are partial characterizations of abstract data types. The notation allows for machine processing, verification, analysis, and so on. The traits can be reused, inherited, and specialized. At the second

"Location is undefined and the target record doesn't appear on the list"

"Location is defined and the target record doesn't appear on the list previous to location"

"If result isn't undefined then ((it isn't on the list and target isn't on the list) or (result specifies the first target record on the list))"

**F I G U R E 4-29**   ASSERTIONS FOR VERIFYING SOFTWARE

```
structure BTREE
  declare  CREATE( ) → btree
           ISMTBT (btree) → boolean
           MAKEBT (btree, item, btree) → btree
           LCHILD (btree) → btree
           DATA(btree) → item
           RCHILD(btree) → btree
  for all  p, r ε btree, d ε item let
      ISMTBT (CREATE):: = true
      ISMTBT (MAKEBT (p, d, r)):: = false
      LCHILD (MAKEBT(p, d, r)):: = p; LCHILD(CREATE):: = error
      DATA(MAKEBT(p, d, r)):: = d; DATA(CREATE):: = error
      RCHILD(MAKEBT(p, d, r)):: = r; RCHILD(CREATE):: = error
  end
end BTREE
```

**F I G U R E 4-30**   AXIOMS FOR A BINARY TREE

level of specification, IO interfaces that service the traits can be defined in any of several Larch interface languages, each of them used with a particular implementation language like Pascal or Ada. This two-tiered structure, a common core for ADTs and separate variant languages for IO, allows for specifications to be transformed into individual implementation languages, despite the radical differences of the latter.

*Entity-relationship* diagrams ([CHE76]) represent database relationships between individual data items. In Figure 4-31, we see a part of the student registration system again. The rectangles represent entities in the database, and the diamonds are relations of entities. For example, there is a 1-1 relationship between classes and time slots — each class occupies a single slot. However, each room has many slots associated with it; hence, we find the M-1 relationship indicated in the diagram. Normally, each class has a single professor, but in special situations (team teaching) there may be several professors. Therefore, in the first instance, the instructor relationship indicates one professor may instruct many classes but in the second, many professors may instruct many classes.

### 4.3.4 Specification Tools

The notations of the Sections 4.31 to 4.33 may be used as the basis for a formal specification language which, in turn, can support various software tools. Recall that specification tools are generally used to understand, analyze, or transform the specifications.

The simplest of tools for understanding is the *cross-reference generator*, which allows us to trace connections within the specification itself. This provides us with an index of references for the definition and use of terms. In a similar vein, the *data dictionary* is able to bring together and organize all the definitions of data items within the specification. This allows us to visualize the relationships and dependencies between data entities.

Only slightly more complex are the various *graphics capabilities* that allow us to edit and to present data flow diagrams, entity-relationship diagrams, Petri nets, and the

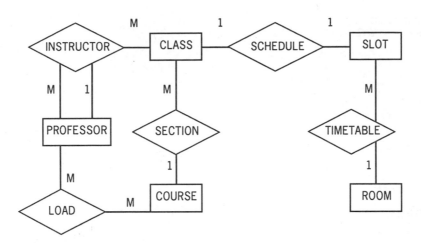

**FIGURE4-31**   ENTITY-RELATIONSHIP DIAGRAM

like. These are usually provided with special shapes and symbols that have meaning in the context of those specification methodologies that depend on graphic presentation. A good tool can be tailored, allowing us to design and to use our own set of shapes and connection techniques. Such tools also allow us to include text in the graphics.

Another, very useful tool for understanding is one that supports the *execution of specifications*. If we can execute specifications directly, then we are able to experiment with them and to validate their correctness more fully, both in terms of their feasibility and their acceptability to the user. Specification errors and misconceptions can be caught early, allowing us to avoid costly rework. This tool obviously supports the rapid prototyping model of the development process. In a slightly different vein, a *paraphraser* makes it possible to translate specifications back into English, for the purpose of user inspection and validation of the specifications.

The most complex understanding tools, from a technical point of view, are those that allow us to input and to translate natural language specifications into formal language specifications. Such a tool automates the major task of specification, and thus provides significant savings of labor costs. Of course, the inherent ambiguity and imprecision of natural languages means that tools of this kind only represent semi-intelligent assistants in the process of creating specifications. The actual process has to be guided interactively by software engineers. Nevertheless, even this amount of automation is very worthwhile.

The second kind of tool is used for analysis of specifications, particularly to determine whether they exhibit the characteristics of Section 4.2.2. The very fact that a particular specification is done in a formal language tends to corroborate its *structuredness, minimality,* and *verifiability* — attributes that flow directly from the character of the specification language. The specification language will impose whatever structure is inherent within its syntax. (Of course, this makes it vital that we choose the specification language that provides the best structure for the kind of system we are trying to represent.) Irrelevant or premature detail probably cannot be expressed,; hence, requirements will be minimal. The syntax for stating constraints or functions should impose sufficient rigor to ensure their testability.

*Consistency* can be analyzed by extending the cross-reference capability mentioned in the previous section. A consistency tool would analyze, for instance, different appearances of a data item within the specifications; its usage should always be consistent. If it were a string, its length should always be the same; if it were a record, it should always have the same subfields. Similarly, the output specifications of a process would be matched to the input specifications of the next process(es) in the data flow diagram; the actual data flow, as it is seen exiting from one and entering the others, should be identical. Consistent use and interpretation of data can be fostered by data dictionaries and semantic annotations. Consistency questions related to timing and synchronization are more difficult, but can often be settled by specification simulation or execution.

Completeness has two different meanings in specifications. *External completeness* means that everything that is important has been mentioned. No tool can guarantee this. But *internal completeness* means that there are no undefined references within the specifications. Internal completeness can be analyzed by differentiating definitions of terms from references to terms in the formal specification language and then extending the indexing capability to see that there are no references to undefined objects. However, a specification tool should not enforce completeness and consistency to the extent that it refuses to allow the temporary incompleteness and inconsistency that inevitably occur during development of the specifications. The tool should point these problems out, but should continue to function in a reasonable way despite them ([ARA88]).

*Structure* can be evaluated as well as guaranteed. Data flow diagrams or Petri nets can be analyzed for anomalies, like excessive complexity or overlarge input or output flows. Regular expressions can be analyzed for simplification possibilities and entity-relationship diagrams can be evaluated for normality. Most formal specification languages provide for top-down techniques; that is, specifications represent a hierarchical ordering, with more general aspects at the top, and more detailed aspects descending from them. Anomalies in this structure, like heavy or light branching, can also be found, if they represent potential problems.

Finally, the degree of *interdependence* in the specifications can be measured with a software tool that assesses the amount of modularity of the specifications. A high degree of interconnection will work against the modifiability of the requirements, as well as all subsequent work products.

Much of the current research in specifications methodology deals with software tools that transform specifications into design or code. The discussion in Chapter 1 about the operational development process model talked about the importance of automated transformation of specifications into other work products. The ultimate goal is to provide an *environment* in which user requirements automatically become a software product with a minimum of human intervention. Obviously, realization of this goal is still far in the future, but efforts in its direction are sure to pay handsome dividends.

One of the difficult concepts encountered by students who are just learning to program is the absolute need to foresee all aspects of the software before submitting code to a compiler. Some of these students continually complain that "the computer ought to know how to handle *that.*" In a similar way, it is difficult to understand the degree of careful planning that would allow a software engineer to fully develop a software product in the specifications. There is no doubt that specifications that are to be automatically transformed into code require much more effort than those that are manually extended through the design and implementation phases. Some recent experiences ([MIL87] and [MYE87]), however, have indicated that the total effort put into meticulous specification followed by transformation is less than the total effort required when one uses more commonplace techniques.

Such a system would not only shorten the development effort, but maintenance would become much less labor intensive. Most maintenance today is carried out at the code level, with designs and specification being subsequently modified to match code changes. This is a wrong-headed way of doing things, since it usually attacks the symptom rather than the source of the problem, and can lead to a degradation in the overall quality of the product. A specification transformation system would allow us to trace the observed failure back to the specification that gives rise to it and to correct the problem at its root, using a more natural description of it. Thus, using the specifications as the primary software object is more reasonable than using code; as Sievert and Mizell put it, "the cause of the software crisis is code" ([SIE85]).

In fact, the traceability feature of a good project database system provides for automated assistance in a number of aspects of even the *manual transformation* of specifications. For instance, the maintenance problems mentioned above, of fixing code before specifications, can be alleviated by providing an automatic link from code to the relevant specification.

Traceability also helps us utilize tools to aid in the *formal verification* of software (explained in Section 4.4.2). In this instance, requirements can be embedded as comments in design and code. Thus they help in the manual or automatic formulation of appropriate intermediate assertions, from which the correctness of the code may be derived.

Some limited automatic transformation tools are already common. In the case of compiler construction, *Lex* and *Yacc*, available with Unix systems, allow transformation of regular expressions and production grammars into significant portions of the desired compiler. *Applications generators* like database systems and spreadsheet packages do much the same. Although these examples tend to be rather limited in their usefulness, more general transformation systems are under development.

## 4.3.5 Specification Environments

*SADT* (System Analysis and Design Technique) is an older manual methodology, which has recently been automated ([ROS85]). SADT flow diagrams were described in Section 4.3.1. In addition, there are complementary data diagrams, which represent data elements as bubbles and put processes on the arcs. This tool makes the pre- and post-conditions for any process explicit, thus aiding in subsequent formal verification of requirements. One of the major benefits of the SADT tool is a very tight control over work products and their review. The control mechanism makes it easy to practice top down specification. SADT is a product of Softech, Inc., of Waltham, Massachusetts.

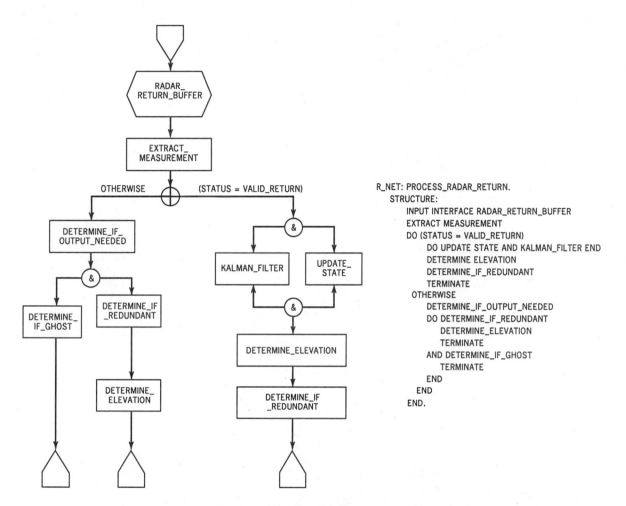

R_NET: PROCESS_RADAR_RETURN.
    STRUCTURE:
        INPUT INTERFACE RADAR_RETURN_BUFFER
        EXTRACT MEASUREMENT
        DO (STATUS = VALID_RETURN)
            DO UPDATE STATE AND KALMAN_FILTER END
            DETERMINE ELEVATION
            DETERMINE_IF_REDUNDANT
            TERMINATE
        OTHERWISE
            DETERMINE_IF_OUTPUT_NEEDED
            DO DETERMINE_IF_REDUNDANT
                DETERMINE_ELEVATION
                TERMINATE
            AND DETERMINE_IF_GHOST
                TERMINATE
            END
        END
    END.

**F I G U R E 4-32**   SREM REQUIREMENTS AS RSL TEXT AND R-NET GRAPHICS (Bell et al., "An Extendable Approach to Computer-Aided Software Requirements Engineering,' *IEEE Transactions on Software Engineering*, copyright © 1977, IEEE.)

*SREM* (Software Requirements Engineering Methodology) is another specification tool, directed especially toward the specification of real-time software. It was developed by Thompson-Ramo-Wooldridge for Department of Defense and for aerospace applications. Alford has given a recent update on the status of the tool in [ALF85]. A case study in the use of SREM can be found in the same issue ([SCH85]). SREM uses a textual requirements specification language, (RSL), but the requirements can also be represented graphically, as is shown in Figure 4-32. SREM provides automated analysis of RSL specifications, browsing capabilities within the specifications, and specification analysis and simulation.

```
Parameters: DB=-EXBDB NAME=hourly-employee-processing NOINDEX
  NOPUNCHED-NAMES PRINT EMPTY NOPUNCH SMARG=5 NMARG=20 AMARG=10
  BMARG=70 CMARG=1 HMARG=60 NODESIGNATE SEVERAL-PER-LINE      DEFINE
  COMMENT NONEW-PAGE NONEW-LINE NOALL-STATEMENTS COMPLEMENTARY-
  STATEMENTS LINE-NUMBERS PRINTEOF DLC-COMMENT
```

```
 1   PROCESS                          hourly-employee-processing;
 2    /* DATE OF LAST CHANGE - JUN 26, 1976, 13:56:44 */
 3   DESCRIPTION;
 4   this process performs those actions needed to interpret
 5   time cards to produce a pay statement for each hourly
 6   employee.;
 7   KEYWORDS:  independent;
 8   ATTRIBUTES ARE:
 9       complexity-level
10                     high;
11   GENERATES: pay-statement, error-listing,
12             hourly-employee-report;
13   RECEIVES: time-card;
14   SUBPARTS ARE: hourly-paycheck-validation, hourly-emp-update,
15             h-report-entry-generation,
16             hourly-paycheck-production;
17   PART OF:   payroll-processing;
18   DERIVES:   pay-statement;
19   USING:     time-card, hourly-employee-record;
20   DERIVES:   hourly-employee-report;
21   USING:     time-card, hourly-employee-record;
22   DERIVES:   error-listing;
23   USING:     time-card, hourly-employee-record;
24   PROCEDURE:
25       1. compute gross pay from time card data.
26       2. compute tax from gross pay.
27       3. subtract tax from gross pay to obtain net pay.
28       4. update hourly employee record accordingly.
29       5. update department record accordingly.
30       6. generate paycheck.
31   note: if status code specifies that the employee did not work
32   this week, no processing will be done for this employee;
33   HAPPENS:
34       number-of-payments TIMES-PER pay-period;
35   TRIGGERED BY:    hourly-emp-processing-event;
36   TERMINATION-CAUSES:
37             new-employee-processing-event;
38   SECURITY IS:     company-only;39
40   EOF EOF EOF EOF
```

**F I G U R E 4-33**   A PARTIAL PSL SPECIFICATION (Teicherow and Hershey, "Structured Documentation and Analysis," *IEEE Transactions on Software Engineering,* copyright © 1977, IEEE.)

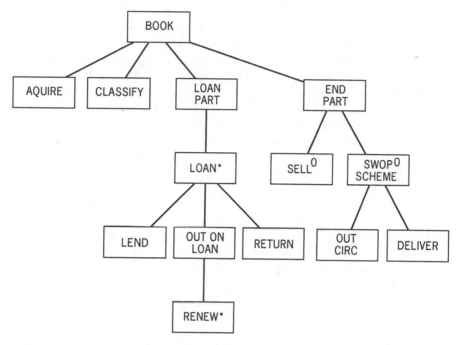

**F I G U R E 4-34**  A JSD ENTITY STRUCTURE DIAGRAM (Cameron, "An Overview of JSD," *IEEE Transactions on Software Engineering*, copyright © 1986, IEEE.)

In the article mentioned above, Alford also describes an extension of SREM, called SYSREM, which provides for specification of entire software systems, as opposed to the single processes of SREM. SYSREM supports decomposition and interface description, specification of exception handling, and inclusion of constraints in the formal specifi-

**SAFE/TI**                                    **ISI/USC**
natural language specifications are transformed; formal specifications are analyzed; interactive modification; product control; transformationinto code

**PSI/CHI**                                    **Stanford & Kestrel**
specification in natural, formal, graphic and example languages; transformation into code; optimization

**PDS**                                        **Harvard**
interactive specification; specification analysis; transformation into code; product control

**Programmer's Apprentice**                    **MIT**
interactive specification and amplification of specification and design

**Dedalus**                                    **Stanford**
formal, mathematical specification; transformation into LISP; correctness analysis

**F I G U R E 4-35**  SOME EXPERIMENTAL SPECIFICATION ENVIRONMENTS

cation. It provides a series of separate languages for the specification (and design) of modules and distributed processing and tasks.

The TAGS environment, described in [SIE85], implements many of the features of the operational model of software development. With TAGS, the formal notation is used to specify, analyze, and validate the software through simulated execution of the specifications; once this has been completed, the specifications are transformed, or allocated, as code. Any optimization that may be required is done as tuning of the allocation, without affecting the specifications at all. The graphic/tabular notation, IORL, allows modeling of both data and control flows while representing decomposition, component timing and relationships, and logic flow for processes.

The previous tools all tended to promote a single design methodology, using data flow techniques. A more general tool for specification was developed during the ISDOS project at the University of Michigan ([TEI77]), which provides a problem statement language, *PSL*, and an analysis and control tool, *PSA*. These are modeled on a general systems concept, without any software specificity. PSA not only analyzes requirements stated in PSL but also provides a high level of product control. An example of part of a PSL specification is given in Figure 4-33.

The *Jackson System Development* (JSD) methodology starts out with no functional requirements. Instead, it models a real-world system and then, in elaborating the model, adds such functions as may be required. The first two JSD steps correspond most closely to the specification stage. First is the "entity action" step, in which the system is modeled by entities (or components within the system) and actions (the interactions between components). Next, in the "entity structure" step, the entities are modeled throughout their lifetime by showing the actions that occur. Figure 4-34 shows an entity structure diagram for BOOK, an entity in a library system. Boxes at the same level indicate actions in the order in which they occur. Boxes at a lower level represent a more detailed description of their parent action. Asterisks represent repeated actions, and circles represent alternatives.

In addition to these commercial products, there are a number of well-publicized experimental environments, which have seen limited use in designing full software products. Most of these include transformation capabilities, which support semiautomated design and implementation. Figure 4-35 lists some of these environments, their capabilities, and their origin.

## 4.4 FOSTERING QUALITY DURING SPECIFICATION

As the technical foundation of software development, the specification work products should exhibit the highest quality possible. Unfortunately, research on specification has tended to lag behind the other development stages. Hence, not as much can be said about metrics, verification/validation, and management as they apply specifically to this stage. On the other hand, since all other work products are formally verified against the specifications, it is appropriate to consider here the groundwork necessary for future verification of design and code against specifications.

## 4.4.1 Specification Metrics

There are few metrics that are used for the Software Requirement Specification. The first measure is simply whether it *conforms to the standard* that has been accepted by the software organization. This requires a simple checkoff procedure to determine whether each part of the document required by the standard is actually present, whether standards in notation and style are met, and so on.

The most obvious metrics for specifications are the *attributes* that are listed in Figure 4-9 and are discussed in Section 4.2.2. Analysis tools will tell us whether they are consistent and internally complete. Such analysis will also determine what portion of the specifications are traceable to the user requirements.

The degree to which specifications are either formal or, at least, conform to the rules in Section 4.2.1 for natural language specifications, can be used as a measure of their formality, minimality, unambiguity, and verifiability. Modifiability can be estimated on the basis of the organization and modularity of the specifications.

Correctness and external completeness can be evaluated by execution of the specification, either in prototype or directly, by the software team and especially by the client. Indeed, *client understanding* of the specifications will give a good measure of how well they are written.

The principle measure of the Software Verification Plan is simply that each of the requirements in the Software Requirements Specification has a *corresponding* section in the verification plan. In addition, each such section should be examined to make sure that it is detailed, precise, and free from ambiguity. Additional characteristics of good verification will be given in Chapter 8.

The preliminary User's Manual should be measured against the *standards* accepted by the organization for user documentation. Use of a style-checking tool will evaluate the manual for conciseness, clarity, and writing style. It should also create a vocabulary of the manual, which can be considered for its level and use of undefined or overly technical terms. Finally, typical users can be surveyed to determine the *comprehensibility* of the manual.

## 4.4.2 Verification and Validation

Verification of the Software Requirements Specification is not a very formal activity, since there is no prior technical document with which to compare it. Nevertheless, it is possible to compare the requirements in the Project Plan with the specifications, point by point, to estimate the correctness and completeness of the translation that has been carried out. As has been mentioned, specifications are validated primarily by allowing the user to read the document and to execute the specifications or to use any prototypes that may exist.

Formal verification is a technique of mathematical reasoning in which we attempt to prove "theorems" or assertions about the product. In its most usual form, this means that each function required by the user is shown to change the state of the software system in just those ways that are dictated by the specifications. To formally verify this, we must describe the important facets of the system state before and after execution of the function, and then show that the function, as it is described in this stage of its development, will effect a transformation from the prior to the following state.

In Chapter 6 we will learn how to prove that a given design of a function satisfies this requirement. During specification, we can define the preassertions and postassertions that describe the system state before and after execution of the process that embodies the function. These assertions represent constraints on the functions and should be carefully composed so that they express no more than is actually required, but at the same time they should prevent the product from entering an incorrect state.

Since the specifications represent a substantial commitment to the entire course of development, there should be a careful review of the document, once it is complete. This is a technical review, conducted by the software team itself, although customers and marketing people should be included. The review should be conducted formally and should give all the participants an opportunity to raise issues of importance. All issues raised during the review should be resolved before proceeding with the design stage.

In a special manner, the specifications are of vital interest to the quality assurance software engineers. Their verification and validation tasks will always come back to the specifications as the standard measure of quality and hence, they must be very sure that the document meets all of the quality attributes that have been presented. In addition, they must be totally in agreement with the Software Verification and Acceptance Test Plans, since they have primary responsibility for carrying these out.

### 4.4.3 Management

Management tasks tend to be somewhat uniform throughout the entire development process. For instance, there is seldom a clear-cut division between one stage and the next. Of course, there will be a review of the major product of a stage, but as we work into the next stage, unforeseen problems will arise. These will force a return to the products of the previous stage, in order to make what we hope to be minor adjustments. It is the task of project management to ensure that such backtracking occurs only when it is truly justified, that proper product control insures the integrity of all the adjusted products, and that work on the current stage continues in a timely fashion.

There are also a few management chores specific to the specification stage. The most important is just to be sure that standards for both the specification process and products are met. There is a common impatience among software engineers with this stage; all too frequently their tendency is a rush to design before specifications have been sufficiently developed. In consequence, confusion and errors increase, and time is wasted at later stages.

It is also important at this point to plan for the acquisition of the additional personnel needed during the design, implementation and testing stages. Since staffing needs increase dramatically toward the middle of design, scheduling within the parent organization or hiring outside it should already begin. Luckily, the qualifications for the new personnel tend to be rather generic, so that they can be more easily acquired than those who are already on board.

Productivity can best be assured during specification by the use of appropriate software tools. Productivity for the entire project will be improved if we take the time to do the specifications right. Once again, the natural tendency is to rush ahead to design, but this will simply cost us more in the end.

Pragmatism is served at this stage by making sure that the customer and users have every opportunity to validate the specifications. This will tend to minimize the likelihood of disappointment and rework. In addition, difficult functions and tight constraints should be investigated by the software team through the use of prototypes and analyses.

## 4.5 A SPECIFICATION EXAMPLE

We give here an example of specification stage documents for the small example product we have been following. The EDCA package is a rapid-development, in-house product, but even so we are not able to include all of the documentation because of its bulk. We display here a full, but "low-tech," Software Requirements Specification, together with small sections of the Software Verification Plan and the preliminary User's Manual. These are sufficient to act as guides, however.

### 4.5.1 Software Requirements Specification

# 1 INTRODUCTION

## 1.1 Problem Overview

Data files are stored on magnetic tape. These are pure binary files, containing a fixed-format header with information entered by the operator at the time of capture, followed by the data stream as provided by the receiving station. The header's structure is defined elsewhere, but header information is not used by this product. It is simply to be passed through. The data stream should be organized into fixed-format frames, but these frames may be invalidated as a result of their being produced during a reset period or because of the existence of gaps in the data caused by overflow in the receiving station memory. There is no guarantee that the data stream portion of the file will start or end on frame boundaries. Subsequent portions of data stream processing will require files containing a sequence of at least 350 valid frames, with unnecessary data eliminated. This portion of the software must accept a data stream with at least 350 consecutive valid frames and must purge all invalid frames while preserving the header and at least 350 consecutive valid frames.

## 1.2 Application Environment and User Characteristics

This software will be run in-house on a single minicomputer. Operation will be batch mode. Problems should be logged to validate processing and to alert the operator to the occurrence of unexpected difficulties. No expertise should be required of the operator.

### 1.3 Notations Used in the Specification

These are standard mathematical operations and formulas, regular expressions (*Introduction to Computer Theory*, Cohen, page 38), and Mealy machines (Cohen, page 158) modified to allow actions more complex than output on the transitions. This is in the spirit of associating semantic rules with productions in context-free grammars used in compiler definition (*Compilers*, Aho, Sethi, Ullman, page 33)

### 1.4 Goals

The software should be developed quickly (total product should be done by July 1), should be table driven to respond to possible modifications in the hardware design for the receiving station, and should be highly modular to promote reuse and modifiability. Compiler methodology should be applied where appropriate.

## 2 SOFTWARE FUNCTIONS

### 2.1 Process Descriptions

#### 2.1.1 Synchronization and Cleaning

key:    sb1 = synch byte 1
        sb2 = synch byte 2
        sb3 = synch byte 3
        sb4 = synch byte 4
        ss = the sequence sb1,sb2,sb3,sb4
        vf = a validated frame
        eof = end-of-file mark
        op = open a data file
        re = rename the data file using the time field
        de = delete the data file
        cl = close and save the data file
        wf = write a frame to the data file
        wh = write the header to the data file

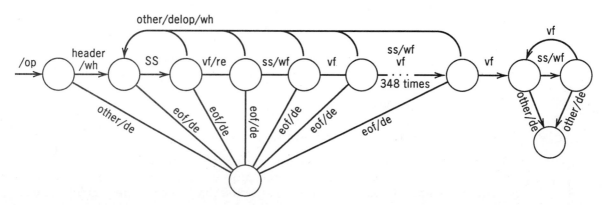

## 2.1.2 Format

There are four formats used on output: hexadecimal, decimal, floating point, and scaled floating point. The transformation of input data stream fields to hexadecimal and decimal format will use the format capabilities of the language to produce integer values in either hexadecimal or decimal form. Floating point values will be converted according to the formula:

$$\text{output} = \text{input} * 10.0 / 32768$$

where the input is understood to be a 2-byte 2's complement integer value. Scaled floating point values will be converted using the following formulas and table

|   | V < 1.1 | 1.1 <= V < 1.3 | 1.3 <=V |
|---|---------|----------------|---------|
| A | 416.2   | 2193           | 17.6    |
| B | -216.3  | -4101          | 23.9    |
| C | -29.9   | 1219           | -47.2   |

Subsequent output will use the language format for reals.

## 2.1.3 Logging of Events

The following events will be logged to a disk file:

Mounting tape #n.
Opening tape file #n.
Creating output file name streamdddhhmmss.dat, where dddhhmmss are the data
    stream time in the first frame; this happens at action re in 2.1.1.
Closing output file streamdddhhmmss.dat; this happens at action cl in 2.1.1.
The following events may be logged to the disk file and to the console at the
    discretion of the operator:

Frame synchronization at byte #n of tape file.
Loss of synch signal at byte #n of tape file.
Loss of housekeeping dataword id at byte #n of tape file.
Loss of time sequence at byte #n of tape file.
The following event may be logged to the console at the discretion of the operator:
    failure to synch reading byte #n, value zz.

## 2.2 Function Pre- and Postassertions

### *Preassertion*

The input file will be at least 2200 bytes long.

### *Postassertions*

The input file will not be modified in any way.

If the input file contains at least 350 consecutive valid frames (defined in 2.4) within
    350 x 40 = 14,000 bytes, starting at a byte with offset greater than 2200 and

followed immediately by a 4-byte synch signal (4B 96 97 AF), then an output file will be created. If this condition is not met, no output file will be created.

If an output file is created, then its first 2200 bytes will be identical to the first 2200 bytes of the input file.

If an output file is created, then the data following the first 2200 bytes will be identical (except for a change of format as defined in 2.1.2 and excision of each synch, gimbal status, reset, and blank field as defined in 2.3) in content and order to data in the input file.

If an output file is created, the data in the output file following the first 2200 bytes will correspond to data in the input file in the first sequence of at least 350 consecutive valid frames starting at a byte with offset greater than 2200 and followed immediately by a 4 byte synch signal (4B 96 97 AF), which in turn is the start of an invalid frame.

## 2.3 Data Descriptions

Key: h = 2200-byte header
p = a string of fewer than 40 arbitrary bytes
f = a valid input data stream frame
o = an output frame
The input data stream should have the form $h(p*f*)*$
The output data stream should have the form $ho^{350}o*$

Valid input frames will satisfy the conditions listed in 2.2 and will have the following structure:

| Starting Byte | Length | Description | Output Format |
|---|---|---|---|
| 0 | 4 | Synch (4B 96 97 AF) | None |
| 4 | 2 | Gimbal status | None |
| 6 | 2 | Housekeep. data id | DEC |
| 8 | 2 | Housekeep. dataword | HEX |
| 10 | 2 | Day | DEC |
| 12 | 2 | Hour | DEC |
| 14 | 2 | Minute | DEC |
| 16 | 2 | Second | DEC |
| 18 | 2 | Heading | FP |
| 20 | 2 | Reset (00 00 for no FF FF for yes) | None |
| 22 | 2 | Detector 1 reading | SFP |
| 24 | 2 | Detector 2 reading | SFP |
| 26 | 2 | Detector 3 reading | SFP |
| 28 | 2 | Detector 4 reading | SFP |

| | | | |
|---|---|---|---|
| 30 | 2 | Detector 5 reading | SFP |
| 32 | 6 | Blank (no data) | None |
| 38 | 2 | Noise monitor | SFP |

The header will be a 2200-byte block with no apparent internal structure. Output frames will consist of those fields of the input frame that are listed as having an output format, in the same sequence.

## 2.4 Data Relationships

The housekeeping dataword id, day, hour, minute, and second fields of a frame are called id,d,h,m,s, whereas those of the previous frame are called pid,pd,ph,pm,ps. Validation of frames will be through determining that the following logical expression is true:

the value of the reset field is 00 00&
id = (pid + 1) mod 55&
((d=pd) & (h=ph) & (m=pm) & (s=ps)) or
((d=pd) & (h=ph) & (m=pm) & (s=ps+1)) or
((d=pd) & (h=ph) & (m=(pm+1)mod60) & (ps=59) & (s=0)) or
((d=pd) & (h=(ph+1)mod60) & (pm=59) & (ps=59) & (m=0) & (s=0)) or
((d=pd+1) & (ph=23) & (pm=59) & (ps=59) & (h=0) & (m=0) & (s=0))

## 2.5 Priorities for Implementation

The processes listed in 2.1.1 and 2.1.2 have equal priority, whereas that of 2.1.3 has lower priority.

# 3 CONSTRAINTS

**3.1** The software must be written in Fortran77 and run on the lab's minicomputer in batch mode.

**3.2** Software operation will be unattended except for the mounting of new tapes, the need for which will be signaled by a continual bell character at the console.

**3.3** The software must require fewer than 512k bytes of internal memory.

**3.4** The software must require fewer than 50 megabytes of external memory.

**3.5** The software must have a throughput of at least 3k bytes per second.

**3.6** The only security needed can be provided by daily backing of the output disk files to tape.

# 4 EXCEPTIONS

**4.1** Recovery from hardware failure is by reset or repair of the hardware, followed by continued processing of the input data tape from the start of the file that had been open at the time of the failure.

4.2 Recovery from software error is by discovery and elimination of the fault by the software team.

4.3 Recovery from full disk conditions will be by backing up and deleting disk files, followed by continued processing of the input data tape from the start of the file that had been open at the time of the failure.

4.4 There will be no recovery from corrupted file structure on input tapes.

# 5 SOFTWARE LIFE CYCLE

5.1 The software will be table driven to the maximum extent reasonable.

5.2 Compiler methodologies for recognition of the data stream will be used if possible.

5.3 Data flow techniques will be used in the early design stage.

5.4 Prototypes will be developed and evaluated by the users before commitment to a final product.

5.5 Company code standards, and low-volume documentation standards will be in force.

5.6 The trainee will be responsible for maintaining frozen documents; authorization for change will come by unanimous vote of the software engineers.

# 6 REFERENCE

*Documents*
**Introduction to Computer Theory,** *D.I.A. Cohen, Wiley, New York, 1986.*
**Compilers: Principles, Techniques and Tools,** *Aho, Sethi,*
*and Ullman, Addison-Wesley, Reading, MA, 1986*
*Document B3-17-1988 rev A, Recorded Signals*
*Document B3-25-1988, Design Problems in Receiving Station Memory*
*Document B3-22-1988, EDCA Project Plan*
*Validation of the RB3 Detector Data Stream, United Engineering Consultants*

*Glossary*
*(Definition of phrases like throughput, full disk condition, frame, console, etc.).*

## 4.5.2 Software Verification Plan

Plans for only two of the many requirements shown above are given here.

**Requirement** Section 2.3

**Design Verification Methodology** Ensure that in the architectural design, a bubble labeled "validate" is in every path from a bubble labeled "get frame" to one labeled "write frame," Ensure that in the detailed design, the logical formula in Section 2.3 appears verbatim in the pseudocode for the process "validate."

**Schedule and Responsible Party** Before preliminary design review and critical design review, respectively. Trainee.

**Code Verification Methodology** Ensure that the logical formula in 2.3 can be transformed into a condition in the code for "validate" by substitution of logical and relational operators and variable names.

**Schedule and Responsible Party** Before unit test for the function "validate." Trainee.

**Test Data and Responses** Data representing each combination of Boolean values for the conditions in the logical formula in 2.3 can be found in the 17 sets of test data now available. They are documented in the independent consultant's report, page 93. The function "validate" will produce values "true" or "false" in agreement with the "Y" and "N" entries in the table on page 93 in the report.

**Schedule and Responsible Party** Before integration testing involving "validate." Trainee.

**Requirement** Section 3.4

**Design Verification Methodology** In the detailed design document, ensure that the fields Synch, Gimbal status, Reset, and blank are not being output.

**Responsible Party and Schedule** Before the critical design review. Trainee.

**Code Verification Methodology** Examine code and the minicomputer documentation to determine that the output frame record is less than 40 bytes long and that the maximum content of a recorded input tape with no record structure (a single long block) is less than 48 megabytes.

**Responsible Party and Schedule** Before any unit testing. Trainee.

**Test Data and Responses** The integrated software will be run against the tape of test data prepared by the independent consultant and against a full tape obtained from the calibrated source. The size of the corresponding sets of output disk files will be obtained by listing the directory involved, and this will be less than 50 megabytes.

**Responsible Party and Schedule** Before acceptance testing. Trainee.

### 4.5.3 Preliminary User's Manual

In keeping with the low level of documentation required on this project, the preliminary user's manual is quite short. Below is one section, detailing a single specific function.

**Amplified Logging** If there is some suspicion about the quality of data stream capture or synchronization and cleaning, additional information can be obtained to monitor the input data stream and the software function. This is done by attaching the option -a or -d to the clean command.

The effect of the -a option is to provide, both in the disk log file and on the screen, the following information:

Frame synchronization at byte #n of tape file.
Loss of synch signal at byte #n of tape file.
Loss of housekeeping dataword id at byte #n of tape file.
Loss of time sequence at byte #n of tape file.

The first message indicates the location of a synch signal (4 consecutive bytes, 4B 96 97 AF) in the input file, as well as the offset of the 4B byte from the beginning of the file. This message may be followed by the second, indicating a failure to find an expected synch signal at the byte indicated. The first and second messages may then alternate, indicating periodic capture and loss of synch.

The third and fourth messages indicate failure to find an acceptable frame id (given by the housekeeping dataword number) or timestamp in a synchronized frame. Like the second message, they indicate a loss of synchronization, and may be followed by a message of type 1, indicating synch reestablishment.

The effect of the -d option is to provide, on the screen only, a listing of every byte (with its offset) encountered in the input data stream following any one of the three types of losses of synchronization shown above.

Failure to synch reading byte #n, value zz.
Failure to synch reading byte #n, value zz.
Failure to synch reading byte #n, value zz.

Since this listing appears very quickly, the scrolling control signals (control-s and control-q) should be used to allow the operator to view them.

Neither of these options should be used during batch operation of the software.

## 4.6 SUMMARY

We have seen the value of careful specification of the software product; it provides the precise, technical foundation needed to carry out the rest of development without confusion and misunderstanding. By spending more effort in the specification stage, we will almost certainly improve the quality and increase the dependability of the final product; we may actually decrease its cost.

One of the primary attributes of a good specification is the formality of the language in which it is written. Not only does this avoid ambiguity and provide clearer understanding, but it lays the groundwork for the use of methodologies and tools that will aid in transforming requirements into software and in verifying the correctness of the transformation. We have seen several different notations now in general use for specification. The most useful of these tend to be graphical in nature.

Notations can be classified as to their aptitude for the representation of processes, data structure, and data relationships. Additional methodologies for the automatic transformation of specifications into design and code show great promise for the future. Tools for implementing these methodologies, both generic and specific, have been described.

With our specification completed, and the accompanying Verification Plan and preliminary User's Manual provided, we are ready to go ahead with the design stage. For most software engineers, this represents the most enjoyable stage of the project — between the unloved details of planning and specification and the pressure of implementation and testing. But first, we will take a detour through the external design phases, which frequently bridges the specification, design, and implementation stages.

# BIBLIOGRAPHY

[ALF85]    Alford, M.W., "SREM at the Age of Eight," *Computer*, 18(4):36 – 46.

[AND81]*   Anderson, T., and P.A. Lee, *Fault Tolerance: Principles and Practices*, Prentice-Hall, Englewood Cliffs, NJ.

[ARA88]    Arango, G., and P. Freeman, "Applications of Artificial Intelligence to Software Specifications," *Software Engineering Notes*, 13(1):32 – 38.

[AVI85]    Avizienis, A., "The N-version Approach to Fault-Tolerant Software," *IEEE Transactions on Software Engineering* 11(12):1491 – 1501.

[BAB80]    Babb, R., and L. Tripp, "Toward Tangible Realization of Software Systems," *Proceedings of the 13th Hawaii International Conference on Systems Science*.

[BAL85]*   Balzer, R., "A 15 Year Perspective on Automatic Programming," *IEEE Transactions on Software Engineering*, 11(11):1257 – 1268.

[BER82]*   Berg, H.K., W.E. Boebert, W.R. Franta, and T.G. Moher, *Formal Methods of Program Verification and Specification*, Prentice-Hall, Englewood Cliffs, NJ.

[BER85]    Berzins, V., and M. Gray, "Analysis and Design in MSG.84 — Formalizing Functional Specifications," *IEEE Transactions on Software Engineering*, 11(8):657 – 670.

[BOE81]*   Boehm, B.W., *Software Engineering Economics*, Prentice-Hall, Englewood Cliffs, NJ.

[BOR87]    Borning, A., "Computer System Reliability and Nuclear War," *Communications of the ACM*, 30(2):112 – 131.

[BRI87]    Brilliant, S.S., J.C. Knight, and N.G. Leveson, "The Consistent Comparison Problem in N-Version Software," *Software Engineering Notes*, 12(1):29 – 34.

[BRU88]*   Bruyn, W., R. Jensen, D. Keskar, and P. Ward, "ESML: An Extended Systems Modeling Language Based on the Data Flow Diagram," *Software Engineering Notes*, 13(1):58 – 67.

[CHE76]*   Chen, P.P., "The Entity-Relationship Model: Toward a Unified View of Data," *ACM Transactions on Database Systems*, 1(1):9 – 36.

[COH86]    Cohen, D.I.A., *Introduction to Computer Theory*, Wiley, New York.

[DAV88]*   Davis, A.M., "A Comparison of Techniques for the Specification of External System Behavior," *Communications of the ACM*, 31(9):1098 – 1115.

[DEN76]    Denning, P.J., "Fault-Tolerant Operating Systems," *Computing Surveys*, 8(4):355 – 389.

[DEM78]*   DeMarco, T., *Structured Analysis and System Specification*, Yourden Press, New York.

[FRE85]*   Frenkel, K.A., "Toward Automating the Software Development Cycle," *Communications of the ACM*, 28(6):579 – 589.

[GOO75]    Goodenough, J.B., "Exception Handling: Issues and a Proposed Notation," *Communications of the ACM*, 18(12):683 – 696.

[GUT85]    Guttag, J.V., J.J. Horning, and J.M. Wing, "The Larch Family of Specification Languages," *IEEE Software*, 2(5):24 – 36.

[HAY86]    Hayes, I.J., "Specification Driven Module Testing," *IEEE Transactions on Software Engineering*, 12(1):124 – 133.

[HUM89]*   Humphrey, W.S., *Managing the Software Process*, Addison-Wesley, Reading, MA.

[IVE80]*   Iverson, K.E., "Notation as a Tool of Thought," *Communications of the ACM*, 23(8):444 – 465.

[KIM84]    Kim, K.H., "Software Fault Tolerance" in *Handbook of Software Engineering*, C.R. Vick, and C.V. Ramamoorthy, eds. Van Nostrand Reinhold, New York.

[KNI86]    Knight, J.C., and N.G. Leveson, "An Experimental Evaluation of the Assumption of Independence in Multiversion Programming," *IEEE Transactions on Software Engineering*, 12(1):96 – 109.

[LUC85]    Luckham, D.C., and F.W. von Henke, "An Overview of Anna," *IEEE Software*, 2(2):9 – 22.

[MEY85]*   Meyer, B., "On Formalism in Specifications," *IEEE Software*, 2(1):6 – 26.

[MIL87]*   Mills, H.D., M. Dyer, and R.C. Linger, "Cleanroom Software Engineering," *IEEE Software*, 4(5):19 – 25.

[MYE87]*   Myers, W., "Ada: First users — pleased; prospective users — still hesitant," *Computer*, 20(3):68 – 73.

[MYE88]    Myers, W., "Shuttle Code Achieves Very Low Error Rate," *IEEE Software*, 5(5):93 – 95.

[MYE89]    Myers, B.A., "User-Interface Tools: Introduction and Survey," *IEEE Software*, 6(1):15 – 23.

[PAR83]*   Parnas, D.L., "A Technique for Software Module Specification with Examples," *Communications of the ACM*, 26(1):75 – 78.

[PET81]    Peterson, J.L., *Petri-Net Theory and the Modeling of Systems*, Prentice-Hall, Englewood Cliffs, NJ.

[POS85]    Posten, R.M., "Preventing Software Requirements Specification Errors with IEEE 830," *IEEE Software*, 2(1):83 – 86.

[POS87]    Posten, R.M., and M.W. Bruen, "Counting Down to Zero Software Failures," *IEEE Software*, 4(5):54 – 61.

[RAN78]*   Randell, B., P.A. Lee, and P.C. Treleaven, "Reliability Issues in Computing System Design," *Computing Surveys*, 10(2):123 – 165.

[REE74]    Rees, R.L.D., *Software Reliability*, Infotech, U.K.

[ROM85]*   Roman, G.C., "A Taxonomy of Current Issues in Requirements Engineering," *Computer*, 18(4):14 – 23.

[ROS85]    Ross, D.T., "Applications and Extensions of SADT," *Computer*, 18(4):25 – 34.

[SCH85]    Scheffer, P.A., A.H. Stone, and W.E. Rzepka "A Case Study of SREM," *Computer*, 18(4):47 – 54.

[SIE85]    Sievert, G.E., and T.A. Mizell, "Specification-Based Software Engineering with TAGS," *Computer*, 18(4):56 – 65.

[SWA82]    Swartout, W., and R. Balzer, "On the Inevitable Intertwining of Specification and Implementation," *Communications of the ACM*, 25(7):438 – 440.

[TEI77]    Teicherow, D., and E. Hershey, "PSL/PSA," *IEEE Transactions on Software Engineering*, 3(1):41 – 48.

[VER78]    Verhofstad, J.S.M., "Recovery Techniques for Database Systems," *Computing Surveys*, 10(2):167 – 195.

[VES86]    Vessey, I., and R. Weber, "Structured Tools and Conditional Logic: An Empirical Investigation," *Communications of the ACM*, 29(1):48 – 57.

[WAR74]    Warnier, J.D., *Logical Construction of Programs*, Van Nostrand Reinhold, New York.

[WUL75]    Wulf, W.A., "Reliable Hardware/Software Architecture" *IEEE Transactions on Software Engineering*, 1(2):233 – 239.

[YOU79]    *Yourden, E., and L. Constantine, *Structured Design*, Prentice-Hall, Englewood Cliffs, NJ.

[ZAV88]    Zave, P., "Assessment," *Software Engineering Notes*, 13(1):40 – 43.

## PROBLEMS

**1** Design $N$-version software to find the roots of a cubic equation.

**2** Design a recovery block to find the roots of a cubic equation.

**3** Read the articles by Avizienis [AVI85] and by Knight and Leveson [KNI86]. Who do you think is right, and why?

**4** What procedures can be undertaken by a software organization to minimize the cost of repairing long-term errors when they do occur?

**5** Specify the process for registration at your university by means of a data flow diagram.

**6** Make a transition table for a recognizer for the FORTRAN real number notation.

**7** Make a decision tree for locating hardware faults in a microcomputer. Use the troubleshooting" section of its user's manual for information.

**8** Give a regular expression for the FORTRAN real number notation.

**9** Use an entity-relationship diagram to represent a typical university information system, with transcripts, student registration, information about students, information about faculty, course lists, and section rolls.

**10** Develop a data dictionary for the university information system of Problem 9.

**11** Read about, or experiment with, one of the requirements environments listed in Section 4.3.5. Report your findings.

**12** Read Meyer ([MEY85]), and use the comments to write complete specifications for the Naur text-filling function. These specs should not be simply functional descriptions but a full specification.

**13** Rewrite the EDCA synchronization and cleaning process specification as a Petri net.

**14** Specify the "string" abstract data type.

**15** Select some subset of the project you worked on in Problem 21 of Chapter 3 and write specifications for it. The subset should probably represent between 10% and 50% of the project, depending on which one you worked on.

**16** Give an example of a reusable software specification component.

**17** Write performance, security, reliability, and accuracy constraint specifications for the student registration system.

**18** Write an acceptance test plan for the requirements specified in Problem 17.

**19** For each of the fault tolerance measures (restart, modularity, error handling procedures, checkpointing, careful replacement, handshaking, self-identifying structures, $n$-version software and recovery blocks) give an example of a software product that would require that measure.

**20** What are the advantages of the SADT notation over the general data flow diagram?

# CHAPTER 5

## THE EXTERNAL DESIGN PHASE

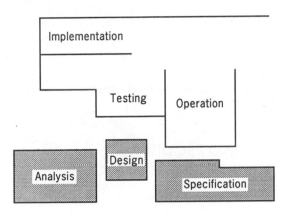

The first, or external, design effort concentrates solely on the interface between the software and its operational environment. The most complex part of the environment, of course, is the human user of the product. The focus in this case is on ensuring that the user interface connects the software structure to the real-world application in a natural, effective and understandable way. To do this, we must understand the user's needs, his psychology, and the principles by which the flow of information at the computer-human interface can be improved.

Since the external design interfaces to such a complex and insufficiently understood component (a human being), careful specification and design are inadequate approaches. Instead, we will depend heavily on the exploratory and illustrative power of prototyping. The high number of iterations of user interface design recommended by current practice make it difficult to contain external design within any one of the development stages. Rather, it starts during analysis and continues in parallel with the development of other components of the product well into the implementation stage. We can only afford to leave this design flexible if the user interface is isolated from the rest of the product. But this flexibility does have the advantage of allowing us to incorporate many of the most typical customer change requests without serious disruption of the development process.

Because of the out-of-step development of external design, the title of this chapter refers to a "phase" rather than a "stage." The use of "phase" may be a little confusing, since "phase" is often used as a synonym for "stage" in the software engineering literature. Besides that problem, the literature frequently restricts external design to lie entirely within a single stage, either analysis, specification, or design. Our approach will be that this is the most changeable part of the product, and that it should be modularized by separating it partially from the mainstream of development, while allowing it plenty of time to mature.

This makes management of the process somewhat difficult ([ROS88]). Mantei and Teorey even suggest in [MAN88] a separate life cycle model for external design. We would be mistaken in minimizing the importance of the external design phase just because it is difficult to manage, however. After all, insofar as the user is concerned, the user interface *is* the product ([GOU85]). When external design is complete, the result is a single module representing a well-defined, compartmentalized interface between the environment and the functional product.

## 5.1 THE EXTERNAL DESIGN PROCESS AND PRODUCTS

Remember that there are always three components to any computerized system — hardware, software, and people. Figure 5-1 ([BO 82]) shows the central position at the intersection of these three of human-computer interaction. That is where all our effort comes together, and it is our challenge to design this area so that each component can

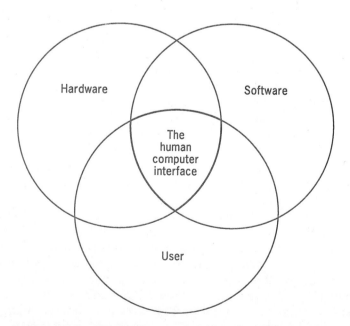

**FIGURE 5-1**  THE CENTRAL ROLE OF THE USER INTERFACE (Kelll, Bo, "Human-Computer Interaction," *Computer*, copyright © 1982, IEEE.)

exercise its full capability in synergy with the other two. In particular, we need to let people do what they do best, while the software helps them in their task.

When we complete the specification stage, external design has already been going on for some time. Designing for interfaces to file systems, operating systems, and hardware is usually clear cut and, although important, requires relatively little effort. Our major challenge is to ensure that the user interface conforms itself to the real world by modeling the problem environment. This adaptation should be such that the software can be used to solve the problem without confusing or irritating the user and without requiring a significant alteration of the environment.

Functional and data requirements have been developed during the analysis and specification stages with this goal in mind. The most significant part of analysis, for the purpose at hand, is a census of potential users of the product. This profile includes information about their experience and background, the tasks they will be performing with the aid of the product, how often they perform these tasks, how important the tasks are, the frequency with which they will use the product, and the psychological characteristics of user activities.

External design will review this existing information and possibly amplify it. Although the specifications should be complete, they might, for instance, specify the different fields in user-input data, without mentioning their placement, the use of highlighting techniques, or the labels which identify the fields. These details will all be needed at some time, and external design is the point at which they should be solidified.

The typical products of the external design phase are file definitions, syntax for system service calls, hardware specifications, descriptions of operational procedures, command language definitions, menu structures, and screen layouts. We may also create keyboard templates and mockups of terminals or other interface devices. An important part of the external design is a categorized list of the errors that the user can encounter during product use, together with error messages and recovery procedures. Finally, we need to design on-line help facilities and information.

This is also a period of time in which the user interface can be prototyped and evaluated by the customer. Some customer suggestions can be handled without modification of the specifications or central design of the product, whereas others will require a short iteration of the appropriate stage while we rework the documents. We would like to avoid rework, since it represents a loss of effort, and so we attempt to separate the user interface design from the rest of the product as much as we can. The external design phase allows the customer to have primary control in the design of that part of the product with which he will be in the most direct contact.

Current practice dictates a rapid, intense, and extended prototyping schedule for the user interface ([GOU87]). We should be willing to keep trying until the user is *completely* satisfied with what is seen in our prototypes. Each successive attempt may vary only slightly from the previous one, however, so that the amount of effort is not as great as it might seem. We have to look at this design paradigm as one of relatively slow convergence, rather than as predictable linear progress.

## 5.2 EXTERNAL DESIGN PRINCIPLES

Ten principles of external design are outlined in [CAR83] and are shown in Figure 5-2. First, the software engineer must know who the user is, what skills and understanding he brings to the task, what types of software behavior is likely to produce confusion or anxiety, and so on. As part of the project plan, developed during analysis, a profile of the potential users of the product was formulated.

In addition, the composition of the user population (for instance, managers, secretaries, engineers, and accountants) is described in the planning document. It is usually appropriate to provide three levels of expertise within the population. We should design interfaces appropriate for novice users, for knowledgeable but occasional users, and for frequent users. These levels might differ in the amount of prompting provided, the degree to which commands can be abbreviated, the amount of reassuring feedback provided to the user, the rapidity of response to user actions, and the extent to which the user is protected from possible errors.

In particular, Carroll and Carrithers suggest in [CAR84] that the entire user interface for novices be simplified, and perhaps standardized. Such a "training wheels" interface can be designed to prevent the most frequent beginner panics and dead ends from even occurring. These errors can be determined by prototype testing of the user interface. Going further, it might be reasonable to provide a fixed, simple interface for beginners to use with *all* software products. The specialized, more complex interface designed for a specific product would be made available only after the learning period.

It is also necessary to analyze the kinds of tasks that will be carried out by software users. The most frequent tasks should be the easiest to accomplish, and the most risky should entail the greatest degree of fault tolerance. Again, analysis should have determined what tasks are to be performed, how often they are required, and how smaller tasks are put together to compose larger ones. This breakdown of a task into subtasks defines the method by which a task is accomplished.

During specification, we must give detailed requirements for performance and the methods, or actions needed, for completing user tasks. However, there is probably not

- Consider the psychology of the user.
- Specify performance requirements.
- Specify the user population.
- Specify the tasks.
- Specify the methods for accomplishing the tasks.
- Describe the methods in enough detail for complete design.
- Allow expert users to take shortcuts and combine tasks.
- Clearly delineate alternative methods.
- Design error recovery methods carefully and completely.
- Be careful about the effect of incorrect assumptions.

**FIGURE 5-2**   PRINCIPLES OF EXTERNAL DESIGN

enough detail in the specification to make a full design possible; hence, additional method analysis may now be necessary. In particular, we must decide on default settings and meanings, and design techniques for batching commands, creating macros, and abbreviating commands. These will aid the expert user in rapid execution of tasks.

When errors do occur from which the software cannot recover, adequate information to the user is vital. During external design, error message format should be determined; a single format should be followed throughout the product. Error messages should be understandable and specific. They should contain information about this event ["Pointer out of range (62198) in record 417"] rather than just generic text ("Value out of range"). Where possible, the user should be provided with suggested strategies for error correction. This information should be provided either by the software as it dies or in easily used documentation about recovery methods.

Finally, we must be cautious about blindly accepting the assumptions we have made. If our understanding of user psychology is incorrect, the user interface we design can be irritating, frustrating, error-prone, or even unusable. If our assumptions are wrong, the users may react by abandoning the system, ignoring parts of it, pushing use off onto other people, finding workarounds, enduring extra work, or even sabotage ([POT87]). Once again, there is no substitute for prototyping and field study of user interfaces.

### 5.2.1 Goals for External Design

Each ambitious software engineer must surely ask: "What factors cause one product to be successful; what factors cause other products to fail?" Our academic training leads us to suppose that efficiency or elegance are the keys to success. Perhaps the million-seller used particularly complex and subtle data structures. Maybe the program that bombed took five times as long to carry out a particular function.

The truth of the matter is that although the million-seller probably exhibited careful design and good throughput, neither of these was the most important factor in its success. Rather, it sold because users liked the way it looked and handled. They found input natural and easy to formulate; they understood the output at a glance; they were never frustrated or frightened when they used the product. In a word, the deciding factor in success is not functionality, but usability ([GOO87]). In fact, unusable functionality is like a buried treasure; it's no good if you don't know how to find it. Gould and Lewis ([GOU85]) believe that the primary quality attribute of the user interface is its usability — that is, how easily the user can learn, remember and use the product.

Granted, there are a lot of programs that, in terms of speed and power, plod along like sick oxen, when users demand thoroughbreds. These will obviously fail in a competitive market. But there are always several thoroughbreds competing for a market niche. The deciding factor for them will be the quality of the user interface.

As an example of poor design, in a certain operating system popular 15 years ago, the command to delete all files on a tape was

```
PIP/DE *.*.
```

whereas the command to show a directory of all files on a tape was

```
PIP/DI *.*.
```

For years software engineers suffered the mishap of deleting all their backup files when they just wanted to see the file names. The company did finally add a confirmation request ("Do you really want to do that?"), but that was simply an acknowledgment of failure in user interface design.

### 5.2.2 Characteristics of Good External Design

One of the main goals of good external design is to create an environment in which the user can accomplish tasks with a minimum of anxiety, frustration, confusion, fatigue, boredom, and mental overload. These are factors that are detrimental to human performance (see Section 5.2.3). Although some of these problems are inherent in the task itself (as would be true, say, for an air traffic controller), it is up to the software engineer to ensure that the software does not add to the user's difficulties. Some specific characteristics of a well-designed product are shown in Figure 5-3.

In addition, the software engineer should strive to provide an interface that minimizes the likelihood of errors and the harmful consequences of those errors that do occur. This goal can be achieved, in part, by simplifying the user interface to the maximum degree that is still compatible with the performance goals of system users. In particular, at any given moment we should present inexperienced users with a restricted set of safe and appropriate actions or objects of manipulation. It is hard to crash such a system.

Another principal characteristic of external design is to provide an interface that will allow users to employ the software in a natural fashion, without requiring any knowledge of how the hardware functions or how the software is implemented. Of course, the user will have to know how to accomplish the tasks that the software was designed to assist; but no specialized or technical knowledge should be required.

One contribution toward achieving all of these disparate design goals is to give all the external design task to a single person or small team. When the detailed definition of the user interface is split along the same lines as the detailed design of function modules, it is likely that the resulting software will appear inconsistent, confusing, and illogical to the user ([MOR83]).

- The user is given sufficient information for task accomplishment.
- The user can control the pace of interaction.
- The user is given feedback about the current state of the process.
- The user can correct errors easily.
- Software performance conforms to user expectations.

**FIGURE 5-3** CHARACTERISTICS OF GOOD EXTERNAL DESIGN

### 5.2.3 User Psychology

**User interface** refers to several different aspects of software that are directly visible to the user and that influence the user's ease, comfort, security, and productivity. Human-computer interaction is usually carried out for three different purposes: data input, data presentation, and interactive data manipulation. Specifically, the user interface can be divided into the input interface, the output interface, and system dependability. These are considered in Section 5.3 following after a discussion of those psychological traits of the user that a software engineer must understand and design for.

Shneiderman ([SHN87]) cites a number of *human processes* and the factors that can influence performance. These are listed in Figure 5-4. All of those processes must be considered and planned for as we design software for human interaction, although many of the factors are beyond our control. However, software engineers should be careful to design so that mental load, monotony, and anxiety are reduced, whereas arousal and knowledge of results are increased. In addition, the possibility that these factors might reduce user performance must be included in our design so that we can reduce the likelihood of disastrous mistakes.

Software engineers must always try to design the user interface of their product to match the *mental strength* of the user. This entails many things: the difficulty of the interface cannot exceed the understanding of the user; the complexity of the interface should be minimized while preserving functionality; and the demands of the interface ought not to surpass the patience of the user. One of the best ways for determining the actual match between an interface design and user needs is through empirical measurement of the performance of and satisfaction with prototypes. This kind of prototype evaluation may even be superior to full specification in designing the user interface ([DRA85]).

| Processes | Factors |
|---|---|
| Short-term memory | Arousal and vigilance |
| Long-term memory, learning | Fatigue |
| Problem solving | Perceptual (mental) load |
| Decision making | Knowledge of results |
| Attention and set | Monotony and boredom |
| Search and scanning | Sensory deprivation |
| Time perception | Sleep deprivation |
|  | Anxiety and fear |
|  | Isolation |
|  | Aging |
|  | Drugs and alcohol |
|  | Circadian rhythm |

**FIGURE 5-4**   HUMAN PROCESSES AND FACTORS INFLUENCING PERFORMANCE

The user needs to:
- Manipulate objects directly, in a natural fashion.
- Use language in a conversational manner.
- Work out of short-term memory as much as possible.
- Control the pace and duration of the interaction.
- Break long tasks down into more manageable size.
- Experiment without making a final commitment.
- Wait for the system only as long as seems reasonable.
- Organize objects, processes, and ideas into logical groups.
- Judge values by comparison within a context.
- Control, or, at least, accurately predict, response time.
- Experience a consistent, rational environment.

**F I G U R E 5-5**   PSYCHOLOGICAL NEEDS OF USERS

During *empirical measurement*, user interaction with a prototype interface is evaluated. This prototype might actually be simulated through printed displays, mockup keyboards, simulation of computers by a hidden human operator, and so on, or it might really be software controlled. User reaction, in terms of learning time, performance, error rates, satisfaction, and retention of skills is measured by using the standard techniques of cognitive science. These results, along with application needs and human-computer interaction theory, should be carefully studied to guide further external design ([POT87]).

However, Thomas and Kellogg warn that we must be careful that results drawn from the artificial prototyping environment are representative of the real environment in which the software will function ([THO89]). There are four ways in which the laboratory and the field experience differ: (1) the users may not be representative; (2) the tasks tested may not be realistic; (3) the system context can be spurious; and (4) the work context may present an incorrect view of pressure, deadlines, and the like. In particular, we may succumb to the temptation to test knowledgeable users on clear-cut tasks. This is not wrong, but we should also test some ill-trained or nontarget users, and present them with confusing tasks.

Figure 5-5 lists some of the specific psychological traits that need to be evaluated in designing software.

When the interaction between user and computer is visualized by the user in terms of actions on objects, the user should be shown such an action on the screen. For instance, several icon-oriented window systems allow files to be represented by **icons**, or small representative graphic symbols. The process of deleting a file is then represented by selecting the file icon with a mouse and moving it to a pictorial representation of a trash can. In a similar vein, the user may set the sensitivity of the cursor to motion of the mouse by sliding a graphic button to an appropriate level along a graduated scale.

In these examples, the user is *directly manipulating* the objects represented by the icons in the same way that he manipulates real objects. Since the actions and the visual response on the screen so closely model real-life actions, the likelihood of confusion, misunderstanding, and mistakes are greatly reduced. In addition to providing a "world" that mirrors the real world in a visual and operational sense, direct manipulation allows the user to exercise motor skills, to "show" rather than to "tell." These skills were the first ones learned during infancy, the ones with which the user has the most practice and experience and that are still frequently used during adulthood. For the user, knowing how to accomplish the task is enough; he doesn't have to know how to tell a computer how to do it.

An example of the "user friendliness" of direct manipulation is a typical full-screen display text editor. Text is presented in a stable, consistent format, as if it were a printed sheet, and the user can move the center of attention (cursor) at will. Erasure, insertion, text movement, and other small, familiar actions are immediately echoed in the screen's appearance in a natural way. Mistakes can easily be reversed. Users even talk about "picking up a paragraph and putting it at the end" as if they were physically performing the act. In effect, the software has disappeared, leaving the user to interact directly with the task, thus providing a degree of satisfaction and even excitement not experienced with line-oriented editors.

In a similar fashion, command languages that enable the software to interpret expressions formed in a *natural language* as part of a conversation with the user provide a friendlier and more intuitive environment. In its purest form, communication between user and software would be carried on through the channel of voice synthesis and recognition hardware (see Figure 5-6). However, since natural language provides a much richer and more complex background for interaction than a set of windows with a few icons, the potential for confusion and doubt is much higher. This means that the software must be designed to check carefully the correctness of its interpretation of commands before taking action.

**FIGURE 5-6** NATURAL LANGUAGE INTERFACE (Doonesbury, copyright © 1984, G.B. Trudeau. Reprinted with permission of Universal Press Syndicate. All rights reserved.)

One advantage of using direct manipulation and natural language is that the user need not learn an artificial command language in order to control software. Even with the best of intentions, these languages frequently appear arbitrary and illogical to the user, whereas the amount of detail that must be acquired may require extensive memorization or practice ([SHN87]). The problem is compounded when the language is not structured properly, demanding different responses in various places to effect similar results. In the extreme, even trained software engineers may require years of experience with a command language like JCL before they can use all its capabilities.

Direct manipulation has the additional benefits of being easy to learn and to retain and has a high level of user acceptance and satisfaction. On the negative side, both the natural language and direct manipulation interaction styles are difficult to provide in software and may require specialized hardware like high-resolution displays, pointing devices, and voice synthesizers. Natural language has the potential for ambiguity and the corresponding need for clarification, as well as being verbose.

*Short-term memory* contains those things you are thinking about *right now*. The items in short-term memory do not need to be recalled by association or conscious effort; they are present. In this sense, these items correspond to the contents of registers in modern computers, and they have equal value. A computer program will be much more efficient if it can operate by using only data found in registers. A computer user will be much more efficient if he can work by using only the contents of short-term memory.

There are some clear limitations involved here. Generally, short-term memory is thought to be limited to about seven distinct items, and it will not store an unused item for more than two seconds. This means that the user interface must lead the user in a gradual flow, requesting data and decisions that are closely associated with the previous data and decisions.

In contrast, there is also a long-term memory, which stores our "real" memories, things that we have memorized and can recall more or less at will. Accessing informa-

You may see a shape in the clouds,
but when you look away and back
again, you will have lost it.
Shapes seen in clouds are as
evanescent as short–term memories.

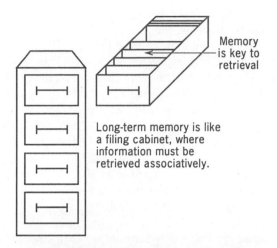

Memory is key to retrieval

Long-term memory is like a filing cabinet, where information must be retrieved associatively.

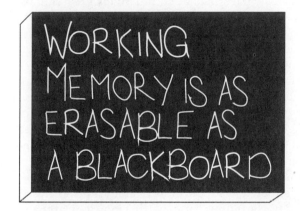

WORKING MEMORY IS AS ERASABLE AS A BLACKBOARD

tion in long-term memory may result in significant delays; therefore it is important that software not require this any more than is necessary. However, there is a third category —working memory. This consists largely of those parts of long-term memory that have already been activated and are much more accessible or "closer to the surface." Users employ working memory for planning, problem solving, and decision making.

The distinction between recognition and recall is similar to that between short- and long-term memory. Recognition is the process of being presented with an object, and using it to retrieve information about it. Recall is information retrieval about an object without any associated sensory cues. Bo points out ([BO 82]) that recognition is about twice as effective as recall. For this reason, interfaces that provide direct manipulation or, at least, menus or prompts are more user friendly than interfaces that depend on the user to formulate commands on his own.

Interruptions, delays, and confusion tend to erase the contents of short-term memory. The information can be recovered from working memory. This, however, lowers user performance and increases error rates during rote or repetitive tasks, since it requires a constant "reorientation." Software should be designed so as to promote constant attention on the user's part. This means that it should be pleasing, enjoyable to use, and interesting — insofar as possible.

On the other hand, users do not want to be pushed by the software to perform more quickly than is natural. Error rates climb, especially for nonrote tasks, when there is no time to react to feedback and to plan further action. If correction of errors is quite simple, there is still a tendency to want all response times to be in the subsecond range. However, if it is difficult to undo errors, most users would prefer longer delays, which would give them time to think before acting.

Besides the question of needing slower pacing during thoughtful as opposed to routine tasks, there is also a need for software to adapt the *pace of interaction* to the level of sophistication and experience of the user. Card et al. ([CAR83]) indicate that there may be an order of magnitude difference between the speeds of the least and the most expert users of software. To accommodate the fastest user, the amount of feedback in the way of messages, menus, screens, and reassurance will have to be user modifiable.

Computer users are daunted by tasks that cannot be *subdivided*. Even though the effort involved in doing a job by parts may be cumulatively greater, most users would prefer to have it this way. The feeling of having no reasonable points at which to stop and relax is distressing to users. This has been the subject of numerous studies, which have clearly shown that user well-being depends on the ability to pace, to control, and to interrupt the flow of interaction.

*Experimentation*, or probing, is one of the most productive decision making strategies for users. It should be fostered in the interface by allowing for conditional decisions and by making backtracking easy when the decision turns out not to be appropriate. An "undo" command will help encourage the user in his exploration of the system. This principle has contributed to the recent astonishing success of "spreadsheet" software. For the same reason, using a text editor is much more pleasant than creating a file simply by typing it in from a keyboard.

Computers are ideally situated to support this strategy, and software should make the most of it. Users should not be required to construct long logical chains of reasoning in order to give their next input. Instead, they should be assisted in working through the decisions one small step at a time. On the other hand, an alternative approach that moves in much larger steps should also be acceptable as input to the software, to satisfy the needs of the expert user.

All people experience a reaction called **closure**. This is the degree to which some action just completed represents the end, or closure, of a task. The amount of closure we feel depends on the size of the task completed. This can range from the nonexistent closure of typing one more character on a line to the very significant closure of typing the last character in a book.

One of the most disconcerting things software can do to people is to delay *response* to an action far beyond what seems reasonable in terms of the sense of closure they feel. One would like an instantaneous response to typing another character (for people, that probably means seeing the character echoed within 0.2 seconds). A longer delay can be irritating, whereas having to wait 5 seconds can destroy our train of thought (i.e., replace the contents of our short-term memory) (see Figure 5-7).

If the character we typed was a request to display a disk directory, we feel good about waiting 2 or 3 seconds for the display, since we have completed a command and would like to rest a moment before making whatever decision depends on the contents of the directory. If the character was the last in a command to compile a large program, we know that we have moved from one big task (editing a large program) to another and feel that we could well take a few minutes off. But a 5 minute delay for a small compilation would be frustrating, because our perception of closure is completely out of line with the delay.

Shneiderman suggests some general rules of thumb relating closure to acceptable delay ([SHN87]). First, users will not generally notice response time if it is within 50% of their expectations. Nonclosure actions, like typing a single character of text, should show no delay. Small closures, like giving an immediately executed command, should not be delayed longer than 2 seconds. If delays are double the expected amount, users will begin to get frustrated; they will panic if delays amount to eight times the expected amount. They will also panic for very short delays ($\frac{1}{4}$ second when they were expecting 2 seconds).

*Organization* is the principal technique we use to allow us to deal with more information in our environment than we can handle. The organization may be simply mnemonic, as when we memorize a long list by putting the words in alphabetical order. More often, organization means grouping individual items of information logically, then replacing the group in our mind with a name for the group. The name is much easier to remember, but from it the entire group can be reconstructed. This is the essence of the abstraction technique that we use to such good effect in software engineering. The "quantum grouping" operation is frequently called **chunking**.

As an example, consider the string of bits at the top of Figure 5-8 which, you would say, is just about impossible to memorize. However, if you divide (organize) the bits into groups of four and translate them (give names to the groups) into hexadecimal, you would get something that you might be able to memorize. If you further group the

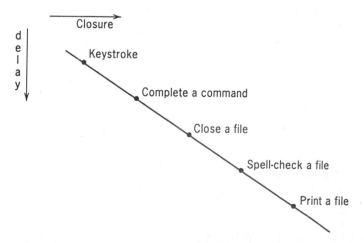

**FIGURE 5-7**   TOLERABLE DELAYS DEPEND ON THE AMOUNT OF PERCEIVED CLOSURE

```
00010100000000000101010101010001001000010010

0001  0100  0000  0000  0101  0101  0101  0001  0010  0001  0010

  1     8     0     0     5     5     5     1     2     1     2

              1-800-555-1212
```

**F I G U R E 5-8**   ORGANIZATION, OR CHUNKING, IS AN AID TO COMPREHENSION

digits using dashes as shown, you will probably have no trouble at all in memorizing them, at least, if you use the U.S. telephone system much. And if someone asked you for the original string of bits right now, you could roll them off, which you would have thought impossible just a minute ago.

If you have fed a young child vegetables, you have been told that his portion is "too big." It doesn't look too big to you — in fact your own portion is probably much larger. But big and small have no meaning unless they are placed in a context. Putting values in a context often permits *comparative judgment*, which requires much less thought than the analytic judgment that might otherwise be necessary. Are 4 ounces of lettuce a lot of lettuce? You would have to see it on a plate to know. Comparative judgment often benefits from some kind of graphical display, as when you compare the pile of lettuce to the plate it sits on. It makes good use of our ability to form overall impressions ([SOM89]).

Each person needs to feel that he is in *control*, or, at least, that he has an accurate idea of what will happen. The unpredictable behavior of a computing system will render the system useless — not because useful work can't usually be done but because nobody trusts it any more. When there is no feeling of security, people will unreasonably avoid the system. A lack of confidence in a computing system can have a dramatic effect on user productivity.

*Consistency* is also a prerequisite for user productivity ([GUY88]). Let me illustrate this with a personal experience. I have two apparently identical keys on my key ring. They open two different categories of doors, and neither key can be inserted in the other kind of lock. When I had only one key, I always succeeded in inserting the key into the locks. Now, you might expect that with two keys, and not being able to tell which is which, I would get the right key immediately half the time, and succeed on the second attempt the other half of the time. However, it frequently takes three, and sometimes four tries to decide which is the right key for a lock. Previously, if a key didn't slip immediately into the lock, I readjusted it till it did, because I *knew* that it fit. Now I am a prey to doubts. If the key doesn't slip in, I think it's the wrong one, whether it is or not.

Similarly, users who have lost confidence in a system spend a great deal of time worrying, and sometimes they foolishly and needlessly kill jobs, back up backed-up files, and agonize over commands. For example, suppose a user runs a program, gives some input, and then waits for what seems a long time for a response. The user who's confident of the software will simply wait for a response. But the user who has lost faith will panic. What's happening? Is the system busy? Maybe the system is down. Maybe he should call the operator. Perhaps the data caused the software to hit an infinite loop. Perhaps it's erasing files.

All of these psychological needs are important. The software engineer will ignore them at his peril, or use them profitably.

## 5.3 EXTERNAL DESIGN METHODOLOGIES AND TOOLS

The following sections concentrate on four aspects of external design. First, we need a way to determine what the user really needs if he is to solve his problems by using our software. Second, we must design an input interface that will allow the user to communicate information to the product. Third, an output interface, including general system characteristics that affect the user, has to be designed. Fourth, we must determine what kinds of errors the user is likely to make, design provisions for handling these, and create a set of error messages.

A great deal of effort is currently being expended in producing *user-interface development systems* (UIDSs), which incorporate tools for producing all of these aspects of the external design. Myers gives a list in [MYE89] of the currently available UIDSs. The run-time support libraries for these interfaces are called user-interface management systems (UIMSs). Among the tools that might be part of a UIDS are graphics generators, form management systems, and window systems.

### 5.3.1 User Needs Assessment

There is a temptation for software engineers to judge users in terms of themselves and their own limited experience. To avoid this, external design should be based on a rational methodology. Gould et al. ([GOU87]) propose three principles: (1) design focus should concentrate on users and the tasks they must perform; (2) design should be evaluated empirically from the very start; and (3) an iterative set of prototype designs are needed to converge on the optimal final product.

Based on their experience in designing a message system, Gould et al. believe that even the best task analysis cannot be depended on to indicate how users will really use an existing system. For this reason, they recommend that from the very beginning of external design, prototypes must be delivered to representative sets of users for evaluation. This evaluation should be done through scientifically conducted experiments.

The point is that external design must be user centered. In the past, it has been software (and software engineer) centered. We have thought of the external design of interactive software as describing the interface that the user encounters while operating the product. But Draper and Norman point out ([DRA85]) that we might just as well consider the user-software relationship from the inverse viewpoint: the external design describes to the software how the user interface "runs" on people. From this angle, we see many familiar problems. First, we are faced with the problem of balancing the trade-off between ease of learning and use, on one hand, and convenience and speed, on the other. Second, we encounter the familiar need for methodology, tools, and metrics for evaluating users. Third, this user, which represents a coroutine with our software, is often incompletely specified.

Because of its dual nature, the user interface should be encapsulated away from program design. The picture at the top of Figure 5-9 is wrong, since it shows the user interface as a primary and public interface in the design of the software. The picture at the bottom of the same figure represents a modular and hidden user interface, which can be modified or replaced with little effect on the rest of the software ([GOU85]).

In effect, we are creating two dialogues: an external dialogue between the user and the user interface, and an internal dialogue between the user interface and the product ([HAR89]). Hartson states that the user interface should contain a substantial functionality separate from the product — enough to accept, parse, and validate input, to map input to internal functions and parameters, and to report success or errors back to the user. However, it is important not to allow the functionality of the user interface to become so rich that it drowns in its own complexity.

Some of the issues seen by Draper and Norman in designing the user interface include workspace size, response time, menu structure, command language design, primary dependence on keyboard or pointing device for commands, and ease of learning and use. They point out that there is a general failure to specify the user interface carefully. A good specification might be this one from Shneiderman ([SHN87]): "After 75 minutes of training, 40 typical users should be able to accomplish 80 percent of the benchmark tasks in 35 minutes with fewer than 12 errors."

The interface must be prototyped and tested to measure user performance and satisfaction. An instrumentation capability, which can capture information about error frequency, time to formulate commands and accomplish tasks, access to help facilities, and the like will be invaluable in painting a true picture of the user's reactions to the software.

Prototype interfaces can include user instructions sheets, mockup keyboards, and displays and human intervention simulations as well as actual software/hardware systems. Experimental subjects can be obtained from other divisions of an organization, from paid subject pools, or even from volunteers. It is possible to use a "hallway" design, in which the software is made available to random passersby in a public area. Some passersby may become so interested in the system as to provide a valuable different viewpoint on the software — especially if they accept the challenge of trying

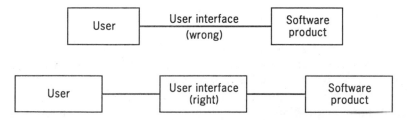

**FIGURE 5-9**  CORRECT ENCAPSULATION OF THE USER INTERFACE

to "break" it. Data collected from dozens of these ensuing prototype experiments can be used to gradually optimize the user interface while other design activities proceed.

## 5.3.2 The Input Interface

There are two classes of interaction between computer and user. In the first , the course of the interaction is guided by the software. The user is asked to input data, or is given a very limited choice from a menu. Extreme instances of this are the video game and the data input program, in which the software demands input of a specific nature in a preselected sequence. But one of the first principles of input interface design is to automate as much of the data capture as possible ([BO 82]). This means that A/D converters should replace human fingers.

In the second class, the control over processing is exercised by the user, who issues instructions to the system from a complex menu, or in a command or natural language, or by direct manipulation. Typical examples here are operating systems, software engineering environments, and text or graphics editors. One significant difference between the two classes is that the first merely requires the user to select actions by recognizing them, whereas the second requires the user to recall commands.

Shneiderman suggests ([SHN87]) that the most frequent tasks, or those associated with a high degree of closure, might be invoked with the help of a special function key. These have the advantage of providing a distinct single keystroke action, separate from that of the data keys. Special functions can be identified for novices by using templates, key caps or flexible overlays, or screen displays. Less common actions may utilize shift- or control-key combinations. These are somewhat more convenient than special function keys in that they do not require movement of the fingers off the home position on the data keypad. Rarer activities might require a command name (like DELETE), while the rarest could require a series of steps to change the interaction mode. Pointing devices are effective for certain kinds of tasks. They are most often used to indicate position on a display, or to select an item from the display. But they can also be used to connect items, to trace lines, to surround and select areas, and to indicate direction.

Prompting for input can be by a simple character for command language interaction. But when the software is guiding the interaction and the user has to conform exactly to rigid input formats or limited selections, prompting must be much more elaborate. First, in deference to the user's short-term memory problems, the prompt must include sufficient information to know what data is required and what form it must have. The software engineer can, for instance, request a social security number with this kind of prompt:

`social security number:  |_  -  -   |.`

Of course, we have to monitor the input and issue a beep instead of echoing nondigit characters typed in response. In fact, it is worthwhile to develop a template for procedures to perform this kind of prompt-input-test operation.

Additional effort would allow the designer to produce a software product that displays an entire form on the screen, with default values in some or all fields (see Figure 5-10). This can be filled with data by the user. Such a form allows the user even

```
┌──────────────────────────────────────────────┐
│                                                │
│   Name:                Age:      Sex:          │
│                                                │
│   Street Address:                              │
│                                                │
│   City:              State:      Zip:          │
│                                                │
│   Manager:                                     │
│                                                │
│   Grade:        Hourly Pay:    Insurance:      │
│                                                │
│   Years Employed:   Union:                     │
│                                                │
│   Comments:                                    │
│                                                │
└──────────────────────────────────────────────┘
```

**FIGURE 5-10**   FULL SCREEN PERSONNEL FORM

greater ability to control, pace, and retry. It also represents a limited form of direct manipulation, since it imitates the actions of filling in a printed form by hand. In addition, there are many form generation and presentation tools available. One disadvantage of form fill-in is that it fills up the screen very quickly.

Thought should be used in designing menus. Menus jog the user's memory by showing a short list of possible selections, perhaps contained in the prompt itself, or on a 25th line, which on many terminals is a window that the cursor will not enter and that is unaffected by scrolling. Although beginning users may appreciate standard large menus, which require rewriting the screen, after a while these become a time-consuming bore. A good technique is to allow the user to display a menu, either by typing "?" to ask for a help page explaining the currently valid options, or by pointing to a pull-down or pop-up menu. This satisfies the user's need to experiment and to explore the current environment. Another technique is to automatically display an appropriate help screen when the user hesitates for more than a specified number of seconds.

If a full menu is displayed, selection from it can be made by using a pointing device, by using cursor control keys, or by typing a single key. For some menus, it is appropriate to accept multiple selections; a type-style menu might allow turning on or off bold, underline, caps and reverse in a single menu reference. Multiple keystrokes are usually an irritation. Function keys and control or alphabetic characters can be used, depending on the application. If alphabetic or control characters are used, be careful to make them mnemonic. Avoid listing thoughtless options like those in Figure 5-11.

The entire issue of the size, placement, wording, and design of menus, along with the method for entering, changing, and backtracking through multiple menus deserves careful attention during external design. Shneiderman ([SHN87]) cites data to indicate that when multiple menus are required, there should be about eight entries in each menu. This may correspond to the postulated short-term memory limit of seven.

In terms of organization, it appears that user performance will be best when the

Type **A** to **D**elete

Type **B** to **A**ppend

Type **C** to change **B**uffers

Type **D** to **C**opy

Type "1" for "Yes" and "0" for "No".

**F I G U R E 5-11**   BAD MENU CHOICES

menu items are listed in a natural order (like earliest to latest) or in alphabetic order, or grouped functionally. Of course, success with alphabetic ordering depends on choosing predictable and memorable names for entries. These names should clearly delineate the difference between the various selections. For intermenu organization, tree-structured, or hierarchical menu systems should title each menu by using the entry word found on the parent menu.

In the second kind of interaction, the kind guided by the user, the software has much less control over the course of processing. Shneiderman also suggests that if an extensive menu tree, consisting of many different menus, is used, users will be helped by some kind of menu map. Presenting menus in overlapping windows has the effect of providing just such a visual trace of the path by which the user arrived at a point. Navigation through a complex of menus can be aided by giving each menu a title and by letting the user open a menu by typing the name. Alternatively, the user might type a string of selecting codes to describe the path to the menu of choice. It should also be possible to back out of menus by typing or selecting a code to return to the previous level.

Menus have the advantage of being quite natural and of giving the software engineer strong control over the course of decision making performed by the user. There are a number of excellent tools for menu construction and display. Menus have the disadvantage of being slow and verbose, and of becoming confusing when giving access to large, hierarchical software products.

Within a reasonable software engineering or programming environment, one should have the use of the interface generator that supports the environment ([RAM86], [STO88]). Such a tool aids in the automated creation of prompt, menu, form or window-based software, using keyboards or pointing devices for input. An interface generator also provides capabilities for command combination into macrocommands and interaction with input command scripts or output history files. But if an interface generator is not available, it is up to the software engineer to design these capabilities directly.

A command language, in one form or another, is often the vehicle of communication for the user. This kind of interaction has the appeal of allowing a high degree of experimentation and control on the part of the user. It also makes task division and control of the pace of the interaction easier. Command languages can usually be customized by providing a macro facility, by which the user can define a single command that represents an entire series of previously defined commands. This type of flexibility and power can be very attractive to the experienced user.

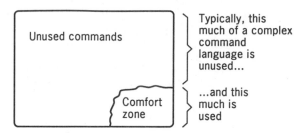

**FIGURE 5-12**    USERS TAKE ADVANTAGE OF ONLY A SMALL PORTION OF THE COMMANDS

Although command languages give the user more control over the sequence of actions, they also require the memorization of syntactic rules. The syntax of the language can range from the very simple, single-verb type, through complex combinations of verbs, parameters, and qualifiers, to English (or other natural language) interactions. The least and most complex of these are generally the easiest to use because of their naturalness or their familiarity. Writing software to correctly interpret complex English-like commands is, granted, quite difficult. Complex, but nonnatural, command languages often provide more functionality than users can handle. Experienced users usually settle on a subset of preferred commands, representing perhaps 20% of the total (Figure 5-12).

Certain rules should always be observed in defining the syntax of a command language. First, the commands themselves describe their function; it often helps to use a less common and more technical word, since these usually have a more sharply defined meaning. Second, there should be a single syntactic rule defining the ordering of commands, arguments, and options. Such consistency is of great importance.

Third, commands should be organized in such a way as to facilitate their use. In single-keystroke languages, this can take the form of prefixing all cursor movement commands with one stroke, all block commands with another, all file commands with a third, and so on. Another important organization technique is to provide identical structure for parallel operations. Thus, commands that output data to a screen, a printer, or a plotter should be identical except in specifying the destination device.

For the middle case between user- and computer-dominated interaction, complexity can be offset by a judicious choice of default parameters and qualifiers. This allows the command language to naturally tailor itself to the novice as well as to the expert user. The novice specifies a verb with no qualifiers and perhaps no parameters — this results in the expected, standard action of the verb. On the other hand, an expert can specify any one of a number of qualifiers that will result in tailored, special, and nonstandard actions. Of course, the expert has to know and to remember more than the novice, but that's what being an expert is all about.

The ability to abbreviate verbs and parameters is related to the use of defaults and is equally important to users. The novice will likely spell things out in full, whereas the expert will learn and use very short abbreviations or mnemonics. It is up to the interface designer to choose command names that make abbreviations unique. Experts are also more likely to make use of function keys, to combine several commands or operations on one line, or to construct conditional commands and macros.

The help facility for command language interaction is of necessity more complicated. Since the user is in control, he may legitimately want to get help on a wide variety of subjects. Thus, there must be a way of displaying quickly a large amount of information, allowing the user to select topics for further consideration, and permitting the user to navigate the help database. We should remember that ease of access to information is as important as the information itself ([DRA85]). It is useful to make the help facility context sensitive, displaying information appropriate to the current state of the software or mode of user interaction.

## 5.3.3 The Output Interface

There are probably two principles of good output interface design: organize the output carefully, and communicate as clearly and quickly as possible.

Organization is aided by grouping related output together and separating it from unrelated data. Another aid is the use of consistent notation. Input and output data should be presented in the same format, where possible, and common features of different screens and windows (prompt placement, window identification, menu style, and so on) should be presented in the same way on all screens. Figures 5-13 and 5-14 contrast two approaches (bad and good) to the problem of organizing. The first shows the output from a debugger using standard line-oriented output, which is controlling a program that does the same. The second shows a debugger using a window interface and running a window-oriented version of the program.

Most terminals today allow the designer to address positions on the screen. This permits us to avoid the scrolling problem shown in Figure 5-13. Instead, we create windows, that is, independent sections of the screen, each containing related data. Within windows, we may again avoid scrolling by having a static display, like the code

```
DBG>step
Stepped to line 9
TYPE *,"What is the speed?"
DBG>step
What is the speed?
stepped to line 10
ACCEPT *, SPEED
DBG>step
75
stepped to line 11
TYPE *,"What is the wind vector?"
DBG>examine widn
Unknown identifier-widn
DBG>
```

**FIGURE 5-13** BADLY CONSTRUCTED SCREEN

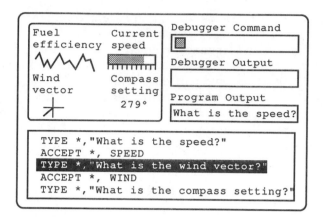

**FIGURE 5-14**   WELL DESIGNED SCREEN

window in Figure 5-14. The stability thus created allows the user to know where to look for a specific piece of information rather than having to scan through a past history, as in Figure 5-13.

Good screen design will avoid busyness in several ways: no extraneous information will be presented; unnecessary motion in the form of scrolling and display refreshing will be minimized; and wide separation of windows will eliminate the problem of reading a densely packed screen. These principles provide aids to the short-term memory problems as well as assisting the user in organizing data and tasks. Where possible, it is also wise to allow the user an option to control the amount and presentation style of data. This will permit individuals to tailor displays for maximum personal efficiency and to satisfy their need to control the environment.

The principle of clear and quick presentation of data dictates the use of graphic representation of data wherever possible. This includes the use of familiar shapes like the dials and arrows of Figure 5-14. *Limited* use of icons, colors, highlighting, reverse and blinking video, special fonts, and sound is valuable. These help in the selection of the most important data from the display or to provide visual clues to the meaning of the data. Boundaries and graphs assist in comparative judgment, again, as shown in Figure 5-14.

The bandwidth of graphic presentation of information is much higher than that of textual presentation. Our brains are able to extract patterns from visual fields quickly ([BO 82]), and our eyes are set up for real-time processing ([FEL87]). Humans identify and react to shapes and motion in one fiftieth of a second, whereas reading and reacting to an equivalent written stimulus might take more than 1 second. In addition, we have random access to a field of view. For this reason, visual, graphic display of information, where possible, improves the performance of computer users ([UMA88]).

The software engineer should specify a reasonable level of user reassurance and feedback to keep users' confidence. This could include messages like "About to update files," or "working on block 17" updated each time through a loop, or a target and completion bar graph that looks like this

| .............................                                                            |
0%                                                                              100%

and is updated at appropriate moments. Only very reliable software with very naïve or trusting users can leave a screen dead for minutes at a time.

Every effort should be made to maintain low variability in the time used to complete user requests. This does not mean that all instances of a task have to have the same response time, although rumor has it that a major manufacturer issued software which, if it completed more quickly than worst-case time, simply went to sleep until that time arrived. Instead, if the software detects that extraordinary measures (and processor time) will be required, an initial response of the type "this will take longer than expected, please stand by" should be given. If the required time is again longer than the reasonable response time, additional reassurance messages must be given.

## 5.3.4 Dealing with User Errors

Users will display greater acceptance of software that is robust. This means that efforts should be made to "bullet proof" the product in terms of handling badly formatted and out-of-range data. No software should die, perhaps destroying many minutes of work, because a user hit the "e" key instead of the "3" key. When commands are input that have drastic effects (like PIP/DE *.* in Section 5.2.1), the command language should be designed to require extra effort from the user to formulate the command properly and then may still have to request from the user confirmation of the command.

Designing the user interface to minimize the occurrence of user errors is an important part of good software engineering. Error reporting should be tailored to the level of user experience and the context of user operations. Remember that direct manipulation and menu systems are safer than other command interfaces, since they present only relatively safe choices. Command languages allow more latitude, but this includes the possibility of errors.

Norman suggests ([NOR83]) that there are four kinds of errors that may occur (see Figure 5-15). *Mode* errors happen when a command is issued that is inappropriate for the current command mode (e.g., file system commands during text editing). Mode errors can be minimized by giving plenty of visual cues to keep the user aware of the current mode. It is also important to ensure that a command does not have two distinct

Error Types

| | |
|---|---|
| Mode | Inappropriate command |
| Description | Ill-formed command |
| Capture | Thoughtless command |
| Activation | Incomplete or interrupted command |

**FIGURE 5-15**   COMMAND ERROR CATEGORIES

meanings in two distinct modes. Otherwise, a mode error might result in a mistaken and possibly disastrous error instead of a simple error message.

It is good to minimize the impact of modes, inasmuch as possible, by having a common set of commands with identical meaning in all modes, even though they may have some context-sensitive variations in the different modes. Among the commands that ought to be always present are those that *interrupt* the interaction ([PER88]): HELP, QUIT, SUSPEND (for later resumption), UNDO, REDO (if the user missed what was happening).

*Description* errors occur when the user formulates a command incorrectly: reversed parameters, unrecognized synonyms (remove instead of delete), and use of an altmode where a control key was needed are all examples. These errors can be reduced by using direct manipulation or menu interfaces, especially when their structure truly mirrors the underlying system. If a command language is consistent in its rules for parameter and option specification and command abbreviation, users will make fewer description errors. This consistency also allows user to learn by analogy.

It is also possible to reduce some description error rates by using multiple synonyms (aliases) for commands ([FUR87]). Since the command names used by designers may not be obvious, or even appropriate, we can obtain a set of words that users would choose for the function being invoked. The software would then react to each such command alias just as it would for the command name. Aliases can be derived from existing vocabulary databases or can be captured by the software when an unrecognized command is finally resolved by the user. We might even go to the extent of taking a set of common words and mapping all of them to the most appropriate command function(s), rather than trying to think up a name and a few aliases.

Using aliases is most important when dealing with infrequent or naïve users. When a dozen or more aliases are available, first-time success in giving a command can rise from around 15% to 80%. In case of possible ambiguity in an alias, the system can present the various sets of mutual aliases, and let the user pick the right category. The fact that common words tend to have multiple and contradictory meanings indicates that in nonaliasing command languages, less common (and more precise) names should be chosen for commands.

*Capture* errors occur when the user gives a habitual, rather than intended, command response. In defense, the software engineer should make certain that plenty of feedback is provided at points in which standard and nonstandard commands branch away from each other. If an action is dangerous, it should be difficult to formulate and implement. This goes beyond a request for confirmation; Newman says that people often react to requests for confirmation by saying "yes, yes, yes, yes. Oh dear!." Some kind of "undo" capability should be provided if this might happen to a user.

Finally, Norman describes *activation* errors in which the user forgets what he intends to do. Visual reminders about what has been going on (like overlapping open windows) are one way of solving the problem. Shneiderman [SHN87] suggests 3 ways to reduce the likelihood that users will commit certain kinds of activation errors: automatic completion of unmatched pairs, task sequence completion, and command correction.

Unmatched pairs occur when the command syntax requires two elements like opening and closing parentheses or apostrophes, or perhaps markers like underline-on and underline-off. At the least, the software should provide error messages flagging the unmatched element of the pair. A better solution is to create the closing half automatically whenever the opening half of the pair is entered, with further text being placed between them until the user escapes the pairs by some special keystroke.

Task sequences may be incomplete because the user becomes confused in the middle of the process, forgets how to complete the task, or is interrupted. In the easiest case, it should be possible for the user to pre-specify the intended sequence of a given task. Then a problem can be alleviated by suggesting this completion path. It may also be that the sequence is dictated by the syntax of the command language. For instance, an operating system might require the COPY command to be followed by two parameters. If the user forgets their order, he could type COPY and strike return, at which point the system software would prompt for the source files and then the destination filenames.

Users may also be aided by creating a template within which to work when an identifiable task is initiated. A language-oriented editor could respond to the word IF by echoing

```
IF <condition> THEN
        BEGIN
        END
ELSE
        BEGIN
        END;
```

and placing the cursor on the condition. The user could complete the task by fleshing out the template.

Command correction is needed when an incompatible or badly constructed command is issued. In its best form, this provides a DWIM (do what I mean) command correction and confirmation system. At a minimum, some indication should be given of the problem. Error messages should be nonjudgmental; otherwise, it may seem to the user that the product is usurping control of the interaction. A condemnatory message like "Bad Command — DEELTE" should be rewritten as "System can't process DEELTE: possible replacement is DELETE." If it is impossible to suggest one or two replacements, then a list of all acceptable commands at this point can be displayed, allowing the user to select one of them by pointing. In the same vein, a missing file error can be corrected by presenting a list of all files in the directory for selection.

Although it may be impossible to predict, *a priori*, which errors will be committed by users, we can get a good estimate from experimentation with prototypes. Even after the software is in use, it can be instrumented to gather information about the frequency with which different errors occur. By gathering and analyzing the information produced at individual sites by the instrumentation, designers can take steps to optimize both error messages and error handling procedures.

## 5.4 FOSTERING QUALITY DURING EXTERNAL DESIGN

For the external design, Shneiderman [SHN87] suggests five possible metrics (Figure 5-16).

Additional metrics from Perlman ([PER88]) include the frequency of use of the help facility or the manual, location, and duration of eye fixation, and subjective ratings of ease of use, ease of learning, throughput, and esthetics.

These metrics should be determined through controlled experiments, using system prototypes, simulations, or models. Of course, the degree of skill and experience of these experimental subjects should be recorded as factors in the data, since we want to measure the software, not the users. Because these metrics have a "psychological" flavor to them, Curtis ([CUR87]) suggests that the techniques of cognitive science, statistics, and psychology should be used in determining these measurements. Even then it is dangerous for novices in these sciences to use measurements as absolute explanations; instead, the measurements should be used as diagnostic indicators.

Another set of metrics for screen design are proposed by Tullis in [TUL84]. They are overall density (percentage of total character positions that are nonblank), local density (in a circle whose diameter measures 5 degrees of visual angle), grouping (size of a group where distance between adjacent characters is less than half the width of boundaries surrounding the group), and layout complexity.

The principal validation effort during external design is simply that of trying out the user interface prototypes on users to determine whether the prototypes are acceptable. Sommerville ([SOM89]) suggests providing a "gripe button" to allow users to record their reactions immediately as they occur. In terms of verification, there is a two-way process of comparing specifications against external design and external design against specifications.

The management challenges of this phase are not great. If we are able to conduct the entire activity with a small, cohesive group, our communication and product control problems will be reduced. It is sometimes difficult to find people with sufficient training in computer science, cognitive science, *and* software engineering, however.

## 5.5 AN EXTERNAL DESIGN EXAMPLE

In keeping with the exploratory nature of external design, this section is written as a sort of journal in which experience, commentary, and documentation are combined. Actual specifications and design are generally italicized.


- Time required to learn to use the software for a given task.
- Speed at which the user can carry out a given task.
- Rate of errors by users in carrying out a given task.
- Subjective satisfaction users feel for the software.
- Retention of knowledge and skills by users over time.

**FIGURE 5-16**   METRICS FOR ETERNAL DESIGN

### 5.5.1 File Format

The specifications did not make clear what the exact structure of the output file is to be. Note, however, that the specifications imply that data will be output encoded in ASCII characters, since there would otherwise be no distinction between the HEX and DEC formats. On the other hand, to thus encode the data, and still meet the requirements that a cleaned frame occupies "less than 40 bytes," we would only be able to represent the floating point values with three digits of precision, a significant loss.

We decide that the *output will be in binary, rather than ASCII-encoded, form*, requiring a nonessential change in the specifications for this part of the software and for other parts as well. Since this change will improve processing times by avoiding encoding and decoding data in successive steps, we decide to modify the specifications. This change is approved unanimously by the software team and the customer.

The output file format will be a 2200 byte header followed by at least 350 whole frames. *Each frame will include the following fields of binary encoded data:*

| | |
|---|---|
| Housekeeping data identification number | 1 byte |
| Housekeeping data word | 2 bytes |
| Day | 2 bytes |
| Hour | 1 byte |
| Minute | 1 byte |
| Second | 1 byte |
| Heading | 4 bytes |
| Detector readings, 1 through 5 | 5x4 bytes |
| Noise monitor reading | <u>4 bytes</u> |
| **Total** | 36 bytes |

### 5.5.2 Operator Interface

During analysis the software team decided to estimate the speed with which a single byte will be processed by the software. This was done by calculating the time required to read an "average" sized block (1K bytes) from the tape, doubling this for processing, then dividing by 1K to get a per-byte time expenditure. It was obviously well within the acceptable limits for processing speed. But, in fact, it indicated that bytes would be processed at a rate of 45 per second. This raises concerns about the acceptability of the scrolled message screen interface, controlled by control-s and control-q keystrokes. Even though the users suggested this interface, no one on the software team thinks they will be happy with it.

To explore this question, an event-driven simulator is built. Its effect is to schedule various events, listed as follows, and then to display the specified messages on the screen. The timing of elapsed bytes is controlled at 45 per second by a null loop. Events Acquire and Lose refer to acquisition or loss of synchronization.

| At Event | Schedule Event | After Delay (bytes) | With Probability |
|---|---|---|---|
| Start | End of File | 1,500 | 0.1 |
| | | 2,500 | 0.1 |
| | | 18,000 | 0.5 |
| | | 40,000 | 0.2 |
| | | 80,000 | 0.1 |
| Start | End of Header | 2,200 | 1.0 |
| Ready or end of head | Reset | 10,000 to 20,000 | Uniform |
| Reset | Ready | 4,000 to 6,000 | Uniform |
| Acquire or end of head | Lose | 0 | 0.1 |
| | | 1,000 | 0.1 |
| | | 3,000 | 0.1 |
| | | 7,000 | 0.1 |
| | | 13,000 | 0.1 |
| | | 16,000 | 0.5 |
| (reported cause of loss ) | | Synch signal | 0.34 |
| | | Frame ID | 0.33 |
| | | Time stamp | 0.33 |
| Lose | Acquire | 0 to 2,000 | Uniform |

As expected, both the software team and the users find that they cannot capture information in a usable form when it is scrolled at realistic rates. In the process, they also note that the specifications are inadequate in that they fail to *report loss of usable frames due to a reset event*. The specifications are altered to include this additional event.

### 5.5.3 Screen Design

The next step is to design a screen on which information can be displayed in a stable, organized, and readable fashion. It is decided that some peripheral information can be included at no cost. The *designed screen's appearance is*

```
               Starting Frame Timestamp DDD HH:MM:SS
                    Current Timestamp  DDD HH:MM:SS

                   Now Processing...CURRENT DATATYPE

      Last Event...................LAST EVENT...at byte BBBBBBBB

      Current Value..........................XX....at byte BBBBBBBB
```

The possible values for CURRENT DATATYPE are "Header," "Valid Frame #######," "Bonus Frame #######" (used when the consecutive sequence of valid frames has exceeded 350 in number), "Reset Frames" (used when the value of the reset signal is not 00 00) and "Garbage" (used when synchronization has been lost). The possible values for LAST EVENT are "Valid Sequence Begun," "Frame Synch Signal Lost," "Frame ID Lost," "Timestamp Lost," "Entered Reset," "End of File in Header," "EOF-No Valid Sequence," "EOF-File

*Created," and "Synch Lost-File Created." The Current Value line is only displayed when the user has specified the -d option.*

After experimenting with this screen layout, the users are happy, except that use of control-s and control-q keystrokes are not adequate to stop the flow of data in time to capture the information that triggered the desire to stop it. Also note that painting the screen without the Current Value line does not significantly slow down the simulated processing.

### 5.5.4 Screen Control

In the next interface prototype, it is decided to alter the user options to -d and -s, standing for data logging and single step. *When no option is specified, the screen as shown above, without the Current Value line, will be updated without any possibility of pausing. With the -d option, the LAST EVENTs will be written to a disk logging file as they are displayed. With the -s option, disk logging will occur as with -d and the processing will proceed in single steps, with the user striking any key to proceed to the next step, and the Current Value line will be displayed.*

After experimenting, we decide that standard mode is working fine, but that the -s mode is too slow to be acceptable. In thinking how the stepwise processing mode might be used, we decide that it will only be used to debug bad data streams and that the user will be able to capture an approximate byte location for the problem in standard mode and then rerun the processing in -s mode with a breakpoint set. The next version *allows the user to start the software with an option of -s BBBBBBBB. Processing will proceed in standard mode until the processing of the specified byte, at which time processing will continue in single-step mode as before.*

The users are happy with this compromise, but they point out that if the operator is not paying attention, he may miss the LAST EVENT that causes termination of processing, as the batch job initiates processing of a new file and overwrites the old screen. We decide that *upon termination the software will issue five distinct BELL characters and then pause for 30 seconds so that the screen will be seen by the operator if he desires. The software team asks about the possible use of blinking, reverse video, and the like. It is decided to reverse the fields labeled CURRENT DATATYPE, LAST EVENT, XX and BBBBBBBB in the screen layout above.*

Appropriate changes are made to the Preliminary User's Manual, including a definition of the meaning of all messages, with suggestions for user action in error cases. Plans are made to continue to test the interface for tuning purposes as the actual software becomes available to replace the simulation. Once the interface has become validated, actual dumps of the various screen states will be made for inclusion in the User's Manual.

## 5.6 SUMMARY

The external design phase defines the interface between the software and its environment — human, operating, software, and hardware. This phase generally extends across various life cycle stages (analysis, specification, design, and implementation). However, we want to complete most external design activities before the beginning of the implementation effort. To allow for isolation of the changes that may occur after architectural design has started, the appropriate interfaces have to be heavily encapsulated in separate modules.

This same modularity makes it possible for us to design and tune the user interface by means of a sequence of many prototypes. Since we are usually dealing with an incompletely understood element (the user), exploratory prototyping is frequently the most effective, and sometimes the only method for developing a correct design. But before we strike off into our prototyping efforts, we must develop a thorough profile of users determining their needs, the tasks they will accomplish with the software, their experience and training, and their psychological needs and limitations.

In general, the user interface should be designed to provide a natural, dependable, productive, and pleasant computational environment for the user. This will involve the careful design of input techniques, with a selection of methods from among full screen forms, menus, command languages, natural language, and direct manipulation. The output interface will likely depend on simple, stable, and graphically oriented screen designs. It should take advantage of the high bandwidth provided by visual information transmission. We must also take into account user reactions to response time and processing speed.

Another important aspect of the user interface is the management of errors. To be done properly, this requires knowledge of the classification of errors, a study of what error conditions might occur during the execution of the product, decisions about what response should be given to errors, and design of a comprehensive set of error messages.

People don't like to be put into uncertain, stressful or difficult situations. They don't even like to wonder which of two keys is the right one to use in a door. If their software isn't friendly to them, then it is in jeopardy. Proper external design is the key to *that* door.

## BIBLIOGRAPHY

[BO 82]     Bo, K., "Human-Computer Interaction," *Computer* 15(11):9 – 11.

[CAR83]*    Card, S.K., T.P. Moran, and A. Newell, *The Psychology of Human-Computer Interaction*, Lawrence Erlbaum Associates, Hillsdale, NJ.

[CAR84]     Carroll, J.M., and C. Carrithers, "Training Wheels in a User Interface," *Communications of the ACM*, 27(8):800 – 806.

[CUR87]     Curtis, B., "Foundations for a Measurement Discipline," *IEEE Software*, 4(6):89 – 92.

[DRA85]*    Draper, S.W., and D.A. Norman, "Software Engineering for User Interfaces," *IEEE Transactions on Software Engineering*, 11(3):252 – 258.

[FEL87]*    Feller, P.H., "User Interface Technology Survey," *Software Engineering Institute*, CME/SEI-87-TR-6, Pittsburgh, PA.

[FUR87]* Furnas, G.W., T.K. Landauer, L.M. Gomez, and S.T. Dumais, "The Vocabulary Problem in Human-System Communication," *Communications of the ACM*, 30(11):964 – 971.

[GOO87] Goodwin, N.C., "Functionality and Usability," *Communications of the ACM*, 30(3):229 – 233.

[GOU85]* Gould, J.D., and C. Lewis, "Designing for Usability," *Communications of the ACM*, 28(3):300 – 311.

[GOU87]* Gould, J.D., S.J. Boies, S. Levy, J.T. Richards, and J. Schoonard, "The 1984 Olympic Message System: A Test of Behavioral Principles of System Design," *Communications of the ACM*, 30(9):758 – 769.

[GUY88]* Guynes, J.L., "Impact of System Response Time on State Anxiety," *Communications of the ACM*, 31(3):342 – 347.

[HAR89] Hartson, R., "User-Interface Management Control and Communication," *IEEE Software*, 6(1):62 – 70.

[MAN88] Mantei, M.M., and T.J. Teorey, "Cost/Benefit Analysis for Incorporating Human Factors in the Software Lifecycle," *Communications of the ACM*, 31(4):428 – 439.

[MOR83] Morland, D.V., "Human Factors Guidelines for Terminal Interface Design," *Communications of the ACM*, 26(7):484 – 494.

[MYE89]* Myers, B.A., "User-Interface Tools: Introduction and Survey," *IEEE Software*, 6(1):15 – 23.

[NOR83]* Norman, D.A., "Design Rules Based on Analyses of Human Error," *Communications of the ACM*, 26(4):254 – 258.

[PER88]* Perlman, G., "User Interface Development," *Software Engineering Institute*, SEI-CM-17-1.0, Pittsburgh, PA.

[POT87] Potosnak, K., "Where Human Factors Fit in the Design Process," *IEEE Software*, 4(5):86 – 87, 4(6):90 – 92.

[RAM86]* Ramamoorthy, C.V., V. Garg, and A. Prakash, "Programming in the Large," *IEEE Transactions on Software Engineering*, 12(7):769 – 783.

[ROS88] Rossen, M.B., S. Maass, and W.A. Kellogg, "The Designer as User," *Communications of the ACM*, 31(11):1288 – 1298.

[SHN87]* Shneiderman, B., *Designing the User Interface*, Addison-Wesley, Reading, MA.

[SOM89] Sommerville, I., *Software Engineering*, Addison-Wesley, Reading, MA.

[STO88] Stott, J.W., and J.E. Kottemann, "Anatomy of a Compact User Interface Development Tool," *Communications of the ACM*, 31(1):56 – 66.

[THO89] Thomas, JC, and WA Kellogg, "Minimizing Ecological Gaps in Interface Design," *IEEE Software*, 6(1):78 – 86.

[TUL84] Tullis, T.S., "Predicting the Usability of Alphanumeric Displays," Ph.D. dissertation, University of Kansas, Lawrence, KS.

[UMA88] Umanath, N.S., and R.W. Scamell, "An Experimental Evaluation of the Impact of Data Display Format on Recall Performance," *Communications of the ACM*, 31(5):562 – 570.

## PROBLEMS

1  Design and write general code to accept as a parameter some data structure consisting of a 24x80 character form, default values for some fields, and data validity assertions for all the fields of the form. Your software should display the form and allow a user to fill it out. It should warn the user of invalid data and allow him to correct data through use of an erasure key (backspace or delete), and also by using cursor control to move to a field and enter data over the data in the field. You might use COBOL's PIC as a guide to data validity categories.

2  Write code to experiment with the differences in time required to form absolute and comparative judgment. Test the code on at least 10 other people and report the results with the code.

3  Write code to experiment with the duration and capacity of short-term memory. Test it on at least 10 other people and report the results with the code.

4  Design a code segment to prompt, input, and test a four-digit hexadecimal number between -20,000 and 20,000 inclusive. The code should require the user to either supply a correct value or terminate this portion of processing. No incorrect characters should be echoed to the screen.

5  Why is external design not a part of the specification stage?

6  Sketch a prototype "training wheels" interface for text editors. Validate it by means of a hallway survey.

7  Select a single function from the project you worked on in Problem 15 in Chapter 4. Develop the external design, including the input and output interfaces, error message lists and display, and constraints on timing and response.

8  Write code for a command language shell that can be run as the interface to an existing operating system on a fast computer. Put in busy-wait loops that will delay echoing of keystrokes, as well as loops to delay the system's response to commands. Set the delay loop defaults to be fairly slow but allow users to speed up echo and response incrementally by issuing two distinct, special single keystrokes. Keep track of, and report on, the rates that users consider to be optimal for echoing and for each command. How do they differ for different types of commands?

9  Give examples of mode, description, capture, and activation errors that occur during the use of a word processing product with which you are familiar.

10  Describe a command language for a software project database.

11  Describe a menu system for a software project database.

12  Do a task analysis for students using the student registration system.

13  Some users of window-based operating systems complain that they are slower in using them than they are in using command language-based operating systems.

Devise an experiment to confirm or refute this.

**14** Give examples of software products for which the external design is a relatively unimportant activity.

**15** Evaluate three journals that concentrate on computer-human interaction.

# CHAPTER 6

# THE DESIGN STAGE

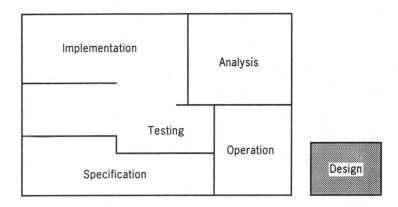

Design, as a general activity, is defined by Nobel laureate Herbert Simon as "devising artifacts to attain goals." Devising is not manufacturing; the end result of design is not a usable product, but rather a plan or outline for creating a usable product. It is important to note in Simon's definition that the likelihood of attaining our goals is the primary measure of good design. Finally, the end result of design will be an artifact, the product of skilled workmanship. It is not simply an artistic effort, although the results are often artistic.

Freeman thinks that design is the integrative activity that lies at the core of software engineering ([FRE87]). In other words, all other software-related activities can be seen as either preparation for, or completion of, design. To carry out effective design, we must understand not only the technical design process, but we must also have extensive knowledge of other areas of computer science like algorithm analysis, data structures, programming languages, or human — computer interaction. Design is the crux of software engineering (Figure 6-1).

The software design stage continues to build the software product by transforming the specifications into a detailed design. There are three levels of design, each using its own notation(s): external, which we have already examined, architectural (sometimes called preliminary design), and detailed. The design notations of the work products

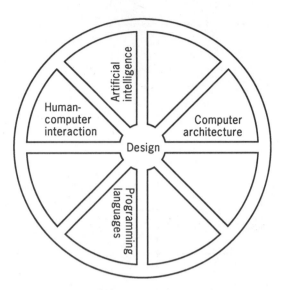

**F I G U R E 6-1**    DESIGN IS THE HUB ON WHICH THE COMPUTER SCIENCE WHEEL TURNS

should be sufficiently formal to allow for automated support of the design process. The detailed design will be a conceptual model of the actual code, which will be produced at the following stage of the software life cycle.

## 6.1 THE DESIGN PROCESS AND PRODUCTS

During design we need to integrate a body of knowledge that is both technical and general, software engineering- and application-oriented, practical and creative. We will use this knowledge to shape the product. Starting with specifications, which are amorphous insofar as the internal workings of the product are concerned, we end up with a detailed conceptualization of the data structures and procedures that constitute the software. This is done by developing a series of approximations of the whole product. The final step concentrates on actions wholly hidden to the user, each one so specialized that not even the other parts of the software need to know what is going on. As a result, the final part of design can be divided among independent detail workers.

Although the design stage is carried out at three levels, the process is actually a stepwise movement from one extreme to the other. The number of intermediate steps depends basically on the size of the product. As shown in Figure 6-2, we go from the external design to the detailed design by way of a number of ever more detailed architectural designs. At each of these intermediate stages, the same sequence of events is repeated: decompose an existing component conceptually, describe an interface between the new, smaller components, and finally define the smaller components formally. We always settle on an interface before defining the exact nature of the components.

**FIGURE 6-2**   THE STRUCTURE OF THE DESIGN STAGE

The design process within the entire context of the software life cycle is outlined by Kant in [KAN85] as consisting of the following steps. First, we must *understand* the problem (analysis and specification). Next, we *plan* a solution based on a central idea and *refine* that solution by elaborating this concept. This step probably represents architectural design. The third step is to *execute* the partially specified solution in order to analyze its behavior (prototyping). Following this, we deal with any *difficulties and opportunities* that the prototype has disclosed. Finally, we *verify* the correctness of the solution and *evaluate* its performance. If the solution is not satisfactory, we iterate the entire design process.

Software engineers should possess several important design skills according to Kant (listed in Figure 6-3). These skills imply the possession of a wide range of knowledge, both in software engineering and the application area; an ability to manage several viewpoints and diverse acceptability criteria at the same time; and mental agility in recognizing potential solutions by considering all of the alternatives and thinking through the algorithmic process.

## 6.1.1 Purpose of the Design Stage

The purpose of the design stage is to describe completely the "how" of the software. During the process we will first subdivide and organize the software into interconnecting components. This is done for purposes of comprehension, reusability, division of effort among software engineers, error confinement, and establishment of intellectual control over the host of details that will shortly be introduced. Next, we will introduce those details, designing the exact processes and data structures necessary to provide the software product specified by the user.

A software engineer should be able to:
- Search for a good design when one is not self-evident.
- Evaluate/investigate solutions from several viewpoints.
- Recognize potential design solutions.
- Execute solutions in his head.
- Have a large repertoire of algorithms.
- Understand the application domain.
- Estimate the efficiency of solutions.
- Generate comprehensive examples and test cases.

**FIGURE 6-3** TRAITS OF A GOOD SOFTWARE DESIGNER

Designers face a number of problems, but one of the most significant is that of maintaining intellectual control over the complexity of the design of large products. Good methodology and notation will allow a designer to carry design further before becoming lost in complexity. At some point, the design task will probably be subdivided among independent groups or individuals. However, the product will be of higher quality if its design is under single control until its philosophical and stylistic unity has been guaranteed. If this occurs, both users and maintainers of the product will have an easier time understanding it.

Where possible, the point at which we pass from architectural to detailed design should coincide with the point of subdividing work to separate groups. This isn't feasible with very large products, however. In any case, the hallmark of architectural design is that it focuses on abstractions and on the interfaces between the components that embody these abstractions. The architectural product is still entirely conceptual and possesses as yet no procedural detail. The structure and organization of this web of interacting components are the special concern of architectural design.

The detailed design level adds all of the particulars of procedural control and data structuring but does not include any implementation-specific minutiae. A good detailed design can be coded later into any programming language on any computer system that provides the basic system capabilities envisioned in the design. Portability of the detailed design maximizes the possibility of its reuse, as well as increasing its understandability by avoiding inessential system-dependent distinctions. The detailed design is still conceptual to this degree.

## 6.1.2 Activities During Design

The guiding principle of design is to consider all of the different facets of the software: function, data, and control. For the function and data facets, we start with their definitions as they appear in the specifications. We then establish a conceptual organization that subdivides *function* into a hierarchy of subfunctions and clusters them around natural *data* entities. These subdivisions are usually called **modules,** which means that they are well-defined, independent units. When the conceptual structure is complete, we proceed to define the details of procedural *control* that will allow the function to be performed. We also describe the structural details of *data* entities that will enable the execution of the procedure.

The process of transforming one architectural design into the following, more elaborate, design is based on the division of a software module, with a well-defined interface to its environment, into several submodules with newly defined interfaces between them. Each of these modules is defined by function and data clustering. Our stepwise design process creates an increasing refinement of the modules.

Hoare gives an interesting example in [HOA87] of how this process of intermediate designs can be viewed, not as successively more detailed versions of the same basic design, but as successive prototype designs of differing nature. In fact, he shows the initial specifications of a subroutine successively in the form of a logic program (e.g., in Prolog), an algebraic-style specification, a functional or applicative program, an optimized functional program, and finally as a detailed procedural design. At each step, mathematical analysis is used to verify correctness and to assess the efficiency of the design.

Detailed design is carried out when the functionality of the modules has been completely developed. At this point, the design methodology shifts from emphasis on function and data clustering to emphasis on control and data structuring. It is likely that the methodologies used in external, architectural, and detailed design will be distinct as a result of these shifts in viewpoint.

Since the main function of architectural design is to create modules and interfaces, we ought to say a little more about these two concepts. A module is supposed to be a well-defined and independent unit. In electronics, we expect that modules can be removed and replaced by others that conform to the same interface standards and provide the same functionality. In particular, *we do not have to know what is going on inside a module to use it.*

As a result of the historical quirks of the development of software engineering, use of the word "module" calls up the idea of a subprogram, a procedure to provide some specific function. However, data can exhibit modularity just as a function can. Thus, by all rights, a module should equally call to mind the idea of an abstract data type.

Just as we understand that the subprogram will provide internal data structuring to act on the actual data passed to it through its interface, so an abstract data type should provide internal procedures to act on the functional requests passed to it through its interface. There is a fundamental duality between data and function: each can be expressed by modularity, each can be passed through interface connections, each can be the central concept of a design methodology (Figure 6-4).

Because of our software cultural heritage, we frequently concentrate too much on the design of control and function at the expense of data. However, the functional requirements are no more important than the data dictionary; and the same efforts should be expended in cataloging and analyzing the data requirements as the functional requirements. Indeed, many users consider data to be the fundamental issue (hence, the use of the term "data processing" rather than "computing") and are better served by concentration on data.

In the analysis stage, we adopted a solution strategy and established standards. One part of that strategy was a decision to use a specific design methodology; it defines the balance of emphasis between data and function. On their part, the standards will

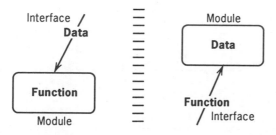

**F I G U R E 6-4**  THE DUALITY OF FUNCTION AND DATA

determine the kind and degree of modularity to be developed in the software. These criteria will permit us to evaluate the quality of the architectural design, as well as to determine the point at which we can switch over to detailed designing.

As we start architectural design, we need to identify the major modules (probably not more than 10) and the interfaces between them. These modules should be chosen rationally, with an eye to optimizing the structure of relationships they represent. If we are taking a function-oriented approach, optimization will concern itself with the relationship of invoked and invoking procedures, and with the sharing of data (see Figure 6-5). If we are taking a data-oriented approach, optimization will be concerned with the clustering of functions with data entities and with the visibility of one entity to another. When the optimization is complete, we need to formalize the structure, that is, the description of the interfaces and the definition of the modules. If adequate tools are available, we can use them to evaluate the consistency of the interfaces and the modularity of the modules.

Assuming that each of the major modules is too large, we now have to apply the same process recursively. Instead of the entire software package, we concentrate on a major module and identify the major submodules and the interfaces between them. Again we attempt to optimize the substructures and then the full structure, before continuing with the process. Next, we formalize the interface description and module definition. The recursion stops when modules are suitable for detailed design. This point can be determined by using the cohesion and decoupling metrics explained in Section 6.4.1.

Mills gives an alternate definition of architectural design in [MIL85] by suggesting that our concern should be for exploratory analysis of design issues and feasibility at the top level. Initially, a software system architect should be concerned with the shape

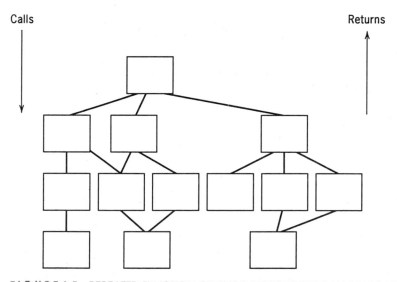

Calls                                                                                                            Returns

**F I G U R E 6-5**   REPEATED FUNCTION-ORIENTED DESIGN YIELDS AN INVOCATION HIERARCHY of the system as a whole, the order of development of the system and the direction it should take. Many of the more detailed concerns of architectural design should then be left to subordinate designers.

We started out by saying that design developed function, data, and control. We have said very little about control so far. In fact, the invocation structure represented by functional module refinement and the visibility structure represented by data module refinement are two kinds of control structure, and their creation is an important part of architectural design. Within modules, and during detailed design, we can create procedural control. **Procedural control** is the use of control constructs like iteration, selection, and sequencing, which allow the migration of a locus of control from one primitive operation to another. These control constructs will be represented in the eventual implementation by loops, if-then-else's, and so on.

Remember that a module may be data- or function-centered, but all modules contain both: procedures (or algorithms) for the implementation of function and data structures to be manipulated by the procedures.

It is obvious that, in detailed design, we are drawing near to the stage of actually implementing the software in some programming language. The question often arises: "Why not carry out detailed design by actually implementing the module?" First, the module may turn out to be rather large in terms of the number of lines it represents in the eventual language. In fact, it may still contain a number of different subprograms. It may require too much additional structuring before implementation is possible.

Second, the product may need to be implemented in several different languages for several different environments. To conduct detailed design in one language might require a later effort in reverse engineering to provide a basis for an equivalent implementation in another language.

Finally, there is still a great benefit to be derived from deferring details. There are many details required in implementation that are irrelevant to design. They represent no design decisions, but instead conformity to the peculiarities of languages and equipment. It is best to finalize the design before becoming enmeshed in this kind of detail.

Detailed design will be completed when the design decisions have all been made. Usually, this happens when we stop asking procedural kinds of questions (Should I use a case structure or an if structure?) and start to wonder about syntax (How many statements will this take?; Will I use a flag or a complex condition?). Typically, the volume of a detailed design is about one-fifth that of the final product; each design statement expands to five programming language statements.

During detailed design, we seek to optimize data structures and algorithms to achieve the goals stated in the project plan. In one instance, we might find that the performance of the product is primary; hence, elaborate algorithms and structures have to be devised to achieve blazing speed or incredible compactness. In another instance, a desire for cost effectiveness might lead us to choose data structures and algorithms that are easily implemented in a particular programming language on a particular machine. In still other cases, the need for a high level of maintainability might limit our choices to the most standard and easily understood options.

Whatever our goals are, we do our best to achieve them. But we should always govern our decisions by our goals and not by our predilections or prejudices. There is no point in optimizing detailed design for an attribute that is irrelevant to the goals of the project. This will only serve to expend effort without accomplishing an end that has been judged to be worthwhile. If we believe that the goal *is* worthwhile, then we can remember to include it in the plans next time.

Introduction
    Problem overview
    Application environment, user characteristics
    Notations used in the design
    Goals of the project
Review of Specifications
    Software functions
    Data descriptions
    Data relationships
    Priorities for implementation
    Constraints
    Exceptions
    Predicted modifications and maintenance
Architectural Design
    Hierarchical module and interface diagrams
    Function/data cluster description
    Interface specifications
Detailed Designs
    For each module:
        Module description
        Interface specification
        Process description
        Data structure definitions
        Initialization requirements
        Exception handling specification
Alternatives
    For each rejected architectural and detailed design:
        Brief description
        Reason for rejection
        Conditions that might favor it
Reference
    Documents used in developing the design
    Glossary of terms

**FIGURE 6-6**  THE DESIGN SPECIFICATION

## 6.1.3 Design Documents and Deliverables

The most important design stage work product is the Design Specification itself. Figure 6-6 shows an outline of its contents.

Quality assurance personnel can be looking forward to the time when implemented code needs to be tested. Actual data will be needed to test the software, and the data should exercise the code in as many ways as practical, to detect any possible residual errors that were not caught by reviews and inspections. Some of the data will be developed with an eye to the specific procedures and control flows represented by the detailed design. These will be applied to individual modules, and conformity to the predicted results will be assured. This kind of test is called a **unit test**, since it is carried out on an individual module, and the data and expected results for them are put into Unit Test Plans. The Unit Test Plans may be expanded as needed during implementation.

Unit tests fail to test the validity of interfaces between modules. This can best be done by combining several modules and observing their combined action on specially designed data. Here, the data are designed not so much to exercise specific loops or conditional branches as to test the connection and consistency of interface definitions. This kind of testing is called **integration** testing, and these plans are added to the Software Verification Plan.

To properly plan for integration testing, it is important to determine the order in which modules will be accreted to form larger subsystems, until they come together into the entire software package. This **integration sequence** also needs to be determined by quality assurance personnel during the design stage.

Besides Unit Test Plans, an augmented Software Verification Plan, an integration sequence, and the review minutes, the design stage should provide a User's Manual. After external design, the external behavior of the product is set, and it should be possible to describe it fully to the user. After the Critical Design Review, we would expect no substantive changes in the software's external behavior to be allowed; hence, it is safe to finalize the preliminary user's manual.

## 6.2 DESIGN PRINCIPLES

Design is a legitimate topic independent of its specific application, whether software, furniture, engines, or clothing. A survey of the general principles of good design should be interesting to any software engineer, but this kind of survey goes beyond the scope of this book (see [CRO84] and [JON70]). However, some of those general principles include functionality, minimality, and unity. These are all attributes that have been mentioned in connection with specification and design. Our major goal during the design stage is to produce a quality design in the context of a quality process. A set of attributes for both the designed software product and the software design process is given in Figure 6-7. These attributes are explained more fully in Section 6.2.1.

We may suppose that a good design methodology is one that implements the underlying principles of design and promotes both the process and product attributes

Product
    Realism (conformity to the real world)
    Modifiability
    Unity
    Clarity
    Reusability
Process (it allows us to:)
    Evaluate
    Integrate (with other stages)
    Automate
    Divide (effort among many people)
    Duplicate (can transfer methodology to others)
    Control (the conceptual complexity of the product)

**FIGURE 6-7**   SOME ATTRIBUTES OF GOOD SOFTWARE DESIGN

listed in Figure 6-7. Six attributes that characterize good design methodologies are discussed in Section 6.2.2. These attributes are not disjoint, however; they are ordered in a way that each tends to depend on, but augment, the previous one.

### 6.2.1 Goals for the Design Stage

We saw in Chapter 1 that the growing cost of maintenance for our base of current software products is a major problem. One of the reasons for the tremendous cost of maintenance is the effort expended by maintenance personnel in recapturing the concepts and decisions of the original design from the code itself, which is often the only document available to them. We must avoid the problem by producing and maintaining a complete, understandable, and well-organized design document (Figure 6-8).

The code is usually too large, complex, and interwoven to allow software engineers to modify it without incurring the risk of unwanted side effects. To maintain large products, we have to go back to some more abstract representation, at the level of design or specifications, to comprehend the implications of a change. It is then necessary to trace forward, following the effects of the change and thus locating all parts of the code that need modification to accommodate the change properly. A complete, up-to-date design document is necessary.

Thus, the maintenance software engineer needs to understand the original design just as well as the designer did. If that design was developed by using some kind of nonstandard notation or technique, the task of understanding it becomes much harder. When we are familiar with the design technique, we find ourselves repeating "Yes, I see, yes, uh-huh, yes." If the design is not methodical, or represents an unknown methodology , then we find ourselves asking "Why did he do that? Now what? What's he doing?" Understandable design documentation saves a great deal of time.

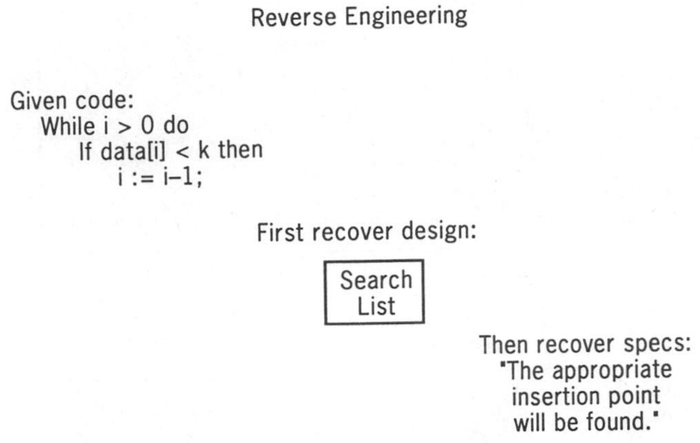

Reverse Engineering

```
Given code:
    While i > 0 do
        If data[i] < k then
            i := i–1;
```

First recover design:

```
┌──────────┐
│  Search  │
│   List   │
└──────────┘
```

Then recover specs:
"The appropriate
insertion point
will be found."

**FIGURE 6-8**   RECAPTURING DESIGN INFORMATION FROM CODE

Not only must a maintainer understand the design, he also has to duplicate it. The use of standard methodologies furthers this goal. When a software product experiences repeated modifications that are designed in a different way than the original, it begins to resemble a patchwork quilt. Additional maintenance faces the problem of dealing with a confusing variety of incompatible design styles, and the product degenerates to the point that it can no longer *be* maintained. On the other hand, to preserve the unity of style and philosophy in the software, which will enhance its future maintainability, we have to be able to design modifications by using the original methodology. This may be difficult if that methodology is nonexistent or is not standard.

Of course, tools and automation depend on the existence of well-defined standards, both in technique and notation, and their use is impossible without standards. Finally, most ad hoc designs end up being based on specific programming languages; portability is sacrificed when this happens. Opportunities to reuse design components are equally narrowed.

All this means that using standard design methodologies (which necessarily constrain creativity and elegance) provides us with important dividends: understandability, duplicability, automation, design portability and design reuse (Figure 6-9).

Two different value systems are at conflict during the design stage. On the one hand, practical values call for methodology, system, process efficiency, and automation. On the other hand, aesthetic values call for insight, creativity, elegance and craftsmanship. The question of the appropriate balance between these two value systems probably cannot be settled. Our attitude favors a pragmatic approach that stresses methodology and process efficiency.

One reason for this is that our software assembly line will come to a sudden halt if we abandon the principles of maximum use of tools and methodology. Second, quality assurance requires measurable criteria with which to work, and aesthetic values are usually a matter of taste rather than science. Finally, experience indicates that creative designers will still find scope for creativity within the framework of a methodology,

Design                                    Is supported by
                                              tools

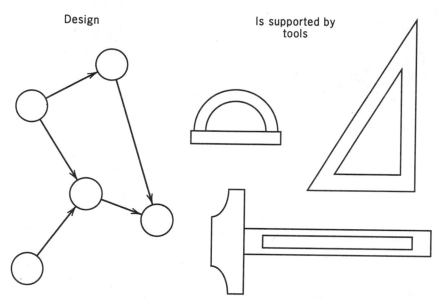

**FIGURE 6-9**   TOOL USE SUPPORTS GOOD DESIGN

whereas methodical designers are less likely to maintain productivity and discipline under rules that establish no guidelines except elegance (Figure 6-9).

Quality assurance during the design stage should verify that the work products meet their specifications, at the same time ensuring that the design standards established during planning are met. Thus, it is necessary that alternative designs be measured against the quality assurance standards to evaluate the degree with which they display the attributes of good design. This is not the only reason for the selection of one design over another, but it is a significant factor in such decisions.

Another goal of design is to use methodologies that are based on strong theoretical foundations. Dijkstra, Wirth and Mills are all contributors to design theory. One such theoretical technique has been proposed by Hoare et al. ([HO87a]). Their suggested Laws of Programming are used in conjunction with a design notation that is, in fact, a programming language. They find that three primitive operations are sufficient: assignment, halt, and abort (there is no I/O). These operations can be combined using sequence, conditional selection, iteration, recursion or nondeterministic choice.

At various levels, this notation can support both specification and design activities as well as implementation. Although the system gives a rational basis for design and a mathematical precision in verification, it is not practical at this time for large-scale software. One of the insights provided by this theory is a reason why design is difficult: design can be composed from simpler design but not in a way that mirrors specifications. We can break down specifications as a conjunction of simpler specifications. On the other hand, even if we create several designs, one for each simple specification, the conjunction of those designs will not satisfy the conjunction of the specifications. *Design decomposition is not guided by specification decomposition.* It is a much more complex issue.

Even though we are as methodical and controlled as we are able to be during design, it is frequently impossible for design to follow an entirely rational course. Parnas and Clements ([PAR86]) point out a number of factors that upset our design plans and methodologies: customer ignorance, the need to experiment with solutions, the burden of large software, changes to specifications, human error and prejudice, and pragmatic imperatives. Traces of these problems will no doubt be visible in our work products. Nevertheless, there may be some worth in going back through a less-than-rational design and explaining what should have been done (rationalizing, or making reasonable, the documentation) to provide guidance to future maintainers and to evaluate the quality of our work.

### 6.2.2 Characteristics of Good Design

Figure 6-10 shows the interaction between the attributes of a quality design process and product, listed in Section 6.2, and the attributes of good design methodology outlined below. An x at the intersection of any methodology attribute and product or process attribute means that the methodology helps provide the attribute of the product or process. Notice that good design methodologies are best at providing intellectual control, reusability, division of labor, and clarity.

A good design notation supports understanding (both of the product and the process), automation, and duplication of the methodology. A carefully chosen notation will support the smooth transformation of specifications into the design and the design into code. Thus, it provides help for both the verification and integration of software development.

Recall the quotes from Whitehead and Babbage in Section 3.3.2. Their import was that a carefully chosen notation compresses meaning, facilitates reasoning, and frees

| Provides | Notation | Expansion | Abstraction | Modularization | Organization | Encapsulation |
|---|---|---|---|---|---|---|
| Realism | | | X | | X | X |
| Modifiability | X | X | | X | | X |
| Unity | X | X | X | | | |
| Clarity | X | X | X | X | X | X |
| Reusability | X | X | X | X | | X |
| Evaluate | X | X | X | X | | |
| Integrate | X | | | | X | X |
| Automate | X | | | X | X | |
| Divide | X | X | X | X | X | X |
| Duplicate | X | X | | | X | X |
| Control | X | X | X | X | X | X |

**FIGURE 6-10**   RELATIONSHIP BETWEEN DESIGN QUALITY AND METHODOLOGY

Notation

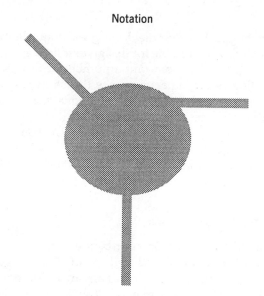

the brain to concentrate on essentials. All of these are important if we are to maintain control of the tremendous complexity of the developing design of a large product. In fact, the problem of comprehending complexity was viewed by Brooks as the primary limit to our ability to increase our productivity ([BRO87]).

Expansion

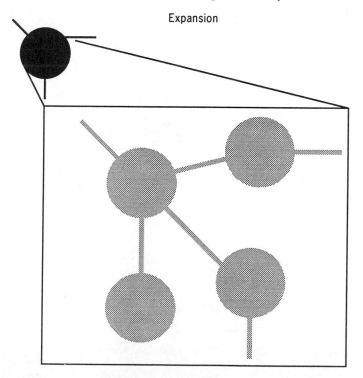

Most techniques for evaluation of software design, if they are to rise above a matter of personal taste, must depend on our ability to measure and analyze. This, in turn, means that standard notations have to be used in expressing design. When a product is too big for any one person to carry it to conclusion, it has to be divided up. To avoid inconsistency and incompatibility, the various designers and implementors have to be working with a lingua franca of some kind. Again, the design must be expressed in a standard notation. Finally, reuse becomes difficult when the reused component is expressed in a variant and incompatible notation. In addition, the classification of design components, in support of browsing and location of candidates for reuse, must be dependent on an appropriate notation for the designs.

In keeping with the oft-stated principle that there is great power in being able to defer details, it is important for any design methodology to allow us to postpone design decisions until they really need to be made. One way of doing this is to have design proceed in small steps, with incremental *expansion* by that amount of detail that must be added. This slowly expanding design fits in with the notions expressed in Figure 6-2. Architectural design should continue until modules are subdivided to the point that they express unitary functionality and atomic data clustering. Then detailed design should continue until implementation-specific details have to be considered.

Another benefit of this gradual extension of design is that we are able to limit the size and impact of decisions that are made at each step. The effort expended in one step, the complexity of the questions under consideration, and the difficulty in verifying the additional design components being added are all reduced by taking many small steps rather than one huge stride. Along with this comes an increased opportunity to isolate design decisions and to analyze arguments for accepting one alternative instead of another. This allows us to *rationalize* the design process by providing reasons for what we do.

The task of a maintenance software engineer, attempting to understand the design of a product, is facilitated by a stepwise expansion of the design. Likewise, it is easier to choose an intermediate spot, where the critical design decision was made, at which to start maintenance modifications. The same can be said for positioning the exact point at which insertion of a reusable component or division of the product occurs. With the increased resolution of small steps, these can be done at optimal points.

If we were to rewind an expanding design process, so that in reverse it becomes a contracting design, then at each step a set of decisions and components would collapse into a single decision or component. This is the process of *abstraction* — consolidating an entire set of detailed attributes by using a few central traits, or even a single name, to represent them ([SHA85]). When used in forward gear, abstraction allows us to concentrate first on the details we will emphasize, while ignoring the rest. This permits us to represent, without actually enumerating, aspects that are peripheral to the fundamental concept. It is a way of dealing with complex systems while avoiding stifling detail.

As an example, consider the concept of "structure." It communicates the same basic message to most people. It could be used at a stage in the design, say, of a software engineering methodology (perhaps during the step that introduces formalism, deferral of detail, and verification). Still, the concept isn't sufficiently strong for the design of a

Abstraction

real, working methodology. It would eventually have to be expanded into its constituents: subdivision, connectivity, nesting, and the like. "Structure" is good to work with until further detail is needed.

Shaw notes in [SHA85] that abstraction corresponds to the analytic form of scientific understanding. A physical scientist might observe some phenomenon, hypothesize the laws governing it, construct an experimental apparatus, predict the results of the experiment, and then evaluate the results. Similarly, a software engineer will conduct requirements analysis and specification (observation), design (hypothesis), implementation (construction), prediction, and evaluation (software validation). Abstraction is the key to controlling the complexity of all of these activities. In particular, strong abstraction facilitates the formal verification of design ([BER86]).

In software design, we find ourselves abstracting the three facets of software mentioned earlier: function, data, and control. Functional abstraction is often achieved through the use of descriptive titles; we might call the process of eliminating partial data stream frames, either leading or trailing, "synchronization." Similarly, the elimination of invalid sequences of frames, starting at a gap in the data stream, could be called "cleaning." Often we characterize functional abstractions as data transforms, state machines, and so on.

Data abstraction is the central topic in data structures texts; it is the process of taking some complex structure of primitive data items, like an array of values and an accompanying array index variable, and consolidating them into a simpler idea, "stack." Included in data abstractions might be functional methods applied to data structures, like "push" and "pop."

Control abstraction occurs at the detailed design level when, for example, "the complex of steps necessary to repeat a segment of code some specified number of times while providing an indicator of progress through the iteration" is turned into "counted loop."

At the architectural level, control abstractions provide us with templates for "recursion" or "concurrency" or "invocation."

One of the ways to make abstractions work harder for us is to reuse them as generic concepts, which through parameterization can be specialized to the situation at hand. In our example, there might be some universal definition of "___ structure," which could be made more specific by the inclusion of parameters, like "data structure," "architectural structure," "program structure," and the like. To get down to the case of software engineering, we may want to parameterize abstractions like "stack of ___" or "___ sorting procedure" to obtain instances like "stack of activation records" or "stable sorting procedure."

To provide the realism that is a hallmark of good software design, abstractions should always be suggested first by the structure of the real world environment. If banks provide paper receipts to their customers to verify deposits, then a software product dealing with deposits should have a corresponding record representing the transaction. If a physical stream of signals is created by the cyclic transmission of several individual signals in the same order each time, the software design to handle the data stream should reach the abstraction of "frame" at some point.

The use of abstraction goes hand in hand with the use of appropriate notation in freeing our brains of the burdens of detail, while permitting them to penetrate to the core of the concept at the same time. Abstraction facilitates the kind of browsing through a design that is necessary to maintenance personnel and detail workers alike.

*Modularity* in design, which creates large products by composing smaller, independent products together, using the glue of interfaces, has been a very fruitful design technique indeed. It has made today's technological society possible, and not just from the standpoint of providing equipment. In a sense, even services have become modular. If a field engineer trained to repair IBM 4341 computers gets sick at a critical

Modularity

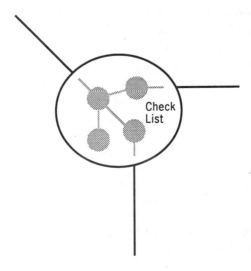

moment, another one can be shipped in to take his place temporarily and with little delay or loss of continuity. Of course, individuals can be composed into interchangeable teams, like emergency medical teams or fruit-picking teams.

The principle of expansion says that design should proceed in small steps until it is done. Modularity tells us that the criteria for "doneness" are that.

- The total complexity of interfaces between the modules begins to balance approximately the complexity of procedural and data structure within the modules.
- Modules begin to exhibit **cohesion**, which is the quality of hanging together, a kind of atomicity that makes further division difficult.
- Modules are still **decoupled** — they are relatively independent and their individual interfaces are relatively simple.

The second criterion, cohesion, usually forces modules to center around a single major data entity, or to implement a single functional abstraction. To satisfy the third criterion — decoupling — it is necessary at each step of expansion to draw the division lines between newly created abstractions, or modules, through "gaps" in which their interconnectedness is simple, thus providing small interfaces.

Myers et al. in [STE74] originally defined most of the following kinds of modular cohesion:

*Functional* The module performs a single, well-defined function.

*Informational* The module performs several functions on the same shared data structure or database.

*Sequential* The module performs several functions, which are constrained to occur in sequence by the real world model or specifications.

*Communicational* The module performs several functions on the same body of data, which is not organized as a single type or structure.

*Procedural* The module performs several functions that all relate to a general procedure effected by the software.

*Temporal* The module performs several functions that all relate to a particular portion of the execution of the software (e.g., initialization).

*Logical* The module performs several functions that bear a superficial similarity (e.g., screen output).

*Coincidental* The module performs several functions that have been grouped together by chance or caprice.

Myers also lists the varying types of *coupling* that can occur between different modules (see Figure 6-11):

*Independence* No coupling at all.

*Data* Data are passed in the finest resolution possible on a well-defined interface and on a strict "need to know" basis.

*Stamp* Data on the interface are made available as part of a larger structure; thus, unneeded data are also presented to the module.

*Control* Data are passed that will control the execution of some other module (e.g., flags).

*External* Aside from the internal interface, modules communicate through external lines, usually by means of files.

*Common* Modules may communicate without the medium of an explicit interface, by accessing global data structures.

*Content* Modules can access and change each other's internal data state or procedural state.

Highly modular design provides several important benefits. First, the verification task is simpler. Decoupling means that modules can largely be verified without a lot of concern for interactions with other modules. Cohesion means that modules have a single purpose, nature, and function and that they probably correspond to one, or a very few, requirements. For the same reasons, maintaining a modular design is easier — there are few side effects to worry about, and the individual module is not overly complex. The fact that modules can easily be extracted and replaced means that reuse at the design and code level is much easier when the modular design principle is followed.

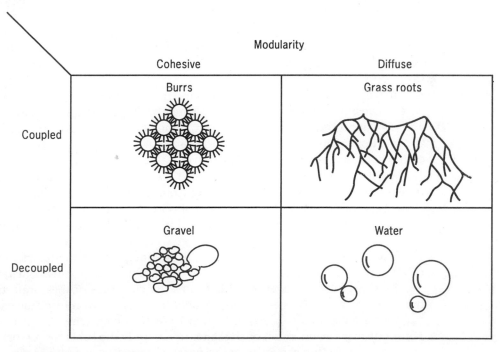

**FIGURE 6-11** EXAMPLES OF DECOUPLING AND COHESION

Modularity can exist for data, function, and control and for logic as well. We have already seen examples of the first three: subprograms, abstract data types, and control structures. But consider the case of table-driven software. We might be able to design a functional module that analyzes separate Boolean conditions and carries out actions in response to them. This procedure would be completely generic. Now, we can feed to this generic procedure a single decision table and get an implementation of the logic represented by the table. Feed it another decision table and it embodies a separate logic. The logic is modularized into the table itself.

In fact, the division of functional, data, control, and logic abstractions into separate and independent modules is a powerful method for designing generic components and software tools. Parser generators work in this fashion, by separating function from logic. In a similar way, user interface generators treat function, data, and control as three separate modules.

Modules and interfaces are dual entities. Correct definition of modules ensures cohesion, by including just the right abstraction. Correct definition of interfaces ensures decoupling, by controlling the amount and kind of interaction between modules. This duality can combine with that of function and data. We may assume that functionality resides in modules, data being passed back and forth between them via interfaces. We may also assume that data resides in modules, with the requests for function passing between them on the interface. But the important thing to remember is that both data and function are modular — neither is to be shared in an indiscriminate or uncontrolled way. Appropriate interfaces and protocols should always be established. In particular, this means that as little data as possible should be the common or global possession of many functional modules.

Modularization is perhaps the most important of all software design methodology attributes. It makes all of the previous attributes (notation, expansion, abstraction) necessary and leads easily into the two we have yet to consider. When we are careful to remember the dual nature of data and function, and to pay as much attention to data modularity and abstraction as to procedural modularity and abstraction, we are almost sure to design a good product. Nevertheless, the principle is neither universally accepted nor universally applied. In fact, some design methodologies purposely avoid the creation of modules. Although these methodologies work well in appropriate circumstances, they are not generally applicable.

Once the software design is assumed to be made up of a large collection of independent modules, connected through interfaces, it is evident that some orderliness must be established to turn a mere collection of abstractions into a meaningful structure, exhibiting significant relationships and interactions between its components.

In fact, the process of *organization* has already begun with modularization. The very fact that we are clustering certain data and function together establishes structure and relationship. But organization adds to this the closeness of the connection between modules, the control of one module by another, the access one module has to another, and the nested structure of modules, which creates a hierarchy. Parnas et al. ([PAR85]) point out that this module, or package, structure is the basis for a work assignment organization, defining specific tasks to be assigned to specific software engineers.

Organization

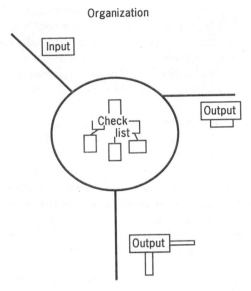

Beyond this, functional modules are also organized by means of the call relationship. For nonconcurrent software, if we neglect the possibility of indirect recursion, this call relation is bound to create a tree, or hierarchical ordering of modules. (For concurrent software, there is a third, runtime, hierarchy consisting of processes.)

Data modules can similarly be organized into a graph, representing the visibility relationship, in which certain data are allowed to interact with other. Data and function can be clustered together, and usually are, on the basis of what interactions are most frequent and natural.

There are two particular suggestions dealing with the structure of the invocation hierarchy or call tree. The scope of control of any module in the tree is defined to be the subtree that is rooted in that module—everything it calls, everything they call, and so on. The scope of effect of a single module (A) is the set of modules in which certain procedures may be executed, or not, depending on the execution details of A. To improve decoupling and to diminish the possibility of troubling side effects, the scope of effect of a module should be limited to its scope of control ([STE74]).

The second suggestion is that the nature of modules should change as we move down from the top to the bottom of the invocation hierarchy. At the top, modules tend to be managers. They don't cause anything to happen directly but, instead, call on other modules to act as their surrogates. At the bottom of the tree, modules are agents—they carry out direct action, without thinking a lot about it. This means that we will question a design in which top-level modules in the invocation tree directly manipulate the fundamental data entities of the software. It also means that we will think twice about including a large amount of decision logic in modules that are located at the bottom of the tree.

It is most natural for us to define the top-level, or control modules, first, and then to continue the design by selecting an individual action call and expanding it in terms of a compound of additional action calls. This process, going from the control to the action level as an organizational technique, is called *top-down* design. Top-down design makes it fairly easy to ensure that our developing software continues to meet its specifications. However, it is relatively difficult to subdivide a top-down design into several parallel efforts until we get to the lowest levels of the tree. This inefficiency can be ameliorated by a strict division of the software on a modular, or package, basis. Top-down design of any kind tends to be rather unforgiving if poor initial decisions are made ([RAJ85]).

The dual concept, *bottom-up* design, starts with a definition of the lowest level (in the invocation hierarchy) modules, and then builds control modules on top of them. Bottom-up design requires foresight, since in some sense it proceeds by "deferring abstraction" rather than deferring detail. It is most often used in conjunction with the reuse or prototyping process models. It has the advantage of allowing us to verify (often with a prototype) actions first, rather than building an entire design structure on the supposition that some action design will be possible. Since most tightly-constrained designs fail at the action levels, this is a way of reducing the risk of botching the design and having to rework it. On the other hand, fitting two incompatible action modules under a single control module may sometimes be possible only by creating a fragmented or even incoherent design, thus sacrificing clarity and unity. As a result, bottom-up design is not easily subdivided among different software engineers, and often fails to match its specifications exactly (see Figure 6-12).

As further examples of organization, data entities are structured as composites of simpler types during detailed design; and the structure of control is exhibited by the

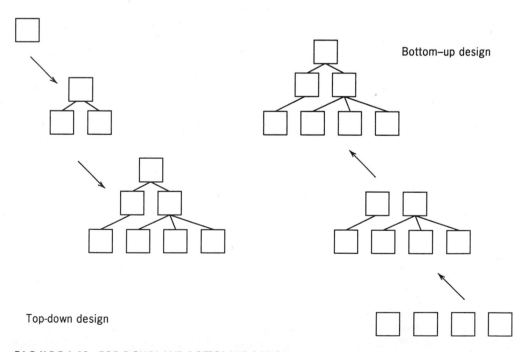

Bottom–up design

Top-down design

**FIGURE 6-12**  TOP-DOWN AND BOTTOM-UP DESIGN

individual control structures of iteration, selection, and sequence at the detailed level and by the invocation hierarchy at the architectural level.

In discussing the benefits of modularization, it was noted that verification and understanding were both easier, since concern about side effects and coupling were minimized. This would allow us to concentrate on a single *encapsulated* module without concerning ourselves with what might be taking place elsewhere. Being able to think about just one little thing at a time is a way of reducing the complexity of any process. Rajlich put it in a different way ([RAJ85]) when he said that good decomposition creates a module whose interface is simpler than its details.

This principle can be strengthened, going on the belief that "ignorance is bliss," by stating that, in fact, we should be encouraged to ignore the secondary aspects of other modules by hiding away all of the information about their internal structure. This will certainly guarantee the decoupling of modules, since the only thing we will still know will be the publicly available description of their function (an abstraction of their actual procedural or data structure) and the formal definition of their relatively simple interface. This principle provides dependability by protecting us against unforeseen and disastrous side effects.

In fact, Parnas recommends in [PAR85] that this be the basis for drawing the boundaries between modules. A module should be defined at any point that there is a design decision that needs to be hidden from the other modules. By following this pattern, we restrict all possible interaction between modules solely to their interfaces. We also guarantee that any module can be replaced by another that will provide a compatible interface and the same functionality. The actual design decisions — is the stack implemented as an array or a linked list, for instance — are totally irrelevant.

Not only does encapsulation minimize coupling, it also tends to maximize cohesion. The only software components that go into a module are those that are so closely intertwined that they depend on the same design decision. This is an ideal way to implement abstract data types, which are discussed in Section 4.3.3. Thus encapsula-

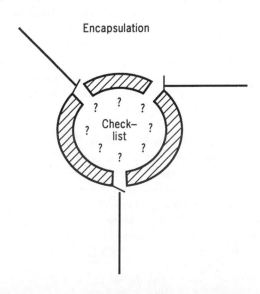

Encapsulation

tion provides a reason for clustering the basic data structure and all of its operations into a single module. Designers who use the structure simply generate requests for the operations that manipulate that structure and send them to the module itself. Encapsulation is a particularly good way to design software that works in an environment that is strongly data oriented.

Another use of encapsulation is to protect the stability of the entire software package from those parts of it that are very likely to change. Some instances of this are the following:

- Very difficult modules, which are likely to contain errors or to be the subject of additional design efforts, or for which the specifications are still fluid.
- Kernels, or machine specific data or procedures (like the escape sequences needed to generate certain effects on a screen), called hardware-hiding in [PAR85].
- Specific data or procedures (like data types or the procedures for changing character case, buffering or system generation), called software decision hiding in [PAR85].
- The specific functionality of the product, called behavior hiding in [PAR85].

In each of these situations, anticipated changes, like augmenting the functionality of the product, porting the software to a new machine, or correcting faults in the difficult design, can be carried out without modifying any other modules *if the modules are encapsulated.*

## 6.3 DESIGN METHODOLOGIES AND TOOLS

The importance of using a fixed design notation and a design methodology was pointed out in Section 6.1.1. We discussed a number of attributes of good design methodology in Section 6.2. It still remains to consider some specific notations and methodologies in action, and to determine some of the criteria for choosing one in preference to another. In fact, there are many published software design methodologies, more than 100 (see, for instance, [WEB88]). They are not all entirely distinct, but it is surprising how many really different ideas have been proposed.

This multiplicity arises, in part, from the actual variety of different software applications. Many of the design techniques are explicitly or implicitly aimed at specific kinds of applications in specific sorts of environments. Thus, one way of selecting a methodology is on the basis of the specific application area in which we are working.

In this section, all of the methodologies presented have an extensive and successful track record. Some, like structured design, Box-structures, layers of abstraction, object-oriented design, and table-driven design have coped with some very large or complex applications. Nevertheless, two generally useful design methodologies are highlighted: structured design (shown here for architectural design) and stepwise decomposition (shown for detailed design). Each of these *can* be used in both the architectural and detailed design processes, but they are particularly suited to employment as illustrated in Sections 6.3.1 and 6.3.2.

### 6.3.1 Architectural Design

The major purpose of design notations is to provide media for recording, understanding, transmitting, and transforming architectural and detailed designs. Notations are frequently the outgrowth of specific methodologies, but this does not mean that a designer is constrained to use a notation exclusively in the context of the methodology for which it was developed. Ideally, any notation can be used with any methodology if such a marriage is beneficial to the design process. Of course, software tools usually provide a single notation to be used in conjunction with the techniques they automate.

About 10 years ago there was discussion as to whether flowcharts, a traditional way of expressing detailed design, or pseudocode, a newer textual design notation, was the better option. In part, the choice depended on the orientation of the designer, whether textual/linguistic or graphic/visual. However, most designers probably favored pseudocode because it was easily integrated with existing software and hardware tools like keyboard-based terminals, editors, formatters, and high-level language compilers. Some research has indicated that pseudocode is a more valuable notation than the relatively weak flowchart graphical notation ([RAM83]).

More recently, the advent of high-speed workstations with large memories and high-quality graphics has given impetus to the design of similar graphic editors and even visual programming language compilers. It now appears that graphical notations are favored over textual in most industrial environments where they are both available. This is probably related to issues of direct manipulation and to the high bandwidth of visual communication. Although there may be a simple element of trendiness involved, on the whole, graphical notations have more to recommend them, particularly at the architectural design level.

The basic role of architectural design notations is to facilitate mapping of functional and data specifications into individual modules. In addition, the invocation hierarchy, the flow of data or messages between modules, the definition of module interfaces, and the conditions that trigger invocation or activation of a given module all need to be represented. Many of the most used notations for this purpose are presented in Chapter 4.

The most frequently used category of architectural design notations is that of directed graphs. These include data flow diagrams, SADT diagrams, ESML diagrams, Petri nets, and all of their cousins (see Section 4.3.1). Trees are also useful in picturing the invocation hierarchy or composite data structures, as with the Jackson entity structure diagram (see Section 4.3.5). For modelling data on interfaces, Warnier diagrams and data dictionaries (treelike) and regular expressions and production grammars (textual) can be useful (see Sections 4.3.2 and 4.3.3). Entity-relationship diagrams (graphs), which are the data counterpart of the procedural data flow diagram, can also be useful in outlining software architecture. Several recent attempts have been made to define specialized notations for object-oriented design, (e.g., [WAS89]).

Our first architectural design methodology, *structured analysis and design*, is due to Constantine ([STE74]) but has been further developed by many others ([YOU78]). It exhibits the benefits listed in Figure 6-13. It uses the data flow notation that is presented in Chapter 4. Since the architectural structure of the software is defined by data flows,

- An appropriate emphasis on data in the design process.
- A natural approach to modularization.
- A semialgorithmic way of defining software organization.
- A natural and widely understood notation.
- Easy integration with specification and detailed design.

**FIGURE 6-13**   BENEFITS OF STRUCTURED DESIGN

which are usually modeled on the real world, it offers an understandable and realistic way of representing software. Its specific attention to modules and interfaces promotes the divisibility of design.

Structured design starts with a high-level data flow diagram of the proposed software. Figure 6-14 shows two different examples of such a diagram. Notice that the diagram on the left represents a relatively unified flow, particularly on the output side, with a single possible output flow resulting from two concurrent input flows. The diagram on the right, however, shows many possible alternative processing and output flows.

These two types of flows — transform and transaction — are treated in a slightly different way by the methodology. The first step, of course, is to label the process bubbles and data flows with as detailed a description as is currently possible. In this abstract example we use only letters and numbers for process and data flow identification.

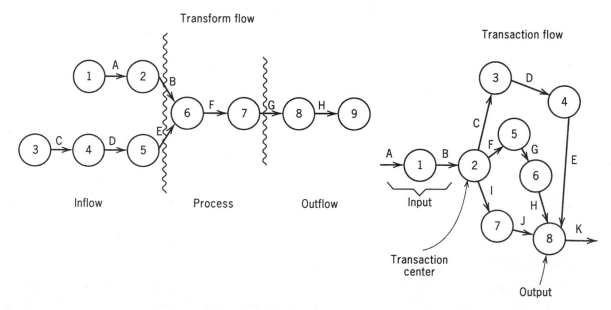

**FIGURE 6-14**   INITIAL DATA FLOW DIAGRAMS

Processes should be evaluated for the degree of decoupling they exhibit. If processes are too interdependent and interconnected, the bubbles should be redrawn to provide simpler interfaces. Data flows should be examined to see whether they represent an excessively complex data definition. If there are any evident problems, the single arc representing the flow should be divided into two or more; or, perhaps, the diagram should be redrawn.

The next step is to divide the flows into regions. For a transform flow, this is done by tracing the input flows, which may be undergoing successive stages of abstraction and filtering, to the latest point at which the input data streams are still distinct and recognizable as abstractions of the original input. This is the input region. Similarly, the output flow is traced backward to the earliest point at which it assumes the basic outlines of its final shape, however abstractly this may be. This is the output region. In between the two is the transform region, where the input data is processed in such a way that the output data is produced.

For a transaction flow, the input region is located in a similar manner. The input region feeds into the transaction center, where one of several different action paths is selected. Depending on the complexity of any action path, it can be treated as an output region, or as an entire transform or transaction flow, which will need to be reanalyzed by itself. Transaction flows are frequently encountered in the design of menu-based transaction systems, where individual action paths come together at a common final update and output process. If this is the case, the update/output region should also be located.

Using the regions defined in the data flow diagram, we are now in a position to organize the software into an invocation hierarchy. For a transform flow, this is accomplished by "hinging" the flow at the input/transform and the transform/output junctures. The resulting tree has a controlling module, at the root, and three subtrees representing input, transform, and output. Notice that the earliest input and the latest output are located at the lowest levels of the tree. Of course, if there are multiple input or output flows, they each occupy a different subtree.

Figure 6-15 shows an invocation hierarchy for the transform flow in Figure 6-14. Each data flow is represented by a module, labeled "get," and the subsequent process bubble is represented by a separate, and sibling, module called "transform."

For a transaction flow, we again create a hinge where the input flows into the transaction center; the center itself is represented by a dispatcher with a number of subtrees, one for each action path. If there is a common update/output process, it is shown as a common leaf at the bottom of all of the action path subtrees. Figure 6-16 shows the call tree that results from the transaction flow of Figure 6-14.

To give a more concrete example, let us consider the student registration system described in Section 4.3.1. The node in that data flow diagram labeled "Create Student Schedule," since it represents the interaction with a student who is adding a course, might be expanded into the data flow diagram shown in Figure 6-17. The first step is to translate the course names, as given by the student, to the index numbers for the actual courses. In processing each request to add a course the software must determine whether the student has a high enough grade point average (e.g., over 1.5), is sufficiently advanced in class standing (e.g., at least a Junior), is majoring in an

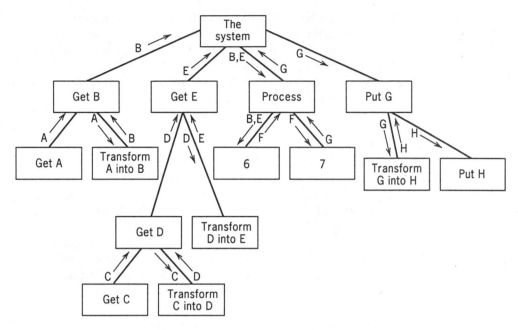

**FIGURE 6-15**  INVOCATION HIERARCHY FOR A TRANSFORM FLOW

appropriate subject (e.g., only CS or EE in Compiler Construction), and has taken the prerequisite courses (e.g., Differential Equations only after Linear Algebra) (see Figure 6-17).

Next, the class rolls are checked to determine which sections of the course are not in conflict with the student's current schedule, and whether they have space for another student. If so, a temporary registration is created, a confirmation of registration is sent to the student, and a bill is calculated and sent to the cashier. If the student pays the tuition fees, then the cashier transmits a payment record and the temporary registration becomes permanent.

We must now determine which parts of the data flow diagram represent input, output, and processing. Input consists of the Get Student Input, Get Index Numbers, and Get Cashier Input nodes, while output consists of the three Print nodes. The other nodes are processing transforms. The resulting invocation hierarchy is given in Figure 6-18.

You may have noticed that the original data flow was designed to provide good interfaces and module decoupling but not cohesion. In all likelihood, a data flow small enough to be analyzed according to the rules we have given is not large enough to represent an entire software product. Modules that are highly cohesive can be left as they are, but we must expand each noncohesive module (like Create Student Schedule) as an independent data flow, repeating the structured design process. The root of the resulting tree will replace the single module in the higher level call tree. In particular, the transform center is likely to require additional expansion before we can start with detailed design.

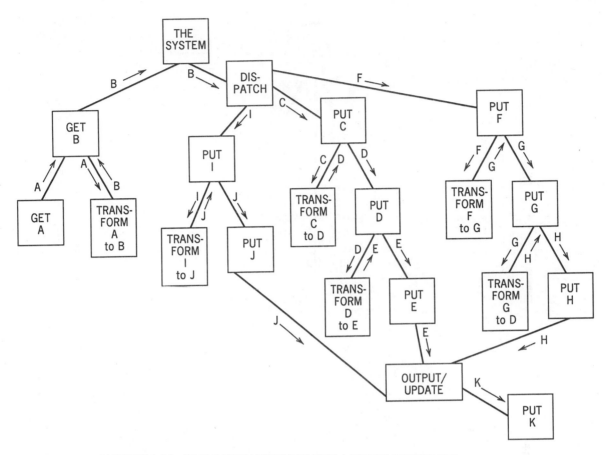

**FIGURE 6-16**   INVOCATION HIERARCHY FOR A TRANSACTION FLOW

Structured analysis and design can be assisted by tools, principally graphics editors with access to a data dictionary and some analysis tools. In particular, the quality and consistency of the interfaces can be evaluated. Structured design is fairly methodical. If we assume that the initial data flows are part of the specification, then independent designers tend to use them to produce very similar invocation hierarchies without a great deal of trouble. In terms of the six principles of good design, structured design shows strength in the first five.

The strengths of structured design are its data orientation and its general applicability. It is weak on encapsulation and is only semi-automatable, since it relies heavily on heuristic knowledge and intuition. As a methodology, structured design does allow for significant insertion of creativity and insight. Whether this is a benefit or a drawback depends on one's point of view. Structured design should be chosen for architectural design when no more specialized design methodology exists for the application, and when the flow of data can reasonably be used as the unifying principle of the software.

*Object-oriented design* is a newer methodology, particularly favored for real-time,

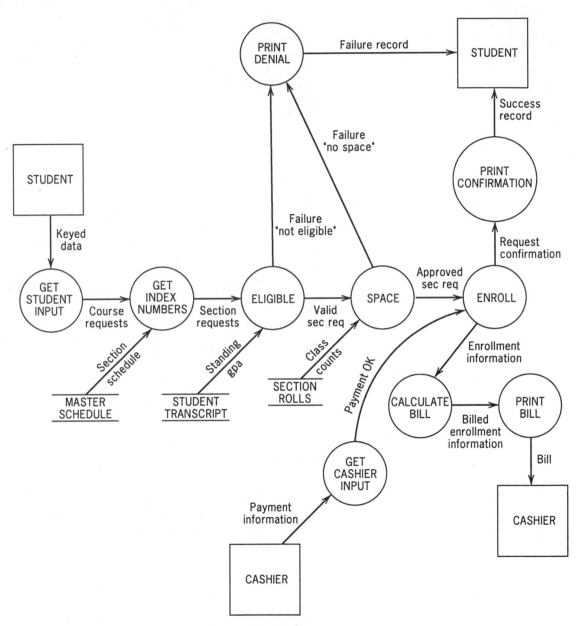

**FIGURE 6-17** STUDENT REGISTRATION SUBFLOW

parallel, and visual-interface systems. The Smalltalk-80 environment is the prototype of object-oriented tools. The object-oriented design methodology takes classes representing abstract data types as its fundamental principle.

In fact, object-oriented design can be seen as the current culmination of an evolution that begins with procedural programming, which concentrates on process description

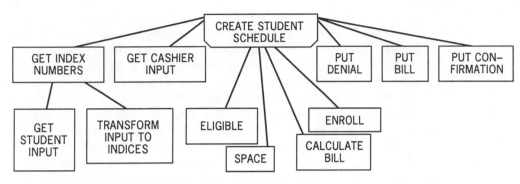

**F I G U R E 6-18**   STUDENT REGISTRATION SUBHIERARCHY

to create monolithic algorithms utilizing the simplest of data types. From this level we have seen progress through modular design and data abstraction to full object-oriented design ([STR88]). In this final evolutionary stage, we concentrate on objects, which are autonomous instances of abstract data types, together with their interactions, in the same way that the earlier stages concentrated on specific processes as instances of more abstract algorithms. The hallmark of object-oriented design is the concept of inheritance, in which specific objects are grouped into *classes*. Each class is a general type, and individual subclasses may not only *inherit* all the characteristics of the parent class but may also possess other characteristics defined for them individually (Figure 6-19).

In fact, Halbert and O'Brien claim in [HAL87] that these classes or types are the major organizing principle for object-oriented design. Although individual objects provide specific behavior, types capture common object characteristics. To allow this, a class may incompletely specify certain details, which would then be settled within the subclass. These partial types may permit incremental growth as new functions are added to them, or they may provide the basis for entirely new types (which would inherit their characteristics). This latter approach is more appropriate if the added

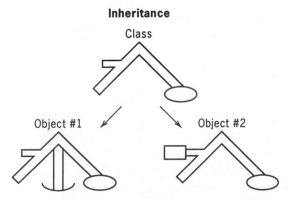

**F I G U R E 6-19**   INHERITANCE PRESERVES TRAITS BUT ALLOWS FLEXIBILITY

functions and characteristics provide an object type that would likely be reused.

The basic elements of an object-oriented design are, of course, objects. An object is a module that usually embodies an abstract data type; but it is also possible for a process to be an object. Objects generally encapsulate both state and behavior. This means that an object contains some data structure, which stores data, process state, or other persistent aspects of the system, together with methods, or procedures for implementing the allowed operations on the data structure. Exactly what implementations are used to structure either data or function is immaterial to the design technique.

The interface between objects (modules) is represented by communication paths along which messages can be sent from one object to another. These messages are requests that specific operations be carried out. The sequencing of events is created by chains of messages, each triggering the next. Although the internal structuring of an object, its private part, is hidden from all other objects, the external view, or shared part, is generally available and very precisely defined. This strong encapsulation leaves the detailed design as unconstrained as possible by the architectural design. To enhance maintainability, and strong modular decoupling, individual methods should only export data that are part of their received messages or are instances of the class of objects to which they are attached ([LIE88]) (Figure 6-20).

Booch ([BOO86]) suggests that objects, their attributes, and the operations that can be applied to them are implicit in the functional requirements. If these are stated in a natural language like English, then we scan the requirements, locating nouns, which have the potential of becoming objects. Similarly, adjectives modifying the object-

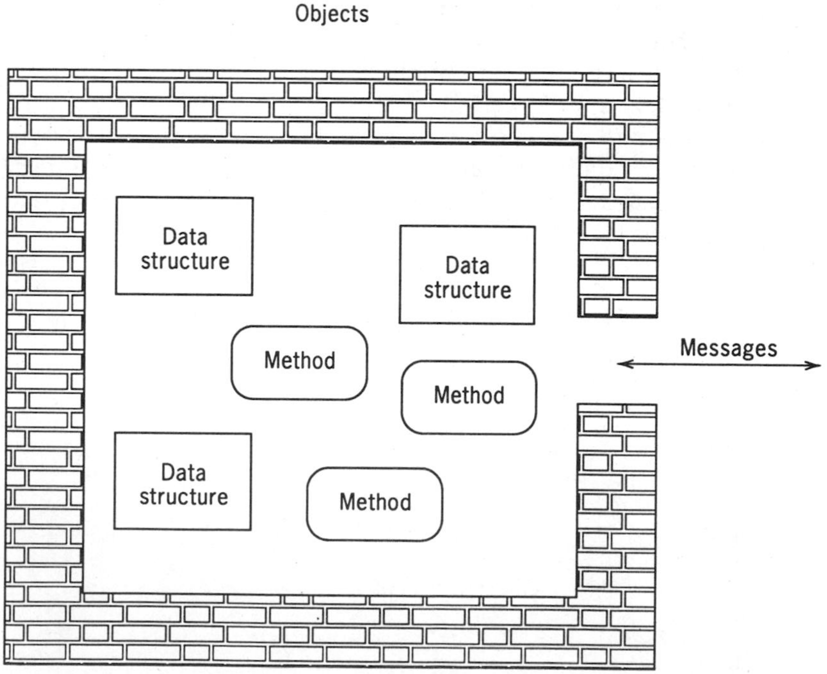

Objects

**FIGURE 6-20**   OBJECTS ARE HIGHLY ENCAPSULATED

nouns may become attributes, whereas verbs with object-nouns as objects are operations, and verbs with object-nouns as subjects generate messages, representing the visibility of objects to other objects. This visibility, together with the definition of messages, represents the interface between objects. Timing and other constraints can be included in the definition of operations and messages.

For instance, reading subsection 1.1 of section 4.5.1 might suggest that we consider "data file," "header," "data stream," "frame," "output file," and "process" (portion of software) as objects. Frames could have the attributes "valid," "invalid," "(created during) reset," and "consecutive." "Preserve" and "purge" messages could be sent from process to output file and data stream and would trigger delete and append operations within these two objects.

The design methodology then calls for drawing a network of objects connected by messages, which can be compared back to the original specifications. It is frequently possible to prototype the design by reusing and composing existing objects, in order to validate it. If it cannot be shown that the design meets the requirements, optimization or redesign must occur. Similarly, it is possible (although not as likely as in some other design methodologies) to decompose a single complex object into a network of simpler sub-objects.

A valid object is generally characterized by a state and associated operations; it is an instance of a class, which instance is denoted by a name; it has restricted visibility; and it can be viewed by specification (the public part) or implementation (the private part). The operations (actions or methods) are typically of three different kinds: *constructors*, which alter the state of the object; *selectors*, which evaluate the state of the object; and *iterators*, which visit the components of the object. Specific internal functions can include creation, initialization, construction, access, traversal, value storage, input, output, testing, insertion, deletion, and measuring. Objects are denominated *actors* when they are never the target of actions by other objects, *servers* when they operate on no other objects, or *agents* when they both operate and are operated on.

Object-oriented design benefits from the naturalness of modeling the objects on real world entities, concrete or abstract, and is well adapted to representing parallelism, since different objects could be allocated to different processors. It tends to be more maintainable because of the strong encapsulation of data and relatively weak coupling represented by messages. The final designs usually support concurrency easily and tend to be similar to levels of abstraction, because of the composition of object classes. Object-oriented design differs from data-structure design in its use of inheritance and its emphasis on actors ([BOO86]).

Obviously, object-oriented design promotes reuse at the design level, with objects being the reusable component. In fact, the methodology also promotes a kind of parameterization that allows us to reuse components more easily. We can suppose that each class represents an entire set of subclasses of specialized objects (or instances) of the original. Each instance inherits the attributes and operations of the parent class but is specialized by adding more attributes or operations. This is the parameterization step.

Among the weaknesses of object-oriented design are the fact that the design is implicit in the original description of the system, which is manipulated in a relatively

## Levels of Abstraction

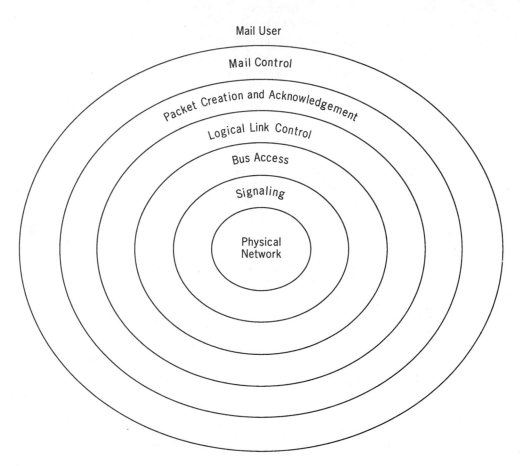

**FIGURE 6-21**   LEVELS OF ABSTRACTION FOR ELECTRONIC MAIL

unmethodical fashion, and the fact that implementations in many common languages will not be able to reflect all of the features of the design.

Dijkstra proposed the *levels of abstraction* design technique in conjunction with the design of an operating system. In contrast to structured design, it starts with those modules at the lowest levels of invocation and builds up from them. For an operating system this corresponds to taking the physical machine as the basic structure on which the software rests and then determining the most fundamental operating system capabilities or services in order to compose level 1.

This level 1 is composed of individual software modules instead of hardware capabilities. Nevertheless, it could be viewed by a user as a more powerful machine, with the new services replacing, amplifying, or augmenting those available from the physical machine itself. Thus, from the user's point of view, the software layer, together with the hardware beneath it, represents a virtual machine ([PAR79]), probably presenting its services at a more abstract level; hence, the term "levels of abstraction."

Each layer consists of a set of related services at about the same level of complexity. Each level of capability views the boundary below it as the "skin" of a virtual machine, and issues calls to lower level services as if it were executing instructions on a physical machine. In addition, each level probably controls a particular class of resources, which are available to higher levels only through invocation of services at this level, directly or indirectly.

As an example, consider a local area network, on which we wish to provide for communication via electronic mail. At the lowest level, we have the physical network, made up of workstations, servers, ethernet boards, and cables. The lowest level software capabilities provide for sending and receiving signals on the network. At the next level, these signaling features support protocols governing which nodes can access the transmission capabilities of the network under what conditions. In turn, logical link modules provide for the establishment of connections between nodes, the logical routing of information, and the dismantling of connections. These features are the foundation of modules that allow for the division of user files into packets and the sending and acknowledgement of packets. Above all this is the user interface that allows the user to send information as mail. These levels are shown in Figure 6-21.

The levels of abstraction design methodology creates a highly organized and encapsulated structure among the layers. However, this structure is rather coarse, representing no more than 10 layers. Finer-grained modularity is not directly supported by levels of abstraction, although, when modules are created, they tend to be quite autonomous. There is no particular notation associated with the technique. Like all bottom-up design methodologies, it requires a lot of foresight. The fine structure of an individual layer can be expanded one layer at a time; but the overall structure of the layers needs to be understood beforehand.

Some software architectural design can be modeled on mathematical *function applications*. In this situation, specifications are frequently written by using mathematical notation. So far as architectural design is concerned, there is no real need to represent control at all. Functional design can use data flow or Petri diagrams, with the data flows or tokens carefully described. Processes are heavily encapsulated with any needed local data structures. The software is made up of totally independent modules, with the possibility of connecting them whenever their interfaces agree. The only architectural structure is represented by the set of connections of the data flow or Petri diagram.

*Real-time* design, as proposed by Mellor and Ward ([WAR86]), is an extension of structured design in which data flowing from one node to another is classified as either discrete or continuous. Discrete flows are data flows as we have seen them before; a process can simply wait for discrete data to arrive. Continuous flows are flows that must be continually monitored by the process; they are usually those data that require special handling to maintain the real-time quality of the software, and they often involve special hardware capabilities.

The data flows are also augmented to represent the flow of control information representing events. State transition diagrams describe which events trigger changes in the state of the software, and what actions are taken as a result. Timing information is also included in the design ([WAR86]). The augmented data flow diagram can then be expanded much as is done with structured design. The ESML notation has been developed for real-time design.

### 6.3.2 Detailed Design

Detailed design notations should be capable of representing the step-by-step flow of atomic actions, the specific definitions of objects, and functional relationships. The most appropriate notations for step-by-step flow are pseudocode and flowcharts. *Pseudocode* is an abstracted programming language that possesses the standard data types and control structures but allows for some looseness in the syntactic details of IO and assignment statements and declarations. An example of a pseudocode design of CREATE STUDENT REQUESTS will be given shortly.

*Flowcharts* are flow diagrams in which different shaped boxes are used to indicate decision points and the various activities of input, output, invocation, assignment, and the like. However, data are represented separately from the flowchart; what flows along the arcs is control. The Nassi–Shneiderman chart, shown in Figure 6-22, is generally preferable to the flowchart, since it enforces the use of standard control structures that have a single entrance and exit and permit only nonoverlapped nested control structures.

It is possible to represent very perverse control structures with a flowchart. Hence, those who use them should try to restrict themselves to standard control structures. One result of this restraint will be improved comprehension of the design. A modularity analyzer is useful for both pseudocode and flowchart notations. This tool indicates whether the module is sufficiently cohesive or needs to be subdivided further.

*Nassi–Shneiderman* charts are a flowchart variant in which control structures are restricted to simple sequence, if-then-else, while, repeat, and case ([YOD78]). Here, rather than using separate nodes to represent the as-yet unrefined tasks in the module, we fit these into rectangles embedded within control shapes. These shapes are chosen to allow the composition of tasks according to standard control constructs and without needing the use of any of the "goto" arcs found in flowcharts. There is evidence ([BAS81]) that this kind of structured control provides greater design integrity. The Nassi–Shneiderman chart in Figure 6-22 is accompanied by a parallel pseudocode design.

Specific data objects in a detailed design can be defined by using the techniques already mentioned in connection with architectural level interfaces: Warnier diagrams, regular expressions, and production grammars. Implicit in these last two may be rules for the process of recognizing correctly formed objects.

Functional relationships can be represented either as the total definition of a finite function from constant values, or as a combination of previous functions, particularly by using mathematical formulas. Truth tables, transition tables and diagrams, decision tables and trees, and event tables all represent total definitions of functions (see Section 4.3.1). Sentences in the predicate logic can also be used to define logical values, and together with truth, decision, and event tables allow us to test conditions for the

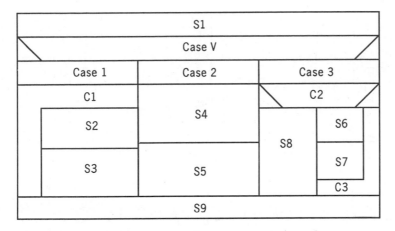

**FIGURE 6-22**  NASSI–SHNEIDERMAN CHART AND PSEUDOCODE

application of rules. These notations have wide applicability ranging from business data processing to logic programming in Prolog.

*HIPO* charts are a notation useful for both architectural and detailed design. The term "HIPO" stands for Hierarchy, Input, Process, Output; the charts are simply a combination of two different views of the software. Hierarchy is a graphic representation of the invocation hierarchy as a tree (perhaps broken into subtrees to fit a large structure onto individual screens). Process consists of individual procedural module descriptions that are based on structured natural language, a kind of pseudocode. Attached to the process descriptions are specific lists of Input and Output, which define the module's interface. Figure 6-23 shows an architectural Hierarchy chart, as well as one individual IPO chart.

Like HIPO charts, the *SARA* notation represents both design levels. Architectural design is shown in a form based on electronic logic diagrams, with chips, pins, and connections. These diagrams represent modules and interfaces. Two other graphs, essentially data flow and Petri nets, are used to show the flow of data and control and represent detailed design.

*Stepwise refinement* is the formalization of the natural, top-down design methodology mentioned in section 6.2.2. As originally enunciated by Wirth, stepwise refinement consists of the following:

1 Decompose each task and data description into several components by making appropriate design decisions. Attempt to maximize modularity between the components. Postpone inessential and representation detail as long as possible.

1a Repeat step 1 by decomposing the same tasks and descriptions by means of other design decisions. Do this as many times as appears to be fruitful.

2 Evaluate these rival refinements in terms of correctness, clarity, efficiency, regularity, modularity, and so on. Choose the refinement that best meets your goals. If no refinements have sufficiently high quality, back up to reconsider the design decisions representing previous (coarser) refinements.

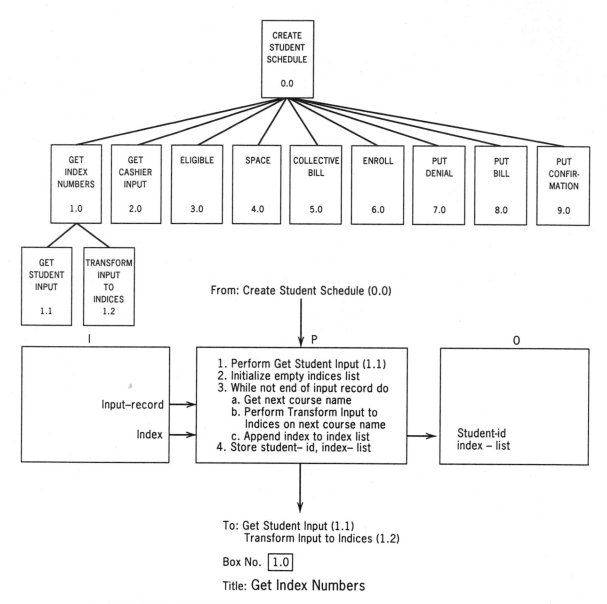

**FIGURE 6-23** HIPO CHARTS

3  As the refinement draws closer to the implementation stage, gradually bring the notation in which the refinements are expressed closer to the eventual implementation language.

This technique remains valid almost two decades later. Of course, Wirth didn't invent it; it is a standard problem-solving methodology that people have been using from time immemorial. Stepwise refinement is natural and familiar, and is, by all odds, the predominant detailed design methodology in use today. Its only rival in frequency of application is a nonmethodology: start at the beginning and stop when you get to the end.

Consider again the student registration system and how stepwise refinement might be used to design that portion of Create Student Course Requests that constructs the counts of how many students request a course and the conflict matrix of joint requests for pairs of courses. By using pseudocode notation, we can begin the design of this function with

```
INITIALIZE
CREATE MATRIX
STORE MATRIX
```

Really, no design decisions have been made here. At the next level, however, we get

```
INITIALIZE
    GET COURSE DATA
    OPEN REQUEST FILE
    ZERO MATRIX
CREATE MATRIX
    FOR EACH STUDENT
        GET INDIVIDUAL STUDENT'S REQUESTS
        TALLY INDIVIDUAL STUDENT'S JOINTLY REQUESTED COURSES
STORE MATRIX
        CLOSE REQUEST FILE
        OPEN CONFLICT FILE
        WRITE MATRIX TO CONFLICT FILE
        CLOSE CONFLICT FILE
```

Now we have decided that files will be used to store both the input and output. In addition, the structure of the input REQUEST file will be sequential, with each record containing the multiple course requests of a single student; and the output CONFLICT file will have a structure appropriate for storing a conflict matrix.

At the next level of refinement, we must first decide how to obtain the necessary course data. This will include both the number of courses and the way they will be identified. We can assume that student requests at this point will be in terms of course index numbers: therefore, we develop a file structure for courses:

```
COURSE FILE
    NUMBER OF COURSES
        SMALLEST INDEX NUMBER
        NEXT SMALLEST INDEX NUMBER
        . . .
        LARGEST INDEX NUMBER
```

These data will be read from the file and stored in an array. To commit to as little detail as possible, we do not assume the array to be standard. Instead, we just assume the availability of an INDEX function that can locate an appropriate location for storage and retrieval. The refinement is

```
GET COURSE DATA
  OPEN COURSE FILE
  READ NUMBER_OF_COURSES
  FOR SINGLE_COURSE = 1 TO NUMBER_OF_COURSES
    READ THIS_INDEX
    STORE THIS_INDEX IN COURSE_ARRAY AT INDEX(SINGLE_COURSE)
    CLOSE COURSE FILE
```

We fix in our minds at this time that the index numbers we read are not consecutive. This allows the registrar to impose structure by allowing the first two digits to be the code of a department and to leave sufficient gaps to accommodate additional offerings within this structure. But it means that we will have to translate these index numbers to the internal index numbers of our matrix as we read student information.

At the same level, as we try to define ZERO MATRIX, we come face to face with the need to decide on the structure of the conflict matrix, which will govern the steps used to initialize it. Some investigation reveals that the number of requests for a single course can amount to 1000. Therefore, we will be using a two-byte integer to store the counts in the array. There are typically about 2500 courses offered each semester and hence, a full matrix will require about 13 megabytes, which exhausts the 8 megabytes of main memory available on the machine. We are concerned about slow processing if we resort to too much paging on the machine and are equally concerned about the performance of a linked list implementation of the admittedly sparse conflict matrix.

The final design decision is based on the fact that the number of conflicts of course A with course B is the same as the number of conflicts of course B with course A. For this reason, we only need half of a matrix. Consequently, we will use a triangular matrix as illustrated in Figure 6-24. Since the matrix is not a normal, two-dimensional array, we will need a special index function, TINDEX. The figure shows the total enrollments for the courses on the diagonal (17 for course A....19 for course E). Tallies of joint enrollment for individuals are shown at the appropriate intersections of rows and columns. For instance, 12 people wanted to take both course C and course B. The total

|   | A | B | C | D | E |
|---|---|---|---|---|---|
| A | 17 |   |   |   |   |
| B | 5 | 23 |   |   |   |
| C | 8 | 12 | 18 |   |   |
| D | 0 | 0 | 0 | 23 |   |
| E | 2 | 0 | 1 | 17 | 19 |

**FIGURE 6-24**  TRIANGULAR CONFLICT MATRIX

size of an 2500x2500 triangular matrix is 6.3 megabytes.

The refinement of ZERO MATRIX now becomes

```
ZERO MATRIX
   FOR ROW = 1 TO NUMBER_OF_COURSES
         FOR COLUMN = 1 TO ROW
                VALUE OF CONFLICT_MATRIX AT TINDEX(ROW,COLUMN) = 0
```

We next expand GET INDIVIDUAL STUDENT'S REQUESTS. Again, the structure of the file must be designed, and we decide on the following:

```
REQUEST FILE
   STUDENT ID
   NUMBER_OF_REQUESTED_COURSES
         REQUEST WITH LOWEST INDEX
         REQUEST NEXT LOWEST INDEX        repeated for each student
         ...
         REQUEST WITH HIGHEST INDEX
```

Remembering the need to translate from the registrar's to our internal index numbers, the refinement then becomes

```
GET INDIVIDUAL STUDENT'S REQUESTS
   READ STUDENT ID
   READ NUMBER_OF_REQUESTED_COURSES
         FOR SINGLE_COURSE = 1 TO NUMBER_OF_REQUESTED_COURSES
                READ SINGLE REQUEST
                FIND INTERNAL INDEX OF REQUEST BY BINARY SEARCH OF
                                                       COURSE_ARRAY
                STORE INTERNAL INDEX IN REQUEST_ARRAY AT
                                       INDEX(SINGLE_COURSE)
```

We refine TALLY INDIVIDUAL STUDENT'S REQUESTS in the only apparent way allowed by our past decisions:

```
TALLY INDIVIDUAL STUDENT'S REQUESTS
      FOR FIRST = 1 TO NUMBER_OF_REQUESTED_COURSES
        INCREMENT CONFLICT_MATRIX AT TINDEX(FIRST,FIRST)
      FOR SECOND = 1 TO FIRST-1
             INCREMENT CONFLICT_MATRIX AT TINDEX(FIRST,SECOND)
```

The exact structure of the triangular matrix has not yet been decided. Instead, we have assumed the existence of an index function, TINDEX. This is expanded by using the normal addressing scheme for two-dimensional rectangular matrices as a guide:

```
TINDEX(ROW,COLUMN) = (ROW-1)*ROW/2 + COLUMN
```

Finally, WRITE MATRIX TO CONFLICT FILE becomes

```
WRITE MATRIX TO CONFLICT FILE
  FOR ROW = 1 TO NUMBER_OF_COURSES
       FOR COLUMN = 1 TO ROW
             WRITE VALUE OF CONFLICT_MATRIX AT TINDEX(ROW,COLUMN)
                                               TO CONFLICT FILE
```

Wirth suggested stepwise refinement as a unified design technique for both the architectural and detailed levels, and it is often used in that way. In practice however, stepwise refinement seems to suffer at the architectural level from limited modularity. This reduces the designer's ability to compartmentalize concerns and to control the intellectual complexity of the software. As Cameron ([CAM86]) points out, the most far-reaching decisions have to be made initially, when we are most ignorant of their implication.

The other weakness of stepwise refinement during the detailed, and especially during the architectural step, is that notations like pseudocode and flowcharts tempt designers to concentrate on the structure of functional processes at the expense of considering the structure of data. This results in simplistic data structures that inadequately support the embellishment of overly elaborate algorithms. The optimal strategy for detailed design is to structure and to refine data and process simultaneously. Stepwise refinement should only be used at the architectural level when the algorithmic structure of the process is highly constrained or already specified.

When stepwise refinement is used for both the architectural and detailed design steps, and taken to an extreme, it becomes the *integrated top-down* design methodology. In this technique, the detailed design, implementation, and unit testing of a module is completed before one continues with the architectural design of the lower levels of the invocation hierarchy.

For the student registration example, this might mean that we have coded Create Student Course Requests as a very simple module consisting of

```
INITIALIZE
  GET COURSE DATA (*)
  OPEN REQUEST FILE
  ZERO MATRIX (*)
CREATE MATRIX
  FOR EACH STUDENT
       GET INDIVIDUAL STUDENT'S REQUESTS (*)
       TALLY INDIVIDUAL STUDENT'S JOINTLY REQUESTED COURSES (*)
STORE MATRIX
  CLOSE REQUEST FILE
  OPEN CONFLICT FILE
  WRITE MATRIX TO CONFLICT FILE (*)
  CLOSE CONFLICT FILE
```

and tested it with stubs representing all of the calls marked (*) by integrating it directly into the higher level modules of the entire system. Only after this testing was successful would we begin to design the modules indicated by (*) above.

Integrated top-down design is a very risky methodology, since design errors can lead to rework of not just the design, but the implementation and testing as well. It should be used only when the application is very familiar and the design path appears clearly set.

Mills has described *Box-structures* ([MIL88]) as the basis for a methodology that allows for simultaneous specification and design of software with strong potential for formal verification. There are three types of box-structures: black box, state box, and clear box. Initially, a composite of black boxes is defined, each of which represents an external, or functional, description of a data abstraction.

Each black box is then clarified a bit by transforming it into a state box in which permanent data states are included to capture the past history of stimuli to the black box. In this way, the combined effect of current stimulus and execution history is made explicit. There is an algorithmic method for verifying the correctness of this step, which collapses the state information back into the black box.

Next, the state box is further clarified to clear box status by implementing the state transition function as a single control structure, either sequence, selection, iteration, or concurrency. In this process, it is also necessary to condense the abstract state of the state boxes into a set of specific data abstractions, and to determine exactly which boxes make use of them. This concentration on specific data puts the box-structure design technique in the realm of object-oriented design. Again, the state to clear box transformation is verified by formally collapsing the control structure and data abstraction back into the state box.

The process is continued by stepwise refinement, with each clear box now being represented as a set of black box functions. Prototyping of the specification/design is helpful for validation purposes, and all box elaborations must be verified immediately. Although the box-structure design methodology is not as clear-cut as Jackson design, it does allow for greater flexibility and use of expertise. It also meets most of the concerns for good design within the framework of traditional design techniques.

The programming language *Ada* is sometimes used as the vehicle for design as well as for implementation of software. Because Ada packages have shared and private parts, with the interface defined in the shared part, and also because they allow some amount of parameterization, Ada is a good implementation language for object-oriented design. In fact, the shared parts can be used as the abstract description of modules and can form the notation for architectural design.

Functional descriptions of modules can be represented at the architectural level by the appropriate naming of identifiers, as well as by comments in the shared part. Detailed design can be done in a pseudocode based on Ada control structures. Non-Ada statements can be written as comments and can survive as internal documentation in the final implementation.

As is mentioned in Section 6.2.2, it is possible to represent procedural details in tables, such as transition tables for finite state machines, decision tables, and event tables. These tables abstract the logic of individual procedures and can be executed by generic modules. In effect, the generic module becomes a general-purpose virtual machine (finite state, or whatever), and the table becomes the program for that machine.

*Table-driven* detailed design of modules consists in simply putting together the rules expressed in the table. Usually, the table provides a methodical and easily understood framework that makes the design process manifest. Certainly, the use of table-driven design allows for easy understanding and maintenance of the software.

In the chapter on specifications, we considered the first few steps of the *Jackson System Development* technique. At that point, we obtained an entity structure diagram, as illustrated in Figure 4-34. The next three steps, corresponding to architectural and detailed design, are the initial model step, the function step, and the system timing step. Notation for the initial model step is shown in Figure 6-25.

During the *initial model* step, architectural structure is represented by a System Specification Diagram, a distributed network of processes similar to a data flow diagram, which connects entities with the real world via communication media and interconnects entities with internal data flows ([CAM86]). There are two types of media and flows: data streams or messages, which are assumed to be infinitely buffered and

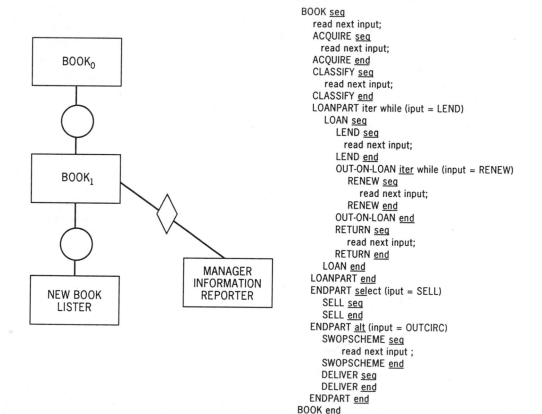

**FIGURE 6-25**  THE JSD INITIAL MODEL STEP (John Cameron, "An Overview of JSD," *IEEE Transactions on Software Engineering,* copyright © 1986, IEEE.)

strictly time sequences (represented by circles), and state vector inspection, which is an unbuffered inspection of one entity's state by another (represented by diamonds). Communication with the outside world requires two process bubbles, one, subscripted 0, in the real world, and one, subscripted 1, in the software. Of course, the real world process is not a software process.

In the initial model step, detailed design is indicated by transforming the entity structures into structure text. This is a straightforward pseudocode transcription of the entity structure diagram, using the string *itr* for the iteration * and the strings *sel* and *alt* for the selection o. The transformation can be deduced easily by comparing Figures 4-34 and 6-25.

During the *function* step, the functions represented by structure text are added to the model. In some instances, this may be done by inserting the function into an existing model process, if the function's inputs and outputs correspond to those of the process. If this is not the case, then the function is inserted separately into the model and is connected appropriately by means of data streams or state vector inspection. Other functions may include interactive feedback and error handling.

Functions are considered to be time-persistent processes; they are active for the entire duration. Figure 6-26 shows the same model of Figure 6-25 with new functions, ACK, which sends an acknowledgement slip when a book is returned to the library, and NEW, which informs the new book lister of the acquisition of a book, inserted into the model. The double lines crossing the data stream represent a many–one connection: many data streams coming out of BOOK are merged as input to NEW BOOKS LISTER.

As a final design step before implementation, the JSD model should be analyzed for constraints. This *system timing* step deals with synchronization, timing constraints,

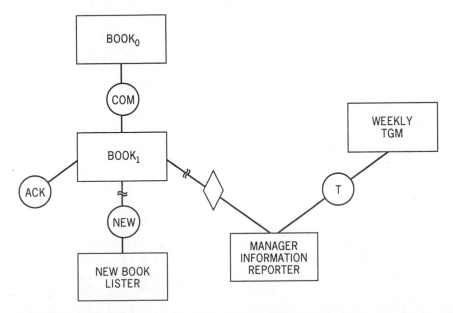

**FIGURE 6-26**  THE JSD MODEL AFTER THE FUNCTION STEP (John Cameron, "An Overview of JSD," *IEEE Transactions on Software Engineering*, copyright © 1986, IEEE.)

initial conditions, and the like. One technique for introducing synchronization is the creation of time grain markers, shown in Figure 6-26 as a data stream (T) of periodic signals, generated by WEEKLY TGM, to trigger the weekly production of management lists.

The JSD methodology, in common with the older JSP (Jackson Structured Programming (see [ING86]), technique, has the advantage of being quite algorithmic. It also relies heavily on modeling the solution on real world data (or entities), which provides an easy starting point and appropriate emphasis on data. Like object-oriented design, JSD methodology tends to proceed by composition of simpler parts rather than by decomposition of the product as a whole.

However, in circumstances in which it is not immediately evident how processing transforms one entity structure into another, it is difficult to come up with either an appropriate model or structured function texts. Thus, the methodology is most useful for relatively straightforward processing applications. Jackson would say, and with perfect accuracy, that most applications are of that nature.

*Higher Order Software* (HOS) is a methodology developed by Hamilton and Zeldin and now marketed commercially as an environment. It is a true specification transformation system. The specifications, built by the software engineer and customer using an interactive graphics tool, are a hierarchy of functions with control notation and a set of composite data types. Data interfaces, using the defined data types, are indicated in the control map or tree. The functions in the tree, and the control forms available, are carefully constrained to allow automated analysis of the specification for correctness and consistency.

Once validated, the specification is automatically translated into code. This can be tested, and the specification can be modified in a prototyping fashion. The system handles incomplete specification by simulating missing components. When the complete final product is built, some documentation is automatically produced.

Among the other design methodologies currently being promoted are *rules-oriented, access-oriented,* and *data-structure-oriented* design ([HAL86]). Rules-oriented design is typified by the Prolog/expert system environment. Specification is carried out by stating the constraints that a solution will have to meet. A set of rules is automatically searched to put together a solution that meets the constraints. Access-oriented design represents actions as side effects of the access or storage of data. Data-structure-oriented design attempts to fit all problems into the context of a single data structure, like lists or arrays, and the existing operations on the structures. It is somewhat similar to functional design.

### 6.3.3 Assertions and Formal Verification

Although verification is important at all stages of software development, at the end of the design stage we have a major opportunity to check the *'how'*s developed during architectural and detailed design against the *'what'*s produced during specifications. Since the design stage causes by far the greatest transformation in the product, verification is both more useful and more necessary following this period than at the end of any other period.

Formal verification of detailed design is an attempt to press the proof methods of mathematics into the cause of showing that software is error free. Two related techniques are used: **input-output assertions** and **structural induction**. Input-output assertions take advantage of the obvious formal nature of detailed design languages to treat them like statements in mathematical logic, the proofs of which are susceptible to mechanical verification.

Structural induction seems more familiar to many software engineers; it uses the principle of mathematical induction in much the same way as it might be applied in algebra. Proofs by structural induction tend to be more informal than proofs from assertions. Another method, proposed by Mills ([MIL88]), applies the concepts of mathematical functions and relations to programs. It will not be treated here but can be read about in [MIL88].

An **assertion** is simply a statement that represents, as precisely as possible, some claim about the relationship of variable values in the system state at a particular moment during execution. The technique of input-output assertions attempts to show that if the input assertion is true at the beginning of the execution of a procedure, then the output assertion will necessarily be true at the end of execution ([SAI84]). If the procedure is of significant size, the step from beginning to end will be too complex to verify directly and, hence, other intermediate assertions will be added at points in the procedure to provide more manageable steps.

There are three rules of deduction and an axiom used in proving that an assertion follows from the previous one. The axiom expresses the nature of the assignment operation. The first rule is the standard chain rule of mathematical logic and represents the effect of sequential (program) statements. The last two rules are for while loops and if-then-else statements. Here we use P, Q and R to represent assertions which are true before or after the execution of the statements S in a program. The notation

$$\{P\}S\{Q\}$$

means that we can prove that if P is true before execution of S, then Q is true afterward. The notation

$$\frac{XXXXX}{YYY}$$

means that from XXXXX we can logically deduce YYY.

The assignment axiom takes the form $\{P(expr)\}x := expr\{P(x)\}$ and means that if the assertion P is true of some expression and $x$ is assigned the value of that expression, then P is true of $x$.

The chain rule is

$$\frac{\{P\}S_1\{Q\}, \{Q\}S_2\{R\}}{\{P\}S_1; S_2\{R\}}$$

allowing us to deduce bigger logical steps from a chain of small ones.

The loop rule is

$$\frac{\{P\&B\}S\{P\}}{\{P\}\text{while B loop S; endloop}\{-B\&P\}}$$

and indicates that an assertion P is invariant under the action of a loop; that is, if P is true before execution of the loop, P is true after execution as well.

The rule for selection is

$$\frac{\{P\&B\}S_1\{Q\}, \quad \{P\&-B\}S_2\{Q\}}{\{P\}\text{if B then }S_1;\text{ else }S_2;\text{ end if}\{Q\}}$$

and indicates that Q follows P no matter which branch is taken to get there.

Because this is an introductory text, even formal verification is treated somewhat informally here. A mathematician would still find fault with the following proof because we will use rules not included above. In part, these rules cover the fact that logic, independent of program semantics, can be used with validity, and that assertions that do not refer to variables affected by a program statement are themselves unaffected by the statement.

To illustrate the technique, consider the program in Figure 6-27. (In fact, we should only be verifying its detailed design at this stage. A similar verification of the program should be part of the implementation stage. But formal verification is appropriate for a detailed design and should be presented at this stage. On the other hand, this abstract example becomes a little more concrete if it is presented in a real implementation language like Pascal.) The assertions are assumed to be already present. The program implements an easy and familiar function, finding the first node in a linear linked list containing a particular target value. Although it is a simple task, programmers often create errors as they implement it. This is, in part, due to some of the shortcomings of Pascal. In particular, this design requires the use of a shortcircuit *or* condition. This is a logical operator in which, if the first disjunct is true, no attempt is made to evaluate subsequent disjuncts. Since it isn't available in Pascal, it is necessary to define a function or_else. Such language drawbacks make the logic of a program harder to verify. That is the reason for implementing the function in Pascal here. You will see an Ada program that is considerably cleaner.

To deduce that P6 (see Figure 6-27) follows from P1, we build up larger steps incrementally.

**P4 —> P5:**  By the selection rule, we must show that P5 follows from P4 no matter which branch is taken. If the true branch is taken, NIL and NODE are unaffected by the statement and RESULT is true because the condition of the selection statement was true and we can substitute result for p by the assignment axiom. If the false branch is taken, then either there is a next node in the list and thus NODE remains true since target was not at that node either, or there is no next node and thus NIL is true, since target had not appeared by the last node. RESULT, in turn, is true because it is unaffected by the change in p.

```
function or_else(a,b:boolean):boolean;
begin or_else := false; if a then or_else := true
                             else if b then or_else := true; end;
```

{In the following, we abbreviate statements:
    NIL is "p is nil and target doesn't appear on the list"
    NODE is "p points to a node and target doesn't appear in a
    previous node"
    RESULT is "if result isn't undefined then ((it is nil and
    target isn't on the list) or (result points to the first node
    on the list containing target))"}

```
function search(head_of_list:nodeptr; target:integer):nodeptr;
var undefined,p,result:nodeptr;
begin
                {P1: head_of_list is nil or points to the first node
                in a nonempty linear list whose last node points to
                nil}
p := head_of_list;
                {P2: NIL or NODE}
new(undefined);
result := undefined;
                {P3: ((NIL or NODE) and RESULT)}
while result = undefined do
begin
                {P4: ((NIL or NODE) and RESULT) and (result is
                undefined)}
if or_else(p = nil,p^.value = target) then result := p
                                      else p := p^.next
                {P5: (NIL or NODE) and RESULT}
end;
                {P6: ((NIL or NODE) and RESULT) and (result is
                defined)}
search := result;
dispose(undefined);
end;
```

**F I G U R E 6-27**   A PASCAL LINEAR SEARCH

**P3 —> P6:**   By the loop rule.

**P2 —> P3:**   By logical deduction, including the fact that a logical implication is true
if the antecedent is false and the assignment axiom.

**P2 —> P6:**   By the sequence rule.

**P1 —> P2:**   By the assignment axiom and the fact that there are *no* nodes previous to the first node in a linear list.

**P1 —> P6:**   By the sequence rule.

Finally, if at P6 we combine the fact that result is defined with RESULT being true, we see that if p originally pointed to the first node in a (possibly empty) list, the first occurrence of target (or nil if there is none) is returned by search.

Interestingly enough, we can also show that this particular procedure terminates. This is not always possible. The execution must lead into the loop body, and as we loop around again within the body we always move to a new node. This is because the list, being linear, has no cycles. (This follows from the preassertion, P1.) Since any list stored in a computer must be finite, we will eventually find the target or reach the last node, which points to nil (P1 again). Thus, we will surely exit from the loop and the procedure will terminate.

Structural induction is a technique that uses the method of mathematical induction as it is applied to data structures that have some kind of size, like the length of a list or the height of a tree ([BER82]). It is also applicable to recursive procedures, since they themselves are defined inductively

Structural induction can be used to show that the search function works correctly. The induction proceeds on the length of the list. The desired conclusion is the operant part of assertion P6:

**Hypothesis**:   (result is nil and target is not on the list) or (result points to the first node on the list containing target), when the length of the list is $n$.

**Basis**:   The list is of length 0; it has no elements and head_of_list is nil. In the only execution of the loop body, result is set to nil. Of course, target does not appear in the empty list. Thus, the hypothesis is true if $n = 0$.

**Induction**:   Let the list be of length $n+1$. Suppose the induction hypothesis is true for lists of length n. Consider the action of the function on a separate list made up of the first $n$ elements of this list. If target is found on the shorter list, it will be found in exactly the same place on this list, by the induction hypothesis. If target is not found on the shorter list, but is at the last node on this list, then it will be the first occurrence and will be returned. If target is not found on the shorter list, or at the last node of this list, then it is not on the list and nil will be returned. Thus, the hypothesis is also true for $n+1$.

**Conclusion**:   For a list of any length at all, the hypothesis is true.

Consider this simple Ada function to calculate a factorial:

```
function factorial(n:natural) return natural is
      begin
      return(if n = 0 then 1 else n*factorial(n-1));
      end factorial;
```

We can show by structural induction that factorial($n$) equals $n!$ for all $n$ such that $n! <=$ integer'last.

**Hypothesis**:      if $0 < n! <=$ integer'last then factorial($n$) = $n!$

**Basis**:           $n = 0$. factorial($n$) returns 1 and $0! = 1$.

**Induction**:        if $0 < (n+1)! <=$ integer'last then factorial($n+1$) returns $(n+1)$\*factorial($n$), which by the induction hypothesis is $(n+1)$\*$n!$. But $(n+1)$\*$n! = (n+1)$\*$(n$\*$((n-1)$\*...\*$1))$.)., which by the commutativity and associativity of integer arithmetic, is $(n+1)!$

**Conclusion**:     Within expected ranges, factorial ($n$) is correct.

You may already have gotten the idea that formal verification is difficult and tedious. This is true to such a degree that it remains more a classroom exercise and laboratory experiment than a practical part of software engineering. The consensus is that no software product of significant size has been fully verified, despite the fact that considerable effort has been expended on verification for many years ([PAR85a]). The effort needed to verify the correctness of a 500-line program is generally far greater than the effort of designing the correct program. The effort of verifying a 500,000-line program boggles the mind. Even the existence of automated verification tools eases the problem only slightly. This situation is only partially mitigated by the fact that successful verification substantially reduces the testing effort. The real problem is that the job just seems too difficult and the complexity too great to cope with.

The problem here is specifically that of finding loop invariants. A **loop invariant** is an assertion that can be used as assertion $P$ in the loop rule of deduction ([SAI84]); it is true at the entry to, and the exit from, the loop. As one can see from the rule, $P$ is true before, during, and after the execution of the loop and, hence, the name invariant. It is sometimes quite a trick to find the right invariant for a loop. Of course, one could choose any number of true invariants, like sum = sum, but they are useless in verifying the correct function of the procedure. Nor is it possible for all of the relevant invariants to be generated automatically. So, in the end, it is up to the individual to utilize insight and skill to provide a proof (Figure 6-28).

Along the same lines, it is difficult to verify any segment of a design if we start with too weak a preassertion. Simply put, this will not have enough power to provide the results we want. For this reason, a theory exists for deriving the *weakest precondition* for the postcondition we desire — a theory that will guarantee its achievement ([DIJ76], [HO87a]). It may also occur that there are hidden assumptions, used implicitly by the proof, but absent in the assertion.

Another of the several potential problems in formal verification arises from the existence of the Halting Problem set: it is formally impossible to show in general that a procedure will terminate for given input. Thus, whenever one works with assertions, one must claim that *if* execution reaches this point, the assertion will be true. Of course, never getting into an infinite loop is one of the things that we really need to verify, and it just is not possible in the general case.

Still another problem is that in actuality we are simply verifying that the procedure meets its specifications, in the form of preassertion and postassertion. There is no

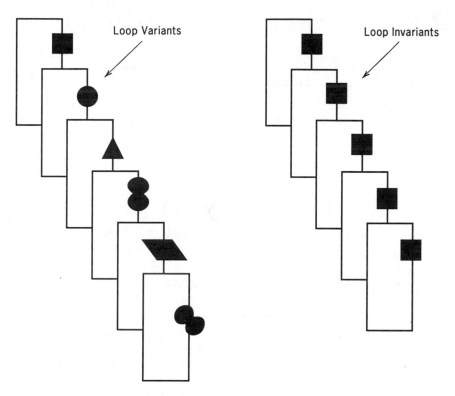

**FIGURE 6-28**   LOOP VARIANTS AND INVARIANTS

guarantee that the specifications really meet the intention of the customer, analyst or designer. Something might be wrong with the specification; more likely, the specification is incomplete. In fact, if the assertions do not match the design exactly, a correct proof may be given mistakenly for another design, one that does match.

Since the difficulty of formal verification rises sharply with procedure size, it is common to see exception conditions ruled out during proofs of correctness. For instance, the Pascal linear search above could fail if no space were available to create the dynamic entity "undefined." This issue was ignored in the verification, however. Of course, exception handling can be defined, and can itself be verified, but the size of the code and the difficulty of the verification increases dramatically. Add to that the problems of verifying concurrent procedures communicating through message passing and verifying the performance of real-time software, and it becomes apparent that there are strict limits to the kind of verification task that can be reasonably undertaken.

Finally, one always runs the risk that the same kinds of mistakes that occur in designing and implementing software will also occur in "proving" the correctness of the software. Gerhart and Yelowitz give numerous examples of incorrect and incomplete "proofs" of correctness ([GER76]), and ([DEM79]) points out that the mathematical proof environment works only because large numbers of experts examine proofs carefully. It may be true that just as more errors are introduced in a program while correcting errors, so also more errors in a verification are created while those concerned attempt to prove that there are none. Mills and Linger believe that these errors can be avoided if we restrict ourselves to the use of simple and well-understood data abstractions like sets, stacks and queues ([MIL86]).

### 6.3.4 Verification-Driven Design

There is, however, one reasonable way of using verification to provide better software, and it has been advocated for a long time by many people. The technique is simply to design software so that it can be easily proved ([DIJ72], [GRI81], [HO87a], [MIL88]). Consider how the program of Figure 6-27 was developed. The first step was to come up with the postassertion, which was the then part of RESULT. Next, a simple algorithm was sketched that, it was hoped, would derive the postassertion. The algorithm was

```
initialize p at the beginning of the list
loop: for each node p^, if p^.value = target
                        then search := p and exit
```

Since the algorithm consists largely of a simple loop, the next step was to find an appropriate loop invariant. This required a couple of refinement steps, as it turned out. It was evident that the exit in the loop would have to be effected through some kind of flag value to be tested in the loop condition. It seemed reasonable to use a separate pointer that would be undefined until the "exit" instruction was to be performed. It also seemed reasonable to let the extra pointer carry the return value. The first attempt at an invariant was "if result is defined then either result is nil and target was not found or result points to target."

This was, in fact, fairly close to the final form of the invariant, with the significant omission of any notion of result pointing to the *first* occurrence of target on the list. When an implementation was written, it became apparent that to prove anything it would be necessary to involve the "first occurrence" concept and to prove things about both result and p. This complication again derives from the design of Pascal and would not have been necessary in Ada.

The incrementation in the loop, p := p^.next, was obvious and unavoidable. There is simply no other way to traverse the list. Once an invariant was in place, it remained to establish the termination condition for the loop. Again, this was essentially constrained by our need to execute some kind of "exit" statement. Finally, it was necessary to provide a preassertion that would ensure that the loop invariant would be true after initialization. It had been anticipated that pointing to the beginning of the list would be sufficient. The subsequent proof of termination showed that it would be necessary to specify that the list was "linear" as well.

Given this framework, it became quite easy to implement and prove the "correct" procedure search. However, the proof ended up glossing over questions like "what if, for some reason, the value stored in the target field of some node isn't a valid integer?" and "what if the new allocation can't be completed?" As is the usual situation, the proof of correctness was incomplete but was judged sufficient for the purposes at hand.

It is also true that the Pascal implementation is about as clean and understandable as one is likely to see. This tends to support the idea that the need to provide a proof not only promotes correct software but also results in clear and efficient software.

Dijkstra was one of the first to advocate that the demands of formal verification should guide us in the design of the software ([DIJ72]). Since then, many others have reiterated the same imperative. The article by Mili, Desharnais, and Gagne ([MI86a]) represents a recent and extended treatment of the same idea.

## 6.4 FOSTERING QUALITY DURING DESIGN

Freeman ([FRE87]) is at least partially right — if design is not the unifying activity of software development, it is certainly the pivotal one. A lack of quality in the design process can invalidate an otherwise good specification and can make correct implementation impossible. For this reason, we must take special care to ensure that the design process is carried out correctly.

Luckily, there are many useful metrics for evaluating design at all three levels. In fact, this book lists more metrics for the design stage than for any other. As we have just learned, there is also a strongly developed verification technology for detailed design (and implementation). On the other hand, there is not enough that is new to be said about management of the design stage to merit mention.

### 6.4.1 Design Metrics

To evaluate design, it is necessary to choose a set of design attributes that will be measured, along with some objective metrics, which can be applied in a procedural way to the design. There should also be a procedure for combining individual metrics to evaluate overall design quality. As a warning, one should remember that any of the proposed metrics are based on introspection and have intuitive appeal, but research has failed to support their claim that they really measure important attributes like clarity, maintainability, or proclivity to error ([KEA86]).

In using metrics, it is important to realize just what we are trying to measure. Some design metrics evaluate the complexity of the design process, whereas others are more oriented to determining the difficulty of maintenance. If we are measuring design effort, then we must take into account contributing factors like experience, ability, and environment ([KEA86]). Waguespack and Badlani ([WAG87]) have recently published an annotated bibliography that gives access to most of the literature on metrics for design and other stages.

For architectural design, we take the invocation hierarchy of software that has no indirect recursion and represent it as a true directed graph, where procedures called by more than one procedure are represented by one node with several incoming arcs. The *depth* of this graph, the length of its longest path, can be easily determined. This metric roughly correlates with the size and complexity of the product.

In a similar fashion, the *shape* of the graph can be evaluated. Typically, the upper levels of the graph should show substantial fan-out (number of modules invoked), perhaps in a ratio of 1:4, whereas the lowest levels should show fan-in (number of invoking modules) to, at least, that degree. Although the exact ratios are project dependent, attention to them fosters a design in which there are a number of well-chosen utility modules, whose effects can be combined by midlevel control modules to provide a much higher degree of versatility. Of course, there would also be a few high-level control and interface routines. Such a graph would exhibit a somewhat oval shape.

In an object-oriented design, the *visibility* of an object can be taken as a measure of the degree to which it is global to the entire system. Generally, a high level of visibility is desirable for no more than a few objects in the design, and then only those most central to the software.

When modules are highly decoupled, we generally have a better architectural design. The spectrum in Figure 6-29, due in part to Myers ([STE74]), provides a comparative metric by arranging coupling types from best to worst. To evaluate decoupling by the above criteria, we need to know something about the internal function of modules as well as the interfaces between modules. Internal function can be estimated by examining functional descriptions from the specifications or we may wait until detailed design is complete. The latter, however, is somewhat risky, since discovery of an error in the architectural design might require the rework of parts of the detailed design.

In any situation, the quality of the architectural design can be measured by assigning a value, from 0 to 6, to the decoupling of each module, and then evaluating the frequency with which different values occur as well, perhaps, as an overall average.

*Cohesion* is also an important attribute of good modularity ([STE74]). The cohesiveness of the modules in an architectural design can be measured in the same way as their degree of decoupling. If we are basing ourselves on the functional descriptions, and if they are expressed in something like natural language, then we can scan them for words like "next" or "after" to detect sequential cohesion, for words like "object" or "operation" to detect informational cohesion, for multiple verbs to detect anything less than functional cohesion, and so on.

| **Coupling** | **Good** | **Cohesion** |
|---|---|---|
| Independence | ↑ | Functional |
| Data | | Informational |
| Stamp | | Sequential |
| Control | | Communicational |
| External | | Procedural |
| Common | | Temporal |
| Content | ↓ | Logical |
| | Bad | Coincidental |

**F I G U R E 6-29**   SPECTRA OF MODULE DECOUPLING AND COHESION

Note that modules defined at the design stage may never achieve better than informational cohesion. True functional cohesion is often too fine grained to show up until we begin to package code into individual procedures during implementation.

Li and Cheung ([LI 87]) classify different detailed design metrics into Control Organization, Volume, Data Organization, and Hybrid measures. The control organization metrics measure the control structure of processes. Volume metrics measure the size of the detailed design. Data Organization evaluates the usage, interactions, and visibility of data. Of course, hybrid measures attempt to combine the influences of the separate aspects of detailed design into a single normative value.

The first control organization metric for detailed design, due to McCabe, is called the *cyclomatic complexity* of a procedure. Graphically, it is represented, as in Figure 6-30, by the number of different regions of the plane created by the arcs of a flowchart for the process. Actually, it is measured by calculating the number of binary decisions in the module and then adding 1.

In general, a detailed design that exhibits a complexity below 3 is either insufficiently developed or a candidate for inclusion in some other module. Similarly, a design whose complexity exceeds 7 is a candidate for further modularization. (McCabe suggested 10 rather than 7, but this may allow too deep a nesting of control structures.)

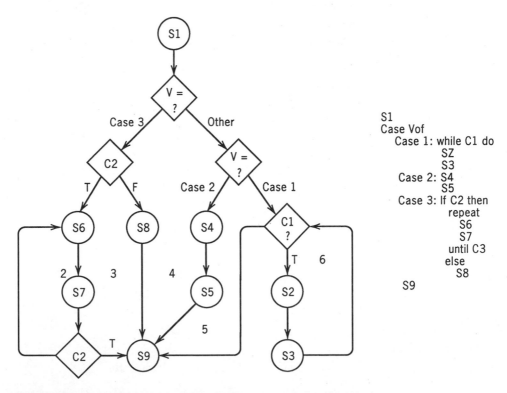

**FIGURE 6-30** CYCLOMATIC COMPLEXITY OF A DETAILED DESIGN

However, if the complexity is due solely to a well-constructed CASE structure, it can be discounted.

The *reachability* of a sequence of statements that includes no control statements (a block or segment) can be evaluated by counting the number of different control paths that reach the segment. If the segment is subsequent to a loop, there are two paths that correspond to execution or nonexecution of the loop body. The average reachability of all segments in the entire module can also be calculated. In general, high reachability numbers indicate an overly complex module that is ripe for further modularization.

Another control organization metric, discovered by Gilb, counts the number of *binary decisions* (if-then-else's and iteration statements) in a module. It may be desirable to augment this count by the number of procedure and function invocations in the module. In turn, these numbers can be given in absolute or relative terms, the latter found by dividing the number of decisions (plus calls) by the total number of statements.

The easiest volume metric, *size*, of detailed designs can be measured in terms of pseudocode statement or Nassi–Shneiderman box counts. Once again, if the size of an individual module exceeds 10, the module is probably too complex. However, we can also calculate mean size of all modules in the product design.

Data organization can be measured by techniques proposed by Yin and Winchester (see [NAV87]). They use both a control and a data flow chart to measure *intermodule coupling*. When this is normalized by the size of the module, there is a high correlation with errors. The Henry and Kafura information flow metric, described in the same article, uses both global and local data flows to measure *complexity*, which is proportional to the size of a module and to the square of the product of inflow and outflow. A complex module is called a stress point. High inflow and outflow is a symptom of lack of cohesion or a lack of refinement. Poor module construction is signaled by a high global data flow combined with low complexity, whereas low global flow and high complexity indicate poor decomposition.

It is also possible to evaluate the overall quality of design by assigning numeric values to degrees of the various attributes that have been previously introduced in this chapter (clarity, encapsulation, and the like) and for which no other metric is available. These values will serve as rough metrics for those attributes. We can also assign relative weighting to each attribute, measuring its relative importance in achieving the goals of the project. The weighted average of all metrics then provides a single hybrid measure of design.

### 6.4.2 Verification and Validation

During design, quality assurance personnel must verify that the design is in conformity with the specifications. They will be assisted in this task by the use of notations and methodologies that provide a basis for the smooth transformation of specifications into design. Lacking this, quality assurance is provided by careful inspections of the developing design.

The design process can be assured as well. One way is to verify conformity to established standard methodologies and notations. A second way would be to require the completion and approval of all planned work products. A third way applies some appropriate metrics to measure the fundamental attributes of the design.

There will be two major reviews during the design stage. They will be conducted in a formal fashion, with many participants, and they represent points at which development activities pass important milestones. It is possible that the project might be canceled as a result of either of these design reviews; however, it is more likely that the result will be a freezing of the design at that point, to the extent that only minor modifications will be considered in the future.

The first review, called the **Preliminary Design Review**, occurs at the point when the design task is divided, passing from the responsibility of a single person or group to many people. The design at this point will have progressed down through several levels of refinement. For large software products, which may employ a number of architectural designers, the participants might prepare for this review by walking through their designs with one or more of their peers.

Some of the questions asked at the preliminary design review are shown in Figure 6-31. The review may not be favorable, in which case a large amount of rework on the design will be necessary. Even if the review is favorable, some minor problems with the design will probably be discovered. Correction of these will be verified during the Critical Design Review.

The **Critical Design Review** occurs when all detailed design is complete. The same questions are asked again, and once again there is a possibility of extensive rework if the review is not favorable. Minor change orders can be recorded and verified before implementation begins on that portion of the product.

The low-level walkthroughs mentioned above are more informal inspections in which a designer explains his work to some peers by walking through the process, data flow, logic, or some other organizing principle. The peers are on hand to catch errors, evaluate decisions, and clarify imprecision. Questions are usually recorded and responded to at a later date. Every significant design effort should be evaluated by a walkthrough.

Finally, the quality assurance group must help develop and approve the Unit Test Plans, the Integration Test Plans, and the Integration Sequence.

- Are all functional specifications being met?
- Are the performance, dependability, and exception-handling requirements of the software achievable with this design?
- Is the user interface acceptable to the customer?
- Does the design provide for early completion of high-priority functions and addition of probable enhancements?
- Have previously chosen design standards been met?
- Has the design been fully inspected through low-level walkthroughs?

**FIGURE 6-31**   QUESTIONS TO BE ASKED DURING THE DESIGN REVIEWS

## 6.5 A DESIGN EXAMPLE

This section does not provide an entire design document; instead, it exemplifies some of the design steps. It should not be too hard to understand how to put a design document together from the examples.

### 6.5.1 Architectural Design of EDCA Synchronization and Cleaning

In terms of data design, the external data are already fully defined. Internally, data will be most naturally represented as a stream of bytes on the front end, or a stream of frames (with a possible header) on the rear end. These streams will either be represented by true sequences, say, of bytes, or by blocks of memory designated by starting address and byte length. There will be some additional messages passed between modules. These will be represented by character strings (see Figures 6-32 through 6-35).

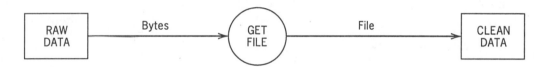

**FIGURE 6-32**   A PRELIMINARY DATA FLOW DIAGRAM FOR THE SOFTWARE

**FIGURE 6-33**   THE SECOND EXPANSION OF THE DIAGRAM

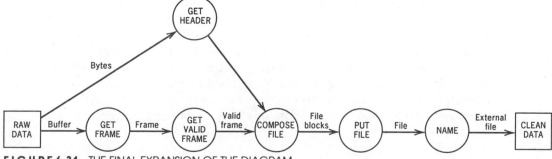

**FIGURE 6-34**   THE FINAL EXPANSION OF THE DIAGRAM

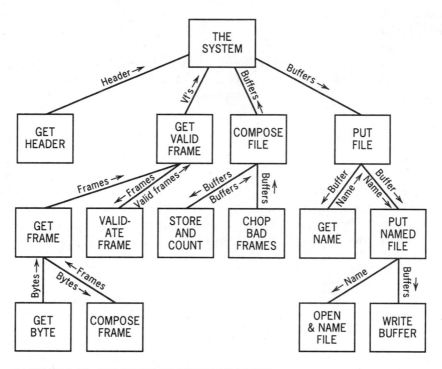

**F I G U R E 6-35**   THE RESULTING STRUCTURE CHART

## 6.5.2 The Detailed Design of Compose File

We start with a detailed pseudocode design of STORE AND COUNT. This module is supposed to accept header and validated frames, count the frames, and store them until, at least, 350 valid frames are accumulated. It will then provide the header and valid frames to THE SYSTEM.

The fundamental data structure is the buffer for holding the header and frames. We decide to make this a fixed length buffer. Upon consideration, it is realized that it only needs to be long enough to hold the header and 350 frames (16,200 bytes). When it has been filled to that point, a valid file has been composed, and the buffer can be flushed. Additional valid frames can still be stored and flushed when the buffer is full or when the sequence of valid frames is broken. There will have to be a pointer to the first free byte in the buffer.

The question arises whether there should be any handshaking (see section 4.2.4) to determine that the buffer has been flushed before more data are appended to the store. The decision is to let THE SYSTEM handle that problem.

Beside the header and frame structures, the interface will also carry in the commands "store" and "flush" and the completion code "full," indicating that the buffer is full. The interface structure will be

```
command, inbuffer, outbuffer, and completion code.

        If command is "store" then
              append inbuffer to store
              update pointer
              If pointer beyond buffer-end then
                    code = "full"
                    outbuffer = store
                    move pointer to buffer-start
        else {command is "flush"}
              outbuffer = store
              move pointer to buffer-start
```

For the CHOP BAD FRAMES module, the function should reset the store pointer so that only the header precedes it. The interface consists of two completion codes, "done" and "failed." Failed occurs when there is insufficient data in the store to make up a header.

```
        If pointer before header-end then
              code = "failed"
        else
              move pointer to header-end
              code = "done"
```

Since CHOP BAD FRAMES is so small, and uses the same structure as STORE AND COUNT, the two should probably be merged.

## 6.6 SUMMARY

We have seen that design is a mixture of methodology and creativity. The creativity makes it fun, but the methodology makes it profitable. To reap the full benefits of methodology, tools, and analysis, we should accept the need to use formal design notations.

Design is a stepwise process, and good methodologies aid in the expansion of the design through abstraction, creation of modules, organization of modules, and hiding of design decisions. The preferred architectural design methodology is structured design, whereas the preferred detailed design methodology is stepwise refinement. Object-oriented, levels of abstraction and box-structured design are among the most useful of the remaining design methodologies, but there are any number of different methodologies and environments for design that can be chosen according to the particular application and training of the designer. There are also some tools for evaluating design, which depend on the metrics available.

Formal verification can be effected in several ways. Proofs of correctness allow us to use mathematical proof techniques on programs, whereas structural induction uses proof by induction on data structures. Both are difficult to perform correctly and have been applied in the past only to relatively small products. However, the exercise of designing modules with proof requirements in mind may well produce cleaner and more efficient code.

Our next step will be to transform the detailed design in executable code.

# BIBLIOGRAPHY

[BAS81]     Basili, V.R., and R.W. Reiter, "A Controlled Experiment Quantitatively Comparing Software Development Approaches," *IEEE Transactions on Software Engineering*, 7(3):299 – 320.

[BER82]*    Berg, H.K., W.E. Boebert, W.R. Franta, and T.G. Moher, *Formal Methods of Program Verification and Specification*, Prentice-Hall, Englewood Cliffs, NJ.

[BER86]     Berzins, V.M., M. Gray, and D. Naumann, "Abstraction-based Software Development," *Communications of the ACM*, 29(5):402 – 415.

[BOO86]*    Booch, G., "Object-Oriented Development," *IEEE Transactions on Software Engineering*, 12(2):211 – 221.

[BRO87]*    Brooks, F.P., "No Silver Bullet: Essence and Accidents of Software Engineering," *Computer*, 20(4):10 – 19.

[CAM86]     Cameron, J.R., "An Overview of JSD," *IEEE Transactions on Software Engineering*, 12(2):222 – 240.

[CRO84]     Cross, N., *Developments in Design Methodology*, Wiley, New York.

[DEM79]     DeMillo, R.A., R.J. Lipton, and A.J. Perlis, "Social Processes and Proofs of Theorems and Programs," *Communications of the ACM*, 22(5):271 – 280.

[DIJ72]*    Dijkstra, E., "The Humble Programmer," *Communications of the ACM*, 15(10):859 – 866.

[DIJ76]     Dijkstra, E., *A Discipline of Programming*, Prentice-Hall, Englewood Cliffs, NJ.

[FRE87]*    Freeman, P., "Essential Elements of Software Engineering Education Revisited," *IEEE Transactions on Software Engineering*, 13(11):1143 – 1148.

[GER76]*    Gerhart, S.L., and L. Yelowitz, "Observations of Fallibility in Applications of Modern Programming Methodologies," *IEEE Transactions on Software Engineering*, 2(9):195 – 200.

[GRI81]*    Gries, D., *The Science of Programming*, Springer-Verlag, New York.

[HAL86]     Halpern, B., "Multiparadigm Languages and Environments," *Software*, 3(1):6 – 9.

[HAL87]*    Halbert, D.C., and P.D. O'Brien, "Using Types and Inheritance in Object-Oriented Programming," *IEEE Software*, 4(5):71 – 79.

[HOA87]*    Hoare, C.A.R., "An Overview of Some Formal Methods for Program Design," *Computer*. 20(9):85 – 91.

[HO87a]     Hoare, C.A.R. et al., "Laws of Programming," *Communications of the ACM*, 30(8):672 – 86.

[ING86]     Ingevaldsson, L., *JSP: A Practical Method of Program Design*, 2nd ed., Chartwell-Bratt Ltd., London.

[JON70]     Jones, J.C., *Design Methods: Seeds of Human Futures*, Wiley-Interscience, New York.

[KAN85]     Kant, E., "Understanding and Automating Algorithm Design," *IEEE Transactions on Software Engineering*, 11(11):1361 – 74.

[KEA86]     Kearney, J.K., R.L. Sedlmeyer, W.B. Thompson, M.L. Gray, and M.A. Adler, "Software Complexity Measurement," *Communications of the ACM*, 29(11):1044 – 1050.

[LIE88]     Lieberherr, K., I. Holland, G. Lee, and A.J. Riel, "An Objective Sense of Style," *Computer*, 21(6):79 – 80.

[LI 87]*    Li, H.F., and W.K. Cheung, "An Empirical Study of Software Metrics," *IEEE Transactions on Software Engineering*, 13(6):697 – 708.

[MIL85]     Mills, J.A., "A Pragmatic View of the System Architect," *Communication of the ACM*, 28(7):708 – 717.

[MIL86]*    Mills, H.D., and R.C. Linger, "Data Structured Programming," *IEEE Transactions on Software Engineering*, 12(2):192 – 197.

[MI86a]*    Mili, A., J. Desharnais, and J.R. Gagne, "Formal Models of Stepwise Refinement of Programs," *Computing Surveys*, 18(3):231 – 276.

[MIL88]*    Mills, H.D., "Stepwise Refinement and Verification in Box-Structured Systems," *Computer*, 21(6):23 – 36.

[NAV87]     Navlakka, J.K., "A Survey of System Complexity Metrics," *Computer Journal*, 30(3):233 – 238.

[PAR79]*    Parnas, D.L., "Designing Software for Ease of Extension and Contraction," *IEEE Transactions of the ACM*, 5(2):128 – 138.

[PAR85a]*   Parnas, D.L., P.C. Clements, and D.M. Weiss, "The Modular Structure of Complex Systems," *IEEE Transactions on Software Engineering*, 11(3):252 – 258.

[PAR85b]*   Parnas, D.L., "Software Aspects of Strategic Defense Systems," *Communications of the ACM*, 28(12):1326 – 1335.

[PAR86]     Parnas, D.L., and P.C. Clements, "A Rational Design Process: How and Why to Fake It," *IEEE Transactions on Software Engineering*, 12(2):251 – 257.

[RAJ85]     Rajlich, V., "Paradigms for Design and Implementation in Ada," *Communications of the ACM*, 28(7):718 – 727.

[RAM83]     Ramsey, H.R., M.E. Atwood, and J.R. Van Doren, "Flowcharts Versus Program Design Languages: An Experimental Comparison," *Communications of the ACM*, 26(6):445 – 449.

[SAI84]     Saib, S.H., "Formal Verification" in *Handbook of Software Engineering* by G.R. Vick and G.V. Ramamoorthy, Van Nostrand Reinhold, New York.

[SHA85]*    Shaw, M., "Abstraction Techniques in Modern Programming Languages," *IEEE Software*, 1(4):10 – 27.

[STE74]*    Stevens, W., G. Myers, and L. Constantine, "Structured Design," *IBM Systems Journal*, 13(2):115 – 139.

[STR88]*    Stroustrup, B., "What is Object-Oriented Programming," *IEEE Software*, 5(3):10 – 20.

[WAG87]*    Waguespack, L.J., and S. Badlani, "Software Complexity Assessment: An Introduction and Annotated Bibliography," *Software Engineering Notes*, 12(4):52 – 71.

[WAR86]*    Ward, P.T., "The Transformation Scheme," *IEEE Transactions on Software Engineering*, 12(2):198 – 210.

[WAS89]     Wasserman, A.I., P.A. Pircher, and R.J. Muller, "An Object-oriented Structured Design Method for Code Generation," *Software Engineering Notes*, 14(1):32 – 55.

[WEB88]*    Webster, D.E., "Mapping the Design Information Representation Terrain," *Computer*, 21(12):8 – 23.

[YOD78]     Yoder, C.M., and M.L. Schrag, "Nassi-Shneiderman Charts: An Alternative for Design," *Proceedings of the ACM Quality Assurance Workshop*, 386 – 393, Association for Computing Machinery, New York.

[YOU78]     Yourden, E., and L. Constantine, *Structured Design*, Yourden Press, New York.

## PROBLEMS

1    Write a program to calculate the average of 100 integers in an array. Prove that it is correct.

2    Write a program to find the largest integer in a linear linked list. Prove that it is correct.

3    Write a recursive subprogram to print out the integers found at the nodes of a binary tree, using the inorder traversal pattern. Prove that it is correct by structural induction.

4    Read [FRE87] and evaluate Freeman's claim that design is the central topic of software engineering.

5    Apply JSD to the EDCA project. Are the results more natural?

6    Write abbreviated detailed designs for individual modules to represent all of the levels of cohesion mentioned in Section 6.2.2.

7    Write abbreviated architectural designs to represent all levels of coupling listed in Section 6.2.2.

8    Rank the design methodologies in the order of the strength of their realism.

9    Rank the design methodologies in the order of their ability to partition design.

10   If structured analysis and design is used for the university information system of Problem 9 in Chapter 4, should we use the transform or transaction model? Why?

11   List the major objects and associated messages and actions of the university information system of Problem 9 in Chapter 4.

12   What portions of the university information system of Problem 9 in Chapter 4 would most benefit from strong encapsulation?

13   Draw a Nassi–Shneiderman chart for this quicksort.

```
procedure quicksort(list,m,n);
begin
    if m < n then
            begin
            i := m; j := n+1; k :=list[m].key;
            repeat
                    repeat i := i+1 until list[i].key >= k;
                    repeat j := j-1 until list[j].key <= k;
                    if i < j then interchange(list[i], list[j]);
            until i >= j;
            interchange(list[m], list[j]);
            quicksort(list,m,j-1);
            quicksort(list,j+1,n);
    end; {of if}
end; {of quicksort}
```

**14** Calculate the cyclomatic complexity of the quicksort of the previous problem.

**15** Prepare HIPO charts for the EDCA synchronization and cleaning function.

**16** Conduct a walk-through for one of your designs with your classmates. Submit the minutes.

**17** Show that sequence, selection, and iteration are sufficient to implement any flowchart. *Hint*: an article by Bohm and Jacopini shows you how to do this.

**18** Develop the architectural and detailed designs for the function you used in Problem 7 of Chapter 5.

# C H A P T E R 7

# THE IMPLEMENTATION STAGE

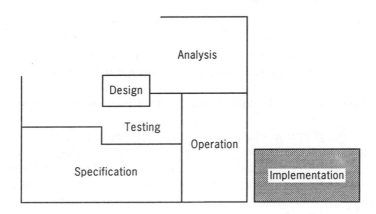

During the implementation stage, we convert the detailed design into code in a programming language. At this stage, the detail workers contribute most of the effort. The major product of the implementation stage—source code—is the ultimate goal of the entire software development process. There is a real sense of accomplishment when the software reaches its deliverable form. Executable code seems much more immediate, real, and exciting than specifications or designs. Nevertheless, implementation is *not* the culmination of our efforts. We must still test the source code to determine that it meets the specifications, and that it satisfies the needs of the user.

## 7.1 THE IMPLEMENTATION PROCESS AND PRODUCTS

Although implementation is the fruition of the chain of effort starting with analysis, it is not the most demanding stage in the software life cycle. In fact, if detailed design has been done properly, thought and creativity are less needed than persistence, accuracy, and attention to detail. It is for this reason that detail workers are frequently drawn from the ranks of new, or less fully trained, employees.

In the following sections, we first examine the purpose of the implementation stage, which is to faithfully translate the design (and specifications) into executable code. Next we consider implementation activities, such as design translation, code reading and reuse, informal code inspection, formal verification, and code prototyping. Finally, we outline the format and content of the documents and deliverables produced during the implementation stage.

### 7.1.1 Purpose of the Implementation Stage

The primary purpose of the implementation stage is to transform the detailed design into code in such a way that is consistent with the design as well as the nonfunctional constraints contained in the specifications. This source code is used in two ways: first, it is the basis for compiling the executable code—the fundamental component of the entire software product; second, it is a text document for future use by software engineers as they maintain the software and as they reuse parts of the source code in other products.

For this reason, it is important that the code not only express the design in its operation but also as text. The code should be written, formatted, commented, and laid out in a way that allows the design to show through and promotes its readability. Source code is not just an intermediate step on the way to executable code—it is a document which is important in and of itself. It deserves enough thought and care to make it useful to its readers.

Another purpose of the implementation stage is to prepare for unit testing and debugging. This can best be done by documenting the code carefully, as described in Section 7.3.1. It may be that some of the data required by the unit test plans—which were developed in the detailed design phase—will actually be accumulated or formulated during the implementation stage in parallel with creation of the code.

An indirect goal of implementation is the training of new employees. Because of the relatively simple nature of transformation of a detailed design into source code, and the natural mentor/student relationship of the designer to the detail worker, implementation is an ideal vehicle for introducing a newcomer to the activities, standards, products, and policies of the organization. Since it requires very little real world experience, implementation can easily be carried out by those who have recently completed their schooling (Figure 7-1).

# Translating
# Coding
# Documenting
# Preparing to test
# Learning

FIGURE 7-1   IMPLEMENTATION ACTIVITIES

## 7.1.2 Activities during Implementation

The primary activity during implementation is writing source code from the detailed design of each module. This is usually accomplished by a direct translation of the constructs of detailed design and external design—control structures, parameter lists, and screen layouts—into the programming language selected for the implementation. In some instances, implementation may require familiarity with simple plans or templates, like traversal of lists, summing arrays, or validating input data.

Although the major product created at this stage is written in a specific programming language, knowledge of the syntax of that language is not a detail worker's primary qualification. Of course, the programmer must know it, but an experienced software engineer can learn a language's syntax in a few days. It is more important to be familiar with the style of current programming practice in a given language. When one sees an advertisement wanting "a C programmer", it really means "a programmer aware of the accepted mechanisms, methods and representations used in commercial C programs".

Most important of all, surpassing a knowledge of the syntax or style of a language, are the general experience, ability, and background of the detail worker. Even though implementing a good detailed design is relatively straightforward, the work will be speeded or slowed in accordance with the worker's familiarity with the task at hand.

Along with writing code, the detail worker will probably *read* a lot of existing code, as well as browse through component libraries for possible ready-made implementations of the detailed design ([WEI87]). Reading code written by colleagues will also be necessary during informal verification of the source code, carried out by inspections and walkthroughs. Software engineers who are able to establish systematic comprehension strategies for code reading obtain better understanding of the code than engineers who just cast about in the code at random ([SOL88]).

There is much to be learned from the expert work of other programmers. More experienced colleagues can fill this need; but it is also useful to learn from source code produced by the best in the field. An exploratory environment in which the code of the environment's implementation is available to the programmer ([GOL87]) promotes software reuse by furnishing a built-in source code library. These code components may be adopted as complete modules or subprograms; or they can be extracted as smaller code segments; or they can simply be read for ideas. In this way, new plans and templates for common activities may be adopted by detail workers.

Informal verification of source code consists of examination by peers. It is important to avoid inclusion of managers or supervisors at this point, since the purpose of the walkthrough is to find errors, not judge the detail worker. Since implementation is carried out on isolated design units, special care should be taken to verify that interface design has been faithfully observed.

Formal verification is performed exactly as it was described for the detailed design in Section 6.3.3. Generally, the same assertions that were used for the detailed design remain valid for the implementation. Additional details may have to be checked, if they have been inserted during the transformation into source code. This would possibly require the formulation of additional, intermediate assertions.

Unit Status
   Sign-off sheets
   Planning and actual schedules
   Acquisition of reusable components and tools
   Effort Expended
Relevant Specifications
Relevant Design
   External design
   Architectural design
   Detailed design
Operational Information
   Notes and plans
   Instructions
   Alternate implementations, feasibility, rationale
Source Code
Test Plans
   Facet, feature or path to be tested
   Person responsible and date scheduled
   Tools or auxiliary code needed
   Test data and instructions
   Expected test results
   Actual test results; analysis (if needed)
   Corrections schedule and signoff (if needed)
      (the above section is repeated many times)
Software Problems
   Report
   Analysis
   Action
      (the above section is repeated many times)
Audits and Reviews

**FIGURE 7-2**   THE UNIT FOLDER

Prototype coding furnishes product validation through cycles of use and modification. Validation may show that time or space constraints are being met; or it may demonstrate the acceptability or utility of the user interface. Sometimes a code prototype may be implemented in a VHLL. Once a prototype's functionality is proved, it can be rewritten in the ultimate implementation language.

Validation can be simplified by a system that permits execution of partially complete code. It is easier to experiment with a small portion of the entire package without constructing elaborate scaffolding. In particular, user interfaces can easily be made more visible for purposes of evaluation in such a system.

### 7.1.3 Implementation Documents and Deliverables

The most important implementation document is the Unit Folder. It may actually be a physical document stored in a three-ring binder. In that case, it should contain the parts of the Project Plan, Software Requirements Specification, and External and Architectural Design Documents that constrain this particular program unit. Of course, in addition to this, the Unit Folder should contain the detailed design and code for the program unit, as well as the Unit Test Plans (see figure 7-2).

One of the important functions of the Unit Folder is to allow a software engineer to determine the current stage of any software component. For this reason, it is best managed as an on-line document, part of the project database. It may be helpful to display the source code by using color or intensity cues to categorize parts that are recent, unverified, or temporary ([GOL87]). Of course, configuration control is applied to the folder, with signoffs after inspection and freezing of completed units.

The Unit Folder contains minutes of the various inspections carried out at this stage. Besides the folder, implementation generates numerous management progress reports and analyses. The folder will continue be the major document of the testing stage. During that stage, the folder will be completed as unit test results are added.

In a good software engineering environment, the project database relieves us of the necessity of storing all this information physically, or of extracting information pertinent to a single unit from prior work products. The database provides the necessary pointers and connections to allow us to browse through documents reviewing just those parts that relate to a single unit.

## 7.2 IMPLEMENTATION PRINCIPLES

As always in software engineering, the use of a rational methodology is a fundamental principle of implementation. However, because of the relative simplicity of the task (assuming the existence of a detailed design), there are few methodologies available. Indeed, the transformation of detailed design into code is one of the most automatable of the software development processes. Nevertheless, there are some methodologies in which a standard detailed design is not present (e.g., Jackson System Design) and in which implementation provides more of a challenge. As another example, the profiling and tuning of source code for performance can be considered an important implementation methodology.

The primary characteristic of a good implementation is that it fulfill the design accurately. This means that many design characteristics, like abstraction, modularity, encapsulation, and usability, should also be present in the source code. In addition, there are some newly important characteristics, like portability and efficiency.

It is important that the major product of the implementation stage be maintainable and verifiable. These attributes can be enhanced if care is taken to make the implementation as easily understood as the design. It is also necessary to make sure that the correspondence between design components and code components is perfectly clear.

The correct choice of a programming language appropriate for our application can make it significantly easier to achieve the goal of implementation quality. We will analyze the important software engineering aspects of languages in general, and Ada in particular, to aid in making that choice.

### 7.2.1 Goals for the Implementation Stage

The first goal of implementation is to provide a faithful translation of design. This is easier if we choose an implementation language that includes the various control constructs, data types, and syntax features that we wish to use. However, we may face restrictions: customer specification of a suboptimal language, cost of obtaining compilers or environments, lack of experience with the most appropriate languages, or the need for compatibility with existing products. As a result, the choice of a language is pragmatic, governed by a mixture of theoretical needs and practical constraints.

Working within this less-than-perfect language, we still need to make sure that the design is evident in the code, and that each code unit can be traced back to the originating design component and specification. Whatever techniques are appropriate for approaching this task in a methodical way should be adopted.

Good software should avoid any semantic gap between design and code. This is particularly important for reuse of a component or for maintenance work that will require tracing the connection of design to code. One solution to this problem is to put comments in the code that reproduce *in situ*, or refer back to, portions of the design. This effort can be avoided if the project database provides traceability from implementation to design automatically.

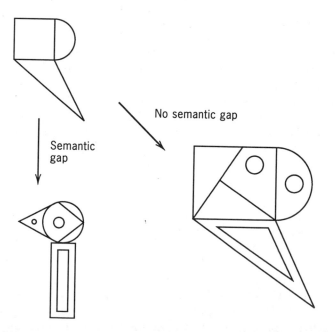

**FIGURE 7-3** SEMANTIC GAP BETWEEN DESIGN AND IMPLEMENTATION

Another technique for tracing design in the code has been provided by Knuth ([BEN86]). The WEB system allows programs to be structured, not according to the shape of the eventual object code, but according to the conceptual design. One objective of this "literate" style of programming is to make programs more readable by allowing the reader to start out by seeing the forest, and then later be introduced to individual trees. In fact, it is a text presentation technique that promotes browsing.

The next stage in the software life cycle is testing, and the implementation is the major work product validated during that stage. It is advantageous to perform the implementation in such a way as to support the testing process. This means that the code should be structured to permit quick location of errors; that it should be uniform, reducing the number and complexity of separate test cases; and that it should be understandable, so that testing personnel can comprehend the design behind the code.

Comprehensibility, modularity, and straightforwardness are just as important during maintenance as in testing. The implementor must learn to put himself in the place of the maintenance worker. Tricky code, obscure names, and a multitude of interconnecting threads running through the code are a disaster for maintenance. Since maintenance is the longest stage, and usually consumes the most effort, extra care during implementation can pay off in dramatically reduced *lifetime* software costs.

Although implementation is by far the most straightforward of the stages (assuming that design is done properly), it cannot be carried out by untrained personnel proceeding intuitively and carelessly. As at any other stage, using appropriate methodology, planning, and tools will produce better work at less cost. Significant improvement can be obtained from a good programming environment that provides fast context switching between edit, compile, execute, and debug operations as well as access to a component library and product control services.

### 7.2.2 Characteristics of Good Implementation

The first set of important, higher level features for languages deals with abstraction, modularization, and encapsulation capabilities. If these were worthy attributes for a design, they continue to be worthy for code. In fact, producing code from a design is easier when the code continues to support design characteristics (Figure 7-4).

**Abstraction**     **Dependability**
**Modularization**     **Maintainability**
**Encapsulation**     **Portability**
**Concurrence**     **Efficiency**
**Verification**     **Performance**

**FIGURE 7-4** IMPLEMENTATION QUALITY ATTRIBUTES

***Abstraction*** Abstraction deals with the ability of an implementation to allow the programmer to ignore that portion of detail that is not important at the current level of consideration. Each of the three kinds of abstraction—control, data, and process—should be present in the code. We are then able to control the intellectual complexity of the implementation by substituting a single abstract description (like "initialization loop," "queue of processes," or "zeta function") for an entire block of statements.

Control abstraction resides in the ability to block individual instructions together and then apply standard control to them (see Figure 7-5). Blocking is typically done by isolating instructions into a subprogram or by enclosing the instructions between "begin" and "end" or similar tokens. There are four kinds of control that can be applied to such blocks of code:

- *Sequence*: execution of each block once in order.
- *Selection*: conditional execution of some blocks.
- *Iteration*: repeated execution of a block.
- *Invocation*: execution of a named block at some other point in the code, possibly with parameters.

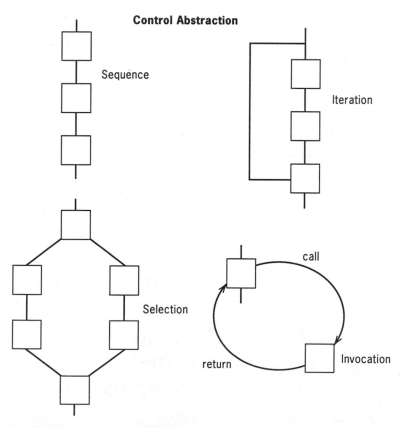

**FIGURE 7-5**  CONTROL STRUCTURES

The first three control types are sufficient to implement any flowchart ([MIL86]). Typically, selection is represented by an "if..then..else" construct, whereas iteration is represented by "while..do..". Control types may be amplified by "case," "repeat," and "for" structures. In each instance, these control structures have a single point of entry and a single point of exit. This fact provides a mini-modularity, with a single thread of control connecting each "module" or controlled block of code. Software written in this structured fashion is much easier to understand and thus to maintain ([GIB89]).

It is this reduction of program flow of control to a set of nested sequences of blocks, each controlled in a regulated way by a fixed, simple iteration or selection, that enables us to apply the principles of formal verification to source code. The same structure and simplicity that allow verification also promote the understandability of the code.

Since data abstraction is as important as control abstraction, we want our program to use it freely; data abstractions will have to be implemented in terms of the primitive data types provided in the language. We can compose simpler data types into more complex ones, usually in a stepwise fashion. This graduated composition is smoother if we can declare data *types* as well as variables.

Another part of data abstraction is the definition of operations on the data in a natural fashion. These operations should include the extension of familiar operations to appropriate new data types, or combinations of data types. In addition, other, novel operations on the new data types should be as easily represented.

Process abstraction should be used in implementation by naming and referencing separate blocks of executable statements that incorporate the process. In general, such processes, either sequential or concurrent, are program units that mirror the modules of the design. Here again, process abstraction aids in the understanding process that is vital to effective program maintenance ([GIB89]).

**Modularization**  Modularization requires us to partition the implementation, with each abstraction occupying its own separate and identifiable unit. Control structure blocks can be more clearly delineated by naming, or at least by using, comments or blocked indentation; data abstractions should be formally composed as records, arrays, or the like, with separately named types instead of just informal aggregations.

We should make extensive use of procedures and functions, including parameter lists, to decrease coupling. Isolating abstractions into separate components promotes the understandability of the product; more importantly, it facilitates division of labor, maintenance by component modification, and reuse. It is helpful to provide macro expansion as an alternate modularization technique.

**Encapsulation**  Care should be taken to truly hide details within a module while implementing a design. Too often, encapsulation in the design is sacrificed to expediency in the code. In particular, encapsulating a data structure is usually more difficult than creating a control block or a subroutine. Therefore, we need to take particular notice of data encapsulation. At the same, time the interface of the hidden type or mechanism should be carefully crafted to make it appear both natural and useful to the rest of the code. Promoting the graceful incorporation and reuse of the component is the other side of encapsulation.

Parameters usually compose the visible interface of an encapsulated process. We need the capability of designating parameters as input or output or both, and the

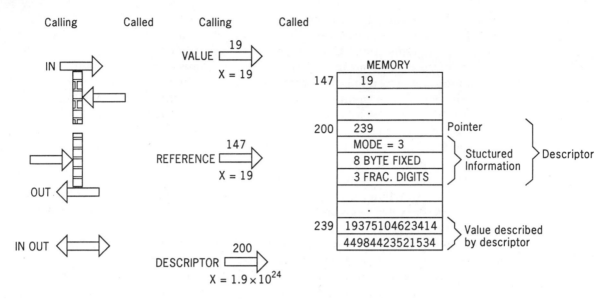

**FIGURE 7-6** FORMS OF PARAMETER PASSING

language should provide parameter passing by value, reference, and descriptor. A **descriptor** is a fixed length structure with information about, and a pointer to, the parameter (see Figure 7-6). Another possible parameter passing technique—passing by name—is not so useful.

*Verification* Assertions used during formal verification of the detailed design should be included as comments, at least, in the source code. The same verification process can be repeated on the code, perhaps by an automated assertion checker. The requirements of proving correctness should guide implementation just as they guide design. In particular, verification is inhibited by stratagems like untyped pointers, shared use of memory by two variables of different type (FORTRAN equivalence or Pascal variant records), or transfer of values between variables of different type.

*Dependability* We can make use of type checking in some languages to guard against software errors. For instance, if "temperature" and "velocity" are both declared to be real types, it would be within the capability of the hardware to substitute a temperature value with a velocity value. However, it would not be sensible to do so, since the physical realities being expressed by the types cannot be interchanged in this way. A careful software engineer can avoid such faults simply by creating two derived types—temperature and velocity, each based in the real type—and letting the compiler signal any inadvertent errors in data usage.

Exceptions (error conditions) interrupt the normal flow of execution at unpredictable times and places. They must be handled in some appropriate fashion, after which we might be able to resume normal processing. At a minimum, we would like our implementation language to permit us to define and to react to exceptions in the code; we should make full use of these capabilities.

*Maintainability/Portability* An important implementation goal is to improve maintainability of the code. Careful documentation and the extensive use of abstraction provide greater comprehension for the maintenance worker. Standard (template) coding techniques are also worthwhile. Avoiding nonstandard constructs in whatever implementation language is chosen increases the portability of the product; encapsulation and isolation of hardware-specific code have a similar effect.

*Efficiency* **Code tuning** is optimizing the code for efficiency. In the old days, when hardware was very limited and expensive, it made sense to concentrate on machine efficiency as a primary goal in software development. Specifically, algorithms and data storage organizations were carefully designed and more carefully implemented to get the job done in the fewest CPU seconds, using the fewest kilobytes of memory. This often went under the name of optimization. Nowadays, these results may be obtainable automatically from a code optimizer, part of a compiler that restructures object code for maximum efficiency with respect to the target machine. In extreme cases, an optimizer may take the source code and may produce correct executable programs that improve its run time by an order of magnitude over non-optimized code.

Today we are faced with relatively plentiful hardware resources, combined with a scarcity and rising cost of labor. Optimization, which means designing and implementing to best achieve the goals of the project, may not have anything to do with fast or compact code; instead, we may choose to shorten software development time. If this is our goal, then our effort is optimized when we choose the easiest implementation available to us, including the reuse of available code. In the long run, we may optimize our effort by spending time now in creating a general library of reusable components (see Figure 7-7).

We may also want to minimize coding effort. The simplicity and familiarity of the implementation language will be our guides here. Specifically, we should attempt to choose implementation techniques that allow a nearly automatic translation of detailed design into code. This is frequently made possible by the use of a programming environment and its constituent tools. Another optimization choice can be dependabil-

**Development effort**
**Project duration**
**Maintainability**
**Dependability**
**Code speed**
**Code and data size**
**User effort**

**FIGURE 7-7** OPTIMIZATION GOALS

ity. Then we should choose to spend time on careful design and validation of exception handlers and fault-correction features in the code. Another choice is to optimize our maintenance effort. This is done by concentrating on modularity and understandability and by providing a high level of documentation.

### 7.2.3 Programming Language Issues

The most important attributes of a good programming language, according to Shaw ([SHA84]), should be to facilitate simple implementation of design, to interface smoothly with formal specification and verification techniques, and to support effective cost control measures. Besides enabling the programmer to represent mathematical functionality, Shaw believes that a language should provide synchronization mechanisms as well as flow control mechanisms.

Some additional desirable properties of languages are suggested in [STR88]. First, the advanced features of the language should be cleanly integrated so that they are natural to use. Next, all aspects of the language should work together in synergy, making solutions easier to implement. Languages should be lean, avoiding the bells and whistles that too often appear; advanced features should be avoidable when not desired, and should add no overhead when unused. The issues discussed in this section are couched in terms of traditional procedural languages, but usually have equal importance for logic, functional, object-oriented, or other types of nonprocedural languages.

*Abstraction* Besides the regular control abstractions of sequence, iteration, selection, and invocation, many languages have provided a *goto* statement that performs an unconstrained transfer of control. One basic reason for **structured programming**, restricting ourselves to use of the standard control structures and avoiding an uninhibited using the "goto" statement, is to facilitate the verification and understanding of the code. An entire program, or any of its constituent blocks, written with standard control can be viewed as a sequence of block abstractions. This means that the flow of control through the program is clearly reflected in the code itself ([WIR74]). With the program's dynamic behavior closely modeled by its static structure, we are better able to understand and to inspect it ([DIJ68]).

In contrast, a program that makes use of "goto" statements cannot be viewed as a sequence of instructions that will be executed linearly. To understand and inspect unstructured code, we must follow many possible loci of control; usually, rather than understanding the situation, we become thoroughly confused. Research indicates that structured programming, the dependence on sequence, iteration, selection, and invocation as the only control structures, results in better program integrity and improves productivity by reducing the incidence of errors ([BAS81]).

"Goto" statements usually make formal verification infeasible unless the "gotos" are restricted to occurrences that fit in with the verification methodology. As it happens, and not accidentally, the standard control structures are usually the ones that do fit in. Thus, together with the sufficiency of the structures for implementing any flowchart, verification is a powerful argument for restricting ourselves to these alone without using the "goto."

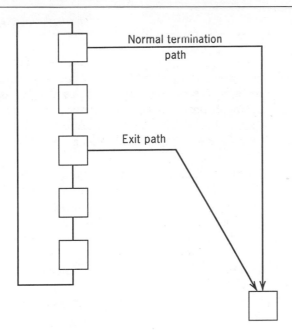

**FIGURE 7-8** THE EXIT CONTROL STRUCTURE

This is not an overwhelming argument, however. There are several legitimate constructs that become much more complex when they are forced into the straitjacket of the standard control structures. For instance, we frequently encounter a condition in the middle of a loop body that requires us to bypass the rest of the statements in the loop body and to cease further iteration altogether. This can be done with an "if..then" statement, the null "else" branch representing the bypassing operation.

There are some problems with this approach, however. First, the "if" statement is no clearer, but somewhat bulkier, than an **exit** statement, which would cause us to leave the loop. Second, if there are several such points in a loop body, the nesting of "if" statements becomes confusing. Third, there are circumstances in which the natural loop control condition cannot be tested after such an exit point without generating some kind of fatal error. In that instance, we must complicate the control condition by inclusion of additional Boolean flags.

The case for the existence of an "exit" statement or use of a "goto" in such circumstances seems clear. The loop is terminated and control passes on to the next statement so that understanding the code does not become more complex. Manual verification is no worse than it would be with the more complicated termination condition. The code is easier to read (see Figure 7-8).

There is no need to uncompromisingly prohibit the use of the "goto" statement simply because it is not necessary and can get us into trouble when it is badly applied. Instead, we should establish standards defining those circumstances in which "goto," or any other disputed language capability, can be used. If we follow these standards in a disciplined way, we will ensure the real goal of high quality without artificially restricting our options in reaching that goal.

The two data abstraction capabilities we want in a language are declaration and composition of types. This means that we can create a basic type by enumerating the different values that it might have, by restricting existing types to subranges of their current ranges, and by composing types into vectors, arrays, records, sets, bags, sequences, maps (finite functions), and so on. The ability to define linked structures and use language-supported heap management for dynamic allocation is also very important.

We have already mentioned the importance of extending familiar operations to new data types or mixed data types. In the first case (new types), called *overloading*, we use the same function identifier to represent many different functions, each with a distinctive set of parameters. For instance, we might want to overload the symbol "+" to mean addition of matrices or vectors as well as reals and integers. In the second case (mixed types), called *coercion*, we define the strongest of the mixed types and transform all others to it. We then perform the action appropriate for that type. In the case of calculating the maximum of 43.32, -5, and $7.2 - 0.6i$, we would first transform them into $43.32 + 0.0i$, $-5.0 + 0.0i$ and $7.2 - 0.6i$, and then obtain the value with the maximum modulus, $43.32 + 0.0i$.

As a relatively minor feature, it is important to declare and to use constants in code. These values should be protected by the compiler from alteration during execution, but they should have the same scoping rules as variables. They should also be usable in the declaration of other types.

**Modularization** Procedural languages usually provide a block structure as the basis for control modules. Each block is a sequence of statements in the language delimited by "begin" and "end" or by some similar pair. Data modules are typically formed by composition of simpler data types into more complex ones. Storage and compilation modules are normally formed by dividing code into files or libraries.

The principal intermediate-scale module, between the control block or data structure and the file, is the subprogram. Subroutine invocation should be either by macro expansion or by invocation. It is often natural to use recursive calls, which puts special requirements on the compiler. This is because nesting of n invocations of a subroutine creates the need for n different activation records, each with different values for the parameters and local variables. Nevertheless, the value of recursion makes it worthwhile to look for a language that supports it.

One technique for providing parameterization of reusable code, and for avoiding the overhead of subprogram invocation, is supporting macro expansion in code. For example, we might expect that reference to "$\sin(x)$" in code would generate commands to push a process activation record on a stack, with the value of $x$ stored in it, and then jump to the code for calculating a sine. After execution, there would be a jump back to the original code and the activation record would be popped. But with macro expansion, the code for calculating a sine value would be included directly at the point of use. The code would be parameterized by substituting "$x$" for a generic argument. Macro expansion usually trades off space for time. Multiple occurrences of the code segment are created, thus increasing the size of the code, while the overhead of call activation is eliminated. But even when the code segment will be executed only once, macro expansion still provides a technique for instantiating a generic module (Figure 7-9).

```
For i: := 1 to n do              For i := 1 to n do
    begin                            begin
    For j := 1 to i-1 do             For j := 1 to i-1 do
      Replace(data[i],data[j], ≤);     If data[i] ≤ data[j] then
    data[1] := data[j];                  data[i] := data[j];
    end;                                 else data[j] :=data[i];
    Replace(data[1], data[j] ,≥);    data[1] := data[i];
                                     end;
    Defmac Replace(x, y, op)         If data[1] ≥ data[j] then
      If x op y then x := y            data[1] := data[j]
        else y := x;                   else data[j] := data[1];
```

**Unexpanded Code**                       **Expanded Code**

**FIGURE 7-9**   MACRO EXPANSION IN A HIGH-LEVEL LANGUAGE

Programming languages can provide additional modularization by allowing components to be grouped into packages. Thus, an object can be packaged by combining a data structure, auxiliary variables, operations, and utility routines. The entire abstraction is then a module composed of other modules.

***Encapsulation***  Modules should permit the declaration of static variables whose values will persist from one invocation of the subprogram to the next. This allows the creation of abstract data types whose state is stored within the module itself. Encapsulation is further enhanced if the implementation of the operations and the data structure supporting the abstract type can be hidden from the rest of the software. This can be done by locating them in a private part of the module. Code and data in the private part are totally local—there is no way to export them to the rest of the software. Separate compilation provides an additional degree of hiding by allowing components to be used without ever revealing the implementation source code at all.

To provide operations on the data type, modules must provide a public interface that includes the data type and functions that furnish the operations. These operations should provide implementation-independent access for the purpose of iteration, data storage and retrieval, synchronization, and the like. For instance, an iteration operator would allow us to visit all nodes of a tree, without any notion of whether it is implemented as a sequential structure in an array or a linked structure in a heap.

To facilitate incorporation of user-defined data types into the code, it is not enough just to encapsulate the type with its operations. We should also be able to *declare* objects of that type rather than being required to call a "create_object" routine. This means that data abstractions will have an instantiation that is provided directly by the compiler and probably implemented automatically by some initialization code at program startup.

***Concurrency***  We frequently require a language to provide ways of controlling concurrent processes. This concept is an important abstraction of the locus of control. Support for concurrency will ease the transformation of designs for concurrent

- Invoke a procedure and continue execution rather than wait.
- Send or receive a message.
- Select and accept a service request from a concurrent process.
- Terminate execution of another dependent or parent process.
- Create resources for and share data with an invoked process.
- Sychronize and control access to shared resources.

**FIGURE 7-10** CONCURRENCY FEATURES

software into code. Figure 7-10 lists necessary concurrency features; they are more easily used if the implementor finds them available as separate language capabilities, rather than having to build them up out of synchronization or message-passing primitives.

**Verification** Programming languages, by proscribing features like "goto," untyped data, or shared space, can significantly simplify verification. Of course, this trend can by carried further by eliminating constructs, like pointers (the "goto" of data structures), that are normally accepted as reasonable. Ada and PL/I are frequently criticized as being "too rich" to ensure the verifiability of code written in them. On the other hand, some experimental languages have been specifically designed to promote verification.

**Dependability** Using an "exit" statement to get out of a loop when some condition arises is a special example of the more general problem of error handling. There are some specific questions about exception handling that we should consider. For instance, since an exception may occur at unpredictable times, we have to be able to declare an exception and its handler to be in effect throughout an entire scope. We will need some way to delimit this scope in the code. In fact, since we might want to turn exception handling on and off and on again, we would like the definition of the exception and its handler in a part of the code to be separated from its scope.

The levels of abstraction design methodology views each module as utilizing the capabilities of some lower level virtual machine. If an exception occurs in that machine, we do not want our software to just crash Hence, it is necessary to be able to signal exceptions back up through the levels. This implies that we will need a way for a software module in the virtual machine to *terminate* (or, at least, to interrupt) its own execution and signal to another software module. Such a signal has to be outside the interface used in normal processing (Figure 7-11).

We must decide whether to allow *resumption* of normal processing following an exception that the exception handler within a module has dealt with. One might argue that a called module does not understand the full implications of an exception arising from data sent to it, so that the best technique is to unfailingly terminate execution of the called module and to inform the calling module that the exception occurred. If it desires to resume processing, it can reinvoke the module in which the exception occurred.

On the other hand, the levels of abstraction model puts the module in which the exception occurs within a virtual machine. We do not expect a machine fault (say, a

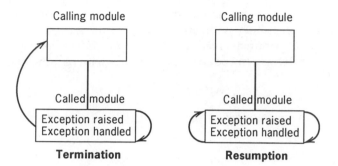

**FIGURE 7-11** EXCEPTION HANDLING MODES

page fault) to be signaled to software if that fault can be corrected by the machine. Our software becomes much more complex if we are required to pay attention to all the exceptions that might occur and be corrected without our intervention. But passing control "laterally" from a called procedure to an exception handler, with no intervention by the calling module, is an example of control coupling. The difficult decision whether to use a termination or resumption model for exception handling must be made for all methodologies, not just for levels of abstraction.

Some languages have no capability for declaring or raising exceptions. In that instance, we need an implementation standard that all procedures and functions return a parameter representing a success/error code. Every procedure call would be followed by statements that check the code and call an appropriate exception handler if needed. Going further, some standards require all procedures and functions to be implemented as functions which return the success/error code as their value.

In much the same way, procedures in these languages should always check their preassertion immediately on invocation and should exit at once with an error code if the preassertion is not satisfied by the parameters. At the end of procedure execution, the postassertion should be checked, and any error should either be corrected inside the procedure (resumption mode) or signaled by returning an appropriate error code (termination mode).

Besides declaring types, we need to be able to enforce appropriate use of typed data. In its simplest form, this means that the compiler signals an error when an attempt is made to assign a value of one type to a variable of another type. This should even be the case when two different derived types have the same underlying structure. It is also valuable to be able to include run-time type checking procedures when these are vital to the dependable function of the product. The passing of parameters needs to be carefully monitored at compile time for type correspondence. Checking for correspondence problems like those encountered in the use of variant records or programmer manipulated pointers is beyond the capability of compilers; but the compiler could be directed to insert correspondence-checking code for execution whenever correspondence is in doubt.

Sometimes a language that appears to protect the programmer through strong data typing actually has some holes in its armor. For instance, Pascal allows a variant record to change its structure during program execution but does not require that use of the record be checked for consistency with its *current* structure. Also, Pascal, as originally defined, allows a formal parameter, call it A, of procedure B to be itself a procedure. Then within the body of B there can be an invocation of A with parameter C of type real:

```
A(C);
```

On the other hand, a separate procedure might call B with procedure D as an actual parameter:

```
B(D);
```

The question is, does D have to have a single argument of type real? The answer is no ([FAI85]).

***Maintainability/Portability*** A language that supports encapsulation and separate compilation promotes easier maintenance, since components can be replaced more easily, and since a maintenance worker only needs to comprehend a limited scope within the product to effect a single change. It is also important for a language to encapsulate hardware dependencies into machine-specific file packages, I/O packages, memory word size constants and the like. If the original implementation language promotes the use of standard control structures and programming practices, porting a product to another language will be easier; perhaps, this can even be accomplished by automatic translation. Languagewide standards for I/O device and file system access, mathematical, database, and graphics libraries, and information representation will also greatly improve portability.

We cannot overemphasize how vital language standardization is to true source-code portability. The first issue is whether a true standard for the language exists at all; the second is whether the compiler being used observes the standard. It may not be necessary for the compiler to enforce language standards strictly. Rather, the ability of giving a compiler directive to flag all non-standard usages may provide the programmer desirable flexibility.

***Efficiency*** Reuse will be easier if it is possible to parameterize modules. This does not refer to the use of formal parameters. Rather, it is a technique by which modules representing a class of types or functions, like stack or output, can be specialized or instantiated, giving stack of reals or screen output. The language and compiler should support such instantiation directly, without any need for re-editing the existing component. Languages can also be the basis for general-purpose libraries of reusable subprograms. These can be amplified with more specialized routines that are developed within the software organization.

Languages that are planned to match a specific design methodology, or around which a programming environment has been established, make implementation quicker and less error prone. Syntax-directed editors are also a minor aid in translating design into a particular language.

There are two broad categories of higher-order languages: "general-purpose" languages like Ada, C, Pascal, Modula-2, FORTRAN, COBOL, PL/I, and Lisp; and "specialized" languages like Prolog, APL, and FORTH. The specialized languages can be used to implement a wide variety of applications. Among the specialized languages are the so-called "little languages" ([BE86a]). These are very focused in their applicability and are often used for prototypes or exploration.

Another broad distinction can be made between proscriptive and permissive languages. In designing a proscriptive language, an attempt is made to prohibit practices that have been shown to be generally harmful in terms of good software engineering methodology. Pascal is a prime example of such a language—problems are avoided by not allowing them to occur. A permissive language takes the opposite viewpoint—good programmers will stay out of trouble and may need flexibility in achieving optimal implementations. The popularity of C with many professionals is because of its undemanding rules.

In developing software, it is frequently necessary to fit the product in a matrix of people, existing products, and equipment; thus, using correct methodology in the implementation context may be difficult. This means we may decide to use a language that is less than ideal, because it is an organization standard, because we are more familiar with it, or even because it is the only way to link to another program. Figure 7-12 shows some of the practical and theoretical grounds for selecting a programming language in which to implement a design. While the theoretical reasons focus on the nature of the language itself, the practical constraints arise from the environment in which we are working.

Practical considerations usually outweigh theoretical ones in selecting a language. For instance, Hoare points out that implementations in specialized functional or logic programming languages often match specifications much more closely than in procedural languages ([HOA87]). Although the compiled version of such code is likely to be too inefficient to be acceptable, such an implementation might serve as a prototype. In general, language suitability has priority, and an appropriate language specialized to the application should always be chosen if practical considerations do not prohibit it. But, they usually do. In that instance, we choose the general language that satisfies the practical constraints and represents the highest level of capability available.

| Practical | Theoretical |
|---|---|
| Customer requirements | Suitability for application |
| Organization standards | Level of language |
| Compiler availability | Abstraction capabilities |
| Component library availability | Execution of partial code |
| Tool availability | Separate compilation |
|    optimizer | Exception handling |
|    analyzer | Concurrency mechanisms |
|    debugger | Portability |
|    pretty printer | Hardware interface |
| Worker experience | Interface to other languages |

**FIGURE 7-12** CRITERIA FOR CHOOSING AN IMPLEMENTATION LANGUAGE

```
1   if (error .lt. errlim) goto 2
        oldtmp = tmprtr
        tmprtr = estmp(oldtmp)
        error = abs(tmprtr-oldtmp)
        goto 1

2   ...
   emulation of "while error >= errlim"

        parameter (reclim = 1000)
C       record
            character*25        name        (reclim)
            real                balanc      (reclim)
            character           status      (reclim)
C       end record
            emulation of "array of record"
```

**FIGURE 7-13** EMULATION OF LANGUAGE FEATURES

A less important practical consideration, like worker experience, can sometimes be sacrificed to an important, higher level theoretical criterion. This should only be done, however, if the decision promotes the goals of the project. Since most software is still written in general-purpose procedural languages, some discussion of appropriate language features has been given in Section 7.2.2.

Sometimes practical constraints make it necessary to choose a language with lower level capabilities. In this instance, we should do our best to emulate the missing higher level capabilities so as to meet appropriate coding standards. For instance, Figure 7-13 shows some of the ways in which FORTRAN-77 can emulate missing language features. This sort of emulation may be coded directly, or we may code in an extension to the language and then translate to the actual language by means of a preprocessor prior to compiling.

## 7.2.4 The Case for Ada

In 1974, the U.S. Department of Defense publicly recognized what had been evident for some time: it was deeply involved in the software crisis. Out of this recognition came several initiatives to improve software procurement and use. One plan was to develop a single, high-level language to be used in all real-time and embedded software developed for the Department of Defense. The Department hoped that this language would serve to improve the methodology of the average programmer as well as to provide access to important tools ([ICH83]). Although this might not reduce implementation costs, the costs should be lowered over the entire software life cycle. Current experience indicates that this indeed will be the case ([MYE87]).

The Ada programming language is the result of this initiative ([SAM86]). Its characteristics were largely determined by the problems it was to solve, and these were the same problems attacked by software engineering. As a natural result, Ada includes features intended to provide many of the success factors for software development. The language was developed in an atmosphere of extensive public discussion and incorporates suggestions from many sources. In particular, a wide range of capabilities and a high level of code reliability are hallmarks of Ada.

*Abstraction* Control abstraction is provided by Ada through a full set of standard control statements—block, case, if, basic loop, for loop, while loop, and goto—as well as an exit statement. Ada supports complete capabilities for declaring and compounding data types. Operators and functions can be overloaded. Automatic and user-defined coercions are available as well as specific overriding of the prohibition on value transfer between incompatible types. The data abstraction capability is completed with the possibility of symbolic constant declaration and data initialization.Process abstraction is provided by Ada units (procedures, functions, and tasks). Tasks are concurrent program units, and procedures and functions can be recursive.

*Modularization* Ada allows for the creation of separately compiled modules and libraries. It supports a form of macro through the generic unit. Generic units can be instantiated with specific types or values. Subprogram parameters can be designated "in" if they are called by value, "in out" if they are called by reference, or "out" if their values are provided by the subprogram itself.

*Encapsulation* Encapsulation is furnished by Ada packages; these packages are divided into public and private parts, to allow hiding. Data can be statically or dynamically stored. Within packages, procedures and functions provide a finer-grained resolution of package-level encapsulation. Interfaces are fully defined, can be separately declared, and are carefully controlled. Packages provide a convenient way for managing an entire abstraction when it is to be incorporated as an object into the implementation. See Section 7.5.1 for an example of a package.

*Concurrency* Concurrent and real-time programming are supported in Ada by the rendezvous, which provides both synchronization and communication ([BAK85]). Data are passed through a formal parameter list in a simultaneous two-way manner ([NIE87]). A process requiring service from another concurrent process, or wishing to pass a message to it, simply invokes the process by name (like a subroutine) as an entry, using the parameter list to pass or receive information (Figure 7-14).

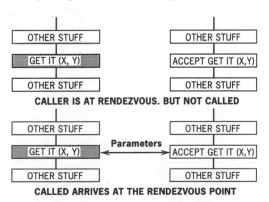

**FIGURE 7-14**  AN ADA RENDEZVOUS

The invoked routine (a server) has no knowledge of who did the calling (the client), unless this information is inserted into the parameter list. The routine simply executes an accept statement to receive the parameter list and then continues processing. If there is no call pending, the accept statement causes it to block and wait. However, a select statement guarded by a "when" clause will allow the called routine to avoid blocking. The asymmetric form of call versus accept allows callers to be anonymous (allowing service utilities) and permits utilities to select which of many concurrent callers to serve. The terminate statement allows a task to commit suicide, whereas the abort statement permits a task to murder another task that is visible to it. A delay statement allows a task to suspend itself until it is wakened by successful synchronization of a rendezvous or until a specific amount of time has passed.

*Dependability* Exceptions in Ada can be declared, signaled, and handled, and exception handlers have scopes. Exceptions in Ada are handled in termination mode ([BAK86]). Thus, even if a local exception handler is able to deal with the exception effectively, it is still necessary to inform the calling procedure that it occurred. If there is no handler present, the exception will continue to propagate along the dynamic links to higher level calling routines. Section 7.3.5 has examples of exception handling in Ada, which has very strong type checking.

*Maintainability/Portability* Ada is highly standardized, since the name itself is copyrighted. This gives the Department of Defense's Ada Joint Program Office the power to forbid attaching the name "Ada" to any compiler that has not been validated through their extensive test suite. Testing not only ensures that required features are present, but also disqualifies compilers that have extended the language beyond its specifications. Thus, the portability of any Ada program to any compiler should be guaranteed. The long-standing problem of proliferation of different dialects of a single high-level language should be solved by this enforced standardization ([ICH83]).

Internally, many hardware dependencies are either accessible by or transparent to the programmer. Attributes of data types can be determined by the software through use of the many predefined constants. For instance, INTEGER'LAST has the value of the largest representable integer, P'FIRST_BIT gives the offset of a field (P) within a record, measured in bits for a particular machine implementation, and REAL'MACHINE_MANTISSA shows the number of digits in the mantissa of a machine representation of a base-P floating point number (Figure 7-15). In a similar

| | |
|---|---|
| WALNUT'FIRST | — minimum value of the enumeration type WALNUT |
| FOOD'BASE'FIRST | — same as WALNUT'FIRST |
| REAL'DIGITS | — precision of type REAL |
| PLAT'LAST(2) | — upper bound of the second dimension of PLAT |
| PLAT'RANGE(1) | — index range of the first dimension of PLAT |
| CONTEXT(I)'TERMINATED | — TRUE if task CONTEXT(I) is terminated |
| PERSONNEL'SIZE | — number of bits for records of type PERSONNEL |
| DOCUMENT'ADDRESS | — address of the record variable DOCUMENT |

**FIGURE 7-15**   SOME ADA REPRESENTATION ATTRIBUTES

manner, the KAPSE (see Section 7.3.4) carries predefined I/O packages to provide input/output capabilities in a selectable and machine-and-operating-system independent fashion. All of these capabilities enhance portability. Maintainability is supported by encapsulation, abstraction,and generic packages.

*Efficiency* Each Ada implementation is accompanied by a standard library of services, which also eliminates the problem of the nonportability of file system and other system calls; by a facility for adapting software automatically to varying hardware capabilities; and by a minimal programming support environment (MAPSE), which provides a standard minimal set of tools, like an editor, linker, configuration manager, and so on. These tools, and the language as a whole, have been designed to provide a programming environment that fosters productivity ([WOL85]).

With their strong modularity, Ada programs are fairly easy to develop as the end result of their design by expansion and abstraction. Indeed, Ada design methodology recommends top-down design at the architectural level, using the public part of package declarations as the design notation. Detailed design would then continue by using a mixture of subprogram declarations, comments, and Ada code. As a result of generic packages, and of the rich variety of different program units with encapsulation furnished by public and private parts, software reuse is quite easy in Ada ([GAR87]). Ada has been proposed as a possible language for implementation of object-oriented designs. Generic packages are used to implement classes, whereas actors are represented by tasks ([BOO86]). The public/private division in packages provides the strong encapsulation needed for objects.

Of course, practically every standard is old-fashioned as soon as it is adopted, and Ada is no different. There have been concerns ([WEG84]) that Ada is a language for the 70s which will be affecting what we do in the year 2000. In particular, Ada supports the traditional model of software development much better than others like the prototyping model. On the other hand, it is the only widely used language that is an integral part of an entire, well-developed software methodology.

## 7.3 IMPLEMENTATION METHODOLOGIES AND TOOLS

We have said that there are not many methodologies that deal purely with implementation. Some specific challenges do have solutions, however. One of them is to use appropriate programming *style*. This term refers to the way in which we name identifiers, lay out our code, introduce comments, and organize modules.

Other methodologies include code *packaging*, which deals with the problem of clustering modules into effective groupings for understanding, processing, and storage, and code *tuning*, which deals with techniques for code modification to maximize run-time performance. Jackson System Design also provides a unique implementation methodology.

Many tools are available for the implementation stage. These tools are as numerous as for any other stage and probably more sophisticated. They range from the simple text comparison tool to the most complex optimizing compiler and from the limited pretty printer to the overarching programming environment.

### 7.3.1 Implementation Style and Documentation

The principal goal of a good programming style is to make code understandable and maintainable. Like nontechnical writing, code is best understood when it is simple, direct, well organized, well paced, and meaningful. Some people have used terms like "literate programming" or "esthetic appeal" to describe the best aspects of programming style. In general, clarity and simplicity should be the watchwords during implementation.

Six qualities of programming style are suggested in [RED86]: economy, modularity, simplicity, structure, documentation, and layout. Modularity and structure are more a part of design than implementation, although it is necessary to make sure that they are faithfully translated from the design into the code. Documentation refers to the use of comments and identifier names to convey information to the reader, whereas layout refers to the use of blank lines, indentation, paging, varying type styles, and the like.

Economy is usually achieved by choosing the least complex form of implementation within the context of the given programming language. For instance, an array of Booleans is a more economical representation of a bit map than is a string of bits that is concatenated from an array of integers, even though the former may occupy more space.

Simplicity is the semantic analogue of the syntactic concept of economy. Case statements are often simpler than the equivalent cascaded if statements. In a similar way, an infinite loop with an Exit statement in the middle may be simpler than a While loop preceded by a section of priming code, and with the same priming block of code terminating the loop body. Simplicity is increased when only one procedure or function is displayed on each screen or page.

The nesting structure of control structures in the detailed design should be mirrored in the indentation of the code. This means that loop bodies or selection branches are indented to the right of loop or selection statements. In a similar manner procedure and

```
procedure push(stack:stack_of_chars; value:char);
  var p:header_ptr; temp:node_ptr;

  begin
  p := start;
  while (p <> nil) and (p^.value <> stack) do p :=p^.next;
  if p<> nil then
        begin
        temp := P^.top;
        new(p^.top);
        p^.top^.value := value;
        p^.top^.next := temp;
        end;
  end;
```

**FIGURE 7-16**   CODE INDENTATION

function bodies are indented from the procedure or function statement itself, and declarations can be aligned by type and use, and so forth. An indentation of two to four columns per level is probably optimal ([MIA83]). Special indentation should be used for full-line comments so that they do not obscure the flow of control of the code. Long statements should be indented according to their structure on subsequent lines. No more than one statement should appear on a given line, unless the statements are very closely related (Figure 7-16).

Chunking should be created in code by separating different code segments by blank lines. This means that there will be a separation between a procedure header declaration and the subordinate declarations within the procedure between declarations and executable statements and between major code segments like multiline loops or cases. Begin and end statements should not appear on the same line as code statements. Comments can be used to tag the beginning and end of blocks if the language does not allow block naming. Comment blocks can be surrounded by borders in order to make them stand out.

Extra emphasis can be given within code by repeated characters or double spacing, as in this line:

```
******** W A R N I N G — D O   N O T   M O V E ********
```

The same or a stronger effect can be obtained by the use of colored or bold or underlined characters. Spacing and parentheses can also be used to clarify the meaning of arithmetic expressions.

Besides the structure and layout of the code, documentation appearing within the code itself improves its clarity and understandability. By incorporating as much documentation as is feasible into the code, we obtain several advantages. First, the documentation is directly available, side by side with the code. This improves the reader's ability to make connections and to combine the two streams of information into one. Second, documentation is more likely to be updated at the same time that code is, ensuring that they will be constantly synchronized. Third, tags or keywords that appear in internal documentation can assist in browsing through the code or in extracting information for external documentation.

The simplest kind of internal documentation is obtained by careful choice of identifier names. Programmers should always resist the temptation to choose short names, like "x," for variables. They provide very few clues about the code to readers. A programmer who really thinks that too much time is wasted by typing long names can always use short ones, and then take advantage of the replacement capability of an editor to change them to something more reasonable.

Names of variables should always connect to the real world entity that they model. Procedures and functions should be named with verb phrases to describe their action, whereas larger packages, which usually represent an abstract data type or a group of related operations, should be named by noun phrases like "Activation_Stack" or "Tax_Procedures." Generic packages should be given simpler names, like "Stack," and tasks should be named as agents, like "Scheduler" or "Interrupt_Monitor."

Code ought to be free of literal constants, which give little or no hint of their meaning. For example, software written to do accounting for a company with 12 sales districts might be sprinkled with "12." If the company splits a district, a maintenance software engineer would have to scan the code carefully to see which 12's related to sales districts and which related to months of the year, changing each occurrence of the former but none of the latter. On the other hand, a declared symbolic constant, "Number_Sales_Districts = 12," could be changed in one spot and understood throughout the code without effort. Once again, this is a form of parameterization.

Comments are an obvious and ubiquitous type of internal documentation. Individual statements or blocks in the code can be accompanied by a comment if they would otherwise be difficult to understand. It is certainly not necessary to comment on every statement. Comments should be avoided if they don't add to understanding. A comment like

```
Total_Guests := Reservations*2 {multiply Reservations by two}
```

is worthless, whereas

```
Total_Guests := Reservations*2 {each reservation is for two people}
```

helps a little more. In general, comments should explain the real world meaning of the code, rather than the technical (or worse, syntactic) meaning.

Comments should also be attached to the declarations of individual variables and formal parameters. These declarations should appear one per line and in columns to allow the reader to scan quickly and find the name, type, and meaning of each entity. Although it is not necessary to comment each statement, it is important to comment each variable. Once again, the language of comments should be that of the real world problem being solved by the software; it should explain what these data "really are" or "really do."

It is particularly important that modifications to code be documented with the reasons for and the nature of the change. These comments should be flagged as changes by using a tag with that specific meaning. Other blocks of code, particularly those

```
MODULE NAME:
FUNCTION:
INTERFACE PARAMETERS AND MODES:
PREASSERTION:
POSTASSERTION:
GLOBALS AND SIDE EFFECTS:
IMPORTANT INTERACTIONS:
EXCEPTIONS:
HARDWARE AND OPERATING SYSTEM REQUIREMENTS:
CREATION AND MODIFICATION HISTORY:
ALGORITHM:
MAJOR DATA STRUCTURES:
CALLED BY:
CALLS:
```

**FIGURE 7-17**   A MODULE PROLOGUE

representing activities that are difficult to understand, can be set off as paragraphs in the code and can be preceded by a more extensive comment explaining their purpose and clarifying their action.

Each module should start with a prologue comment that defines its function, interface, derivation history, pre- and postassertions, exception conditions, structure, and so on. These prologues may well begin life as text attached to the module during architectural design and then be expanded during detailed design. An example of a prologue template is given in Figure 7-17.

Although it may seem to some detail workers that the time spent in commenting code is unproductive, the assessment from industry shows a net gain in productivity as a result of comments, even during the first stages of development ([GLA82]). The gains realized during maintenance are even more striking. Soloway et al. ([SOL88]) point out that code understanding depends on abstracting familiar "plans" embedded in it, and that in large products these plans are often broken up and distributed over large areas. The information contained in the prologue's important interactions section can help to clarify this situation to a maintenance worker. There are many detailed suggestions for improving commenting, and programming style in general, in [KER78], a book that is both profitable and entertaining.

## 7.3.2 Code Packaging

Code can be organized in various ways: design modules can be broken up or combined as they are transformed into an actual code module and; functional code units should occupy single subprograms, either procedure or function. But these code units may be combined into larger groupings for the purpose of accessing a common data structure to form an abstract data type; in Ada, these larger groupings are called packages. On the other hand, if the actual size of a subprogram exceeds one printed page (or even one terminal screen), this may be a signal that we should reconsider the design for the possibility of further decomposition.

Combining code modules into packages often has two objectives: it reinforces encapsulation, and it simplifies the externally visible interface of the package. Any time that we observe very complex interfaces in the code, we should consider the possibility of either packaging several functions or packaging the data on the interface into a larger and conceptually simpler structure.

One purpose of this kind of packaging is to propagate the benefits of modularity and encapsulation from design into code. In particular, maintenance will be easier and unwanted maintenance side effects fewer if we decouple independent code segments by placing them into separate modules. Another benefit of packaging is that reader understanding is increased if we amplify the chunking effects mentioned in the previous section by modularization.

There are other reasons for packaging code in a particular way. For instance, memory restrictions on a nonvirtual memory machine may require us to form overlays. If so, a decision needs to be made—which code segments and data structures will be packaged into a common overlay? On a virtual memory machine, it may be beneficial to cluster code segments onto a single page; again, this is a packaging question.

In the external file system or, if available, project database, code will be stored in many different files or persistent objects. Several code modules may be packaged in one file, if they are used together or have a high degree of logical connection. This will simplify the database as a whole. When code is organized into libraries, it should again be packaged so that the proximity of different modules aids in transporting, browsing and understanding.

One rule for packaging that is suggested in [GAN86] is to restrict visibility of other packages to the lowest possible levels within any given package. This will place knowledge of interfaces to other modules where it is needed, and hide it where it is not.

### 7.3.3 Implementation Methodology

Some implementation methodologies, like structured programming, concurrent programming, and the declaration and use of exceptions, are discussed elsewhere in this chapter. Methods for improving style, like formatting, packaging, and documentation could also be considered implementation methodologies. Formal verification is sometimes considered to be purely an implementation technique, but it more properly starts at the detailed design level and was presented in Chapter 6. In general, translating a detailed design into code is quite straightforward, and any problems that exist tend to be specific to a single implementation language and inappropriate for consideration here.

There is little use of prototyping during implementation, but a choice might be made, investigated, and later reversed on experimentation. For instance, deciding whether to implement a multiway choice as a IF-THEN-ELSEIF-...-ELSE-END or a CASE statement can legitimately wait until the implementation stage, and they can be decided on the basis of style, clarity, or efficiency.

However, in a larger sense, source code is an inevitable part of every prototype design. For this reason, sometimes it may be most effective to create a relatively "quick and dirty" implementation to proceed to an inevitable next version. We must be careful, however, that any such substandard code is not an end product, and in fact it should have a lifetime measured in weeks at the most.

One way to improve code efficiency is to use in-line expansion of code instead of subprogram invocation. This will trade off decreased CPU time against increased code size, and is a useful technique in real-time programming. We can often depend on an optimizing compiler to choose the most efficient machine language implementation of our code, without the need for human intervention. But sometimes the optimizer does not do as well as we want.

In such situations, *code tuning* is an important technique associated with the implementation of a design. Although analysis, specifications, and design have all been concerned with the ultimate efficiency of the software, computer systems and user behavior are so complex that one can not be certain that even the best theoretical analysis of a program's run-time behavior will be correct. Thus, it is necessary to instrument the code in some way to determine where time and space are actually being used. **Instrumentation** is the inclusion of additional code that tells us how the original code is behaving. A profiling tool can be used to automatically instrument code and report on it.

We may choose to wait until a fairly complete prototype of the product is available and to use a profiler to instrument the code and to locate those parts of the code that experience the highest traffic. They aren't always obvious beforehand, but these hot spots promise the best return on our manual optimization investment. Sometimes, we might even wait for an opportunity to profile a delivered product under actual use, and thus to carry out optimization as a maintenance activity and to deliver optimized code as an updated version of the product.

Bentley points out in [BEN87] that significant improvements, sometimes on the order of doubled speed, can be obtained by a very modest tuning effort. Usually this would involve a small redesign of the software or a change to a more machine-oriented implementation (perhaps in assembler) ([BEN82]). In this way, tuning can be considered an application of profiling to implementation and, perhaps to design.

Since the JSD methodology bypasses the more traditional forms of detailed design, we ought to mention its last step, *implementation*, at this point. The structure text obtained during design was modeled on the actual real world entity lifetime. Since this modelling represented the normal course of events for the entity, JSD has no direct way of producing designs for exceptions. For this reason, it is necessary to design and to insert exception handling during the implementation stage.

Related to this problem is the fact that JSD assumes that all control information necessary to process a data record is available before the start of processing. In particular, if two variant records with the same initial fields exist, it is impossible to directly translate structured text into code and have it function properly. The problem of getting some distance into processing and finding that we are using control information for the other kind of record produces a situation much like an exception. These can both be solved by a backtracking technique in which intermediate data are stored that allows us to undo actions, and to return to a point where proper processing or exception handling can be integrated into the structure text.

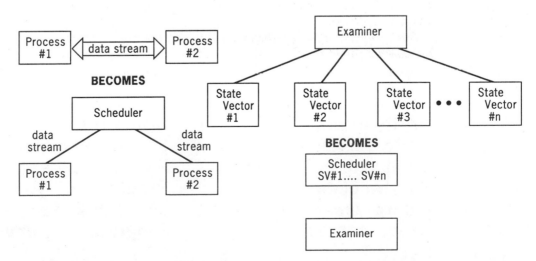

**FIGURE 7-18**   JSD CODE OPTIMIZATIONS

Another problem in implementing JSD designs comes from the fact that each defined process is supposed to be an independent concurrent task. This might be achieved on a single-processor system by providing one subroutine per process and using suspend and resume capabilities. But if there are too many tasks for efficient performance of code based directly on this design, it will be necessary to reduce their number. In cases where processes communicate via a data stream, the two processes at either end of the data stream can be made into modules called by a new, third module, which is their scheduler. The data stream is now represented by the interface between the scheduler and the called modules. Jackson calls this technique process inversion (Figure 7-18).

Sometimes many different, but identically structured, state vectors are examined by a single process communicating with many identical but separate processes. This might be true if we were modeling many equivalent entities, like customers. Then the actual implementation code may have a single scheduler holding many separate state vectors (one per customer). The scheduler repeatedly calls a single process that would be passed to the state vector of one specific customer as a parameter. This technique is called state–vector separation ([CAM86]).

### 7.3.4 Implementation Tools and Environments

*Pretty printers* furnish automatic formatting of code. Not only will they create an appropriate indentation and paragraphing pattern in the code, but they may also print different syntactic items in different cases or fonts. For instance, pretty code might show all identifiers in uppercase, operators in bold type and reserved words in lowercase. Such an embellisher may also have an interactive mode for insertion of module prologues(Figure 7-19).

*Code auditors* can be used to analyze adherence to coding standards and coding style. Auditors detect improperly structured code, excessive nesting of control structures, excessive fan-out or fan-in of the invocation hierarchy, inconsistent indentation, missing module prologues, excessively long or short modules, overcomplicated interfaces, and the like.

*Syntax-directed editors* assist in creating and manipulating source code in a specific high-order programming language. Unlike normal text editors, which see text as composed of individual characters, sentences, paragraphs and pages, syntax-directed

**Pretty printer**                  **Optimizer**
**Code auditor**                    **Separate compilation**
**Syntax–directed editor**          **Partial code execution**
**Source code browser**             **Profiler**
**Macro expander**                  **Static analyzer**
**Cross–compiler**                  **Programming environment**

**F I G U R E 7-19**   IMPLEMENTATION TOOLS

editors allow the programmer to treat text on the basis of syntactic units. Thus, such an editor recognizes the beginning and ending of a controlled block and can prompt for the different components of an if-then-else statement. It is important, however, that the editor not enforce this level of resolution uniformly, since the detail worker will sometimes want to deal with characters and words as well.

Raeder points out that syntax-directed editors tend to reduce the effort and the number of errors made during source code creation ([RAE85]). Syntax-directed editors provide immediate identification and correction of syntax errors, thus reducing the time spent in switching context between an editor and a compiler. Syntax-directed editors allow for natural manipulation of the code *as code*, rather than as word or line-oriented operations. For example, searches can be bounded by controlled blocks or subprograms.

It is natural for such editors to promote certain stylistic standards and, in fact, they can automatically provide the services of a pretty printer by creating indentation, spacing, and other layout patterns as code is keyed in. Finally, since a syntax-directed editor parses code anyway, it is able to provide the necessary hooks for structural representation of code, symbolic debugging, code animation, and partial code execution.

*Source code browsing* systems are in some ways similar to text editors. Source code browsing provides on-line access to text, with keyword search and pattern matching capability. They also allow the user to extract portions of the code into separate files. But beyond this, browsers have to give a sense of structure to a large body of software.

This can be done by representing a product graphically as a module or an invocation hierarchy to see the connections between its different components. Individual components can be abstracted in this representation by showing just their interfaces. It is also necessary to provide tracing between the code and prior work products, particularly the design. All this can be founded in the project database.

Another capability of browsers is expanding program information on a microscale. For instance, if the user were to select an identifier name in the text, then a window might be opened showing the declaration of the identifier ([SHN86]). On the other hand, selecting a keyword or system-defined utility routine might provide a window containing the appropriate information from the language manual.

Traditionally, the greatest reuse of software occurs during implementation, when existing code components are plugged into the software directly or in a slightly modified form. Methodologies for reuse were discussed in Chapter 1 and are not repeated here. These components are usually organized into *libraries* of some kind, which provide a classification scheme and permit a moderate amount of browsing in order to enable the software engineer to choose the best module for the job.

Since these libraries are frequently purchased rather than developed by the software organization itself, it is important to consider a few factors before investing in one. First, we should examine the cost of purchase plus anticipated modification of the components compared with the cost of creating the software in-house. Of course, the anticipated modification will depend on both the generality with which the library components have been written and the degree to which they meet the foreseeable needs of the software organization. It is usually better to build than to buy if the costs are comparable; on the other hand, the cost of a library is usually much less than the cost of in-house development.

It is also important to investigate the degree of support provided with the library, including documentation, consultation, and customization. If this support is limited, the library may turn out to be nothing but a heap of unusable components. Finally, the dependability of the components has to be assessed. Some providers are able to document dependability directly. More often, it is necessary to infer dependability from the frequency and extent of new version publication and from the experience of other users.

A *macro expander* allows for the abstraction of a program unit to a single identifier. As with subprograms, a macro can be parameterized, but unlike them it is expanded (or inserted with parameter substitution) in-line. This eliminates the need for call/ return time and stack overhead, but increases the size of the code itself. It also reduces the modularity of the unit. More sophisticated macro expansion allows for compile time execution of programmed logic, which allows the programmer to customize code semiautomatically.

*Cross-compilation* is simply the use of one machine to compile high-level code into object code for a different machine. Usually, the development, or host, system provides an environment that makes it particularly attractive for software production. Most often, the product is targeted for many different hardware systems, so that, although it might be developed on one of them, it is still necessary to cross-compile to the rest.

In other cases, the target machine, on which the software will eventually run, may have too little memory to allow it to host the compilation, or may use ROM (read-only memory) as its only primary store. Perhaps it is an embedded system, without I/O devices that could support a user environment or secondary storage to hold files. These situations all require compilation of code on some machine other than the target machine that will execute it.

*Optimization* of object code, which is a function of an optimizing compiler, attempts to modify the compiled version of software so that it runs faster, uses less memory, or calls less often for resources like disk blocks and I/O cycles. Some optimization is machine dependent, like register allocation or selection of especially efficient machine idioms (sequences of instructions). Other optimizations are machine independent. They include detection of common subexpressions, elimination of dead code, loop overhead reduction, use of algebraic identities, and loop rewriting ([AHO86]).

Languages can expand modularity features in several ways. The most important is to provide *separate compilation* for individual modules. This facility supports a less expensive modification and recompilation of code; it also allows us to reuse executable software components. However, there is a natural conflict between separate compilation and enforcement of type correspondence: the compiler needs to see both modules together to verify correspondence. How can they be separated? One way is to include in other modules a copy of the public part of the separately compiled module. It is up to the linkage software, which will put the separate modules together into an entire package, to verify that the public part of module B as referenced from module A corresponds to the actual public part of module B as it was compiled.

A similar facility, which is very useful in prototyping and the growth model, is *execution of partial code*, where the interpreter or compiler or linker allows execution of code with unresolved references to missing modules. As long as no attempt is made to enter those modules, the code behaves normally. An attempt to use a missing module may cause program termination, or in an appropriate environment may allow the software engineer to specify the location of the module, or even create it, and then continue with the interrupted execution.

A *profiler* allows us to examine the run-time performance of code. It will certainly provide information about CPU time usage for individual modules. In addition, profilers can provide counts of how many times individual modules are executed, how many times selection of a specific branch occurs, and even how many times a variable is read or assigned a new value. Profilers are used to spot errors in the code, like branches that can never be selected, as well as hot spots.

*Static analysis* examines the code as written, rather than following its dynamic execution the way a profiler does. Among the problems that can be located by static analysis are interface incompatibility, unreachable code, use of uninitialized variables, and values assigned to variables but never referenced. Static analysis can also generate a cross-reference of all variable declaration, assignment and reference, and all subprogram invocation. Lint is a static analysis tool for applications written in the C language in the Unix environment.

*Programming Environments* are the broadest of all implementation tools, and were described in Section 1.2.6. They frequently combine all the tools listed here, as well as communication, product control, testing, and design tools. A full programming environment is usually specific to a single programming language and a single design paradigm, so that the chosen development model and methodologies must be matched before a programming environment can be acceptable. At best, a programming environment improves productivity and detail worker satisfaction very significantly.

In some instances, the programming environment is attached directly to the language. For instance, each Ada compiler should come with an APSE that meets standard specifications. To diminish the cost of transporting the APSE, many of the features that vary between machines or operating systems are made uniform. This is done by making it a layers of abstraction structure that rests on a central kernel of implementation-specific code (the KAPSE, "K" for kernel). The KAPSE provides database primitives, device drivers, and a run-time library as services to the rest of the APSE, which is thus system independent.

## 7.3.5 Dependability in Source Code

Suppose we have a linked list containing sampled experimental data, one part of which is a temperature reading expressed as a real number. The recording devices may fail at some point, and this will be signaled by a temperature below absolute zero. These data and all that follow in the list should then be ignored. Suppose further that we want to calculate the variance in the temperature readings, defined by

```
variance =  sum of (temperature − average temperature)²
           ─────────────────────────────────────────────
                        number of nodes
```

However, we find an alternate, and more efficient, formula:

$$\text{variance} = \frac{\text{sum of temperature}^2 - \dfrac{(\text{sum of temperature})^2}{\text{number of nodes}}}{\text{number of nodes} - 1}$$

We have already designed a function that will traverse the list, and calculate the variance. The design seems straightforward, but at some point we need to consider what might go wrong.

1  The list might be empty, in which case variance is not defined, or might contain only one node; in each case, the formula would cause a divide-by-zero error.
2  The sums may cause a numeric overflow.
3  The process of squaring a number close to zero may cause a numeric underflow.
4  The pointer from some node might be mistakenly misdirected back into the list itself, so that traversal becomes an infinite loop.
5  The pointer from some node might be messed up and point to data that does not actually comprise part of the list.

Some possible responses to these errors would be the following:

1  Check to determine if the number of nodes is zero or one, in which case write an appropriate message to a log.
2  Overflow is much less likely to occur with the first formula; however, it is less efficient. Use the recovery block pattern, with overflow during the calculation of the second formula causing the first to be calculated instead. In case of overflow in the first formula, return the variance for the first part of the list, and log this fact.
3  The error caused by underflow will be quite small, so log it when it occurs, but continue with the calculation.
4  Include a Boolean value in the node that will allow us to mark the node as we process it and to detect possible looping. If we want to use the mark again for other purposes, we can wait until we get to the end of the list, then retraverse it, unmarking the nodes. Return the variance for the first part of the list and log this event.
5  Let the list be self-identifying, by including a string field containing some hopefully unique value, like "tmprtr". Return the variance for the first part of the list and log this event.

Ada code for the implementation of these ideas is shown in figure 7-20.

## 7.4 FOSTERING QUALITY DURING IMPLEMENTATION

We once again consider the appropriate metrics for the stage, the verification and validation activities, and the special management concerns.

```
-- these types define the structure of the linked list and its nodes
type node; type nodeptr is access node;
type node is record
                seen:              boolean;       -- marks nodes to detect cycles
                id:                string(1..6);  -- self-identifying label
                temperature:       float;         -- data collected by device
                next:              nodeptr;       -- pointer to next node in list
            end record;
standard_id: constant string(1..6) := "tmprtr";  -- self-identification


-- MODULE NAME: sum_squares
-- FUNCTION: This function takes a list, the number of nodes already seen
-- on the list and the sum of the temperatures in those nodes as
-- arguments.  It calculates the variance for those nodes.
-- The function is called by alt_variance.  It is an abstraction
-- of the clean-up calculation that must occur after various
-- exceptions occur in alt_variance.
-- INTERFACE PARAMETERS AND MODES:
--              head_of_list;                       nodeptr;       IN
--                    sum;                          float;         IN
--              number_of_nodes;                    natural;       IN
-- PRE-ASSERTION: none
-- POST-ASSERTION: if the list is non-empty and each node contains a valid
--                 float value, then the function returns the sum of squares.
--                 Otherwise, it returns 0.0
-- GLOBALS AND SIDE EFFECTS: none
-- EXCEPTIONS: divide-by-zero or invalid float
-- HARDWARE AND OPERATING SYSTEM REQUIREMENTS: none
-- CREATION AND MODIFICATION HISTORY: author, Bob Willis, 6/14/88
-- ALGORITHM: standard summation loop
-- MAJOR DATA STRUCTURES: a linked list headed by the node accessed by
--                                             head_of_list
-- CALLED BY: alt_variance
-- CALLS: nothing

function sum_squares(    head_of_list:    in    nodeptr;  -- points to first node
                         sum:             in    float;    -- sum of data in nodes
                         number_of_nodes:in    natural)  -- number of nodes
                         return float is               -- variance
            i: natural := 1;        -- loop counter
            mean: float;            -- average of data at nodes
            sumsq: float := 0.0;    -- sum of terms (temperature - mean)²
            p:nodeptr;              -- points to successive nodes


begin
            mean := sum/float(number_of_nodes);
            p := head_of_list;
            while i <= number_of_nodes loop
              sumsq := sumsq + (p.temperature - mean)**2;
              p := p.next;
              i := i+1;
            end loop;
            return sumsq/float(number_of_nodes - 1);
            exception
              when numeric_error =>
                if i > 1 then return sumsq/float(i-1); else return 0.0; end if;
end sum_squares;
```

```
-- MODULE NAME: alt_variance
-- FUNCTION: This function calculates the variance of the nodes on a list
-- using the simpler and more costly technique.  It is, however,
-- more immune to overflow, and is called when an overflow exception
-- occurs in the function variance.  Alt_variance calls sum_squares
-- to finish the calculation of the variance of a partial list
-- when an exception occurs.
-- INTERFACE PARAMETERS AND MODES: head_of_list; nodeptr; IN
-- PRE-ASSERTION: none
-- POST-ASSERTION: if the list has at least two nodes, but is not infinite,
-- the variance is calculated.  If underflow or overflow occurs, then 0.0
-- is returned instead.
-- GLOBALS AND SIDE EFFECTS: none
-- EXCEPTIONS: bad head pointer, circular list, numeric_error
-- HARDWARE AND OPERATING SYSTEM REQUIREMENTS: none
-- CREATION AND MODIFICATION HISTORY: author, Bob Willis, 6/14/88
-- ALGORITHM: standard statistical formula
-- MAJOR DATA STRUCTURES: a linked list headed by the node accessed by
--                                           head_of_list
-- CALLED BY: variance
-- CALLS: sum_squares

function alt_variance(   head_of_list:   in nodeptr)  -- points to first node
                      return float is              -- safer variance
         absolute_zero:constant   float := -273.1; -- physical constant
         number_of_nodes:         natural := 0;    -- size of list
         sum:                     float := 0.0;    -- accumulates temperatures
         p:nodeptr;                                -- points to successive nodes
         infinite: exception                       -- circular list condition
         bad_pointer:exception;                    -- pointer to non-node condition

begin
         p := head_of_list;
         loop
           exit when p = null;
           if p.seen then raise infinite; end if;
           p.seen := true;
           if p.id /= standard_id then raise bad_pointer; end if;
           exit when p.temperature < absolute_zero;
           number_of_nodes := number_of_nodes + 1;
           sum := sum + p.temperature;
           p := p.next;
         end loop;
         if number_of_nodes < 2 then
           put(log,"alt_variance isn't defined, number of nodes = ");
           integer_io.put(log,number_of_nodes); new_line(log);
           return 0.0;
         end if;

         exception
           when bad_pointer =>
             put(log,"bad pointer in node ");
             integer_io.put(log,number_of_nodes); new_line(log);
             if number_of_nodes > 1 then
               return sum_squares(head_of_list,sum,number_of_nodes);
             else return 0.0; end if;
           when infinite =>
             put(log,"circular pointer in node ");
             integer_io.put(log,number_of_nodes); new_line(log);
             if number_of_nodes > 1 then
               return sum_squares(head_of_list,sum,number_of_nodes);
             else return 0.0; end if;
           when numeric_error =>
             put(log,"alternate variance calculation overflow at node ");
             integer_io.put(log,number_of_nodes); new_line(log);
             if number_of_nodes > 1 then
               return sum_squares(head_of_list,sum,number_of_nodes);
             else return 0.0; end if;
end alt_variance;
```

```
-- FUNCTION: This function calculates the variance of the temperatures in a
-- linked list.  It attempts to calculate the variance in an
-- efficient manner, but may encounter several exception
-- conditions: the list may  be too short for a variance, the
-- list may not be linear, the list may be corrupted, or underflow
-- or overflow may occur.  All these exceptions are handled in
-- variance except for overflow, which requires the help of
-- alt_variance.
-- INTERFACE PARAMETERS AND MODES: head_of_list; nodeptr; IN
-- PRE-ASSERTION: none
-- POST-ASSERTION: if the list has at least two nodes, but is not infinite,
-- the variance is calculated.  If underflow or overflow occurs, then 0.0
-- is returned instead.
-- GLOBALS AND SIDE EFFECTS: none
-- EXCEPTIONS: bad head pointer, circular list, numeric_error
-- HARDWARE AND OPERATING SYSTEM REQUIREMENTS: none
-- CREATION AND MODIFICATION HISTORY: author, Bob Willis, 6/14/88
-- ALGORITHM: standard statistical formula
-- MAJOR DATA STRUCTURES: a linked list headed by the node accessed by
--                                                 head_of_list
--
-- CALLED BY: anonymous
-- CALLS: alt_variance

function variance(        head_of_list:nodeptr)   -- points to first node
                          return float is          -- faster variance
          absolute_zero: constant  float := -273.1; -- physical constant
          number_of_nodes:         natural := 0;    -- size of list
          sum, sum_of_squares:     float := 0.0;    -- accumulates temperatures
          old_sum_of_squares:      float;           -- for comparison
          p:                       nodeptr;         -- points to successive nodes
          numeric_error:           exception;       -- over- or under-flow condition
          infinite:                exception;       -- circular list condition
          bad_pointer:             exception;       -- pointer to non-node

begin
          p := head_of_list;
          loop
            exit when p = null;
            if p.seen then raise infinite; end if;
            p.seen := true;
            if p.id /= standard_id then raise bad_pointer; end if;
            exit when p.temperature < absolute_zero;
            number_of_nodes := number_of_nodes + 1;
            sum := sum + p.temperature;
            old_sum_of_squares := sum_of_squares;
            sum_of_squares := sum_of_squares + p.temperature**2;
            if p.temperature /= 0.0 and old_sum_of_squares = sum_of_squares then
              put(log,"underflow at node ");
              integer_io.put(log,number_of_nodes); new_line(log);
            end if;
            p := p.next;
          end loop;
          if number_of_nodes < 2 then
            put(log,"variance isn't defined, number of nodes = ");
            integer_io.put(log,number_of_nodes); new_line(log);
            return 0.0;
          end if;
          return (sum_of_squares - sum/float(number_of_nodes)*sum)/
                    float(number_of_nodes - 1);
```

```
exception
  when bad_pointer =>
    put(log,"bad pointer in node ");
    integer_io.put(log,number_of_nodes); new_line(log);
    if number_of_nodes > 1 then
      return (sum_of_squares - sum/float(number_of_nodes)*sum)/
        float(number_of_nodes - 1);
      else return 0.0; end if;
  when infinite =>
    put(log,"circular pointer in node ");
    integer_io.put(log,number_of_nodes); new_line(log);
    if number_of_nodes > 1 then
      return (sum_of_squares - sum/float(number_of_nodes)*sum)/
        float(number_of_nodes - 1);
      else return 0.0; end if;
  when numeric_error =>
    p := head_of_list;
    for i in 1..number_of_nodes loop
      p.seen := false;
      p := p.next;
    end loop;
    return alt_variance(head_of_list);
end variance;
```

**FIGURE 7-20**  AN ADA PROGRAM

## 7.4.1 Implementation Metrics

There are several useful implementation metrics for code (Figure 7-21). Code size, measured in KDSI, is an obvious and basic measure. This metric has some obvious shortcomings (discussed in Chapter 1). Boehm mentions that KDSI does not provide uniform resolution—some instructions are more complex than others ([BOE87]). KDSI also suffers from measuring volume rather than quality. Gaffney suggests that the inherent compactness of VHLLs makes the object code resulting from compilation a better measure of actual software functionality ([GAF86]).

Other metrics are the kind measured by static analyzers: structuredness, nesting, fan-out and fan-in, module size, interface structure, and the like. The cyclomatic complexity of code can be measured automatically using the principles outlined in Section 6.4.1. Likewise, function points analysis can be applied to code as well as specifications.

Another set of metrics, developed by Halstead, is shown in Figure 7-22.

One should realize that $E$ is measured in the total number of elementary mental discriminations needed to generate the code, not in person-months. The Stroud number measures how many discriminations can be made in a second, so $T$ is measured in seconds. Halstead verifies a pair of estimates: $L$ is approximately equal to $2(n_2/n_1)N_2$ and $B$ is approximately equal to $E^{2/3}/E_0$.

The relative size ($V$) and difficulty ($D$) metrics can be especially useful in measuring code. Some of the metrics do seem to have empirical validity, especially $N$, $D$ and $E$ ([SHE83]). However, the theoretical basis in psychology for some of the Halstead metrics has been called into question ([COU83]). The validity of Halstead's metrics for time, effort, and delivered bugs has recently come under attack.

Source code size                    Function points
Object code size                    Halstead metrics
Conformity to standards             Use/Access ratio
Nesting depth                       Need-to-know/Access ratio
Fan-in/Fan-out                      Error rates
Module size                         Recompilation rates
Interface complexity

**FIGURE 7-21**   IMPLEMENTATION METRICS

The effectiveness of data hiding via encapsulation can be measured ([GAN86]) by a pair of ratios. First, the ratio of modules that actually use a given module, against those to which it is visible, can give a measure of the real utility of what is assumed to be a general service module. Second, the ratio of the number modules from which it is visible against the number of those where it must be visible gives a measure of the effectiveness of information hiding in the code.

Finally, there are several metrics that can be gathered by the project database management system as statistics for the implementation stage. For instance, the ratio of compiler-detected errors per line of code in a module can indicate careless or

| | |
|---|---|
| $n_1$ | Number of unique operators in code |
| $n_2$ | Number of unique operands in code |
| $N_1$ | Total occurrences of operators |
| $N_2$ | Total occurrences of operands |
| $n_1 + n_2 = n$ | Vocabulary size of code |
| $N_1 + N_2 = N$ | Length of code |
| $N + \log_2 n = V$ | Volume of the code |
| $V\star$ | Potential volume, measured by the smallest possible encoding of code |
| $V\star / V = L$ | Program (succinctness) level |
| $1/L = D$ | Code difficulty |
| $LV^2 = ll$ | Language level |
| $V/L = E$ | Effort |
| $S$ | Stroud number, about 15/sec |
| $E/S = T$ | Time |
| $E_0$ | Constant (about 3000) |
| $V/E_0 = B$ | Deliverd bugs |

**FIGURE 7-22**   HALSTEAD CODE METRICS

incompetent coding, as can the total number of compile/modification cycles for the module. Counts of departures from coding style standards may indicate hurried or sloppy work.

### 7.4.2 Verification and Validation

During implementation, quality assurance efforts focus on verification that code is being produced in compliance with the design and specifications. Since different detail workers are involved in different parts of the code, inspection activities are fragmented into parts that correspond to individual code authors. Most inspections will be either (1) walkthroughs, in which peers (not managers) examine an author's product as he explains it; or (2) formal inspections, in which code is audited for compliance to standards. If a physical Unit Folder exists, inspection results and signatures should be stored in it along with other materials. If an automated project database is used, then the inspection results and approvals will be stored appropriately.

Because of the fragmentation of coding effort, it is particularly important to verify interfaces between different code modules. This can be done by ensuring internal interface consistency, that is, by inspecting invocations and the corresponding formal parameter lists. This can be done automatically by the compiler or linker, or by a separate analysis tool. Of course, formal verification should be performed on actual code whenever possible.

More importantly, modules also interface through access to global data and external files. Each such external reference in each module must be carefully examined to ensure that it does not create undesirable side effects in the context of other modules. If any unneeded references to global data exist, they should be reimplemented in a more controlled way.

### 7.4.3 Management

There are three major management concerns during the implementation stage. The most significant is product or *configuration control*. This is a time of rapid expansion of the major work product, possibly under the hands of a many detail workers. Each of them may be generating new code, updated code, alternative code and partial code. A flexible but general framework for keeping track of all of these different parts of the product is vital.

The next management concern is for the *visibility* of the product at this stage. This can be provided within the structure imposed by product control. In essence, it is necessary to determine which of the design modules have been implemented and the degree of completion of partially finished modules. It is, of course, insufficient to ask a detail worker how close he is to concluding his work. The answer will always be, "I'm about 90% of the way there."

This brings up the third management activity during implementation. We have to establish individual *accountability* for each detail worker's performance. One way of

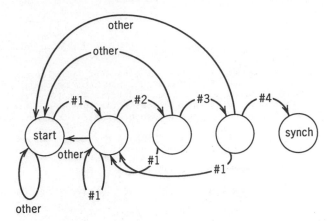

**FIGURE 7-23**   THE FINITE AUTOMATION WHICH RECOGNIZES SYNCHRONIZATION

doing this is by determining the correspondence between visible progress and schedule. Another measure of effort is obtained from various analyses of code quality, including conformity to standards, stylistic analysis, and peer reviews via code walkthroughs.

## 7.5 AN IMPLEMENTATION EXAMPLE

In Sections 7.5.1 and 7.5.2, the same detailed design is translated into two different implementation languages: Ada and FORTRAN-77. As they are examined, it should be evident that the Ada code is cleaner and easier to read. Among other things, strong typing, user-declared types, reasonable identifier names, exception handling, and structured control are used in the Ada code, but are missing in FORTRAN-77.

At one point the design for the module made use of the table-driven methodology. This required structures representing the synchronization signal bytes and the transition table of a finite automaton (Figure 7-23) that recognizes the synchronization signal. A small while loop then interprets the table. In fact, it would have been possible to structure the signal, its length, and the transition table together in a single record, rather than having them appear separately. This record could serve as the parameter for the generic package "synch_signal_recognizer."

In the FORTRAN code, the SAVE declaration ensures that the value of STATE is static, that is, that its value persists from one invocation to the next. This allows some encapsulation, since otherwise STATE would have to be in a COMMON block.

## 7.5.1 Ada Code

```
package Frames is

    type Command is private;
--  Refill    : constant Command; -- buffer is exhausted, provide more data
--  Lost_synch: constant Command; -- synch signal has been lost
--  Compose   : constant Command; -- synchronized frame found and returned
--  Reset     : constant Command; -- start looking for synchronization signal
--  Continue  : constant Command; -- assume synch signal will be at frame end

    Procedure Compose_frame(Buffer   :in      Byte_array;   -- data stream
                            Last_byte:in out Index;                  -- index of
final byte
                            Frame    :    out Index;             -- start of
found frame
                            Frame_end:    out Index;             -- end of found
frame
                            Code     :in out Command);          -- initiation,
result

private

    type Command is (Refill, Lost_synch, Compose, Reset, Continue);

end Frames;


package body Frames is

    Frame_size        : constant integer  := 36;
    Synch_signal_length: constant integer  := 4;
    Number_of_states  : constant integer  := Synch_signal_length+1;
    Finish            : constant integer  := Number_of_states;

    subtype      Symbols is integer range 1..Synch_signal_length+1;
    subtype      States  is integer range 1..Number_of_states;
    type Signal  is array(1..Synch_signal_length) of Byte;

    State:States; -- finite automaton state
            --  1         - have seen no usable synch signal bytes
            --  2         - saw synch signal byte 1
            --  3         - saw synch signal bytes 1,2
            --  4         - saw synch signal bytes 1,2,3
            --  ...
            --  Finish - saw complete synch signal

    Synch_symbols: constant Signal                  -- the synch signal
            := (16#4B#,16#96#,16#97#,16#AF#); -- in hexadecimal bytes

    Table: constant array(States,Symbols) of Byte := ((2,1,1,1,1), -- transition
                                                       (2,3,1,1,1), -- table for
                                                       (2,1,4,1,1), -- finite
                                                       (2,1,1,Finish,1),
                                                       (Symbols => Finish));
                                                                    -- automaton
```

```
-- MODULE NAME: Compose_frame
-- FUNCTION: This module locates a synchronization signal in the data stream
--    provided in Buffer.  Once located, the module provides whole frames of
--    data until the synchronization signal is lost.
-- INTERFACE PARAMETERS AND MODES:
--   Buffer      in          contains a segment of the data stream
--   Last_byte   in out      on input the number of data stream bytes in Buffer
--                           on output the last byte processed in Buffer
--   Frame       out         an index showing the byte in Buffer at which the found
--                           frame starts (the first byte of the frame)
--   Frame_end   out         an index showing the byte in Buffer at which the found
--                           frame stops (the last byte of the frame)
--   Code        in out      passes status information with the following meaning:
--               in          Reset  - start looking for the first synch byte
--               in          Continue - continue in the same state as when
--                                    Compose_frame was exited
--               out         Refill - move the bytes from Last_byte+1 to the end of
--                                    Buffer up to the beginning and fill the rest
--                                    of the buffer with data stream bytes
--               out         Lost_synch - the synchronization signal was not found
--                                    where expected, assuming a frame started
--                                    at Frame
--               out         Compose - the bytes from Frame to Frame_end are a
--                                    synchronized frame
-- PRE-ASSERTION: Last_byte >= Frame_size + Synch_signal_length and Last_byte =
--                length (buffer) - 1; that is, the buffer holds enough bytes
--                to make up at least one frame plus synchronization signal and
--                Last_byte is the index of the last byte in the buffer.
-- POST-ASSERTION: when Code is Refill, further processing requires more bytes
--                when Code is Lost_synch, the data stream synchronization was
--                 lost somewhere after the byte indicated by Last_byte and
--                 the byte at Last_byte + Frame_size + Synch_signal_length
--                when Code is Compose, the block of bytes between Frame and
--                 Frame + Frame_end are surrounded by two valid
--                 synchronization signals
-- GLOBALS AND SIDE EFFECTS: none
-- EXCEPTIONS: unknown input code
-- HARDWARE AND OPERATING SYSTEM REQUIREMENTS: standard Ada compiler
-- CREATION AND MODIFICATION HISTORY: author Sam Washington, 2/19/88
--                                   auditor Jeanie Krowalski, 2/23/88
--                                   modifications:
-- ALGORITHM: the first part of the procedure acts as a finite automaton
--            looking for the synch signal.  In continuation mode, if the
--            finite automaton state indicates that a synch signal has been
--            found, the first part of the procedure is bypassed.  The second
--            part skips ahead to the predicted location of the next synch
--            signal and outputs a frame if the signal is there.
-- MAJOR DATA STRUCTURES: Table is a transition table for the finite automaton
--                        looking for the synch signal.  Synch_symbols is the
--                        synch symbol string.
-- CALLED BY: Get_Frame
-- CALLS: Error_report
```

```
Procedure Compose_frame(Buffer    :in      Byte_array;
                        Last_byte:in out Index;
                        Frame     :    out Index;
                        Frame_end:     out Index;
                        Code      :in out Command) is


   This_byte: Index := 0;  -- points to byte in Buffer under consideration
   Symbol:    Symbols;     -- encodes symbol types for finite automaton; codes 1 to
                           -- Synch_signal_length are for the synchronization signal

                           -- bytes, code Synch_signal_length+1 is for any other
byte
   Bad_code, Out_of_data, Synch_lost: Exception;

   begin
           -- are we starting the finite automaton or continuing it?
   if (Code = Reset) then
      State := 1;
   elsif (Code = Continue) then
      State := State;
   else
      raise Bad_code;
   end if;

   while State /= Finish loop
      if This_byte = Last_byte then raise Out_of_data; end if;
      This_byte := This_byte + 1;
          -- use a linear search through the array synch_symbols in order to
          -- translate the byte into an input symbol for the finite automaton
      Symbol := 1;
      while Symbol <= Synch_signal_length and then
            Buffer(This_byte) /= Synch_symbols(Symbol) loop
               Symbol := Symbol + 1;
      end loop;
               -- finite automaton switches to the next state
      State := Table(State,Symbol);
   end loop;

-- synchronization established, exit finite automaton, recognize full frames

   if This_byte + Frame_size + Synch_signal_length > Last_byte then
      raise Out_of_data;
   end if;

   for n in 1..Synch_signal_length loop
      if Buffer(This_byte + Frame_size + n) /= Synch_symbols(n) then
         raise Synch_lost;
      end if;
   end loop;
                        -- synchronization signal found
   Frame := This_byte + 1;
   Frame_end := This_byte + Frame_size;
   Last_byte := This_byte + Frame_size + Synch_signal_length;
   Code := Compose;

   Exception
      when Bad_code =>
      Error_report("Compose_frame", "Bad code request", code);
      when Out_of_data =>
         Code := Refill;
         Last_byte := This_byte;
      when Synch_lost =>
         Code := Lost_synch;
         Last_byte := This_byte;
end Compose_frame;
end Frames;
```

## 7.5.2 FORTRAN-77 Code

```
c MODULE NAME: CPSFRM
c FUNCTION: This module locates a synchronization signal in the data stream
c    provided in BUFFER.  Once located, the module provides whole frames of
c    data until the synchronization signal is lost.
c INTERFACE PARAMETERS AND MODES:
c    BUFFER      input       contains a segment of the data stream
c    ENDBUF      in/out      on input the number of data stream bytes in BUFFER
c                            on output the last byte processed in BUFFER
c    FRAME       output      an index showing the byte in BUFFER at which the found
c                               frame starts (the first byte of the frame)
c    ENDFRM      output      an index showing the byte in BUFFER at which the found
c                               frame stops (the last byte of the frame)
c    CODE        in/out      passes status information with the following meaning:
c                in          RESET  - start looking for the first synch byte
c                in          CNTINU - continue in the same state as when CPSFRM was
c                                        exited
c                out         REFILL - move the bytes from ENDBUF+1 to the end of
c                                        BUFFER up to the beginning and fill the rest
c                                        of the buffer with data stream bytes
c                out         UNSYNC - the synchronization signal was not found where
c                                        expected, assuming a frame started at FRAME
c                out         COMPOS - the bytes from FRAME to ENDFRM represent a
c                                        synchronized frame
c PRE-ASSERTION: ENDBUF >= FRMSIZ + SNCLEN; that is, the buffer holds enough
c                   bytes to make up at least one frame plus synchronization
c                   signal
c PRE-ASSERTION: ENDBUF >= FRMSIZ + SNCLEN and ENDBUF = length (BUFFER); that
c                      is, the buffer holds enough bytes to make up at least one
c                      frame plus synchronization signal and ENDBUF is the index
c                      of the last byte in the buffer.
c POST-ASSERTION: when code is REFILL, further processing requires more bytes
c                   when code is UNSYNC, the data stream synchronization was lost
c                      somewhere after the byte indicated by ENDBUF and the byte at
c                      ENDBUF + FRMSIZ + SNCLEN
c                   when code is COMPOS, the block of bytes between FRAME and
c                      FRAME + ENDFRM are surrounded by two valid synchronization
c                      signals
c GLOBALS AND SIDE EFFECTS: none
c EXCEPTIONS: unknown input code
c HARDWARE AND OPERATING SYSTEM REQUIREMENTS: ANSI standard Fortran-77
c CREATION AND MODIFICATION HISTORY: author Sam Washington, 2/19/88
c                                    auditor Jeanie Krowalski, 2/23/88
c                                    modifications:
c ALGORITHM: the first part of the procedure acts as a finite automaton
c               looking for the synch signal.  In continuation mode, if the
c               finite automaton state indicates that a synch signal has been
c               found, the first part of the procedure is bypassed.  The second
c               part skips ahead to the predicted location of the next synch
c               signal and outputs a frame if the signal is there.
c MAJOR DATA STRUCTURES: TABLE is a transition table for the finite automaton
c                           looking for the synch signal.  SNCSYM is the synch
c                           symbol string.
c CALLED BY: GETFRM
c CALLS: ERROR
```

```
      SUBROUTINE CPSFRM(BUFFER, ENDBUF, FRAME, ENDFRM,CODE)

      PARAMETER(REFILL = 0, UNSYNC = 1, COMPOS = 2, RESET  = 3,
     -          CNTINU = 4, FRMSIZ = 36, SNCLEN = 4,
     -          NMSTAT = SNCLEN + 1, FINISH = SNCLEN + 1)

      INTEGER CODE, ENDBUF, FRAME, ENDFRM
      CHARACTER BUFFER(1:ENDBUF)
c     THSBYT      integer     index, points to byte in BUFFER under consideration
c     SYMBOL      integer     encodes symbol types for finite automaton; codes 1 to
c                             SNCLEN are for the synchronization signal bytes, code
c                             SNCLEN+1 is for any other byte
c     STATE       integer     finite automaton state
c                             1       - have seen no usable synch signal bytes
c                             2       - saw synch signal byte 1
c                             3       - saw synch signal bytes 1,2
c                             4       - saw synch signal bytes 1,3,4
c                             FINISH - saw complete synch signal
      INTEGER THSBYT, SYMBOL, STATE
      SAVE STATE
      CHARACTER SNCSYM(SNCLEN)
      INTEGER TABLE(NMSTAT,SNCLEN+1)

c remember that Fortran stores in column order, so this table appears to
c be flip-flopped, with rows where columns should be.
      DATA TABLE
     -    /    2,      2,      2,      2,         FINISH,
     -         1,      3,      1,      1,         FINISH,
     -         1,      1,      4,      1,         FINISH,
     -         1,      1,      1, FINISH,         FINISH,
     -         1,      1,      1,      1,         FINISH/

c initialize synchronization byte values
      SNCSYM(1) = CHAR(75)
      SNCSYM(2) = CHAR(150)
      SNCSYM(3) = CHAR(151)
      SNCSYM(4) = CHAR(175)

c get a buffer of bytes
      THSBYT = 0

c are we starting the finite automaton or continuing it?
      IF (CODE .EQ. RESET) THEN
          STATE = 1
      ELSE IF (CODE .EQ. CNTINU) THEN
          STATE = STATE
      ELSE
          CALL ERROR('CPSFRM','Unknown service request code',CODE)
      END IF

c while we have not established synchronization
1     IF (STATE .NE. FINISH) THEN
c    get a byte; exception -> request buffer refill
          IF (THSBYT .EQ. ENDBUF) GOTO 99
          THSBYT = THSBYT + 1
c    use a linear search through the array sncsym in order to
c    translate the byte into an input symbol for the finite automaton
          SYMBOL = 1
2         IF (BUFFER(THSBYT) .EQ. SNCSYM(SYMBOL)) GOTO 3
              SYMBOL = SYMBOL + 1
              IF (SYMBOL .LE. SNCLEN) GOTO 2
3         CONTINUE
c    finite automaton switches to the next state
          STATE = TABLE(STATE,SYMBOL)
          GOTO 1
      END IF
c synchronization established, exit finite automaton, recognize full frames
```

```
c get a frame's worth of bytes; exception -> request buffer refill with
c partial frame moving to the front
        IF (THSBYT + FRMSIZ + SNCLEN .GT. ENDBUF) GOTO 99

c if synchronization is maintained then return frame
c else signal loss of synchronization
        CODE = COMPOS
        DO 4 SYMBOL = 1,SNCLEN
            IF (BUFFER(THSBYT + FRMSIZ + SYMBOL) .NE. SNCSYM(SYMBOL)) THEN
                CODE = UNSYNC
            END IF
4       CONTINUE
        IF (CODE .EQ. COMPOS) THEN
            FRAME = THSBYT + 1
            ENDFRM = THSBYT + FRMSIZ
            ENDBUF = THSBYT + FRMSIZ + SNCLEN
        ELSE IF (CODE .EQ. UNSYNC) THEN
            ENDBUF = THSBYT
        END IF
        RETURN

99      CODE = REFILL
        ENDBUF = THSBYT
        END
```

## 7.6 SUMMARY

We produce source code during the implementation stage. The bulk of our discussion has focused on the nature of programming languages and how their attributes can improve productivity at this stage. We looked at Ada as a particular example of a language that supports the aims of software engineering.

Among the methodologies appropriate for implementation, we examined programming style, code packaging, and code tuning. There are a multitude of small tools that support a multitude of additional, small methodologies. We looked at methods for ensuring the dependability of code through the intelligent use of exceptions.

With our implementation complete, we can now proceed to test the code. We assume that it is free of syntax errors but, of course, there will be more serious faults. These will be discovered first during unit testing, and then during integration testing. The completed product will then be ready for acceptance testing and installation.

## BIBLIOGRAPHY

[AHO86]    Aho, A.V., R. Sethi, and J.D. Ullman, *Compilers: Principles, Techniques and Tools*, Addison-Wesley, Reading, MA.

[BAK85]*   Baker, T.P. and G.A. Riccardi, "Ada Tasking," *IEEE Software*, 2(2):34–46.

[BAK86]*   Baker, T.P. and G.A. Riccardi, "Implementing Ada Exceptions," *IEEE Software*, 3(5):42–51.

[BAS81]    Basili, V.R. & R.W. Reiter, "A Controlled Experiment Quantitatively Comparing Software Development Approaches," *IEEE Transactions on Software Engineering*, 7(3):299–320.

[BEN82]      Bentley, J., *Writing Efficient Programs*, Prentice-Hall, Englewood Cliffs, NJ.

[BEN86]*     Bentley, J., "Literate Programming," *Communications of the ACM*, 29(5):364 – 369.

[BE86a]      Bentley, J., "Little Languages," *Communications of the ACM*, 29(8):711 – 721.

[BEN87]*     Bentley, J., "Profilers," *Communications of the ACM*, 30(7):587 – 592.

[BOE87]*     Boehm, B.W., "Improving Software Productivity," *Computer*, 20(9):43 – 57.

[BOO86]*     Booch, G., "Object-Oriented Development," *IEEE Transactions on Software Engineering*, 12(2):198 – 210.

[CAM86]      Cameron, J.R., "An Overview of Jackson System Development," *IEEE Transactions on Software Engineering*, 12(2):222 – 240.

[COU83]      Coulter, N.S., "Software Science and Cognitive Psychology," *IEEE Transactions on Software Engineering*, 9(2):166 – 171.

[DIJ68]*     Dijkstra, E., "Go To Statement Considered Harmful," *Communications of the ACM*, 11(3):147 – 148.

[FAI85]      Fairley, R.E., *IEEE Software Engineering Concepts*, McGraw-Hill, New York.

[GAF86]      Gaffney, J.E., "The Impact on Software Development Costs of Using HOL's," *IEEE Transactions on Software Engineering*, 12(3):496 – 499.

[GAN86]      Gannon, J.D., E.E. Katz and V.R. Basili, "Metrics for Ada Packages: An Initial Study," *Communications of the ACM*, 29(7):616 – 623.

[GAR87]      Gargaro, A. and T.L. Pappas, "Reusability Issues and Ada," *IEEE Software*, 4(4):43 – 57.

[GIB89]      Gibson, V.R. and J.A. Senn, "System Structure and Software Maintenance Performance," *Communications of the ACM*, 32(3):347 – 358

[GLA82]*     Glass, R.L., *Modern Programming Practices*, Prentice-Hall, Englewood Cliffs, NJ.

[GOL87]      Goldberg, A., "Programmer as Reader," *IEEE Software*, 4(5):62 – 70.

[HOA87]*     Hoare, C.A.R., "An Overview of Some Formal Methods for Program Design," *Computer*, 20(9):85 – 91.

[ICH83]*     Ichbiah, J., "Ada: Past, Present, Future," *Communications of the ACM*, 27(10):990 – 997.

[KER78]      Kernighan, B.W. and P.J. Plauger, *The Elements of Programming Style*, second edition, McGraw-Hill, New York.

[MIA83]      Miara, R.J., J.A. Musselman, J.A. Navarro and B. Shneiderman, "Program Indentation and Comprehensibility," *Communications of the ACM*, 26(11):861 – 867.

[MIL86]*     Mills, H.D., "Structured Programming: Retrospect and Prospect," *IEEE Software* 3(6):58 – 66.

[MYE87]      Myers, W., "Ada: First users—pleased; prospective users—still hesitant," *Computer*, 20(3):68 – 73.

[NIE87]      Nielsen, K.W. & K. Shumate, "Designing Large Real-Time Systems with Ada," *Communications of the ACM*, 30(8):695 – 715.

[RAE85]      Raeder, G., "A Survey of Current Graphic Programming Techniques," *Computer*, 18(8):11 – 26.

[RED86]      Recish, K.A. and W.F. Smith, "Program Style Analysis," *Communications of the ACM*, 29(2):126 – 133.

[SAM86]*     Sammet, J.E., "Why Ada is not Just Another Programming Language," *Communications of the ACM*, 29(8):722 – 732.

[SHA84]*     Shaw, M., "Abstraction Techniques in Modern Programming Languages," *IEEE Software* 1(4):10 – 27.

[SHE83]    Shen, V.Y., S.D. Conte and H.E. Dunsmore, "Software Science Revisited," *IEEE Transactions on Software Engineering*, 9(2):155 – 165.

[SHN86]*   Shneiderman, B., P. Shafer, R. Simon and L. Weldon, "Display Strategies for Program Browsing," *IEEE Software*, 3(3):7 – 15.

[SOL88]    Soloway, E., J. Pinto, S. Letovsky, D. Littman and R. Lampert, "Documentation to Compensate for Delocalized Plans," *Communications of the ACM*, 31(11):1259 – 1267.

[STR88]*   Stroustrup, B., "What Is Object-Oriented Programming," *IEEE Software* 5(3):10 – 20.

[WEG84]*   Wegner, P., "Accomplishments and Deficiencies of Ada," *IEEE Software*, 1(3):39 – 42.

[WIR74]*   Wirth, N., "On the Composition of Well-Structured Programs," *Computing Surveys*, 6(4):247 – 259.

[WEI87]    Weiser, M., "Source Code," *Computer* 20(11):66 – 73.

[WOL85]    Wolf, A.L., L.A. Clarke and J.C. Wileden, "Ada-Based Support for Programming-in-the-Large," *IEEE Software* 2(2):58 – 71.

## PROBLEMS

1   As a class, design several radically different applications, then implement each in three different languages, say, C, COBOL, and assembler. Measure the ratio of the volume of each (measured in executable statements) to the generated object code. Explain the variation between applications.

2   Rewrite one of the applications in Problem 1 as a "literary" work. Submit both versions.

3   How can true modularity be provided in COBOL?

4   Evaluate a language other than Ada in terms of its support of abstraction, modularization, encapsulation, verifiability, dependability, maintainability, portability, and efficiency.

5   How could we best provide an abstract data type, like a queue, in FORTRAN? What about instantiation, encapsulation, and shared access to the common data structure for different operations?

6   Outline the concurrency services provided by a commercial-grade operating system like VMS. Evaluate their accessibility from within some implementation language usable on the system. How would use of such services affect portability?

7   Use Ada rendezvous constructs to provide an "answering service" that would connect a process on a time-share system to a specified user, if logged on, for message interchange, or to a message storage and retrieval facility if the user were not logged on.

8   Analyze the exception handling capabilities of BASIC.

9   Instrument, implement and profile the design of Problem 3 in Chapter 6. Tune the implementation and use the new profile to evaluate the success of the optimization.

**10** Add a full spectrum of exception handling in the code of Problem 9.

**11** Apply the Halstead metrics to the code of Problem 10.

**12** Describe appropriate layout and format rules for Lisp.

**13** What are the strengths and weaknesses of pointers in C, from a software engineering standpoint?

**14** Implement the designs you created for Problem 18 in Chapter 6.

**15** Inspect the code in Sections 7.5.1 and 7.5.2.

**16** Develop test cases for the code in Sections 7.5.1 and 7.5.2.

**17** Conduct reverse engineering on the code in Section 7.5.1 to recapture the detailed design.

**18** Conduct an inspection to determine whether the code in Section 7.5.2 is a direct translation of the code in Section 7.5.1.

# CHAPTER 8

# THE TESTING STAGE

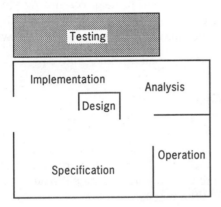

Testing is the last stage of software development before we release the product to the customer. During testing we try to make sure that the product does exactly what it is supposed to do. It is the culmination of our efforts to produce a high-quality product, and it depends on work products reaching back to the standards and verification plans we developed during the analysis and specification stages.

Sometimes we make the mistake of thinking that the purpose of testing is to make certain that the software is error free. However, this is usually an impossible task. In fact, verifying that code in general contains no errors at all (including failure to terminate execution) reduces to the halting problem and is thus mathematically impossible ([HOW85], [HAM88]). Luckily, the formal correctness of the software is of far less interest to the customer than its functionality and dependability ([MUS87], [MIL87]), and we do have many techniques for guaranteeing these attributes.

For this reason, customers will not be impressed with counts of errors found and corrected during testing. What they want to see is an estimate of the system's *reliability*: how often they can expect to see failures while they are using it ([BEI84]). Eliminating an error that would probably occur once every 1500 years will not sell the product to anyone ([MIL87]). Many of the testing activities are aimed at convincing the customer, through demonstration and actual use, that both the product and the process that created it are of high quality.

Of course, requiring a higher degree of dependability in the software, in this case by means of extensive or even exhaustive testing, increases the cost of development. This is complicated by the fact that software is discontinuous—99.9999% of the bytes in the executable code might be correct, but the one incorrect byte can still cause performance to be 100% wrong. The bright side of this is that operational costs are reduced for highly dependable products (because of fewer corrective changes and fewer customer complaints and damage claims). The optimal level of dependability will minimize the sum of the costs of development and operation. This level should have been decided during the analysis stage; a commensurate level of testing can then be planned.

Testing is emotionally difficult—it recalls all the tests we took in school, with every bad connotation of those experiences. But testing is not as bad as issuing flawed software and having to live with the consequences. Keep reminding yourself that a good test is not one that the software passes, since that just means the error that probably resides in it was missed. A good test is one that reveals an error, which we can then remove.

## 8.1 THE TESTING PROCESS AND PRODUCTS

We first examine the basic outline of the testing stage, and then consider testing principles and methodologies in later sections. Of course, the major pragmatic reason for testing is to eliminate as many errors as possible from the product. By doing so, we will be protecting the user from loss of time, effort, and money. We will also protect our own reputation, as well as our share of the market.

Naturally, we hope that our ongoing verification activities, as well as the attention we have shown to the quality of the development process, have minimized errors in the software. Nevertheless, experience shows that there will still be many problems, and we are prepared to spend up to 40% of total development effort in solving them during the testing stage.

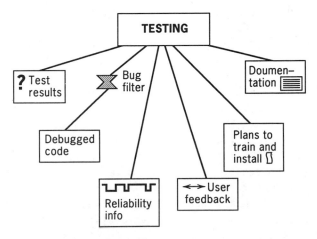

**FIGURE 8-1**   PRODUCTS OF THE TESTING STAGE

Besides error-removing activities, which will proceed by testing individual program units first and then build to the full product, the testing stage provides another opportunity to validate that the software will answer the customer's needs. We can also take advantage of this period to plan for training customer personnel and for installation of the product when it has been released for use, and to finish up the final details of user documentation.

The principal documents of the testing stage will be the results of the actual testing of the product, together with the modified specifications, design, and code that we obtain by correcting the errors we find. The testing results will be added to the Unit Folder, or to the Software Verification Plan (Figure 8-1).

### 8.1.1 Purpose of the Testing Stage

Testing is the final verification and validation activity within the software organization itself. The testing stage has several purposes: to affirm the quality of the product (and indirectly the process), to find and eliminate any residual errors from previous stages; to validate the software as a solution to the original problem, to demonstrate the presence of all specified functionality in the product, and to estimate the operational reliability of the system ([MIL81]).

It is inevitable that any significant software product will contain errors. An organization's reputation depends on the following question: How many and how severe are the errors? Typical industry standards are about 10 errors per KDSI. Most of these errors are expected to be minor. High-quality software will probably have an error rate of 1 per KDSI, whereas exceptionally reliable software may reduce this to 0.1 per KDSI. It should be noted, however, that most of the errors will be in portions of the code that are seldom executed. An average of one error in every 100 lines does *not* mean that the software fails every 100 microseconds.

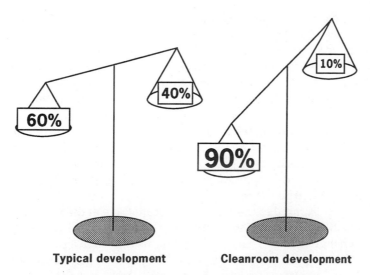

Typical development          Cleanroom development

**F I G U R E 8-2**   ERROR ELIMINATION RATES DURING TESTING

Whereas error discovery and removal have traditionally consumed the bulk of the effort expended during the testing stage, Mills points out in [MIL87] that about 40% of the errors in a typical product escape the process and are uncovered during the actual use of the product by the customer. He proposes that this situation be remedied by using specification and design techniques that support the formal verification of the product and by requiring multiple inspections of work products. Error detection and removal would thus be restricted to the pretesting stages. Testing then becomes a simple process of running the software and logging failures so as to obtain a statistical estimate of its reliability. In practice, this "cleanroom" software technology improves error results to one-half as many error-producing faults and gives an elimination rate among these of 90%, compared with the traditional 60% (Figure 8-2).

## 8.1.2 Activities during Testing

Many of the activities on which testing depends were carried out previously. During specification we decided on the level of dependability we had to meet and formulated plans for software verification. The design and implementation stages provided unit and integration test definitions. In fact, since we may be operating in a mode of parallel stage execution by independent teams, testing of one unit can overlap coding and even design of others.

During testing, the major activities are centered around the examination and modification of source code. We proceed in levels from individual program units to the entire software system. At one end, we attempt to exercise small units in all possible ways so as to detect any errors. From there, we advance through larger and larger aggregates of units, called *builds* or *threads*, testing both their detailed structure and their function. In the end, we ignore the internal structure of the software and concentrate on how it responds to the typical kind of operations that will be requested by the user.

These three phases of testing are usually referred to as *unit testing, integration testing* and *system testing*. As the tests are conducted, substantial efforts are required in recording and interpreting test results. When these indicate the presence of errors that, in the opinion of the change control board, must be removed before the software is released, then the errors are tracked down through the *debugging* process (Figure 8-3).

In fact, errors located during testing may fall into several categories ([DEU82]). Those that merit immediate attention are usually of a nature that they crash the software under consideration; testing cannot continue until they are removed. Other errors need to be corrected before testing is complete but can be ignored during the immediate testing schedule. In general, the importance of removing an error is proportional to its severity, the frequency with which it will occur, and the degree to which the customer will be aware of it ([BEI84]). There are errors that may be acceptable to the user when compared to the cost of correcting them at the moment; these will be held until some future release date or until the customer becomes concerned enough to request a change. Finally, there are errors, usually nonreproducible, for which insufficient evidence exists to evaluate them. They are flagged for ongoing considera-

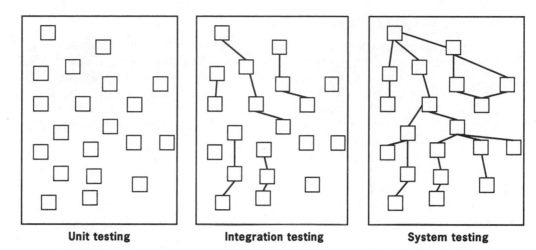

**FIGURE 8-3**  THE THREE TESTING PHASES

tion until they become more tractable. Nonreproducible errors are a frequent problem with concurrent software.

When the software is modified, we start at the point in the work products (analysis, specification, design, or code) where the error was first manifested. Of course, auxiliary work products like documentation may also require a parallel modification. Configuration control activities are vital during the testing stage, since different versions of the product can proliferate. After modification, software is subjected to all of the tests it has passed to this point (*regression testing*) to make certain that no additional errors have been introduced. Then testing can continue.

Along with testing, test documentation, and product modification, there are other activities that are probably occurring. These include polishing user documentation, discussions with the customer to schedule installation and training, and the preparation of installation and training materials. When the product has finally been released by the quality assurance group at the end of testing, we want to move immediately into the installation portion of product delivery.

Thus, there is plenty of activity for every member of the software team during testing. Detail workers will be heavily involved in unit testing and debugging, whizzes will be helping them with their head scratching, and designers will work in integration and system testing. Quality assurance people will focus on integration and system testing, on recording test data, in the application of all the relevant metrics, and evaluating the degree of quality that the process has instilled in the product. Management types will be busy keeping everybody on track and on schedule, whereas writers will be finishing off documentation and analysts will be planning installation and training.

### 8.1.3 Testing Documents and Deliverables

Documentation of the activities outlined in this chapter appears in various work products. Test results and error removal for unit testing will be included in Section 6 of the unit notebook. Results of integration testing will be appended to the respective test plans. Management information about the incidence of errors, the time spent in removing them, and so on, will go into the project legacy. Finally, installation plans will be added to the project plan, whereas training documents will stand alone as part of the user documentation.

As a reminder, the form of the Verification Plan and Section 6 of the Unit Folder are reproduced in Figure 8-4, with a further refinement of the test results section for unit testing. It is important that these be electronic documents wherever possible, to facilitate the modification of test plans in response to changing specifications ([OST88]).

## 8.2 TESTING PRINCIPLES

Testing has been the object of concern, attention, and discussion since the very inception of computing. *Ad hoc* suggestions have predominated over organized and

Requirement (restates specification)
Design verification methodology, schedule,
    responsible party
Code verification methodology, schedule, responsible
    party
Test data and responses, schedule, responsible party

Test Plans
    Facet, feature, or path to be tested
    Person responsible and date scheduled
    Tools or auxiliary code needed
    Test data and instructions
    Expected test results
    Actual test results; analysis (if needed)
            Date
            Operator
            Computing environment
            Description of deviation from expectation
            Was the result reproducible?
            Analysis of possible causes
    Correction schedule and signoff (if needed)
            (the above section is repeated many times)

**FIGURE 8-4**   TEST DOCUMENTATION

well-founded methodologies, however. Hamlet complains that when we begin testing a software product we don't know where the errors are or how to search for them; we don't know how to evaluate the test case data and we don't know when we can stop testing and still guarantee our goals ([HAM88]). There is, he says, very little science exhibited in the typical software testing process, and practically none when the software is developed with functional or logical design paradigms. The use of effective existing tools is also resisted, as usual.

Nevertheless, there are proven techniques for testing. Some of the most productive of these fall into the realm of software project management making sure that a broad variety of tests are planned, carried out, evaluated, and acted on. Many deal with techniques for designing a sufficiently comprehensive set of test cases to locate all significant errors in the product. Others provide metrics that allow us to determine the degree of testing effectiveness that we have attained. Finally, there are categorizations of different methods of testing and the order in which they should be applied.

There are three basic ways in which software can be tested, and they correspond roughly to the three different testing phases. *Structural* testing techniques (commonly utilized during unit tests) view the software in terms of its detailed design and attempt to exercise it so that we can certify the correct behavior of every statement or every decision or every path through the code. Structural testing is possible during the unit test phase, but the growing complexity of the integrated product soon outpaces our ability to focus on microscopic details. Structural testing is sometimes referred to as *program-based* testing and tests the product for conformity to our view of it at the detailed design stage.

*Functional* testing techniques (commonly utilized during integration tests) avoid the detailed point of view. Instead, these techniques take a macroscopic approach—they look at the functions specified for the product, and see if they are indeed implemented satisfactorily. Specified functions are frequently so widely divided among different units that functional testing is impossible during unit tests;. however, it becomes very practical during integration. Functional testing is also called *specification-based* testing, and tests the product for conformity to our view of it at the specification and architectural design stage.

*Pragmatic* testing techniques (commonly utilized during systems testing) attempt to model the actual usage that the software will encounter after it is released to the customer ([PET85]). The concern here is more for the usability and reliability of the software than its universal correctness. This form of validation tests the product for conformity to our view of it at the analysis stage. Pragmatic testing is a kind of superpowered acceptance testing. It is usually much more extensive than acceptance testing and is planned and conducted by the software organization. Since acceptance testing directly involves the customer, we will postpone consideration of it to Chapter 9 (Figure 8-5).

Some attempts have been made to bridge the gap between unit and integration testing, so that the testing point of view can expand smoothly from structure to function ([HOW87]). This sort of *error-based* testing looks for common errors, and designs test cases to disclose them. Although perfect disclosure of all errors is a theoretical impossibility, the hope is that perfect disclosure of *some* classes of errors *will* be possible.

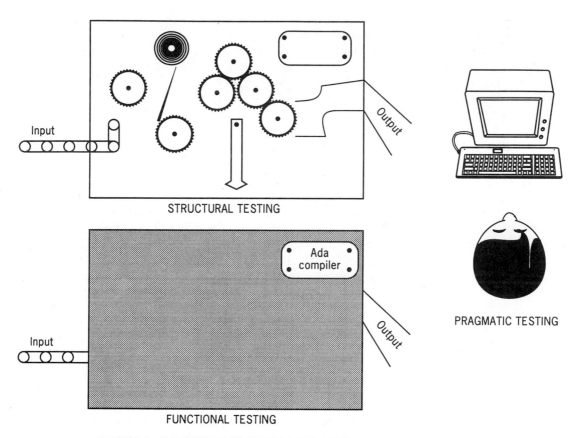

STRUCTURAL TESTING

PRAGMATIC TESTING

FUNCTIONAL TESTING

FIGURE 8-5   THE THREE BASIC WAYS TO TEST SOFTWARE

## 8.2.1 Goals for the Testing Stage

Among the legitimate goals of the testing stage are the detection and elimination of errors, the prevention of additional errors during software modification, the validation of the product ([GEL88]), and the release of the product on the scheduled date. These goals may conflict with each other, however; validation means finding no errors, whereas error detection means finding errors. Careful modification can mean late delivery. The possible conflict among our goals can cause confusion in the trenches and can lead to irrational decision making.

Indeed, the pressure of being in the last stage of product development can cause the software team to make some serious mistakes. On the one hand, we might resolve to correct every error that testing uncovers. Although this is a laudable goal in theory, being penny-wise about minor errors may lead us to be pound-foolish about contract penalties, or to lose out on a window of opportunity in the market. On the other hand, bowing to the schedule and hurrying testing to the point that we fail to detect and to correct serious errors may incur other contract penalties or the loss of our reputation as a source of high-quality products.

We really we need to have some predetermined goals for testing—just how much dependability the product requires, just how important the schedule is, and so on. A cost-benefit analysis will indicate the best balance of testing effort. Once this decision has been made, it is up to project management to make sure that the selected goals do indeed guide the actions of the individuals carrying out testing activities. Since the testing stage probably consumes the greatest single block of effort during development, it is especially important that the process remain under firm management control.

In terms of the validation function, we must be certain that the software is tested in a realistic setting. Notwithstanding all of the theoretical means of choosing test cases, the only way to be sure that software is satisfactory to users is to exercise it extensively in the same way that users are expected to do.

## 8.2.2 Characteristics of Good Testing

As usual, a good testing process is well planned and methodical—methodical in the sense of being carefully controlled, but more importantly in that it depends on some rational and well-founded techniques. The two best-developed methodologies for the testing stage deal with methods for selecting test data and, when the data reveal software failures, methods for locating the errors that have given rise to them.

In terms of test data selection, the fundamental attribute of quality is whether test cases are **adequate** to uncover all of the errors of the specific types that we are concerned with. Since it is theoretically impossible for testing to display symptoms of *all* errors, we have to narrow the scope of our efforts to cover at least those possibilities that are most menacing to the product.

Another characteristic of good testing is the amount of control over its progress that is exerted by project management. As will be discussed in Section 8.4.3, it is frequently possible to predict the success or failure of a product on the basis of the rate at which testing and debugging progress. These, in turn, depend partly on the quality of product as it has been developed to this point, and partly on the intelligent application of resources to the testing process itself.

In particular, good testing makes full use of the large variety of software tools which are now available and will be described in Section 8.3.5. The psychological threat of exposing their faults sometimes leads software engineers to want to privatize testing, and keep it under their personal control as much as possible. Tools are then seen as threats to personal control of the process, and tool use is frequently avoided for that reason. Besides, if tools amplify the scope of the testing, the probability of exposing faults will be greatly increased.

Another characteristic of a good testing process is the existence of a dependable **test oracle** ([HOW85]). This is a method for determining what the correct response to input test cases should be. Although responses to functional testing can often be obtained by analyzing the specifications of the function being tested, unit testing may depend on a human being to determine the desired outcome. This is a significant bottleneck in the use of massive test cases, and we should make use of any possible automation of test script composition.

### 8.2.3 Test Case Design

Since testing depends on the controlled execution of code, we must provide input values for the code to run on. We may be executing an individual program unit or aggregates of several modules or the entire program or system. Each set of data for execution, together with the correct results of execution with that data, is called a **test case**. It is necessary that we develop a large enough and broad enough set of test cases to find as many errors as possible, and to verify the presence of all the software functionality that was originally specified.

There are many techniques for discovering and developing test cases. Some depend on static analysis of the code and the previous design and specification documents. Others require that we investigate the dynamic behavior of the code as it is executed, either directly or symbolically. Of course, the simplest procedure is to allow the tester just to make up data and to use these data. This will work more or less well, depending on the skill and understanding of the tester, and on blind luck; but intuition is not a good basis for complete testing of a software product. A list of this and other possible methods of selecting test cases is shown in Figure 8-6.

The second method listed in Figure 8-6 is to test the software by using all possible data. Although this is easily managed, this technique is not practical; there are usually far too many possible data points to allow us to test them individually. For instance, suppose we want to test software that looks for patterns within a string. If each test of a pattern and string pair took only a microsecond, and we restricted ourselves to patterns and strings of length at most four and made up of only the standard printable characters, the time for an exhaustive data test would still exceed 100 years.

Data that are intuitively appealing to the tester.
An exhaustive set of all possible data.
Data that represent all possible data.
Data that represent anticipated actual use of the product.
Data that cause a desired special effect.
Data that cause each statement to be executed.
Data that cause each branch to be followed.
Data that are close to the data that have already been effective.
Data that cause all possible combinations of predicate values
    in the evaluation of conditions.
Data that cause each path to be followed.
Data that cause a flow of control from each value definition to each use.
Data that cause a flow of control from some value definition to each use.
Data that represent a domain of equivalent points.
Data that cause the execution of specific functions.
Data specified to be unprocessable.

**FIGURE 8-6**   DIFFERENT KINDS OF TEST DATA

Faced with the need to choose a few test cases among all of the possible data, we must select our testing goals. If we have no particular concerns or goals, then it might be enough to select representative data that are randomly distributed over the set of all possibilities. The distribution could be uniform, or exponential, or any other that might seem appropriate. This technique does surprisingly well—it may catch 60% of the errors in the software. In addition, little more than a pseudo-random number generator and a test oracle are required for automated testing on a massive scale. Of course, defining an effective oracle may be a very difficult task. Another non-automated alternative in choosing numeric data is to select it along a gradient of maximum variation in the function being evaluated.

On the other hand, if we do have a goal and it is to determine how the software will behave during use, we can choose data that are typical of actual usage patterns. This can be determined by going back to the analysis documents or we may actually be able to capture data from the system currently being used.

Although this is not perfect, for practical purposes this is probably the most convincing kind of test, since using realistic input data has the advantage of providing test case data that are distributed statistically according to the **execution profile**, which describes the actual frequency of various classes of user inputs. This provides more assurance that the reliability of the code, as measured by the occurrence of failures during testing, truly mirrors the reliability of the product during customer use ([MIL81]).

A special effect is just an output or a system state that we have selected as important in testing the software. We can work back from the effect to the data that might cause it by using cause/effect analysis. This is covered briefly in Section 8.3.2, and more thoroughly in [MYE79]. Another way of viewing special effects is to enumerate the more common possible errors and to try to create them. There are many of these for which we can test, for instance infinite loops, array indices out of bounds, overflow and underflow, initialization failure, incorrect control flow, and incompatible interface semantics. In particular, it is good to test all exception handling states as special effects.

One guide to itemizing special effects is a categorization of error types. Two of these categories, for instance, are computation errors and domain errors. The former deals with incorrect composition of expressions, whereas the latter means that incorrect logic formulation causes us to take the wrong path.

Clearly, execution of each module statement is advisable and under usual circumstances is achievable. Branches are the edges in a program flowchart. If-then-else statements have two internal branches, whereas loops have an exit branch and a branch through the loop body and back to the test and so on. It is possible to have full statement coverage but incomplete branch coverage, for instance, in cases where if-then-else statements have no "else" part. We might thoughtlessly slip by this circumstance, reasoning that an empty block does not need testing anyway. But consider the following situation:

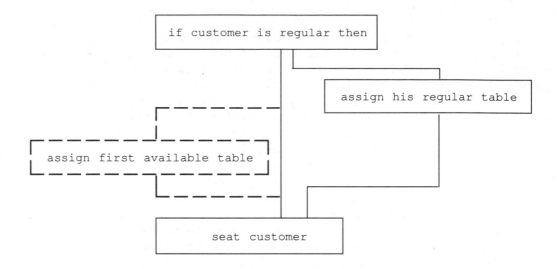

Our test might always be for regular customers, and thus would never demonstrate that new customers are never assigned a table, presumably an error.

Full branch coverage means, for condition-controlled loops, that the body of the loop is executed at least once in one of the tests, and that the loop always terminates. But it is particularly important to test the effect of zero-repetition, that is, never executing the loop body at all. Additional confidence can be gained by requiring longer and longer ranges of execution, although zero, one and two repetitions are often perceived as sufficient.

We are frequently able to build new test cases by adapting existing ones. Prather and Myers suggest a "path prefix" strategy for obtaining branch coverage quickly ([PRA87]). It consists of starting with intuitive test cases, then examining their dynamic trace to find the first branch point encountered for which the other branches have not all been followed. The data are then modified to cause another branch from this point to be followed. All of this can be done fairly rapidly with the aid of a software tool.

In developing a broad range of test data, we may be guided by the need to cause variation in each expression (arithmetic, Boolean, string, and so on) in the code. There is really little we can deduce about the correctness of an expression we have created if we cannot see it changing as a result of the change in data. Weiser, Gannon, and McMullin go further in [WEI85] by suggesting that we need to modify test data for each expression until we have found a point for each of its subexpressions that causes the value of the expression to vary from the value of the subexpression. This ensures that the part of the expression not contained in the subexpression is not meaningless. Once again, the appropriate adaptation of data sets can find useful new data cases.

Continuing on in the same vein, we may test both branches of an if statement and still find that errors are masked by the combination of predicates in the condition. For example, in the software for a small store's credit department, we want to allow credit for adults with a minimum yearly wage and disallow it for other people. Suppose the resultant code were as follows:

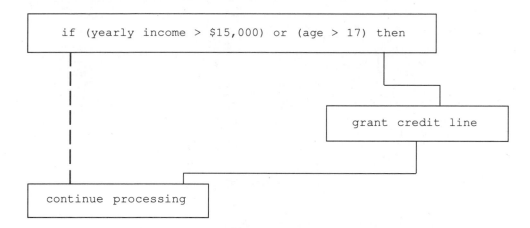

We might conduct a large number of tests by using data representing people with incomes above $15000 who were adults (older than 17 years of age). These would function correctly. We could also test for penniless 2-year-olds, exercising the other branch, and the tests would again be correct. Even though these tests were branch complete, they test only the T-T and F-F combinations of predicate values. If we were to test all of the predicate combinations, we would quickly find that the "or" should be an "and." Decision tables or decision trees can be a valuable aid in developing test cases for full branch coverage.

Finally, a path is a single locus of execution through a procedure. Code that contains an if-then-else statement embedded in a loop that is executed four times has 16 paths. These can be calculated in terms of which branch is taken on each of the four traversals: F-F-F-F, F-F-F-T, ... T-T-T-T. In general, the number of paths rises exponentially as more control structures are added to a procedure, and Tai has shown that the minimum set of test cases needed to exercise these adequately for full path coverage also rises exponentially ([TAI80]). If the loop is indefinite (a while or until loop with no limit on the number of repetitions), there can be an infinite number of paths.

Of course, some of these paths may be infeasible; that is, the conditions that must be true at a branch point may be incompatible with the condition that must be true at a following branch point on the path. A tool or technique for eliminating infeasible paths can reduce the number of cases to be tested for complete path coverage. If possible, path analysis should interface with the test data generator to avoid an attempt to create impossible data. Even so, full path testing is not possible under normal circumstances.

Theoreticians claim that another drawback of path testing is its total independence from the program's specifications. Both the path explosion and the independence problems can be answered in part by using data flow rather than control flow (path) criteria for selecting test cases. In this technique, we use static analysis, similar to that performed by optimizing compilers, to locate all execution paths between a variable definition (storage of a value) and a use (retrieval of the value) of the same variable. The logic is that we aren't sure the right value was calculated and stored unless it is used

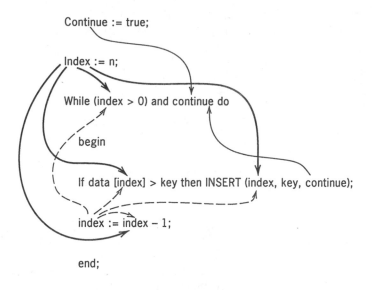

Continue := true;

Index := n;

While (index > 0) and continue do

  begin

    If data [index] > key then INSERT (index, key, continue);

    index := index − 1;

  end;


If continue then INSERT (0, key, continue);


readln(key);

**FIGURE 8-7**   DATA FLOW ANALYSIS OF CODE

again (see Figure 8-7). We choose to execute these data flow paths ([WEI85]). Data flow paths are frequently fewer in number than decision paths, and they are more closely tied to software function.

In fact, [FRA88] lists an extensive repertoire of different data flow criteria that can be used in testing. One additional data flow method requires that a set of contexts be constructed for each statement that uses data. Each context is an alternate path through definitions of all the values being accessed. The context paths are then tested ([HOW87]).

Given that intuitive testing and branch-complete testing are far from adequate, and that full path testing is both theoretically and effectively incomplete, how do we choose our test data? Howden, in his proposal for functional testing ([HOW85]), suggests a pragmatic technique, which is based on the assumption that almost all errors are of a rather predictable nature and occur during the process of synthesizing larger structures from smaller ones. This assumption is a form of the "competent programmer hypothesis": programmers don't make mistakes that are wild or unpredictable. Instead, programmer faults are simple slips, resulting in code that is very close to what it should be.

Howden's technique is to exploit the model of the module generated by the specifications and design, using it to show how the module's components are composed of smaller components. Next, we test exhaustively for the predictable errors that might occur at each composition step ([HOW87]). The composition techniques (during which errors are assumed to occur) are algebraic (use of arithmetic, relational, logical, string, and so on, operators), use of selection and iteration, and control (composition of individual nodes to form finite state diagrams).

It turns out that there are a number of the "special case" variety of test cases, like boundary vicinities, fixed size random sets, and nonzero values, which provide very good test coverage for the kinds of errors Howden is looking for in the algebraic, selection, and iteration compositions. Thus we are able to trade off the size of the test set against the breadth of the errors that will be disclosed by it ([HOW87]).

For control composition, it is necessary to insert all possible functions (determined by examining the specifications and design) on the arcs in the state diagram to form "mutants" and then to trace the execution of all of the mutants, hoping that the tester will be able to recognize the right one. Although this technique helps solve the problem of missing code, it also represents a nonautomatable burden on the tester's time.

For those who believe that errors are not all *that* predictable, the domain viewpoint of test data is available. A domain consists of a set of input data combinations that should be indistinguishable insofar as the software is concerned. Thus, if we can define a domain, it should be possible to select a single data point to represent all the others. Symbolic execution can help in finding domains defined by the structure of the code, as will be seen in Section 8.3.5.

Of course, domains can be constructed in such detail as to enumerate all paths or to achieve full path coverage, but we have already decided that this is infeasible. The capability of selecting just one point from a domain for test purposes does not solve the path explosion problem, since a distinct domain is defined by each different path. It does relax the requirements of exhaustive testing from the need to look at *all* data, but that isn't enough.

The truth is that mutation (see below), branch, path, and data flow testing are not perfect. There can be significant errors left in the software even after all conceivable tests of these kinds have been successfully passed ([HAM88]). In particular, missing code/function errors will never be reliably caught by structural testing of any kind ([WEI85]).

Nevertheless, domain analysis will allow us to use structural knowledge about the implementation to form some larger domains of interest, and to define other, separate domains on the basis of functional knowledge about the specifications. These two distinct partitions of the input space can be intersected to form a finer partition. A single point can then be selected from each cell of this finer partition as a test case.

Although domain testing can not guarantee perfect testing, it is possible to construct **revealing** subdomains that will disclose all errors of the type for which the subdomain was constructed ([WEY80]). This is, in fact, one of the motivating ideas of Howden's functional testing, of structural coverage techniques, and of special effects testing.

Ostrand and Balcer claim in [OST88] that structural coverage is not as important as testing all the functionality of the software; and that these tests should maximize the likelihood of finding errors. In place of the usually fuzzy criteria for selecting functional test data, they suggest a careful investigation of specifications (formal specifications are useful for this) to form domains based on all functions and the parameters and environmental contexts that govern their execution. Special cases can then be constructed on the basis of these domains.

In testing special cases we often want to consider the boundaries of those domains of which we are aware, and then test in the vicinity of the boundary. By vicinity, we mean the boundary value as well as the values just above and below it—as close as we can come within the resolution of that particular data type. These boundaries can occur at the limits of counted loops, on the edges of regions defined by Boolean predicates, at the limits of the sizes of arrays or strings, and so on. For instance, if the statement

```
if age > 17 then permit(age); else exclude(age); end if;
```

appeared in a program, then it would be wise to test for age = 17 and 18.

It is also important to test extreme values (the largest possible value, largest minus one, the smallest, smallest plus one, empty files, empty strings and empty lists, and so on) and values at boundaries which select different portions of code. Loops should be traversed zero, one, and two times, as well as the maximum and maximum minus one times. We should investigate the situations in which the data are the first or the last in a looping process or represent a control break. Finally, a special attempt should be made to test for infinite loops by trying to deduce what circumstances might cause a loop condition to be constantly true or false.

Sometimes software provides more functionality than was specified—it processes data that it shouldn't. For this reason, it is particularly important to test with formally unacceptable data as well as processable data. This might be viewed as another instance of exception handler testing under special effects data, but instead of just obtaining the effect once, in this situation we want to test a wide range of representative "bad" data.

There is an entire branch of testing theory that deals with the question of whether a set of test cases is **adequate**, that is, sufficient to exhibit errors of certain types in the product. Generally speaking, we attempt to evaluate the adequacy of a set of test cases to disclose *errors of a fixed kind*. It is impossible to construct test data to disclose all errors, hence, we limit our goals to some recognized class of common errors, and then attempt to define criteria for test set construction that will guarantee catching at least these kinds of problems.

Weyuker, for instance, proposes a set of axioms that describe acceptable test case completeness criteria ([WEY88]). In brief, these axioms state that adequate criteria should require test cases that take implementation structure into account, and in particular that they need to cause every statement to be executed. It is also necessary to test interfaces and interactions between already tested units, and to take into account the context within which a unit will be used. Finally, a criterion that does not make it harder to test complex software than it is to test simple software is not adequate.

Program *mutation* is another method for evaluating the completeness of test cases ([ADR82]). As originally envisioned ([DEM78]), the technique calls for the code to be modified in certain predictable ways, thus forming a large set of nearly identical mutants. Mutants are produced by replacing one variable name by another, one loop limit by another, one pointer expression by another, and so on. As one can imagine, the full set of mutants is enormous. The set of test cases is then thought to be adequate if each mutant, which contains one of the errors thought to be possible, is caused to behave differently than the original program by at least one of the test cases. In other words, the test cases are complete when every mutant error is revealed, or disclosed, by at least one among them.

Among the weaknesses of program mutation are the difficulty of dealing with the huge set of mutants, the fact that it presupposes the competent programmer hypothesis (in that it checks for simple slips rather than deep errors of comprehension), and that it assumes that compounded, multiple-error failures can be uncovered by simple, single-error test cases. In an attempt to ameliorate some of these difficulties, Howden proposed *weak mutation* in [HOW82].

In weak mutation evaluation, very low level errors are targeted, like storing or retrieving the wrong variable or using the wrong arithmetic or relational operator. Figure 8-8 shows code with each "weak gene", or mutation point underlined. A mutant is formed by altering just one of these. For instance, we might change the "and" in line 3 to "or." The number of mutants thus produced is smaller than in the case of program mutation, whereas an adequate test set as demonstrated by weak mutation is probably much stronger than a set that guarantees full branch coverage. On the negative side, weak mutation still shows no relationship to specified function, the set of mutants is still very large, and the apparent failure of a test set to be adequate may in fact be caused by program errors ([HOW85]).

## 8.3 TESTING METHODOLOGIES AND TOOLS

Techniques for generating test cases surely represent one of the most important of testing methodologies. Others will be outlined in Sections 8.3.1 to 8.3.5. Unit testing, which depends on the exact form of the implementation, will be considered first. Structural testing can be seen as the most powerful form of verification of the implementation and detailed design. It concentrates on the details of program execution rather than on the interactions of modules or the broad sweep of software function.

As unit testing reveals failures in code execution, we often decide that these are severe enough to justify modification of the product to eliminate them. This is not just a question of kludging a patch to the code, but of going back through all the work

```
Continue := true
Index := n;
While (Index > 0) and Continue do
  begin
  If Data[Index] ≥ Key then INSERT(Index, Key, Continue);
  Index := Index - 1;
  end;
If Continue then INSERT(0. Key, Continue);
Readln (Key);
```

**FIGURE 8-8**   WEAK GENES FOR WEAK MUTATION

products and changing them. But first it is necessary to locate the error behind the failure; sometimes this is an obscure problem that takes considerable tracking. This debugging technology will be even more useful as we proceed with testing and begin to encounter errors caused by the complex interactions of the whole system.

Integration testing is the process of checking interfaces and interactions between modules. The best methodology for integration is adding a single program unit at a time to a growing base of debugged modules. At the end of integration we have a full system, which can then be tested in a functional sense. This is a validation step in which we attempt to demonstrate that the product can really do the intended job.

Testing methodologies are important, but it is not a good idea to allow the entire validation and verification process to depend on them alone. After all, even with the best test sets, it is still necessary for the oracle (usually the tester) to notice the failure that testing discloses. But there is evidence that as many as 30% of all failures are not noticed ([BAS87]). Tools can help with this problem, and testing's effectiveness will be multiplied if quality control has been fully exercised at previous life cycle stages.

For instance, code walkthroughs and inspections are another way of eliminating errors, and should already have been used. Basili again notes that code reading can be as effective in catching errors as any of the other methods commonly used. Code reading is particularly effective in allowing experienced testers to discover interface problems. In addition, an error discovered by reading has *already been located*.

### 8.3.1 Unit Testing

Unit testing is the process of taking a program module and running it in isolation from the rest of the software product by using prepared input and comparing the actual results with the results predicted by the specifications and design of the module. One purpose of testing is to find (and remove) as many errors in the software as practical. There are three reasons for testing units, as opposed to testing the entire product:

1  The size of a single module is small enough that we can locate an error fairly easily.
2  Confusing interactions of multiple errors in widely different parts of the software are eliminated.
3  The module is small enough that we can attempt to test it in some demonstrably exhaustive fashion.

These ideas reinforce some of the specification and design goals presented earlier. Obviously, low coupling of modules will make it more feasible for us to test individual modules in the absence of others and to eliminate multiple error interactions. High cohesion will tend to limit the size of individual modules and to make the task of predicting correct outcomes easier. Thus the same methods that allow us to control the complexity of design also give us enough control to improve testing. The use of functional specifications will again aid in predicting outcomes, since the oracle may already be spelled out in them.

The reverse side of this logic is that modules that do not demonstrate principles of good design are not only likely to contain more errors, but the errors will be harder to find. Any of the detailed design metrics could be used to measure the complexity or structure or cohesion of a unit and thus to predict difficulty of testing. In particular, the McCabe cyclomatic complexity measure has been used to good effect to pinpoint testing "hot spots."

Structural testing is based on the dynamic analysis of code execution, which requires that it be instrumented to allow the tester to see into its progress at a level of detail that goes far beyond just looking at the output ([MIL81]). This may be taken to the extent of examining an entire dump of all values and paths during the execution, but is more likely to involve the checking of certain data values and relationships as well as logging the flow of control as it passes designated points.

In doing this, we can make use of the assertions that were developed during formal verification of the design and code and that should be present as comments of some kind in the code. These assertions can be manually instrumented as conditional statements—if they are not true, then the location and appropriate data values are output and logged. An automatic assertion checker can be valuable for minimizing the amount of handwork required in dynamic analysis ([STU77]).

One problem with testing a module in isolation may already have occurred to you. How do you run a procedure without anything to call it, to be called by it or, possibly, to output intermediate values obtained during execution? One approach is to construct an appropriate driver routine to call it and, simple stubs to be called by it, and to insert output statements in it. This overhead code, called *scaffolding*, represents effort that is important to testing, but does not appear in the delivered product (Figure 8-9). A second, and much better, approach is to generate the scaffolding automatically by means of a **test harness**. A test harness, among other things, allows us to run a single unit in isolation, while simulating the rest of the software system environment by providing appropriate input, output, parameters, and interaction for the unit. Test harnesses are discussed below in Section 8.3.5. A third and rather ineffective technique is to omit unit testing per se and simply to allow incremental addition of modules to

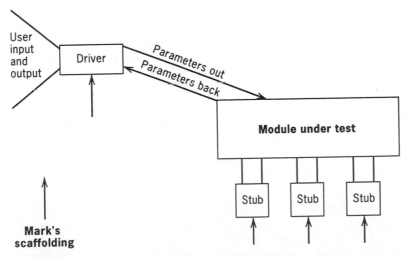

**FIGURE 8-9**  SCAFFOLDING REQUIRED TO TEST A PROGRAM UNIT

a partially integrated product, hoping that the integration testing will also provide sufficient coverage of the module's structure. This technique is usually inadequate, but nevertheless it is often recommended in the literature.

The set of test input data, together with the results, will be recorded in the Unit Folder. Test data are also saved in computer-accessible files, called a **test suite**. During maintenance, when it is time to modify a module, the set of all previously passed tests will need to be run again, and the results compared with the previous results. This regression testing ensures that inadvertent errors are not introduced as we make our modifications.

The basis for choosing a representative set of data is usually the structure of the code itself. Choosing data to fit program structure is also called *white-box* testing. A white box, as opposed to a black box, is one we can see the insides of. The unit test will usually start with the simplest kind of data, representing the standard operation of the module. As testing and error-removal progress, more complex and unusual test data will be tried.

Generally, our initial choice of test data is relatively intuitive, governed first by what we consider to be the priorities among the different cases that might occur. For this reason we select standard operations to test first, and will probably spend the most time on these. We will also test more heavily what we consider to be the weak parts of the design or the portions of code where failure could be most devastating.

If we attempt to define a path-testing test case strategy, we can probably expect to catch about 35% of the errors in the software. Adding other intuitive, random, and structural test cases may bring unit test effectiveness to the point of catching 65% of the errors ([BEI84]). Of course, it is always possible that errors will be revealed by the test cases but will not be noticed by the tester.

### 8.3.2 Debugging

Error removal, frequently called **debugging**, is the process of locating and correcting the errors in software by using information we gather from failures exhibited during testing. Error removal occurs during original development and subsequent modifications and can comprise up to 40% of the total cost of software. Of course, that is too much to pay for an essentially unproductive activity, and many of the techniques presented in earlier chapters are important because they reduce the eventual cost of error removal.

The primary characteristic of design and implementation that makes for easy fault location and removal is understandability. This is provided in part by decomposition, clustering of related components and separation from unrelated ones, careful selection of names for software entities, and full documentation. Of course, tools that make it possible to execute code under full control and with full visibility are also important ([COM80]).

The related methods of modularity, data hiding, and abstraction are important because they allow a complex product to be viewed as a system of relatively simple and independent units that communicate over a tightly controlled and easily monitored interface. Structured programming has much the same role within program units, with its insistence on single-entrance and single-exit blocks of code. As a corollary, debug-

1  Detect a failure in the test results.

2  Find a set of test data that will allow you to reproduce the failure at will.

3  Localize the error and deduce the corresponding fault.

4  Correct the error, in *all* work products, starting with the document in whose creation the fault occurred.

5  Retest the modified code with all applicable tests that have been passed thus far.

6  Log the fault, recording the phase in which it occurred, its type and context, whose fault it was, how it might have been discovered earlier or avoided altogether, and how it was found.

**F I G U R E 8-10**   SEQUENCE OF ACTIVITIES FOR ERROR REMOVAL

ging concurrent and distributed software can be extremely difficult. In concurrent systems, the nondeterminacy of selection operations and of system changes due to other processes may make it very difficult to reproduce a fault for study. In distributed systems, the time delay in the communication network makes it difficult to correlate the fault with the error that gave rise to it.

The general pattern of error-removal activities is shown in Figure 8-10. Step 2 might not be as easy as it appears. Failures could, after all, be hardware rather than software induced. This means that they might depend on the temperature, voltage variations, or other unpredictable causes. Even software-caused failures might depend not on the software under test but on operating system initialization procedures or the interference of other concurrent processes. Note that test sets for exhibiting failures for debugging should not be made intentionally extensive, as is done with regular testing. Rather, they should be fine-tuned to help pinpoint the problem efficiently.

As mentioned earlier, Step 3 is made much easier if we utilize structured and modular design and programming techniques. The high cohesion we expect to find will give strong hints as to where the error occurs, whereas the low coupling will allow us to easily monitor interfaces to verify these suppositions.

Steps 4 and 5 almost represent a litmus test for professionalism among software engineers. First, there is the temptation of expediency to which many amateurs succumb: if the fault is not immediately evident, experiment with various kludges that will mask the symptoms of the error. If one is found, go on. Second, self-discipline is needed to determine carefully the true fault and correct it, both at its source and in its subsequent effects.

Regression testing must be used to determine that the change did not actually degrade the product. Some research has shown that the probability of a change being an improvement is below 50%. Here again, modular software should be largely impervious to changes in the implementation of any module; hence problems due to side effects generated by a correction occur much less frequently in modular code.

Step 6 is important for the systematic management of software projects. Self-assessment and planning are the only way to spiral up out of a never-ending round in which we commit the same errors over and over. It might be mentioned here that errors tend to cluster. Therefore, one way to find errors is to investigate a vicinity in which errors have already been found.

Remember that error removal can be psychologically difficult. It requires humility to even admit the possibility of errors in the code we have created and requires an open mind that is willing to see what the software actually *does* rather than what it *should* do. Error removal requires persistence to continue to test until all errors have been found, as well as the integrity to resist the pressure to do a slipshod job and get on with other things. It also requires serenity to work with elusive errors without falling prey to frustration. And speaking of prey, it doesn't hurt to have some of the intensity of a hunter on the spoor.

There are two strategies for tracking down errors once a failure has been observed. The first, called backtracking, involves tracing step-by-step backward from the failure, at each step examining the system state to locate a deviation from the intended state. Eventually we reach a statement that inherits a correct state and produces an erroneous one. This is our quarry.

The second strategy is cause postulation. This involves an examination of the nature of the failure and a hypothesis of possible cause. It uses a combination of (1) inductive thinking, in which we analyze the nature and pattern of individual failures and then decide what might have caused these specific results, and (2) deductive thinking, in which we consider all possible causes and eliminate some that could not, in fact, produce the erroneous results.

Cause postulation has the potential for being a faster technique than backtracking, since it allows us to jump directly from effect to cause. However, it is often impossible to come up with a single postulated cause on the basis of a single example of a failure, Therefore, we may be forced to develop additional test sets to confirm or to discard hypotheses until only one is left. For a highly modular and relatively short piece of code, backtracking with a good tool may actually turn out to be faster.

We have three different windows into the nature of the software. First, we may examine the code itself. Program analysis of this kind is particularly suited to the cause postulation strategy. The static analysis tools mentioned in Section 8.3.5 can be very helpful when one uses examination. But the methods are essentially intellectual, since they do not depend on the dynamic behavior of the software.

The next window is an execution history of an instance of a failure. If the code is sufficiently instrumented to allow us to examine the relevant parts of the system state at each step, we can deduce the relationship of failure to error and eventually locate the error. This window is particularly suited to the backtracking method.

Finally, we may be able to interactively control and trace execution of the software. This is similar to the execution history technique, since it provides insight into the dynamic behavior of the software. It has the advantage of making the flow of control much clearer and of allowing us to modify the system state to cause certain reactions in the software. The disadvantage is that we have to guess in advance what will happen rather than backtrack from what *did* happen. Of course, hindsight is a lot clearer than foresight.

When the specific erroneous code statement has been located, correction depends on tracing back through the detailed design, architectural design, external design, and specifications to find the point at which there was a deviation from the intended function. The context of the statement must be carefully examined so that changes will not create side effects. The proposed change should be in keeping with the overall design of the system.

### 8.3.3 Integration Testing

The purpose of unit testing is to determine that each independent module is correctly implemented. This gives little chance to determine that the interface between modules is also correct, and for this reason integration testing must be performed. One specific target of integration testing is the interface: whether parameters match on both sides as to type, permissible ranges, meaning, and utilization ([COL88]). Another way of stating this is: module testing assures us that the detailed design was correctly implemented; now it is necessary to verify that the architectural design specifications were met.

Our hope is that the modules exhibit a low degree of coupling; hence we should be working with an interface that is dependent on the call and parameter list mechanisms alone. Since these mechanisms were already exercised by the test harnesses, integration testing should proceed smoothly and quickly. For some reason, it never does.

Sometimes, because of the lack of a good test harness tool, the software team will decide to use the upper-level modules as drivers in testing the lower-level modules, or the lower level as stubs for the upper. This kind of testing verifies modules as they are integrated into the system. The problem with it is that interface errors are detected in the same process as intra-module errors, and it is frequently difficult to separate their effect. This only confuses the issue. It is strongly recommended that module and integration testing be separate.

During integration, we choose portions of the structure tree of the software to put together. Each subtree should have some logical reason for being tested: it may implement a single function; it may be a particularly difficult or tricky part of the code; or it may be essential to the function of the rest of the product. As testing progresses, we find ourselves putting together larger and larger parts of the tree, until the entire product has been integrated.

There are several classical integration strategies, that really have little basis in a rational methodology. Top-down integration proceeds down the invocation hierarchy, adding one module at a time until an entire tree level is integrated; it eliminates the need for drivers. The bottom-up strategy works similarly from the bottom, and has no need of stubs. A sandwich strategy runs from top and bottom concurrently, meeting somewhere in the middle (Figure 8-11).

There has been a lot of discussion about whether top-down, bottom-up, or sandwich integration is best. Most of this concern is driven by the need to mix module testing into integration, because of a lack of test harnesses. When the lack disappears, then the concern is no longer significant. But there are a few principles that should guide integration.

First, if we are going to overlap module testing and integration testing, then we will find that not all modules will be ready for integration at the same time. If there is a preferred integration pattern, the scheduling of unit testing should have the modules that are to be integrated first available the soonest.

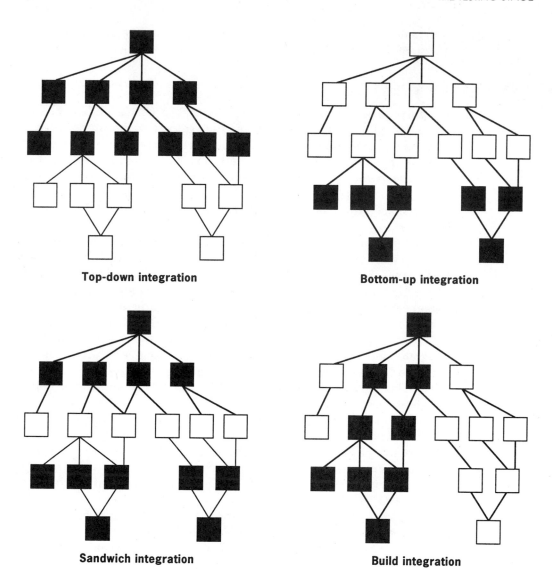

**Top-down integration**  **Bottom-up integration**

**Sandwich integration**  **Build integration**

**FIGURE 8-11** FOUR DIFFERENT INTEGRATION PATTERNS

Integration should follow the lines of first putting together those subsystems that are of greatest concern. This prioritization might dictate top-down integration if control and the user interface were the most worrisome or complex part of the software. This can occur, for instance, if the customer is anxious to see a "running" program early in the testing phase.

In another situation, the machine interface and performance might be of special interest, and then bottom-up integration would be dictated. With bottom-up integration we stand a better chance of experiencing a high degree of concurrency during our integration, so that more separate efforts could be under way. It has also been said that top-down integration is an exercise in faith that everything will work out well, whereas bottom-up integration shows that things really do work.

One of the principles of integration testing is to add to the complexity of that portion of the product under test gradually and in a controlled manner. This is probably best done by attempting to integrate along branches of the structure tree rather than by levels. This allows us to expand the details of a particular portion of the functionality of the software rather than expanding detail of all the software at once.

One technique for this kind of rational integration involves creation of **threads** within the entire product ([DEU82]). A thread is associated with a particular function provided by the software. It may run through a considerable part of the product, traversing many modules from input to output. Any one module may form part of several threads. These threads can be the basis for testing a whole function rather than the structure of individual units. Separate but related threads can be braided together to form **builds**, which prototype the entire system in its different aspects. Adding threads to a build can mirror a form of the program growth development model. The principle is to maintain control of the testing process by attaching just a little more functionality each time.

With integration testing we move slowly away from structural testing and toward functional, or *black-box* testing, which treats a module as an impenetrable mechanism for performing a function. As the aggregated modules become larger and larger, we lose our ability to think about path coverage and domains and must be satisfied with simply determining that the product seems to do what we intended. That is, we treat the product as a black box and verify that specified inputs produce appropriate outputs, without concern for the internal structure of the software. However, even in functional tests we can and should continue to choose test data that represent important, boundary, or unusual conditions.

In attempting to bridge the gap from small units to a large software system, we may not be able to jump from structural tests to specification-oriented functional tests immediately, while maintaining the principle of adding one unit at a time. One way of testing intermediate levels of the product is to isolate utility, or internal, functions defined during the architectural design stage and to use them as the basis for functional testing. A second method is to use Howden's concept of functional testing, with its structural elements, which encompasses many program units and is modeled by finite state machines ([HOW87]).

Functional testing is a way of determining that the specifications of the software are being met. Thus, the specifications and the user's manual become the standard against which to compare the software. Of course, we must test functions by using a reasonable variety of data, both correct and incorrect, as before.

## 8.3.4 System Testing

The primary activity in system testing is to determine whether specified *functionality* is indeed present in the software. Compatibility with the operational environment of the software system should also be verified during these tests. Test case techniques for system testing include causing special effects or invoking a specific function. A specification-based analysis, such as the one described in [OST88], can provide a highly structured method for producing test cases. If conducted by an independent tester, this may also be as a check on architectural design, since both involve a decomposition of the product in terms of its function.

There are many types of specifications, and we should be aware of them as we perform our integration testing. For instance, there may be a specified level of *performance* required of the software. This may involve measurement of response time under various loads and operating conditions. It may also require measurement of main and disk memory usage.

*Stress* testing entails operating the product at full capacity for an extended period of time and introducing momentary overloads. These might take the form of exceptional conditions, incorrect sequences of commands, failure of devices, requests made to the product that go beyond its stated limits, contention for or depletion of resources, and so on If the product is meant to run in a multi-programming environment, then other processes must also be executing during the stress test. Software may not be able to fully deal with the problems arising either from processing at maximum specified volume or from these overloads. Failures arising from specified load must be dealt with; catastrophic failures caused by overload may also give reason for one to believe that there are errors in the design or specifications.

Most software products are designed to run on a variety of hardware *configurations*. The software should actually be tested on many different hardware setups, although the full range of memory, processor, operating system, and peripheral possibilities may be too large for complete testing. As an example, an Ada compiler is validated for individual hardware configurations, not generically. During configuration testing we must include a special evaluation of concurrent software to investigate possible resource contention, race conditions, deadlocks, and faulty interrupt handling or synchronization.

Finally, software *reliability* should be measured during all other tests of the integrated product. If minimum and average up-time behavior of the product were specified, then these should be met. The time and effort needed to recover from failures should also be recorded and compared with specifications (Figure 8-12).

# System Testing Goals
## Is the product........?
### Correct
### Efficient
### Stable
### Versatile
### Dependable

FIGURE 8-12  SOFTWARE QUALITIES DETERMINED BY SYSTEM TESTING

# Targets for
# Pragmatic
# Testing

## Function versus structure
## Old versus new
## Usual versus exotic

**F I G U R E 8-13**   PRAGMATICALLY, WHICH FUNCTIONS SHOULD BE TESTED?

Toward the end of system testing, there is a period during which the product should be tested not against the specifications but rather in the light of the customer's original goals and expectations. Obviously, the specifications *should* represent the customer's wants and needs; but now that we have a running system, we can try to see if the requirements and specifications really *do* coincide. This pragmatic testing is done with the complete product, as it will be delivered, and should be carried out from the point of view of the user.

Petschenik gives some guidelines for choosing test cases during system testing in [PET85]. The first is that "testing the system's capabilities is more important than testing its components." This implies that failures that are catastrophic should be looked for, whereas failures that are merely annoying need not worry us. The idea is that a user can deal with a badly formatted report, but probably cannot deal with a complete inability to obtain the report.

Petschenik's second rule is that testing the usual is more important than testing the exotic. This can be accomplished by subjecting the software to the kind of use that is representative of actual use, as described in the operational profile. The customer may be able to help with this kind of testing. In fact, software engineers may exhibit blind spots that cause them to notice exotic problems, while they ignore problems that customers would spot immediately.

Third, if we are testing after modification of an existing product, we should test old capabilities rather than new ones. The rationale here is that the user is not depending on the new functions of the software, and won't be paralyzed if they aren't right. But a failure in the old functionality could do just that–paralyze the customer's entire operation (Figure 8-13).

The rationale for Petschenik's pragmatic testing priorities is that exhaustive testing of functional capabilities is incompatible with the kind of short update cycle imposed on many software products. Just as dependability is more important to the user than total correctness, so also do basic and existing functionality weigh much more heavily than total functionality. Foremost we should avoid disrupting current usage by introducing a new release of the product that won't support current functions. He reports that, in his experience, while about 75% of errors are caught by the end of pragmatic system testing, about 90% of *serious* errors, the kind that disrupt, are eliminated before release.

| Usable | Is the product convenient, clear, and predictable? |
| Secure | Is access to sensitive data restricted to those with authorization? |
| Compatible | Will the product work correctly in conjunction with existing data, software, and procedures? |
| Dependable | Do adequate safeguards against failure and methods for recovery exist in the product? |
| Documented | Are manuals complete, correct, and understandable? |

**FIGURE 8-14**   QUALITIES IMPORTANT TO SOFTWARE OPERATION

During system testing, we should evaluate a number of attributes of the software that are vital to the user (listed in Figure 8-14). They represent the operational correctness of the product and may have been part of the software specifications.

## 8.3.5 Testing Tools

Deutsch points out that automation of testing activities provides a number of benefits: activities can be organized and tracked, measurement can be carried out easily, good methodology can be fostered and, most especially, the raw power needed to execute many test cases becomes available ([DEU82]).

There are a number of very useful tools to have around when it comes time to test your software. Some of these are outlined in Figure 8-15. Testing is probably the most automatable of the phases of software development, and good tools can make a tremendous difference in productivity. The figure has been organized with the most important tools at the top and the least important at the bottom. Many of the testing tools perform dynamic analysis of the code. These include debuggers, profilers, coverage analyzers, assertion checkers, symbolic executors, and test harnesses ([HOU83]).

The *test harness* is the fundamental tool used in testing. It provides stubs to replace all of the missing procedures and functions called by the module under test, as well as a main routine to acquire data and feed it to the module. Of course, the stubs may need to provide data as well. The test harness should be configurable for either interactive or batch use. Batch use would presumably be controlled by scripts written in the interactive command language.

The test harness should either generate test data directly or should interface to a test data generator. Input of domain information should be possible, in which case specific data points in the vicinity of domain boundaries would be selected by the tool ([OST88]). It is also useful to provide a technique for constraining certain combinations of data to occur or from occurring.

Another way of generating data is by capturing keystrokes. Correct output can be captured in a similar manner, and the context in which certain behavior has been demonstrated may need to be saved to reproduce errors ([CHA82]). The test harness should furnish extensive and detailed reporting, and may even be able to assist in the

Interactive debugger to analyze dynamic behavior.

Test harness to run a single module in isolation.

Test database manager with statistical reporting.

Test data generator to provide input data to module.

Static analyzer to examine code for simple mistakes.

Test coverage analyzer to help track testing progress.

Comparator to analyze and to certify module output.

Symbolic executor to define test cases and to clarify actual software function.

Profiler to determine resource usage for optimization.

Simulator to take the place of missing devices or environment.

Assertion checker to output failure of verification assertions.

Execution history database manager for backtracking analysis.

**FIGURE 8-15**   USEFUL TESTING TOOLS

management of testing by flagging units containing detected errors and prohibiting further compilation or execution until the flag has been manually reset.

One way to improve the quality (and quantity) of testing is to make the process as pleasant as possible for the tester. This means that commands to the test harness should be as concise, powerful, and natural as possible. This is a circumstance where the user is an expert so that power and functionality are more important than friendliness. Expected result values for the test should be stored directly in the scripts to allow them to be easily modified ([DON88]). If the test harness has enough intelligence to ignore inessential differences between expected and actual results, so much the better ([CHA82]).

Testing a large program can involve incredible amounts of data to organize. A *test database manager* will provide a method for correlating test data with results, keeping track of changes, and reporting progress of the testing phase. The progress reports will involve coverage of individual modules achieved, error discovery rates, adherence to schedule, and so on.

A *test data generator* allows data to be created according to specification, usually by a pseudo-random number generator working in conjunction with a probability distribution. Specifications for test data usually come from consideration of test case definitions, although we may decide to depend blindly on luck and be satisfied with simply generating a lot of test data. A generator is particularly handy when system testing may require large volumes of data in order to test the software under operational loads.

The purpose of a *static analyzer* is to provide mechanical checking of source code. It can detect type mismatches, uninitialized variables, and unused values, as well as indicate inconsistency in the declaration and use of parameter lists and nonconformity to design or coding standards. The static analyzer may also provide various aids to debugging, like data flow maps, a cross-reference chart, a software structure chart, a control flow graph, a data flow graph and a call graph ([HOU83]).

Since the amount of coverage obtained is a principal method for deciding when to quit testing, it is handy to have the code instrumented to record different kinds of coverage in permanent files. This instrumentation, as well as the reporting of coverage, can be obtained from a *coverage analyzer*.

If there are considerable test data, simply comparing expected with actual results can be a serious task. A *comparator* can help with this by automating, or at least assisting, the comparison. Assistance can be obtained through techniques like split-screen presentation, whereas automation requires that there be an oracle, a certified method of calculating correct results. However, this is frequently not available.

*Symbolic execution* involves the use of a special kind of interpreter, that stores symbolic rather than numeric values for variables ([HOW77]). This means that execution of the code segment

```
get (a);
get (b);
a := 2*a-b;
```

would leave "$2*a_0-b_0$" as the value of a, where $a_0$ and $b_0$ represent the input values of a and b. Since there are no real conditions that control branch points, Boolean conditions in the code cannot be evaluated. This means that the symbolic executor is in fact following all possible branches in parallel and is generating a tree of possible execution paths as shown in figure 8-16. The interpreter will substitute appropriate expressions during any assignment statement and will attempt to carry out algebraic simplification of expressions as they are generated. Consequently, each possible path through the code will be labeled with the test domain conditions for that branch. This, in turn, allows us to choose test data to exercise a given path rather easily. In fact, the process of finding domain points or boundary points is easily automated. Figure 8-17 shows the domains for the three paths in Figure 8-16.

Elimination of infeasible paths can occur when the domain predicate defined by symbolic execution is self-contradictory. Symbolic execution can also aid us by allowing comparison of the actual results of following a path with those that were

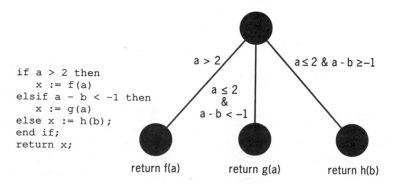

**FIGURE 8-16**  SYMBOLIC EXECUTION TREE

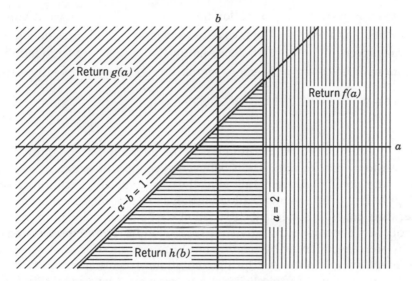

**FIGURE 8-17**   DOMAINS FOR THE CODE IN FIGURE 8-16

specified. On the other hand, symbolic execution loses effectiveness when the code contains pointer references or array references controlled by symbolic values ([HOW87]).

A *profiler* instruments code to determine how much CPU time is being spent in a given code segment. As a side benefit, it may give an execution trace of the software. Although this is not useful in determining that the functionality of the code is correct with respect to specifications, it is useful to measure conformity to performance specs. Thus, if we find that a module is too slow, or if during integration testing we find that one module is consuming too much of the total CPU time, we are able to modify the code to bring it into conformity. A profile may also reveal abnormally low or high use of certain modules, which can be symptomatic of software faults.

When executing a module in isolation, it may be very difficult to provide some of the conditions or input that would be expected in the environment. One example would be signals from a device that is not present in the system. To obtain a realistic testing atmosphere, it may be necessary to *simulate* the environment. Such a tool for simulation allows generation of interrupts and other real-time effects where needed.

An *assertion checker* would simply validate the code by making use of assertions in the code about relationships between data. These may be left over from the formal verification of the code, or may be inserted for testing purposes. The code is run under the control of the checker, and if at any time an assertion is not true, the event is output and logged ([STU77]). This tool allows us to isolate errors quickly, as well as to check on the reliability of semiformal verifications.

Probably the most familiar of the debugging tools is the *interactive debugger*. Although it can vary considerably in its capabilities, desirable features are shown in Figure 8-18. Not only are debuggers familiar, but they are extremely useful. The software engineer should become an expert in their use.

| Step-by-step control | Execution trace | Snashot dump |
| Statement breakpoint | Data/code examination | Session logging |
| Data breakpoint | Data/code editing | Macrodefinition |
| Conditional breakpoint | Memory search | Friendly commands |

**FIGURE 8-18**   DESIRABLE DEBUGGER FEATURES

Step-by-step control is the foundation of interactive debugging. It causes the program to pause for interaction between execution of program statements. Two useful extensions of this are: (1) allowing the user to specify execution of some number of steps before pausing and (2) allowing steps to be defined by machine instructions rather than program statements. Execution trace allows the user to trace the flow of control. It can be provided by indicating source code line numbers or statements during step-by-step execution, or by echoing line numbers, module names, block names, or other identifying information during continuous execution. When flow is nondeterministic (as with an Ada select statement), there must be a capability for forcing the trace onto a chosen flow. Of course, nondeterminism makes it very difficult to repeat errors and thus to locate them.

Breakpoints are a particularly useful capability, since they allow us to adjust the resolution of step-by-step control to meet the needs of our particular debugging problem. We can, for instance, specify a statement breakpoint for a particular statement of which we are suspicious or that represents the end of a loop cycle. We can then instruct the debugger to execute the program continuously, which it will do until it reaches the breakpointed statement. Data breakpoints establish stopping conditions when the value of a particular variable is altered. Conditional breakpoints permit breakpoints to be conditioned on assertions. For instance, suppose you have an array index that is going out of bounds. The VAX debugger would allow a command of the form:

```
set watch indx when (indx .lt. lower_bound .or. indx .gt. upper_bound)
```

Continuous execution would follow, with all changes to the variable indx being traced. Execution would stop when indx strayed from its bounds, with information about the old and new values of indx as well as the next source code instruction to be executed and its line number. Such a capability parallels the activity of an automated assertion checker.

One of the fundamental capabilities of any debugger is to examine the values in memory. These should include both data values and code. Likewise, we ought to be able to modify both data and code during the debugger session. An additional useful feature is searching through a block of memory for a particular pattern of data. Once we find a segment of memory of special interest to us , or a set of variable values, we may want to dump these to a file for later off-line examination. In fact, it is more useful still if we can create a permanent log of all the commands given to the debugger and its responses. In this instance, a standard script might be generated to dump the selected information.

Such an action of dumping selected variable values to a log can be streamlined if we are able to define macro commands in the debugger command language. These can also be attached to breakpoint definitions so that the macro command will be executed whenever the breakpoint is triggered. In general, we should look for all of the user-friendly features in debugger command languages that we have grown accustomed to in other command language interfaces.

The foregoing discussion of debuggers has ignored one question: How does a program, being executed as a sequence of machine language instructions, allow the user to work with it in its source language form? We want to refer to variable indx, not memory location B67F2; we trace line numbers, not code storage addresses; and we need to see character data as characters, not ASCII hex codes.

One solution to this problem is to build the debugger as an interpreter of the high-level language. This greatly simplifies the tasks of tracing, examining and modifying data (and especially code) and step-by-step control. On the other hand, execution performance may be seriously degraded. Even more serious is the possible masking of errors created by the particular semantics of compiler translation of the source code into machine code. That is, we are testing another program, that although closely related to the compiled version we want to obtain may, in fact, differ in just those subtle areas that are already hard for us to find.

Another solution is to have the compiler save sufficient information to be able to determine the correlation between machine and source versions of the program and then execute the machine version. This can be particularly tricky when the compiler optimizes the code by moving statements or using registers. Of course, we might be able to compile in nonoptimizing mode for debugging, but this too might mask errors. There are no easy answers to these problems.

Recently, a number of visual debuggers have come onto the market. They use different windows for displaying data values, debugger input–output, program

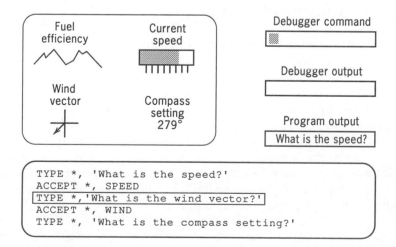

**FIGURE 8-19** A VISUAL DEBUGGER OUTPUT INTERFACE

input–output, source code, and debugger environment setup. Figure 8-19 (repeated from Chapter 5) gives an example of such a visual debugger's output interface. Users generally tend to be more productive when they are using this kind of system, since the windows organize and present information in a more comprehensible form.

A related capability is provided by a *program animator*. This tool provides a graphic trace of the operation of the software, in terms of both the flow of control as well as the modification of selected values. The animator displays information in a visual rather than textual fashion and depends on debugging hooks or on execution monitoring by a separate process(or) ([LON85], [ISO87]). Program animation is also useful for performance evaluation, documentation, demonstration, and understanding.

There has also been significant recent research in automating the debugging process by introducing expert-system technology into debuggers ([SEV87]). We can all imagine the value of a "debugging assistant" that would analyze our code to look for weaknesses, design test data and study the execution history for them, trace control flow in the same cases, localize the error, and then hand control over to us with the error highlighted and a suggested correction provided. Such capabilities are as yet available only for very limited application, but perhaps in the future we will all have our automated assistant.

The second major debugging tool is an *execution history database manager*. This package provides techniques for instrumenting the code to provide incremental dumps of control information and data modification as execution progresses. It then allows the user to navigate the execution history by tracing values forward or backward at will and correlating changing data values with the program statements that were executed. The advantage of an execution history tool is that it provides backtracking capabilities; the disadvantage is that the user canot interact with and modify the execution of the software. Since both interaction and backtracking are important, it would be wise to have both tools available to you.

## 8.4 FOSTERING QUALITY DURING TESTING

Testing is the final quality-instilling activity of software development and perhaps the most important. Although testing does not directly produce the attribute of quality, it makes sure the product is reworked until quality is present. The final verification and validation of the product occur during testing. Metrics can be used to determine the quality of the testing process, to decide when enough testing has been done, to evaluate the adequacy of test cases, and to provide management data for future projects.

Not only do we verify the software, but we should also verify the testing. This is because the pressures of approaching delivery deadlines may cause us to skip some important activities, or even to introduce errors while attempting to eliminate them. The management challenges during testing amount to the difficulty of keeping everything on track when so much is happening.

### 8.4.1 Testing Metrics

There are four major uses for testing metrics. The first is to determine the effectiveness of the process, and in particular to decide when we bring the stage to a halt. Of course, the effectiveness of testing depends entirely on the level of testedness we think is necessary ([MIL84]), and this is a management decision. The second is to measure the probable reliability of the product during its operational phase. This will help in planning for maintenance activities. The third use of metrics is to evaluate the adequacy of test sets; we will be able to choose the kinds of errors that most concern us, and then tell if our test data are likely (or even sure) to reveal them. Test case adequacy was discussed in Section 8.2.3. Fourth, we gather information about the incidence and nature of discovered errors in order to pinpoint weaknesses in the development process and to initiate management activities that will enhance future projects. This will be discussed in the next chapter.

There are six common methods of deciding when testing should come to an end:

1  We have achieved a predetermined level of coverage (statement, branch, path, and so on.).
2  We have found a predicted number of errors.
3  The error-discovery rate has dropped off.
4  A fixed proportion of seeded errors has been found.
5  An acceptable level of reliability has been achieved.
6  We have exhausted the time available for testing.

The first method has been described above, and is the most quantitative of all. It allows us to establish the target level of coverage for the module, measure the actual coverage, and finish when that target has been reached.

Experiments have shown that intuitive testing will exercise only about 75% to 90% of the module's statements and about 50% of its branches; but 100% of statement and branch coverage is essential. All loops should be executed at least 0 and 1 times. Full predicate combination coverage may be impossible, but the most questionable or important combinations should be tested. Path coverage will be minimal, and again we must test those paths that are questionable or frequent or vital to test.

Unfortunately, the 50% coverage obtained by the use of intuitive test cases is nowhere near adequate. There are a number of levels to which testing can be taken.

Execute $n$% of module statements at least once.

Cause $n$% of branches to be followed.

Cause $n$% of combinations of predicate truth values within selection and loop conditions to be tested.

Cause $n$% of condition-controlled loops to be executed $0,1,2,\ldots$, and $k$ times.

Cause $n$% of paths through the code to be followed.

Cause $n$% of paths from some value definition to each value use to be followed.

**F I G U R E 8-20**  POSSIBLE TEST COVERAGE CRITERIA

Some of them are necessary, others advisable, still others are unreachable. In a rough hierarchy, they are shown in Figure 8-20.

With these coverage guidelines we can either design test cases to guarantee the coverage or else can use statistics and history to generate data and then monitor coverage until we have reached the appropriate levels. It is likely that errors are more frequent in very complex portions of the code. We can utilize design complexity metrics to indicate which modules are likely to need stringent test coverage criteria.

Howden suggests an alternative technique for measuring the amount of testing needed to disclose software errors that will lead to eventual failures ([HOW87]). Assuming the competent programmer hypothesis and that test data are distributed according to the execution profile, we can ensure that the probability of missing an error is less than $1/N$ if the number of our tests cases exceeds $\log(N)/(\log(N)-\log(N-1))$. For instance, if we want the probability of an error to be less than 1%, we will need at least 459 tests.

Another coverage metric is to measure what percentage of expression values have been caused to diverge from each of their respective subexpression values at one or more data points ([WEI85]).

The second of the six techniques for determining when testing is complete requires that we have a way to calculate the likely number of errors to be found in the software module. This can be done in a number of ways. For instance, Halstead gives a formula based on $N$, the total number of occurrences of operators and operands in the module, and $n$, the total number of distinct occurrences of operators and operands. Halstead estimates the number of bugs to be

$$B = (N * \log_2(n))/3000$$

This is one of the most disputed of Halstead's metrics, however. Shooman gives a statistical approach, indicating that we might expect about 10 errors per thousand for large programs, and 20 errors per thousand for small programs. Of course, experience

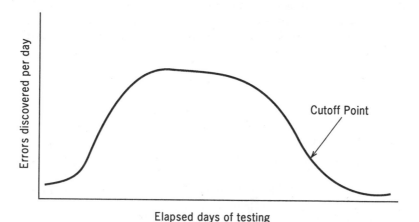

FIGURE 8-21    THE RATE AT WHICH ERRORS ARE FOUND

within a particular software organization might allow us to fine tune such numbers. This is one of the reasons for a project postmortem.

The third approach is based on a supposition that the graph of the rate of error discovery will look like that shown in Figure 8-21. We recognize that we are at the end of testing when we have turned the "elbow" of the graph and reached an area of diminishing returns on our testing investment. This decision is essentially intuitive, although we may decide beforehand to stop, for instance, when n hours of testing have revealed no additional errors.

Mills suggests that the completeness of our testing can be measured by artificially **seeding**, or introducing, errors into the software (thus creating a single, multigene mutant). This should be done by someone other than the person responsible for generating test data so that the test data are not unintentionally designed to catch the seeded errors. The degree to which our test cases reveal the seeded errors is then used to predict the number of real errors that still exist in the software. Mills gives the formula:

$$\text{total errors} = \frac{\text{indigenous errors found} * \text{total errors seeded}}{\text{seeded errors found}}$$

for an estimate on the total number of errors in the module. Of course, we probably should continue testing until all the seeded errors have been found by our tests.

Another metric of significance obtained during testing is reliability. Shooman defines reliability as the probability of failure-free performance for a specified period of time ([SHO83]). Another frequently used indication of reliability is the mean time to failure, (MTTF). This is the average time that elapses between starting software (initially or after correction of a previous failure) and the occurrence of another failure.

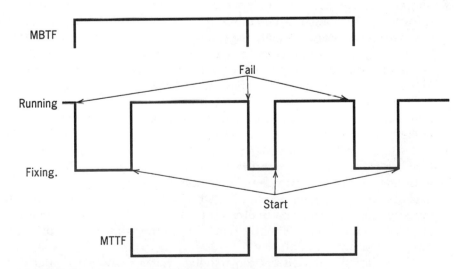

**FIGURE 8-22**   MEAN TIME TO (AND BETWEEN) FAILURE

Another common metric, mean time between failures (MTBF), adds the time required to correct or reset to the MTTF (Figure 8-22). During the operational period, software is usually restarted immediately and runs for long periods compared with down time, hence MTTF and MTBF are essentially the same.

Mean time to failure can be estimated by mean times to failure during testing if the test data are generated according to the execution profile ([MUS89]). We can terminate testing when a predetermined level of reliability is reached; we must be careful to use truly representative input data. Standard test cases intentionally stress the software and artificially decrease the MTTF. In the same way, we should use CPU time for measurement, since some software may get as much use (and, hence, failure) during a week of testing as it would during a year of operation. But the rate of failure would be consistent in both instances when it is measured in CPU time.

Reliability can be estimated by much more sophisticated techniques than an average of running time between failures during testing. Some of these reliability models can be found in [MUS87], [SHO83], and [MIL87]. They mainly require a familiarity with probability theory and statistics, which goes beyond the scope of this text. However, some of the questions involve what kind of time (execution or calendar) is to be used in calculations; how we calculate remaining errors on the basis of errors found to date; and how closely test data mirror the execution profile ([MIL87]).

The last method, running out of time, is probably used more than any other, but it is totally inadequate and it perpetuates the view that testing is an add-on feature—nice but not really vital in software development. At the same time, it ignores the software engineer's professional responsibility to verify and to validate the quality of his product.

### 8.4.2 Verification and Validation

The testing stage consists largely of the final verification and validation activities of the software project. But an old dictum states that somebody must "watch the watchers"; we need to verify and validate the testing process itself. One aspect of this is simply controlling the process to make sure that every test planned earlier was indeed executed and documented. Another is the application of testing metrics, as described in the previous section, to determine the adequacy of the testing effort.

Evaluating the effectiveness of the test process and test case data is difficult. Hamlet remarks that it is usually impossible to determine what part of testing success is due to methodology, to tester skill, and to luck. On the other hand, it is also hard to show that success in testing a program against artificial test data equates to success in running the same program in a real world environment ([HAM88]).

Besides recording coverage and other metrics, we should keep track of the ranges of data obtained during test execution ([DEU82]). These will provide us with a basis for investigating errors that may still crop up during the maintenance phase, since we may be able to determine whether the data causing the problem have driven the software into a tested state or not.

The redesign and modification activities that occur when we decide to remove a documented error from the product must also be carefully verified. Ironically, the code produced to correct errors is much more likely, on a line-by-line basis, to introduce errors than is the original code. Wolverton estimates that modified code has only a 50-50 chance of being correct. Therefore, all of the verification procedures that apply to specification, design, and coding need to be applied to changes, along with regression through all the tests required of the software. Where appropriate, design of additional tests covering the new portions of the product should be required.

### 8.4.3 Management

The biggest management challenge of the testing stage is ensuring that all standards and planned activities are indeed implemented. Since this is the last stage before delivery, there is a tendency to want to make up for any schedule slippages by taking shortcuts. But sloppy testing and code modification carry their own penalty ([EVA83]) and may actually lengthen, rather than shorten, the testing stage. Even worse, they may create time bombs that will produce great damage to the organization during maintenance.

Usually these bombs take the form of hasty design decisions that turn out to be inflexible and thus not maintainable. These may be poorly thought-out choices, or they may be kludges that were consciously chosen to meet a deadline, but that later become so embedded in the product that they are an albatross around its neck. In other instances, time bombs are simply short-term but suboptimal solutions that were chosen to meet the immediate need of getting the software out the door; the developer is fully aware that additional, compounded effort will be required later to fix this mess.

As part of the product visibility component of management, it is necessary to keep tabs on the status of testing. Beizer notes that research indicates three periods of test-case completion. During the first, errors that are found tend to be obstructive, so that testing proceeds slowly as we fix each error in order to continue with the plan. During the second period, errors do not obstruct the continuation of testing, and error removal can proceed in parallel with testing. These errors are also less fundamental and easier to correct and so error discovery speeds up. During the third stage, we have to look harder for more obscure errors, and discovery again slows down ([BEI84]).

It appears that the point during the testing schedule at which we arrive at stages two and three determines whether the product can be delivered on schedule and whether it will be an ultimate success. Figure 8-23, based on data from 23 separate projects ([BEI84]), shows that in a successful project the first period occupies about 15% of the schedule and the second period about 57%. Problem or failed projects are also pictured—they lag behind, in that the intensive first period lasts longer.

Collofello suggests in [COL88] that the degree of testing of a product during integration testing can be measured by coverages. As in statement coverage, we may determine whether every module has been invoked at least once. Corresponding to branch coverage, every module should have been invoked by all possible callers. Finally, similar to path coverage, we might want all possible invocation sequences to be executed.

Periodic reliability measures can also be used to determine the progress of testing. We should find that periods between failures are becoming longer and longer.

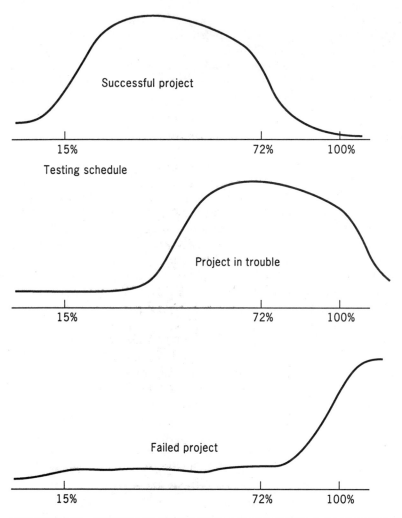

**FIGURE 8-23** TEST COMPLETION SCHEDULES FOR GOOD AND BAD PROJECTS

Reliability can also be used to estimate the amount of effort that will be needed to maintain the product, the staffing that will be required and the price that ought to be charged. Finally, reliability can figure into a calculation of the potential liability which the organization may incur by releasing the product.

## 8.5 A TESTING EXAMPLE

As an example of unit testing, consider the following Ada code, repeated from Section 7.5.1. We will develop unit test data first, guided by the list found in Figure 8-6.

```
package Frames is

   type Command is private;
-- Refill    : constant Command; -- buffer is exhausted, provide more data
-- Lost_synch: constant Command; -- synch signal has been lost
-- Compose   : constant Command; -- synchronized frame found and returned
-- Reset     : constant Command; -- start looking for synchronization signal
-- Continue  : constant Command; -- assume synch signal will be at frame end

   Procedure Compose_frame(Buffer   :in       Byte_array;    -- data stream
                           Last_byte:in out Index;               -- index of
final byte
                           Frame   :    out Index;             -- start of
found frame
                           Frame_end:   out Index;             -- end of found
frame
                           Code    :in out Command);           -- initiation,
result

private

   type Command is (Refill, Lost_synch, Compose, Reset, Continue);

end Frames;


package body Frames is

   Frame_size         : constant integer    := 36;
   Synch_signal_length: constant integer    := 4;
   Number_of_states   : constant integer    := Synch_signal_length+1;
   Finish             : constant integer    := Number_of_states;

   subtype      Symbols is integer range 1..Synch_signal_length+1;
   subtype      States  is integer range 1..Number_of_states;
   type Signal  is array(1..Synch_signal_length) of Byte;

   State:States; -- finite automaton state
                 --   1      - have seen no usable synch signal bytes
                 --   2      - saw synch signal byte 1
                 --   3      - saw synch signal bytes 1,2
                 --   4      - saw synch signal bytes 1,2,3
                 --  ...
                 --  Finish - saw complete synch signal

   Synch_symbols: constant Signal               -- the synch signal
                := (16#4B#,16#96#,16#97#,16#AF#); -- in hexadecimal bytes

   Table: constant array(States,Symbols) of Byte := ((2,1,1,1,1), -- transition
                                                      (2,3,1,1,1), -- table for
                                                      (2,1,4,1,1), -- finite
                                                      (2,1,1,Finish,1),
                                                      (Symbols => Finish));
                                                                   -- automaton
```

```
-- MODULE NAME: Compose_frame
-- FUNCTION: This module locates a synchronization signal in the data stream
--   provided in Buffer.  Once located, the module provides whole frames of
--   data until the synchronization signal is lost.
-- INTERFACE PARAMETERS AND MODES:
--   Buffer      in          contains a segment of the data stream
--   Last_byte   in out      on input the number of data stream bytes in Buffer
--                           on output the last byte processed in Buffer
--   Frame       out         an index showing the byte in Buffer at which the found
--                              frame starts (the first byte of the frame)
--   Frame_end   out         an index showing the byte in Buffer at which the found
--                              frame stops (the last byte of the frame)
--   Code        in out      passes status information with the following meaning:
--               in          Reset  - start looking for the first synch byte
--               in          Continue - continue in the same state as when
--                              Compose_frame was exited
--               out         Refill - move the bytes from Last_byte+1 to the end of
--                              Buffer up to the beginning and fill the rest
--                              of the buffer with data stream bytes
--               out         Lost_synch - the synchronization signal was not found
--                              where expected, assuming a frame started
--                              at Frame
--               out         Compose - the bytes from Frame to Frame_end are a
--                              synchronized frame
-- PRE-ASSERTION: Last_byte >= Frame_size + Synch_signal_length and Last_byte =
--                length (buffer) - 1; that is, the buffer holds enough bytes
--                to make up at least one frame plus synchronization signal and
--                Last_byte is the index of the last byte in the buffer.
-- POST-ASSERTION: when Code is Refill, further processing requires more bytes
--                 when Code is Lost_synch, the data stream synchronization was
--                    lost somewhere after the byte indicated by Last_byte and
--                    the byte at Last_byte + Frame_size + Synch_signal_length
--                 when Code is Compose, the block of bytes between Frame and
--                    Frame + Frame_end are surrounded by two valid
--                    synchronization signals
-- GLOBALS AND SIDE EFFECTS: none
-- EXCEPTIONS: unknown input code
-- HARDWARE AND OPERATING SYSTEM REQUIREMENTS: standard Ada compiler
-- CREATION AND MODIFICATION HISTORY: author Sam Washington, 2/19/88
--                                    auditor Jeanie Krowalski, 2/23/88
--                                    modifications:
-- ALGORITHM: the first part of the procedure acts as a finite automaton
--            looking for the synch signal.  In continuation mode, if the
--            finite automaton state indicates that a synch signal has been
--            found, the first part of the procedure is bypassed.  The second
--            part skips ahead to the predicted location of the next synch
--            signal and outputs a frame if the signal is there.
-- MAJOR DATA STRUCTURES: Table is a transition table for the finite automaton
--                        looking for the synch signal.  Synch_symbols is the
--                        synch symbol string.
-- CALLED BY: Get_Frame
-- CALLS: Error_report
```

```
Procedure Compose_frame(Buffer    :in      Byte_array;
                        Last_byte:in out Index;
                        Frame     :    out Index;
                        Frame_end:    out Index;
                        Code      :in out Command) is


    This_byte: Index := 0; -- points to byte in Buffer under consideration
    Symbol:    Symbols;    -- encodes symbol types for finite automaton; codes 1 to
                           -- Synch_signal_length are for the synchronization signal

                           -- bytes, code Synch_signal_length+1 is for any other
byte
    Bad_code, Out_of_data, Synch_lost: Exception;

    begin
            -- are we starting the finite automaton or continuing it?
    if (Code = Reset) then
       State := 1;
    elsif (Code = Continue) then
       State := State;
    else
       raise Bad_code;
    end if;

    while State /= Finish loop
       if This_byte = Last_byte then raise Out_of_data; end if;
       This_byte := This_byte + 1;
            -- use a linear search through the array synch_symbols in order to
            -- translate the byte into an input symbol for the finite automaton
       Symbol := 1;
       while Symbol <= Synch_signal_length and then
             Buffer(This_byte) /= Synch_symbols(Symbol) loop
                Symbol := Symbol + 1;
       end loop;
                -- finite automaton switches to the next state
       State := Table(State,Symbol);
    end loop;

-- synchronization established, exit finite automaton, recognize full frames

    if This_byte + Frame_size + Synch_signal_length > Last_byte then
       raise Out_of_data;
    end if;

    for n in 1..Synch_signal_length loop
       if Buffer(This_byte + Frame_size + n) /= Synch_symbols(n) then
          raise Synch_lost;
       end if;
    end loop;
                        -- synchronization signal found
    Frame := This_byte + 1;
    Frame_end := This_byte + Frame_size;
    Last_byte := This_byte + Frame_size + Synch_signal_length;
    Code := Compose;

    Exception
      when Bad_code =>
      Error_report("Compose_frame", "Bad code request", code);
      when Out_of_data =>
         Code := Refill;
         Last_byte := This_byte;
      when Synch_lost =>
         Code := Lost_synch;
         Last_byte := This_byte;
end Compose_frame;
end Frames;
```

There are no global variables in this code, and only three input parameters. We will avoid testing cases in which Last_byte is different from the index of the last byte in Buffer, since this is contrary to the stated preassertion of the procedure. Thus there are only two test data items, Code and Buffer. In the following, we will let the letters A through F stand for these byte sequences, and use the notation (*nn*X) to mean *nn* repetitions of the sequence X.

| | |
|---|---|
| A | 4B 96 97 AF (the synch signal) |
| B | 4B 96 97 00 |
| C | 4B 96 00 |
| D | 4B 00 |
| E | 00 |
| F | 4B |

The first set of test data is that which "appeals" to the tester:

| Code | Buffer | Reason |
|---|---|---|
| Reset | A(36E)A | Simple, acceptable buffer |
| Reset | A(36E)AE | Acceptable, longer than minimum |
| Reset | A(36E)B | Incorrect trailing synch |
| Reset | B(36E)A | Incorrect leading synch |
| Reset | A(36E)C | Shorter buffer than needed |
| Reset | (50F)A(36E)A | Longer, correct buffer in reset mode |
| Reset | EA(36E)AE | Longer, acceptable, extra bytes at end |
| Reset | (20B)D | No initial synch signal found |
| Reset | EA(36E)B | Longer, no trailing synch signal |
| Continue | (36E)A | Simple, acceptable buffer |
| Continue | (36E)B | Incorrect trailing synch |
| Continue | (35E)A | Buffer shorter than needed |
| Continue | (36E)AE | Acceptable, longer than minimum |

The second criterion is to use all possible data. This cannot be done, given the unbounded size of Buffer. But we could use all possible codes:

| | | |
|---|---|---|
| Refill | A(36E)A | Incorrect code |
| Lost_synch | A(36E)A | Incorrect code |
| Compose | A(36E)A | Incorrect code |

The third criterion, special effects, including raising all exceptions, seems to be covered by the cases already chosen, except for those cases in which we enter in Continue mode with a value of State which is different from Finish. This seems more like a problem in the calling routine, so it won't be tested. Obviously, if such a circumstance occurs, the output of Compose_Frame would be a frame if the appropriate 40 bytes were present at the beginning of Buffer.

The fourth and fifth criteria—statement and branch coverage—are met by the existing cases. Path coverage is impossible, since we are dealing with an unbounded iteration, but could be easily obtained by limiting the number of initial, nonsynch bytes for testing in the Reset mode. Data flow and domain coverage also appear to be present.

The data types of Code and Buffer make it impossible to test for unprocessable data, and the only function performed by the procedure is tested. But there are some special cases, that try to trick to finite state machine.

| Reset | (4F)(36E)A | Almost correct, repeat symbol number 1 |
| Reset | CE(36E)A | Almost correct, two wrong symbols |
| Reset | DEE(36E)A | Almost correct, three wrong symbols |

The adequacy of these data can be tested by using weak mutation with 78 mutants. This number could be significantly reduced by using more derived types, thus restricting many identifiers to be the only one of their type.

## 8.6 SUMMARY

The testing stage is for verifying code against the design and specifications, and for validating the entire system against the customer's requirements. The definition of test case data that will allow this is a significant challenge, but there are many techniques for doing so.

Unit testing involves execution of an individual module in isolation from all the other modules of the product. Most unit tests are structural, that is, they are conducted to exercise specific parts of the code within the module. The extent to which structural testing is exhaustive depends on the criterion being used. In particular, full path coverage is not achievable in any realistic situation. Nonetheless, there are guidelines for choosing appropriate test cases and deciding when testing is sufficiently complete.

Integration testing is a test of the interfaces between modules that have already been tested as units. It is a functional rather than a structural process. Integration patterns should be flexible enough to meet the specific goals of testing. At the end of this phase, we test the system as a whole from a pragmatic user's viewpoint.

Throughout testing, we must remove errors as they are detected. Strategies for debugging include backtracking and cause postulation, and debuggers and execution history tools help automate the process. Since error-correcting changes to software frequently generate further errors, it is necessary to maintain a high degree of quality control during these debugging activities.

Testing is one part of the development process that is successfully automatable, and the software engineer should take advantage of the many software tools available for testing. The most important are the test harness, the test database manager, and the test data generator.

When testing is complete, we are ready to prepare the entire product (software plus documents) for delivery to, and use by, the customer. Although the long development process is over, the operational stage ahead is much longer. There will be a wide variety of activities in this period, some of which recapitulate development and some of which are entirely new.

# BIBLIOGRAPHY

[ADR82]     Adrion, W.R., M.A. Branstad and J.C. Cherniavsky, "Validation, Verification and Testing of Computer Software," *Computing Surveys*, 14(2):159 – 192.

[BAS87]     Basili, V.R., and R.W. Selby, "Comparing the Effectiveness of Software Testing Strategies," *IEEE Transactions on Software Engineering*, 13(12):1278 – 1296.

[BEI84]*    Beizer, B., *Software Testing and Quality Assurance*, Van Nostrand Reinhold, New York.

[CHA82]     Chapman, D., "A Program Testing Assistant," *Communications of the ACM*, 25(9):625 – 634.

[COL88]     Collofello, J.S., *Introduction to Software Verification and Validation*, SEI-CM-13-1.1, Software Engineering Institute, Pittsburgh, PA.

[COM80]     Compton, M.T., "Easing Fault Location in Large Systems," *Communications of the ACM*, 23(8):440 – 443.

[DEM78]     DeMillo, R.A., R.J. Lipton, and F.G. Sayward, "Hints on Test Data Selection: Help for the Practicing Programmer," *Computer*, 11(4):34 – 43.

[DEU82]     Deutsch, M.S., *Software Verification and Validation*, Prentice-Hall, Englewood Cliffs, NJ.

[DON88]     Donnelly, K.F., and K.A. Gluck, "Pastel and Astra: A Case Study in Test Environment Evolution," *Software Engineering Notes*, 13(1):22 – 28.

[EVA83]     Evans, M.W., P.H. Piazza, and J.B. Dolkas, *Principles of Productive Software Management*, Wiley-Interscience, New York.

[FRA88]     Frankl, P.G., and E.J. Weyuker, "An Applicable Family of Data Flow Testing Criteria," *IEEE Transactions on Software Engineering*, 14(10):1483 – 1498.

[GEL88]*    Gelperin, D., and B. Hetzel, "The Growth of Software Testing," *Communications of the ACM*, 31(6):687 – 695.

[HAM88]*   Hamlet, R, "Special Section on Software Testing," *Communications of the ACM*, 31(6):662 – 667.

[HOU83]*   Houghton, R.C., "Software Development Tools: A Profile," *Computer*, 16(5):63 – 70.

[HOW77]    Howden, W.E., "Symbolic Testing and the Dissect Symbolic Evaluation System," *IEEE Transactions on Software Engineering*, 3(4):266 – 278.

[HOW82]*   Howden, W.E., "Weak Mutation Testing and Completeness of Test Sets," *IEEE Transactions on Software Engineering*, 8(4):371 – 379.

[HOW85]*   Howden, W.E., "The Theory and Practice of Functional Testing," *IEEE Software* 2(5):6 – 17.

[HOW87]*   Howden, W.E., *Functional Program Testing and Analysis*, McGraw-Hill, New York.

[ISO87]     Isoda, S., T. Shinomura, and Y. Ono, "VIPS: A Visual Debugger," *IEEE Software*, 4(3):8 – 19.

[LON85]     London, R.L., and R.A. Duisberg, "Animating Programs Using Smalltalk," *Computer*, 18(8):61 – 71.

[MIL81]     Miller, E.M., "Introduction to Software Testing Technology," in *Software Testing and Validation Techniques* by E.M. Miller and W.E. Howden, eds., 2nd ed., IEEE, New York.

[MIL84]     Miller, E.F., "Software Testing Technology: An Overview" in *Handbook of Software Engineering*, C.R. Vick and C.V. Ramamoorthy, eds., Van Nostrand Reinhold, New York.

[MIL87]*    Mills, H.D., M. Dyers and R Linger, "Cleanroom Software Engineering," *IEEE Software*, 4(5):19 – 25.

[MUS87]*    Musa, J.D., A. Iannino, and K. Okumoto, *Software Reliability*, McGraw-Hill, New York.

[MUS89]*    Musa, J.D., and A.F. Ackerman, "Quantifying Software Validation: When to Stop Testing?" *IEEE Software*, 6(3):19 – 27.

[MYE79]*    Myers, G.J., *The Art of Software Testing*, Wiley-Interscience, New York.

[OST88]*    Ostrand, T.J., and M.J. Balcer, "The Category-Partition Method for Specifying and Generating Functional Tests," *Communications of the ACM*, 31(6):676 – 686.

[PET85]*    Petschenik, N.H., "Practical Priorities in System Testing," *IEEE Software*, 2(5):18 – 23.

[PRA87]    Prather, R.F., and J.P. Myers, "The Path Prefix Software Testing Strategy," *IEEE Transactions on Software Engineering*, 13(7):761 – 766.

[SEV87]    Seviora, R.E., "Knowledge-Based Program Debugging Systems," *IEEE Software*, 4(3):20 – 32.

[SHO83]*    Shooman, M.L., *Software Engineering*, McGraw-Hill, New York.

[STU77]    Stucki, L.G., "New Directions in Automated Tools for Improving Software Quality," in *Current Trends in Programming Methodology*, R.T. Yeh, ed., vol. 2, Prentice-Hall, Englewood Cliffs, NJ.

[TAI80]*    Tai, K., "Program Testing Complexity and Test Criteria," *IEEE Transactions on Software Engineering*, 6(6):531 – 538.

[WEI85]*    Weiser, M.D., J.D. Gannon, and P.R. McMullin, "Comparison of Structural Test Coverage Metrics", *IEEE Software*, 2(2):80 – 85.

[WEY80]*    Weyuker, E.J., and T.J. Ostrand, "Theories of Program Testing and the Application of Revealing Subdomains," *IEEE Transactions on Software Engineering*, 6(3):236 – 246.

[WEY88]*    Weyuker, E.J., "The Evaluation of Program-Based Software Test Data Adequacy," *Communications of the ACM*, 31(6):668 – 675.

## PROBLEMS

**1**   Describe structural, functional and pragmatic testing of an automobile. Can you think of another kind of test applied to an automobile and describe a corresponding software test?

**2**   Give the symbolic execution tree for this insertion sort of five items.

```
list[0].key := -maxint;
for j := 1 to 5 do
   begin
      k := j-1;
      while unsorted[j].key < list[k].key do
        begin
        list[k+1] := list[k];
         k := k-1;
      end;
   list[k+1] := unsorted[j];
   end;
```

**3** Perform static analysis for the code of Problem 2.

**4** Hand instrument the insertion sort of Problem 2 to give coverage statistics.

**5** Design a stress test for the insertion sort of Problem 2.

**6** Design an adequate set of test cases for Problem 2. What is your criterion for adequacy?

**7** How many paths are there in the code for Problem 2?

**8** Petschenik suggests that system testing should be carried out by a different team than the one that does integration testing. What are some good reasons for this?

**9** Report on the capabilities of the debugger available to you for your class work.

**10** Assess the validity of Howden's claim ([HOW87]) that the composition techniques of functional testing are sufficient to represent real software.

**11** How can design attributes facilitate debugging?

**12** Is there any relationship between cause postulation and formal verification? Explain your answer.

**13** Describe the basic elements for defining test domains and test cases in an interactive test harness command language.

**14** Insert two sets of two errors in the code for Problem 2. Consider the first set to be indigenous and the second to be seeded. Run the code on randomly generated sequences of data. How well does the disclosure of failures due to seeded errors correlate to the disclosure of failures due to indigenous errors?

**15** Is it reasonable for the project database to store a new version of a program unit every time that a bug is discovered and corrected? If not, then how do we decide the frequency for recording new versions?

**16** Test the implementation you derived in Problem 14 of Chapter 7, including stress and performance tests. Can you draw any conclusions from the pattern of occurrence of errors in the code?

**17** Submit installation and training plans for the code tested in Problem 16.

**18** Test the Ada code in Section 8.5 using the test data there.

**19** Evaluate the adequacy of the test data in Section 8.5 by code mutation.

**20** Test the FORTRAN code of Section 7.5.2 using the data in Section 8.5.

# CHAPTER 9

# THE OPERATIONAL STAGE

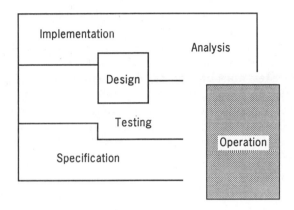

We now reach the point when the software product, so long in development, will really be used. Although it may seem like the end of a long road, the product, in fact, is just getting off to a start. Unless we have made a serious error in analysis, our software will most likely be used for 5 to 10 years before it is retired. Indeed, if we have done a good job, some of the product's components should live on far beyond the 10 year mark.

However, this does not mean that we can now ignore the product. On the contrary, we will be modifying the software constantly, as long as it is worth maintaining. Recall that the three kinds of maintenance are the following: corrective, in which we remove errors; adaptive, by which we port the product to a new environment; and perfective, which adds additional performance. Software that is no longer growing is on its way to being discontinued. The maintenance task demands the *largest* effort of the life cycle.

The difference between perfective maintenance and an entirely new development effort is a subtle one. After all, upgrading the product is logically indistinguishable from creating a new product with a high degree of component reuse, with the components coming from the previous version. Perhaps talking about program "evolution" rather than maintenance, or agreeing that we are using the program growth or incremental model of development, could clarify the distinction ([BEN87]). In fact, it should be recognized that changes to work products occur during all stages of the life cycle, not just during the operational stage.

Distinguishing enhancement from further development is especially important when maintenance work is covered by an existing contract, whereas new development would require the negotiation of a new contract (and fee). If such changes are viewed as perfective maintenance, then we must be sure to limit them so that our current maintenance budget can support the effort ([GLA81]).

## 9.1 THE OPERATIONAL PROCESSES AND PRODUCTS

There are five distinct processes that occur during operation.

1 Software delivery to the customer. The responsibility for this activity falls on the analyst, in the instance of contract software, or on the sales department for packaged software. An acceptance test must be performed in the first case by the customer or in the second by the sales staff or the management of the software organization. The analyst may participate in the physical installation of the product and the training of customer personnel in the use of the software. The major documents produced by this process are the minutes of the acceptance test, together with a log of the installation process (Figure 9-1).

2 A short-lived review of the project's history and the gathering of information. This is conducted under the direction of the project management and the quality assurance group. A structured study of the technical and managerial procedures employed and an evaluation of their effectiveness provides insight into the project. Relevant data on the product, a narrative of the project, and analyses of its success are stored as part of the project database. Successful procedures and management techniques are recorded by the quality assurance personnel for future use. Potentially reusable components developed during the project are stored in the reuse libraries.

3 Actual use of the software by the customer.

4 In conjunction with the third process, within the software organization the customer support department is responsible for answering questions, helping to handle crises, providing additional documentation and training, fielding requests for modifications, and delivering updated versions of the software to the customers. The major products of this process are the records of correspondence and surveys of customer wants, needs, complaints, and suggestions.

5 Maintenance. This is the responsibility of the organization's maintenance staff and includes an analysis of customer complaints, problem reports, surveys, and suggestions to determine what modifications to the product might be in the best interests of the software organization. Modifications that qualify are handled either as new development or as maintenance. If they are maintenance, then assignments must be made for carrying them out. The major products are the updated versions of the software and accompanying documentation and the maintenance plan that governs the entire process.

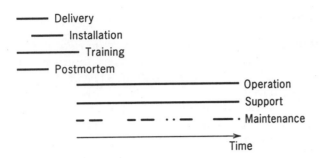

**FIGURE 9-1**  OPERATIONAL ACTIVITIES

### 9.1.1 Purpose of the Operational Stage

The major purpose of the operational stage of the software life cycle is also the overall purpose of the software. It was built to be used, and this is the period of its use. The utilization of our product should be a source of both satisfaction and pride to us, and is one of the major, although frequently unmentioned, compensations for all of the effort that software development requires.

A more mundane purpose of the early operational period is the simple satisfaction of our contractual obligations to the customer and the receipt of payment. The mechanism for this is the acceptance test, which should embody all of the original requirements specified by the user. If we pass the acceptance test, we have redeemed our pledge and deserve to be paid.

The major purpose of the software engineer's operational activities is to prolong the useful lifetime of the product. This is done by additional development and maintenance activities, as well as by supplying exceptional service in the form of customer support. We have made a substantial investment in the product, and only by promoting its widespread and extended use can we collect additional dividends beyond the selling price. On the customer's side, a long and productive lifetime means that his investment was also well repaid; our own reputation and market strength are thereby enhanced.

It is vital that we get off to a good start at the beginning of the operational period. This puts a special emphasis on garnering customer goodwill during installation and training activities. It is unfortunate that software often encounters substantial resistance on the part of users and operators, who may be familiar and comfortable with existing procedures or tools. They are ready to accept any hint of difficulty, incapacity, or undependability as proof that the product won't work and should be abandoned. We, in turn, must *sell* the software to them and convince them that its value justifies their effort in learning to use it.

Finally, the operational period is a time in which we can gather information about the effectiveness of our analysis of user needs and our design of a product to meet these needs. Careful attention to user reactions, observation of problems and location of the faults in the development process that gave rise to them, and analysis of the strengths of successful competitors will teach us how to do a better job next time.

### 9.1.2 Activities During the Operational Stage

For a brief period of time, we will be involved in the *delivery* of the product. During delivery, the software moves from the development environment to the application environment. The first step is passing the acceptance test. This happens when the customer has been satisfied that the software meets the original description found in the Project Plan and the Software Requirements Specification.

Next, the software will be transported to the user environment, where it will be installed on the user's equipment. For contract software, this happens only once, but it is an ongoing process for a packaged product. In addition, documentation needs to be provided, databases have to be converted, and backup procedures must be initiated. Operations will then be shifted from the previous system to the new one, which is based on the new software product.

As the final act of development, we need to conduct an *evaluation* of the software project. During this **post mortem**, or **debriefing** examination, we will be interested in what went right (or wrong) with the development process. The lessons learned from the previous stages of the life cycle need to be recorded in such a way that they will be available in the future. Here is our opportunity to learn, not just earn, from the development process.

At this point, we cannot rest on our laurels. If the lifetime of the product is to be extended as far as it is reasonable for us to expect, we have to support our customers in any problems that they may have with it, as well as respond to their evolving needs. One of the software organization's continuing responsibilities is to *support* users in the operation of the software. In parallel with acceptance, installation, and conversion, customer personnel are trained in the use of the new product. Preparations for this training period may have begun previously, however, since materials and techniques may require extensive preparation.

In all likelihood, users will discover errors or shortcomings in the product, which will require that it be modified. Changes may also be necessary in response to alteration of the environment in which the software is used, or to the users' evolving need for additional features. All of these changes come under the title of *maintenance*. To keep the proliferating versions of the product (new, old, modified, specialized, and the like) organized, we will need to exercise some kind of *configuration management*.

Even with the best design, management, and maintenance, we eventually come to the point where software faces *retirement*. This decision is reached pragmatically by weighing the potential benefits to the software organization of further work against its cost. Of course, that does not mean that the product is dead yet, but merely that it has stopped growing. Loyal users (or those who have provided themselves with no alternate avenues for upgrade) will continue to use it for a year or two. As they find other systems that satisfy their needs better, however, they will abandon the product as we have done. In the end, *demise* is the inevitable result.

### 9.1.3 Operational Documents and Deliverables

The Acceptance Test Plan, the Installation Plan and the Training Plan, together with training materials, comprise the bulk of the operational documents for the initial part

Title and description of product
Product profile
   Functions
   Application area
   Size
   Complexity
   Development model
   Design paradigm
   Tools used
   Success level
Management and team organization
Personnel
Project narrative
Product and process measurements
Problems and analysis
Recommendations
Location of reusable components (stored elsewhere)

**F I G U R E 9-2**   THE PROJECT LEGACY

of the period. The Project Legacy shown in Figure 9-2 becomes part of the software organization's history and serves to educate coming generations of software engineers, as well as to refresh the memory and to guide the future decisions of those who participated in the development project.

The fundamental maintenance document is a Maintenance Plan, shown in Figure 9-3, which outlines the management structures that will support the maintenance effort.

Individual problems and requests for changes will be documented in forms like the one shown in Figure 9-4.

When a change has been fully implemented, a document like the one shown in Figure 9-5 ([TUR84]) should be issued.

Projected major modifications and extensions.
Planned revision cycle schedule.
Known problems and reliability estimates.
Maintenance organization structure and staff.
Error report procedures
Change request procedures
Revision distribution procedures

**F I G U R E 9-3**   SOFTWARE MAINTENANCE PLAN

SOFTWARE PROBLEM REPORT

SPR No. _____

**PROBLEM: (Prepared by User)**

Originator _____ Phone No. _____
          (Name)           (Organization)

System, processor, or
Component Failing _____ Computer _____ System Version ID _____ Test Case or Program ID _____
or Project Involved

Description of Problem 9attach additional pages if
necessary – include numbers or other identification
of offending statements or data)

Classification                                              Enclosures

☐ Minor or Not to Specs _____  ☐ Program Listings
☐ Major or Missing _____  ☐ Run Deck
☐ Information _____  ☐ Run Instructions
☐ Revision Request _____  ☐ Storage Map Listings
☐ Software Addition _____  ☐ Data Listings
           Correction Required By _____  ☐ On–Line Output
                       (Date)

Authorizing Signature _____ Date _____ Time _____
                  (Name)          (Organization)

**ANALYSIS: (Prepared by organization responsible for software)**

Received Date _____ Time _____ Charge Number _____

☐ Software in Error     Explanation _____ Analysis Time Expended:
☐ Software Not in Error            _____ Man Hours _____
   Explain and Return to          _____ Computer Hours _____
   Originator                _____ Computer _____
☐ Insufficient Information      _____ Estimated Cost of Solutions:
   for Analysis. See          _____ Man Hours _____
   Explanation            _____ Computer Hours _____
☐ Error Previously         _____ Planned _____
   Reported on SPR No.                           Correction Date
☐ Others, Explain
☐ Not Approved
☐ Approved for Correction
   or Change

Signature _____ Date _____ Time _____
             (Name)          (Organization)

**CORRECTION: (Brief description of work performed, including test cases used to confirm correction)**

Solution: _____  Modules Changed:

_____
_____
_____  Correction Time Expended:
_____  Man Hours
_____  Computer Hours
_____  Submitted to

Work Performed by (Signature) _____ Date _____ Time _____

**CONFIRMATION: Corrections Veri fied by CCB/CPL**

Signature _____ Date _____ Time _____
CTF No(s) _____
Available in (VersionID) _____ Date Returned to Originator _____ Time _____

**F I G U R E 9-4** SOFTWARE CHANGE REQUEST. (Bruce and Pederson, *The Software Development Project*, copyright © 1982, John Wiley & Sons, Inc., New York.)

Scope
Change summary
   New features
   Problems fixed
   Restrictions removed/capacities enlarged
Known problems
   Bugs
   Restrictions
Hardware and software compatibility requirements
Cross reference to relevant documentation
Detailed functional changes
Directory of packages on the distribution medium
Installation procedures

**FIGURE 9-5**   SOFTWARE RELEASE NOTICE FORMAT

## 9.2 OPERATIONAL STAGE PRINCIPLES

It is unusual to see an advertisement for an automobile that stresses the quality of its design and manufacturing. The selling points are usually its operational characteristics: how fast it goes; how economical it is to operate; how dependable it is; how cheap and easy it is to maintain. This does not mean that quality development is unimportant—it means that customers are interested in something else.

The same could be said for almost anything that people buy. True, there are snobs who are interested only in who produced a work of art or an article of fashion clothing and do not care about its utility or beauty. But generally customers are interested in functionality, dependability, usability, economy, and easy maintenance.

These software attributes obviously depend in large part on the quality of the development process, but we can enhance them by the planning we conduct, and the service we render during the operational phase. The sections that follow will discuss some of the specific goals of the operational processes and desirable operational characteristics of software. We will then discuss some of the factors that make it difficult, in principle, to maintain software.

### 9.2.1 Goals for the Operational Stage

The major goals of the maintenance activity are to preserve the product's market viability and longevity and to limit the cost of current and future maintenance effort. This can be done by utilizing the best methodologies, as well as by exercising management control. Indeed, management problems are more serious in the operational phase than are technical problems.

Control support expenses

Control maintenance expenses

Distinguish between maintenance and revision

Keep customers happy

Preserve software quality

Keep track of the marketplace

Improve staff morale

## Goals During Operation

**FIGURE 9-6**  SPECIFIC OPERATIONAL GOALS

Specifically, we want to use management principles to gain control over the cost of the customer support and maintenance process, over the flow of communication to and from the customers, over the direction in which modifications to the product take it, and over the multitude of different components of the various product versions. These goals can be achieved by using the following: a careful approval process for any modification, including a cost/benefit analysis; a set of formal procedures for receipt of customer calls and letters, the transmission of responses, and the distribution of product documentation and revisions; and configuration control tools.

As part of the control of maintenance costs, there must be a mechanism in place for distinguishing between modifications that legitimately fall into the category of maintenance and can be handled as such, and the ones that represent a major revision of the product and should be handled as a new development effort. Since maintenance is frequently performed on a fixed yearly cost basis, making a mistake in this decision can be devastating to the software organization.

Another goal of the operational stage is to create a sense of satisfaction and success in the users. This is done by starting out with a successful installation and training period, and is continued by providing satisfactory customer support. Paradoxically, we are usually most successful in satisfying the user when we convince him that he is able to handle almost all of his problems alone. Thus, high-quality training and documentation, combined with simplicity in using the product, and amplified by its dependability, will allow the user to be successful.

We must be particularly careful to avoid product decay through our control over modifications to the product. Product decay may be caused by modifications that reduce the product's maintainability and generality, increase its complexity, or introduce additional errors. We must thoughtfully select the modifications we undertake and then monitor the quality of the process by which the modifications are carried out.

The operational period is also a time for observing the market and the success of our product in order to plan for the future. Thus, we should not only handle customer communications on an individual basis but try to abstract the meaning and trends that underlie them. Of course, a list of those customers who have received the product is very useful if we are gathering information by surveying users.

Finally, a major goal of the operational stage is simply to keep the staff happy. For all its importance, there is little glamour or status to be gained from technical support and maintenance. This puts the manager in the uncomfortable position of running a very important enterprise with unmotivated workers. However, it is possible to do a good job by careful planning, by choosing workers with the right temperament for the job, and by isolating maintenance workers from the worst pressures of the process.

### 9.2.2 Operational Characteristics of Good Products

The most desirable operational characteristics of software are its functionality, friendliness, dependability, and simplicity. These attributes all have their foundation in quality development and they can be enhanced or diminished by the kind of maintenance the product receives. Complexity, lack of modularity, and size are important indicators of maintainability problems. Experience indicates that a module that utilizes a large amount of data, or that contains deep, complicated logic, is likely to be more costly to maintain ([SHE85]).

One of the major operational characteristics of a product, which has been stressed throughout this book, is its completeness. Remember that a software product consists not only of code, but also of all of the work products from all stages of the life cycle, together with all of the supporting documentation. If shortcuts have been taken, by skipping some of the life cycle stages or by omitting some of the documentation, then maintenance will be severely impaired ([GLA81]). In fact, Belady and Lehman estimate that maintenance effort decreases exponentially with improved documentation.

A particularly severe problem is encountered when code is so interconnected that a change in one spot may cause unwanted side effects almost anywhere else. Such a product is said to lack stability. This *ripple-effect* can be controlled by modularity and encapsulation in the original design ([YAU85]). It is equally important that modifications during maintenance should not create strands of interdependent segments running throughout the code that will increase the ripple effect problem later on. This is one of the reasons that maintenance should touch all documents, starting with the specifications; we will then be able to preserve a rational architectural design.

The programming language used to implement the product may contribute to or detract from its maintainability. On the one hand, structured languages contribute to the self-documenting aspects of the code, as well as make dispersion of logic less likely. On the other hand, some nonprocedural languages or VHLL's may implement unclear data flows and communication modes, thus impeding maintenance ([SCH87]).

### 9.2.3 Maintenance Challenges

*Maintenance* usually represents the bulk of the cost of the operational stage. Indeed, it is the dominant part of *all* costs for a software product; maintenance consumes about 60% of the total effort of the life cycle ([SCH87], [LIE81], [GLA81]). In its turn, perfective maintenance constitutes about 60% of all maintenance effort, with corrective and adaptive maintenance splitting the remainder pretty evenly (Figure 9-7).

High costs
Increasing software inventory
Low productivity
Heavy workloads
Lack of tools
Customer dependence
Customer demands
Alien code
Incomplete documentation
Aged code
Intertwined code

**Maintenance Challenges**

**FIGURE 9-7**  MAINTENANCE CHALLENGES

Lientz and Swanson ([LIE81]) indicate that the growth rate of a product is about 10% per year, with a lifetime of five years. This means that the product will be 61% larger at the end of its lifetime than it was when first delivered. On the other hand, Lientz [LIE83] claims that the maintenance effort in the average organization is *not* increasing, which apparently means that organizations are retiring products, or are choosing not to update them, in order to keep the maintenance burden under control.

Other problems gathered from surveys by Lientz and Swanson are low maintenance productivity (due in part to the amount of handwork required), heavy work loads, and lack of hardware and software tools ([LIE81]). The maintainers' primary complaint, however, is the insistence of user demands for service, coupled with user ignorance about the current function of the product ( often because they do not read the manual).

Statistics like these represent the average situation over the entire industry. Individual experience can be much worse. Boehm, for instance, cites the case of one product developed for the U.S. Air Force. Although the initial cost of development was only $30 per line of code, the maintenance cost was $4000 per line of code. In this case, maintenance consumed more than 99% of the total software budget, an absolutely intolerable state of affairs. A more graphic illustration of the need for good maintenance methodology is hard to imagine.

The primary challenge in maintenance technology, as has already been stated, is acquiring or keeping knowledge and insight. These elements permit us to make modifications that are consistent with the original product, without degrading it in any way. Frequently, we have the additional problem of tracing our way from the symptom of an error, manifested as a failure in operation, all the way back to the original software engineering fault that gave rise to it. This problem is ameliorated when the maintenance personnel are part of the original development team and when complete documentation is available. It is aggravated when we attempt to modify badly documented code or code that is **alien**, that is, produced by some other organization. This can occur when the customer organization undertakes maintenance of a product they purchased elsewhere, or when a third party receives the contract for maintenance.

A secondary, but related, problem in maintenance is that of the ripple effect. We may create a separate problem by modifications that are meant to (and often do) correct the initial problem. Some such side effects might be the modification of the interpretation of control codes in some places, but not all; the unexpected change of a variable's value, the change of an array's bounds, or the removal of an apparently senseless but actually vital piece of code.

It is quite possible that modifications to a product can blur its originally clean lines, distort its structure, invalidate its goals, or muddy the purity of its methods. Aging code of this kind is much more difficult to maintain ([COL87]). To avoid this problem, the maintenance worker needs to recapture the technical and the management information of the original team. The same plans and goals should continue to guide the course of additional development. If this is not done, then a product can, quite literally, be "maintained to death."

## 9.3 OPERATIONAL STAGE METHODOLOGIES AND TOOLS

The major operational processes all have their own methodologies and specific tools and are outlined in the following sections. First, we need to find out how to conduct an acceptance test, install the product, and convert procedures and the database to the new system. Then we will see how to conduct a project evaluation, and why it is essential to the continued success of the software organization.

Training and general customer support techniques are covered next. Other than the functioning of the product itself, training and support have the greatest impact on the user. Maintenance and configuration management are discussed in Sections 9.3.4 and 9.3.5.

### 9.3.1 System Delivery

***System Acceptance*** Passing the acceptance tests represents the fulfillment of the software organization's contractual responsibilities to the customer. In other words, this is the moment at which we prove that we have really done what we promised to do. The acceptance test is not merely a demonstration—it is very serious and formal. The customer needs to be sure that everything about the software is correct. On the other hand, acceptance testing is not the same as the testing conducted in the previous stage of the life cycle, since we involve the customer and intend that the tests disclose *no errors at all*.

The characteristics of the software that need to be demonstrated were outlined during the planning stage and formalized in the specifications. The Acceptance Test Plan was also finalized at that time. It may contain all of the actual test data and expected results. However, it is also possible that the customer will include test conditions and data that the software organization has never seen. Of course, these will fall within the specified operating conditions and behavior of the software. But the purchaser may demand that the software pass tests of which the software organization knows neither the questions nor the answers beforehand.

In fact, it is possible that the customer might contract with an entirely different organization to conduct the acceptance tests. This would allow an unbiased but expert third party to evaluate the quality of the product. This option can be continued by allowing for third party training, delivery, and support of the software.

There are three major kinds of acceptance test patterns that are most commonly used. *Benchmark* testing utilizes a predetermined set of test data meant to evaluate the software in certain areas, including correctness, accuracy, speed, dependability, and the like. The response to the test data is compared to the predicted response based on the specifications, and the software passes the test if it conforms within permissible limits. Benchmark tests are by far the most common acceptance tests.

*Parallel* testing is used when the new software reimplements an existing system, either manual or automated. Both systems are executed with a common set of data, and the correctness of the new software is determined by the degree to which it conforms to the existing system's responses. The test data can either be preselected or obtained by capturing actual input data to the existing system.

*Beta* testing is the process of using software in the application environment and monitoring it for anomalies or errors. In benchmark and parallel tests, we assume that correct responses are known (benchmarks) or determined by an ideal (existing) system. In beta testing, we presume nothing about the data or the correct responses before the test is conducted. Instead, we observe the software as it functions, hoping that any problems will be manifested. Obviously, if the customer challenges the product's operation, it will be necessary to determine objectively what the correct behavior should have been. When beta testing is specified for acceptance, we must also specify those objective rules for judging behavior.

A full log of acceptance test results must be kept and, on satisfactory completion of the test, the customer signs off on the software, thus agreeing to pay the stipulated price. If the software fails to pass the acceptance test, it may be rejected outright, or may be sent back for redesign, reimplementation, and subsequent testing, or may be accepted for provisional use, provided that the development team agrees that problems will be completely corrected within a specified time. Figure 9-8 shows that the actual acceptance test can be performed at either the development site or the customer's site.

For packaged software, there is no customer to conduct the acceptance testing. Integration and system testing as described in the preceding chapter may be sufficient. Alternatively, the software organization's marketing or management personnel may take on the role of customers for the purpose of conducting an acceptance test.

**System Conversion** Sometimes people see things from diametrically opposed points of view. When they try to work together, it is likely that confusion, disagreement, and unhappiness will result. System conversion is a critical time during the software life cycle, since it is one of those situations which can give rise to diametrically opposed viewpoints. From the software organization's point of view, all the work is done, the product is finished, and there is nothing more to worry about. From the customer organization's point of view, the work is just starting and everything can go wrong.

To avoid customer resentment and user resistance, software engineers must curb their natural desire to be done with the project and focus on the problems of integrating the software product into the customer environment. The person designated to provide customer support, frequently the analyst, takes the lead in this task. However, the rest of the software team may well become involved.

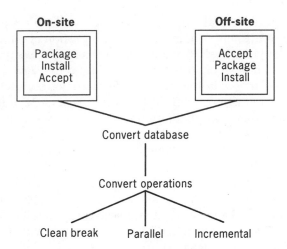

**FIGURE 9-8**  INSTALLATION SEQUENCES

The first task is the installation of the software. This starts with packaging all of the software on media and checking that the proper configuration of software components is present. Next, all the appropriate documentation, support, and training materials have to be gathered. After a physical configuration audit, these are delivered to the user site and the software is installed on the user's media. Finally, an installation test is run to ensure that everything is working properly. At this point, we may note some software deficiencies that would necessitate a return to the software organization site for further work. It is also possible that user hardware and supplies might need some alteration before the software system can function properly.

Following installation, it is necessary to convert operations from whatever system was being used previously. There are several conversion modes, and any one of them can be chosen according to the needs of the user. The first mode is *"cold turkey"*: operations under the old system cease, a total conversion to the new system is effected, and then operations under the new system commence. The advantages of this mode are that a clean break is made between the two regimes, responsibility for ensuing problems is clearly defined and the new software can be used as soon as possible. The disadvantage is that errors in the software may throw the user organization into chaos.

Another installation mode is *parallel operation*. In this situation, both systems are used simultaneously. Users gain confidence in the new software as they see that it functions correctly, but they also have full backup if there are any serious failures. The disadvantage is confusion and the need for additional effort and hardware to support the use of two systems at once.

The third mode of conversion is *incremental*. Here we install only a small portion of the new system, which runs in conjunction with the old system until the customer is confident that it works correctly and is accustomed to using it. In succession, additional portions of the new system replace parts of the old one, until the new system is entirely installed. Although this mode avoids much of the danger of cold turkey installation and the added effort of parallel installation, it only works if there are a number of interfaces at which a part of the new system can replace a portion of the old.

During conversion it may be necessary to change the format of an existing database, to modify the procedures and paper forms in use, to tune the new software for maximum efficiency in the user environment, and, of course, to train the users in its operation. This is really one of the most critical stages of the life cycle. If users have a bad experience at this point, they may abandon the product; hence all the work and effort of development may be wasted.

This makes conversion a particularly challenging stage for packaged software. The customer is probably converting alone, and there are no support personnel present during conversion. Also, the software is probably not tailored to the customer's environment, thus necessitating more change and adaptation on the user's part. For this reason, documentation of packaged software must be exceptionally complete and must include detailed installation instructions. It is also wise to provide free phone-in support for new users of a software package.

### 9.3.2 Project Evaluation

Brooks ([BRO75]) quotes a Dutch proverb, "A ship on the beach is a lighthouse to the sea", meaning that when we see the remains of a disaster, we should be careful not to make the same mistakes. Unfortunately, there is a tendency to be ashamed of mistakes, and so most of our "shipwrecks" are dealt with in secrecy. Although this may make us look better and feel better, it does not help us to learn from our errors.

The purpose of project evaluation is to record our experiences with software development and to organize this information in such a way as to provide guidance during future projects. Part of this information, particularly as it relates to project cost, schedule, and the occurrence of errors, is integrated into our project database system. Potentially reusable software components have to be classified and inserted into the reuse libraries, but most of the information will be in the form of a project narrative.

The narrative is created by the manager or the quality assurance personnel and is stored in a database under quality assurance's control. Writing the narrative requires that the software team postpone the parties and vacations for a day or two to record their experiences while they are still fresh in their minds. User reactions to the software, as far as they are known, should be included. Future user feedback should be added to the narrative as it becomes available.

One purpose of the narrative is to allow software engineers to reflect on and evaluate their experience. Engineers need to draw conclusions about the effectiveness of the methodologies, the tools, the process models, the management techniques, and the team organization. An effort should be made to highlight the differences between the expected and the actual results of using these techniques. Such conclusions will form the basis for decisions made in the analysis of future software development projects.

In order to make the narrative accessible, it is necessary to create a profile of the project. This profile is based on the profile developed during planning; it classifies the product according to its function, application area, size, complexity, and the like. In addition, the profile should categorize team organization, development success,

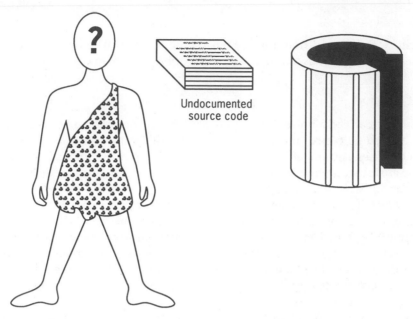
Undocumented
source code

**FIGURE 9-9**   TRYING TO MAINTAIN SOFTWARE WITHOUT A PROJECT HISTORY

process model, user reaction and satisfaction, management techniques and tools. The profile will serve as a set of keys by which the narrative will be accessed.

We often hear a quote from George Santayana: "Those who cannot remember the past are condemned to repeat it". It seems like a pleasant bromide, but people who lived in prehistoric times were in just that situation. With only an oral tradition to record their successes and failures, they were caught on a treadmill, with generation after generation showing slow, uneven progress. We, however, can chronicle the events of our lives and quickly learn from our own and others' experience.

The problem with this attitude is that most software engineers continue to live in prehistory. The idea of recording the successes and failures of our professional lives is at best distasteful. In fact, there is no need to do so (we feel), since the next project we will work on will be the one where everything goes right. It will be exciting, satisfying and profitable, and there is no need to dwell on negative ideas and past failures.

Hence just like prehistoric hunter-gatherers, many of us spend our lives on a treadmill repeating the same mistakes over and over again and wondering why our work is not exciting, satisfying, or profitable (Figure 9-9). Few software engineers are willing to admit that keeping a personal journal of our professional activities is one of the very best ways to spend our time. More organizations are now beginning to keep a group history, although their efforts are often spotty. A software engineer moving from one organization to another, however, must depend on his personal journal if he wants to carry history with him.

Researchers like Barry Boehm and T. Capers Jones have accumulated databases of information about software projects. These are used to develop cost estimation models, risk analysis techniques, metrics, productivity analyses, and the like. Similar chronicles can be produced within any organization, which would then allow organizational history to be used fine-tuning their methodologies. The best way to improve is to analyze the past, discern the source of trouble, and plan corrective action.

### 9.3.3 Customer Support

We have already presented arguments for the importance of customer support for packaged software, and this also applies, with perhaps more force, in the contract software environment. In that case, because of the close contact between the software and customer organizations, there is often a greater tendency for the users to come back to the software engineers for help.

In fact, it is wise to state precisely in the contract the degree to which support can be expected. Many customers disagree on the fine line between training and ongoing support, or between the correction of unacceptable errors and the enhancement of a satisfactory software product. Entering into a clear-cut agreement before misunderstandings occur may help avoid disappointment and resentment later on.

*Customer Training* Training has a public goal—to enable the customer's personnel to operate and to use the software product—and a private goal—to convince the customer's personnel that the software is worth what it cost. It is also possible that the users have a hidden agenda for training; they may want to prolong it indefinitely, thus depending on the software organization to handle their problems and to direct their work. For this reason, it is always wise to specify the software organization's responsibilities with respect to training and to agree on a fee schedule for training services that go beyond these responsibilities.

Training can be delivered in several ways. The most common is the classroom *lecture* environment. Although most of us are comfortable with this instructional mode, having experienced it in our own education, it is not very effective. People have the tendency to understand, but not retain, what is said in a classroom. Retention can be improved by the use of standard instructional media, like manuals, illustrations, quizzes, and the like.

A more effective training environment is found in the *laboratory*. Here, customer personnel are allowed to operate the software in a controlled and directed pattern. Because of their involvement—doing as well as hearing—both retention and compre-

# Training Modes

## Lecture
## Laboratory
## Tutorial
## CAI
## Consultation
## Documentation

**FIGURE 9-10**   DIFFERENT VEHICLES FOR DELIVERING TRAINING

hension are improved. The laboratory method can be modified still further to provide a *tutorial* mode of training, in which there is no predetermined body of training information and the order of learning and the subject matter are governed by the particular level of comprehension and needs of a single user. This is a very effective training environment, but it is also costly, since all interaction is one on one.

If the sales volume of a product is sufficiently large, we may be able to automate the tutorial mode by providing *computer-aided instruction* (CAI). Although it is never as effective as a true tutorial, if CAI is sufficiently extensive it may combine the attributes of greatest satisfaction with lowest cost. Production of on-line tutorials is simplified when we have tools for CAI development at our disposal. Of course, the effectiveness of on-line tutorials is enhanced when there is some contact, either direct or via telephone, with a human consultant.

In the case of packaged software, most of our contacts with customers should be indirect, through documentation and updates of the product. As mentioned earlier, if we do a good job of documentation, the amount of direct support through correspondence and telephone calls will be minimized. Of course, it is a challenge to document a product enough to answer most users' legitimate questions, without making it too easy for competitors to acquire all of our techniques.

We should be prepared to provide some legitimate call-up and correspondence consultation. The people designated in our organization for this task must combine an ability to deal with the public and a high level of technical competence and familiarity with the product. It is also important to maintain continuity of support over the lifetime of the product. If the cost of consultation becomes too great, then support contracts or fees can be offered to users.

Training in the use of packaged software again depends largely on documentation. When the software is sold through some marketing organization, training is amplified by the services of a salesperson. It is important to determine the quality and professional ability of salespeople in any organization that we allow to sell our software. Word of mouth may condemn a software product when, in fact, the fault lies with an incompetent computer store.

Support for a product also takes the form of making newer versions available to purchasers. A mailing list of purchasers can provide an opportunity to advertise updates as well as to inform users of errors in the software and of potential applications of which they are unaware. The same mailing list can be used to advertise related new products.

The principal postdelivery support activities are listed in Figure 9-11. The first two are the most routine: answering questions and clarifying the operation of the software. If the software is as dependable as it should be, there will be few customer emergencies. However, customers can still find ways to misuse even the most bulletproof software, and it is during emergencies that support is most vital to them. Support personnel must be able to respond quickly and to bring a high degree of expertise to bear on problems. The quality of support received in a crisis has a tremendous influence on future software purchases. It can damage both reputation and profitability if the management control system is so ponderous that emergency aid cannot be provided to the user.

Answer questions.

Clarify operations.

Help in dealing with exceptions.

Receive information on errors.

Accept requests for modification and enhancements.

Provide feedback on progress of requested maintenance.

Deliver and install updates.

**FIGURE 9-11**   CUSTOMER SUPPORT ACTIVITIES

One form of help in an emergency can be a temporary fix to the product or the procedures for using it. A **patch** is not a regular modification to the software for correction. Rather, it is a solution that we hope will allow the user's operations to continue, without creating any other problems. Because patches are rough and ready, hurried and unmethodical, they should be avoided if possible. Patches must always be replaced by carefully thought-out modifications as soon as a solution is devised.

Sometimes the support person can come up with an alternative method for achieving customer processing without modifying the code. A **workaround** provides another procedure to allow the system to continue working in a manner not envisioned in the original design. Since a workaround is probably illogical, unhandy, and difficult, a proper modification will likely be needed as soon as possible. When our software has an open architecture, we may be able to provide sufficient tools and documentation to allow the customer himself to provide a workaround. This is the quickest method and is usually satisfactory to the user. However, it is still necessary to maintain a reporting system for problems.

The support organization that receives reports of errors and requests for software maintenance acts as an intermediary between the customer and the maintainers. This buffer is important, because direct contact and pressure on maintenance software engineers tend to cause a short circuit in what should be a very controlled process. The support people should be able to gather all of the information possible (including copies of data that generate software failures) for transmission to the maintenance organization. This is a vital responsibility, since nothing is more frustrating than trying to deal with a report of a failure that we are unable to re-create.

On the other hand, customers hate to send in information and requests only to have them not acted on. The support personnel need to provide feedback and to indicate the status of requests and the projected delivery of updated software. This kind of considerate attention promotes both security and confidence in the customers and makes for a more successful product. When updates become available, it is up to the support people to inform customers of their availability and to provide means for delivery and installation. It might be worthwhile to implement some electronic means of downloading updates directly.

## 9.3.4 Maintenance Techniques

The size of the maintenance problem has been repeatedly emphasized throughout this

# Maintenance Activities
### Plan changes
### Predict consequences
### Modify code
### Eliminate side effects
### Test resulting software
### Distribute new versions

**FIGURE 9-12**   MAINTENANCE ACTIVITIES

book. It constitutes a major part of the software crisis and can be so overpowering as to divert all attention from the development of new products. For this reason, specification, design, and implementation techniques have all emphasized the importance of developing software with maintainability as a primary goal.

These techniques include the use of formal specifications, transformation tools and methodologies, clear and standard design procedures, and carefully documented implementation. One source of maintainability is the complete documentation of the development effort. Probable enhancements to the software should be planned in advance, during regular development, so that the necessary "hooks" for the expanded capabilities already exist when it becomes necessary to implement them.

The general list of maintenance activities includes determining what changes will be made to existing products, understanding the structure and purpose of the affected components, modifying them to meet new requirements or to correct errors, eliminating any unwanted side effects resulting from the modification, testing the resulting product to verify the correctness of the changes, and controlling the distribution of new versions to customers ([YAU85]) (Figure 9-12).

Maintainers try to eliminate bottlenecks and roadblocks in customer operations and either to introduce innovations or to customize current software capabilities in an attempt to improve the service for which the product was originally developed ([BEN87]). This facilitation of customer activities is a fundamental goal of the operational period.

Three different types of changes are made to a software product during the maintenance stage:

1 The **corrective** change, which has the same effect as changes during the testing stage: it eliminates deviations from the specifications.
2 The **adaptive** change, which responds to alterations in the hardware or operating system environment, in other related software products, or in the operational or legal requirements of the customer.
3 The **perfective** change, which augments the performance of the product beyond what was envisioned in the original specifications.

Generally, corrective changes dominate in the period just after delivery of the product, whereas perfective changes dominate later on. In fact, we can think of the initial and successive versions of the product as representing a single development using the program growth model.

In a way, the tools and techniques for maintenance are the same as those used previously. Corrective maintenance is largely indistinguishable from debugging during testing, whereas adaptive and perfective maintenance are very similar to the whole development process. We reemphasize that *all* stages are involved; any modification to code comes only after modification of specifications and design. Likewise, all modified code must be tested thoroughly, as it is more likely to contain errors than the original code. Adaptation of code, particularly for changing hardware environments, need not reach deeply into the specification and design stages if careful encapsulation was practiced originally. It may be possible to excise old hardware descriptions and to to replace them with new ones at very little cost.

There is one significant difference between original development and maintenance, however. During maintenance, considerable time must be spent in recapturing knowledge about the original plans, goals, intentions, and methods of the software team. This is the reason why full documentation is so important to the maintainer. Tools that support the traceability of software working products are invaluable during this process.

We listed a number of maintenance problems in Section 9.2.3: alien code, decay, side effects, cost, discouragement, and inadequate tools. The alien code problem can be attacked by a process of reverse engineering, in which we take the code and develop the rest of the missing documentation from it. This is a time-consuming task, that should be started before an emergency occurs. When the pressure is on, our tendency is to try to patch the obvious symptoms of the error and then hope for the best. Usually we will only be making things worse. Sometimes, even code produced by one's own organization that predates the establishment of good development practices and standards can seem pretty alien.

The core of reverse engineering technology is the abstraction of code into design concepts ([BRI86]). From this point, we can both work backward to specification and forward, through redesign, to a better implementation. This can be difficult, however, when clues to the design are scattered in threads throughout the implementation, or when optimization in the code obscures the design ([ARA86]). Previous maintenance can also hide the lineaments of the original design.

To detect decay in the structure, organization, and understandability of a product, metrics, like the McCabe cyclomatic complexity or the cohesion/coupling levels, can be applied to the affected parts before and after modification. If the metrics indicate that the quality of the software is degenerating, then the cause of this decline must be isolated and eliminated. The standard quality assurance auditing must also be applied to modifications, and all documentation must be brought up to date before any changes are distributed to users.

Sometimes, we think we need only to modify the major documents, like the specifications, design, code, and user's manual, but there are also other effects to worry about. In particular, there is usually a host of subsidiary work products, like command files and test data, that must be updated as a result of changes. Surely we must apply all existing tests to the modified code—regression testing—to be sure that we have not destroyed something of its function in the alteration. But we must also add new test data to cover new function, or to modify existing test data to match adaptation.

One of the techniques of development that we might employ is systems analysis—going back to the users to determine what changes are needed. This should be done with caution. At the simplest level, we can profile use of the product to determine what parts could benefit from some kind of optimization, an action that is always appropriate.

At the next higher level, we must respond in some way to requested changes that are submitted through the customer support group. These can be evaluated in terms of their impact on the overall functionality and marketability of the product and the availability of maintenance personnel to implement them. They will be either accepted or rejected in accordance with their benefit *to the software organization* rather than to the user.

The ripple effect problem can be largely avoided by good development practices and fully documented products. When this is done, the code is traceable to design and specifications, and vice versa, which will make clear the reasons for code segments as well as the ramifications of changes to them. If the development practices or documentation are poor, then all one can do is proceed with extreme caution.

One possible solution to the staffing problem is to transfer some of the development staff into maintenance, or to periodically rotate all development people into maintenance. This is likely to provide needed experience and knowledge, as well as an incentive for development people to design for maintainability. After all, they might have to solve their own problems in a little while. One of the worse policies is to staff maintenance solely with the newest employees. True, this does provide a training effect, familiarizing them with the company's products. But maintenance is far too important a task to be totally given over to those least qualified to undertake it.

A browser that will allow us to look at just the modifications that have been made within a given period time can help us to see the changes that have occurred during the operational stage. A static analyzer may be able to trace data flows, which will help if reverse engineering is needed. A translator that will turn code written in one implementation language into another or will structure unstructured programs can dramatically cut the cost of adaptation to a new machine or environment ([SCH87]).

### 9.3.5 Configuration Management During the Operational Stage

Product control was discussed in Chapter 2, but some topics relate more specifically to the operational stage of the life cycle. Product control continues to fall under the responsibility of the quality assurance group. The obligations of configuration managers are generally to identify different work products, to audit their quality, to account for their current status, and to control their modification and distribution. Recall that the different activities of configuration management are component identification, control, auditing, and accounting ([BER84]).

Software product versions are commonly identified by a pair of numbers, like 4.2, representing major and minor releases of new configurations. Usually, a major release involves significant changes in the function and internal structure of the software, whereas minor releases concentrate on correction of errors and small improvements. Sometimes these two numbers are referred to as level and update numbers or version and revision numbers as well. It should be noted that even "minor" revisions can be very expensive when they are propagated to all the documentation and all the customers.

It is normal to batch several different modifications of a product into a single release, so that they all make their first appearance under a single new identification number. We can either wait until sufficient changes have taken place to warrant a new release or plan to have releases at fixed intervals.

Additional information may be included in version numbers. For instance, V4.2 might indicate the standard software configuration, whereas S4.2 could be a specially modified version, and X4.2 might be an internal, unreleased, or unsupported version. T4.2 can designate a temporary version, for example, a patch sent to the user to keep the operation going while a methodical correction is being prepared.

Individual work products within the entire software product can have subidentification numbers; specifications could be called V4.2SP. If these are so large that they need to be stored in separate documents, then the tree-level numbering system could be used. Thus the third subsubsection of the fifth subsection of the second section of the specifications might be identified as V4.2SP2.5.3. Auxiliary products, like test plans or command files for rebuilding versions of the product after a maintenance cycle, need to be identified and controlled in the same way as the mainline work products.

Part of the challenge of component identification is knowing how the various components must be put together to form a deliverable product. There will likely be a number of different configurations in actual use, and their architecture will determine how systems are to be built. Configuration management needs to understand this model of each separate product constructed from the pool of components, as well as their dependencies. It is particularly important that variant versions of a module be isolated and identified ([LEB87]).

The auditing function has already been discussed. Not only is it necessary to ensure that all standards for the different products have been met by their modifications but also to see that all work products have in fact been modified in coordination. An important part of auditing is ensuring that documents reflect the product as it really turned out to be, not as it was planned. Thus, documentation for previous and unimplemented versions of the product are superseded by *as built* documentation.

In status accounting our task is to identify any work that is currently being undertaken on the product, to be able to distinguish those work products that belong with any given version from those corresponding to previous or subsequent versions, and to divide temporary from permanent versions.

The control function of configuration management deals with enforcement of the various policies outlined in the preceding discussion. For instance, the original permission to make modifications and the decision to release them to the customers are part of the control responsibility, and there should be explicit procedures for arriving at such determinations. Archiving and providing baseline versions of any work product is another such responsibility; in fact, deciding when to allow a temporary product to pass from an individual software engineer and into the sphere of configuration management must also be made by the product control people.

Since it may be difficult to comprehend all the consequences of modification to a complex software product, it is up to the configuration managers to notify members of the software organization (and perhaps users as well) of requested changes in a product. If any disagreement appears likely, sufficient time must be allowed for everybody to comment on the changes before they are authorized.

The task of tracing all possible ramifications of a modification is greatly simplified by a good project database system, or another configuration control tool like Make and SCCS (Unix tools that ensure that object code is consistent with source, and that keep track of modifications and version numbers) or CCC, DSEE, RCS, Domain, or MMS/CMS (commercial products). These tools allow us to locate other modules that depend on the module that has been modified so we can make additional required modifications as well as recompilations.

The database system must also have to recognize the commonality of variant modules that have the same fundamental purpose. These may be automatically grouped into families on the basis that they share the same functionality and templates ([NAR87]). This could open the way for a single modification to their common function, which would be automatically propagated through each member of the family. Commonality also makes it possible for variant modules to be stored as "delta" files, containing only the information in which they vary from the base file. These differences can then be merged automatically with the base file to produce the full variant.

Another useful service of an all-inclusive database would be to inform the responsible party about any reported problem in the software. This capability could be integrated with electronic mail, which can also be a vehicle for distributing Engineering Change Notices and Software Release Notices.

## 9.4 FOSTERING QUALITY DURING THE OPERATIONAL STAGE

The length of the operational stage, the volume of the communication between the organization and the customers, and the diffuseness of the maintenance task all combine to make control of the process difficult. Thus, quality control must be more strictly and carefully applied than at any other time. The biggest challenges are to perform customer service and maintenance within cost and in a timely manner, to prevent the product from decaying into a heap of disorder, and to provide visible measures of the entire process.

Operation and maintenance provide the principal source of feedback into the development process. Observing customer reactions and problems, performance and error characteristics of the product, and the nature of requested enhancements can provide information that will benefit new projects within the organization. In a sense, the quality assurance group represents the collective conscience of the software organization. By carefully weighing the mistakes of the past and the needs of the present, they can help the organization to seize on the opportunities of the future.

Error density of each module.

Originating causes of errors.

Categorical description of errors.

Severity of errors.

Effort/schedule for types of maintenance.

Product complexity before and after maintenance.

Number of unresolved problems.

Duration of unresolved problems.

Percentage of modifications introducing errors.

Time lapse in acknowledging customer problem report.

Time lapse in resolving customer problem report.

Customer downtime, losses, and reinstallation costs.

Number of modules modified to implement one change.

Correlation of development methodology with maintenance cost.

Trends and correlations among all of the above.

**FIGURE 9-13**   OPERATIONAL METRICS

## 9.4.1 Operational Metrics

Since the operational stage usually consumes more than one half of the total software budget, we must gather all the information we can about its effectiveness. In addition, many indicators of the quality of the original development effort will only become visible during the operational stage. Grady suggests a number of possible metrics that might be used during the operational period ([GRA87]). These are listed in Figure 9-13.

One particular metric that interests Grady is the seriousness of user problems. These ratings are given by the customers themselves (and probably govern the charges for modifications not covered by a contract). Serious or critical problems cause the customer site to be put onto an "alert" list. If no quick patch or workaround is found, the site goes onto a "hot" list. Alert and hot indexes for a problem can then be calculated by summing the number of weeks each site reporting the problem has been on the list (see figure 9-14).

Yau and Collofello propose a *stability* metric to measure the resistance of code to the ripple effect ([YAU85]). This metric is rather limited, but it basically counts the number of modules that might be affected by changes within the module about to be changed. It does not measure ripple effect within a single module. The stability measure can be used to choose between alternative redesigns as well as to evaluate the quality of modules and systems.

An estimate of the maintainability of code can be obtained prior to any actual maintenance experience by analyzing its structure automatically. Rombach reports favorable experiences with this type of metric ([ROM87]). It can be used to plan the cost of maintenance, and thus the appropriate price of maintenance contracts, as the product is first released.

We may be able to gather useful information about the operational profile of the software by instrumenting it and gathering usage, CPU, and error statistics from our customers (perhaps during an update process). Similarly, we might automate the gathering of information about user satisfaction and suggestions.

### 9.4.2 Verification and Validation

Tight control of verification and validation activities is vital to the operational period ([GRA87]). Since the incomplete knowledge of the maintainer is more likely to foster errors in code modifications, and since errors will affect users immediately upon release of an update, error minimization during the operational stage is both more difficult and more important.

Brooks indicates that there is a 20% to 50% probability that any modification to a product will itself be in error ([BRO75]). Collofello and Buck claim that as many as 65% of modifications will be wrong at the first try, and that 17% of all modifications contain undetected errors ([COL87]). If this is true, it means that the rate of errors in modified code is much higher than in original code and that the testing requirements for modifications should be much more stringent. Of course, regression testing is conducted on all modified modules, and on the integrated whole. Of course, new tests should be devised for new functions and enhancements. However, it is also necessary to test modules and functions that *should not* have been changed in the modification,

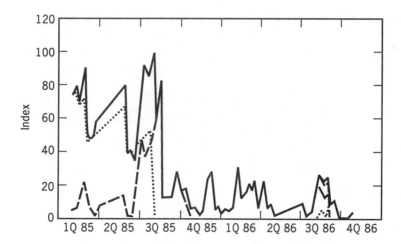

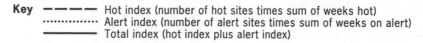

Key ――――  Hot index (number of hot sites times sum of weeks hot)
............  Alert index (number of alert sites times sum of weeks on alert)
――――  Total index (hot index plus alert index)

**FIGURE 9-14**  TRACKING THE SEVERITY OF A PROBLEM. (R. Grady, "Measuring and Managing Software Maintenance," *IEEE Software*, copyright © 1987, IEEE.)

since the ripple effect may, in fact, have propagated the change to them. This is most often the result of incorrect logic in the original modification.

Error-prone modules should also be singled out for special testing and perhaps for preventive maintenance. Preventive maintenance is the replacement of a suspect module before it has been reported as the source of a problem. The number of individual data items utilized within the module, together with the cyclomatic complexity of the logic in the module, can be indications of its error-proneness ([SHE85]).

One unavoidable consequence of introducing errors into modifications—"breaking" the software as we attempt to fix it—is that less than perfect error detection and correction in the future will guarantee that the total number of errors in the product will increase over time. In the long run, this is another source of product decay.

Maintenance personnel can take a proactive approach to eliminating some of the difficulties that they experience as a result of inferior work by careless developers. They can be given a voice, perhaps through the quality assurance organization, in the original design of the product ([SCH87]).

The permanence of the software and hardware environment is an overriding factor in the maintainability of a product. Thus, an evaluation of the permanence of a market niche is an appropriate factor in the decision whether to enter it at all. We can increase the likelihood of an equable maintenance experience by choosing not to move into a volatile product environment.

### 9.4.3 Management

Since maintenance can usually be viewed as a repetition of development, and since other operational processes include few technical activities, the major new challenges of the operational stage are more managerial than technological. At this point, the users learn how to operate the product, and their suggestions become more explicit and

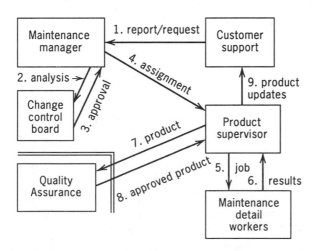

**F I G U R E 9-15**   A MAINTENANCE ORGANIZATION

demanding. If the product is marketed, then we must deal with the thousands of customers who replace one marketing department, which acted as their surrogate during development. Considerable organizing is necessary to keep from bogging down in the mass of detail. The manager may react to the challenge by shifting into a reactive mode: he spends his time running from problem to problem putting out fires.

What kind of organization should be established to manage maintenance? We might decide to continue as in development by putting maintenance of a particular product under a (perhaps actually the same) project manager. This person has ultimate responsibility to both management and users for the product. An alternative to the project pattern would be to take the model of the departmental organization, perhaps allowing a product to pass to a final maintenance department after it leaves the development stages. For a small product, it might be unnecessary to provide any management—a single worker could undertake all maintenance efforts. A typical departmental organization is shown in Figure 9-15.

Obviously, the original development staff provides a good place to look for the most qualified people for maintenance. If a chief programmer team has been used, then the alter ego might be an ideal product supervisor ([MCC81]). This is the typical model of maintenance in Japan ([SCH87]), where it is expected that lifetime maintenance of a product will be conducted by members of the development staff. Perhaps if people know they will have to live with their mistakes for years, they will be more careful in their initial efforts. Grady suggests that development personnel maintain the product for at least the first six months of its operational period. One thing is clear, however. Whether we choose a project, departmental, or individual model, there must be a permanent responsibility vested in someone to see that modifications to a product are carried out in an orderly and controlled fashion. Figure 9-16 lists some of the different management activities during maintenance.

To plan the staffing and budget needed for maintenance of a new product, a manager may use one of the formulas presented in Chapter 3. A rule of thumb suggested in [LIE81] calls for one detail worker for each 40K lines of code to be maintained, but a manageable load can vary by a factor of 10, depending on the quality of the product under maintenance. It has been suggested that the Rayleigh curve, the basis for the Putnam estimation technique, is only valid in modeling corrective maintenance ([WEI84]). For this and other reasons, we might do well to plan adaptive

Capture and rating of error reports/change requests.

Assessment of impact and cost of modifications.

Approval of changes to the product.

Assignment of work to individuals.

Application of quality assurance to the modifications.

Release of the updated product to customers.

Evaluation of the maintenance product.

Retirement of outdated products.

**FIGURE 9-16**  MANAGEMENT ACTIVITIES IN MAINTENANCE.

and perfective maintenance and enhancements as if they were new product developments.

We learned in Section 9.3.3 that requests for modifications to the product, as well as reports of errors in the product, should be channeled through the user support group. This protects the maintenance organization from pressure to provide unwarranted services. These reports and requests can be forwarded to the maintenance manager by using a form like the one shown in Figure 9-4.

Upon arrival of the change request, the maintenance manager must determine the nature of the problem and rate the urgency of the request. Some serious problems need to be solved as soon as humanly possible; others are given priority over less important work but do not require heroic measures like overtime. Requested changes might be scheduled for the next update release or they might be put into a holding pattern, pending the availability of additional resources or a demonstration of interest on the part of more customers. This initial rating of seriousness is mainly for expediting urgent problems. The rating of nonemergency requests can be changed when a more complete appraisal of the request is made.

The maintenance manager supervises the maintenance department over the long term. One of the tasks is estimating the budget, independent of individual change requests. The overall maintenance cost of the organization will depend on the volume of activity in the products under its supervision. This is, roughly, the percentage of change in the products in a year's time. For individual products, we must assess the costs and benefits of the requested modification.

First, an investigation of the product determines the impact of the change in terms of the amount and the complexity of code and other documents and products to be modified. Next, the degree to which other users would benefit from the change has to be determined. Finally, we estimate the benefit to the software organization in terms of income, utilization of free personnel, creation of reusable components, and creation of customer goodwill.

This kind of analysis can be carried out by using the same methods and tools that were used in the planning stage. We may use actual experience with this product to estimate effort and schedule. Thus if the change will augment the code by 10%, we can estimate the cost at 10% of the cost for development of the product, adjusted to compensate for the relearning that might be required. We may additionally adjust the effort estimate if the product has aged through previous maintenance to the point where its integrity and unity have been degraded.

Following this planning ministage, the maintenance manager's findings are sent to the change control board, a management unit that decides whether the requested modifications are justified in terms of the software organization's plans for growth, development, and overall goals, as well as the desires of users. This board works not as a committee but as an advisory group to one of its members, who has the total responsibility for making decisions ([HAR86]). Of course, there should also be some mechanism for appealing the decision of the board.

It is quite possible that pressures for a new product have caused personnel to be shifted to development, so maintenance will be postponed or eliminated ([GRA87]). Figure 9-17 lists several factors to be considered in making the decision. The same

- Urgency of requested changes.
- Availability of resources.
- Disruption of other projects.
- Cost of installation.
- Modify existing/create additional product.
- Amount of user retraining/retooling required.
- Degree of product decay introduced by changes.
- Expected lifetime of these changes before product demise.
- Additional configuration management cost for variant products.

**FIGURE 9-17**   FACTORS IN DECIDING TO APPROVE MAINTENANCE

criteria should be used in making the decision to *eliminate* unwanted or outdated portions of the product.

Unless a contract exists that specifies the software organization's responsibility for additional development, it has no obligation to satisfy additional user desires, since there is no arrangement for fixed payment for modifications in this circumstance. For this reason, it is unwise to encourage the user to dream up new ideas for an existing product, that must be implemented through uncontracted maintenance.

Other questions that need to be considered before embarking on enhancements are shown in Figure 9-18 ([MCC81]).

If the requested changes are approved, then it is up to the maintenance manager to schedule the work and the resources needed to complete it. One method of controlling the cost of enhancements is to postpone them until correction or adaptation of the corresponding modules is also necessary. This allows us to make the same time and energy investments serve more than one purpose. It may also be useful to schedule alterations so as to make the easiest changes first.

Responsibility for carrying out the modifications is given to a product supervisor, who has ongoing oversight of all changes to this particular product. The supervisor acts as project manager for the modification and directs the efforts of maintenance workers if they are required. The supervisor will frequently produce the specification and design modifications while the detail workers carry out detailed design, implementation, and unit testing.

- Can users tolerate the current level of service?
- Do we have enough personnel free and other resources at the moment for this project?
- Will these changes disrupt user operations?
- How much retraining and rewriting of manuals will be required?
- Are we painting ourselves into a corner with these changes?
- Does the anticipated useful lifetime of the product justify the expense?
- Does the customer fully understand the magnitude of the project?

**FIGURE 9-18**   DECISION CTRITERIA FOR MODIFYING THE PRODUCT

The software organization's quality assurance group will conduct regression testing, as well as ensure that all documentation has been brought up to date and that standards have been met. In this function they perform essentially the same role as they would for an initial development effort. When all work is done, the change control board will examine the results and then, if no problems are seen, authorize distribution of the modifications.

Project management needs to enhance the status of maintenance and maintenance workers in the organization; ensure that products are well documented; and choose personnel who are flexible, patient, self-motivated, and organized ([GLA81]). Thus, the software organization should make it a goal to provide high-quality training, to insulate the maintenance worker from customer harassment, and to provide as many hardware and software resources for maintenance as for development.

It is difficult to provide sufficient numbers of well-trained and motivated software engineers to meet the maintenance needs of an organization. Maintenance is not usually seen as a particularly glamorous or rewarding task. Schneidewind ([SCH87]) claims that being a maintainer is "akin to having bad breath" in terms of esteem. Maintainers support the work of other people or fix their problems rather than do something creative themselves. Maintenance is sometimes seen as a dead-end job, but this can be offset by improving the salaries and by rotating the assignments given to maintenance people.

Another concern of the maintenance manager is the quality of maintenance service. One measure of quality is the amount of elapsed time between receiving a maintenance change request or error report and releasing the modified software for use. Another concern is the percentage of total maintenance effort expended in learning about the software as opposed to doing productive work with it. Still another measure is the comparison of software quality before and after modification.

Finally, it is important for management to assess the temper of the software marketplace. This is done by periodic surveys, which determine the level of customer satisfaction, how the product compares with its competition, its level of usefulness as perceived by the customer, and customer plans for its continued employment.

At some point in each product's lifetime, the maintenance manager will decide that it has reached a point where no further effort should be expended on it. Although customers may continue to buy and to use such software thereafter, from the software organization's point of view, the product has died. The decision to suspend mainte-

- Product has decayed, is no longer maintainable.
- Product is no longer competitive in marketplace.
- Application environment is disappearing.
- Hardware/operating environment is disappearing.
- Modification will compromise performance.
- Modification will compromise dependability.
- Product no longer serves software organization goals.

FIGURE 9-19   REASONS FOR PHASING OUT A SOFTWARE PRODUCT

nance is generally made when it appears that possible future benefits will not outweigh the costs. Several factors in arriving at this decision are outlined in Figure 9-19.

However, as Schneidewind points out in [SCH87], even a dead product can be useful. We should take the time to harvest useful components for reuse in other contexts. Old code can be a treasurehouse of plans, strategies, and algorithms that may not have been noticed, particularly if it was developed before the organization paid much attention to reuse. In a real sense, programs never really die; they continue to live on as components of other programs and as integral parts of the professional experience and shrewdness of software engineers.

## 9.5 SUMMARY

The operational stage is the longest and most costly in the software life cycle. It is dominated by managerial as opposed to technical problems. It spans acceptance, installation, training, support, and especially maintenance. The operational stage is also the time for project debriefing to evaluate the development experience.

From the software engineer's point of view, the purpose of the operational stage is to keep the product viable, attract new customers, and determine the quality of our, as well as our competitor's, product. However, from the point of view of the user, this is the *only* important part of the entire life cycle. For the user, the product must be constantly supported, and the software organization must be responsive to his changing needs.

Maintenance is by far the dominant activity during operation, and we have discussed a number of maintenance principles. They all come down to control: we need rational processes to decide what changes will be made, to collect customer requests and disperse new software, to modify and retest the software and, finally, to retire it. A stable organization of support personnel is necessary to provide this kind of control, as well as timely response to customer needs.

No less than at any other stage, methodology, tools, management skills, pragmatism, and quality assurance guarantee our success during software operation. In fact, these elements have been the foundation for success during all stages of the software life cycle. This truth simply reflects, once again, that software engineering goes far beyond "programming" in its scope.

## BIBLIOGRAPHY

[ARA86]*  Arango, G., I. Baxter, P. Freeman and C. Pidgeon, "TMM: Software Maintenance by Transformation," *IEEE Software*, 3(3):27 – 39.

[BEN87]  Bendifallah, S. and W. Scacchi, "Understanding Software Maintenance Work," *IEEE Transactions on Software Engineering*, 13(3):311 – 323.

[BER84]*  Bersoff, E.H., "Elements of Software Configuration Management," *IEEE Transactions on Software Engineering*, 10(1):79 – 88.

[BRI86]   Britcher, R.N. and J.J. Craig, "Using Modern Design Practices to Update Aging Software Systems," *IEEE Software* 3(3):16 – 24.

[BRO75]*  Brook, F.P., *The Mythical Man-Month*, Addison-Wesley, Reading, MA.

[COL87]*  Collofello, J.S., and J.J. Buck, "Software Quality Assurance for Maintenance," *IEEE Software*, 4(5):46 – 51.

[GLA81]*  Glass, R.L. and R.A. Noiseux, *Software Maintenance Guidebook*, Prentice-Hall, Englewood Cliffs, NJ.

[GRA87]*  Grady, R.B., "Measuring and Managing Software Maintenance," *IEEE Software*, 4(5):35 – 45.

[HAR86]   Harvey, K.E., "Summary of the SEI Workshop on Software Configuration Management," *Software Engineering Institute*, CMU/SEI-86-TR-5 Pittsburgh, PA.

[LEB87]*  Leblang, D.B. and R.P. Chase, "Parallel Software Configuration Management in a Network Environment," *IEEE Software*, 4(6):28 – 35.

[LIE81]*  Lientz, B.P. and E.B. Swanson, "Problems in Application Software Maintenance," *Communications of the ACM*, 24(11):763 – 769.

[LIE83]*  Lientz, B.P., "Issues in Software Maintenance," *Computing Surveys*, 15(3):271 – 278.

[MCC81]   McClure, C.L., *Managing Software Development and Maintenance* Van Nostrand Reinhold, New York.

[NAR87]   Narayanaswamy, K., and W. Scacchi, "Maintenance Configurations of Evolving Software Systems," *IEEE Transactions on Software Engineering*, 13(3):324–334.

[ROM87]*  Rombach, H.D., "Impact of Software Structure on Maintainability," *IEEE Transactions on Software Engineering*, 13(3):344 – 354.

[SCH87]*  Schneidewind, N.F., "The State of Software Maintenance," *IEEE Transactions on Software Engineering*, 13(3):303 – 310.

[SHE85]   Shen, V.Y., T.-J. Yu, S.M. Thebault and L.R. Paulsen, "Identifying Error-Prone Software," *IEEE Transactions on Software Engineering*, 11(4):317 – 324.

[TUR84]   Turner, R, *Software Engineering Methodology*, Reston, Reston, VA.

[WEI84]   Weiner-Ehrlich, W.K., J.R. Hamrick and V.F. Rupolo, "Modeling Software Behavior in Terms of a Formal Life-Cycle Curve," *IEEE Transactions on Software Engineering*, 10(4):376 – 383.

[YAU85]   Yau, S.S., and J.S. Collofello, "Design Stability Measures for Software Maintenance," *IEEE Transactions on Software Engineering*, 11(9):849 – 856.

## PROBLEMS

1  Talk to a systems programmer or contact a software supplier to find out about the rules, methods, and cost of software support.

2  Give a rule of thumb for distinguishing between perfective maintenance and software development that involves extensive enhancements to an existing product.

3  Compare the benefits and drawbacks of a free product support policy and one that charges customers for support.

**4** Perform an acceptance test for the software product tested in problem 16 in Chapter 8.

**5** Perform a project debriefing for the software product accepted in Problem 4. How does your project compare with others in your class in terms of effort, success, and error rates? Can you explain this?

**6** Develop a maintenance plan for the product accepted in Problem 4.

**7** Prepare a product survey for the product accepted in Problem 4.

**8** Perform a minor modification on the product accepted in Problem 4.

**9** Perform a minor modification on the product of another student.

**10** Modify the code of Section 7.5.1 or 7.5.2 to change the size of frames to 44 bytes and the synch signal to 4B 96 97 AF FF. How much design information were you able to recover? Could the design or code have been improved to make these changes easier? Was it difficult to obtain a new test data set?

**11** Describe a manual configuration management system that will ensure product integrity and change control during the operational stage. Include error reporting and update distribution mechanisms.

# APPENDIX 1

# COURSE PROJECTS

It has been my experience that a course project greatly enhances the depth of learning of the principles of software engineering. It gives the students a chance to do instead of listen, which aids in the transfer of the theory into practice. Students tend to enjoy the experience; they particularly express appreciation for the principles of software engineering after having a semirealistic project involvement. Time after time one hears the comment, "I didn't really understand why the things you were teaching me were important until...."

Project courses are popular, and are further discussed in the articles listed in the bibliography. I particularly recommend [KAN81], but they are all worth looking into. The suggestions I give are a mixture of my own experience and information culled from them.

1 The project should come after the theory, in a separate quarter or semester.
2 Teams should consist of four to six persons, organized in an anarchistic or democratic team.
3 The instructor can serve as the client, unless the work is being done for a real client, for example, the computer science department or another university unit, a community organization, a research group, or the like.
4 If needed, teaching assistants can play the part of team managers, but then they should do so in all teams to avoid feelings of unfairness.

456

**5** If the project's duration is long enough, it can be useful to transfer a member from each team to another about half-way along; but this may cause too much disruption for a short project.

**6** It is very useful to assign projects that involve maintenance activities on projects from previous years; but be sure to obtain every former student's permission to do this. It can also be worthwhile to have a team conduct only testing or only specification of a larger product.

**7** The Software Hut game, which involves different teams producing duplicate portions of the entire project and then bartering them to each other, can introduce fun and a sense of economic realism into the process.

**8** Special care should be taken to emphasize the importance of the process, and especially of documentation, so that this does not become just another "programming" project.

**9** Teams should be given group, rather than individual, grades. It can be effective to have the entire course population vote on the quality of projects and then to take peer approval into account in assigning grades. (In all fairness, [COL85] and some others recommend that individual evaluation of effort is better.)

**10** The instructor should make every effort to avoid becoming entangled in personal disputes. Once it becomes clear that students will either live with their differences or resolve them on their own, they almost always do the latter.

**11** It is possible to have students all work on the same project, in which case they get a chance to see the different, but valid, approaches that can be taken. There is, however, some danger of collusion between teams or individual members of different teams. More objective comparisons are possible when all products are supposed to be the same, but this demands careful attention on the part of the client during the analysis and specification stage.

**12** The instructor must insist that milestone documents be submitted according to the schedule set up during analysis. Students may not understand the seriousness of schedule slips but poor grades will drive the message home.

The following suggested projects are stated not as specifications but as initial concepts. It is up to the team to conduct an analysis of requirements, specify the product, design and implement it, test it, and install it.

*Plagiarism Checker*  A tool to detect plagiarized source code. It should look for simple substitution of identifiers, structural similarities, and similar McCabe, Halstead, or other code measures.

*Memo Filter*  A tool to analyze memos received through electronic mail in order to prioritize and sort them according to the individual's interests and duties. Memos must be identified through some classification scheme, but memo contents should also be scanned for keywords.

*Estimation Tool*  A tool to estimate effort, duration and manpower for software projects. It can be based on COCOMO or any other pricing model.

*Cross-reference Analyzer* A tool to create a cross-reference table for a text document. It should attempt to distinguish definitions from uses of terms, as well as eliminate words that appear in a common, nontechnical vocabulary.

*Flowchart Generator* A tool to create an on-line flowchart from pseudocode. It should provide scrolling capabilities for flowcharts whose size exceeds the screen.

*Syntax-Directed Editor* A tool for input of source code in a specific implementation language. It should provide structure templates with defaults, automatic indentation, prologue creation, syntax-checking, visual distinctions between key words and identifiers, and creation of intermediate code.

*Test Harness* A tool to allow the execution of single program units in some implementation language. It should allow its user to generate scripts that will contain specific test cases and anticipated results, or specifications of test case domains for which the harness will randomly generate data and display results.

*Profiler* A tool to instrument source code in some implementation language. It should monitor execution of the object code under user control and then provide tables, statistics, and graphs indicating traces, branch and program unit execution counts, CPU time expenditure, and so on.

*Form Generator* A tool to allow a programmer to specify the appearance of a screen, the format and validation assertions for the input, and the format of an output file to be created.

*Spelling Checker* A tool to compare a text file, word by word, to a standard dictionary and a personalized dictionary, locating unknown words and allowing the user to skip them, edit them, or exchange them for one of a list of suggested replacements produced by the tool.

*Code Standards Auditor* A tool to examine code in a specific implementation language and flag nonstandard usage, style, layout, and so on.

*Scheduler* A tool to assist in the creation of PERT and Gantt charts, that will subsequently produce charts comparing scheduled and actual activities and effort.

*Advisor* An interactive program to give information and advice about a student's status regarding graduation requirements. This product should be able to interface to a departmental database containing individual transcripts, schedules for future course offerings, and graduation requirements.

*Bulletin Board* A product to facilitate communication and interchange of information and data between students served by a local-area network. This product should have sufficient safeguards to avoid some of the well-known abuses of bulletin boards.

*Macro Expander* A preprocessor to expand named and parameterized macros in a specific programming language. This product should be able to implement preprocess-time logic.

*Departmental Calendar* An interactive product to manage the scheduling calendars of a group. It should provide a daily tickler, journal capabilities, electronic reminder calls, patterned exclusion of blocks of time (office hours, classes, and the like) and scheduling of meetings in common free time.

*Interface Checker* A tool to verify the syntactic and semantic consistency of interfaces during architectural design.

*Program Animator* An interactive tool to allow the user to specify portions of source code that are to be animated during execution. This product should have default representations for objects, values, flows, and so on, but should also allow the user to customize representations.

*Slide Show Generator* An interactive text/graphics editor with multiple font capability and sound generation. The product should allow for the creation of each slide and for the sequencing, timing, and conditional display of a set of slides.

*Browser* An interactive tool that allows a user to roam through source code and interfaces to the project database. When a portion of code is selected, a window gives information about it. The information can be about syntax, specifications, design, testing, and the like.

*Structure Extractor* A tool to extract from source code an invocation hierarchy, data flow diagram, object visibility chart, Nassi-Shneiderman chart, and so on.

## SOFTWARE ENGINEERING PROJECT BIBLIOGRAPHY

[BEN87]* Bentley, J.L. and J.A. Dallen, "Exercises in Software Design," *IEEE Transactions on Software Engineering*, 13(11):1164 – 1169.

[BIC85] Bickerstaff, D.D., "The Evolution of a Project Oriented Course in Software Development," *ACM SIGSCE Bulletin*, 17(1):13 – 22.

[BOE81] Boehm, B.W., "An Experiment in Small-Scale Application Software Engineering," *IEEE Transactions on Software Engineering*, 7(5):482 – 493.

[BUR87]* Burns, J.E. and E.L. Robertson, "Two Complementary Course Sequences on the Design and Implementation of Software Products," *IEEE Transactions on Software Engineering*, 13(11):1170 – 1175.

[CAR85] Carver, D.L., "Comparison of Techniques in Project-Based Courses," *ACM SIGSCE*, 17(1):9 – 12.

[COL85] Collofello, J.S., "Monitoring and Evaluating Individual Team Members in a Software Engineering Course," *ACM SIGSCE Bulletin*, 17(1):6 – 8.

[FAI85] Fairley, R.E., *Software Engineering Concepts*, pp. 341 – 349, McGraw-Hill, New York.

[HEN83] Henry, S., "A Project Oriented Course on Software Engineering," *ACM SIGSCE Bulletin*, 15(1):57–61.

[HOR77]* Horning, J.J. and D.G. Wortman, "Software Hut: A Computer Program Engineering Project in the Form of a Game," *IEEE Transactions on Software Engineering*, 3(4):325 – 330.

[KAN81]* Kant, E., "A Semester Course in Software Engineering," *Software Engineering Notes*, 16(4):52 – 76.

[LEV87]*    Leventhal, L.M. and B.T. Mynatt, "Components of Typical Undergraduate Software Engineering Courses", *IEEE Transactions on Software Engineering*, 13(11):1193 – 1198.

[MAZ81]     Mazlack, L.J., "Using a Sales Incentive Technique in a First Course in Software Engineering," *ACM SIGSCE Bulletin*, 13(1):37 – 40.

[MCK87]*    McKeeman, W.M., "Experience with a Software Engineering Project Course," *IEEE Transactions on Software Engineering*, 13(11):1182 – 1192.

[SHO83]     Shooman, ML, "The Teaching of Software Engineering," *ACM SIGSCE Bulletin*, 15(1):66 – 69.

[WAG84]     Waguespack, L.J. and D.F. Haas, "A Workbench for Project Oriented Software Engineering Courses," *ACM SIGSCE Bulletin*, 16(1):137 – 145.

[WEI87]*    Weiss, D.M., "Teaching a Software Design Methodology," *IEEE Transactions on Software Engineering*, 13(11):1156 – 1163.

[WOO82]     Woodfield, S.N. and C.S. Collofello, "A Project-Unified Software Engineering Course Sequence," *ACM SIGSCE Bulletin*, 14(1):13 – 19.

[WOO83]     Woodfield, S.N., Collofello, C.S. and Collofello, P.M., "Some Insights and Experiences in Teaching Team Project Courses," *ACM SIGSCE Bulletin*, 15(1):62 – 65.

[WOR87]*    Wortman, D.B., "Software Projects in an Academic Environment," *IEEE Transactions on Software Engineering*, 13(11):1176 – 1181.

# APPENDIX 2

## DOCUMENT TEMPLATES

## PROJECT PLAN

**Introduction**

Description of the problem
Description of the problem environment
Client and software organization goals
Proposed solution and its scope

**Proposal**

Functions provided through the proposed solution
General strategy for developing the solution
Role of users and hardware in the solution
Advantages and drawbacks of the solution

**Constraints**

Customer priorities
Profile of users
Expected lifetime of the product
Reliability requirements
Performance requirements
Existing data interface and hardware environment
Future extensions of the product
Required implementation language (if any)
Training, installation, and documentation requirements
Availability of customer environment
Alternative solutions
Feasibility of proposed and alternative solutions

**Estimates**

Schedule
Staffing and organization
Budget
Cost/benefit analysis
Risk analysis
Deliverable documents
Software tools needed
Facilities and hardware needed

**Procedures**

       Process model

       Methodologies and notations

       Standards and quality assurance

       Accountability monitoring

       Product control

       Testing and source of test data

       Acceptance criteria and method of payment

**Reference**

       Documents used in developing the plan

       Glossary of terms

       Proposed contract (if any)

## Software Requirements Specification

Introduction
      Problem overview
      Application environment, user characteristics
      Notations used in the specification
      Goals of the project

Software Functions
      Process descriptions
      Function pre- and postassertions
      Data descriptions
      Data relationships
      Priorities for implementation

Constraints
      External interfaces (hardware, operating system, user, data, network)
      Compatibility with previous products
      Timing and processing rates
      Code and data size, and processing volume
      Reliability
      Accuracy
      Maintainability
      Security

Exceptions
      Hardware failures and responses
      Software faults and responses
      Data faults and responses

Software Life Cycle
      Process model, standards, and methodologies
      Predicted modifications and maintenance

Reference
      Documents used in developing the specifications
      Glossary of terms

## Software Verification Plan

Requirement (restates specification)
Design verification methodology, schedule, responsible party
Code verification methodology, schedule, responsible party
Test data and responses, schedule, responsible party

**User's Manual**

Introduction
> Purpose of the software product
> Operating environment
> General functionality
> Special features
> Limitations
> Conventions used in this document

Installation
> Physical requirements
> Copying and backing up
> Software installation procedures
> Customizing the product

Tutorial
> Walkthrough of an example
> Explanation of the example
> Elaboration of the basic example
> Use of on-line help package and manuals

Detailed Instructions
> Output of the product
> Input to the product
> Operation of the product
> Error handling
> Specific functions
>> How to invoke this function
>> Input data needed
>> How to interpret the results

Technical details
> Principles of operation
> Advanced features
> Major algorithms
> Major data structures
> Modification of the product
> How to get support and further information

## Design Specification

Introduction
      Problem overview
      Application environment, user characteristics
      Notations used in the design
      Goals of the project
Review of Specifications
      Software functions
      Data descriptions
      Data relationships
      Priorities for implementation
      Constraints
      Exceptions
      Predicted modifications and maintenance
Architectural Design
      Hierarchical module and interface diagrams
      Function/data cluster description
      Interface specifications
Detailed Designs
      For each module:
            Module description
            Interface specification
            Process description
            Data structure definitions
            Initialization requirements
            Exception handling specification
Alternatives
      For each rejected design:
            Brief description
            Reason for rejection
            Conditions that might favor it
Reference
      Documents used in developing the design
      Glossary of terms

## The Unit Folder

Unit Status
     Sign-off sheets
     Planning and actual schedules
     Acquisition of reusable components and tools
     Effort expended

Relevant specifications

Relevant design
     External design
     Architectural design
     Detailed design

Operational information
     Notes and plans
     Instructions
     Alternate implementations, feasibility, rationale

Source Code

Test Plans
     Facet, feature or path to be tested
     Person responsible and date scheduled
     Tools or auxiliary code needed
     Test data and instructions
     Expected test results
     Actual test results; analysis (if needed)
     Correction schedule and sign-off (if needed)
        (the above section is repeated many times)

Software Problems
     Report
     Analysis
     Action
        (the above section is repeated many times)

Audits and Reviews

## A Module Prologue

```
MODULE NAME:
FUNCTION:
INTERFACE PARAMETERS AND MODES:
PREASSERTION:
POSTASSERTION:
GLOBALS AND SIDE EFFECTS:
EXCEPTIONS:
HARDWARE AND OPERATING SYSTEM REQUIREMENTS:
CREATION AND MODIFICATION HISTORY:
ALGORITHM:
MAJOR DATA STRUCTURES:
CALLED BY:
CALLS:
```

## Test Documentation

Requirement (restates specification)

Design verification methodology, schedule, responsible party

Code verification methodology, schedule, responsible party

Test data and responses, schedule, responsible party

Test Plans
    Facet, feature or path to be tested
    Person responsible and date scheduled
    Tools or auxiliary code needed
    Test data and instructions
    Expected test results
    Actual test results; analysis (if needed)
        Date
        Operator
        Computing environment
        Description of deviation from expectation
        Was the result reproducible?
        Analysis of possible causes
    Correction schedule and sign-off (if needed)
        (the above section is repeated many times)

## The Project Legacy

Title and Description of Product
Product Profile
    Functions
    Application area
    Size
    Complexity
    Development model
    Design paradigm
    Tools used
    Success level

Management and Team Organization

Personnel

Project Narrative

Product and Process Measurements

Problems and Analysis

Recommendations

Location of Reusable Components (stored elsewhere)

**Software Maintenance Plan**

Projected Major Modifications and Extensions

Planned Revision Cycle Schedule

Known Problems and Reliability Estimates

Maintenance Organization Structure and Staff

Error Report Procedures

Change Request Procedures

Revision Distribution Procedures

**Software Release Notice Format**

Scope

Change Summary

      New features

      Problems fixed

      Restrictions removed / capacities enlarged

      Known Problems

      Bugs

      Restrictions

Hardware and Software Compatibility Requirements

Cross-reference to Relevant Documentation

Detailed Functional Changes

Directory of Packages on the Distribution Medium

Installation Procedures

## Software Change Request

<table>
<tr><td colspan="2" align="center">SOFTWARE PROBLEM REPORT</td><td>SPR No. _____</td></tr>
</table>

**PROBLEM: (Prepared by User)**

Originator _____ Phone No. _____

(Name)                              (Organization)

System, processor, or
Component Failing          _____ Computer _____ System _____ Test Case or
or Project Involved                                          Version ID          Program ID _____

Description of Problem 9attach additional pages if
necessary – include numbers or other identification
of offending statements or data)

**Classification**

☐ Minor or Not to Specs     _____
☐ Major or Missing          _____
☐ Information               _____
☐ Revision Request          _____
☐ Software Addition         _____

Correction Required By _____

(Date)

**Enclosures**

☐ Program Listings
☐ Run Deck
☐ Run Instructions
☐ Storage Map Listings
☐ Data Listings
☐ On–Line Output

Authorizing Signature _____ Date _____ Time _____

(Name)                              (Organization)

**ANALYSIS: (Prepared by organization responsible for software)**

Received Date _____ Time _____ Charge Number _____

☐ Software in Error               Explanation _____        Analysis Time Expended:
☐ Software Not in Error                        _____        Man Hours _____
   Explain and Return to                       _____        Computer Hours _____
   Originator                                  _____        Computer _____
☐ Insufficient Information                     _____        Estimated Cost of Solutions:
   for Analysis. See                           _____        Man Hours _____
   Explanation                                 _____        Computer Hours _____
☐ Error Previously                             _____        Planned _____
   Reported on SPR No.                                             Correction Date
☐ Others, Explain
☐ Not Approved
☐ Approved for Correction
   or Change

Signature _____ Date _____ Time _____

(Name)                              (Organization)

**CORRECTION: (Brief description of work performed, including test cases used to confirm correction)**

Solution: _____ Modules Changed:
_____
_____
_____  Correction Time Expended:
_____  Man Hours
_____  Computer Hours
_____  Submitted to

Work Performed by (Signature) _____ Date _____ Time _____

**CONFIRMATION: Corrections Veri fied by CCB/CPL**

Signature _____ Date _____ Time _____

CTF No(s) _____

Available in (VersionID) _____ Date Returned to Originator _____ Time _____

# INDEX